THE CAMBRIDGE HANDBOOK OF LITERARY AUTHORSHIP

This handbook surveys the state of the art in literary authorship studies. Its 27 original contributions by eminent scholars offer a multi-layered account of authorship as a defining element of literature and culture. Covering a vast chronological range, Part I considers the history of authorship from cuneiform writing to contemporary digital publishing; it discusses authorship in ancient Egypt, Greece, Rome, early Jewish cultures, medieval, Renaissance, modern, postmodern, and Chinese literature. The second part focuses on the place of authorship in literary theory, and on challenges to theorizing literary authorship, such as gender and sexuality, postcolonial and indigenous contexts for writing. Finally, Part III investigates practical perspectives on the topic, with a focus on attribution, anonymity and pseudonymity, plagiarism and forgery, copyright and literary property, censorship, publishing and marketing, and institutional contexts.

INGO BERENSMEYER is Professor of Modern English Literature at the University of Munich and a visiting professor at Ghent University. His previous publications include *Mendacity in Early Modern Literature and Culture* (co-edited with Andrew Hadfield, 2016), and over seventy essays in collections and journals, including *New Literary History, Poetics Today, Studies in English Literature 1500–1900, Anglia,* and *Poetica.*

GERT BUELENS is senior full Professor of English and American Literature at Ghent University. His previous publications include *The Future of Trauma Theory* (co-edited with Durrant and Eaglestone, 2013), and over sixty essays in collections and journals, including *Dickens Quarterly, Wallace Stevens Journal, Modern Philology, Texas Studies in Literature and Language, Diacritics, Studies in the Novel, Textual Practice, Criticism,* and *PMLA.*

MARYSA DEMOOR is senior full Professor of English Literature at Ghent University and a life member of Clare Hall, Cambridge. She is the author of *Their Fair Share: Women, Power and Criticism in the Athenaeum, from Millicent Garrett Fawcett to Katherine Mansfield, 1870–1920* (2000) and the editor of *Marketing the Author: Authorial Personae, Narrative Selves and Self-Fashioning, 1880–1930* (2004). With Laurel Brake, she edited *The Lure of Illustration in the Nineteenth Century: Picture and Press* (2009) and the *Dictionary of Nineteenth-Century Journalism* (2009).

THE CAMBRIDGE HANDBOOK OF LITERARY AUTHORSHIP

EDITED BY

INGO BERENSMEYER

GERT BUELENS

MARYSA DEMOOR

CAMBRIDGE
UNIVERSITY PRESS

CAMBRIDGE
UNIVERSITY PRESS

University Printing House, Cambridge CB2 8BS, United Kingdom

One Liberty Plaza, 20th Floor, New York, NY 10006, USA

477 Williamstown Road, Port Melbourne, VIC 3207, Australia

314–321, 3rd Floor, Plot 3, Splendor Forum, Jasola District Centre,
New Delhi – 110025, India

79 Anson Road, #06–04/06, Singapore 079906

Cambridge University Press is part of the University of Cambridge.

It furthers the University's mission by disseminating knowledge in the pursuit of
education, learning, and research at the highest international levels of excellence.

www.cambridge.org
Information on this title: www.cambridge.org/9781107168657
DOI: 10.1017/9781316717516

First published 2019

Printed and bound in Great Britain by Clays Ltd, Elcograf S.p.A.

A catalogue record for this publication is available from the British Library.

ISBN 978-1-107-16865-7 Hardback

Contents

Figures

Contributors

CHRISTIAN BADURA, Free University of Berlin, Germany

MITA BANERJEE, University of Mainz, Germany

INGO BERENSMEYER, University of Munich, Germany

HANS BERTENS, University of Utrecht, The Netherlands

GERT BUELENS, Ghent University, Belgium

JOHN BURROWS, University of Newcastle, Australia

KANG-I SUN CHANG, Yale University, New Haven, USA

MORDECHAI Z. COHEN, Yeshiva University, New York, USA

DANIEL COOK, University of Dundee, UK

HUGH CRAIG, University of Newcastle, Australia

MARYSA DEMOOR, Ghent University, Belgium

KEVIN DUNN, Tufts University, Boston, USA

ALEXIS EASLEY, University of St. Thomas, Minnesota, USA

MARGARET J.M. EZELL, Texas A&M, College Station, USA

BENJAMIN R. FOSTER, Yale University, New Haven, USA

ROBERT J. GRIFFIN, Texas A&M, College Station, USA

ANDREW KING, University of Greenwich, UK

ANDREW KRAEBEL, Trinity University, San Antonio, USA

SEAN LATHAM, University of Tulsa, USA

ANTONIO LOPRIENO, University of Basel, Switzerland

JACK LYNCH, Rutgers University–Newark, USA

MELANIE MÖLLER, Free University of Berlin, Germany

JAMES PHELAN, Ohio State University, USA

JASON PUSKAR, University of Wisconsin, Milwaukee, USA

TREVOR ROSS, Dalhousie University, Halifax, Canada

BETTY A. SCHELLENBERG, Simon Fraser University, Canada

RUTH SCODEL, University of Michigan, Ann Arbor, USA

JAKOB STOUGAARD-NIELSEN, University College London, UK

ADRIAAN VAN DER WEEL, Leiden University, the Netherlands

DIRK VAN HULLE, University of Antwerp, Belgium

CHANTAL ZABUS, University Paris 13 – Sorbonne Paris Cité, France

Acknowledgments

The editors are grateful to Ghent University's Special Research Fund for a grant that enabled us to focus on the topic of literary authorship for a number of years, and to the young scholars who worked with us on this project: Isabelle Clairhout, Yuri Cowan, Gero Guttzeit, Sören Hammerschmidt, Alise Jameson, Jasper Schelstraete, Birgit Van Puymbroeck, Marianne Van Remoortel, and Lisa Walters. We would also like to thank our advisory board for steering us wisely during the early stages of the project: Odin Dekkers, Brean Hammond, Betty Schellenberg, Joanne Shattock, Clifford Siskin, Wendy Wall, and Martha Woodmansee.

We want to express our gratitude, above all, to our contributors, who not only took on this assignment in an increasingly busy academic world but also delivered their chapters on time (well, mostly) and responded quickly and effectively to any query we threw back at them. For their invaluable assistance with textual editing, we would like to thank Liza Bauer and George Rainov. Any remaining errors should of course be blamed entirely on us.

At Cambridge University Press, thanks are due to Linda Bree for commissioning this handbook, and to Tim Mason, Emily Hockley, and Victoria Parrin for their help in guiding us to the finish line. Mark Fisher provided expert copy-editing, Jim Fuhr a professional index. Last but not least, we are grateful to our families for their loving support, patience, and endurance.

Abbreviations

EETS	Early English Text Society
es	Extra Series
fr.	fragment
JEGP	*Journal of English and Germanic Philology*
LCL	Loeb Classical Library
ME	Middle English
MLN	*Modern Language Notes*
MS	manuscript
NLH	*New Literary History*
ns	New Series
os	Original Series
pl.	plate

CHAPTER I

Introduction

Ingo Berensmeyer, Gert Buelens, and Marysa Demoor

Why do texts and readers need authors? Why is "authorship talk" so prevalent in literary conversations – whether at book fairs, book clubs, or readers' groups, in literary magazines, newspapers, university seminars, or social media? These questions may seem absurd, at least to those who are blissfully unaware of, or have happily moved on from, twentieth-century debates about "the intentional fallacy," "the death of the author," or indeed his or her "return."[1] But, as we hope to show in this handbook, these questions have a relevance for literary studies that transcends the theory wars of the past or the narrow confines of the discipline itself. They are – or should be – central to the field if only because questions of authorship are of great popular interest, given the media attention devoted to, for instance, celebrity authors and the size of their advances, accusations of plagiarism, the gender of an anonymous author, or the Shakespeare authorship cottage industry.[2]

We Call upon the Author to Explain

Perhaps, first and foremost, "we call upon the author to explain," as a Nick Cave song has it.[3] Fittingly, Cave leaves unspecified what exactly needs to be explained, and who is supposed to do the explaining, the author or "we" – presumably, readers and critics who invoke the author to justify how they make sense of textual meanings, or indeed of ambiguities such as the one contained in this very phrase. The song touches on various aspects of authorship, ranging from the author as a figure of explanation to one of authority and responsibility not only in literary but also in economic and legal terms. For example, it refers to God as the ultimate "author" responsible for an imperfect creation, but it also compares a trio of male American literary heavyweights (Bukowski, Berryman, and Hemingway) and quotes an unattributed line from Wallace Stevens's poem "Dry Loaf," thus implicating another American poet in the lyrics. The song also comments on literary publishing and on an author's or editor's task of revising the "prolix" effusions of authorial expression: "Prolix! Prolix! Nothing a pair of scissors can't fix!"[4]

Despite, or perhaps because of, its ironic and self-referential manner, this song provides a useful starting point to this handbook, since it may serve as a reminder of some of the many aspects involved in the term "authorship," or more narrowly and specifically, "literary authorship." To explicate but a few, literary authorship can be or has been understood, among other things, as:

- the practice or activity of (literary) writing, especially of writing for publication;
- a creative activity shaping not only words but also turning the author's life into an artistic experiment that (re-)shapes both life and work, style and man; a romantic but also classical Roman notion of authorship (see Christian Badura and Melanie Möller's chapter "Authorship in Classical Rome");
- a form of textual control that involves cutting and taking away as well as adding: something a pair of scissors can fix; editorial and censorship practices that shape an author's work and/or image in the field of production and reception (see Trevor Ross's chapter "Censorship");
- a complex of values and moral rights associated with individual creative acts in literature, such as responsibility, authority, sincerity, authenticity, which entail certain legal rights and obligations, as mandated by copyright and libel laws, such as rules for quotation and acknowledgment (see Jack Lynch's chapter "Plagiarism and Forgery," Alexis Easley's chapter "The Nineteenth Century," and Daniel Cook's chapter "Copyright and Literary Property").

Since all of these aspects are interlinked and historically and culturally complex, it is perhaps impossible to unite them into a single, coherent narrative – as in "the history of literary authorship" – or a unified "theory of literary authorship." It is easier to dismiss authorship talk entirely from literary studies and just focus on texts or readers, as the New Criticism and reader-response criticism tended to do (see Jakob Stougaard-Nielsen's chapter "The Author in Literary Theory"), but this neglect leaves out an essential aspect of literature – its creation – and willfully reduces the scope of the field, leaving the study of literary creation and production to sociologists, with the exception of landmark studies such as Harold Bloom's *Anxiety of Influence*, whose (all-male) major poets create by misreading and revising the work of their precursors, or Sandra Gilbert and

Susan Gubar's *The Madwoman in the Attic*, which revived interest in authorship by women.[5] Yet, since the turn of the millennium, there have been a number of important shifts and changes in the field of literary studies, as well as in literature itself, that have brought authors and authorship back into focus. For decades now, the "return of the author"[6] has been an undeniable phenomenon not only in literary studies, book history, and related disciplines but also in literature itself, in such practices as autofiction, for example, which closely links novelistic narrative with the author's personal life, as in Chris Kraus's *I Love Dick* (1997), Dave Eggers's *A Heartbreaking Work of Staggering Genius* (2000), or Karl Ove Knausgård's *Min Kamp* (2009–2011) (see Hans Bertens's chapter "Postmodernist Authorship"). The revelation of the (putative) real name behind the pseudonym "Elena Ferrante" and the media storm surrounding this journalistic scoop, in 2016, showed again that there is a deep-seated public desire to relate the work of a writer to that writer's identity, age, gender, and her/his life story; also, perhaps, that women writers, even in the twenty-first century, are often denied the privileges of anonymity, privacy, and impersonality – that most modern of literary credos – that the wider public ungrudgingly grants to their male colleagues (see also Robert J. Griffin's chapter "Anonymity and Pseudonymity" and John Burrows and Hugh Craig's chapter "Attribution").

After decades of neglect and poststructuralist posturing about the "death" or, at the very least, utter irrelevance of the author as a critical concept, authors have returned to the focus of attention not only of readers – who never relinquished their attachment to authors, real or imagined – but also of professional critics and scholars. This is not an uncritical return to biographical criticism or to the much-disputed "implied author" of Booth's *Rhetoric of Fiction*,[7] nor a backlash against reader-response theory or deconstruction so as to reinvest interpretative authority in the author. The rise of what one might call "authorship studies" in recent decades is not merely driven by the common-sense notion that texts require somebody (or, indeed, some machine) to write them. It is, rather, part of a wider development in literary studies to take into account not only texts and readers but also authors among other agents within what Robert Darnton has called "the communications circuit."[8] This development builds on recent trends in a range of fields and subfields: actor-network theory; attribution studies and stylistics; bibliography and textual studies; book history; periodical studies; cultural archaeology and cultural memory studies; gender and sexuality studies; literary sociology; narratology; the New Historicism; the New

Materialism; media history; performance and performativity studies; rhetoric; new methodologies of research made possible by databases, personal computers, and the Internet; to name but the most obvious ones.[9]

If these new "authorship studies" for the twenty-first century are as yet vaguely defined, the present volume sets out to present a – somewhat selective – survey of historical, systematic, and practical perspectives on literary authorship on which to build future inquiries. Even with the generous space granted in this handbook, it is not possible to cover all the aspects and perspectives of this burgeoning field of research. Despite its broad historical range, from about 3000 BCE to the contemporary world, and its disciplinary plurality, from Chinese studies to digital media studies, there were practical limits to what we were able to include, and – with some, we hope, notable exceptions – the focus is, by and large, Western and predominantly Anglophone. Nevertheless, the handbook's obvious geographical and cultural limitations should be understood not as arising from ignorance or willful neglect; the fact that we include a chapter on China, for instance, but none on India or Japan, is not meant to signal any judgment of relative importance on our part. Rather, these obvious lacunae should be viewed as invitations for future endeavors by *migliori fabbri*.

This introduction is not the place to delve into the long history of authorship concepts from antiquity to the present (which is the subject of the first part of this handbook), nor into the intricate and hard-fought battles about authorship in twentieth-century literary theory (these are examined in part two, especially in Jakob Stougaard-Nielsen's chapter "The Author in Literary Theory and Theories of Literature"). Even less space is there for a precise definition of *literary* authorship – a term that might be even more contentious than authorship *per se*, especially in pre-modern contexts. The adjective is there because without it, the term "authorship" would have a much wider remit, a conceptual horizon – or conceptual baggage – that is frequently evoked in discussions of literary authorship but that would have led us too far away from our principal interest in literature. For the "author" in a broader sense of "original creator," some languages have a special term, such as the German *Urheber*, whereas the literary "author" can also carry a narrower meaning and just be a synonym for "writer" (*écrivain, Schriftsteller, scrittore,* писатель, etc., vs. *auteur, Autor, autore,* автор). "Literary authorship," then, should be understood as limiting authorship to the literary field, however culturally and historically defined, and as invoking an area of social practice as well as scholarly study in which authorship, more or less sharply defined, figures strongly in various forms and meanings and in connection with related and contrasting terms such as writer, poet, playwright, novelist, scribe, hack, agent, editor, publisher, ghostwriter, translator, commentator, plagiarist, secretary, biographer.

Nothing a Pair of Scissors Can't Fix

Summing up the debates about authorship in literary studies, mostly in the twentieth century, Peter Lamarque makes a useful distinction between three major conceptions of literary authorship:

- contextualism (connecting a work essentially to its author: in this view, it really makes a difference if you know who the real Elena Ferrante is);
- institutionalism (defining literature as a practice with norms and conventions that define what readers and authors are and do); and
- expressivism (regarding an author's intention as the ultimate authority over textual meaning).[10]

The New Critics famously denounced the cult of personality surrounding authors. Although they acknowledged the fact that "a poem does not come into existence by accident"[11] (see Jakob Stougaard-Nielsen's chapter "The Author in Literary Theory and Theories of Literature"), they effectively cut off a long-standing Romantic tradition of the poet as genius or "sage"; genius, as defined by Kant, meaning "the exemplary originality of the natural endowments of an individual in the *free* employment of his cognitive faculties."[12] The works of a genius, according to this eighteenth-century definition, are not the result of an imitation but an object of emulation, whose purpose is to wake up other, later geniuses, according to Kant. Since the Romantics, this has developed into the expressivist theory of authorship that closely relates authors' lives to their works. As Lamarque shows, there are numerous problems with this view, not least in "the paradoxes of inspiration and expression":[13] is the poem that derives from inspiration the experience that the poet has before writing it down, so that the written text is only a copy of the experience, or is the linguistic expression identical to the poet's inspiration, and thus something given to the poet by a higher power than his/her "own voice," not an act of self-expression at all? In that case, "genius" would be defined as heteronomous rather than autonomous, and characterized by "impersonality" rather than a unique and original personality.[14]

These questions also then extend to the concept of style in literature; is style an expression of the author's personality or rather a social (and political) relation, determined as much by social circumstances such as class, gender, and education as by something as difficult to pinpoint as "personality"?[15] Finally, debates about intentionalism and anti-intentionalism pivot on the question whether literary works can, as it were, speak for themselves or should, must, or must never be related to what the author (might have) intended. These questions affect not only literary theory but also critical understandings of attribution studies and textual editing (see John Burrows and Hugh Craig's chapter "Attribution" and Dirk Van Hulle's chapter "Authorship and Scholarly Editing") as well as wider social conceptions of reading and writing, the issue of censorship, and the intricacies of literary publishing and marketing (see Jason Puskar's chapter "Institutions: Writing and Reading," Trevor Ross's chapter "Censorship," and Andrew King's chapter "Publishing and Marketing"). After the poststructuralist deflation of the expressivist concept of the author-genius, more modest recent authorial self-descriptions are eager to resist the honorific implications of the term "author." As the novelist Tom McCarthy professes, "an author is more like a by- or waste-product of the work, and of literature in general."[16] Yet such a view ignores the fact that there is now an industry concerned with the marketing of "name-economy" authors as media products, hosting professional author websites and creating social media "buzz" to generate maximum profit.[17] The social and economic conditions of how authors are made invite closer analysis and contextualization, including the question whether writers whose work – for whatever reason – is not published should count as authors.

These ramifications should make clear that literary authorship, whether as a privileged origin or a "waste-product" of literature, cannot be understood outside of larger institutional settings in which literary writing and its dissemination among readers are situated. This is the domain of reader-response criticism, for example, as in Stanley Fish's idea of "interpretive communities" that determine textual meanings,[18] but also the context of literary history and book history. These wider contexts allow us to view literary authorship under at least two different aspects: as an *activity* (something that writers do) and as an *ascription* (something that writers are thought to do or to be). To perform authorship means to write as an author, certainly, but this is more than a mere tautology – it also means to follow certain rules or protocols that define authorship. This notion of "performativity" derives from speech act theory and cultural studies and is inspired by Judith Butler's description of social protocols shaping gender and sexual identity.[19] In other words, authors are, to some extent, free to follow or ignore these protocols, but when it comes to the field transition from writing to publishing, they ignore them at their peril. Even though writers commonly – if not exclusively – write alone, this powerful myth of authorial individuality, loneliness, and freedom obscures a common reality of social bonds and connections, educational and collegial support networks, and the power of audience and market expectations.[20]

There are interesting limit cases of authorship, when a writer's work is published posthumously or is continued by other writers, in the form of sequels, prequels, or fan fiction (e.g., Stieg Larsson), or cases where authors stop writing or publishing during their lifetime while their status as authors remains unchanged or their reputation actually grows because of the "mystery" of their silence (e.g., J. D. Salinger or Wolfgang Koeppen). Such cases illustrate the fact that authorship and the act of writing, although necessarily related, are not identical and should not be confused.

As both an activity and an ascription, authorship is a crucial part of the literary field, and it would be difficult to imagine literary studies without a concept, or concepts, of authorship. Hence it is not merely worthwhile but imperative for scholars of literature to think as systematically about authors and authorship as they have thought, and are still thinking, about readers and reading, and about texts and their various contexts. For literary studies, authors are more than merely providers of one more (biographical) context for a poem, play, or novel. They serve as crucial anchor points for textual meaning, if only to exclude historically impossible meanings in interpretation (because a particular reading would not have been available during the author's lifetime)[21] or to locate a text within a particular period or cultural moment (as is common practice, for instance, in the New Historicism) or in an author's nationality, race, or gender (see Mita Banerjee's chapter "Postcolonial and Indigenous Authorship" and Chantal Zabus's chapter "Gender, Sexuality, and the Author: Five Phases of Authorship from the Renaissance to the Twenty-First Century"). The ways in which authors are invoked and the purposes they serve in more or less institutionalized and formalized, culture- and class-specific routines and conventions, still remain underexplored.

Finally, the choices made by authors (or the choices they ascribe to themselves or that others ascribe to them) also depend on media-historical configurations: orality or literacy, clay tablet or papyrus, manuscript or print or digital text, book or periodical. They depend, not least, on available literary forms. As Raymond Williams reminds us, "anyone who has carefully observed his [*sic*] own practice of writing eventually finds that there is a point where, although he is holding the pen or tapping the typewriter, what is being written, while not separate from him, is not only him either, and of course this other force is literary form."[22] Literary genres have their own protocols of authorial performativity, throwing into relief the manifold ways in which literary creation is enabled and constrained by existing media and publishing formats, forms, and formulae (see, amongst others, James Phelan's chapter on "Authors, Genres, and Audiences"). Finally, while authors may have (good) intentions, they cannot control what others (editors, publishers, readers' groups) will make of their texts, and they have few or no opportunities to determine where their texts will be placed in the fields of production and reception: drawer or award, backlist or bestseller list, oblivion or canon.

Expressivism, contextualism, and institutionalism as the three major strands of conceptualizing literary authorship are all, explicitly or implicitly, covered and questioned in the contributions to this volume. Their historical roots are laid open in part one; their systematic implications for literary theory and criticism are explored in part two; and their practical effects in the fields of production and reception are discussed in part three. This handbook attempts, in its first part, to map something akin to a global cultural history of the conditions that, in different circumstances, determine how writers become – or are turned into – authors; how this origin of textuality, the "zero point" of literary communication,[23] has been envisaged, understood, and constrained throughout history. The second part presents established and emerging systematic perspectives on this much-contested category of literary discourse, from rhetoric and poetics to feminist and postcolonial criticism. The third part engages with a set of concepts and problems relating to authorship in literary and scholarly practice, ranging from new methods in authorship attribution studies (computer stylistics) and scholarly textual editing to questions of publishing and marketing that influence how literary authorship "works." Authorship may well be a key category in literary creation, but it also plays – or assumptions about it play – a central role in the fields of production and reception, from antiquity to the present and, it is safe to say, the future.

Notes

1. W. K. Wimsatt and Monroe C. Beardsley, "The Intentional Fallacy," in *The Verbal Icon: Studies in the Meaning of Poetry*, ed. W. K. Wimsatt (Lexington: University of Kentucky Press, 1954), pp. 3–20; Roland Barthes, "The Death of the Author" (1967), in *Image–Music–Text*, trans. Stephen Heath (London: Fontana, 1977), pp. 142–48; Seán Burke, *The Death and Return of the Author: Criticism and Subjectivity in Barthes, Foucault and Derrida* (Edinburgh: Edinburgh University Press, 1998).

2. See James Shapiro, *Contested Will: Who Wrote Shakespeare?* (New York: Simon and Schuster, 2010).

3. Nick Cave and the Bad Seeds, "We Call Upon the Author," from the album *Dig, Lazarus, Dig!!!,* Mute, 2008.

4. Lyrics as published on www.nickcave.com/lyrics/nick-cave-bad-seeds/dig-la zarus-dig/call-upon-author/; all caps changed to lowercase letters and number of exclamation points reduced. Last accessed 4 January 2018.

5. Harold Bloom, *The Anxiety of Influence: A Theory of Poetry* (1973), 2nd edn (New York: Oxford University Press, 1997); Sandra Gilbert and Susan Gubar, *The Madwoman in the Attic: The Woman Writer and the Nineteenth-Century Literary Imagination* (1979), 2nd edn (New Haven, CT: Yale University Press, 2000). For an impressive sociological study of the "life cycle" of a novel from creation to reception, see Clayton Childress, *Under the Cover: The Creation, Production and Reception of a Novel* (Princeton, NJ: Princeton University Press, 2017), on authorship and authorial careers in the US in particular pp. 17–58.

6. Burke, *Death and Return*; see also Fotis Jannidis et al., eds., *Rückkehr des Autors: Zur Erneuerung eines umstrittenen Begriffs* (Tübingen: Niemeyer, 1999).

7. Wayne C. Booth, *The Rhetoric of Fiction* (1961), 2nd edn (Chicago: University of Chicago Press, 1983); Tom Kindt and Hans-Harald Müller, eds., *The Implied Author: Concept and Controversy*, trans. Alastair Matthews (Berlin: de Gruyter, 2006).

8. Robert Darnton, "What is the History of Books?," *Daedalus*, 111.3 (1982), 65–83.

9. For a more ambitious systematic outline, see Ingo Berensmeyer, Gert Buelens, and Marysa Demoor, "Authorship as Cultural Performance: New Perspectives in Authorship Studies," *Zeitschrift für Anglistik und Amerikanistik*, 60.1 (2012), 5–29.

10. Peter Lamarque, *The Philosophy of Literature* (Malden, MA: Blackwell, 2009), pp. 84–85.

11. Wimsatt and Beardsley, "Intentional Fallacy," p. 4.

12. Immanuel Kant, *Critique of Judgment*, §49, quoted in Lamarque, *Philosophy*, p. 87.

13. Lamarque, *Philosophy*, p. 96.

14. On the formative impact of genius discourse in Europe around 1800, see the landmark essay by Martha Woodmansee, "The Genius and the Copyright: Economic and Legal Conditions of the Emergence of the 'Author'," *Eighteenth-Century Studies*, 17.4 (1984), 425–48, and Betty Schellenberg's chapter "The Eighteenth Century" within this volume. See also Christine Haynes, "Reassessing 'Genius' in Studies of Authorship: The State of the Discipline," *Book History*, 8 (2005), 287–320.

15. On style as a personal quality – predating, in effect, Buffon's *le style c'est l'homme* – in antiquity, see Christian Badura and Melanie Möller's chapter "Authorship in Classical Rome" within this volume. On style as social relation, see Daniel Hartley, *The Politics of Style: Towards a Marxist Poetics* (Leiden: Brill, 2016).

16. Tom McCarthy, "Foreword: On Being the Subject of a Conference or, What Do I Know?", in *Tom McCarthy: Critical Essays*, ed. Dennis Duncan (Canterbury, UK: Gylphi, 2016), pp. 1–2, p. 2.

17. The term "name economy" derives from Brian Moeran, "Celebrities and the Name Economy," *Research in Economic Anthropology*, 22 (2003), 299–324. Cf. Childress, *Under the Cover*, p. 42 for the example of bestselling author James Patterson, who has "a stable of about twenty-five coauthors" and "a sixteen-person team solely dedicated to him at his publisher," allowing him to release as many as eighteen books in a single year (2015).

18. Stanley Fish, *Is There a Text in this Class? The Authority of Interpretive Communities* (Cambridge, MA: Harvard University Press, 1982).

19. See, for example, the chapter on Butler in James Loxley, *Performativity* (Abingdon: Routledge, 2007), pp. 112–138; for a more extended application of performativity theory to authorship studies, see Berensmeyer, Buelens, and Demoor, "Authorship as Cultural Performance." For a related study of (contemporary) authorial performance, inspired by Erika Fischer-Lichte's "aesthetics of the performative," see Sonja Longolius, *Performing Authorship: Strategies of "Becoming an Author" in the Works of Paul Auster, Candice Breitz, Sophie Calle, and Jonathan Safran Foer* (Bielefeld: transcript, 2016), pp. 44–50.

20. Cf. Ernest Hemingway's Nobel Prize acceptance speech (1954), as quoted in Childress, *Under the Cover*, p. 17: "Writing, at its best, is a lonely life … for [an author] does his work alone, and if he is a good enough writer he must face eternity, or the lack of it, each day." Childress rightly calls for a distinction to be made between "the physical act of writing" and "the broader practice" of writing that "snaps back and forth from the individual act [. . .] to the mutually constitutive creative actions that take place in social interactions" (p. 34). A modern institution that supports and conditions literary authorship is the university, in the form of creative writing programs; see Mark McGurl, *The Program Era: Postwar Fiction and the Rise of Creative Writing* (Cambridge, MA: Harvard University Press, 2011).

21. Cf. Carlos Spoerhase, *Autorschaft und Interpretation: Methodische Grundlagen einer philologischen Hermeneutik* (Berlin: de Gruyter, 2007).

22. Raymond Williams, "The Writer: Commitment and Alignment" (1980), in *The Raymond Williams Reader*, ed. John O. Higgins (Oxford: Blackwell, 2001), pp. 208–217, p. 216.

23. Wolfgang Iser, "Auktorialität: Die Nullstelle des Diskurses," in *Spielräume des auktorialen Diskurses*, eds. Ralph Kray and Klaus Städtke (Berlin: Akademie Verlag, 2003), pp. 219–41. On the author as "zero," see also Julia Kristeva, "Word, Dialogue and Novel," in *Desire in Language: A Semiotic Approach to Literature and Art*, ed. Leon S. Roudiez, trans. Thomas Gora, Alice Jardine, and Leon Roudiez (New York: Columbia University Press, 1980), pp. 64–91, p. 75.

PART I

Historical Perspectives

CHAPTER 2

Authorship in Cuneiform Literature

Benjamin R. Foster

The ancient Mesopotamian written culture in cuneiform script on clay tablets, beginning about 3000 BCE and disappearing in the early Christian era, offers abundant evidence for authorship, including individual strategies for remembering the names of people who composed specific literary works and statements about how, why, and when they did so.[1] These stand out because the authorship of most Mesopotamian literary and scholarly achievements was unknown in antiquity and remains so today; amidst such general anonymity some authors clearly made special efforts to ensure that their claims and experiences continued to be associated with their handiwork. A contrasting artifice, use of a pseudonym, was intended to associate a text with some notable figure of the past who had no role in its composition, even if it seems unlikely in most cases that ancient readers took such an attribution seriously. Cases of authors' anonymous self-reference and evident presence in the text may also be suggested, as well as apostrophe, or direct address of the author to the reader.

Explicit Statements of Authorship

At the beginning of any inquiry on Mesopotamian authorship is the extraordinary *oeuvre* of Enheduanna (*c.*2300 BCE), including at least three Sumerian hymn-like narrative poems, of 150 to 270 lines each, about deeds of the goddess of love and conflict, Inanna (in Semitic languages Ishtar), as well as a collection of short hymns in honor of various Sumerian sanctuaries. Enheduanna, daughter of king Sargon of Akkad and high priestess to the moon-god, Nanna-Suen, at Ur, has the distinction of being the first author in world history who can be associated with a surviving literary work. Though some scholars doubt that she really was the author of some or even any of these poems, their highly individual style, autobiographical and historical content, certain spellings and usages, and ancient subscripts to manuscripts of her works naming her as author favor ascribing at least the three long poems to her and perhaps the collection of hymns as well, though with later additions.[2]

In two of the long poems, Enheduanna introduces herself by name, in this instance, *Queen of All Cosmic Powers,* telling of her humiliation during a rebellion against her father's rule:

> Yes, I took up my place in the sanctuary dwelling,
> I was high priestess, I, Enheduanna.
> Though I bore the offering basket, though I chanted the hymns,
> A death offering was ready, was I no longer living?
> I went towards light, it felt scorching to me,
> I went towards shade, it shrouded me in swirling dust.
> A slobbered hand was laid across my honeyed mouth,
> What was fairest in my nature was turned to dirt.[3]

Disillusioned with the inaction of the deity she had served throughout her adult life, Enheduanna prays for help to Inanna-Ishtar. The angry goddess, patron of her father's dynasty, destroys her enemies, including the rebel leader, "who dared approach me in his lust." At the end of her composition, Enheduanna, restored, reveals that she felt this poem stirring inside her: "This filled me, this overflowed from me, Exalted Lady, as I gave birth for you. / What I confided to you in the dark of night, a singer shall perform in the bright of day!"[4]

The notion that a work of art could arise from intimate night-time converse of a human being with a deity was developed independently by a Babylonian poet some 1,500 years later, who likewise introduces himself by name at the end of his poem, *Erra and Ishum.*

> How it came to pass that the god Erra grew angry and set out to lay waste
>   the lands and destroy their peoples,
> But Ishum his counselor calmed him and he left a remnant,
> The composer of the text about it was Kabti-ilani-Marduk, of the family
>   Dabibi.
> He let him see it at night, and, just as he put it in words while he was
>   coming awake, he omitted nothing at all,
> Nor did he add one line to it.
> When Erra heard it he approved,
> What pertained to Ishum his vanguard satisfied him,
> All the gods praised his sign.[5]

The grammatically ambiguous statement about authorship in the fourth line most likely means that the author disclosed his idea to the god, just as Enheduanna "confided" hers to the goddess, then verbalized it, rather than that the god Erra revealed the text to the author, as some scholars believe, but the latter interpretation is by no means excluded and was advanced by the writer himself in his 1991 study of the passage (see endnote 1).

The author's self-reference in *Erra and Ishum* was likely inspired by an earlier, comparable one at the conclusion of the *Babylonian Epic of Creation*, which uses another term for "letting someone see," here translated as "revelation," but the same term for "putting in words," in this case in the presence of Marduk, the chief Babylonian deity and hero of the epic: "The revelation that the first one put in words in his presence, / He wrote it down and established it so that future generations could hear it."[6] The "first one" presumably refers to the unnamed author, the "revelation" to his vision of his poem, and "put in words" to its composition, while "established" points to the same understanding of a complete and authoritative text offered in the preceding example, with nothing added or deleted. The primary form of his poem was in writing; there is no sense of an oral original even if later generations "hear it" rather than read it silently, and this is true of most Mesopotamian literary works.[7]

Another way an author of a literary work could introduce himself into his composition was by asking for a blessing at the end, in the manner of hymns of praise or petitions to deities, which often concluded with an appeal for divine favor for a specific person. Thus the concluding lines of a hymn to the goddess of healing, Gula, beg for mercy, health, and long life for the author, Bullutsa-rabi, "meek and lowly": "Set right his confusion, illumine his darkness, / Let him strip off his mourning weeds, let him put on raiment."[8] An erudite lament about undeserved suffering, dating to the sixth century BCE, concludes in a similar vein: "(This is) the lament of the weary captive, whom a malefactor imprisoned. As he recites it to Marduk, through this lament to Marduk may he be released and may people and land behold his sublimity. (This is) the work of the weary, exhausted Nabu-shuma-ukin, son of Nebuchadnezzar, [king of Babylon]. Let them bear witness to all these misfortunes!"[9] In *The Poem of the Righteous Sufferer*, a work probably known to Nabu-shuma-ukin, the author likewise introduces himself by name in his narrative, but indirectly. In the midst of his maladies, fall from favor at court, and social ostracism, he has a dream vision of a divine exorcist come to cure his ills. This figure announces: "To Shubshi-meshre-Shakkan I have brought a swathe!"[10] This author may be identified with a Babylonian notable of that name of the early thirteenth century BCE.

Authors could also resort to acrostics to embed their names in the body of their work. *The Babylonian Theodicy*, a dialogue on divine justice in twenty-seven eleven-line stanzas, contains an acrostic at the beginning of the lines that reads, "I, Saggil-kinam-ubbub, am adorant of god and king," thereby identifying the author as a distinguished scholar at the Babylonian royal court of the eleventh century BCE, an attribution well in keeping with the recondite style and demanding poetics of the piece.[11] The limits of acrostic were probed in a pair of short prayers to the god of literate scholarship, Nabu, which contain acrostics at both the beginnings and ends of the lines. The beginnings of each line in both spell "Nabu-ushebshi the exorcist," while the ends of the first spell "The servant who proclaims your dominion" and the second "The suppliant servant who reveres you."[12] A ponderous hymn to the Babylonian god Marduk contains an acrostic on the name of the seventh-century BCE Assyrian king Assurbanipal, perhaps an adroit piece of court flattery, though the king, who boasted of his learning, may have written it himself.[13]

Self-Reference of Anonymous Authors

The rhetorical strategy whereby a poet speaks, anonymously, only the opening lines of his work, like Virgil in the *Aeneid*, is first known in Babylonian literature, as in the opening lines of *Anzu*: "The mighty one will I ever sing, divine firstborn of Enlil."[14] Some Babylonian authors, still without naming themselves, express satisfaction at the artfulness of their composition, generally toward the end, using various devices, such as grammatical ambiguity and claims for divine approval of the wording. A hymn to Ishtar, for example, asserts that its art is worthy of the god of magic and wisdom, Ea: "What she (the goddess) desires, a song about her charms, / Is indeed well suited for his (the king's) mouth, he wrought for her what Ea said. / When she (or he) heard her praises, she (or he) was well pleased with him (or it)."[15] Comparable thoughts are found in the *Agushaya* poem, addressed likewise to Ishtar: "As for the king who heard from me this song / Your praise, a sign of your valor, / Hammurabi, in whose reign this praise of you was wrought, / May he be granted everlasting life!"[16] Further in *Agushaya*, this poet returns to this theme, summarizing the story, in which Ea tames the shrewish Ishtar by creating a noxious double, Saltu, for her to contend with. This too resorts to grammatical ambiguity, so the author could be speaking in the first person or could be ascribing his poem to Ea himself:

> Let me praise Ishtar, queen of the gods . . .
> Clamorous Saltu, whom Ea the leader
> Created on account of her (Ishtar),
> The sign of her might I (or he)
> Made all the people hear.
> I (or he) have (or has) made her glorification a thing of beauty.[17]

In the following instance, from *The Babylonian Story of the Flood*, which likewise includes a short summary of the narrative, the final speech by the god of wisdom, Ea, invoking the chief god, Enlil, seems to become the author's own self-statement, thereby implicitly extolling his epic as sublime:

> "How we brought about the [flood]
> "(But) Man survived the [catastrophe] ...
> "At [your] command have I brought a [ ] to be.
> "May the lesser gods hear this my song for your praise,
> "That they extol your greatness, one to the other.
> "I have sung of the flood to all peoples,
> "Listen!"[18]

Association of the god of wisdom, Ea (Sumerian Enki), or other gods of magic, with the wording of texts is common in magic spells, which likewise may conclude with a statement that the words (and recitation) are not the work of the magician but of a god: "This spell is not mine. It is a spell of Ninkilim, master of spells."[19]

Apostrophe

Instances of implied direct address by authors to readers are largely confined to wishes for blessings, as noted above, or admonitions, as in the Babylonian *Epic of Creation*, which states of the fifty names of the god Marduk: "They must be grasped: the first one should reveal, / The wise and knowledgeable should ponder them together, / The master should repeat, and make the pupil understand ... "[20] As in the case of Kabti-ilani-Marduk, it is the author who "reveals," not a god.

An interesting, and far less common, case of interrupting a narrative flow with an abrupt address to the reader occurs in the *Etana Story*. When the perfidious eagle approaches the corpse of a wild ox in which his enemy, the serpent, is waiting for him in ambush, the poet asks, in story-telling mode: "Did the eagle know the evil in store for him? / He would not eat the meat with the other birds!"[21]

Signed Compositions

Because Mesopotamian literary works were copied and edited by scribes and their pupils over many generations, there are almost no instances of a text known as it left the hand of the author, such as would reveal whether or not authors routinely signed their own manuscripts of their works; rather, it was the scribes who signed their copies with their own names. An instance of the author's signature on a unique manuscript is a florid description of Nebuchadnezzar I's invasion of Elam on a stone monument recording a land grant to one of his officers, signed by the author, Enlil-tabni-bullit, who had every reason to be proud of his work.[22]

An autobiographical funerary statue from Alalakh clearly distinguishes the putative first-person narrator, the deceased king Idrimi, from the scribe, Sharruwa, both of whom signed the inscription at the end, with the king's last words carved so that they seem to come from the statue's mouth. The scribe signs first, with a prayer for his own wellbeing: "Sharruwa the scribe, who wrote this statue, may the gods of heaven and netherworld keep him well and watch over him ... "[23] The king's signature reads: "I was king for thirty years. I wrote my tribulations on my tablet, let them remark them and bless me in perpetuity."[24]

An alabaster slab with an inscription of the Assyrian king Tukulti-Ninurta I is signed at the top by the scribe Uprum, presumably because he composed rather than engraved it.[25] So too Nabu-shallimshunu, chief scribe of Sargon II, king of Assyria, signed the great tablet preserving his magnificent account of the eighth campaign of that king, the single most imposing relic of Assyrian commemorative prose.[26]

Pseudonymous Authorship

Complex literary problems are presented by first-person compositions, often of an autobiographical and admonitory character, somewhat in the style of a monumental inscription but written on clay tablets, in the name of famous kings of the past, including Sargon, Manishtusu, and Naram-Sin of Akkad; Shulgi of Ur, and the Kassite kings Agum-kakrime and Kurigalzu.[27] Some of these, such as the *Cruciform Monument of Manishtusu*, a unique instance engraved on stone, would be classed today as deliberate forgeries with the intent of deceit, and evidently did deceive ancient scholars who copied them as authentic relics of the past.[28] Others, such as the *Autobiography of Sargon of Akkad*, may be historical fiction, imaginative works in which the author could expect that his readers would know who the subject was, but would not necessarily believe that the first-person narrator was actually the author.[29]

Special instances are the posthumous commemorative autobiographies of Idrimi of Alalakh, discussed above, and of Adad-guppi, mother of king

Nabonidus of Babylon, carved on stone funerary stelae.[30] Both of these may belong to a North Syrian tradition of funerary monuments in which the deceased speaks in the first person, so were pseudonymous but not intended to deceive.

Divine Speech and Authorship

Mesopotamian compositions in which deities speak in the first person are variously classed today as prophecies or apocalypses.[31] These may be autobiographical, as with the *Marduk Prophecy*,[32] or may, like the *Uruk*[33] and *Dynastic Prophecy*,[34] foretell proleptically historical events that could already have occurred when the text was written. Brief exhortations purporting to be actual divine speech, communicated by ecstatics or in some cases induced by intoxicants, were reported in letters as matters of state interest, since they were typically addressed to kings, but were not otherwise written down or compiled.[35] Oracles, on the other hand, in which deities addressed Assyrian kings directly, sometimes using vivid figures of speech, were written down and preserved in collections.[36] A dialogue between a nineteenth-century BCE king of Assur, Ishme-Dagan, and the god Assur, known from a manuscript of much later date, may belong to this tradition or with the pseudonymous works mentioned above.[37] Letters purporting to be from deities are known from northern Babylonia in roughly the same period.[38]

Letters, Pseudonymous and Historical

Mesopotamian letters normally included the name of the sender and the recipient in the salutation, so they comprise a substantial corpus of material with a certain or putative author. Some are clearly pseudonymous literary works, such as spurious letters of the hero Gilgamesh[39] and of Sargon of Akkad.[40] Numerous letters purportedly written by prominent historical figures of the third to the first millennia BCE, including Sumerian, Babylonian, Assyrian, and Elamite kings, diplomats, and military officers, were copied in later times and in some cases even included in school curricula centuries after their chronological setting. These include some noteworthy for their high literary quality or their dramatic historical content. Decisions for or against their authenticity are often difficult to make. While a few such letters seem to be outright forgeries with intent to deceive, most of them present no obvious reasons for fabrication, and were perhaps copied in later times for their inherent interest.[41]

Other pseudonymous letters written for school exercises use ordinary names that may be fictitious or the names of students in class.[42] What might be called the purely literary letter – one that uses the letter form in an exaggerated manner – was cultivated in Sumerian-language schools in Babylonia in the early second millennium.[43]

Catalogs and Compilation

Mesopotamian scholars of the first millennium interested themselves in the authorship of major works of scholarship and imagination that had come to them from the past, as witnessed by an extensive but fragmentary catalog of texts and authors, known from manuscripts of the seventh century BCE and later.[44] In this, certain divinatory and exorcistic collections are attributed to the god of wisdom himself, whereas other texts, such as hymns, epics, fables, and dialogues, some unknown today, are attributed to human authors, often by name. Some of these seem improbable, such as Enmerkar, an early Sumerian king, or Adapa, an antediluvian sage. In the case of *Erra and Ishum*, the catalog agrees with what is known from the text itself, but in most other instances, even such well-known works of literature as *Etana*, the *Epic of Gilgamesh*, or *The Fox*, there is no way to know or assess the evidence for the attribution of authorship in the catalog.

From a modern perspective, certain people in the list, such as Saggil-kinam-ubbib and Sin-leqi-unninni, were not so much authors – in the sense that they created a work that had not existed before – as they were compilers or editors who integrated disparate swatches or strands of related material into a new text with such success that the resulting product was generally adopted thereafter as standard. For a scholarly reference work such as *Sa-gig*, a diagnostic medical handbook in forty tablets, Saggil-kinam-ubbib as compiler evidently made important decisions about what to include and how to order the contents, beginning with omens the physician observed on his way to the patient; next, symptoms arranged from head to foot; next, when the illness began and how long it had lasted; next, seizures and fevers; finally, pregnancy and diseases thought peculiar to women. According to a scribal note, "Concerning that which from ancient times had not had a revised text, and, taking into account the tangled strands for which no duplicates were available, ... he thought it through carefully, produced a revised text, from start to finish, and established it for knowledge."[45] The word translated here as "had a revised text" seems to mean "plaited anew" in scribal jargon, using a metaphor, like the

English word "text," based on producing cloth, thread, or rope.[46] The same figure was used by Julia Ward Howe, who, like Enheduanna and Kabti-ilani-Marduk, found inspiration in the dark, then, "in the gray of the early morning twilight," the "lines of poetry began to twine themselves together" in her mind. She "sprang out of bed" and wrote them down, thereby producing one of America's best-known songs of the nineteenth century, *The Battle Hymn of the Republic*.[47]

The memory of a singer of laments, editor, and compiler by the name of Sidu, who may have lived at Nippur near the end of the third millennium BCE, was honored in Mesopotamian scholarship well into the Hellenistic period. He was evidently associated with collections of Sumerian proverbs studied in the later second and first millennia BCE, as well as other educational texts sufficient to fill thirty-five tablets.[48]

An editorial presence comparable to that of *Sa-gig* is found in a handbook to teach Sumerian legal phraseology to Babylonian scribes called *Ana ittišu*. Some gifted editor and compiler ingeniously arranged the dry sentences into a loosely structured morality tale, in which a man marries a prostitute off the street, then divorces her, thus introducing the terminology for both marriage and divorce proceedings. The next episode introduces the formal language of adoption documents, quoted here in italics, and has a happier ending:

> After that, having taken (another) prostitute off the street, (the man) married her for love, though she was a prostitute. This prostitute had taken a baby boy off the street and had nursed him. He had no knowledge of his father or mother. (The man) was good to him, did not slap his cheek, and raised him. He taught him the scribal art, made a man of him, and found him a wife. *At any time in the future, if the son says to his father, "You are not my father," they can shave his hair to a slave lock and sell him. If the son says to his mother, "You are not my mother," they can shave half of his head, parade him around the town, then expel him from the house . . .*[49]

The case of the *Epic of Gilgamesh* has attracted much discussion both because of its strong appeal and because important changes and expansions in its structure, artistic purpose, poetics, and development of themes can be documented over its 1,500-year history.[50] Despite its complex evolution and expansion, the latest, or 12-tablet, epic shows an overall artistic unity that suggests the work of one person, identified in the ancient *Catalogue of Texts and Authors* as Sin-leqi-unninni, about whom nothing definite is otherwise known. If, for example, he wished to rework the form of the epic he knew to make it a story of gaining and transmitting knowledge, he could have added the prologue (Tablet I lines 1–28), not present in the much earlier Old Babylonian version, as well as two other important blocks of material, the story of the Flood in Tablet XI, originally a separate composition but, in the epic, retold by the flood hero himself to Gilgamesh, and the account of the netherworld in Tablet XII, a partial translation of an independent Sumerian narrative poem. Thereby, according to this reworking of the text, Gilgamesh attained the alpha and omega of human knowledge: what happened before the Flood brought about universal death and wiped out human memory, and what will happen to the individual person after he dies. To judge from the remains of the Old Babylonian version, its theme was built around Gilgamesh's quest, at once futile and heroic, to escape death, which the gods had decreed for all human beings, so a person should live well the life he is given and seek immortality through his achievements, whatever form those may take.[51]

Other works of cuneiform literature suggest, on formal or stylistic grounds, that they too were reworked and combined from disparate material. A long praise of the goddess Ishtar, *The Queen of Nippur*, for example, was evidently created by sewing together portions of originally separate compositions, in that case hymns, prayers, and litanies, into a poetic pastiche or symphony of about two hundred lines.[52]

Translations

Owing to its bilingual Sumero-Akkadian fabric, cuneiform culture afforded a special place to the art of translation. Of particular interest to an inquiry on authorship are some brilliantly executed Akkadian translations of Sumerian literary works, perhaps done in the mid-second millennium BCE. The resulting Akkadian poems are of very high literary quality and would read well independently, but were always copied with the Sumerian originals. The purpose of these translations was not so much to assist a reader who did not understand the source language as to show the virtuosity of the translator in exploiting the rich resources of the Mesopotamian lexical tradition, to the extent of constructing parallel or possible alternative understandings of the lines before him to test the wits of an educated audience schooled in Mesopotamian techniques of multileveled, associative reading and reflection. Such esteem did these superb renderings enjoy that in later periods their texts were strictly copied but the Sumerian originals were sometimes changed to fit them.[53] These show that, at its best, cuneiform translation was a kind of secondary authorship in which the translator could take pride in his art, ingenuity, and erudition and breathe new life into ancient works of literature by creating a new text from old materials.

Conclusions

Throughout its 3,000-year history, Mesopotamian literary culture engaged with authorship in different ways, drawing attention to the genesis, divine approval, composition, authority, and dissemination of specific compositions. As the examples cited here show, there was a clearly defined notion of individual inspiration and authorship, in which someone visualized a work and put it into words, as well as of a pristine text without additions or deletions that met the standards of the sublime. Authors sometimes stressed the uniqueness and production of their work as the climax of events of cosmic importance. Their authority was thereby peculiarly enhanced because the texts were part of the events they described, and they became sources of blessing, prosperity, security, and wellbeing, as well as of knowledge.

Seen in this light, the author's name can be given as a detail of the circumstances of composition, as in *Erra and Ishum,* or omitted, as in the *Epic of Creation* or the *Flood Story*. Since many texts were presented as a "sign," "praise," or "naming" of a deity, the absence of the author's name gives them the universality they would lack if they were presented as individual efforts or petitions. On the other hand, a desire to perpetuate one's name was seen as a legitimate ambition in cuneiform culture, one of the most effective strategies to achieve it being to use the power of writing to reach across space and time.[54]

Further significance of the absence of an author's name may be recognition that copier, editor, translator, performer, or auditor of a text play roles no less important than that of the author himself. Thus authors urge the importance of dissemination, performance, and understanding of what they have done. Without these, the text is lost and the author's achievement nullified. Just as the text is impossible without its initial moment of inspiration and verbal mediation, so too it is impossible without the participation of succeeding generations. Authors in Mesopotamian civilization well knew and were wont to recall in their texts that composition was an ongoing, contributive enterprise, in which the author, or "first one," was present only at the beginning.

Notes

1. Benjamin R. Foster, "On Authorship in Akkadian Literature," *Istituto Universitario Orientale di Napoli, Annali,* 51 (1991), 17–32; Jean-Jacques Glassner, "Être auteur avant Homère en Mésopotamie?", *Diogène,* 196 (2001), 111–18.

2. Annette Zgoll, *Der Rechtsfall der En-hedu-Ana im Lied nin-me-šara*, Alter Orient und Altes Testament 246 (Münster: Ugarit-Verlag, 1997), with discussion of her authorship on pp. 179–84. English translations of the long poems are in Benjamin R. Foster, *The Age of Agade: Inventing Empire in Ancient Mesopotamia* (London: Routledge, 2016), pp. 331–47. For the temple hymns, see Åke W. Sjöberg and Eugen Bergmann, *The Collection of the Sumerian Temple Hymns*, Texts from Cuneiform Sources 3 (Locust Valley, NY: J.J. Augustin, 1969); in general Joan Goodnick Westenholz, "Enheduanna, En-Priestess, Hen of Nanna, Spouse of Nanna," in *DUMU-E₂-DUB-BA-A, Studies in Honor of Åke W. Sjöberg*, eds. Hermann Behrens, Darlene Loding, and Martha T. Roth, Occasional Publications of the Samuel Noah Kramer Fund II (Philadelphia: University Museum, 1989), pp. 539–56.

3. Foster, *Age of Agade*, p. 333.

4. Ibid., p. 335.

5. Benjamin R. Foster, *Before the Muses: An Anthology of Akkadian Literature*, 3rd edn (Bethesda, MD: CDL Press, 2005), p. 910.

6. Ibid., p. 484.

7. For orality, Marianna E. Vogelzang and Herman L. Vanstiphout, eds., *Mesopotamian Epic Literature: Oral or Aural?* (Lewiston, NY: Edwin Mellen Press, 1992); for reading aloud or silently, A. K. Grayson, "Murmuring in Mesopotamia," *Wisdom, Gods and Literature: Studies in Assyriology in Honour of W. G. Lambert*, eds. A. R. George and I. L. Finkel (Winona Lake, IN: Eisenbrauns, 2000), pp. 301–8.

8. Foster, *Before the Muses*, p. 591.

9. Ibid., p. 856.

10. Ibid., p. 403; see also Benjamin R. Foster, "Self-Reference of an Akkadian Poet," *Journal of the American Oriental Society* 103 (1983): 123–30.

11. Foster, *Before the Muses*, pp. 914–22.

12. Ibid., pp. 704–5.

13. Ibid., pp. 821–26.

14. Ibid., p. 561; see also Claus Wilcke, "Die Anfänge der akkadischen Epen," *Zeitschrift für Assyriologie*, 67 (1977), 153–216.

15. Foster, *Before the Muses*, p. 87.

16. Ibid., p. 105.

17. Ibid.

18. Ibid., p. 253 (corrected).

19. Ibid., p. 77.

20. Ibid., p. 484.

21. Ibid., p. 548.

22. Ibid., pp. 383–84.

23. Gary Howard Oller, "The Autobiography of Idrimi: A New Text Edition with Philological and Historical Commentary," PhD dissertation, University of Pennsylvania, 1977, pp. 129–46; Manfred Dietrich and Oswald Loretz, "Die Inschrift der Statue des Königs Idrimi von Alalaḫ," *Ugarit-Forschungen*, 13 (1981), 201–69 (see p. 207); more recent English version in Tremper Longman, *Fictional*

Akkadian Autobiography: A Generic and Comparative Study (Winona Lake, IN: Eisenbrauns, 1991), pp. 216–18.

24. My translation, BRF. For more information, see the sources provided in note 23.
25. Ernst Weidner, "Hof- und Harems-Erlasse assyrischer Könige aus dem 2. Jahrtausend v. Chr.", *Archiv für Orientforschung*, 17 (1954–56), 257–93, p. 264.
26. Foster, *Before the Muses*, p. 813.
27. For a study of this group of texts, see Longman, *Fictional Akkadian Autobiography*.
28. Edmond Sollberger, "The Cruciform Monument," *Jaarbericht Ex Oriente Lux*, 20 (1968), 50–70.
29. Foster, *Before the Muses,* pp. 912–13.
30. Longman, *Fictional Akkadian Autobiography*, pp. 97–103.
31. Martti Nissinen, with contributions by C. L. Seow and Robert K. Ritner, *Prophets and Prophecy in the Ancient Near East*, ed. Peter Machinist (Atlanta: Society of Biblical Literature, 2003).
32. Longman, *Fictional Akkadian Autobiography*, pp. 132–42.
33. Ibid., pp. 146–49.
34. Ibid., pp. 149–52.
35. Nissinen, *Prophets and Prophecy*, pp. 13–77.
36. Ibid., pp. 97–124.
37. Eckart Frahm, *Historische und historisch-literarische Texte, Keilschrifttexte aus Assur literarischen Inhalts 3*, Wissenschaftliche Veröffentlichungen der Deutschen Orient-Gesellschaft 121 (Wiesbaden: Harrassowitz, 2009), pp. 145–51.
38. Nissinen, *Prophets and Prophecy,* pp. 93–95.
39. Foster, *Before the Muses*, pp. 113–14.
40. Ibid., pp. 1017–19.
41. Piotr Michalowski, *The Correspondence of the Kings of Ur: An Epistolary History of an Ancient Mesopotamian Kingdom* (Winona Lake, IN: Eisenbrauns, 2011); Mary Frazer, "Akkadian Royal Letters in Later Mesopotamian Tradition," PhD dissertation, Yale University, 2015.
42. Foster, *Before the Muses*, p. 225 and its companion piece, Rintje Frankena, *Altbabylonische Briefe in Umschrift und Übersetzung*, vol. 3: *Briefe aus der Leidener Sammlung* (Leiden: Brill, 1968), no. 84; see also F. R. Kraus, "Briefschreibübungen im altbabylonischen Schulunterricht," *Jaarbericht Ex Oriente Lux*, 16 (1959), 16–29.
43. Alexandra Kleinerman, *Education in Early 2nd Millennium BC Babylonia: The Sumerian Epistolary Miscellany* (Leiden: Brill, 2011).
44. Wilfred G. Lambert, "A Catalog of Texts and Authors," *Journal of Cuneiform Studies*, 16 (1962), 59–77.
45. Irving L. Finkel, "Adad-apla-iddina, Esagil-kīn-apli, and the Series SA.GIG," *A Scientific Humanist: Studies in Memory of Abraham Sachs*, eds. Erle Leichty, Maria deJ. Ellis, and Pamela Gerardi (Philadelphia: The University Museum, 1988), pp. 143–59.

46. Marten Stol, "Remarks on Some Sumerograms and Akkadian Words," *Studies Presented to Robert D. Biggs, June 4, 2004*, eds. Martha T. Roth, Walter Farber, Matthew W. Stolper, and Paula von Bechtolsheim (Chicago: The Oriental Institute, 2007), pp. 233–42, pp. 241–42 (who translates "new text"); see also Eckart Frahm, *Babylonian and Assyrian Text Commentaries: Origins of Interpretation* (Münster: Ugarit-Verlag, 2011), pp. 328–29.

47. Elaine Showalter, *The Civil Wars of Julia Ward Howe* (New York: Simon & Schuster, 2016), pp. 164–65.

48. Eckart Frahm, "The Latest Sumerian Proverbs," *Opening the Tablet Box: Near Eastern Studies in Honor of Benjamin R. Foster*, eds. Sarah Melville and Alice Slotsky (Leiden: Brill, 2010), pp. 155–84.

49. Benno Landsberger, *Die Serie ana ittišu, Materialien zum sumerischen Lexikon* 1 (Rome: Pontificium Institutum Biblicum, 1937), pp. 100–2.

50. A. R. George, *The Babylonian Gilgamesh Epic: Introduction, Critical Edition and Cuneiform Manuscripts*, 2 vols. (Oxford: Oxford University Press, 2003); Jeffrey H. Tigay, *The Evolution of the Gilgamesh Epic* (Philadelphia: University of Pennsylvania Press, 1982).

51. George, *Babylonian Gilgamesh Epic*, 1: 28–33; Herman L. J. Vanstiphout, "The Craftsmanship of Sîn-leqi-unninnī," *Orientalia Lovaniensia Periodica*, 21 (1990), 45–79.

52. Foster, *Before the Muses*, pp. 592–98.

53. Stefano Seminara, *La versione accadica del LUGAL-E: La tecnica babilonese della traduzione dal Sumerico e le sue "regole"* (Rome: Università degli Studi di Roma "La Sapienza," Dipartimento di Studi Orientali, 2001).

54. Karen Radner, *Die Macht des Namens: Altorientalische Strategien zur Selbsterhaltung*, (Wiesbaden: Harrassowitz, 2005), with discussion of authorship and signature pp. 167–69.

CHAPTER 3

Authorship in Ancient Egypt

Antonio Loprieno

Authors

Around 1200 BCE, at the height of Egyptian literary culture, a scribe named Mersekhmet wrote a school text in which he praised his own profession as the best one to reach immortality:

> Is there anyone now like Hardjedef, or another like Imhotep?
> None of our contemporaries is like Neferti or Khety, the most famous of them,
> not to speak of Ptahemdjehuty and of Khakheperraseneb!
> Is there another like Ptahhotep or someone as skilled as Kaires?[1]

If this were the only text to survive from Ancient Egypt, we would infer that the civilization behind it must have known an abundant authorial literature. We would assume that at a time preceding the redaction of this text, the mentioned individuals had established themselves as successful authors, unequalled by their followers; that Imhotep, Neferti, or Khety were the Egyptian counterparts of Dante, Shakespeare, or Cervantes. Historically sensitive interpreters would read these lines as the mirror of an Egyptian *querelle des anciens et des modernes*, of a cultural divide between classicist and modernist tendencies in the literature of that period.

The impression generated by this counterfactual scenario turns out to be both very right and very wrong. This passage provides at the same time a *fragment* and a *detail* of Egyptian authorship.[2] Read as a haphazard fragment, it gives us a distorted perspective on the relevance of individual authors (in the modern sense of this term) in Egyptian literary discourse. Egyptian literature was actually among the *least* authorial ones in human history: very few literary compositions can be ascribed to an empirically documented author. But as an encyclopedic detail of Egyptian culture, this passage summarizes in a powerful way the Egyptian view of literary authorship and its transmission in two millennia of literary activity, from about 2000 BCE to Roman times.[3]

Scribes

How do we know that this papyrus was written by Mersekhmet? Because this is what appears in the enigmatic colophon (fol. 7^r,1):

> It has come to a good end for the benefit of Horus who crosses the sky in the horizons, and Ra, the lord of heaven, great of love, and for the benefit of the scribe and draughtsman of Amun, Mersekhmet. He says: "I sing to you, drunk with your beauty, my hands on the musician's harp. I inform the singers' children how to praise the beauty of your face. Reward me with a good burial, because I am a singer who sings for you, so that I may go forth on earth as a good spirit to see the Lord of the gods."

If we continued our exercise and imagined that this colophon were the only extant one, we would be inclined to make generalizations on Egyptian literature that again turn out to be both correct and misleading. Indeed, the colophon very frequently mentions the name of the copyist who wrote down the text and sometimes its beneficiary. Mersekhmet presents himself here as the beneficiary, not as the *agent* of the writing exercise, but there can be little doubt that he was also the copyist. This colophon, however, does not appear at the end of the text, as is usually the case, but within the sequence of textual units: it marks the beginning of a religious hymn, which probably justifies the reference to the "benefit of the gods." This colophon, therefore, is both utterly idiosyncratic, placed as it is in the body of the text, and very telling, because it emphasizes the ideological connection that existed in Egypt between writing literature and seeking immortality.

Writers

So, was Mersekhmet the *copyist* or the *author* of the texts on the recto and verso of Papyrus Chester Beatty IV? This is a thorny issue. While since classical antiquity "to write" and "to copy" have been two separate activities, the best translation of the Egyptian verb *sš* "to write" would be "to write down." The Egyptian evidence does not provide an answer to the question whether the composer of an Egyptian text only wrote it *down* or also *wrote* it. We do know for sure, however, that at least in some contexts, such as the library of Qenherkhepeshef, father of Amennakht[4] (to whom we shall return below), and the *Miscellanies*, the Late Bronze Age texts used for scribal education, the writers of the manuscripts were also their owners.[5]

Unlike Western philology, where the distinction between original composition and later transmission is encyclopedically clear, Egyptian scribal practice was a continuum with blurred transitions. There were two proto-typical, but combinable modes of transmission: (a) the *productive* mode, which allowed for creative contributions to the text on the part of its subsequent authors and was typical for the transmission of literary texts; (b) the *reproductive* mode, in which the divide between "original" and "copy" was adhered to more strictly, and was more typical for religious texts.[6] The Late Period official Ibi (650 BCE) borrows textual models and con-tents from the tomb of a homonym of his who had lived in the very early Middle Bronze Age (*c*.2030 BCE) in Asyut, and invites the visitors to his tomb to do the same, i.e., to copy and transmit texts. The appeal to the living is an example of cross-fertilization between the two prototypical modes:

> If you desire some of these things, write them down on empty papyrus, so that my name may come forth. [. . .] There are many people willing to recite it to the benefit of one of them, so that a mouth can transmit the spell to another mouth when the papyrus is destroyed, and what was found may be transmitted to later times.[7]

Inspiration, Composition, Performance

The putative composer of an original text and the actual copyist who wrote it down represent the two poles of a cultural spectrum from *model authors* to *factual scribes*. Hardjedef and Khety belong to the former type: they are model authors; Mersekhmet belongs to the latter: he is a factual scribe.[8] But the contribution to the text formation provided by the various agencies is independent of their locus on this continuum: we should not assume that authors like Khety only *wrote* and scribes like Mersekhmet only *wrote down* texts. Quite to the contrary: in the instruction attributed to him, known as the "Satire of Trades," Khety praises the privileges of the scribal profession in the same vein as Mersekhmet, which leaves little doubt that the latter was the author of at least some of the compositions on Papyrus Chester Beatty IV.

It may be of interest to observe that five out of the eight names mentioned in Papyrus Chester Beatty IV are known to us through a literary text attributed to them; one (Kaires) may be the author of the *Loyalist Instructions*, and one (Imhotep) is mentioned in the Song of king Intef as author of a wisdom text. Since some of these names are also mentioned in lists of famous authors coming from Ramesside tombs,[9] we may venture to assume that our knowledge of Egyptian literature is in fact quite extensive. Egyptian culture, therefore, placed literary authors in a hierarchy of *authority* rather than of *authorship*:[10]

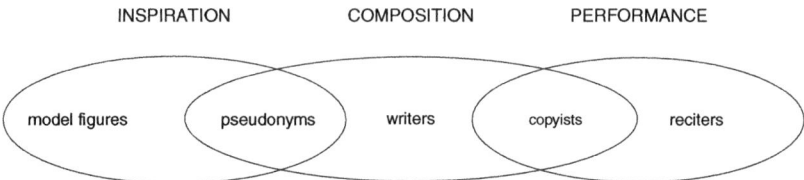

Figure 3.1 Authorship in Egyptian literature.

Between Performance and Search

Egyptian literary authors frequently appear in performative settings in which texts are publicly re-enacted.[11] Instructions display references to their oral transmission, which is also at the roots of the sequential plotlines typical for Egyptian narrative texts;[12] "story tellers" (*sḏd.w*) are mentioned as entertainers for the social elite;[13] structuring points, paragraph markers, and metric devices were used to mark the rhythm of speech;[14] stage directions such as the use of *rubra* or the remark *ḫrw-f m-mitt* "his voice should be accordingly" in the Demotic *Myth of the Sun's Eye* point to the recitation of literary texts.[15] The king appears as the addressee of performative re-enactment, as in the complaints of the *Eloquent Peasant*, whose petitions for justice were secretly recorded in order to be read aloud and stored for him:

> Then the high steward Rensi, son of Meru, said: "Don't be afraid, peasant! I will take care of this matter of yours." But this peasant swore an oath: "I will never again eat your bread and drink your beer forever!" The high steward Rensi, son of Meru, said: "Now wait here and hear your petitions!" And he had every petition read along from a new papyrus roll according to its content. Then the high steward Rensi, son of Meru, delivered them to the now deceased majesty of the king of Upper and Lower Egypt Nebkaure, and they pleased his heart more than anything in this entire land.[16]

On the other end of the continuum we find a non-performative, philosophical literature, of which *Khakheperreseneb* is probably the most explicit representative. He claims that an author should not use the ancestors' words, but try to formulate new ideas that have not been repeated (*wḥm*) before:

A collection of words, a gathering of verses, a quest for utterances with heart searching, made by the priest of Heliopolis, Seni's son Khakheperreseneb, called Ankhu. He says: "Had I only unknown utterances and unexpected verses, in a new language that is not ephemeral, free from repetition and trite speech already spoken by the ancestors! I shall press my body for what is in it and let all my speech free. For what is already said can only be repeated, what is said once has already been said; I shall not make a boast of the ancestors' words that those who come later should also find it good."[17]

Khakheperreseneb may also be the author of a lament in which a man dialogues with his own *Ba*,[18] and is arguably the only representative of an approach to authorship in which writing a text involves creating something *new*. For the vast majority of literati, whether in the context of entertainment (*shmḫ-ib* "pleasing the heart") or of intellectual endeavor (*ḥḫj n ib* "heart searching"), the ultimate goal of literature was to "repeat" the past and foresee the future. Literary texts can be arranged along the two axes of the "event" they elaborate on and of the authorial attitude toward the writing exercise ("heart"):[19]

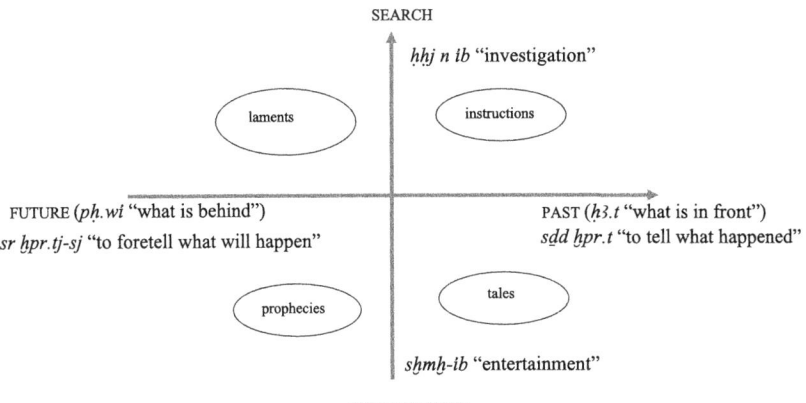

Figure 3.2 Textual "genres" in Egyptian literature.

To emphasize the performative context of Egyptian literary activity means to reacquire consciousness of the fact that language is primarily intended to be spoken, not to be written or read.[20] Egyptian literati were far more conscious than we are of the "pontifical," bridging character of writing at the crossroads of representing language and reproducing reality.[21]

Ethics and Authorship

In general terms, Egyptian literature is more interested in social values than in individual feelings. This is the reason why the "instruction" (*sb3y.t*) is both the most homogeneous "genre" of Egyptian literature until the end of Egyptian literary activity and the only one to guarantee authorial immortality: in the lists of model authors we do not find protagonists of tales.

The ethical ideals transmitted by secular authors are paralleled by the general principle, conveyed in religious texts, of upholding Maat (*m3ᶜ.t* "truth, justice").[22] The overlapping of practical ethics, loyal service to the king, and moral religion is a foundational element of Egyptian scribal education, which can be observed in sources such as the *Loyalist Instructions*, whose model author might be the Kaires mentioned in Papyrus Chester Beatty IV.[23] Here, the tension between borrowing an encyclopedic topic and striving for individual immortality is evident: Sehetepibre, an official of the Middle Kingdom (*c.*1850 BCE), presents himself on his stela (CG 20538) as the author of the text, which is documented during the eighteenth dynasty until its final elaboration in the Ramesside era (*c.*1200 BCE):

> He says as an instruction to the address of his children:
> Let me say something great, and you should listen,
> since I let you know the manner of eternity,
> a matter of living in truth and of proceeding to the blessed condition.[24]

Literary Theory

In the late twentieth century, Egyptology became interested in the features of Egyptian literature as autonomous cultural discourse.[25] Before then, literature in the sense of "fiction" was taken to be alien to a civilization whose texts were read as religious and political institutions or as educational tools for the palace and temple elites.

In an epochal article of 1974, Jan Assmann identified "situational abstractness," i.e., the lack of an immediate functional embeddedness, as the main criterion justifying the attribution of a text to literary discourse.[26] His research inaugurated the scholarly interest for literary theory, mainly within three methodological paradigms:

(1) models drawn from linguistics and semiotics were adopted to determine the formal features of Egyptian literary discourse as opposed to functionally bounded text types;[27]

(2) anthropologically leaning interpretive strategies stressed the impor-
     tance of the visual component and the societal conventions of
     Egyptian literacy;[28]

(3) close readings of Egyptian literary texts devoted particular attention
     to the role of literature as cultural discourse, particularly in the vein of
     New Historicism.[29]

Directly or indirectly, all these approaches questioned the traditional view
of Egyptian literary transmission, which had assumed that Middle
Kingdom authors of instructional texts (*sb3.yt*) such as Ptahhotep or
Khakheperreseneb were read (and misread) in later periods from manuscripts displaying a number of philological mistakes. This linear view is
now no longer tenable without adjustments: contextual as well as linguistic
features suggest that many Egyptian literary texts were composed later than
the period they refer or are ascribed to.[30] Did a factual author named
Ptahhotep ever exist, or is this a *pseudonym* in the vein of the apocryphal
attribution of the Psalms to David and the Proverbs to Solomon?[31] Does
the language of literary texts in classical Egyptian reflect the time of
composition or the form it had acquired at the time of its *redaction*?
Do the plots of *belles lettres* (instructions and tales) echo real historical
events or are they the result of fictional inventiveness?[32] These questions
eschew empirically robust answers: it is only possible to answer them
within the interpreter's own perspective on Egyptian culture.

   In the last fifteen years, to adopt Paul Ricœur's terminology, Egyptian
literary theory has privileged a hermeneutics of *faith* in restoring meaning to
a text over a hermeneutics of *suspicion* in search of disguised meanings.[33]
We can observe on the one hand a return to a meticulous study of the
sources that circumvents purely theoretical issues, the claim being that
a better philological competence can help us avoid the sweeping generalizations of cultural studies. On the other hand, there is an increased interest
in a micro-historical approach to Egyptian literary authorship[34] and to the
contexts of its transmission.[35] To what extent can we recognize true people's
lives behind the names carried by the human agencies of Egyptian literature, especially in view of the very limited number of historical and
geographic contexts that provide a relevant amount of data?[36]

Simulation

While disagreement remains on whether "fiction" and "fictionality" are
relevant categories for Egyptian literature, forty years of Egyptian literary

studies have brought about the consensus that studying Egyptian author-ship automatically entails assumptions about the readership,[37] and that the transmission of literature coincided to a large extent with the transmission of the cultural encyclopedia (or "memory").[38]

Whether in the context of education or of performance, the functional boundedness displayed by Egyptian texts is much higher than in modern literary traditions. This makes the concept of *simulation* a better candidate than *fiction* to describe the relation between Egyptian authors and their real-world experiences.[39] While there is a semantic connection between the two concepts, "fiction" is usually associated with literary creativity, whereas "simulation" is also applied to the scientific visualization and representa-tion of real-world features. By providing visual or mental pictures of real-world settings (both in the visual and in the mental sense of the German word *Bild*), simulation mobilizes emotions by making proximal, and therefore more believable, what is otherwise only representable in a distal, intellectual way. The Egyptian lector-priest, story-teller, or author of instructions simulate real-world events and states, which places them at the crossroads of scholarship and art.[40]

Early Bronze Age (2250–2000 BCE)

The first context of Egyptian literature is the funerary cult. In the ancient world, weddings and festivals were more likely literary settings than fun-erals – one need only think of the biblical Song of Songs. But in Ancient Egypt, the relation between literature and immortality is so intense that the tomb can be seen as the "cradle" of Egyptian literature.[41] The first Egyptian texts to be ascribed to a personal author are autobiographical narratives inscribed on the external walls of Early Bronze Age tombs. Officials such as Herkhuf (*c.*2200 BCE) emphasize the link between following the king, achieving career goals, and reaching immortality, occasionally by reprodu-cing a royal letter or decree to support their claims:

> The Royal seal bearer, Sole Friend, lector-priest, chief of scouts Herkhuf: I have come here from my city, I have descended from my province; I have built a house, set up its doors, I have dug a pool and planted sycamores. The king praised me, my father made a will for me. [...]

> "The King's own seal: year 2, third month on the Inundation, day 15. The king's decree to the Sole Friend, lector-priest, chief of scouts Herkhuf. [...] You say in your present dispatch that you have brought all kinds of great and beautiful gifts, which Hathor mistress of Imaau has given to the benefit of king Neferkare, who lives forever. You say in your present

dispatch that you have also brought a pygmy for the god's dances from the land of the horizon-dwellers, like the pygmy brought from Punt by the god's seal bearer Bawerded at the time of king Isesi. [. . .] His Majesty will provide you many worthy honors for the benefit of your son's son for all time, so that all people may say when they hear what my Majesty did for you: Does anything equal what was done for the Sole Friend Herkhuf when he returned from Yam?"[42]

The autobiography, which combines fictional and functional aspects, eventually becomes the most durable textual genre known from Ancient Egypt.[43] It represents the Egyptian form of the "speaking objects" we find at the origin of literary activity in societies with a low degree of literacy, e.g., in archaic Italy or pre-Roman Gaul.[44] The speaking agency is here the tomb itself, which lends credibility to the posthumous authorship by the tomb owner.

Belles Lettres during the Middle Bronze Age (2000–1500 BCE)

The next step in the evolution of authorship is the appearance in funerary contexts of "harpers' songs"[45] whose pseudonymous authors held an Epicurean world view and were clearly viewed by later generations as model authors in the literary tradition, as in the *Harper's Song from the Tomb of King Intef*:

> Song in the tomb of king Intef, justified, in front of the harper: "This good prince is indeed happy, whereas death is a kindly fate. A generation passes, another stays, since the time of the ancestors. The gods who were before rest in their tombs, and also blessed nobles are buried in their tombs. Yet those who built tombs – their places are gone: what has become of them?
> I have heard the words of Imhotep and Hordjedef, whose sayings are recited completely. What of their places? Their walls have crumbled, their places are gone, as though they had never been! None comes back from there to tell of their needs and to calm our hearts, until we go where they have gone! Hence rejoice in your heart!"[46]

A further Middle Bronze Age innovation is the emergence of literary narratives whose protagonists bear fictitious names such as *Sinuhe* ("son of the sycamore," a name with many phonetic and semantic associations) or *Chuienanup* ("protected by Anubis," the god who grants immortality).[47] Some of these protagonists are presented as *nḏs.w* "lower-class people" in spite of their intellectual achievements. Here is how the lector-priest Neferti, one of the model authors in Papyrus Chester Beatty IV, is presented in a prophecy from the early eighteenth dynasty (*c.*1500 BCE):

Once upon a time, the majesty of king Snefru, justified, was the beneficent king in our entire country. One of those days, the magistrates of the residence entered the palace to offer greetings. [. . .] Then they said to his majesty: "There is a famous lector-priest of Bastet, o king our lord, whose name is Neferti. He is a lower class man (*nds*) with strong arm, a scribe of excellent fingers, a man of greater wealth than any of his peers. Let him be brought to your majesty and see for yourself." His majesty said: "Go and bring him to me." He was brought in to him at once and he prostrated before his majesty. His majesty said: "Come Neferti, my friend, speak to me fine words (*mdw.t nfr.t*), well-chosen phrases likely to entertain my majesty when I hear them." The lector-priest Neferti said: "Of what has already happened or of what will eventually happen, o king, my lord?" His majesty said: "Of what will happen, because as soon as the present comes, it's already gone."[48]

The name Neferti is full of connotations, derived as it is – like the king's name Snefru – from the root *nfr* "good, fine," which is found in the expression *mdw.t nfr.t* "belles lettres." The fictitious lower status of its authors and practitioners allows literature to convey universal values not necessarily linked to specific people or events.[49] With the appearance of *nds.w* protagonists,[50] who in spite of their elusiveness at the micro-historical level are the mirror of sociopolitical changes retraceable in the archaeological record,[51] Egyptian culture comes closer to our own understanding of literature, in which authors are the intellectual owners of their writings.[52] The underlying message is clear: social capital does not derive from a higher status, but rather from cultural competence.

In Middle Bronze Egypt, literature as a body of "cultural texts" at the intersection of scholarship and enactment also provides an encyclopedia that applies to literacy in general: it establishes written models for historical sequencing and causal intelligibility. The distinction between the literary (word-referential) and the non-literary (world-referential) domain, therefore, is blurred.[53] The figure of the literary author is not distinct from the figure of the writer of historical or religious texts, because the same logic of organization of discourse underlies all written genres. What defines literary production is a specific cultural *context*, not a dedicated *poetics*: the literary author is the person who is able to catch the main features of the *Zeitgeist* and at the same time transcend it by making it timeless, i.e., open to reception.

The Personalizing Turn in the Late Bronze Age (1350–1150 BCE)

The Late Bronze Age displays a "personalizing turn" in literature and religion. After Akhenaten had stressed the transcendence and the universality of the sun god, Ramesside Egypt experienced a privatization of religious and literary activity and saw the birth of a new type of authorship, less dependent on pseudonymity. In the *sb3y.t* the authorial name can be substituted by the prototypical nameless *si* "man" (BM 10258, 1):[54] "Beginning of the instruction made by a man for his son. He says: hear my voice, do not avoid my words, do not untie your heart from what I tell you." In the sphere of religion, individual piety adds an emotional and poetic dimension to textual genres such as the autobiography or the letter to the dead. At Thebes around 1250 BCE, Samut ("son of Mut") decided to become a devotee of the goddess Mut and to confide only in her:

> There was a man of southern Heliopolis, a true scribe in Thebes, whose name from his mother was Samut, called Kiki, justified. Now his god noticed him and instructed him about his wisdom; he placed it on the path of life in order to protect his body. The god knew him as a child and he was given abundance and prosperity. He then pondered deeply within himself to find himself a protector and found Mut to be ahead of the other gods: destiny and fate are in her hand, as are also the lifetime and the breath of life. All that happens is under her control. So, he said: "Now, I want to give her all my property and all the produce I have created, because I know that she is effective on my behalf and that only she is excellent. She took my anguish away from me, she protected me in the difficult moments, and whenever I call her name, she comes preceded by the north wind. I am a weakling of her town, a pauper and a beggar of her city, I achieved my goods thanks to her strength, in return for the breath of life. None of my family shall inherit a part of it, for they are reserved as offerings for her *ka*."[55]

At approximately the same time, at Memphis, a widower writes to his deceased wife Ankhiry who appears to him in nightmares, indirectly accusing him of having an affair:

> I am sending you this letter to let you know what you are doing. When you began to suffer from the disease you had, I had a head physician come. He treated you and did everything you asked him to do. When I followed Pharaoh to the south, and then you died, I spent no less than eight months without eating or drinking as a man should do. [. . .] And see, I passed three years until now living alone, without entering any house, although it is not fair that someone like me should be made to do so. But I did it for you, you who does not discern good from bad! One shall judge between you and me. And something else: I have not had sexual intercourse with any of the girls in the house![56]

Therefore, in addition to the model authors of the classical literature in Middle Egyptian, typically transmitted in schools, Late Bronze Age Egypt also knows what Aulus Gellius would call "proletarian" authors, who write in (more vernacular) Late Egyptian and address not so much societal expectations but rather individual experiences.[57] Middle Bronze paradigms are adapted to the individual sphere, as in the fictitious letter of the scribe and draughtsman Menna to his son Pairi,[58] which combines the lament (itself at the crossroads of secular literature and funerary religion),[59] the instruction, and the tale, and echoes the *Shipwrecked Sailor*.

> The draughtsman Menna says to his son and helper, the scribe Pairi: a storm was forecast to you before it came, you shipman of pitiful landing! I have presented to you many words, but look, you simply do not listen! [. . .] People say that if a son listens to his father, this is a great teaching for eternity. But look, you have followed none of the instructions I gave you earlier. [. . .] You are not in your senses, you sea vagabond![60]

Classical paradigms are now challenged in the wake of individual skepticism. Unlike Sinuhe's edifying exile, which ends in his rehabilitation, Wermai's exile in the *Tale of Woe* is only a cause of distress:

> If only there was a piece of news that would let me breathe a sigh of relief, after I have been stranded in injustice! Nobody asked me how I felt after my erring to and fro. Once flesh and bones are lying on the edge of the desert, who will cover them for protection? No news can gladden my heart. Not the dead, not the living: nobody asks after me in my misfortune. But what does this mean when I enter the realm of the dead and find myself in the presence of the god of the horizon?[61]

At the same time, the Late Bronze Age provides more empirical evidence of authorship, which was very elusive in earlier periods. The most tangible example of a micro-historically retrievable Egyptian author is the scribe Amennakht, who lived in Deir el-Medina around 1150 BCE and inherited his father Qenherkhepeshef's monumental library.[62] He personifies the broad spectrum of literary activity in Ramesside Egypt, being the author of a sizable body of administrative and juridical documentation as well as a diverse range of literary texts from instructions to religious and royal hymns. His most famous text is a *sbꜣy.t* from an ostracon in the British Museum:

> Beginning of the Instruction, the verses for the way of life, made by the scribe Amennakht for his apprentice Hormin. He says: "You are a man who listens to a speech to separate good from evil. Attend and hear my speech! Do not neglect what I say! It is very pleasant for a man to be

recognized as someone competent in every work. Let your heart become like a great dyke, beside which the flood is mighty. [...] You shall be a scribe and go around the House of Life – this is how one can become like a chest of writings![63]

Amennakht was also the author of lyrical poetry, a further Ramesside development (ostracon Gardiner 25), and may even be the author of the eulogy of past authors on Papyrus Chester Beatty IV.[64] In this respect, figures such as Amennakht or his colleagues Hori,[65] who operated at the cultural crossroads of creative composition and reproductive redaction, are probably the first *authors* of Egyptian literature in the modern sense of the word.

The End of a Historical Cycle

In the Iron Age, Egypt shares the literary patterns of other regions of the Mediterranean world, but the documentation of literary activity decreases dramatically, due to a decline of the knowledge of classical authors and a resilience of literary texts in later Egyptian.[66] In general, the trend toward the privatization of literary discourse is continued.[67] In the wisdom of *Ankhsheshonqy*, a literary text that embeds a *sb3y.t* into a narrative of kingly favors and human loyalty,[68] writing an instructional text is claimed to be the surrogate for the physical absence of the son as ideal addressee of its original oral performance. But the narrative presents the king as the covert addressee of the literary text – a rhetorical device that points at enactment and reminds us of the Middle Kingdom tale of *Eloquent Peasant*:

> After this, Pharaoh's accession-day occurred and Pharaoh released everyone who was in prison at Daphnae except Ankhsheshonqy son of Tjainefer. His heart sank because of this and he said to the staff-bearer assigned to him: "Please do me a favor and have a palette and a scroll be brought to me, for I have a boy whom I have not yet been able to instruct. I shall write a *sb3y.t* for him and have it taken to Heliopolis to instruct him with it." The staff-bearer said: "I want to report it to Pharaoh first." The staff-bearer reported it to Pharaoh first, and Pharaoh ordered: "Have a palette be taken to him, do not have a scroll be taken to him." [...] Here follow the words that Ankhsheshonqy son of Tjainefer wrote on the jar sherds that were brought to him containing mixed wine, so as to give them as an instruction to his son, and which were reported before Pharaoh and his great men daily.[69]

While already known in the classical period, e.g., in the *Shipwrecked Sailor*, the literary device of the story within a story becomes very frequent in

Demotic literature.[70] Occasionally, the authorship of a nested story is explicitly mentioned, as in the following passage from the *Story of Peteese*:

> He let his son Ptahnefer come to Teudjoi. They signed over to him the portion of the prophet of Amen. The priests took the other 16 portions. They distributed them among the phyles. They amounted to four portions for every phyle. The treasurer said to me: "The tales you are telling me are numerous. Please, go into the house. Have Sematawitaiefnakht give you a sheet of papyrus. Write down everything that has happened to your forefathers since the day when this portion was in their possession! Write down how it and these other portions were taken from your father. Write down the events which have happened to you until today."[71]

With the last author of Egyptian literature, Taimhotep, who was a contemporary of Cleopatra VII, we are taken back to its cradle in the funerary context and to the entire history of Egyptian authorship. Her laments are embedded into an autobiographical narrative that echoes the motives of classical *belles lettres* as well as those of Hellenistic literatures. Only the colophon displays a modern awareness of the difference between commissioning and composing a literary text:

> Year 10, day 16 of Mekhir was the day of my death. My husband [. . .] the high priest Psherenptah brought me to the West. He performed for me all the rites for a worthy deceased. [. . .] O my brother, my husband, friend and high priest! Do not weary of drink and food, of drinking deep and loving! Celebrate the holiday, follow your heart day and night, do not let your heart be troubled, but value the years spent on earth! [. . .] As for death, its name is "it comes": all those that it calls come to it at once, their hearts afraid through dread of it. Neither gods nor men can look at it, yet great and small are in its hand, nobody can restrain its finger from his own kin. [. . .] You all who come to this tomb, give me incense on the flame and water on every feast of the West!
>
> The scribe, sculptor and scholar, the initiate of the House of Gold in Tenent, the prophet of Horus, Imhotep, son of the prophet Khahapi, made this stela.[72]

I shall now follow Taimhotep's model and end this study of Egyptian authorship with a colophon in Egyptian style: "So it came to an end from Imhotep, the mythical authorial figure on Papyrus Chester Beatty IV, to Imhotep, the factual author of a biographical text from the Roman period." The study of Egyptian authorship remains the study of its elusiveness.

Notes

1. Papyrus Chester Beatty IV, fol. 3ᵛ, 5–6; Alan H. Gardiner, *Hieratic Papyri in the British Museum, Third Series: Chester Beatty Gift. Vol. 1: Text* (London: British Museum, 1935), pp. 28–44. Translations are my own unless otherwise stated.
2. For the difference between *fragment* and *detail*, cf. Omar Calabrese, *Neo-Baroque: A Sign of the Times* (Princeton: Princeton University Press, 1992), pp. 72–73.
3. For the New Kingdom and the Late Period, cf. especially Richard B. Parkinson, *Reading Ancient Egyptian Poetry, Among Other Histories* (Chichester, UK: Wiley-Blackwell, 2009), pp. 173–218. The archive of Tebtunis from Roman times also contained a number of tales and teachings, two literary genres that had emerged during the Middle Bronze Age: Friedhelm Hoffmann and Joachim Quack, *Anthologie der demotischen Literatur* (Münster: LIT, 2007), p. 239; Kim Ryholt, *Narrative Literature from the Tebtunis Temple Library* (Copenhagen: CNI, 2012).
4. Parkinson, *Reading Ancient Egyptian Poetry*, pp. 188–90.
5. Ludwig D. Morenz, "Egyptian Life, by and with Literary Texts," in *Ancient Egyptian Literature: Theory and Practice*, eds. Roland Enmarch and Verena M. Lepper (Oxford: Oxford University Press, 2013), pp. 227–50, esp. p. 234.
6. Jochem Kahl, *Siut-Theben. Zur Wertschätzung von Traditionen im Alten Ägypten* (Leiden: Brill, 1999), pp. 283–355.
7. Klaus Kuhlmann and Wolfgang Schenkel, *Das Grab des Ibi. Theben Nr. 36* (Mainz: Philipp von Zabern, 1983), p. 72, pl. 23.
8. For a discussion of these two poles of literary composition, cf. Morenz, "Egyptian Life," pp. 233–41.
9. Jan Assmann, *The Mind of Egypt. History and Meaning in the Time of the Pharaohs* (Cambridge, MA: Harvard University Press, 2003), pp. 276–77.
10. Pascal Vernus, *Sagesses de l'Égypte pharaonique* (Arles: Actes Sud, 2010), pp. 17–22.
11. Christopher J. Eyre, "The Practice of Literature: The Relationship between Content, Form, Audience, and Performance," in *Ancient Egyptian Literature*, eds. Enmarch and Lepper, pp. 101–42; for the role of recitation (*šdj*) cf. Erika Meyer-Dietrich, "Recitation, Speech Acts, and Declamation," in *UCLA Encyclopedia of Egyptology*, ed. Willeke Wendrich (Los Angeles: UCLA, 2010), http://digital2.library.ucla.edu/viewItem.do?ark=21198/zz00252xth.
12. Mark Collier, "The Language of Literature: On Grammar and Texture," *Ancient Egyptian Literature: History and Forms*, ed. Antonio Loprieno (Leiden: Brill, 1996), pp. 531–36.
13. Ipuwer, 4,12–13: Richard B. Parkinson, *Poetry and Culture in Middle Kingdom Egypt* (London/New York: Continuum, 2002), p. 78. The words *sḏd-i* introduce the narrative section of the *Shipwrecked Sailor*.

14. Papyrus Ramesseum II: Ludwig Morenz, *Beiträge zur Schriftlichkeitskultur im Mittleren Reich und in der 2. Zwischenzeit* (Wiesbaden: Harrassowitz, 1996), p. 38.

15. Danijel Cubelic, Julia Lougovaya, and Joachim Friedrich Quack, "Rezitieren, Vorlesen und Singen," in *Materiale Textkulturen*, eds. Thomas Meier, Michael R. Ott, and Rebecca Sauer (Berlin and Boston: De Gruyter, 2015), pp. 651–63.

16. Richard B. Parkinson, *The Tale of the Eloquent Peasant* (Oxford: Griffith Institute, 1991), B2, 122–32; cf. Fredrik Hagen, "Constructing Textual Identity: Framing and Self-Reference in Egyptian Texts," *Ancient Egyptian Literature*, eds. Enmarch and Lepper, pp. 185–209, esp. pp. 186–89.

17. BM 5645 I, 1–4; Richard B. Parkinson, "The Text of 'Khakheperreseneb': New Readings of EA 5645, and an Unpublished Ostracon," *Journal of Egyptian Archaeology* 83 (1997), pp. 55–68.

18. Christophe Barbotin, "Le dialogue de Khâkheperrêseneb avec son Ba," *Revue d'Égyptologie*, 63 (2012), 1–20.

19. Cf. Morenz, "Egyptian Life," pp. 227–50.

20. Jonathan Culler, *Literary Theory: A Very Short Introduction* (Oxford: Oxford University Press, 1997), p. 9. The most forceful reconstruction of the performative context of Egyptian literature is Parkinson, *Reading Ancient Egyptian Poetry*, pp. 41–68.

21. Antonio Loprieno, "Vom Schriftbild," in *Bild Macht Schrift. Schriftkulturen in bildkritischer Perspektive*, eds. Antonio Loprieno, Carsten Knigge Salis, and Birgit Mersmann (Weilerswist: Velbrück Wissenschaft, 2011), pp. 15–36; John Baines, *Visual and Written Culture in Ancient Egypt* (Oxford: Oxford University Press, 2007), pp. 117–45.

22. Nikolaos Lazaridis, "Ethics," in *UCLA Encyclopedia of Egyptology*, eds. Elizabeth Frood and Willeke Wendrich (Los Angeles: UCLA, 2008). http://digital2.libray.ucla.edu/viewItem.do?ark=21198/zz000s3mhn

23. Ursula Verhoeven, "Von der 'Loyalistischen Lehre' zur 'Lehre des Kairsu'," *Zeitschrift für ägyptische Sprache und Altertumskunde*, 136 (2009), 87–98.

24. Georges Posener, *L'enseignement loyaliste. Sagesse égyptienne du Moyen Empire* (Geneva : Droz, 1976).

25. Verena M. Lepper and Roland Enmarch, "Theory and Practice in Ancient Egyptian Literature," in *Ancient Egyptian Literature*, eds. Enmarch and Lepper, pp. 1–8.

26. Jan Assmann, "Der literarische Text im Alten Ägypten. Versuch einer Begriffsbestimmung," *Orientalistische Literaturzeitung*, 69 (1974), 117–26.

27. Gerald Moers, *Fingierte Welten in der ägyptischen Literatur des 2. Jahrtausends v. Chr.* (Leiden: Brill, 2001), pp. 1–17.

28. Baines, *Visual and Written Culture*, esp. pp. 3–30.

29. Parkinson, *Poetry and Culture*, pp. 22–42.

30. Andrea M. Gnirs, "Das Motiv des Bürgerkriegs in Merikare und Neferti. Zur Literatur der 18. Dynastie," *Jn.t ḏr.w. Festschrift für Friedrich Junge*, eds. Gerald Moers et al. (Göttingen: Seminar für Ägyptologie und Koptologie,

2006), pp. 207–65, esp. p. 214; for the linguistic argument, cf. Andréas Stauder, *Linguistic Dating of Middle Egyptian Literary Texts* (Hamburg: Widmaier Verlag, 2013), pp. 3–55.

31. John Barton, "Intentio operis: Reading Anonymous Texts," in *Ancient Egyptian Literature*, ed. Enmarch and Lepper, pp. 11–23.

32. In Egyptian literature, the reference to previous historical periods is highly ideological and exhibits only marginal connections with real-life events: cf. Antonia Giewekemeyer, "Perspektiven und Grenzen der Nutzung literarischer Texte als historische Quellen," in *Dating Egyptian Literary Texts*, eds. Gerald Moers et al. (Hamburg: Widmaier Verlag, 2013), pp. 285–365.

33. Culler, *Literary Theory*, p. 61; Ruthellen Josselson, "The Hermeneutics of Faith and the Hermeneutics of Suspicion," *Narrative Inquiry*, 14 (2004), 1–28.

34. Juan Carlos Moreno Garcia, "Microhistory," in *UCLA Encyclopedia of Egyptology*, eds. Wolfram Grajetzki and Willeke Wendrich (Los Angeles: UCLA, 2018). http://digital2.library.ucla.edu/viewItem.do?ark=21198/zz002kczsg

35. Parkinson, *Reading Ancient Egyptian Poetry*, pp. 219–78.

36. Henrike Simon, "Literatur im Alten Ägypten," in *Grenzen der Literatur*, eds. Simone Winko, Jannidis Fotis and Gerhard Lauer (Berlin: De Gruyter, 2009), pp. 516–544, esp. p. 531.

37. "The author as (re-)productive reader": Morenz, "Egyptian Life," pp. 245–48; Camilla Di Biase-Dyson, *Foreigners and Egyptians in the Late Egyptian Stories* (Leiden: Brill, 2009), pp. 33–42.

38. Aleida Assmann, "Was sind kulturelle Texte?" in *Literaturkanon, Medienereignis, kultureller Text*, ed. Andreas Poltermann (Berlin: Erich Schmidt Verlag 1995), pp. 232–44.

39. Hagen, "Constructing Textual Identity," pp. 186–89; Antonio Loprieno, *Von Fiktion und Simulation als kognitiven Übergängen* (Basel: Schwabe, 2011).

40. Eyre, "The Practice of Literature," pp. 130–36.

41. Jan Assmann, "Schrift, Tod und Identität. Das Grab als Vorschule der Literatur im alten Ägypten," *Schrift und Gedächtnis: Archäologie der literarischen Kommunikation 1*, eds. Aleida Assmann et al. (Munich: Fink, 1983), pp. 64–93.

42. Urk. I, 121–129; Kurt Sethe, *Urkunden des Alten Reiches* (Leipzig: Hinrichs, 1933), pp. 120–31.

43. Elizabeth Frood, *Biographical Texts from Ramessid Egypt* (Atlanta, GA: Society of Biblical Literature, 2007), pp. 2–29.

44. https://it.wikipedia.org/wiki/Testi_latini_arcaici; Pierre-Yves Lambert, *La langue gauloise* (Paris: Errance, 2003), p. 126.

45. Eyre, "The Practice of Literature," pp. 113–22. The literary character of this genre is signaled by the use of hieratic, as opposed to hieroglyphs, to reproduce the harper's song in TT 60: Norman de Garis Davies and A. H. Gardiner, with Nina de Garis Davis, *The Tomb of Antefoker, Vizier of*

Sesostris I, and of his Wife, Senet (No. 60) (London: George Allen & Unwin, 1920), p. 23, pls. xxvii and xxix.

46. Papyrus Harris 500 vi, 2–vii, 3; Miriam Lichtheim, "The Songs of the Harpers," *Journal of Near Eastern Studies*, 4 (1945), 178–212.

47. For a study on Sinuhe's authorship and composition, see Parkinson, *Reading Ancient Egyptian Poetry*, pp. 113–137; for the name Sinuhe, see Edmund S. Meltzer, "In Search of Sinuhe: What's in a Name?" (2007), www .academia.edu/8429555/In_Search_of_Sinuhe_Whats_in_a_Name.

48. Papyrus St. Petersburg 1116B; Wolfgang Helck, *Die Prophezeiung des Nfr.tj* (Wiesbaden: Harrassowitz, 1970).

49. Parkinson, *Poetry and Culture*, p. 76.

50. Stephen Quirke, "Who Writes the Literary in Late Middle Kingdom Lahun?" in *Problems of Canonicity and Identity Formation in Ancient Egypt and Mesopotamia*, eds. Kim Ryholt and Gojko Barjamovic (Copenhagen: CNI, 2016), pp. 127–52.

51. Juan Carlos Moreno Garcia, "Climatic Change or Sociopolitical Transformation? Reassessing Late 3rd Millennium Egypt," in *2200 BC: A Climatic Breakdown as the Cause for the Collapse of the Old World?*, eds. Harald Meller et al. (Halle: Landesmuseum für Vorgeschichte, 2015), pp. 79–94.

52. Morenz, "Egyptian Life," pp. 233–34.

53. Hagen, "Constructing Textual Identity," p. 205.

54. Hans-Werner Fischer-Elfert, *Die Lehre eines Mannes für seinen Sohn* (Wiesbaden: Harrassowitz, 1994), p. 24.

55. TT 409; Pascal Vernus, "Littérature et autobiographie. Les inscriptions de *S3-Mwt* surnommé Kyky," *Revue d'Egyptologie*, 30 (1978), 115–92.

56. Papyrus Leiden I 371; Lana Troy, "How to Treat a Lady. Reflections on the 'Notorious' P. Leiden I 371," in *Lotus and Laurel. Studies on Egyptian Language and Religion in Honour of Paul John Frandsen*, eds. Rune Nyord and Kim Ryholt (Copenhagen: CNI, 2015), pp. 403–18; on gender issues, cf. Terry Wilfong, "Gender in Ancient Egypt," in *Egyptian Archaeology*, ed. Willeke Wendrich (Chichester, UK: Wiley-Blackwell, 2010), pp. 164–79.

57. Antonio Loprieno, "Defining Egyptian Literature: Ancient Texts and Modern Theories," in *Ancient Egyptian Literature*, ed. Loprieno, pp. 39–58.

58. Hans-Werner Fischer-Elfert, "Literature as a Mirror of Private Affairs. The Case of Menna (i) and His Son Merj-Sachmet (iii)," in *Living and Writing in Deir el-Medina*, eds. Andreas Dorn and Tobias Hofmann (Basel: Schwabe, 2006), pp. 87–92.

59. Roland Enmarch, "Mortuary and Literary Laments: A Comparison," in *Ancient Egyptian Literature*, eds. Enmarch and Lepper, pp. 83–99.

60. Ostracon Chicago 12074; Moers, *Fingierte Welten*, pp. 232–45.

61. Papyrus Pushkin 127, 3, 9–13; Ricardo A. Caminos, *A Tale of Woe* (Oxford: Griffith Institute, 1977), pp. 39–43; Moers, *Fingierte Welten*, pp. 273–79.

62. Stéphane Polis, "The Scribal Repertoire of Amennakhte, Son of Ipuy. Describing Variation Across Late Egyptian Registers," in *Scribal Repertoires in Egypt from the New Kingdom to the Early Islamic Period*, ed. Jennifer Cromwell and Eitan Grossman (Oxford: Oxford University Press, 2017), pp. 89–126.

63. EA 41541; Andreas Dorn, "Die Lehre Amunnachts," *Zeitschrift für ägyptische Sprache und Altertumskunde*, 131 (2004), 38–55; Polis, "Scribal Repertoire," pp. 94–95.

64. Polis, "Scribal Repertoire," p. 108.

65. Ostracon Gardiner 2 *recto*: Susanne Bickel and Bernard Mathieu, "L'écrivain Amennakht et son enseignement," *Bulletin de l'Institut Français d'Archéologie Orientale*, 93 (1993), 49–51.

66. An example is the *Tale of Merire* on Papyrus Vandier (*c.*600 BCE), still written in hieratic script but wholly embedded into the cultural horizon of the Late Period: Hoffmann and Quack, *Anthologie der demotischen Literatur*, pp. 153–160.

67. John Tait, "The Reception of Demotic Narrative," in *Ancient Egyptian Literature*, ed. Enmarch and Lepper, pp. 251–260; p. 258: "Whether they belonged to institutions or to individuals, our manuscripts have the look of 'private' copies."

68. Nikolaos Lazaridis, *Wisdom in Loose Form. The Language of Egyptian and Greek Proverbs in Collections of the Hellenistic and Roman Periods* (Leiden: Brill, 2007), p. 224.

69. BM 10508, 4,8–5,17; Stephen R. K. Glanville, *Catalogue of Demotic Papyri in the British Museum. Vol. 2: The Instructions of 'Onkhsheshonqy (British Museum Papyrus 10508)* (London: British Museum, 1955).

70. Examples are the first *Setna story*, the tale of *Avaris and the Sailor*, and the *Story of Peteese*: Tait, "The Reception of Demotic Narrative," p. 257.

71. Papyrus Rylands 9, III 20–IV 5; Günter Vittmann, *Der demotische Papyrus Rylands 9* (Wiesbaden: Harrassowitz 1998).

72. Stela BM 147, 13–21: Eve A. E. Reymond, *From the Records of a Priestly Family of Memphis*, vol. 1 (Wiesbaden: Harrassowitz. 1981), p. 165–79, table 12.

CHAPTER 4

Authorship in Archaic and Classical Greece

Ruth Scodel

Literature and Authorship

Defining "literature" or "*literary* authorship" in the context of ancient Greece is not simple. Classical Greek has no equivalent word. *Mousikë*, the field of the Muses' activity, includes music and dance, and may exclude texts that Greeks treated in ways that moderns would consider literary. The closest is probably *paideia*, "education" or "culture," although it is broader than our "literature." Greeks themselves did not agree about boundaries. Aristotle's *Poetics* excludes philosophy composed in verse from poetry,[1] but if we think of literature as texts or performances that seek to provide aesthetic pleasure and are evaluated for verbal artistry, the range of Greek literature was very wide. In general, Greeks would have regarded as open to aesthetic judgment any text that was not purely technical. Courtroom and assembly speeches were published and studied for style, and the orator Lysias especially was admired for characterization. History was certainly literature. Plato is important in the Greek literary canon, but the surviving works of Aristotle are much less "literary" than some that are not extant. Hellenistic intellectuals wrote scientific treatises, prose works of all kinds, and poetry, and we do not know where they thought literature ended and technical writing began. There were famous poems that could be used as textbooks, especially Aratus' *Phaenomena* (for astronomy). The biographies of poets that have been transmitted with their manuscripts or that appear in the Byzantine encyclopedia, the *Suda*, make no claims to literary status, but Plutarch certainly does, and Satyrus, probably in the late third century BCE, wrote a biography of Euripides in dialogue form that is clearly intended as what we would call literature.

Despite these complexities of definition, Greeks were certainly fascinated by literary authorship and authors, and indeed we could add to a Greek definition of the literary text that it entailed authorship. This fascination manifested itself in a variety of ways. First, authors, especially poets, were sources of wisdom and authority. Throughout the history of Greek literature, Greeks were relentless quoters and anthologizers, almost always citing the author as the source of wisdom. There were collections of single lines of gnomic wisdom from the comedies of Menander taken entirely out of context (and not every line included was actually by Menander).[2] In Plato's dialogues, the elite conversationalists cite and refer to the poets frequently, by name – Homer, Hesiod, Aeschylus, Archilochus, Euripides, Sophocles, Simonides.[3] Plato's characters know a great deal of poetry by heart and most often have evidently mentally filed the quotations under authors' names. While Plato attacks the tradition that gave poets their cultural importance,[4] his texts also show clearly how profound that influence was. Aristotle even comments that some people would not take an argument seriously unless a poet was cited as a "witness."[5]

Second, for Greeks, interpretation was always about the intention of the author. The ancient exegetical commentary on the *Iliad*, whose remains appear as marginal notes in some manuscripts (the bT scholia), constantly reiterates "the poet means . . . " or "the poet teaches" (for example, on *Iliad* 1.5c, 1.193b, 1.430a, 1.512c). Even allegorizing usually defines itself as uncovering the author's disguised intention, his *hyponoia*. Antiquity did not recognize the possibility of authorless texts or resistant reading. Herodotus did not believe that the epic *Cypria* had the same author as the *Iliad* and *Odyssey*[6] and did not know who the author was. From Aristotle onward, those who refer to the poems of the Epic Cycle will often say, for example, "the composer of the *Cypria*."[7] An anonymous author is still an origin. In the Hellenistic period and later, however, as literature acquired its own scaffolding of commentaries, glossaries, plot summaries, and other "subliterary" aids, these often lacked sufficient status to have authors named. The works of famous grammarians were not anonymous, but many other subliterary texts could circulate without an author's name. Authorial texts were certainly not immune to interpolation or other alterations, but their integrity was supposed to be maintained in copying. Authorless auxiliary works lacked such an expectation of integrity in transmission, so that someone copying a text for a particular purpose could add or omit material at will.

Third, authors were typically seen as responsible for everything in their work, and Greeks did not hesitate to praise or blame poets for sentiments expressed in the speeches of characters. Plato was, of course, completely capable of distinguishing the composer of a narrative from a character within it, but even Plato often seems to obscure the distinction, and in

Greek generally, those who cited only occasionally clarify that the character
does not necessarily speak for the poet. A fragment of Simonides from the
end of the sixth or early fifth century BCE declares that the "man from
Chios" said the "one finest thing": "as the generation of leaves, so is that of
men."[8] Although Homer's birthplace was disputed, Chios was a leading
claimant, and the Homeric line (*Iliad* 6.146) was probably famous enough
that nobody would fail to understand that Homer was the man from
Chios. It is irrelevant here that the line in the *Iliad* is spoken not in the
voice of the poet himself, but in that of a character. Plutarch, in his treatise
on "How to Listen to Poetry," urges the reader to consider the outcome of
the plot in evaluating what characters argue, but he is the exception.

Fourth, for the producers of literature, and for audiences, competitive-
ness was often central to authorship, even outside formal competitions.
Corrections of earlier authors or polemic against them are common in both
poetry and prose. The poem of Simonides to Scopas that is debated in
Plato's *Protagoras*[9] itself takes issue with the saying of a traditional wise
man, Pittacus, one of the Seven Sages, and itself becomes the object of
a competitive display of interpretive ingenuity. By the late fifth century,
finding and solving "problems" in Homer was a small industry.[10] Zoilus of
Amphipolis was nicknamed the "scourge of Homer" for his attacks on the
poet, but criticism could only confirm Homer's canonical status.
An epigram attributed to the fourth-century tragic poet Astydamas complained that he could compete directly against the canonical tragedians of
the previous century, unfairly regarded as unquestionably superior (though
Astydamas thereby became proverbial for conceit).[11]

Authors were biographical subjects. The surviving *Contest of Homer and
Hesiod* is from the imperial period, but it depends on the fourth-century
Mouseion of Alcidamas, and Alcidamas seems to have relied on earlier
stories about the ancient poets' lives. Not only poets received biographies –
there were biographies of Thucydides, and Diogenes Laertius's *Lives of the
Eminent Philosophers* clearly depends on a variety of biographical works
(though philosophers were not just authors, but founders of schools and
traditions). The biographies of poets, especially, are wildly unreliable as
history, but reveal how Greeks read and understood. Author and text were
so closely linked that Greeks did not just read literature through their
biographical knowledge, but even more often inferred biographical facts
from their interpretations of literary texts. Homer was always imagined as
blind, reflecting the blindness of the singer Demodocus, whose skill and
accuracy Odysseus praises in the *Odyssey* (8.487–91), and the common
Greek association of physical blindness with powerful clairvoyance and

insight (and also, perhaps, with poverty and dependence).[12] Euripides was torn apart by dogs because, in one of his last and most celebrated plays, *Bacchae*, the protagonist Pentheus is ripped apart by maenads. As this example shows, great poetry could be understood as prophetic even if the poets themselves did not realize its prophetic force. The fourth-century historian Philochorus pointed out that Euripides could not have criticized the Athenians in his *Palamedes* of 415 BCE for the execution of Socrates in 399 BCE, but the interpretation need not have ignored the chronology.[13] Euripides as poet could have anticipated later events, but Greeks never theorized how these prophetic capabilities of poets were related to their intentions.

Fifth, famous authors themselves became significant features of Greek cultural identity. By the late fourth century, there were statues of the three canonical fifth-century tragedians in the theater at Athens. From the third century, scholars associated with the Library in Alexandria edited and commented on earlier literature, but also established a canon of nine lyric poets and of ten Attic orators. Epigrammatists composed poems about poets, both contemporaries and earlier. Tourists visited the cave where Euripides was believed to have worked. In the Hellenistic and imperial periods, familiarity with Homer becomes a significant marker of Greek identity, and Alexandria and Smyrna had temples, *Homereia*, with statues of the poet.[14]

Performance and Transmission

Authorship, then, was central in the reception of literature. It is clear that by the fifth century, both poets and prose writers saw themselves as authors who could hope to join the company of the revered authors of the past. But it is far from straightforward how the first Greek poets whose work survives thought about themselves as authors, or how the manifest fascination with authorship developed. Even a superficial study of Greek literature demonstrates how much modern concepts of authorship depend on particular institutions – the publishing business, copyright, libraries – that archaic and even classical Greece completely lacked (see Andrew King's chapter "Publishing and Marketing" and Jason Puskar's chapter "Institutions: Writing and Reading" within this volume). The printed modern book transformed authorship, especially because it permits relatively reliable paratext (see Margaret J.M. Ezell's chapter "Manuscript and Print Cultures 1500–1700" within this volume). Modern books typically announce their authors, or pointedly avoid doing so. Since the Statute of Anne in 1710, furthermore, states have created legal institutions to provide protection for intellectual property (see Daniel Cook's chapter "Copyright and Literary Property" within this volume). Early Greek poetry – literary prose develops only in the sixth century BCE – was transmitted primarily in performance, formal or informal.

In early Greece, even where written texts existed and could circulate, even where authors used writing in composition, books were not a common way for people to experience and become familiar with literary works. In many genres, the composer was either the first performer, or supervised an initial performance. Yet if a poem was to achieve popularity or enter the informal canon of Greek performance scripts, it had to be re-performed outside the poet's control. Effective authorship, in effect, meant that such re-performance would have a double quality: it would somehow be relevant to the circumstances of this new performance, but it would simultaneously remind the audience that it came from another, earlier context.

So if we consider the poet's perspective, we do not know when poets first sought to achieve the status that they later had. Authors, as opposed to performers of traditional material, would hope to be re-performed in situations remote from themselves in both space and time. Such re-performance would make them authors only if their texts were relatively stable – absolute fixity only became a reasonable expectation much later, and although scholars could try to establish precisely correct texts, these were often impossible under ancient conditions of transmission. An author, though, must have had a text that could be identified and distinguished from others. The author came into being as Greeks developed a shared identity, traveled and traded, attended festivals that brought together audiences from different communities, created educational systems that taught elite men a shared poetic inheritance, and used writing. But in the world of transmission-in-performance, poets had very limited means of attaching their identity to the work.

The complexity of authorship is especially salient because by far the most important Greek author within the history of Greek literature, Homer, is also the most uncertain from a modern perspective. The earliest surviving texts of Greek literature, the Homeric epics, are products of a tradition of composition-in-performance. Greek literature thus presents at its origin a mystery of authorship: a culture that reveres and insists on authorship arose in a tradition in which authorship was impossible. The artificial dialect and complex formulaic system of Greek epic could not have been created by one person. They are the products of a long tradition, in which aspiring performers learned how to sing inherited stories without memorizing a text, by mastering the tales, the specialized language of epic, and the way to accompany the song on the lyre. Performers practice and rehearse, but the exact form of a song is not determined until the moment it is performed. In such traditions (the most thoroughly studied is the South Slavic), mediocre performers will repeat songs almost as they first learned them, but the accomplished will adjust them to the audience, and the strongest tradition-bearers will modify what they have inherited.[15] The repertory is at once conservative and constantly developing. Within such traditions, the individual author barely exists. Strong singers may be profoundly original in both narrative technique and style. They can develop new lines of story and create new expressions, but if their audience feels that they are no longer within the tradition, they are unlikely to be successful. Their performance is not a unique artifact, and while they can teach others to perform in this particular style, they do not imagine that they are creating a text for re-performance. They may be celebrated as singers, but they are not quite authors.

Furthermore, Greek heroic poets mystify the process of turning inherited material into new performances by calling on the divinities who supervise their performance, the Muses. The singers' reliance on the Muses, however, did not limit at all their responsibility for their performance. First, in Homeric epic, at least, the Muses' function is not primarily to make the song aesthetically powerful, but to ensure its accuracy. Second, since in archaic Greek thought any outstanding achievement required divine favor, and that favor was itself typically a response to the excellence of the human agent, the singer who received help from the Muses was even more praiseworthy.

While the conventions of heroic poetry discourage singers from making their innovations too salient, they have some acknowledged autonomy. They select the subject of their performance and decide where the narrative will begin. The genre allows the author/performer a direct voice, but at least in the Homeric epics, this voice is anonymous and universalized – the "I" is the epic performer, without any context outside the epic world. They can invoke or question the Muses and apostrophize characters, but they do not identify themselves. It is impossible to know whether this anonymity was a generic expectation or an aspect of the exceptional ambition of the *Iliad* and *Odyssey*. They may refuse to name or locate their authors so that the poems can more easily travel anywhere. Each performance evoked, not an original authorial moment, but the history of performances.

Yet even if the singers of epic did not present themselves within their performances, they may still have become celebrated for them. The performer-composer was immediately present to an audience, so that the source of the individual song was not just known, but could be praised and rewarded. If singers traveled widely to perform, or performed at festivals where the audience came from different communities, they could be truly famous. In the South Slavic epic tradition, poets claimed to have inherited songs from Ćor Huso, but were inconsistent about which songs they had learned.[16] A great singer could become an authority without being an author in any meaningful way. Similarly, "Homer" became a legendary character. Biographical traditions about him competed with each other. Indeed, the disputes about his birthplace did not just confirm his prestige as an author, but helped establish his universal value, since the different claims confirmed his value, and different audiences could select the biographical tradition they preferred.

Scholars disagree about how the practice of oral performance produced two very long epic poems that survive under the name "Homer." Some argue that the epics were composed by individual singers (not necessarily the same person), and dictated, around the end of the eighth century. "Homer" would then be not just an author created by his reception, but an author, or two authors, the genuine creator of a unique text, though a text deeply traditional in many ways. The strongest counter-argument lies in the difficulty and expense of such an undertaking. The most prevalent alternative view proposes that the epics were shaped by the institutional pressure of performance at festivals, where audiences came from different cities and organizers needed clear rules for competition. These conditions led to gradual standardization, particularly when Homeric poetry became part of the Athenian Panathenaea in the late sixth century.[17] In this view, Homer should not be imagined as an author at all, and indeed many scholars would deny authorship to all archaic Greek literature. The main counter-arguments against this evolutionary approach are the conservatism of Homeric language, which should have continued to evolve until it was textually fixed, and the narrative peculiarities and unity of each epic, which do not look like a product of evolutionary convergence.

However we believe the Homeric poems came into existence, with the development of the (relatively) fixed text, and institutionalized performance at festivals, came a strong idea of authorship. While Greeks debated about whether Homer composed particular poems, by the fifth century they consistently imagined even heroic epics as texts with single and definite authors who created them to fulfill personal intentions, to express individual meanings, at particular times. Homer was an author for others to emulate. Classical authors were often overtly self-assertive. For example, Simonides of Ceos, who was active from the late sixth century BCE and well into the fifth, was remembered as the first poet who could be hired to produce poetry for cash, without the polite evasions of earlier patronage. The process was circular, as the imagined Homer was filtered through contemporary assumptions, and contemporary authors sought the lasting fame of imagined Homer.

From the beginning, different performance situations provided poets with very different conditions for maintaining the connection between a text or performance script and the person who composed it. The composers of recitative poetry (elegiac) and much solo lyric initially sang among friends at symposia (or, in Sappho's case, women's gatherings both ritual and social). Everyone in the first audience knew them personally. The poets, however, had very little control over the transmission and re-performance, except that they could give a written text only to those they chose. Anyone who could memorize a poem after hearing it in performance could repeat it. Anyone who received a written copy could pass it on or allow further copies. The personal relationship between poet/performer and audience member, however, provided a motive for transmission and re-performance to refer back to the composer, and such word-of-mouth made some poems and their authors famous. Public performance, however – especially festival performance, though the audience did not consist of friends who would be motivated to promote the poet – could offer greater potential for celebrity. The poets of choral songs were chosen by cities or patrons, and the poets' fame redounded to that of the sponsor.

Naming and Sealing

However, apart from these mechanisms for promoting authorship, even in the earliest period of extant Greek literature, explicit claims of authorship within literary works were possible outside heroic epic, because different kinds of performance had different conventions about authorial self-presentation. A poet could try to ensure that work would be recognized as his or her own in such performance by including a name or other identifying information within the poem, so that any re-performance would name the absent author.

Such self-identification was never expected, let alone obligatory, but it was not excluded. While the speaker of the Homeric epics is anonymous, a voice of the tradition, in Hesiod's *Theogony* (a poem in the same epic hexameter as Homer that narrates the origins of the gods), the poet narrates at some length how he was initiated by the Muses while watching sheep on Mt. Helicon and names himself. ("Hesiod" may have been a speaking name assumed for performance, but it is still his name.) His Muses are, from the first line, Heliconian, and he enumerates the springs of Helicon where they bathe (ll. 5–6) before identifying them also as Muses of Olympus (l. 53) and narrating their birth on Pieria.[18] These are Panhellenic divinities, but they also visit and receive cult in his region. Similarly, Hesiod precisely locates himself as an individual whose poem addresses an audience that potentially includes all Greeks. In the *Works and Days*, he does not name himself, but in line 11 corrects the *Theogony* in a way that implies that he is the same person who composed that poem.[19] This poem offers various biographical details about the speaker: that he addresses his brother, Perses, that their father came from Aeolic Cyme and settled in Ascra, below Helicon, and that he won a poetic contest at the funeral games of Amphidamas on the island of Euboea. The ferry from the mainland was his only travel by sea. He won a tripod in a contest and dedicated it to the Muses at the site where the Muses had met him. The tripod was a long-lasting sign of his excellence, but it could not travel, and it was probably not inscribed. The power of the dedication as a sign of authorship derives mostly from the text itself. One form of Greek authorship is closely tied to place. Hesiod's poem seeks an audience of any Greeks, but he addresses them from a particular place. This may have been effective precisely because he came from an unimportant village.

Some modern scholars believe that the Hesiod of these poems was an already legendary figure like the later Homer or like Ćor Huso. Many poems that were certainly not the work of this poet were transmitted under his name because they were similar to his in some way and did not include a *sphragis*, or "seal," the claim of authorship incorporated into the poem itself, that would attach them to someone else. However, the autobiographical information supplied by "Hesiod" is surprisingly precise. If the author of *Words and Days* was not the winner of this contest, he is pretending to be a specific person who won that contest. And while the date of Amphidamas's death is unknown, it belongs in the same general period in which we would locate Hesiod, somewhere in the late eighth or early seventh century BCE. So it is the easier hypothesis that these two poems were composed by a man who was named or chose to call himself "Hesiod," who incorporated this name and his home village into his poems. Yet even if we reject any biographical reality behind the Hesiodic poems, ancient audiences fully accepted it. Indeed, the biographical tradition assumed that his victory was a victory over the other great author, Homer.

Thus, even if the composer of these poems was more traditional than he appears to be, and was taking the name of an earlier celebrated poet, he demonstrates the meaning and power of authorship in early Greece. His poems were probably profoundly original. The *Theogony*-poet did not, of course, invent the main relationships of the gods or the narrative that explains them. The poem, however, organizes both deities of actual cult and many divine embodiments of abstract ideas that were never worshiped into a massive and coherent genealogical structure. *Works and Days* combines very traditional teachings about justice with advice (sometimes idiosyncratic) about farming and strictures about ritual purity, and concludes with a catalog of the good and bad qualities of the days of the month. There is nothing like it, so that Hesiod's name was permanently associated with didactic poetry. Although small snippets from this poem were frequently quoted by themselves, they never became independent of Hesiod.

Hesiod surely sought fame for his poems, but his text shows no anxiety about their transmission. The collection of elegiac poetry transmitted under the name "Theognis," however, does. This sixth-century poet was the first to identify himself and speak of a "seal," *sphragis*:

> Cyrnus, as I perform my skill let a seal [σφρηγὶς] lie upon these words, and they will never be stolen unnoticed, nor will anyone trade something worse for the good that is available; and everyone will say: "These are the verses of Theognis, the Megarian, known by name throughout all humanity."[20]

It is significant that he calls himself "of Megara" rather than giving his patronymic or another local identifier – identifying oneself by city immediately makes a claim to Panhellenic attention. It is also worth noticing the competitive tone – change will be change for the worse, although it is not clear whether he means that nobody will vary his poems to render them worse, or that nobody will choose to perform inferior poetry instead of his. Scholars, however, agree that many of the poems in the collection are not the work of Theognis.[21] Some are cited in other ancient sources as the work of another elegiac poet, Solon, sometimes with variation.

This is not surprising. Theognis's poetry consists of a series of short pieces, some but not all thematically connected. Many address a boy named Cyrnus, and Cyrnus's name could also provide a link to Theognis. However, even these poems probably adapted traditional material and were not entirely "original" in a modern sense. At ll. 239–40, the poet promises Cyrnus that he will be sung at banquets to the accompaniment of the pipes, since these poems were intended to be performed at the male drinking-party, the symposium. If the seal consisted in simply inserting his name into one poem, it would have almost no power to associate his name with all his poems, since they would be performed individually. Furthermore, improvisation was part of symposiastic practice, so the poems could easily be adapted for performance on a particular occasion, or performers could simply forget some of the words they had learned and substitute their own. Nothing, however, could prevent someone from improvising a short poem addressed to Cyrnus in the manner of Theognis. Even a written copy would be open to change.

Theognis may have created a book, a copy intended to provide proof that he had composed these poems and not others and to preserve his poems in precisely the form that he desired. The philosopher Heraclitus is said to have deposited a copy of his book in the temple of Artemis at Ephesus, where it would provide a reliable text – but how often would a reader travel to Ephesus to check? The dedicated copy, like Hesiod's tripod in the shrine of the Muses, was a token of authenticity, but not an effective guarantor of it in the wider world.

Poets, however, could use their own names without marking the name as a claim of authorship. Hipponax is a named character in his poems. Archilochus does not name himself in any surviving fragment, but his poems have repeated addressees, targets of abuse, locations, and situations, as those of Hipponax do, too. Archilochus could be identified by an address to Glaucus or abuse of Lycambes or Neoboule, or Hipponax by references to Boupalus. Solon's surviving elegiac poetry does not use his own name or anyone else's, though in an iambic poem he quotes a political criticism: "Solon was not a deep thinker or a good planner."[22] None of this would be surprising from a modern perspective, but in a world where poetry was transmitted mostly by performance, it is impressive that so much survived with the author's name attached. Another surviving fragment by Solon, an Athenian, objects to a sentiment of Mimnermus, who probably lived in Smyrna, across the Aegean, addressing him.[23] The names of poets traveled with their poems.

Similarly, in solo lyric, Sappho puts her own name in poems (four times in the surviving fragments), along with the names of family members and others in her circle, and Alcaeus names himself once. Sappho does not mention her own name as poet or as a signature, however – since there is no indication that the speaker is not the poet – anyone who hears the poem will infer that Sappho is the author; but there is no *sphragis* and no sign that Sappho was concerned that her poetry be marked as hers. Alcaeus, similarly, mentioned and addressed various contemporaries, but no surviving fragment preserves his name. Some beloved poems probably circulated as songs by these authors, and oral tradition maintained the identification. The Alexandrian edition of Sappho filled at least eight rolls. However, there is no reason to believe that either poet prepared an edition. In fragment 55, Sappho tells another woman that she will not be remembered after her death, because she has no share in the "roses of Pieria."[24] Mt. Pieria, birthplace of the Muses, is even farther from Lesbos than from Hesiod's Ascra, and while Hesiod composed in the special dialect of Panhellenic hexameter poetry, Sappho's poems locate themselves as Lesbian by their dialect alone. Later editors seem to have guessed that all poems in Lesbian dialect were by Sappho or Alcaeus, and used content to decide which poems were by which poet (modern editions include fragments whose authorship is undecided between them). Still, she evidently thought of herself as part of Greek poetry, and she expected to be remembered. Perhaps Sappho and Alcaeus, and other early Greek poets also, hoped to be remembered as poets but were not anxious about being recognized for individual poems or, conversely, being falsely believed to be the composers of poems that were not theirs.

In choral lyric, Alcman names himself twice, but most choral poets do not. In some ritual contexts, identifying the poet may have been inappropriate, since the chorus represented the entire community. Yet some poems use a peculiar form of self-identification. Hymns did not generally have a *sphragis*. The *Homeric Hymn to Apollo*, however, concludes its first section, which recounts the gods' birth on the island of Delos, with an address to a chorus of young women on the island, praising them and asking them to tell visitors that their favorite poet is "a blind man, and he comes from rocky Chios."[25] It is impossible to be certain whether the singer was thereby attributing the song to Homer, or whether an actual blind singer from Chios accidentally contributed to the legend of Homer. In the fifth century, however, Pindar and Bacchylides repeatedly identify themselves by their ethnics but do not give their names. Scholars have suggested that they avoid their names in order to facilitate re-performance, but it is hard to see why it would be easier for someone singing an epinician at a symposium in Ephesus to speak as an anonymous Theban rather than as Pindar. It seems to be an expression of supreme confidence. These poets do not need to attach their actual names to their songs, because the ethnic alone will remind audiences of the author – an especially striking move for

Bacchylides, whose uncle Simonides shared his ethnic and had immense Panhellenic fame.

Historians seem to have had less difficulty than poets sealing their works effectively. Hecataeus, the earliest known historian, began "Hecataeus of Miletus narrates as follows,"[26] and Herodotus: "This is the presentation of the researches of Herodotus of Halicarnassus."[27] Although Herodotus evidently gave public readings of extracts from his *Histories*, such prose was not part of the symposiastic repertory and did not circulate as oral performance. Historical authors begin their texts with their own names: Thucydides not only begins his book "Thucydides of Athens wrote up," but concludes each year with the formula "the xth year of the war that Thucydides wrote up," effectively subordinating the war itself to his account. Thucydides famously calls his book (1.22.4) "a possession forever, not a competition-piece for hearing at the moment."[28] He uses his patronymic when he mentions himself as a historical agent at 4.104, even though he also identifies this Thucydides, the general, as the writer – authorship is a Panhellenic status, generalship an Athenian one. Even historians, however, did not always sign their works. Polybius, writing in the second century BCE, engages in extensive methodological discussion and polemic, so that his work is extremely personal, but does not begin with a *sphragis*. By his time, in a world of libraries and book dealers, it probably did not seem as necessary. He was confident that his authorship was secure, and probably supervised the "publication" of his book – that is, he made copies available to the book trade.

In contrast, medical writers in the Hippocratic tradition, although their treatises are often overtly polemical, do not include their authors' names or the names of those with whom they disputed. They are all transmitted under the name "Hippocrates." Philosophers do not generally sign their works. Plato and Aristotle, who created schools that survived them, may have trusted their students to preserve their texts (but some works, perhaps written within those schools, have been transmitted spuriously under their names). Later scientific authors sometimes use epistolary form, but Euclid's *Elements*, for example, seems to have had no signature.

The status of author for poets, however, received a new kind of support from the archaic period onward as competitive festivals were established. A victory gave a poet celebrity – Hesiod boasts of his – and provided a focus for memory. Some festivals were Panhellenic, but some civic festivals sought and could attract wide attention, as the Athenian Dionysia did. Archaic poets also received patronage from tyrants, irregular rulers of Greek city-states. The fame of the patrons made the poets more famous, while their poems celebrated the patrons. Ibycus says that Polycrates, probably the son of the famous tyrant of Samos, will have immortal fame (like a Homeric hero) "to the limit of song and my fame."[29] Comic poets did not generally name themselves (although they freely named other poets, as well as the targets of their mockery). Yet Aristophanes in his first surviving comedy (his third play), *Acharnians* of 425 BCE, claims that the king of Persia has said that whichever side is abused by "this poet" will win the war and claims that the Spartans want possession of the island of Aegina because it is the home of "this poet."[30] Aristophanes was still a young man, and the joke is funnier precisely because he was probably not widely famous outside Athens. *Peace* (421) urges all the bald men in the audience to support him, so that at parties others will give them extra dessert because they resemble the noblest poet.[31]

By the classical period, however, especially at Athens, Greeks recorded the outcome of festival competitions in inscriptions. They could be a matter of significant public record. Athens inscribed the records of the Great Dionysia, the main theatrical festival, and the inscriptions were used by students of Aristotle to generate records in book form, so that it was usually possible to identify when a play was first performed. The dramas also had titles, which gradually supplemented or replaced citation of the opening as a way of identifying a text. These records could not solve all difficulties, however. Euripides, early in his career, composed a tragedy called *Rhesus*. Very few scholars, however, believe that he composed the play of this title in his surviving corpus. The *Rhesus* was probably written in the fourth century. The *Rhesus* of Euripides may have disappeared by the Hellenistic period, but the record of the title survived, so the extant play was assimilated to his corpus. Similarly, most scholars believe that Aeschylus did not compose *Prometheus Bound*, but it may have been produced under his name by his son Euphorion, and so the title appeared in the record as his.

Books

In the fifth century, a genuine book trade began. The Greek book was a papyrus scroll that did not display information about the contents, and for practical reasons it was limited in length, since long scrolls are not easy to use. At about the same time, some individuals began accumulating books in quantity. Euripides is accused in Aristophanes' *Frogs* (produced in 405) of serving his Muse a medication filtered from books,[32] and Euthydemus in Xenophon's *Memorabilia* owns a complete Homer, and many other books besides, including, apparently, treatises on medicine and astronomy.[33] Such a collection would require some system for identifying the rolls.

Books could circulate earlier, and a fragment of a song from Euripides' *Erechtheus* (422 BCE) celebrating the pleasure of reading survives, but someone who wanted a particular text needed to find someone who held a copy and was willing to allow a further copy to be made. The chain from author to reader went through friendship and personal association. We have no evidence that authors made any profit from the copying of a book at any period in ancient history. Like musicians today, some may have encouraged the circulation of copies in order to promote opportunities for profit-making performances, or simply for fame. The professional teachers known as sophists, like Herodotus, gave public lectures, probably both to attract students and to engage and profit from a wider public, most of whom could not afford a full course of sophistic education. Books were a further form of advertising, but only, of course, if their readers knew who wrote them.

A fragment of the comic poet Eupolis (who probably died about 412 BCE) mentions a place "where books can be bought."[34] In Plato's *Apology*, Socrates objects because Meletus says that young men have learned from him views of the scientist and philosopher Anaxagoras, "which it is sometimes possible to purchase for a drachma, at most, in the *orchestra*."[35] It is unclear whether "sometimes" means that the book market itself was only occasional, or whether the availability of any particular book was never certain. We do not know whether the "orchestra" indicates that a book market was held in the theater, or the term referred to some other location. It is, however, certain that by the end of the fifth century there were traders who commercialized the business of books. Presumably the book dealers obtained copies from authors whose works they believed would sell, or made copies of popular texts (such as the Homeric poems). But since books were sold as the works of particular authors, once there was no social connection linking author and reader, the book trade must have required paratextual material of some kind, simply to manage the business. Similarly, as individuals owned more books (Aristotle is supposed to have had an extensive library), they would have needed ways to organize their collections. And, in the third century, the first great royal libraries were created.

In the third century BCE, the poet Callimachus composed a book called the *Pinakes*, "Tablets." It is sometimes called the first library catalog, but although it was surely based on the holdings of the great library at

Alexandria, it was more like a bibliographical handbook of Greek literature and learning. Each entry included not only the author's name, title, and incipit, and the number of lines of text, but a biographical sketch (dating, if discussed, would belong here) and a discussion of authenticity, if appropriate. The *Pinakes* were divided by genres, including at least rhetorical works, laws, epic, lyric, tragedy, comedy, philosophers, historians, medical writers, and miscellaneous. Within the divisions, however, the arrangement was alphabetical by author's name.[36]

By the Roman period, and probably earlier, literary texts had conventional ways of marking authorship, though these were not entirely uniform.[37] A scroll could have a title and author's name (in the genitive) at the beginning, and typically had a sometimes elaborate notation at the end with author's name, title, book number if the work occupied many scrolls, and a decorative marker called a *coronis* – except that texts of the Homeric poems omit the author's name. This fancy title-section would have been useless for finding a book, since when the scroll was rolled up it would be in the center, but it was also the place least susceptible to damage. For finding scrolls, there were external tags with author's name and title. Author and book were closely linked.

Conclusion

Early Greek poetry was transmitted orally, and so the link between composer and text depended on the network of transmission. Even as writing became more important and the book trade developed, Greeks never had robust institutions to protect authorship. Nonetheless, throughout classical antiquity, Greeks revered authors, identifying texts by and with their authors, and establishing canons that later writers hoped to join.

Notes

1. Aristotle, *Poetics* 1447b, LCL 199, pp. 30–33. References are keyed to the Loeb volumes but translations are my own unless otherwise stated.
2. Sebastiana Nervegna, *Menander in Antiquity: The Contexts of Reception* (Cambridge: Cambridge University Press, 2013), pp. 203–12.
3. Dorothy Tarrant, "Plato's Use of Quotations and Other Illustrative Material," *Classical Quarterly*, ns 1 (1951), 59–67.
4. Most famously in the *Republic* 386a–392c5, LCL 237, pp. 220–47.
5. Aristotle, *Metaphysics* 995a7–8, LCL 271, pp. 94–95.
6. Herodotus, *The Persian Wars* 2.117, LCL 117, pp. 408–9.

7. Aristotle, *Poetics* 1459b1, LCL 199, pp. 116: οἷον ὁ τὰ Κύπρια ποιήσας.
8. Fr. 8 West, cited by Stobaeus, *Florilegium* 4.34.28. LCL 476, pp. 510–11.
9. Simonides, fr. 542 PMG; Plato, *Protagoras* 339a–347a, LCL 165, pp. 182–209.
10. N. J. Richardson, "Homeric Professors in the Age of the Sophists," *Proceedings of the Cambridge Philological Society*, 201 (1975), pp. 65–81.
11. Astydamas I in D. L. Page, *Further Greek Epigrams* (Cambridge: Cambridge University Press, 1981), pp. 33–34.
12. Barbara Graziosi, *Inventing Homer: The Early Reception of Epic* (Cambridge: Cambridge University Press, 2002).
13. 328 FGrH F 221= T 33 Kovacs.
14. Lawrence Kim, *Homer Between History and Fiction in Imperial Greek Literature* (Cambridge: Cambridge University Press, 2010), p. 8 on *Homereia*.
15. Albert B. Lord, *The Singer of Tales* (Cambridge, MA: Harvard University Press, 1960), pp. 13–29; John D. Niles, *Homo Narrans: The Poetics and Anthropology of Oral Literature* (Philadelphia: University of Pennsylvania Press, 1999), pp. 173–93.
16. John Miles Foley, "Individual Poet and Epic Tradition: Homer as Legendary Singer," *Arethusa*, 31 (1998), 149–78.
17. Gregory Nagy, *Poetry as Performance: Homer and Beyond* (Cambridge: Cambridge University Press, 1996).
18. Hesiod, *Theogony*, LCL 57, pp. 2–3.
19. Hesiod, *Works and Days*, LCL 57, pp. 86–87.
20. Theognis, elegiac poems, 19–23. LCL 258, pp. 176–79.
21. Extensive discussion in Hendrik Selle, *Theognis und die Theognidea* (Berlin: de Gruyter, 2008); see also Andrew Lear, "The Pederastic Elegies and the Authorship of the Theognidea," *Classical Quarterly* 61 (2011), pp. 378–93.
22. Fr. 33 West, cited by Plutarch, *Solon* 14.6. LCL 46, pp. 440–41; also in LCL 258, p. 155.
23. Fr. 20 West, from Diogenes Laertius 1.60; the extant quotation uses only the patronymic, but earlier lines may have given his name.
24. Sappho, fr. 55 Voigt (cited by Stobaeus, *Florilegium* 3.4.2), LCL 142, pp. 98–99.
25. LCL 496, pp. 84–85.
26. Hecataeus, fr. 1.1 FGrH, cit. in Demetrius, *On Style*, 12, LCL 199, pp. 354–55.
27. *The Persian Wars*, bk. 1, ch. 1, LCL 117, pp. 2–3.
28. Thucydides, *History of the Peloponnesian War*, 1.22.4, LCL 108, pp. 40–42.
29. Ibycus, fragment 282.47–8, LCL 476, pp. 224–25.
30. Aristophanes, *Acharnians*, ll. 649–51, LCL 178, pp. 136–37.
31. Aristophanes, *Peace*, ll. 769–73, LCL 488, pp. 524–25.
32. Aristophanes, *Frogs*, ll. 943, LCL 180, pp. 152–53.
33. Xenophon, *Memorabilia* 4.2.1–10, LCL 168, pp. 280–87.
34. Eupolis, fr. 327, LCL 514, pp. 236–37.
35. Plato, *Apology* 26d, LCL 36, pp. 140–41.

36. Rudolf Pfeiffer, *History of Classical Scholarship: From the Beginnings to the End of the Hellenistic Age* (Oxford: Clarendon Press, 1968).
37. Francesca Schironi, *To Mega Biblion: Book-ends, End-titles, and Coronides in Papyri with Hexametric Poetry* (Durham, NC: American Society of Papyrologists, 2010); despite the title, the book compares other literary papyri.

CHAPTER 5

Authorship in Classical Rome

Christian Badura and Melanie Möller

Even though the modern term "author" is derived from the Latin *auctor*, histories of authorship usually assume a paradigm shift from premodernity to the modern age, with the invention of printing with movable type as a major historical caesura. Yet they also set out from certain author concepts that rely on central premises concerning copyright: notably, the premise that, within a so-called premodern society less concerned with individuality, notions of property were unknown or at least insignificant; and that the entire theoretical baggage that has accrued around authorship in modern times was "naturally" unknown in antiquity and, hence, irrelevant. Two complementary prejudices take effect here: that art and life were supposedly not thought of as distinct before modernity, and that unity and identity, instead of rupture and change, dominated an author's self-image and his or her works. But ancient thinkers were surely able to distinguish between art and life, with the emphasis on a conscious blending of the two rather than their prior unity.

All these preconceptions fall short of the textual evidence. Indeed, not only the Greeks but also the Romans developed more complex author concepts than they are often given credit for. In this chapter, we sketch the literary culture and trace editorial practices in Roman antiquity; next, we address the literary device of the *sphragis* ("seal impression") that Roman writers use to signal their authorship of a text, often in encryption. In section 3, we turn to a history of the term *auctor* in relation to concepts of the *persona*, i.e., role models that authors operate with explicitly and implicitly. A subtle theory of art and life depends on these questions, implying two further central categories: the moral parameters guiding author and reader, and the role of *imitatio*, that is: the self-placement within or outside of literary tradition by explicit or implicit referencing, which is accompanied by a specific form of morally defined imitation, closely tied to the formula *talis oratio, qualis vita* ("the style is the man"), which embodies a central category of Roman literary criticism.

Roman Literary Culture, Editorial Practices, and Authenticity Criticism

What did it mean to be an *auctor* in Rome? The term at first designated someone possessing specific rights, then also legal and other scholars who made their knowledge available in writing.[1] The *Oxford Latin Dictionary* (*s.v. auctor*, 7) adds to this yet another legal dimension, of "a person, thing, or fact that provides evidence or substantiation, a witness, proof, [. . .] authentication"; and also the meaning of (ibid. 10) "the originator, source, author (of information, etc.)." The term is used for a writer in the sense of the original author as distinct from an imitator or adapter, and the technical term for an anonymous book seems to have been *sine auctore*, "without author."[2] The term is also widely used for artists and the relationship to their works in general.

As for other related terms, Roman poetical authors adopted the term *poeta* from the Greek, beginning with Plautus (*c*.250–184 BCE) and Ennius (239–169 BCE). Before that time, they were presumably just called *scribae* ("scribes"). The noun *poeta* denotes a "maker, creator" in the artistic sense at first, but is already charged with a religious undertone by Ennius (cf. Cicero, *Pro Archia* 18). The Roman idea of this sanctified author is captured in the notion of a poetic *vates*, a "herald" of prophecies encountered in Roman divination practice.[3] At first, it is used by Ennius in the proem to book seven of his *Annales* to deride his predecessor Naevius (*c*.265–201 BCE); but later, beginning with Virgil, it is employed affirmatively for authorial self-descriptions of being a "seer" who has privileged access to truth and the gods by way of their and the Muses' inspiration. This changing of poetic titles over time provides a case in point for the process of assimilation from the Greek sphere that Roman literature and culture were to undergo from the third to the first centuries BCE.

Although the term of the literary author thus derives from legal discourse, Roman *auctores* embodied only a weak form of the author in legal and institutional terms.[4] Up to Augustan times, there are hardly any literary (poetic) texts by free-born Roman citizens, and the first authors in Roman literary history, Livius Andronicus, Naevius, and Ennius, were native Greeks from the south of Italy or other Italian regions only loosely associated with Rome. Often (former) slaves, they usually depended on their masters financially; and even in the late Roman republic and during the reign of Augustus, when poets were mostly ranked as knights (*equites*) within the financial census, they were in need of a wealthy patron, preferably from the nobility, in order to perform and spread their work. There even seems to have been a sort of authors' guild sponsored by the rich nobility at this time, a *collegium scribarum histrionumque* datable to 207 BCE, also including actors. The Temple of Hercules and the Muses, dedicated in 187 BCE, played some role in these efforts as the site of the *collegium poetarum*.[5]

In creative terms, most authors tried to control their texts both in form and content. This is manifest from the common literary device of the *recusatio*:[6] while it is from these passages that we can deduce an influence of patrons (such as Maecenas in Vergil and Horace, or Messalla in Tibullus and Ovid) and what kind of poetry they would commission, it is also here that poets state they are going to write differently from what was expected or requested of them, namely panegyric or epic poetry. "Literary circles" involving various authors who knew and named each other in their texts can be identified within the orbit of these patrons.[7] In most cases, the author was both composer and performer of new texts and would earn a reputation, even fame, from entering the highest social spheres. But no one would expect great wealth from book publication itself. This is why most extant Latin prose texts until well into the early empire were written by rich senatorial politicians in their spare time. From Cato the Elder's and Varro's treatises on agriculture or the first annalistic historical writings to Julius Caesar's *commentarii* on his battles in Gaul and Italy or Cicero's philosophical enterprise, these texts were written by established men wealthy enough to have access to private libraries and to afford the leisure of circulating the results among his peers. Cicero and his friend Atticus are good examples, since they both acquired large collections of papyrus scrolls and kept slaves for associated tasks; these activities can be traced in Cicero's letters.[8]

At least from the first century BCE onwards, the emergence of libraries and extensive private book collections points to a type of book trade conducted by booksellers and copyists, who were often the same people offering their skills in providing texts copied on demand. The first "publishing houses" that made texts available on a grand scale were opened by former library slaves (*librarii*) in the first to third centuries CE. Among the most successful publishers in late republican and Augustan Rome are Atticus (Cicero's friend) and the Sosii brothers, who were well acquainted with Horace and Ovid.[9] These copies involved authors closely with their texts by attaching tags (*tituli*) to papyrus scrolls and by including titles at the beginning of a work, naming the author in the genitive case.[10] These tags made sure authors could be identified with their work, rendering textually internal devices of authentication unnecessary in purely institutional terms.

It is in textual criticism that we seemingly enter neutral epistemic ground in pinning down the author, particularly ancient authors, by investigating their authenticity and authorship, and accounting for the texts as we read them today and how they were read in the past. Yet Irene Peirano has recently found textual criticism to be largely led by a drive for biographical knowledge.[11] "Authenticity criticism" can be suspected of constantly making sophisticated attempts to satisfy learned desires for authentication. From Hellenistic times and early Homeric philology onwards, texts were deemed authentic once a certain author could be assigned to them. But aesthetic, often subjective criteria as well as the assumption of a homogeneous authorial entity, projected as a reality *within* the text, have ever since helped philologists to construct unified personalities of authors complete with their individual writing styles. However, there are no final hermeneutic criteria to distinguish "authentic" from "inauthentic" texts; in addition, there are other challenges with regards to the status of ancient texts: Roman authors did not always complete their works before their death, and there are numerous legends on the origins and editions of texts that complicate the picture. The *Aeneid* was unfinished at Vergil's death, as its 57 half-lines testify – and never to be published, if we believe Donatus's *vita Vergilii* (ch. 51): "When he [*sc.* Vergil] felt he was weighed down by an illness, he was going to burn the *Aeneid*; when this was denied to him, he ordered in his testament for it to be burned, as a thing unrevised and imperfect."[12] But according to legend, Augustus had Varius save the papyrus scrolls and edit them. Ovid might just be pointing to this story from exile, when he speaks of his own autodafé in the *Tristia* (1.7.13–30; 3.14.19–24): he burned the "unfinished" *Metamorphoses*, but his attempt to destroy the text was unsuccessful since copies of the *opus magnum* were already in circulation.

The *Sphragis* and Other Forms of Authorization in Roman Literature

The tradition of the *sphragis*, a "seal" and a kind of copyright statement *avant la lettre*, is the most prominent phenomenon of authorization in Latin poetry, adopted from Greek literature. The author marks his or her work at the end with a reference to him- or herself,[13] using a personalized, yet formally conventional signature in order to document his or her claim to ownership by that token. These seals often only consist in short, epigrammatic pieces of data including place and year of birth, along with background information on family and financial means and sometimes also containing encoded specifics only accessible to insiders.[14] Poets usually give their name explicitly (e.g., Hesiod, Vergil) or else use a common epithet. Once this paratextual seal becomes part of the text proper, the "signature" is detached from the signatory it signifies – and at the same time it exerts a certain control on how a text is handled by its readers.[15]

The device originated in Greek archaic poetry, when there was no book trade yet to securely connect authors to their texts. With the Romans, and especially the Augustan poets, it became an entirely literary form of negotiating authenticity and authorial identity. One of the stock motifs of the *sphragis*, the appeal to eternal fame,[16] is especially prominent in Ovid's conclusion to his *Metamorphoses* (15.871–9), itself inspired by a famous epigram about eternal fame by Ennius. Before Ovid, Vergil (70–19 BCE), Propertius (*c*.48–15 BCE, esp. in *carmen* 1.22), and Horace (65–8 BCE, esp. in *Odes* 3.20) made the most of this poetic authorization device. The concluding piece of Horace's first book of verse epistles is a short autobiography addressed to the book itself, which gives typical elements of the ancient *vita* but remains vague in the details:

> When the milder sun brings you a larger audience, you will tell them about me: that I was a freedman's son, and amid slender means spread wings too wide for my nest, thus adding to my merits what you take from my birth; that I found favour, both in war and peace, with the foremost in the State; of small stature, grey before my time, fond of the sun, quick in temper, yet so as to be easily appeased. If one chance to inquire my age, let him know that I completed my forty-fourth December in the year when Lollius drew Lepidus for colleague.[17]

Here, the (eventually empty-handed) attempt of the author's emancipation from his text is indicated by the *lack* of a name, rendering problematic the usual purpose of the *sphragis*, i.e., to ensure authorship. The poetry book, Horace seems to be saying, must stand for itself, and displays a certain distrust of the possibility to represent oneself textually as an author. However, any popular author could count on the fact that even a meager frame of information, a fully alienated sketch, would offer enough features of recognition to the learned audience; authors would also, at times, explore boundaries of workable alienating effects in these passages. While Horace's epistles are deemed "documents of his *ego*" in particular, they should, with regard to the masquerades of their author, be read as artistic efforts of self-construction, indicated already by the use of metrical language. At the end of Vergil's *Georgics*, there is a regular *sphragis* including name and origin of its author and mentioning the earlier *Eclogues*, thus "authorizing" his first two works:

> So much I sang in addition to the care of fields, of cattle, and of trees, while great Caesar thundered in war by deep Euphrates and bestowed a victor's laws on willing nations, and essayed the path to Heaven. In those days I, Virgil, was nursed by sweet Parthenope, and rejoiced in the arts of inglorious ease – I who toyed with shepherds' songs, and, in youth's boldness, sang of you, Tityrus, under the canopy of a spreading beech.[18]

Ovid (43–17 BCE) directly aligns himself with this tradition when he marks the authorship of his literary debut, the *Amores*: in an introductory epigram containing both the genitive of his cognomen (*Nasonis*) to indicate his ownership and the term *auctor* to denote the editorial act of publishing three books of poems instead of a longer version in five books, he presents himself from the start as a poet turning to face his audience: "We who erewhile were five booklets of Naso now are three; the poet has preferred to have his work thus rather than as before. Though even now you may take no joy of reading us, yet with two books taken away your pains will be lighter."[19] In Ovid's poetry, this communicative stance of a self-confident, yet at times also fractured poetical *ego* prevails throughout. He is variously found acting as *poeta, vates* ("seer"), or *magister* ("teacher"), who not only presents his *opus* ("work"), *liber* ("book"), or *carmen* ("poem") to the reader, but also enters into a dialogue with it. This, presumably, is the main reason we find the literary seal as well as the technique of self-naming most often in Ovid.[20] Among these passages, the autobiographical poem *Tristia* 4.10 assumes a peculiar role not only by its length (132 lines) but also by propounding a detailed CV from the cradle to the (anticipated) grave, an account that largely meets the traditional criteria of the genre: it is intended for publication and written in retrospect from a first-person perspective; it follows chronological order and includes gestures of justification. The poet's life and *opus* have coalesced inseparably here: the poem further contains programmatic statements and situates the signature's "I" within a literary, elegiac tradition. But in the course of the poem, this *ego* takes on different masks at will, e.g., the family father or the culprit in a fictive court trial. This elegy as a whole is thus an impressive blend of elements of the poet's life and elements genuinely intrinsic to the poem.

The well-known initial distich of *Tristia* 4.10 contains another formula dear to Roman poets in defining themselves: *ille ego qui*, "the one who I was": "That you may know who I was, I that playful poet of tender love whom you are reading, hear my words, you of the after time."[21] Embedded in these lines, there is always a tension between a continuous authorial identity – "I am still that writer familiar from my past works" – and a newly created, vigorous personality entering the stage in the present. This juxtaposition of pronouns is a concise way of establishing legitimate authorship, yet at the same time it confronts two perspectives: a subjective claim to being an objectified authorial entity on the one hand, and a bold act of self-renunciation on the other.[22] Ovid himself deploys that formula in no less than eight poems,[23] not counting the seal passages. Its occurrences range from funerary epigrams to his wife (*Trist.* 3.3.73–4) to programmatic reflections accounting for his generic experiments (*Fasti* 2.3–8). Whilst a self-assured *persona* appeals to the by-passing wanderer/reader in the first example, asking for acknowledgment, in the latter he addresses his own elegiac verses in the quest for a coherent aesthetics and authorial identity capable of encompassing both love poems and religious didacticism. Strikingly, it is in these very passages that Ovid usually reminds himself of his erstwhile erotic poetry: this manifests a certain reluctance to give up the self-image of the juvenile love poet, much as he may distance himself from his pernicious *Ars amatoria* in the exile poetry.

However, the most famous instance of the *ille ego* formula is found in the spurious pre-proem of Vergil's *Aeneid*: "I am that man who once sang on a slender reed and coming out of the woods forced the neighboring fields to obey their owner, however greedy for gain, a work pleasing to farmers, but now of Mars' bristling arms I sing and the man . . ."[24] In these four lines, which create a sort of retrospective *sphragis*, the three main Vergilian texts with their generic range from bucolic and agricultural didactic to epic poetry are compressed and lined up to form a coherent whole, all the while distinguishing the novel epic *ego* (*Aeneid* 1.1, *arma virumque cano*) from the *ille* of the earlier works. In contrast to the "truthful" authenticating force of the *sphragis* ending of the *Georgics*, this passage attempts to give credibility to a forged set of lines: it is an editorial fake not found in the earliest manuscripts of the *Aeneid*, "interpolated to provide a measure of authorial or narrative continuity between two distinct poems."[25] At this point, form and content as well as the authorial figure converge when a Pseudo-Vergil enters his own fictive world of the shepherd and the farmer. It is a point of continuity and a new beginning for an authorial identity, while establishing a biography of the poet's work that neatly fits the textual material.[26]

Such textual manifestations of authorial identity and ownership need to be evaluated also against their legal background. A copyright law did not exist in Greco-Roman antiquity.[27] Plagiarism (the Latin word is *furtum*, "theft") was frowned upon, but no consequent law suits are recorded. In Martial's *Epigram* 1.52, the book stolen by a literary competitor is likened to a manumitted slave,[28] the rival author to a *plagiarius*, a slave trader or kidnapper (1.52.9). The word is derived from *plaga*, a net or snare by which animals or humans are captured and snatched away. In the poem, Martial seems to allude to a *lex Fabia de plagiariis*, but this seems to have applied only to human kidnapping, not cases of literary authorship.[29]

Autofiction and Authenticity: Identity and Change

As we have seen above, an *auctor*, i.e., someone possessing *auctoritas*, vouches for a truth or an object; he or she sanctions, approves, authenticates. Ever since antiquity, the relationship between art and life has accommodated the prevailing desire of readers for actuality and authenticity in the experience and production of literary texts. Classical texts themselves have never ceased to be read in this way, which holds for lyric and elegy with their "subjective" stance in particular, but also for historiographical and autobiographical, quasi-documentary texts. The desire to equate authors with their work has led to manifold answers, but also to dead ends in the production and interpretation of texts; some of these approaches can be termed merely "biographistic,"[30] while others have led to genuine theories of the authorial self and its relationship to the book and the fictional world inside it.

Early on, classical philology picked up the term and concept of the *persona* ("mask") used already in Latin texts in order to discuss these problems.[31] It derives from the world of drama and clarifies the vicariousness of literary communication: authors use these kinds of masks to distinguish themselves from the protagonists of their texts, to transform distinctive facets of their *ego* artistically, and to keep the reader at a distance. The textual self-encounter of an author often amounts to a masquerade, and whenever that *ego* starts to put on different masks a kind of fragmentation of the authorial self can be observed, which may be counter-acted and veiled, but also embraced and re-enforced.

A Greco-Roman theory of the *persona* can be found in Cicero's *De officiis*. While the first *persona* separates man – understood as rational being – from animal, the second one describes the temperamentally individual character by which people can be distinguished among themselves. The third *persona* suggests the role images of humans shaped through time, environment, and society, whereas the fourth leaves room for the individual choice of the *genus vitae* (e.g., career choice).[32]

Admittedly, the individual is the agent of choice, but not thought of as a "personality" in the modern sense. In Cicero's own works, this is most prominently put into practice in his letters, which are documents of a prolific autobiographical writer. The epistolary form is one of the earliest genres suspected of being autofictional: this impression is suggested, at least, by the omnipresence of the epistolographic topos of the "letter as mirror of the soul," which was already phrased by Demetrios of Phaleron (fourth/third century BCE) in his treatise Περὶ ἑρμηνείας ("On Style").[33] Cicero excels in the skill of adapting his *persona* to the interests of his different addressees. Thus he addresses his particular recipient as friend, politician, teacher, or companion. He strikingly succeeds in creating the impression of presence and authenticity by suggesting closeness between writer and addressee bordering on their identity. The most intimate, "personal" Ciceronian *persona* might be found, paradoxically, where he is seen just on the verge of authorship, when his text is *not* made public, but instead remains *anecdoton* in the literal sense (from the Greek for "not edited"): a secret, personal side of political history only made available to his close friend Atticus.[34]

As for Roman lyric, it is particularly in Catullus's *carmina* (mid-first century BCE) that we find a complex self-conception with important consequences for that of the author. In poem 16, he clarifies the herme-neutic rules of (auto-)fiction, the so-called *lex Catulli* (*carmen* 16.5–6):[35] *nam castum esse decet pium poetam / ipsum, versiculos nihil necesse est* ("for it befits a pious poet to be chaste himself, but it is not necessary for his little verses at all"). Art and life are two conflicting variables, and for that reason it is impossible to express oneself "authentically" in the arts. The analogy of poetry and the life of their author is rejected as a criterion of evaluation for either art or life: it is a claim for aesthetic autonomy and a genuinely poetical existence of the *ego*.[36] That programmatic condition is the founda-tion for the authorial concept in all of his poems.

The game of changing *personae* is especially popular among the satirists, whose texts regularly adopt autobiographical traits. The Augustan poet Horace uses his satires as well as his epistles to present occasional poetry as the result of different configurations of the self. By subtly using authorial "masks," Horace succeeds in reminding the reader that the relationship to oneself cannot be depicted in a direct or straightforward way, since it has always been subject to different communicative discourses and must include these (literary or non-literary) communities in the search for an authorial self. Autobiographical texts within these collections describe, from a certain distance, the emergence of the self from the arts.

The change of genres and topical variations serves as metamorphosis of an *ego* that can only exist in a penmanship from which there is no escape – making the self vanish quite effectively in writing poetry.

In elegiac poetry, the ever-recurring theme of death is taken both from threnody ("mourning song") and the funerary epigram that aims to capture the life of its author in a concise statement of two to about eight verses – in this, it is a lot like the *sphragis*. Roman love elegy is mostly known today for its erotic topics and Hellenistic erudition, but in the works of Propertius especially, the closeness of death stands out whenever he lets his life take shape in a kind of "thanatographical" imagination. The projected lives of all the elegists come in many forms, but it is in Ovid, the Proteus of classical Latin poets, that the withdrawal from biographistic interpretation toward his extra-literary self is most successful. Ovid assumes numerous *personae* in order to slip into one role after another, resulting in a dynamic presentation of a multi-faceted literary personality. This has led many critics to the false assumption that Ovid is the historically most accessible Roman poet, but all of the supposedly biographical information is only immanent in his texts. In his exile poetry, Ovid unfolds this ambivalent relationship to the aesthetics of writing between the poles of *ego* and world by constantly recurring to the same themes and thus giving the impression of a coherent authorial identity.

The authorial *persona* of the novel *Satyricon libri* by Titus Petronius (27–66 CE) has been described as "hidden author" by Gian Biagio Conte: this author has concealed himself with the aim of striking at the vanity of the early empire's cultured scene, lending a voice to his many characters who are all distinguishable by their individual language. The author is "lurking just outside the story"[37] and can be identified mainly in an implicit dialogue with the narrator and protagonist Encolpius, who seems to respond to the design according to the epic-heroic model of Aeneas, a rhetorically determined role offered by "Petronius" in many suggestions of epic mythological situations.[38]

An author is also defined by his or her ability and authority to direct the perception of posterity and to impose one's own perspective on collective memory.[39] Yet rumors and anecdotes as well as social and political interests of biographers and readers are bound to distort this image. The first Roman emperor Augustus (63–14 BCE) was a master in this kind of self-fashioning and succeeds in influencing our view on his reign even today. The "queen of Latin inscriptions," his *Res gestae divi Augusti* (also known as *Monumentum Ancyranum*) is an autobiographical account of his actions that builds on generic precursors. Among these are Sulla's (138–78 BCE) 22 books of self-justification written at the end of his life; or, even before, Scaurus's (163–89 BCE) *De vita sua*, which begins a new culture of auto-biographic publication: the title not only lays claim to objectivity (written as it is in the third person), but also to comprehensiveness in describing the author's life. Augustus is thus part of a tradition, but he stands out even in the very form of publication: the text was distributed while he was still alive, and was carved in bronze as a funerary inscription in front of the enormous mausoleum after his death. The sober account describes how a man of private means rose to the godlike *pater patriae* within a few years and purely out of a desire to save and restore the republic – it is hardly surprising that we only read of the successes of the author in pacifying Rome and conquering the world. His second, "private" autobiography, also titled *De vita sua* but lost except for a few fragments, documents himself as established *exemplum* and exceptional figure.[40] His outstanding *auctoritas*, manifested in the numerous honorary titles and offices he received, enables him to point to what he achieved, in his own view, again and again: having done something for the first and only time. Therefore, his presentation of the deeds and their author are the main focus and amount to a universal testament.[41]

After Augustus's autobiography, a tradition of life descriptions written by emperors themselves is formed, of which we often possess only the titles: Tiberius (14–37 CE) wrote *Commentarii* to justify his actions, as did Claudius (51–54 CE) in an autobiography said to have comprised eight books. From the fragments of emperor Hadrian's (117–138 CE) autobio-graphy, we can confidently reconstruct the fact that the aspect of apology bordering on self-praise remains relevant. Tellingly, Hadrian's text was published under the name of one of his educated freedmen, illustrating the need for an impression of objectification and authentication with regard to an author's self-praise.

In postclassical times, especially in late antiquity, a new kind of biograph-ical or autobiographical literature emerges, which introduces a new relation-ship of author and text and anticipates the modern *Bildungsroman*: so-called "conversion literature." This includes novelesque conversion stories as well as confessional statements. Criticism of the identity concept is common to all of them; self-portrayals had until then been founded on this concept, even if at times *ex negativo*. Augustine (354–430 CE) wrote one of the most influential autobiographical texts both within this genre and outside of it: his *Confessiones* (*c.*397/399 CE) deal with the question of the constitution of self, and have often been called the first "real" autobiography.[42] He analyzes himself psychologically in order to provide an explanation for his own conversion, but at the same time presents this process as an honorable proclamation of God: this semantic ambivalence is already prepared in the title (*confiteri*: "confess/praise"). To Augustine, the dialogue seems to be the ideal literary form for depicting one's inner divisions and changes in all dramatic nuances. It becomes clear that Augustine also counts himself among the addressees of his book: by writing it, he becomes able to (re-) read his life in order to recognize himself. Consequently, the dialogue also deploys a mode of self-distancing.[43] A multilayered *ego* is presented to us, which constitutes itself between the poles of loss of self on the one hand and self-possession on the other. Furthermore, the devotion to God and the appeal to divine truth as reference point functions as part of the authentication strategy and clarifies the author's position.

Referencing Self and Other: *Imitatio Auctorum* and *Imitatio Morum*

The concept of imitation (*mimesis*) is foundational in ancient thinking. The representation of an idea or a thought in works of art, effected by a creative process of artistic expression, is central to Aristotle's *Poetics* and subsequent theorizing, and all ancient thinking about art revolves around this link between art and – idealized – reality. Rhetoric played an eminent role in forming a related mimetic theory about the author, as it did in all other ancient author concepts we have already looked at. One strand of this influence is found in the theory of *imitatio morum* ("imitation of life-style/ moral conduct") and *auctorum* ("imitation of authors"), complemented by a more competitive aspect of literary imitation, so-called *aemulatio* ("emulation"), i.e., the attempt to surpass the imitated author. The person-related form of *imitatio* as mimicry of ethically apt role models often functions as a corrective when a speaker's or author's style becomes too independent of social realities ruled by binding norms. In the rhetorical theories of Isocrates, Cicero, or Quintilian, the relationship between speaker or author as human being and his style of speech is very close and depends on a personal mimetic concept as to how life and speech are related, namely on the basis of similarity: life and art mirror each other. This is concisely expressed in the aphorism *talis oratio – qualis vita* ("the style is the man").[44]

In ancient literary criticism, as well as in the concepts of the author or "authorized" speaker, the analogy of style and man is part of the semantics of society, which lays bare the individual manifestations of art and speech as risk factors for public order. However, the synthesis of individual creativity and public obligation is effected by Cicero himself; Quintilian gives proof of this when he labels Cicero as *eloquentiae nomen,* "the very name of eloquence." This type of humanizing literary criticism prevailed in antiquity and only rarely contextualized or historicized, e.g., when Cicero reflects on Socrates and Cato; a true exception is Catullus's "law" of separation between art and life, discussed in the last section.[45] Cato the Elder's ideal of the *vir bonus dicendi peritus* ("a good man skilled in speaking") points to the interdependence of author and style: the individual as bearer of this ideal is able to represent the *res publica* as a whole. Cato himself becomes the example of his own ideal for Cicero, who states that "so remarkable was his experience of public affairs [...] and [there was] complete harmony between his life and his words."[46] Quintilian also testifies to the popularity and binding force of this requirement of authors. The twelfth book of his *Institutio oratoriae* is dedicated to the ethical foundation of rhetoric and bears largely on this same ideal.[47]

We have already touched on different examples in Roman literature that negotiate this central analogy on the level of the presented characters and the *personae* of the authorial *ego* (as in satire). We have also seen how easily the two levels are confused, and that the lives of authors are often deduced purely from their works (as in Vergil or Ovid). In these cases, art produces the standards for living, not vice versa. For this reason, the analogy is ultimately inadequate as an ethical criterion.

Notes

1. Thomas Seng, "Autor," *Historisches Wörterbuch der Rhetorik*, ed. Gert Ueding (Tübingen: Niemeyer, 1992), vol. 1, col. 1276–81.

2. Cf. Plinius, *Epistulae* 10.96(97).5: *libellus sine auctore* ("an anonymous pamphlet"). LCL 59, p. 286–87. All English translations are taken from the Loeb editions, unless indicated otherwise.

3. On the concepts of *poeta* and *vates* (as well as other denominations such as *scriba* or *dicti studiosus*), see John K. Newman, *The Concept of Vates in Augustan Poetry* (Brussels: Latomus, 1967); Werner Suerbaum, *Untersuchungen zur Selbstdarstellung älterer römischer Dichter: Livius Andronicus. Naevius. Ennius* (Hildesheim: Olms, 1968), pp. 33–34, 261–95; Hellfried Dahlmann, "Vates," in *Kleine Schriften* (Hildesheim: Olms, 1970), pp. 35–51.

4. Extended surveys of Roman literary culture can be found in Clarence E. Boyd, *Public Libraries and Literary Culture in Rome* (Chicago: University of Chicago Press, 1961); Elaine Fantham, *Roman Literary Culture: From Cicero to Apuleius* (Baltimore, MD: Johns Hopkins University Press, 1996); Martin W. Bloomer, *Latinity and Literary Society at Rome* (Philadelphia: University of Pennsylvania Press, 1997).

5. These terms are found in Valerius Maximus (3.7.11) and Festus (Sexti Pompei Festi De verborum significatu quae supersunt cum Pauli epitome; Thewrewkianis copiis usus edidit Wallace M. Lindsay, Leipzig 1913, p. 446). On the literary sociology of early Roman literature, see Werner Suerbaum, ed., *Die archaische Literatur: Von den Anfängen bis Sullas Tod. Die vorliterarische Periode und die Zeit von 240 bis 78 v. Chr.* (Munich: Beck, 2002), pp. 87–92, with references on p. 96, and Suerbaum, Selbstdarstellung, p. 260.

6. See Walter Wimmel, *Kallimachos in Rom: Die Nachfolge seines apologetischen Dichtens in der Augusteerzeit (Hermes Einzelschriften,* 16) (Wiesbaden: F. Steiner, 1960); Alan Cameron, *Callimachus and his Critics* (Princeton, NJ: Princeton University Press, 1995), pp. 454–83.

7. Well-known examples of literary communication between authors are found in Catullus's *carmen* 50 (addressed to Licinius Macer), Vergil's tenth *Eclogue* (to the elegiac poet Gallus), or in Propertius's first book of elegies (poem 4 to Bassus, poem 6 to Tullus, among others).

8. Many of these passages, as well as more information on Roman public and private libraries, can be found in George W. Houston, *Inside Roman Libraries: Book Collections and their Management in Antiquity* (Chapel Hill: University of North Carolina Press, 2014).

9. Cicero, *Ad Atticum* 12.6, Horace, *Ars poetica* 345–6; see Paolo Fedeli, "I sistemi di produzione e diffusione," in *Lo spazio letterario di Roma antica II: La circolazione del testo*, eds. Guglielmo Cavallo, Paolo Fedeli, and Antonella Giardina (Rome: Salerno, 1989), pp. 343–78. Cicero is said to have edited Lucretius's poem *De rerum natura*; cf. Martin Schanz and Carl Hosius, *Die römische Literatur in der Zeit der Republik*, 4th edn (Munich: Beck,1927), p. 280.

10. On forms and uses of the book in Rome, see also Theodor Birt, *Das antike Buchwesen in seinem Verhältnis zur Literatur* (Berlin: Hertz, 1882) and Horst Blanck, *Das Buch in der Antike* (Munich: Beck, 1992), pp. 152–78.

11. See Irene Peirano, "Authenticity as an Aesthetic Value: Ancient and Modern Reflections," in *Aesthetic Value in Classical Antiquity*, eds. Ineke Sluiter and Ralph M. Rosen (Leiden and Boston: Brill, 2012), pp. 215–42. Similar hermeneutical issues surrounding the reception of classical texts and authors are treated extensively in Charles Martindale, *Redeeming the Text: Latin Poetry and the Hermeneutics of Reception* (Cambridge: Cambridge University Press, 1993) and Shane Butler, ed., *Deep Classics: Rethinking Classical Reception* (London: Bloomsbury, 2016).

12. For the Latin text, see Giorgio Brugnoli and Fabio Stok, eds., *Vitae vergilianae antiquae* (Rome: Ist. Poligrafico dello Stato, 1997), p. 101; the translation is our own.

13. Female authors in Rome were scarce and are, in classical times, only found in Sulpicia's name, whose six extant poems are transmitted within the *corpus Tibullianum* (3.13–18). Roman female authorship is discussed in Claire Dean, "Roman Women Authors: Authorship, Agency and Authority," PhD dissertation (Calgary: University of Calgary, 2012), who focuses mainly on later Christian authors.

14. Cf. Walther Kranz, "*Sphragis*: Ichform und Namensiegel als Eingangs- und Schlussmotiv antiker Dichtung," *Rheinisches Museum*, 104 (1961), 3–46 and 97–124, pp. 3–46; Lothar Spahlinger, *Ars latet arte sua – die Poetologie der Metamorphosen Ovids* (Stuttgart and Leipzig: Teubner, 1996), pp. 27–50.

15. See Cédric Scheidegger Lämmle, *Werkpolitik in der Antike: Studien zu Cicero, Vergil, Horaz und Ovid* (Munich: Beck, 2016), p. 59, referring to Gérard Genette, *Paratexts: Thresholds of Interpretation* (Cambridge: Cambridge University Press, 1997). See also Peggy Kamuf, *Signature Pieces: On the Institution of Authorship* (Ithaca, NY: Cornell University Press, 1988), p. 4.

16. For the Greek tradition of the *sphragis*, see Ruth Scodel's chapter "Authorship in Archaic and Classical Greece" within this volume.

17. *Epist.* 1.20.19–28, LCL 194, pp. 390–91.

18. *Georg.* 4.559–566, LCL. 63, pp. 258–59. On this passage and its reception in Vergil's biographer Donatus, see Irene Peirano, "Ille ego qui quondam: On Authorial (An)onymity," in *The Author's Voice in Classical and Late Antiquity*, eds. Anna Marmodoro and Jonathan Hill (Oxford: Oxford University Press, 2013), pp. 251–85, p. 274.

19. Ovid, *Amores*, "Epigramma ipsius," LCL 41, pp. 318–19. See Alan Cameron, "The First Edition of Ovid's 'Amores'," *Classical Quarterly*, 18 (1968), 320–33; Francesca Martelli, *Ovid's Revisions: The Editor as Author* (Cambridge: Cambridge University Press, 2013).

20. E.g. *Amores* 1.1; 2.1; *Remedia amoris* 1.71–2; *Ibis* 4; *Ex Pont.* 1.1

21. *Trist.* 4.10.1–2, LCL 151, pp. 196–97, translation modified. On the formula in general, see Robert G. Austin, "Ille ego qui quondam," *Classical Quarterly*, 18 (1968), 107–15, and Antonio La Penna, "'*Ille ego qui quondam*' e i raccordi editoriali nell'antichità," *Studi italiani di filologia classica*, 78 (1985), 76–91; in Ovid particularly, see Katharina Volk, "*Ille ego*: (Mis)Reading Ovid's Elegiac Persona," *Antike & Abendland*, 51 (2005), 83–96.

22. Scheidegger, *Werkpolitik*, pp. 16–17.

23. *Amores* 2.1.1–2, 3.8.23–4; *Fasti* 2.5–8; *Tristia* 3.3.73–4, 4.10.1–2; 5.7.55; *Ex Pont.* 1.2.33–4, 129–32, 4.3.11–18.

24. *Vita Vergilii Donatiana*, ch. 42; the Latin text is found in Brugnoli and Stok, *Vitae vergilianae*, p. 95; the translation is taken from Peirano, "*Ille ego*," p. 273.

25. Peirano, "*Ille ego*," p. 274.

26. Scheidegger, *Werkpolitik*, pp. 14–16.

27. See the articles in *Der Neue Pauly* on "Urheberrecht" "Plagiat" and "Fälschungen": *Der Neue Pauly*, ed. Hubert Cancik, Helmuth Schneider, Manfred Landfester (all consulted online on 3 January 2018); on plagiarism, see also "Plagiat" in *Paulys Realencyclopädie* vol. 20, col. 1956–1997, esp. 1967–68. See also Wilhelm Kroll, *Studien zum Verständnis der römischen Literatur* (Stuttgart: Metzler, 1924), pp. 139–184 on different forms of imitation in classical antiquity. Modern copyright law and its repercussions in the literary system are described at length by Mark Rose, *Authors and Owners: The Invention of Copyright* (Harvard, MA: Harvard University Press, 1993).

28. For related metaphors (from Renaissance literature onwards) for the book as a child, or the book as real estate, see Mark Rose, "Copyright and its Metaphors," *UCLA Law Review*, 50.1 (2002), 1–15.

29. For an edition of Martial's first book and a commentary on this poem, see Mario Citroni, ed., *M. Valerii Martialis Epigrammaton liber I: introduzione, testo, apparato critico e commento a cura di M.C.* (Florence: La nuova Italia, 1975).

30. Cf. Scheidegger, *Werkpolitik* pp. 52–3 with bibliography on biographism and its problematic hermeneutical presuppositions. On biographism and intentionalism, two sides of one coin, see Carlos Spoerhase, *Autorschaft und Interpretation: Methodische Grundlagen einer philologischen Hermeneutik* (Berlin: De Gruyter, 2007), pp. 68–79.

31. On the theory of the *persona* in antiquity, see Diskin Clay, "The Theory of the Literary Persona in Antiquity," *Materialie e discussioni*, 40 (1998), 9–40; Roland G. Mayer, "Persona(l) Problems: The Literary Persona in Antiquity Revisited," *Materialie e discussioni*, 50 (2003), 55–80; Volk, "*Ille ego.*"

32. Cicero, *De off.* 114–15., LCL 30, pp. 116–17.

33. "Everyone writes a letter in the virtual image of his own soul" (σχεδὸν γὰρ εἰκόνα ἕκαστος τῆς ἑαυτοῦ ψυχῆς γράφει τὴν ἐπιστολήν): Demetrius, *On Style* 227, LCL 199, pp. 478–81.

34. Cf. *Ad Atticum* 2.6.2, 14.17.6.

35. An edition with translation is found in *C. Valerii Catulli Carmina*, ed. R. A. B. Mynors (Oxford: Clarendon Press, 1958).

36. On this analogy in ancient literature, as well as on the *lex Catulli*, see Melanie Möller, *Talis oratio – qualis vita: Zu Theorie und Praxis mimetischer Verfahren in der griechisch-römischen Literaturkritik* (Heidelberg: Winter, 2004), and Melanie Möller, "Subjekt riskiert (sich): Catullus, *carmen 8*," in *Vom Selbst-Verständnis in Antike und Neuzeit. Notions of the Self in Antiquity and Beyond*, eds. Alexander Arweiler and Melanie Möller (Berlin: De Gruyter, 2008), pp. 3–20.

37. Gian Biagio Conte, *The Hidden Author: An Interpretation of Petronius' Satyricon*, trans. Elaine Fantham (Berkeley: University of California Press,1996), p. viii. See also Möller, Talis oratio, pp. 284–94.

38. Conte, *The Hidden Author*, p. 4.

39. On this motif of everlasting fame for an author in ancient up to early modern poetry, see Philip Hardie, *Rumour and Renown: Representations of Fama in Western Literature* (Cambridge: Cambridge University Press, 2012).

40. The modern presumption about the ancient citizen as lacking privacy in the practically unlimited public realm has been productively discussed by Raymond Geuss, *Public Goods, Private Goods* (Princeton, NJ: Princeton University Press, 2001); see esp. pp. 34–54 on the *res publica* of Rome.

41. See Michèle Lowrie, "Making an Exemplum of Yourself: Cicero and Augustus," in *Classical Constructions: Papers in Memory of Don Fowler, Classicist and Epicurean*, eds. Stephen J. Heyworth, with Peta G. Fowler and Stephen J. Harrison (Oxford: Oxford University Press, 2007), pp. 91–112.

42. Even before the *Confessiones*, self-analysis in dialogical form was the basis of Augustine's *Soliloquies* (386/87), and in the *Retractationes* 2.32 he makes use of retrospection to explain his intention for the autobiographical *opus magnum*. See *Sancti Aureli Augustini Retractationes libri duo*, ed. Pius Knöll, 1902; repr. (Wien: Gerold, 1963), pp. 137–38.

43. For the autobiographical pact as a "medium of difference," making life portrayable only "from a critical distance," see Martina Wagner-Egelhaaf, *Autobiographie*, 2nd edn (Stuttgart: Metzler, 2005), p. 114.

44. Cf. Möller, *Talis oratio*, pp. 343–44.

45. Philodemus and Pseudo-Longinus avoid the dominant analogy as well: see Möller, *Talis oratio*, pp. 133–36 and 323–34.

46. Cicero, *De re publica* 2.1, LCL 213, pp. 110–111.

47. See Möller, *Talis oratio*, pp. 143–44.

CHAPTER 6

Conceptions of Authorship in Early Jewish Cultures
Mordechai Z. Cohen

Although early Jewish authors gave thought to the concept of literary authorship, they composed virtually no separate treatises on the subject, nor in fact did they usually address it directly. Their conceptions of authorship were presented implicitly within larger discussions relating to the ultimate form of literature in their eyes, namely the Holy Bible. Sacred Scripture, of course, stood at the heart of Judaism since Antiquity, and its interpretation has always been an essential element of Jewish learning. The science and art of Bible interpretation were systematized in the medieval period by a number of key Jewish scholars, and their writings included sporadic discussions about the nature of the authorship of the various books in sacred Scripture. In what follows, we explore selected statements from this corpus that together offer a representative sample of how literary authorship was perceived in early Jewish cultures.

An exception to the rule mentioned above is the dedicated poetics penned by the medieval Hebrew poet and literary critic Moses Ibn Ezra (c. 1055–1138, Granada) entitled *The Book of Discussion and Conversation.*[1] Thoughts on authorship and the nature of literary expression in general feature prominently in this work, which is a handbook for composing Hebrew verse according to the rules of Arabic poetics, as was the practice of the great authors of the Golden Age of Hebrew poetry in al-Andalus (=Muslim Spain), who fused biblical language and themes into their Arabic-style poetry. In addition to serving as a how-to guide for aspiring Hebrew poets, this work reflects a broad range of intellectual values and spiritual passions of Judeo-Arabic culture at its height in twelfth-century al-Andalus. Among these values was the desire to demonstrate the aesthetic qualities of the Hebrew Bible, which Moses Ibn Ezra did by harnessing the well-developed art of Arabic poetics and using it as a yardstick by which to evaluate the literary achievements of the ancient biblical prophets.

It made sense that Jewish conceptions of authorship were articulated in Muslim lands, where the Jews were particularly receptive to the highly

developed Arabic language arts. This process is already well-attested in the
pioneering works of Saadia ben Joseph al-Fayyumi (882–942), known as
Saadia Gaon. (The Hebrew term *gaon*, literally "grandeur," connotes the
dean of one of the leading great rabbinic academies.) Having emigrated
from his native Fayyum in Egypt in the early tenth century, Saadia rose to
prominence in Baghdad, a cosmopolitan center of Jewish, Christian, and
Muslim scholarship. Drawing upon a broad range of Arabic learning,
including grammar and philology, poetics, qur'anic hermeneutics,
Mu'tazilite thought, and Muslim jurisprudence (*uṣūl al-fiqh*), Saadia composed works on Hebrew language and stylistics, theology, and law, as well
as Bible translations (into Arabic) and commentaries. Saadia's arabophone
model of Jewish learning would be transplanted to al-Andalus within two
generations. Moses Ibn Ezra asserts that the secrets of the ancient Biblical
Hebrew language were revealed to the Jews only once they had become
familiar with the workings of Arabic grammar. In making this claim,
Moses Ibn Ezra was undoubtedly referring not only to the works of
Saadia, but also – and perhaps primarily – to the revolution of Hebrew
grammar and philology by the great Andalusian linguists Judah ben David
Hayyuj (*c.*945–1012; Fez, Cordoba) and Jonah Ibn Janah (*c.*990–1050;
Cordoba, Saragossa). Their work, in turn, served as the basis for the
influential philological Bible commentaries of the eleventh-century
Andalusian exegetes Moses Ibn Chiquitilla and Judah Ibn Bal'am, works
that shaped Moses Ibn Ezra's understanding of the Bible.[2]

Moses Ibn Ezra's literary values are well represented in the following
anecdote he offers, recalling his early years in Granada:

> In my youth, in my hometown, a Muslim scholar [. . .] asked me to recite
> the Ten Commandments in Arabic. I understood his intention, to demon-
> strate the paucity of its rhetoric. I therefore asked him to recite the opening
> (*al-fatiḥa*) of his Qur'an in Latin [. . .] but when he set out to translate it into
> that language its words became ugly and its beauty tarnished. He under-
> stood my intention and released me from his request.[3]

In tri-cultural medieval Spain, where Jews, Muslims, and Christians inter-
acted – not always peacefully – it was of supreme importance to uphold the
Bible's aesthetic pre-eminence.

Saadia and Ibn Janah described the Bible's aesthetic features in terms of
the Arabic notions of *faṣāḥa* ("purity of speech") and *balāgha* ("eloquence"). Moses Ibn Ezra used more specific Greco-Arabic categories to
describe the aesthetic nature of the Bible and to articulate his conceptions
of its authorship:

The art of rhetoric (Ar. *khitāba*) is called *rhetorica* in Greek [. . .] According to the philosopher Aristotle it is speech that persuades [. . .] And rhetorical addresses are found in our sacred prophetic books

The art of poetry (Ar. *shi'r*) is called *poetica* in Greek [. . .] The term for poet (Ar. *shā'ir*) in our Hebrew language is *navi* (=*prophet*) [. . .] For example:

> "a group of *nevi'im*" (I Sam 10:5) – *a gathering of poets*;
> "you shall engage in *nevu'ah* with them" (I Sam 10:6) –
> *you shall extemporize poetry.*[4]

In equating the Arabic term for *poet* (Ar. *shā'ir*) with the Hebrew term for prophet (*navi*), Moses Ibn Ezra reinforces the central role that poetics played in the formation of the Hebrew Bible. In other words, the prophetic authors of the Bible were guided by rhetorical and poetic considerations in composing sacred Scripture.

To assess the Bible's literary elegance, Ibn Ezra likewise turned to the Greco-Arabic aesthetic yardstick:

> In the eighth of his books on logic (i.e., the *Poetics*), the Philosopher (i.e., Aristotle) enumerated the matters in which poetry excels and is beautified, including [. . .] strength of the words, pleasantness of the matters, incorporating many matters in few words, beauty of the comparisons, quality of the metaphors, strength of the correspondence, repetition of the ends and the openings[. . .]. Now the Arabs divided them into many more than this number and scrutinized this matter deeply, as you shall see in this composition when you reach the appropriate place.[5]

Although he regarded Aristotle as a primary authority, it is in fact the Arabic "embellishments" of poetry that he used to define this art form in his *Book of Discussion*.

In the preface to the section of that work devoted to illustrating twenty key "embellishments" defined by Arab experts on poetry, Moses Ibn Ezra writes: "For each [. . .] I cite an example from Arabic verse and juxtapose with it what I find in the Holy Hebrew Scriptures, lest [. . .] it be said that the Arabic language is unique in these embellishments [. . .] and that our language is devoid of them."[6] In Ibn Ezra's opinion, the poetic techniques defined by Arabic theorists had already been applied by the ancient Hebrew authors whose words have come down to us in the Bible.

The perception of the biblical prophets as poets, while stated openly by Moses Ibn Ezra, was actually shared by many authorities within the Judeo-Arabic tradition. Indeed, this perception powered much of the exegetical thinking in the Andalusian school, which was epitomized by Abraham Ibn

Ezra (1089–1164; no relation to Moses Ibn Ezra). Born and educated in Spain where he primarily wrote poetry, Abraham Ibn Ezra emigrated to Italy in 1140. For the remainder of his life, he traveled from town to town in Italy, France, and England, writing Bible commentaries for Jewish audiences in Christian lands unfamiliar with Judeo-Arabic learning. Underlying his exegetical outlook is a fundamental connection between authorial intent and proper Bible interpretation:

> The words of any author, whether a prophet or a sage, have but one meaning, although those with great wisdom (i.e., the Rabbis) augment this and infer one thing from another thing[...] by way of *derash*[...] About this the early Sages, of blessed memory, said: "A biblical verse does not leave the realm of its *peshat*."[7]

Here Abraham Ibn Ezra juxtaposes the two quintessential forms of Jewish Bible interpretation: *peshat* and *derash*, i.e., midrash. The goal of his commentaries was to interpret Scripture according to "the way of *peshat*," i.e., the plain sense, as determined through philological-grammatical analysis. To justify this outlook, Ibn Ezra cites the maxim stated in the Talmud, the greatest source of authority in rabbinic Judaism, "a biblical verse does not leave the realm of its *peshat*."[8] It was necessary for him to offer this apologia because midrash, i.e., creative, even fanciful, readings of the Bible, was the standard traditional Jewish interpretive mode. Abraham Ibn Ezra negotiates the narrow straits between the authority of midrash and the cogency of *peshat* with the following compromise. The *peshat* represents the singular original intent of the ancient biblical prophets, who like any other literary author, must have had one particular meaning in mind when committing their words to writing. On the other hand, when the Rabbis of Antiquity engaged in *derash*, they were not aiming to discern the intention of the author, but rather to make additional inferences from the text of Holy Scripture.

Abraham Ibn Ezra's interpretive theory was prompted, in part, by the need for a bulwark against Karaism. In a movement that gained strength in the Muslim East since the ninth century, the Karaites rejected the Talmud, because its system of halakhah (religious law) was based on midrashic interpretation that seemed haphazard, especially in contrast to the philological methods developed by the Karaites. In particular, the Karaites challenged the rabbinic doctrine that "the Bible has seventy meanings" – a natural result of the open-endedness of midrash. The early Karaite author Daniel al-Qumisi, who emigrated from his native Tabaristan in northern Iran and resettled in Jerusalem in the late ninth century, accused the

Rabbis of distorting the true meaning of the Bible. He derided the notion of the Bible's multiple meanings, and argued instead: "You must know that everything in Scripture has only one interpretation (*pitaron*), and not two. And it is only because people do not know it correctly that one says thus and the other says thus, until the righteous teacher (i.e., the Messiah) will arrive."[9]

In opposition to the Karaites, the Rabbanites, i.e., adherents of rabbinic Judaism, sought to bolster the authority of the Talmud. Abraham Ibn Ezra tacitly accepts al-Qumisi's assumption that only one interpretation accurately reflects the authorial intention of the ancient prophet who penned each verse of the Bible. It is this singular intention that Ibn Ezra identifies as *peshat*. Unlike al-Qumisi, though, Abraham Ibn Ezra allows for the validity of midrash, as long as it is not confused with the original intention of the Bible. As he writes (in the citation above), "those with great wisdom (i.e., the Rabbis) augment this and infer one thing from another thing . . . by way of *derash*." As Ibn Ezra clarifies elsewhere, *peshat* is the "essence," while midrash is "an added idea."[10]

Notwithstanding Abraham Ibn Ezra's adherence to rabbinic authority, his exegetical approach is, in fact, a sharp departure from the Rabbis of the Talmud. Ibn Ezra interpreted Scripture as one would interpret "the words of any author, whether a prophet or a sage"; but the Rabbis presumed that Scripture possesses unique characteristics and requires a special mode of interpretation, i.e., midrash. As James Kugel shows, the first assumption held by the Rabbis of Antiquity – and in parallel by the early Church Fathers – that powered their midrashic interpretation is that "the Bible is a cryptic document. Although Scripture might appear to say X, what it really means is Y, a meaning that is only hinted at."[11] The Rabbis formulated rules for regularizing the derivation of such "hinted at" meanings in lists of *middot* (sing. *middah*; "hermeneutical principle"), best known of which are "the thirteen *middot* of R. Ishmael," and "the thirty-two *middot* of Rabbi Eliezer." The Rabbis, like the Church Fathers, also believed that Scripture is a "Book of Instruction." Everything in it applies to present-day readers and teaches them how to behave and think. Though the events it recounts are historically true, the Bible is not essentially a record of things that happened. As recorded in I Corinthians 10:11, Paul said about the ancient histories of Israel recounted in the Bible: "Now these things happened to them as a warning, but they were written down for our instruction."[12] Adhering to what Kugel characterizes as the doctrine of "omnisignificance," the ancient interpreters assumed that nothing in Scripture is said in vain or for rhetorical flourish: every detail is important;

everything is intended to impart some teaching. Apparently insignificant details in the Bible, such as an unusual word or grammatical form, or any repetition, were all read as potentially significant.[13] All of this explains why the Rabbis were generally uninterested in the "plain sense," i.e., philological, grammatical-literary analysis of Scripture in its historical setting. They mined the sacred text for eternal messages, moral and religious guidance.

A robust alternative to these presumptions emerged among Jewish thinkers in Muslim lands, where a different conception of Scripture and its authorship prevailed. In Islam, it is believed that God's will (*murād Allah*) is conveyed in the Qur'an in clear, plain (*mubīn*) language.[14] Qur'an 3:7 states that "the clear verses (*muḥkamāt*; sing. *muḥkam*) ... are the essence of the Book," which led Muslim interpreters to privilege the apparent, literal sense (*ẓāhir*), and to disparage allegorical interpretation – at least in theory.[15] This orientation was adapted into the Jewish interpretive tradition by Saadia, who argued that one must always posit initially that the language of the Hebrew Bible is clear (*muḥkam*) and be interpreted according to its apparent sense (*ẓāhir*), unless that would create a contradiction with what is known from other sources of knowledge.[16] This perspective of Saadia's prompted the development of a robust Judeo-Arabic tradition of philological Bible interpretation, which Abraham Ibn Ezra termed "the way of *peshat*," privileging it over midrashic interpretation.

Although the medieval *pashtanim* (practitioners of *peshat*) accepted the divine provenance of the Bible implicitly, they tended to focus on the intentions of its human authors – who were inspired by the Holy Spirit. Abraham Ibn Ezra – following a tradition pioneered by Saadia and developed in al-Andalus – explicated the "surface" of the text, its linguistic and literary structures, and poetic style. Aspects of the biblical text that the Rabbis took to "hint at" deeper meanings, such as redundancies and other linguistic anomalies, were explained by the Andalusian exegetes as literary conventions. They replaced the doctrine of "omnisignificance" with a search to identify the literary techniques typically employed by the biblical prophets – who were also poets, as Moses Ibn Ezra and Abraham Ibn Ezra maintained.

Particularly sensitive was the area of halakhah, since the laws of rabbinic Judaism are derived in the Talmud through the midrashic *middot*. Most of the laws are not stated clearly in the text, but are merely "hinted at," and extrapolated through the rabbinic hermeneutical rules that are predicated on the doctrine of omnisignificance. So how did a *peshat* exegete like Abraham Ibn Ezra reconcile his exegetical approach with the Talmud? Following a path forged by Saadia, he argued that the rabbinic "derivations" of these laws are merely second-ary projections onto the text – known as *asmakhta* (lit. "support") – confirming laws that were transmitted orally from the originally Sinaitic revelation.[17] In other words, the laws of rabbinic Judaism were given to Moses originally at Sinai and were not actually authored by the Rabbis. Yet this explanation does not seem true to the Talmud itself – where the *middot* are ostensibly used in a creative manner, i.e., to generate the laws of rabbinic Judaism. Indeed, the Karaites had a point when accusing the Rabbis of constructing a legal system of their own, com-peting with the divine Law stated clearly in the Bible.

A more essential explanation was given by the great talmudist-philosopher Moses Maimonides (1138–1204), an Andalusian émigré (born to a rabbinic family in Cordoba) who fled first to Fez and Palestine but ultimately settled in Fostat. Maimonides did not write biblical commen-taries and is best known for his influential talmudic-halakhic (i.e., legal) works, especially his comprehensive code of Jewish law, *Mishneh Torah*, and his philosophical opus *The Guide of the Perplexed*. Yet Maimonides sought to anchor both his *halakhah* and philosophy in a methodologically correct reading of Scripture and therefore addressed fundamental herme-neutical issues throughout his writings. This included important state-ments about his conception of the authorship of the Bible.

While most practitioners of *peshat* effectively separated exegesis and *halakhah*, Maimonides argued that "the *peshat* of scripture" serves as the fundamental basis of the *halakhah*. This unique view is advanced in his *Book of the Commandments*, a halakhic work that enumerates the 613 commandments (*miṣwot*) traditionally believed to have been given to Moses at Sinai, a genre popular in the Geonic-Andalusian tradition. Earlier "enumerators" of the commandments included laws of rabbinic origin (*de-rabbanan*); but Maimonides insisted on limiting this core group of 613 to those of biblical origin and authority (*de-orayta*) – which he identifies as those stated in Scripture, as opposed to those derived through midrash. To support this claim, he invokes the rule that "a biblical verse does not leave the realm (lit. "hands") of its *peshat*," which he takes to mean that the original meaning and authority of Scripture does not go beyond ("leave the hands of") its *peshat*.[18]

This dichotomy is based on the conception of the authorship of the Bible presented in the introduction to Maimonides' Mishnah commen-tary. There he reconstructs an account of how the Torah was originally given at Sinai:

> Know that every law that God revealed to Moses was only revealed to him with its interpretation. Now God told him the text, and then told him its interpretation [. . .] And they (i.e., Israel) would write the text and commit the interpretive tradition (*naql*) to memory. And thus the Sages, peace upon them, say: the Written Law (*Torah she-bi-khtav*) and the Oral Law (*Torah she-be-'al peh*).[19]

For Maimonides, the Torah was authored by God, and it was His authorial intent expressed in the interpretive tradition given to Moses alongside the written text.

Yet Maimonides makes room for another layer of meaning that could be derived from Scripture. In his opinion, the original interpretative tradition received by Moses was never forgotten or subject to debate. However, "the applications (*furūʿ*) not heard from the Prophet were subject to discussion, the laws being extrapolated by syllogism (or: legal analogy; *qiyās*), with the thirteen rules given to him at Sinai, and they are 'the thirteen *middot* by which the Torah is interpreted.'"[20] In other words, the Sages were authorized to apply midrash to extrapolate additional laws from the biblical text. Maimonides refers to the midrashic *middot* as *qiyās*, a term from Muslim jurisprudence that it connotes legal inferences from the Qur'an beyond what is stated explicitly in the text (*naṣṣ, manṣūṣ*).

The transmitted interpretations define the Law expressed by God in Scripture, whereas the *middot*, like *qiyās*, draw out further legal implications from the text – a process Maimonides describes using the Arabic term *istikhrāj* ("extrapolation"; lit. bringing out).[21] The Pentateuch text and its Sinaitic interpretation embody the original core of laws given at the one-time divine revelation. The derivation of new laws through the midrashic *middot* was a process that began subsequently and continued in each generation through the talmudic era. Maimonides refers to the original laws as the *uṣūl* ("roots") and later derivations as *furūʿ* ("branches").[22]

Already a generation before Maimonides, Moses Ibn Ezra gave credit to the Rabbis for this legal interpretive creativity:

> "A sage is greater than a prophet"[23] – this is because the prophet merely transmits the communication (*risāla*) [. . .] or prophecy (*nubūwa*) [. . .] as revealed to him, whereas the sage – speaking on the authority of the prophets – extrapolates laws (*yafraʿu*) from Scripture in accordance with what the Law allows him to extrapolate (*tafrīʿ*), and he utilizes his own mental capacity, and draws conclusions (*yuntiju*) from his intellectual premises. He has the distinction (*faḍl*) of creative ability (*al-ibdāʿ*).[24]

However, Maimonides draws a conclusion Moses Ibn Ezra did not draw. As mentioned above, in his *Book of the Commandments* he argues that the "branches" do not have biblical authority. In other words, they do not represent the original intent of God, the author of the Torah. The source of their authority is therefore not the text itself, "the *peshat* of Scripture," but rather the subsequent interpretations of the Rabbis. In making this distinction, Maimonides effectively replies to the Karaite critique. It is true, Maimonides openly acknowledges, that most of the laws of Rabbinic Judaism are derived from midrashic interpretation, and not from the text itself – which is the source of only the 613 core biblical commandments. Rather than denying this distinction, as earlier authorities such as Saadia had done, Maimonides accepts it openly as a formative feature of Rabbinic Judaism.

In parallel to the Andalusian exegetical school, a *peshat* revolution took place in northern France, pioneered by Rabbi Solomon Yitzhaki, known as Rashi (Troyes, France, 1040–1105), a key figure among Ashkenazic (Franco-German) Jewry. Living among Christian neighbors, Rashi and his community of scholarship had little access to the writings of their arabophone co-religionists. Yet the practitioners of *peshat* in Rashi's school developed sophisticated conceptions of authorship – perhaps informed by developments in Latin learning around them. The product of Ashkenazic learning in the Rhineland talmudic academies, where he studied in his youth, Rashi penned a supremely influential Bible commentary. Whereas Ashkenazic learning focused on Talmud and midrash, Rashi took a pioneering step within his cultural milieu in privileging *peshat*. Although he himself was immersed in the *aggadot* (midrashic traditions; sing. *aggadah*) of the Rabbis, Rashi presents a new interpretive agenda:

> There are many midrashic *aggadot* and our Rabbis have already arranged them in their appropriate place in *Genesis Rabbah* and other *midrashim*. But I have come only to relate the *peshat* of Scripture and the sort of *aggadah* that settles the words of Scripture, each word in its proper place.[25]

Unlike Abraham Ibn Ezra, Rashi does not exclude midrash from his commentary. Rather, he selectively incorporates into his commentary *aggadot* that "settle" the words of Scripture, in other words, that fit the language and sequence of the text.

The conception of authorship underlying Rashi's novel exegetical program comes into focus in his introduction to the Song of Songs, a collection of love-songs that was interpreted allegorically in midrashic tradition as an expression of the love between God and Israel. Without questioning the allegorical reading, Rashi invokes biblical and talmudic sources to argue that Scripture, in fact, has two meanings, which must be correlated with one another:

> "One thing God has spoken; two things have I heard" (Psalms 62:12) – "One verse can have a number of meanings,"[26] but in the end you do not have a biblical verse that leaves the realm of its *peshat* and literal sense; and even though the prophets uttered their words in allegory, one must settle the allegorical meaning on its basis and sequence, according to the sequence of the verses. Now I have seen many aggadic *midrashim* on this book [. . .] that fit neither the language nor the order of Scripture. I therefore decided to establish the literal sense of the verses [. . .] and the rabbinic *midrashim* I shall set, one by one, each in its proper place.[27]

For Rashi, Scripture cannot be deprived of its *peshat*, by which he means the philological-contextual sense, which must be explored and interpreted fully – to serve as a first point of reference toward the midrashic allegorical sense. However, he also asserts that "the prophets uttered their words in allegory," a key statement about the intentions of the biblical authors that allows for the multiple interpretations of their words – *peshat* and midrash.

Rashi goes on in his introduction to coordinate the two levels of meaning of the Song of Songs:

> Now I maintain that Solomon saw with the Holy Spirit that Israel will be exiled, exile after exile, destruction after destruction, and will mourn in this exile over their original glory, and will recall the original love of God toward them, which made them His chosen among all nations [. . .] and they will recall His kindness and their transgression, and the good things that He promised to bestow upon them at the end of days.
>
> And he composed this book with the Holy Spirit in the language of a woman stuck in living widowhood, longing for her husband, pining over her lover, recalling to Him the love of their youth, and admitting her sin. Likewise, her lover suffers over her pain, and recalls the goodness of her youth and her beauty, and the excellence of her deeds, through which he was tied to her in powerful love, to say [. . .] that her "casting out" (i.e., divorce) is not actual, and that she is still his wife and he is her husband and that he will ultimately return to her.[28]

Rashi here reconstructs how the Song of Songs was first composed: King Solomon envisioned through the Holy Spirit that Israel – centuries after his time – would be exiled and distanced from God, and seek to rekindle their relationship with Him. Rashi casts the Song midrashically as an expression of the people of Israel in his time communicating with God, recalling the days when the Divine Presence dwelt among, and being promised that God will restore them to that former glory. According to Rashi, this alternative to the Christian view that God has abandoned Israel is undoubtedly the essential prophetic message of this biblical book. Yet Rashi also accounts for the literal sense of the Song of Songs and its literary format – the *peshat*. He does so by constructing a persona and setting for the love lyrics in this biblical book within an imaginative literary framework. On his account, we hear in the Song of Songs the voice of an older woman separated from her husband, in what Rashi terms "living widowhood," recalling their youthful love and striving to restore it. As Rashi explains, the love poems in the Song of Songs are retrospective – this older woman reliving the romance of their youth.[29]

Rashi's commentary sparked others within the French *peshat* school. His grandson Rashbam (Rouen *c*.1080–1160), for example, penned a commentary that presupposes the allegorical nature of this biblical book: "King Solomon composed it through the Holy Spirit, for he saw that Israel would grieve in their exile over God, who has become distant from them, as a groom separated from his beloved. He began to sing his song representing the people of Israel, who are like a bride for Him."[30] Yet Rashbam also highlights *peshat* as his objective, writing:

> Solomon wrote (*katav*) his [...] "Song" [...] in the voice of a maiden longing and lamenting the loss of her lover, who left her and went to a faraway land. She recalls him and his eternal love for her, and she sings and says: such strong love my darling manifested toward me when he was still with me. And she [...] recounts to her friends and her maidens: such and such my darling said to me and this is how I responded.[31]

To better capture the spirit of playful, youthful love in the Song of Songs, Rashbam identifies the beloved as a young maiden, not an older already-married woman in "living widowhood." Indeed, Rashbam notes how the beloved

> grieves about her love for her darling, and after recounting [...] her love to her girlfriends [...] they scold her, responding: "Forget his love, because he has scorned you and will not return to you [...]" And she adjures them that they must not speak of this to her because she shall never forsake his love [....]
>
> Likewise nowadays the way of the singers (*trouvères*) is to sing a song that recounts the narrative of the love of a couple, with love songs as is the custom of the world.[32]

True to the midrash, Rashbam goes on to identify the allegorical referent of these "girlfriends" – the Jews' Christian neighbors, who impel them to renounce their faith. Yet Rashbam here makes a striking comment about the literary nature of the Song of Songs, comparing it to contemporary love songs, as he knew from the *trouvères* of his time in France.[33] Rashbam does not cite theoretical works on poetics, as Moses Ibn Ezra did; but he was aware of secular love poetry and identifies this as the literary garb of the Song of Songs.

Rashi had explicitly mentioned the agency of the Holy Spirit when speaking both of Solomon's vision of Israel's future exile and of the human love story that comprises the literary format of the Song of Songs. Rashbam cites the "Holy Spirit" as the source of Solomon's prophetic knowledge of Israel's grief in exile. But when speaking of the imaginative literary framework of this book, i.e., its *peshat*, he omits any reference to the Holy Spirit. Rashbam says simply (in the citation above) that Solomon wrote the "Song" in the voice of a beloved maiden. It would thus seem that the younger *pashtan* considers this poetic garb to be a product of the human ingenuity of King Solomon, as opposed to the prophetic content he received from God.

This innovative conception of biblical literary authorship is taken a step further in an anonymous northern French *peshat* commentary, where the following gloss appears:

> The Song of Songs – the most special of Solomon's poetry (lit. songs), for he wrote many poems, as it is written "his poems numbered a thousand and one" (I Kings 5:12) [. . .]
>
> From among his poems the Wise Men selected these and compiled them, with the intention to instruct about God and the Community of Israel. And this is what the opening verse means: "A poem that was prepared from Solomon's poetry" – that they anthologized his poems and arranged this collection as a testimonial regarding God and the Community of Israel, and the remainder they did not use. For this [poem; or: biblical book] was compiled with the aid of the Holy Spirit and was included in the Sacred Writings, because it is "holy of holies," for the Wise Men compiled the words of Solomon, as it is written: "These are the sayings of Solomon that the men of Hezekiah transmitted" (Proverbs 25:1).[34]

This commentator, using the vocabulary of Rashi and Rashbam, boldly posits two stages in the authorship of the Song of Songs, corresponding to two aspects of the biblical text and its signification. In his view the book is a selection of love poems by King Solomon – what Rashi defined as the *peshat* layer of the book. As love poetry, these "songs" initially conveyed no religious "instruction." However, a later group of editors, Hezekiah's "Wise Men," are responsible for the anthology of poems that make up the Song of Songs in its current form – and they endowed it with its allegorical sense, inspired by the Holy Spirit, and hence its religious "instruction," as required by the ancient rabbinic assumptions about scriptural interpretation mentioned above. Going a step beyond Rashbam, this commentator argues that Solomon himself is responsible solely for the literary format of the Song of Songs, and that the Holy Spirit that endowed the text with its allegorical sense rested upon a later generation of biblical figures.

These developments in the northern French *peshat* school can be compared with the tendency in the Late Medieval Latin learning to attribute the literal sense of Scripture – and its literary form – to the Bible's human authors, as opposed to the spiritual-allegorical sense produced by the Holy Spirit. As Alastair Minnis has shown, this dichotomy empowered a new focus on the agency of Scripture's human authors and their literary creativity. He notes that in the twelfth century Christian commentators "were preoccupied with allegorical interpretation":

> According to Geoffrey of Auxerre (late twelfth century), it is not important to know who wrote the Song of Songs. Perhaps the human *auctor* knew what he was prophesying, but if he did not, the inspirer (*inspirator*) most certainly knew. What matters is the prophecy itself, of the mystical marriage of Christ and holy Church. But in the early thirteenth century, when emphasis came to be placed on the literal sense of the Scripture, the exegetes' interest in their texts became more literary. [...] the emphasis had shifted from the divine *auctor* to the human *auctor* of Scripture.[35]

Although this trend emerged in force only in the thirteenth century, Minnis points to exceptional Latin scholars in Rashbam's time, such as Peter Abelard, who "anticipates literary attitudes which were widely held in the thirteenth century. [He] was [...] interested in the individual literary activity of the human *auctor* of Scripture, especially in the author's intention and the rhetorical force of his writing."[36] Further research is necessary to explore the possibility of influence between Jewish and Christian interpreters in twelfth-century France. Yet it is noteworthy that they manifest similar concerns regarding the relationship among the literal sense / *peshat* of Scripture, its literary form and human authorship, as opposed to its allegorical sense and the role of the Holy Spirit.

The view articulated by Rashi on the Song of Songs that the *peshat* is a stepping-stone toward the proper midrashic interpretation resonated among his students. Most notably, Rashbam remarks:

> Our Rabbis taught us that "a biblical verse does not leave the realm of its *peshat*," even though the essence (*'iqqar*) of Torah comes to teach and inform us of the *haggadot* (traditions, lore), *halakhot* (laws), and *dinim* (regulations) through the hints of the *peshat* [*remizat ha-peshat*] by way of redundant language, and through the thirty-two hermeneutical rules of R. Eliezer [. . .] and the thirteen rules of R. Ishmael. Now the early generations, because of their piety, tended to delve into the *derashot*, (i.e., midrashic interpretations) since they are the essence (*'iqqar*), and therefore they were not accustomed to the deep *peshat* of Scripture [. . .]. Now our master, Rabbi Solomon, the father of my mother, luminary of the Diaspora who interpreted Torah, Prophets and Writings, aimed to interpret the *peshat* of Scripture. And I, Samuel, son of Meir, his son-in-law (of blessed memory), debated with him personally, and he admitted to me that if he had the opportunity, he would have to write new commentaries according to the *peshat* interpretations that newly emerge every day.[37]

Rashbam emphasizes the independence of "the *peshat* of scripture" from "the *haggadot*, *halakhot* and *dinim*" that make up the creed and the laws of rabbinic Judaism. The latter are extrapolated from "the hints of the *peshat*," using the midrashic *middot*. Reflecting on the curriculum of study in his milieu, he notes that the mainstay of Ashkenazic Bible interpretation was a rehearsal of how the Talmud had applied these *middot* to yield the rubric of rabbinic Judaism – until Rashi began to take note of "the *peshat* of Scripture." According to Rashbam, Rashi himself recognized that more work remained to be done to perfect *peshat* exegesis, a project taken on by his students, among them Rashbam.

Although Rashbam devoted his exegetical efforts primarily to explicate "the *peshat* of scripture," he still adhered to the ancient rabbinic conception of the unique nature of Scripture, i.e., that its "essence" lies beneath the surface, and is to be determined through explication of the "hints" within the text that indicate its deeper meanings. This conception is, of course, quite different from that of Abraham Ibn Ezra, who regarded "the way of *peshat*" as "the essence," and relegated midrashic interpretation to an ancillary standing (as mentioned above). On the other hand, Rashbam's thinking can be compared with analogous conceptions articulated by medieval Christian interpreters. A vibrant new interest in the literal-historical sense of the Old Testament emerged among medieval Christian scholars, such as Hugh of St. Victor (*c*.1096–1141), his student

Andrew of St. Victor (*c.*1110–1175), Herbert of Bosham (1120–1194), and, most notably, Nicholas of Lyre (d. 1349). But this hardly implied its superiority over the spiritual senses of the Bible. Quite the contrary, the literal-historical sense remained subsidiary within a scheme that continued to grant supremacy to the Christological "spiritual" interpretation of the Hebrew Bible. The Victorines sought to preserve the integrity of the literal-historical sense of Scripture to serve as a "foundation" (*fundamentum*) for the spiritual senses.[38] As Rashbam's contemporary Hugh of St. Victor conceived it, Bible interpretation is like the construction of buildings: "first the foundation is laid, then the structure is raised upon it"; similarly "you will [not] be able to become perfectly sensitive to allegory unless you have first been grounded in history."[39] As he explains, "history" is "not only the recounting of actual deeds, but also the first meaning of any narrative which uses words according to their proper nature [i.e., literally]. And in this sense of the word . . . all the books of either Testament . . . belong to this study in their literal meaning."[40] Although Hugh's intensive interest in the literal-historical sense was novel, the image of a "foundation" that he used to depict its status was actually traditional. In fact, Hugh explicitly cites its use by Gregory the Great in his *Moralia on Job*; and the image was repeated regularly throughout the Middle Ages, e.g., by Bede (673–735), Rabanus Maurus (780–856), and Rupert of Deutz (1075–1129).[41]

Just as Hugh's interest in the literal-historical sense is part of a hermeneutical system that grants primacy to the Christological spiritual senses, Rashbam regarded midrash as the ultimate meaning of the Bible. In his view, "the essence (*'iqqar*) of Torah comes to teach and inform us – through the hints of (*remizat*) the *peshat* – the *haggadot*, *halakhot* and *dinim* by way of redundant language," as brought out by midrash. For Rashbam, the Pentateuch was a text intentionally studded with irregularities that hint at deeper meanings, which the Rabbis were authorized to extract using the special interpretive keys entrusted to them, i.e., the midrashic *middot*. In doing so, the Rabbis were not merely drawing inferences from the text (as Maimonides would say) but were actually discovering the deep intentions implanted ("hinted at") therein by God Himself.

Rashbam brought the revolutionary *peshat* method to new heights. But he embraced the traditional hierarchy that granted supreme authority to midrash, based on the assumption that the Bible is a cryptic text, unlike normal human literature. Rashbam lived in a Christian milieu where this assumption was never questioned. The Christian parallels cited above are not necessarily intended to suggest influence; they merely illuminate the conceptual hierarchy implicit in Rashbam's exegetical thought. In fact, there is no need to seek external influence for Rashbam's privileging of midrash over *peshat* – an established hierarchy in Jewish tradition.

On the other hand, Jewish interpreters in the Muslim orbit, from Saadia to Moses Ibn Ezra, overturned this hierarchy and tended to conceive of biblical authorship in terms of human literary design. Embracing Muslim conceptions of the clarity of scriptural expression, they privileged the literal sense of scripture and sought to explain away its supposed "irregularities" in terms of literary convention. As a result, midrash was relegated to the status of "an added idea," as Abraham Ibn Ezra would say, distinct from "the *peshat* of Scripture," which is the sole intention of the Divine author. Maimonides took the next logical step of granting unique halakhic authority to *peshuto shel miqra* – which conveys the will of God exclusively.

Notes

1. *Kitāb al-Muḥāḍara wa-l-Mudhākara (Sefer ha-'Iyyunim we-ha-Diyyunim)*, ed. and trans. [Hebrew] A. S. Halkin (Jerusalem: Mekitzei Nirdamim, 1975); ed. and trans. [Spanish] M. Abumalham Mas (Madrid: Consejo Superior de Investigaciones Cientificas, 1985–86). Hereafter, *Book of Discussion*.
2. See Mordechai Cohen, "Rabbanite Judeo-Arabic Bible Exegesis," *Encyclopedia of Jews in the Islamic World*, ed. Norman Stillman et al. (Leiden: Brill, 2010), vol. 1, p. 442–57.
3. *Book of Discussion* 24a.
4. Ibid. 9b–15a.
5. Ibid. 76a.
6. Ibid. 116b.
7. *Yesod Diqduq*, ed. N. Allony (Jerusalem: Mossad Harav Kook, 1985), p. 86.
8. See Mordechai Z. Cohen, *Opening the Gates of Interpretation: Maimonides' Biblical Hermeneutics in Light of His Geonic-Andalusian Heritage and Muslim Milieu* (Leiden: Brill, 2011), pp. 348–56; 495–99.
9. Commentary on Ps 74:5–6, cited in Meira Polliack, *The Karaite Tradition of Arabic Bible Translation* (Leiden: Brill, 1997), p. 29 n.
10. See Cohen, *Gates of Interpretation*, p. 75.
11. James Kugel, *The Bible as it Was* (Cambridge, MA: Harvard University Press, 1997), p. 18.
12. Ibid., pp. 19–20.
13. Ibid., pp. 20–21.
14. See Meir M. Bar-Asher, "'We Have Made It an Arabic Qur'ān': The Permissibility of Translating Scripture in Islam in Contrast with Judaism and Christianity," in *Interpreting Scriptures in Judaism, Christianity and Islam: Overlapping Inquiries*, eds. Mordechai Cohen and Adele Berlin (Cambridge: Cambridge University Press, 2016), pp. 65–68.

15. See Stefan Wild, "The Self-Referentiality of the Qur'an: Sura 3:7 as an Exegetical Challenge," in *With Reverence for the Word: Scriptural Exegesis in Judaism, Christianity, and Islam*, eds. Jane D. McAuliffe, Barry Walfish, and Joseph W. Goering (Oxford: Oxford University Press, 2010), pp. 422–36.

16. See Cohen, *Gates of Interpretation*, pp. 33–43.

17. See Jay M. Harris, *How Do We Know This? Midrash and the Fragmentation of Modern Judaism* (Albany, NY: State University of New York Press, 1995), pp. 76–86; Cohen, *Gates of Interpretation*, pp. 43, 76–77.

18. *Book of the Commandments*, Introduction, Second Principle. See Cohen, *Gates of Interpretation*, pp. 287–293.

19. *Introduction to the Mishnah*, ed. and trans. [Hebrew] Isaac Shailat (Jerusalem: Ma'aleh Adumim, 1992), p. 327 (Arabic); p. 27 (Hebrew).

20. Ibid., pp. 328, 335 (Arabic); 28–29, 36–37 (Hebrew).

21. See Moshe Halbertal, *People of the Book: Canon, Meaning and Authority* (Cambridge, MA: Harvard University Press, 1997), pp. 59–63.

22. See Cohen, *Gates*, pp. 266–68, 466–67.

23. This is a citation from Babylonian Talmud, *Bava Bathra* 12a.

24. *Book of Discussion*, 20a.

25. Commentary on Genesis 3:8.

26. This is a citation from Babylonian Talmud, *Sanhedrin* 34a.

27. Rashi, Introduction to the Song of Songs.

28. Ibid.

29. See Sarah Kamin, *Jews and Christians Interpret the Bible*, 2nd edn, ed. Sara Japhet (Hebrew; Jerusalem: Magnes Press, 2008), pp. 22–57.

30. *The Commentary of Rabbi Samuel Ben Meir (Rashbam) on the Song of Songs*, ed. Sara Japhet (Jerusalem: Magnes Press, 2008), p. 233.

31. Ibid., p. 234.

32. Ibid., p. 250.

33. See Mary J. O'Neill, *Courtly Love Songs of Medieval France: Transmission and Style in the Trouvère Repertoire* (Oxford: Oxford University Press, 2006).

34. Simon Eppenstein, ed., "Fragment d'un commentaire anonyme du Cantique des Cantiques," *Revue des Études Juives*, 53 (1907), 243–44.

35. Alastair Minnis, *Medieval Theory of Authorship*, 2nd edn (Philadelphia: University of Pennsylvania Press, 1988), pp. 38–39.

36. Ibid., pp. 58–60.

37. Commentary on Genesis 37:2.

38. See Henri de Lubac, *Exégèse médiévale: les quatre sens de l'Ecriture* (Paris: Aubier, 1961), vol. 2, pp. 47–50.

39. *The Didascalicon of Hugh of St. Victor: A Medieval Guide to the Arts*, trans. Jerome Taylor (New York: Columbia University Press, 1991), pp. 135–36.

40. Ibid., p. 138.

41. See de Lubac, *Exégèse médiévale*, vol 1, pp. 434–39.

CHAPTER 7

Modes of Authorship and the Making of Medieval English Literature

Andrew Kraebel

One of the most famous statements of scholastic authorial theory occurs in Bonaventure's mid-thirteenth-century commentary on the *Sentences* of Peter Lombard.[1] At the end of his prologue, the Franciscan master takes up the question of whether or not it is appropriate to call Lombard the author of the *Sentences*, a point initially made doubtful by the many quotations of patristic and earlier medieval writers appearing throughout the text. In his reply, Bonaventure describes what he calls the "fourfold way [*modus*] of making a book":

> For someone writes out the words of other men without adding or changing anything, and he is called the scribe [*scriptor*] pure and simple. Someone else writes the words of other men, putting together material, but not his own, and he is called the compiler [*compilator*]. Someone else writes the words of other men and also his own, but with those of other men comprising the principal part while his own are annexed merely to make clear the argument, and he is called the commentator [*commentator*], not the author. Someone else writes the words of other men and also of his own, but with his own forming the principal part and those of others being annexed merely by way of confirmation, and such a person should be called the author [*auctor*].[2]

Lombard does indeed draw on a wide range of writers, but he uses these authorities to support his own arguments, and Bonaventure concludes that he is therefore properly considered the *auctor* of the *Sentences*. Though, as Matthew Fisher has recently noted, the description of these four modes seems to be tailored to fit the "learned Latin theological production" presently under discussion, Bonaventure elsewhere draws on the same distinctions to describe, for example, biblical literature, distinguishing between Solomon's activities as *auctor* of the Sapiential books and those of Philo, "the wisest of the Jews," who later served as their *compilator*.[3] At issue in this distinction, finally, is the question of where to locate authority (*auctoritas*), of how authority is generated and how authoritative texts are produced. Scribes and compilers may copy and assemble the works of others, and commentators may gloss them, but it is the *auctores* who have ultimate responsibility for all authoritative writings. Bonaventure's argument that Peter Lombard (1100–60) should be considered an *auctor* is therefore high praise indeed, reflecting the central place the *Sentences* had attained in the schools in the century since their author's death. As Alastair Minnis has quipped, such scholastic theories suggest that "the only good *auctor* was a dead one," and it seems that, for Bonaventure, Lombard has been buried long enough to earn this title.[4]

To be sure, Bonaventure was hardly the only scholastic to theorize the work done by different kinds of writers, but his categories prove remarkably durable. Other Parisian masters, for example, including Peter Comestor (d. 1178) and Peter the Chanter (d. 1197), sought to delineate more precisely the activities that Bonaventure would later assign, generally, to *commentatores*. Faced with the complicated assemblages of early scholastic biblical commentary, these theorists distinguished between, on the one hand, *expositores*, the patristic and earlier medieval exegetes whose interpretations were assembled in later interpretive compilations, and, on the other, *glosatores* or *ordinatores glosarum*, medieval commentators who tried to make sense of those interpretations.[5] Indeed, the category of the *commentator* could become quite capacious, and, with the translation of Greek philosophical material into Latin (by way of Arabic commentators) in twelfth-century Spain, and more generally the rise of vernacular literature in the later Middle Ages, the work of translating texts was sometimes seen as a form of commentary, what Huguccio of Pisa (d. 1210) called "interpretation by means of another language."[6] The *modus* of commentary, along with that of the *compilator*, could also provide comparatively "modern" writers with a conceptual vocabulary allowing them to justify their new literary productions without directly or explicitly arrogating to themselves the high status of *auctores*. Such strategies proved especially useful for writers working in the vernacular. John Gower (d. 1408), for example, appears to have outfitted his Middle English *Confessio Amantis* with a substantial apparatus of Latin glosses, thereby suggesting the *auctoritas* of his poetic creation, even as one of those glosses describes the poem as a compilation.[7] More straightforwardly, Osbern Bokenham (d. *c.*1464) insisted that he "desire[d] to be holdyn neythur auctour ne assertour" of his *Mappula Angliae*, but "oonly the pore compilatour & owte of Latyne in-to Ynglissh the rude & symple translatour."[8] John Lydgate (d. *c.*1451) likewise describes the process of composing his massive *Fall of Princes* as "the compilacioun off this litil book," while in his *Troy Book* he rather deviously turns this language against the classical *auctoritates*, claiming that Virgil "in worschip of Enee / *compiled* hath" his Latin epic.⁹ The influence of these ideas can also be seen in the authorial self-presentation of Geoffrey Chaucer (d. *c.*1400), informing the incorporation of exegetical material in his translation of *De consolatione Philosophiae* (drawing on Boethius's Latin, the French of Jean de Meun, and the Latin commentary of Nicholas Trevet), and reflected, too, in his description of himself as a "lewd compilator" in the preface to his *Treatise on the Astrolabe*.¹⁰ In a more obviously literary vein, the colophon concluding the *Canterbury Tales* in Ellesmere and other manuscripts, identifying them as "the tales of Caunterbury, compiled by Geffrey Chaucer," cannily picks up on other disavowals of authorial responsibility within the *Tales*, including the inscribed narrator's claim that someone in his position "moot reherce as ny as ever he kan / Everich a word" of his fellow pilgrims' tales.¹¹ With authorship reserved for those (dead) writers whose venerable works were fit to be the subject of academic exegesis, the more inclusive categories of compilation and commentary helped to create the space in which new authors could be made.

In part, such turns to the relatively humbler discourses of compilation and commentary (and, relatedly, translation) were facilitated by the simple fact that much of the literature produced in the later Middle Ages did indeed build on the authoritative precedent of earlier writers. This is not to say that such medieval writing was boringly derivative, but just that, as Lydgate recognized about Virgil, these writers worked with texts they inherited from earlier periods, engaging with them creatively to produce their new materials. "The compiler is positioned," as Fisher writes, "to generate meaning, and to manipulate authorities and authority, in ways consonant with Bonaventure's conception of an *auctor* as the primary shaper of an argument."¹² While it may thus have been relatively easy for medieval writers to envision themselves as compilers and commentators, however, it seems that no one with literary ambition wanted to identify with the first of Bonaventure's modes, that of the scribe (*scriptor*, ME *scrivein* or *scrivener*). Best known in this regard is the single stanza attributed to Chaucer, in which the speaker excoriates the "negligence and rape" of a certain "Adam scriveyn," insisting that he "wryte more trewe" after his "makyng."¹³ Similar carelessness is evoked by Lydgate, who notes that "A skryuener / [. . .] can [i.e., knows] no more what he shal write, / But as his maister beside dothe endyte," while the author of the *Ayenbite of Inwit* complains about "scriueyns" who "sseweth guode lettre ate ginnynge and efterward maketh wycked," decreasing the quality of their work as they proceed.¹⁴ If vernacular authors were willing to see their efforts as compilations or commentaries, they did not want their literary undertakings to be confused with the error-filled and dishonest work of scribes.

Yet scribal practice – that is, the physical writing of texts – is one of the few things common to all four of Bonaventure's *modi*. The Franciscan uses a single verb, *scribere*, to denote the actions of the scribe, compiler, commentator, and author, and, while this word could (in a secondary sense) refer to acts of literary composition, by first introducing it with reference to scribal labor, he seems to emphasize its more concrete meaning, the material aspect of all of these modes of writing.[15] This is, after all, a schema delineating the ways of "making a book," not of making a text – all of these different kinds of writers work, at least in some respects, as scribes. As Fisher observes, despite their belittling remarks about scribal errors, "medieval authors must have been trained as scribes, and [...] nearly all authors were scribes."[16] In recent scholarship, the commonality of scribal practice has most frequently been used to argue for the contributions made by scribes to the works that they copied, choosing to present the text in a particular way or departing from their exemplar and offering what they considered to be corrections or improvements.[17] This focus on "scribal authorship" follows from the intervention of Bernard Cerquiglini, especially his *Éloge de la variante*, and it offers a valuable approach to medieval literature and manuscript studies. Yet comparatively little attention has been paid to a second (and related) implication of scribal authorship, namely the ways in which the material conditions of their work as scribes could have influenced the compositional practices of medieval authors. The reasons for this neglect are perhaps to some degree theoretical, encouraged by Cerquiglini's dubious claim that "the author is not a medieval concept," but they are also quite practical, since relatively few medieval autograph manuscripts (i.e., copies in the author's hand) survive, and these manuscripts would be one of the most obvious places to look for authors responding to the limits (and possibilities) inherent in scribal production.[18] Still, insofar as every scribe has to respond to what he finds in his exemplar(s), it remains possible that some traces of authorial-scribal decisions are preserved in the manuscripts of at least some medieval texts.

One English writer whose works were importantly shaped by his scribal practice is Richard Rolle (d. 1349), the Yorkshire hermit whose Latin writings had become authoritative guides to the religious life by the early fifteenth century, and who, also working in the vernacular, has good claim to the title of "the first real 'author' in Middle English."[19] Lacking recourse to the typical means of literary production – a monastic scriptorium, for example, or a commercial network of scribes – Rolle very likely had to copy his texts for himself, and his works initially circulated as "dispersed autographs directed to specific known audiences."²⁰ As Ralph Hanna observes, this arrangement could help to account for the unusual degree of substantive variation in the Hermit's works, since, if he "retained his own copies, the[se] writings could have remained capable of possible further differently personalized re-promulgations, with tailoring deemed appropriate for a new recipient."²¹ That is, Rolle could have revised his writings with each new copy in light of his changing understanding of the material or what he thought would better suit the new copy's intended reader. The Hermit's work as author and scribe may also explain why various medieval book owners claim not simply to have his texts, but to have them in a loose-bound booklet (*libellus*) or a single quire (*quaternus*), at once reflecting the modest execution of these productions and, insofar as these owners make a point of identifying their copies as autographs, the value associated with Rolle's material writing. An especially revealing claim of ownership occurs in the Office readings apparently prepared by the Hampole nuns in anticipation of Rolle's canonization, where a quotation from *Incendium Amoris* is said to be taken "from the writing of this saint's own hand, found after his death in a booklet compiled [*libello compilato*] from his works."²² The specification that this booklet was a post-mortem discovery suggests that, rather than necessarily being sent to any potential reader, it was kept for Rolle's own use, with the author himself compiling passages from his longer texts. To be sure, no manuscripts of Rolle's works copied in his lifetime survive today, and many of the medieval owners who claimed to possess autographs could have been expressing a pious wish rather than an historical reality. Yet it is still possible to recover at least some details of these autographs from the surviving copies of his works, helping to explain patterns in the dissemination of his writings and even the composition of some of these works themselves.

Consider, for example, one of Rolle's shortest and least studied texts, called *Super Mulierem Fortem* ("On the Strong Woman") in recent scholarship but titled *De vita activa et contemplativa* ("On the active and contemplative life") in the surviving manuscripts.²³ This work is preserved in five medieval copies, in one case as the sole bit of Rolleana in a miscellany of short religious texts (Oxford, St. John's Coll. MS 77, ff. 94ᵛ–96ʳ) and in another toward the end of a massive anthology of Rolle's Latin (now divided between Oxford, Corpus Christi Coll. MS 193 plus BL MS Cotton Tiberius A. XV, ff. 181–94, at Cotton, f. 190ʳᵛ).²⁴ In the three remaining copies, it comes immediately after the same portion of Rolle's *Judica me Deus*: in one instance it is the last Rollean text in the manuscript (Dublin, Trinity Coll. MS 153, pp. 244–52), and in the other two it is the final work in what was once a discrete booklet (Cambridge, Emmanuel Coll. MS 35, ff. 23^r–25^r; New York, Morgan Lib. MS M.872, ff. 119^v–121^r).[25] John Daly's work editing *Judica* indicates that at least Emma and Dublin were closely related, sharing a common exemplar, and, as Hanna notes, this lost antecedent copy was associated with a hermit living in the area of Tanfield, named in the colophon of *Judica* in Dublin and one other copy which also shared this exemplar but lacks *De vita activa et contemplativa* (Oxford, Bodleian Library MS Bodley 861).[26] Since these three copies (excluding Bodley 861) either present different texts right before *Judica* (Dublin and Emma) or give *Judica* and *De vita* in a discrete booklet (Morgan), it seems most likely that the Tanfield hermit's manuscript contained only these two texts – and, indeed, just such a single-quire (purportedly autograph) copy of *Judica* was bequeathed by Henry Scrope, Lord Masham, to Henry FitzHugh, Lord of West Tanfield, in a will proved 23rd June 1415.[27] The Tanfield hermit, in other words, seems to have come into possession of a "tailored" Rolle manuscript, either an autograph itself or copied from one, reflecting the author's decision to write out only one section of *Judica* and to follow it with the even shorter *De vita*.

Of course, the decision to copy his texts in a specific order does not in itself indicate that Rolle's activities as a scribe shaped the content of those works. But there is reason to believe that Rolle was not simply *copying* his *De vita* in the autograph that made its way (whether directly or at one remove) to the Tanfield hermit. It could be that, having written out the desired portion of *Judica*, Rolle was left with some blank pages at the end of the quire, and that he then devised – more or less simultaneously composing and copying – *De vita* as a way to fill that space, giving a summary of his views on ideal contemplation judged to be appropriate for the quire's recipient. Though admittedly speculative, this scenario fits with the internal evidence of *De vita*: this short text appears to have originated as scribal-authorial filler, an unusually perfunctory and (borrowing substantially from his earlier writings) derivative work crafted to fit a specific amount of space.[28]

De vita falls into a series of distinct and uneven sections. After an initial quotation of Proverbs 31.10 ("Who will find a strong woman?") and the claim that "quanto aurum argento est preciosius, tanto contemplatiua vita quam actiua subtilior estimatur" (Morgan M.872, f. 119^v: "as much as gold is more precious than silver, so much is the contemplative life considered subtler than the active"), Rolle immediately offers criticism of, first, feigned contemplatives who fool themselves into thinking they have moved beyond the active life and, second, those who appear to live a contemplative life but have not actually experienced the heavenly sweetness of true contemplation. He then turns to offer two common biblical images for the divide between the contemplative and active life, drawn from Song of Songs 3.10 and Luke 10.38–42, before giving his account of the true life of contemplation, presented as a gloss of Psalm 41.2–5. This is the longest section of the text, developing material that appears in Rolle's Latin commentary on the Psalms, e.g., "Sitiuit anima mea iam tacta amore supernorum non vanis illecebris carnalis vite, sed ad Deum fontem viuum" (Bodley 861, f. 16va: "My soul thirsted, touched by the love of heavenly things, not after the vain allurements of fleshly life, but after God the living stream"), which in *De vita* becomes:

> Fidelis anima tacta siti superne iusticie null[e] presentis vite delectacioni, nullo mundi gaudio, nulli prorsus cupidini se subdit, sed velocissimo cursu ad celeste poculum hauriendum tendit. (f. 120^v)

> The faithful soul, touched by the thirst of heavenly justice, does not submit itself to any delight of the present life, any worldly joy, any lust whatsoever, but on the quickest course strives to drink the heavenly draught.

The work then comes to a quick conclusion, ending with a succinct account of Rolle's vision of ideal contemplation and the spiritual assurances that come with it:

> Ffulget itaque mens nostra splendore eterni luminis, et tanto iocundiori corde amoris dilecti nostri delicias canere reficimur, quanto ad huius vite nostre terminum cognoscimus nos apropinquare. Non terret nos presens miseria nec paupertatis inedia, nec aliqua despeccio, nec a mundo expulsio, quoniam in illo viuere confidimus qui nos f[a]cit vt viuamus. Ipse seruos suos numquam deserit, nec alicu[b]i orphanos relinquit. Vere ergo in gracia perfunditur, qui incessanter amorem Christi querens, nullis prosperis uel aduersis a recta via variatur. (f. 121^r)

> Our mind shines with the splendor of eternal light, and the more we are restored to sing the delights of our dear love with a more jocund heart, the more we recognize ourselves to have approached the end of this life. Present misery does not terrify us, nor the hunger of poverty, nor any kind of disdain, nor expulsion from the world, for we have confidence to live in him who makes us that we might live. That one never abandons his servants, nor does he ever leave them orphans. Truly, then, he is suffused with grace who,

ceaselessly seeking the love of Christ, is turned from the right way by neither prosperities nor adversities.

Here Rolle invokes the mystical experiences that Nicholas Watson associates with his mature writings – the supernal melodies mentioned in the quotation are preceded by references to spiritual heat and sweetness ("dulcifluo ardore . . . ardemus, ardendo requiescimus").[29] Further, the suggestion that Rolle has "approached the end of this life" is tantalizingly similar to the claim, made in one of his assuredly late works, that he was writing at the end of his days ("iam in fine dierum meorum sum").[30] Yet Watson positions *De vita* early in the Hermit's career, citing its hodgepodge structure and the "lack of an explicitly didactic conclusion," which he associates with the major late treatises.[31] Indeed, coming at the end of the peroration, the final sentence of the text seems oddly disconnected from what precedes it, but, like the uneven structure of the work, this ending could be explicable as a symptom *not* of *De vita*'s earliness, but of its origin in an attempt to fill a specific amount of space.[32] The text can be seen as a series of notes on contemplation, and the final awkward sentence may reflect Rolle's decision to use all of the available lines on the page.

In addition to repeating commonplace material and borrowing from his earlier writings, the offhandedness of *De vita* is made clear by Rolle's treatment of the biblical image with which the text opens, the strong woman of Proverbs 31. After this initial quotation, which goes unglossed, Rolle only returns to this image twice, first to denigrate false contemplatives whose "anima mulierem fortem non demonstrat" (f. 119^v: "soul does not display the strong woman"), and again, at the start of the final section, describing the contemplative rapture in which one can truly claim to appear as "mulierem fortem in oculis Saluatoris" (f. 121^r: "the strong woman in the eyes of the Savior"). While the *Glossa ordinaria* (a standard late medieval exegetical reference work) interprets this strong woman as a type of the Church or of an individual Christian, it was hardly a common image for the ideal contemplative, and Rolle's allusions seem to assume some familiarity with his particular reading of it.[33] More specifically, its use here may take for granted that the reader of *De vita* also knows *Contra Amatores Mundi*, where, describing the soul which "at a quick pace rushes to its Spouse," Rolle writes:

> Scripture says, "Who shall find a strong woman? Far and from the uttermost coasts is the price of her." She dressed herself in purple cloth and linen, but she also made herself parti-colored clothing [*vestem strangulatam*; cf. Prov. 33.22]. This woman is not soft like other women, nor did she submit herself

to the pestiferous words of young men, but, great in strength, and having seized divine love, she stood as a man in her strength and will rejoice now that her enemies are defeated.[34]

The strong woman of *Contra Amatores* is developed more fully as a bellicose figure, a conquering contemplative who has defeated her worldly enemies and captured divine love. Intriguingly, Rolle's reference to her clothing creates a contrast where the biblical text offers three complementary images – the Hermit seems to take the unusual *strangulatam* as describing not luxuriously embroidered cloth, but rather a humbler patchwork, potentially reminiscent of the habit he is said to have made for himself from his sister's tunics.[35] Regardless, having developed the image of the strong woman in *Contra Amatores*, Rolle is able to return to it in *De vita* without taking the time to flesh it out, and his allusiveness could indicate that the recipient of the *Judica* and *De vita* quire had already received a copy of this other text as well. This bit of filler might not just be perfunctory and derivative – it may also be personalized.

This sort of personalization, in the form of revision if not wholesale composition, may also be seen in some of the Hermit's English writings. The copy of *Ego Dormio* in Warminster, Longleat House MS 29, for example, contains a lengthy passage occurring uniquely in this manuscript.[36] As Watson notes, Longleat presents a run of Rolle's English works as a discrete unit within the larger volume, framed with rubrics noting that Rolle prepared the sequence "ad Margaretam de Kyrkby reclusam" (f. 30ʳ), i.e., for Margaret Kirkeby, the Hampole nun who was enclosed as an anchoress at East Layton and later at Ainderby Steeple (both in the North Riding of Yorkshire).[37] The exemplar of this section of Longleat, in other words, seems either to have derived from or itself to have been an autograph booklet prepared by the Hermit for his disciple, and its creation presented Rolle with the opportunity to revise his writings, acting at once as author and scribe.[38]

In this more substantial compilation, the decision to present Rolle's texts in a specific order can at times take on greater significance, especially in the case of his vernacular lyrics, where rearrangement can blur into the remaking of texts. A second copy of the lyrics, for example, Cambridge, University Library MS Dd.5.64, part 3, includes three poems in the order "Ihesu Goddes Sonn", "Luf es lyf þat lastes ay," and "I sygh and aob."[39] Longleat, in contrast, begins the sequence with "Lufe es lyf," followed by "Ihesu Goddes Sonn" and then "I sygh and sob."[40] This arrangement is repeated in the only other manuscript to preserve these particular lyrics,

London, Lambeth Palace Library MS 853, pp. 90–102, though here the three poems are run together and written as continuous prose.[41] Certainly, regardless of Lambeth's presentation, all three of these poems can stand on their own. As it appears in Dd.5.64, for example, "Ihesu Goddes Sonn" is a perfectly coherent freestanding unit, related to (though metrically distinct from) a poem Rolle embeds in *Ego Dormio*.[42] Its three opening stanzas each begin with an invocation of the name of "Ihesu," followed by two stanzas expressing the speaker's prayers and continuing to address Christ (e.g., 13: "Wounde my hert within and welde it at þi wille"), after which the poetic voice turns to reflect on these devotional acts and refers to Christ in the third person:

> My sang es in syghyng whil I dwel in þis way,
> My lyfe es in langyng þat byndes me nyght and day
> Til I comm til my king, þat I won with hym may
> And se his fayre schynyng and lyf þat lastes ay. (21–24)[43]

This continues through two further stanzas, and the poem concludes with four stanzas of Passion meditation (one of which incorporates material from a pre-Rollean lyric, "Whyte was his naked breste") and a final injunction to "Gyf al þi hert til Crist, þi qwert [i.e., health], and lufe hym euermare" (48).[44] Likewise, treating "I sygh and sob" as a discrete poem presents no interpretive problems – indeed, by beginning with a vague statement of love-longing ("I sygh and sob bath day and nyght for ane sa fayre of hew"), this lyric cultivates a feigned indeterminacy that is only resolved in its sixth line: "It es Ihesu, forsoth I say." The speaker's lovesick devotion to Christ is described at length, and the final stanza culminates with four anaphoric lines which (like the opening stanzas of "Ihesu Goddes Sonn") each begin with the Holy Name.

If all three of these poems can at least potentially stand on their own, then the key to their various arrangements might be the conclusion of "Luf es lyf þat lastes ay," which seems to introduce the possibility of a framed lyric. After a stanza and two lines that look forward to the Last Judgment (a concluding lyric move with which Rolle would have been familiar from his work with the Psalter),[45] "Luf es lyf" ends with an enjoinder to song:

> If þow wil lufe, þan may þow syng til Cryst in melody;
> Þe lufe of hym ouercoms al thyng: in lufe lyue we and dye. (67–68)

Whether these lines are followed by "Ihesu Goddes Sonn" as in Longleat and Lambeth or "I sygh and sob" as in Dd.5.64, the subsequent stanzas could be seen as providing the contents of such a love song, a kind of devotional-poetic scripting also found in Rolle's prose epistles.[46] "Ihesu Goddes Sonn" begins, as we have seen, with the repeated invocation of the lover to whom Rolle has just (at the end of "Luf es lyf") instructed his reader to sing, and "I sygh and sob" reflects the devout reader's current state of lovesickness and ends with a stanza that parallels and clarifies the opening of the framing poem, "Ihesu es lufe þat lastes ay" (93). The bracketing effect of this echo may suggest that Rolle originally composed "Luf es lyf" and "I sygh and sob" in the arrangement found in Dd.5.64, but it would still be perfectly conceivable that he decided to replace the latter with "Ihesu Goddes Sonn" in a subsequent copy, potentially an autograph prepared for Kirkeby.

This kind of rearrangement and revision is discernible in another set of lyrics in Dd.5.64. Starting on f. 40[v], the scribe first writes one lyric, "All vanitese forsake," and then copies the Hermit's devotional prose provocation, "Ghostly Gladness," to which he adds a rubricated colophon, "Expliciunt cantica divini amoris secundum Ricardum Hampole" ("Here end the songs of divine love by Richard Hampole"). But he does not end there, instead writing, "Item secundum istum Ricardum" ("Also by the same Richard"), and supplying one more lyric, "Thy joy be ilka dele," concluding with another rubricated note, "Al vanites forsake if þow hys lufe wil fele etc., vt supra" (f. 42[v]). These different paratextual notes seem to indicate that this scribe (or the scribe of his exemplar) had finished his work with one manuscript, from which he copied most of the lyrics and "Ghostly Gladness," and was drawing on a second exemplar perhaps in a later stint, which contained "Thy joy" and (again) "All vanitese."[47] These two texts are presented in this order – but as a single lyric, run together without any signs of a break – in the two other manuscripts preserving them, Longleat 29, ff. 53[r]–54[v], and Lincoln, Cath. Lib. MS 91, f. 222[rv].[48] The Dd scribe (or the scribe of his exemplar) seems to have been trying to indicate that "Thy joy" continued, as in Longleat and Lincoln, with the stanzas of "All vanitese" which he had already copied above and did not wish to repeat. Dd.5.64 may present, in other words, evidence of two separate states of this text – one with "All vanitese" existing independently and another with it as the concluding stanzas of a much longer poem, "Thy joy" – and it would be hard to know whether the materials copied by this scribe reflect an excerpting of "All vanitese" from the longer work (and if so, whether by a scribe or the scribal author) or an expansive (more likely authorial) revision, beginning with "All vanitese" and adding more stanzas before it. Both scenarios are possible, but the latter becomes more likely when we note that Dd.5.64 omits three non-consecutive stanzas of "Thy joy" found in the two other copies, perhaps indicating that the work of expansion was done in multiple stages.[49]

The example of Rolle's Latin and English writings should indicate that Cerquiglini goes too far when he claims that "the author is not a medieval concept," and his imagined scene of medieval literary production as "a writing workshop," where "meaning was to be found everywhere, and its origin was nowhere," is surely fanciful exaggeration.[50] At the same time as the scribe of Dd.5.64 preserved what seem to be two versions of a single poem, he was also careful to attribute them both to "Ricardus Hampole," at once apparently acknowledging the variability of pre-print literature and affirming the importance of this *auctor* as an authorizing figure. At least in some cases, then, variability existed alongside a recognition (and even valuing) of the role of authors as the originating agents of literary production. Without giving way to the excavational philology that Cerquiglini decried, it should be possible to study the variability of medieval texts while also attending to the unfolding of that variability in time, in a way that is often, and perhaps to a surprising degree, recoverable. To put it another way, if these variable texts are especially "ripe for a descriptive turn," then that description must take account of the role of history and the directions of change represented in the differing versions of a text (or a clutch of related texts).[51]

Complicating all this is the intersection of authorial and scribal activities. If much medieval literature originated in authorial acts of writing (in a physical sense), then we must be attentive to the ways in which the resulting compositions could be constrained both by the material page and by more abstract scribal conventions. At the same time, though, just as recent work has made it clear that scribes could contribute importantly to the meaning of the works they copied, we should also be mindful of the possibility that the scribal work of authors could enable them to put these material factors and conventions to creative ends, presenting their text in a form that has much more in common with subsequently circulating copies than would be the case with literature in print. Compared to the details of a work's transmission history, these authorial-scribal activities are now much harder to recover – the example of Rolle's Latin filler and his potential reshufflings of his lyrics are certainly exceptional, insofar as we can still perceive in later manuscripts some details of the author's scribal work. But it is nevertheless important for us to keep sight of what would have been the unexceptional quality and potential significance of medieval authors' work as scribes.

Notes

1. For recent discussions of medieval authorship, see Jan Ziolkowski, "Cultures of Authority in the Long Twelfth Century," *JEGP*, 108 (2009), 421–48; Emily Steiner, "Authority," in *Middle English*, ed. Paul Strohm (Oxford: Oxford University Press, 2007), pp. 142–59; Anthony Bale, "From Translator to Laureate: Imagining the Medieval Author," *Literature Compass*, 5 (2002), 918–34. Throughout the following, Latin quotations will only be provided when the source is unedited.
2. *Medieval Literary Theory and Criticism, c.1100–c.1375: The Commentary Tradition*, ed. A. J. Minnis and A. B. Scott, with the assistance of David Wallace, rev. edn (Oxford: Oxford University Press, 1991), p. 229; for the Latin, see *Doctoris Seraphici S. Bonaventurae ... Opera Omnia* (Quaracchi: Typographia Collegii S. Bonaventurae, 1882–1902), vol. 1, pp. 14–15.
3. Matthew Fisher, *Scribal Authorship and the Writing of History in Medieval Literature* (Columbus: Ohio State University Press, 2012), pp. 71–72.
4. A. J. Minnis, *Medieval Theory of Authorship: Scholastic Literary Attitudes in the Later Middle Ages*, 2nd edn (Philadelphia: University of Pennsylvania Press, 2010), p. 12.
5. Beryl Smalley, *The Study of the Bible in the Middle Ages*, 3rd rev. edn (Oxford: Blackwell, 1983), p. 225.
6. Huguccio of Pisa, *Derivationes*, eds. Enzo Cecchini et al. (Florence: Edizioni del Galluzzo, 2004), vol. 2, p. 536. On Greek-Arabic-Latin translations, see Charles Burnett, *Arabic into Latin in the Middle Ages: The Translators and Their Intellectual and Social Context* (Farnham, UK: Ashgate, 2009); on commentary and translation, see Ralph Hanna et al., "Latin Commentary Tradition and Vernacular Literature," in *The Cambridge History of Literary Criticism*, vol. 2, *The Middle Ages*, eds. Alastair Minnis and Ian Johnson (Cambridge: Cambridge University Press, 2005), pp. 363–421, esp. pp. 363–64; Rita Copeland, *Rhetoric, Hermeneutics, and Translation in the Middle Ages: Academic Traditions and Vernacular Texts* (Cambridge: Cambridge University Press, 1991), pp. 87–97.
7. *The English Works of John Gower*, ed. G. C. Macaulay, EETS es 81–82 (London: Paul, Trench, Trübner, 1900–1901), vol. 1, pp. 3–4. On the glosses, see Derek Pearsall, "The Organisation of the Latin Apparatus in Gower's *Confessio Amantis*: The Scribes and Their Problems," in *The Medieval Book and the Modern Collector: Essays in Honour of Toshiyuki Takamiya*, eds. Takami Matsuda et al. (Woodbridge, UK: Brewer, 2004), pp. 99–112.
8. Carl Horstmann, "*Mappula Angliae* von Osbern Bokenham," *Englische Studien*, 10 (1887), 1–34, p. 34.
9. Respectively, *Lydgate's Fall of Princes*, 6.238, ed. H. Bergen, EETS es 121–124 (London: Milford, 1924–1927), vol. 3, p. 680; *Lydgate's Troy Book*, 2.343–44, ed. H. Bergen, EETS es 97, 103, 106, and 126 (London: Paul, Trench, Trübner, 1906–35), vol. 1, p. 154 (emphasis added). For discussion of poetic authority in Lydgate's corpus, see Lois Ebin, *Illuminator, Makar, Vates: Visions of Poetry in*

the Fifteenth Century (Lincoln: University of Nebraska Press, 1988). The example from the *Troy Book* could, alternatively, demonstrate the prestige of the *compilator* at the time Lydgate wrote: see Alastair Minnis, "Nolens auctor sed compilator reputari: The Late-Medieval Discourse of Compilation," in *La méthode critique au Moyen Âge*, eds. Mireille Chazan and Gilbert Dahan (Turnhout: Brepols, 2008), pp. 47–63.

10. On the complex composition of the *Boece*, see *Chaucer's Boece and the Medieval Tradition of Boethius*, ed. Alastair Minnis (Cambridge: D. S. Brewer, 1993); for Chaucer's self-description in the *Astrolabe* treatise, see *The Riverside Chaucer*, gen. ed. Larry Benson, 3rd edn (Oxford: Oxford University Press, 2008), p. 662, ll. 61–62.

11. *Riverside Chaucer*, p. 382 and p. 35, ll. 732–33. See Minnis, *Medieval Theory*, pp. 190–210, and, on the Ellesmere colophon, Stephen Partridge, "'The Makere of this Boke': Chaucer's Retraction and the Author as Scribe and Compiler," in *Author, Reader, Book: Medieval Authorship in Theory and Practice*, eds. Stephen Partridge and Erik Kwakkel (Toronto: Toronto University Press, 2012), pp. 106–53.

12. Fisher, *Scribal Authorship*, 72.

13. *Riverside Chaucer*, p. 650; see further Alexandra Gillespie, "Reading Chaucer's Words to Adam," *Chaucer Review*, 42 (2008), 267–83.

14. Lydgate, *Complaint of the Black Knight*, 194–96, in *The Minor Poems of John Lydgate*, ed. Henry Noble MacCracken, EETS es 107 and os 192 (London: Paul, Trench, Trübner, 1911; London: Oxford University Press, 1934), vol. 2, p. 390; *Dan Michel's Ayenbite of Inwyt*, ed. Richard Morris, EETS os 23 (London: Trübner, 1866), p. 44.

15. *Dictionary of Medieval Latin from British Sources*, eds. R. E. Latham et al. (London: Oxford University Press for the British Academy, 1975–2010), vol. 15, pp. 2980–81.

16. Fisher, *Scribal Authorship*, 6. Of course, at least some authors dictated their writings to secretaries: see Antoine Dondaine, *Secrétaires de saint Thomas*, 2 vols. (Rome: S. Tomasso, 1956), though St. Thomas's work is also preserved in his own hand in, e.g., Milan, Biblioteca Ambrosiana MS F.187.inf, reproduced in Anthony Kenny, *A New History of Western Philosophy*, vol. 2, *Medieval Philosophy* (Oxford: Clarendon Press, 2005), p. 194.

17. See, e.g., Fisher, *Scribal Authorship*, pp. 45 and 26.

18. Bernard Cerquiglini, *In Praise of the Variant: A Critical History of Philology*, trans. Betsy Wing (Baltimore, MD: Johns Hopkins University Press, 1999), p. 8. On autographs, see Richard Beadle, "English Autograph Writings of the Later Middle Ages: Some Preliminaries," in *Gli autografi medievali: Problemi paleografici e filologici*, eds. Paolo Chiesa and Lucia Pinelli (Spoleto: CISAM, 1994), pp. 249–68; Matthew Fisher, "When Variants Aren't: Authors as Scribes in Some English Manuscripts," in *Probable Truth: Editing Medieval Texts from Britain in the Twenty-First Century*, eds. Vincent Gillespie and Anne Hudson (Turnhout: Brepols, 2013), pp. 207–22.

19. Ralph Hanna, "Rolle and Related Works," in *A Companion to Middle English Prose*, ed. A. S. G. Edwards (Cambridge: Brewer, 2004), pp. 19–31, p. 19.
20. Ralph Hanna, "The Transmission of Richard Rolle's Latin Works," *The Library*, 7th series, 14 (2013), 313–33, p. 328.
21. Ibid.
22. *The Officium and Miracula of Richard Rolle of Hampole*, ed. Reginald Maxwell Woolley (London: SPCK, 1919), p. 36.
23. Use of the editorial title has been encouraged by Hope Emily Allen, *Writings Ascribed to Richard Rolle, Hermit of Hampole, and Materials for his Biography* (New York: Heath, 1927), pp. 159–60; Allen notes that John Bale (d. 1552) records a work by this title attributed to Rolle, though the incipit he provides does not match the present text. In light of the discussion below, it is worth noting Allen's conjecture that Bale may have seen "a copy to which some extra material had been added at the beginning" (p. 159).
24. See Ralph Hanna, *A Descriptive Catalogue of the Western Medieval Manuscripts of St. John's College, Oxford* (Oxford: Oxford University Press, 2002), pp. 100–105; R. M. Thomson, *A Descriptive Catalogue of the Medieval Manuscripts of Corpus Christi College, Oxford: Western Manuscripts* (Cambridge: Brewer, 2011), pp. 96–97.
25. For descriptions of Dublin 153 and Morgan M.872, see Marvin Colker, *Descriptive Catalogue of the Medieval and Renaissance Latin Manuscripts: Trinity College Library, Dublin* (Aldershot: Scolar Press, 1991), pp. 270–71, and Hanna, "Transmission," p. 333. Several factors indicate a quire and booklet break at the end of *De vita* in Emmanuel Coll. 35, ff. 23^r–24^v. First, as noted by Michael Sargent, *James Grenehalgh as Textual Critic* (Salzburg: Institut für Anglistik und Amerikanistik, 1984), vol. 2, p. 478, "thread can be seen in the gutter between ff. 20–21 [and] 28–29," suggesting two consecutive quires of four bifolia with f. 24 being the end of the first. Further, Sargent, *Grenehalgh*, vol. 2, p. 483, observes that the lower portion of f. 24^v has been left blank following the completion of *De vita*, and in her edition of *Incendium Amoris of Richard Rolle of Hampole* (Manchester: Manchester University Press, 1915), pp. 14–15, Margaret Deanesly observes that ff. 1^r–24^v and ff. 25^r–58^v are copied in two different hands.
26. *An Edition of Judica me Deus of Richard Rolle*, ed. John Philip Daly (Salzburg: Institut für Anglistik und Amerikanistik, 1984), esp. pp. xxvii and xxviii–xxxi; Morgan was unknown to Daly. Hanna, "Transmission," pp. 321–22.
27. See Susan Cavanaugh, "A Study of Books Privately Owned in England, 1300–1450," PhD dissertation, University of Pennsylvania (1980), p. 774. I am less confident than Hanna that the Tanfield hermit came to possess this manuscript *after* it was bequeathed to FitzHugh, since the colophon in Bodley 861, f. 102^v, dates that scribe's activities to late 1409, before Scrope's will was proved. Perhaps we are dealing with two distinct but related copies, or perhaps Scrope obtained the quire from the Tanfield hermit.
28. See P. R. Robinson, "The 'Booklet': A Self-Contained Unit of Composite Manuscripts," *Codicologica*, 3 (1980), 46–69, p. 48; Ralph Hanna, *Pursuing*

History: Middle English Manuscripts and their Texts (Stanford: Stanford University Press, 1996), p. 30.

29. Nicholas Watson, *Richard Rolle and the Invention of Authority* (Cambridge: Cambridge University Press, 1991), esp. pp. 60–72.

30. *Exposicio super nouem lecciones mortuorum*, 7, in Cambridge, University Library MS Ii.1.26, f. 172^v.

31. Watson, *Invention of Authority*, pp. 103–105.

32. The final sentence could perhaps gesture back to *De vita*'s discussion of Ps. 41: "Ceruus ad [a]quam festin[ans] nulla vi[e] visione retardi nouerit" (f. 120^v).

33. *Biblia sacra cum Glossa ordinaria novisque additionibus*, ed. François Feruardent (Venice: Giuntas, 1603), vol. 3, sig. Ii4^{rv}.

34. *Contra Amatores Mundi of Richard Rolle of Hampole*, ed. Paul Theiner (Berkeley: University of California Press, 1968), pp. 75–76; my translation adapts Theiner's. Note also the echo of the *velocissimus cursus* in *De vita*, quoted above.

35. *Officium and Miracula*, ed. Woolley, pp. 23–24.

36. See *Richard Rolle: Prose and Verse*, ed. S. J. Ogilvie-Thomson, EETS os 293 (Oxford: Oxford University Press, 1988), p. 32, ll. 243–55 (cf. pp. lxxiii–lxxv for discussion).

37. Watson, *Invention of Authority*, pp. 248–49; cf. Elizabeth Freeman, "The Priory of Hampole and its Literary Culture: English Religious Women and Books in the Age of Richard Rolle," *Parergon* 29 (2012), pp. 1–25, pp. 7–8.

38. Ralph Hanna, *English Manuscripts of Richard Rolle: A Descriptive Catalogue* (Exeter, UK: University of Exeter Press, 2010), pp. xxvi–xxvii, queries this conclusion.

39. For a description, see Hanna, *English Manuscripts*, pp. 26–27.

40. Ibid., pp. 209–210.

41. Ibid., pp. 112–13.

42. Cf. *Prose and Verse*, ed. Ogilvie-Thomson, pp. 32–33.

43. Quotations of Rolle's lyrics are based on *Richard Rolle: Uncollected Prose and Verse with Related Northern Texts*, ed. Ralph Hanna, EETS os 329 (Oxford: Oxford University Press, 2007), pp. 24–25, using Dd as copytext.

44. Thus Vincent Gillespie, *Looking in Holy Books: Essays on Late Medieval Religious Writing in England* (Turnhout: Brepols, 2011), p. 271: "By the end of the poem the speaking voice has acquired a teaching authority urging others to follow in the affective path of the lyric." On the pre-Rollean lyric adapted in ll. 37–38, see Ralph Hanna, "Editing 'Middle English Lyrics': The Case of Candet Nudatum Pectus," *Medium Ævum*, 80 (2011), 189–200.

45. Scholastic commentaries on the Psalms frequently read psalms as turning, in their final verses, to the subject of the Last Judgment: see, e.g., Richard Rolle's *English Psalter*, ed. H. R. Bramley (Oxford: Clarendon Press, 1884), pp. 7–8, 12, 23–24, 39–40, etc.

46. See Watson, *Invention of Authority*, pp. 226–32 and 248–55.

47. Hanna's suggestion – that the rubric following "Thy joy" is the scribe's attempt to "indicate that the sixth lyric [i.e., 'All vanitese'] was to follow, not precede, and has probably been misplaced" – does not satisfactorily account for the colophon following "Ghostly Gladness." See *Uncollected*, ed. Hanna, p. lxi.

48. On this manuscript, see Susanna Fein and Michael Johnston, eds., *Robert Thornton and His Books: Essays on the Lincoln and London Thornton Manuscripts* (Woodbridge, UK: Boydell and Brewer for the York Medieval Press, 2014).

49. These being ll. 9–12, 17–20, and 33–36, supplied in *Uncollected*, ed. Hanna, pp. 29–30. Hanna suggests that the first two omissions may be the result of eyeskip, but he concedes that "no such ready explanation appears for the omission of lines 33–36" (p. 178).

50. Cerquiglini, *In Praise of the Variant*, p. 8 and 33.

51. Ardis Butterfield, "Why Medieval Lyric?" *ELH*, 82 (2015), 319–43, p. 328, referring to critical approaches advocated by Heather Love, "Close but Not Deep: Literary Ethics and the Descriptive Turn," *NLH*, 41 (2010), 371–91.

CHAPTER 8

Manuscript and Print Cultures 1500–1700

Margaret J. M. Ezell

Manuscript and Print, 1500–1700: Competing Literary Histories

What significance does having one's writings appear in print as opposed to being handwritten have for an early modern author? The creation and dissemination of printed texts, starting with the books created at the Gutenberg press in Mainz, Germany, in the mid-fifteenth century and continuing over the course of the sixteenth and seventeenth centuries, has been hailed by many scholars as "one of the most effective means of mastery over the whole world," and "inaugurating a new cultural era in the history of Western man."[1] Echoing Francis Bacon's observation in *Novum Organum* (1620) that printing, along with gunpowder and the compass, has "changed the appearance and state of the whole world," classic studies such as Elizabeth L. Eisenstein's *The Printing Press as an Agent of Change* highlighted what she argued was a cultural transformation coinciding with the "shift from script to print" as the dominant media for written communication.[2] She did stress that this change in Europe from a manuscript to a print culture was in many ways "elusive" and that early printers were at pains to reproduce and adapt attractive elements of manuscript works. Nevertheless, Eisenstein and others delineated what they viewed as the fundamental differences between print and manuscript cultures, namely that print culture is characterized and shaped by its standardization, dissemination, and fixity.[3]

Lucien Febvre, Henri-Jean Martin, and Eisenstein's model of a "revolutionary" European transformation also suggested that the older manuscript culture rapidly faded away as authors benefited from the expansion of centers of commercial print culture. This model of cultural change has been modified, refined, and refuted over the last few decades. Adrian Johns, in *The Nature of the Book: Print and Knowledge in the Making* (1998), argued that the conceptualization of print culture as being distinct from manuscript culture by virtue of its authors' desires for the creation of a fixed and stable textual artifact is itself a cultural construction: "early modern printing was not joined by any obvious or necessary bond to enhanced fidelity, reliability, and truth. That bond had to be forged."[4] Likewise, in a lengthy review of Eisenstein's book published in 1980, "The Importance of Being Printed," Anthony Grafton challenged several of its central assumptions, especially her decision not to base her argument on archival, primary documents, what the authors themselves were saying about their books, but instead on existing secondary commentaries; to emphasize the break from scribal to print cultures, "she minimizes the extent to which any text could circulate in stable form before mechanical means of reproduction became available."[5] Grafton was particularly unconvinced by Eisenstein's account of the relationship between author and reader in a manuscript culture, using the example of Petrarch's editing and preparation of his manuscripts for scribal copy to argue strongly against Eisenstein's premise that the "scribal author could not hope that his work would be distributed in anything like a stable form, or even under his name [. . .] nor could he hope to win lasting fame from works that were so unlikely to be preserved."[6]

The second aspect of the shift from manuscript to print implied that print quickly replaced an inefficient older media technology for transmitting and preserving texts, and thus a writer's choice of scribal publication smacked of nostalgia and quaintness. This, too, has been challenged by studies highlighting the presence of robust manuscript cultures in Europe well into the nineteenth century. Roger Chartier declared in 2007 that "with the work dedicated to manuscript production in England, Spain, and France over the past decade, no one today would argue that 'this' (the printing press) killed 'that' (the manuscripts)."[7] Looking specifically at one of the new dominant centers of print publication, Italy, Brian Richardson has argued that while the circulation of manuscript volumes in Italy did decline after the establishment of printing presses, scribal texts continued to have both writers and audiences whose demands and desires print could not satisfy.[8] Scholars working on the social history of literary cultures in "Golden Age" Spain as well as post-medieval Iceland have reached similar conclusions: manuscript as well as oral literary cultures continued to flourish simultaneously alongside the spread of print technology.[9]

Even as the establishment of printing presses in urban centers across Europe increased the number of texts and quantities of copies available for both readers and booksellers, print was not the standard medium chosen by literary authors to reach their readers during the sixteenth and the majority of the seventeenth centuries. The circulation of literary texts in manuscript form remained throughout this period a vital and vibrant practice for authors and readers. Toward the middle and end of this period, we do see writers engaging strategically with the publishing practices of both print and handwritten media. Indeed, the fluidity of the boundaries between print and manuscript cultures as seen in the late sixteenth and early seventeenth centuries have in recent studies posed challenges to our understanding of the nature of literary collaboration and the construction of the concept of the literary author. By 1700, print was beginning to be increasingly available to literary writers as a viable medium for their works because of new publishing formats, such as literary periodicals, which meant an even greater audience for authors who, in a previous generation, might have confined their audiences to social, scribal ones.

Manuscript Literary Authorship: By Necessity

The narrative of the successful rapid spread of print culture in Europe is so dominant that it is easy to lose sight of the importance of location and language to an aspiring literary author. One might easily suppose that after 1550, to be a literary author was by default to be a writer who desired to see his or her name in print. However, to broaden a question I posed in 1999, if one was a young poet or aspiring fiction writer living in rural France, a small village in Spain, on the west coast of Ireland, or a woman living almost anywhere other than London, Paris, Venice, or Antwerp, what did it mean to be an "author" and by what means was it to be accomplished?[10] To participate in manuscript culture required only paper, pen, and inspiration. Two case studies, Ireland and Iceland, suggest how even after the arrival and establishment of printing presses in a country, those whom we consider to be literary authors remained and flourished within manuscript cultures.

Both Iceland and Ireland had important, well-established early and medieval literary cultures. The first produced the magnificent Sagas and Eddas in the thirteenth and fourteenth centuries, and the second boasted perhaps the oldest vernacular prose tradition in medieval Europe, including heroic sagas recorded in the Book of Leinster in the mid-twelfth century and an unbroken history of Gaelic vernacular poetry. The first printing press in Ireland was established in Dublin in 1551 and the first in Iceland at Hólar around 1530.[11] However, the output was meagre: the King's printer in Dublin from 1604, John Franckton, produced only eleven works in fourteen years, several of them broadsides. In both of these countries, the press was under the direct control of the civil and ecclesiastical authorities, and the presses' priorities were in printing texts that served those masters, whether religious texts or proclamations.

In Ireland, literary historians have theorized that a series of inter-related factors may have left printers without the audience and market that they enjoyed in other countries. It took decades to develop an Irish font, which was rarely used, and as Raymond Gillespie notes, "the literary output of Gaelic Ireland remained in either oral or manuscript form with little commercial potential" and "a considerable part of the Irish world was, at least initially, closed to the world of print."[12] As another scholar phrased it bluntly, "the pool of Protestant literati was small, potential patrons were scarce, and the bulk of the population, comprising Old English and Gaelic Catholics, lay outside the pale of potential publishers or readers of items produced by the state printing press."[13]

Thus, well into the eighteenth century, Irish scribal culture was sustained by multiple generations of professional manuscript writers.[14] Not only did these scribes create copies of Gaelic literary works for circulation and preservation, they were also creating copies of printed works in English for individual customers using imported printed texts. If one was writing verse or prose in Gaelic, handwriting was the preferred and most efficient means of both preserving one's texts and also creating copies for social circulation.

The same is true in Iceland, except that the scribes tended not to be professionals clustered in urban areas. In addition to members of the clergy, literate "lay" participants, including farmers and fishermen, were creating scribal copies of vernacular literature, including the Sagas and popular verse rima, well throughout the nineteenth century.[15] Notably, women in Iceland were also active participants in sustaining this social manuscript culture as documented from the seventeenth century onward: while by Icelandic law, real estate such as land and buildings were inherited by men, women inherited money and moveable property, including manuscripts and books.[16] For both Ireland and Iceland in 1500–1700, the presence of a printing press created no revolution in either literary writing or reading; if anything, printed books simply provided more work for the well-established scribal culture, who rendered print works back into handwritten forms for their wider dissemination and preservation.

Manuscript Literary Authorship: By Choice

Even if, by the late sixteenth century into the seventeenth, a poet or writer of fiction had access to a printing press, many literary authors chose to circulate and preserve their writings in manuscript forms. Some religious communities, for example, viewed both the scribal copying and the creation of devotional writings, saints' lives, and religious verse to be part of a communal spiritual life.[17] In seventeenth-century Venice, for example, it has been estimated that over half of the elite women of the city resided in nunneries under strict monastic enclosure. Nevertheless, recent studies have revealed the ways in which these enclosed communities of women participated in secular literary culture as well as that of the convent, creating in their manuscripts formal literary compositions and histories whose physical presentations are found to incorporate both the conventions of illuminated manuscripts and printed books.[18] The English nuns at the Benedictine monastery of Our Lady of Consolation, Cambrai, in the 1640s were likewise notably prolific as a group of communal authors, not only collecting sermons, editing letters, producing translations, but also creating original prose and verse compositions.[19]

Outside the monastic walls, the writing and sharing of one's verses was a common means to cement social ties. Case studies from England and Spain help to highlight similarities in authorship practices and the ways in which scribal literary texts could both circulate within a small group or coterie as well as become a part of a transnational literary exchange, which could ignore print as a vehicle for its texts. It also highlights the range of attitudes found in the author's desire to control both the audience who read his or her work and also the various manuscript formats in which texts were circulated and preserved.

In England, the disdain expressed by a group of early modern authors, male and female, toward print publication forms the basis for a widely cited theory of "the stigma of print," which claims that having one's compositions appear in print was viewed as debasing and immodest. According to this interpretation, English literary gentlemen and -women "shunned print" and embraced manuscript transmission instead.[20] "The manuscript was generally considered the normal medium of publication," and indeed the leading authors of the period, including Wyatt, Surrey, Fulke Greville, and Sir Philip Sidney, "were not addressing the sort of audience a printed book would normally find."[21] George Puttenham, in *The Arte of English Poesie* (1589), certainly seems to support this interpretation of courtly literary culture, lamenting that "I know very many notable Gentlemen in the Court that haue written commendably, and suppressed it agayne, or els suffred it to be publisht without their owne names to it: as if it were a discredit for a Gentleman, to seeme learned, and to show him selfe amorous of any good Art."[22] Hyder Edward Rollins observed in his edition of the 1593 printed miscellany *The Phoenix Nest* that none of the poets in the volume are fully identified by name, explaining that "[s]uch reticence is altogether character-istic of a book of poems written by Elizabethan gentlemen [...] to have made a parade of one's poetical compositions would have been vulgar."[23] Instead, its title page highlighted the well-bred status of the contributors while refusing to give their names: the contents are declared to be by "Noble *men, worthy Knights, gallant Gentlemen, Masters of Arts, and braue Schollers,*" collected by "R.S." himself of the "Inner Temple *Gentleman.*"

Alternatively, the poets in Queen Anne Boleyn's circle in the 1530s appear to have been quite comfortable circulating their poetry among a mixed courtly audience and having them collected into a manuscript volume. The bound quarto volume which began as a blank book was turned into a private anthology now known as the Devonshire Manuscript (British Library Add MS 17492). Originally, the collection was valued by scholars as a key source for poems by Sir Thomas Wyatt, which comprise about one third of the volume, but more recently attention has been given to the multiple authors who contributed their love poems and acted as scribes.[24] The owner of the book itself was Anne Boleyn's cousin, Mary Fitzroy, the wife of the Duke of Richmond. The volume has been described by a recent biographer as "the Facebook of the Tudor court" and indeed includes poems by Lady Margaret Douglas, who was the niece of Henry VIII, Mary Shelton, another cousin of Anne Boleyn, Lord Thomas Howard, and Henry Stuart, Lord Darnley.[25]

The reluctance of aristocratic English male poets to have their poetry appear in print, at least under their names, extended to other European royal courts. Daniel Traister, in revisiting Saunders's essay, points to Spanish Golden Age poets as possibly sharing similar attitudes toward print publication.[26] Among these are Juan Boscán Almogáver (*c.* 1490–1542), who published his translation of Baldassare Castiglione's *Il cortegiano* (1534) but whose poetry was only published by his widow in 1543, along with that of his friend Garcilaso de la Vega (1503–1536), whose poetry helped introduce Italian meters made popular by Petrarch. One of the most celebrated of the Golden Age poets, Luis de Góngora y Argote (1561–1627) did not have his works appear until after his death, although they circulated instead widely in manuscript copies during his lifetime. The dramatist and poet Gil Vincente (*c.*1470–1536?), whose works were published by his children in 1561–2, is another example of a poet whose works appeared either only after their death or were published pseudony-mously in collections. To this list one can add recent studies arguing for the inclusion of Spanish women poets in the canon of Golden Age poetry, for example the never-printed poems of early seventeenth-century poet and dramatist Leonor de la Cueva y Silva, the poems and autobiographical writings Luisa Carvajal y Mendoza (1566–1614), and the manuscript verses of Catalina Clara Ramírez de Guzmán (1611–1684/85).[27]

In England, Sir Philip Sidney (1554–1586) and John Donne (1572–1631) are probably the two most studied examples of literary authors who eschewed print publication for their writings. It is worth adding Esther Inglis (1571–1624) to this group for further insight into the complexities of manuscript literary authorship versus that of print. Sidney, born into a powerful and well-connected family, was the epitome of the Elizabethan soldier, diplomat, and courtier. John Donne was born in London into a recusant Catholic family, and his uncle Jasper Heywood was the head of the Jesuit mission in England 1581–1583; educated at Oxford and at Lincoln's Inn, Donne had a career as a soldier and a secretary before entering the Church of England and becoming a minister, eventually rising to the position of Dean of St. Paul's. Esther Inglis probably was born in London to French Huguenot parents; by 1574 the family resided in Edinburgh, where her father was the master of the French school, and she was taught by her mother, a well-known scribe, the arts of calligraphy. Sidney and Donne are now regarded as two of the most important figures in the English literary canon, even though only one or two pieces by them were printed during their lifetimes; Inglis, in contrast, until recently was regarded as a relatively minor artisan who created exquisite, collectable book art. The authorship practices of the three of them, however, also serve well to illustrate some of the evolving features of what "being an author" might mean and the significance of choosing handwritten forms over printed ones.

Prior to his early and much-lamented death in 1586, Sir Philip Sidney was the patron of many literary figures and, as such, his name appeared in print in dedications in both English and Continental books.[28] His own writings, however, with the possible exceptions of two sonnets attributed to him in Henry Goldwell's 1581 *A briefe declarion of the shews . . . performed before the queens maiestie, and the French Ambassdours*, remained in manuscript until after his death. "The extant evidence," Woudhuysen notes, "shows Sidney's strong attachment to the world of manuscript culture [. . .]. His motives for this were undoubtedly personal and private, as well as social."[29] Within his family, this commitment to handwritten literary authorship over print varied: his older brother Robert Sidney, first Earl of Leicester, maintained very tight control over his writings, creating a collection of his poems that did not appear in print until 1984, while, as we shall see, his sister Mary Sidney Herbert, Countess of Pembroke, employed both print and manuscript for her writings.

Philip Sidney employed scribes to make copies not only of his own works but also of other's printed books and manuscript treatises in multiple languages at the request of friends. Unlike some other contemporary manuscript authors and most print ones, Sidney was not seeking patronage or preferment with his writings. He gave manuscript copies of his own works as gifts, to his close friends and family members, such as the copy of the *Old Arcadia* given to his sister, the Countess of Pembroke, and "[h]is manuscripts had a practical role beyond simply being read for pleasure: they helped to compile other books, to inspire chivalric fantasies, and even to exercise their owners' wit."[30]

Sidney's use of manuscript volumes as gifts brings another dimension of manuscript culture to our attention.[31] From medieval times, wealthy patrons had commissioned beautiful illuminated manuscript volumes, in particular books of hours, to be given as gifts. Esther Inglis, in contrast, came from an educated background whose connections to the royal courts of Queen Elizabeth and King James VI of Scotland were through her creation of exquisitely calligraphed and presented manuscript books, designed for individual patrons. She incorporated the emblems and insignias of the noble person into the cover decoration as well as the textual ornaments; each of her books offered its recipient devotional texts translated into French, Latin, and English while showcasing her abilities as a calligrapher.[32] She was also, as early feminist anthologists noted, a woman writing "professionally, i.e., for profit."[33] Inglis included many of the paratexts we associate with printed literary texts: her books frequently include commendatory verses about her talents by respected male authorities, there are multiple volumes in which she includes a portrait of herself, pen in hand, with the motto "*Vive la Plume*". As she wrote in her dedication to Susanna, Lady Herbert in 1605, "the Bee draweth naught (Most Noble and Vertuous Ladie) hway [honey] from the fragrant herbs of the garding for hir self: no more haue I payned my self many yearis to burie the talent God hes geuen me in oblivion."[34] While the representation of Inglis by herself owes much to the developing conventions associated with literary authors in print format, the appeal of the book is in the culture of the manuscript volume as gift, in this case, to secure the patronage of wealthy and powerful readers.

If Inglis epitomizes the deliberate evocation of manuscript culture's aura of exclusivity, unique texts designed for a special reader, John Donne's varying attitudes toward his literary manuscript texts is illustrative of the multiple ways in which scribal literary culture functioned. "It may be difficult for modern readers to view Donne's poems as coterie social transactions, rather than literary icons," Arthur Marotti observed, "but this, I believe, is necessary since virtually all of the basic features of Donne's poetic art are related to its coterie character."[35] As one of the early editors of the Variorum edition of Donne's poetry noted, only seven poems were issued as "authorized" printings, "appearing at least with his acquiescence if not always with his wholehearted endorsement," out of 187 other known poems.[36] Ted-Larry Pebworth, in 1984, had recorded 246 manuscripts with Donne's verses in them, and Peter Beal observed in his *Index of English Literary Manuscripts* that "probably more transcripts of Donne's poems were made than of the verse of any other British poet in the 16th and 17th centuries."[37] There is no evidence at this point that Donne himself ever collected his own verse.[38]

As Donne scholars have labored to sort through, the poet exercised different levels of control over access to different types of his writings: some of his early lyrics, such as "Song: Sweetest Love" and "Break of Day," were set to music, suggesting a wide circulation of individual pieces without Donne's particular supervision.[39] Donne even laments this outcome in his poem "The Triple Fool": "I am two fools, I know,/ For loving, and for saying so/ In whining poetry" with the result that the lady still does not love him, but that "when I have done so,/ Some man, his art and voice to show,/ Doth set and sing my pain."

Donne was not always so cavalier in his attitude toward his manuscripts. In a letter written in 1619 prior to his travels to Germany, Donne sent a manuscript of his lengthy prose treatise on suicide, *Biathanatos*, to Robert Ker, later the Earl of Ancrum, describing it as being a "Book written by *Jack Donne*, and not by D. *Donne*," and asks him to "reserve it for me." "I only forbid it the Presse, and the Fire," he informed Ker; "publish it not, but yet burn it not; and between those, do what you will with it."[40] As Beal argued, Donne subsequently kept his original manuscript, but also a copy made and sent to Sir Edward Herbert: "Donne is effectively solving his problem of what to do with it by putting a manuscript into the hands of a trusted confidant and arbiter – or, if you will, custodian and library – one who will (a) preserve it, and (b) decide for him who should see it and who not."[41]

Donne also was concerned about the possibility of some of his manuscript texts being read outside the immediate social and patronage relationships in which they were originally composed. Writing in 1614, when he was apparently under some pressure from the Earl of Somerset to print a collection of his verse, Donne wrote to his friend Sir Henry Goodyer that "I am brought to a necessity of printing my Poems, and addressing them to my L. Chamberlain. This I mean to do forthwith; not for much publique view, but at mine own cost, a few Copies."[42] In addition to the dismay of having poems intended for a private and select audience made available to a wide reading public (and at his expense), Donne apparently had not kept copies of all of his verse epistles. "By this means," Donne concludes, "I am made a Rhapsoder of mine own rags, and that cost me more diligence, to seek them, then it did to make them. This made me aske to borrow that old book of you," in hopes that Goodyer might have kept a copy.[43]

By the end of the seventeenth century, one still finds numerous examples of writers who are now regarded as major literary figures but who during their lifetimes either made no attempt to print their works and exercised little control over the circulation of their manuscript texts, or writers who controlled their manuscripts so tightly that the majority were not published until after the author's death. John Wilmot, the Earl of Rochester (1647–1680), left behind for later editors a bewildering mass of both printed and manuscript source texts. Rochester ordered his own manuscripts of his writings to be burnt shortly before his death as a gesture of repentance and, as his most recent editor observed, "the circumstances of scribal publication made it inevitable that there would be severe problems of attribution."[44] Indeed, the complexities of editing Rochester underlay one of the foundational studies of late seventeenth-century manuscript culture, Harold Love's *Scribal Publication in Seventeenth-Century England*. Love described "scribal publication" as existing in three forms: the author's holograph, the copy done by a "specialist scribe," and "the copy made by an individual who wished to possess the text."[45] Like Donne's, Rochester's poems were set to music, circulated in multiple copies incorporating multiple variations and, because of their often-controversial satirical subjects and obscenity, deemed best read in manuscript rather than in print.

The Restoration period in England with its complex political conflicts created a mass of topical satires, lampoons, and libels, most of which enjoyed wide circulation in manuscript copies, occasionally drifted into print, were set to music, and sometimes were collected in commissioned scribal volumes. Unlike Sidney's desire to restrict his writings to a small group of family members and close friends, the design of the almost always anonymous lampoonist was to reach the widest possible readership without being identified and charged with seditious libel. Love's study of clandestine satires and lampoons highlights both the use of professional scribes to create this dangerous body of manuscripts as well as the participation of readers such as Samuel Pepys, eager to obtain a copy for his collection.[46]

Increasing numbers of writers in the sixteenth and late seventeenth centuries were comfortable placing some of their writings in print, whether as single pieces or as part of printed collections, while restricting the readership of other texts. William Shakespeare published two poems, *Venus and Adonis* (1593) and *The Rape of Lucrece* (1594), which went through nine and five editions respectively during his lifetime; his intentions toward the printing of his plays, on the other hand, are less clear. Some have maintained Shakespeare wrote purely for the stage, arguing that he took no interest in the publication of the quartos, while others declare he was intensely invested in becoming a "literary dramatist" and establishing his name as a literary commodity through print publication.[47] John Donne's two poems on the death of Elizabeth Drury, *The First Anniversarie* and *The Second Anniversarie* (1612), have likewise caused scholarly debate about Donne's reasons for printing them, his involvement in the process itself, and his subsequent feelings about their publication.[48] Writing two generations later, Katherine Philips's angry response to the appearance of an unauthorized print collection of her poetry in 1664 – "my imaginations rifled and exposed to play the Mountebanks, and dance upon the Ropes to entertain all the rabble" – has often caused critics to overlook her publication of individual poems under her name in the 1650s in royalist anthologies and her drama *Pompey* (1663), which was performed in Dublin.[49] As Beal has noted, "what we see Katherine Philips doing through her brief life is exploiting to the full the opportunities which each of her available media afford her – yet essentially without transgressing their social boundaries."[50]

Print Literary Authorship: By Choice, for Fame or Fortune

Although many early modern authors did denounce the appearance of their works in print done apparently without their consent or oversight, from the list of European literary masterpieces printed during this period, others clearly embraced this new medium. François Rabelais's multivolume fiction *Pantagruel ... fils du Grand Géant Gargantua* (1532) was published in Lyons by Claude Nourry, Edmund Spenser's *The Faerie Queene* was done by Nicholas Ponsonby in London (1590), and Miguel de Cervantes's *El ingenioso hidalgo don Quixote de la Mancha* was produced in Madrid in 1605 by the king's printer Francisco de Robles. They were all published during their authors' lifetimes and with their permission. Additionally, many of these celebrated printed literary works, including *Pantagruel* and *Don Quixote*, were also translated during this period, creating international literary reputations for the authors. In England alone this period had the folio publication of John Foxe's *Book of Martyrs* (1563), Holinshed's *Chronicles* (1577), Samuel Daniel's *Works* (1601), *The King James Bible* (1611), Ben Jonson's *Works* (1616), Lady Mary Wroth's *Urania* (1621), Margaret Cavendish's *Poems and Fancies* (1653), and John Milton's *Paradise Lost* (1674).[51] Based on this, Steven W. May has argued that the phrase "the stigma of print," "handy and time-honored as it has become, does not square with the evidence." May argues that even by Queen Elizabeth's time there was a growing emphasis among English elite writers on publishing literary works rather than devotional ones; he points to Sir Thomas Hoby's translation of Baldassare Castiglione's printed work *The Courtier* (1561), King James's *Essayes of a Prentise, in the Divine Art of Poesia* (1584) and *His Majesties Poeticall Exercises* (1591), as well as Bacon's *Essayes* (1597).[52]

In contrast to her brother Sir Philip Sidney, Mary Sidney Herbert, the Countess of Pembroke, exploited the ability of the press to create a lasting, fixed monument to her brother's literary fame through assisting in the posthumous printing of his works. As Woudhuysen has discussed, remarkably quickly, "within a dozen years of his death his major literary works were available in print," including the unfinished *New Arcadia, Astrophil and Stella*, and two editions of *A Defence of Poetry*.[53] She also chose print for her own translation of de Mournay's *A Discourse of Life and Death* and Garnier's *Tragedie of Antonie*, both published by William Ponsonby in 1592. Similarly, their niece, Lady Mary Wroth, published her prose romance *Urania* (1621) with its sonnet sequence "Pamphilia to Amphilanthus." It appeared in a folio with an impressive engraved title page that not only announced it was written by Wroth, but that she was the "Neece to the ever famous, and resnowned Sr Phillips Sidney knight. And to ye most exele[n]t Lady Mary Countesse of Pembroke late deceased."

Margaret Cavendish, Duchess of Newcastle, also preferred folios for her publications in the 1650s and 1660s. She commissioned multiple frontis-pieces for her books designed by Abraham van Diepenbeeck when she and her husband were in exile Paris and Antwerp during the Interregnum. The Duchess had several different author portraits that she used in her publications, although her favorite, which was used in several of her publications, has her standing on a pedestal, being admired by classical figures; another shows her seated at a table with pen and paper, gazing thoughtfully at the reader, as she is crowned with laurel by flying putti.

Both the Duke and the Duchess performed authorship in print. The Duke also used van Diepenbeeck for his elaborate illustrations featuring himself for his two treatises on horsemanship, *Méthode et invention nouvelle de dresser les chevaux* (1658) and *A New Method and Extraordinary Invention to Dress Horses and Work them according to Nature* (1667). The Duke also had four of his plays staged in London and subsequently printed, including the popular comedy *The Country Captain* (1649). The Duchess published two folio volumes of her plays as well as her verse, philosophical writings, and a biography of her husband. At this point, there is no evidence that she participated in social or coterie manuscript circulation; she exists now entirely as a print author, as none of her manuscripts appear to have survived. Neither she nor the Duke had any expectation or desire for commercial return on these publications. In her first publication, *Poems and Fancies* (1653), Margaret Cavendish explains that her intent is to build "A *Pyramid* of *Fame*."⁵⁴ Later in her literary career, she declared, "I am not Covetous, but as Ambitious as ever any of my Sex was, is, or can be; which makes, that though I cannot be *Henry* the Fifth, or *Charles* the Second, yet I endeavour to be *Margaret* the First. [...] I have made a World of my own."⁵⁵

The exiled Duke and Duchess of Newcastle were not alone in turning to the press during the 1650s. Ironically, the decade under Cromwell and the Puritan Parliament that had closed the London theaters witnessed a rapid expansion in the printing of English literary texts and translations of continental ones. Publishers such as Humphrey Moseley (c.1603–61) became known for their editions of contemporary literary authors, who very often were members of the losing royalist side. Some of their writings, like Richard Lovelace's *Lucasta*, were collected and published posthumously by their families as a memorial to the poet, while Robert Herrick had printed his collection of verse *Hesperides* after he was ejected from his clerical living by the Puritans. It was also a period in which royalist sympathizers such as Thomas Stanley (1625–1678) retreated to the countryside and occupied their time creating a notable series of translations from classical authors as well as Spanish and Italian romances.

In addition to publishing posthumously Donne's problematic treatise *Biathanatos* and the collected plays of Beaumont and Fletcher, Moseley also shepherded into print the pre-civil war courtier poets who had been social, coterie writers, including William Cartwright, Thomas Carew, Edmund Waller, William Davenant, James Shirley, John Cleveland, and

Richard Fanshawe, as well as the reluctant young Parliamentarian John Milton. Moseley frequently addresses the readers of these volumes, assuring them of his care to obtain "true copies" of the author's manuscripts; it was Moseley's practice to ask the living writers for a portrait and to choose a suitable epigraph for the title page, establishing the paratextual conventions associated with English poets and dramatists.[56] None of these writers would have been anticipating significant financial rewards for appearing in print.

The growing taste for vernacular fiction after the Restoration in the 1660s not only offered English authors a new genre to explore, but also created a source of income for writers employed by English publishers to translate popular foreign romances. In seventeenth-century France and Spain, print was the format for authors of vernacular romances and novels. The picaresque adventures of Diego de Mendoza's *Lazarillo de Tormes* (1554), Mateo Alemán's *Guzman de Alfarache* (1599), and Quevedo's *El Buscón* (1626) were translated into English in the seventeenth century and inspired English authors to imitate them; Richard Head's popular *The English Rogue* (1665) enjoyed multiple sequels and was itself translated into German. Those with a taste for heroic rather than vagabond adventures were gratified by the fictions produced in France, including Honoré d'Urfé's *Astrée* (1607), Madeleine de Scudéry's *Artamène ou le Grand Cyrus* and *Clélie*, both printed in ten volumes in the 1650s, and La Calprenède's *Cassandre* and *Cléopâtra* (1648), translated into English by George Digby between 1652 and 1658. English writers were not slow to respond to and create their own versions of this popular new print fiction format.

One sees in this expansion of English vernacular literary printing in the 1650s the seeds for the development of professional literary careers, such as that of the poet laureate John Dryden (1631–1700). Educated at Trinity College, Cambridge, he held a minor civil servant position under Cromwell; his first important printed work was a eulogy on Cromwell, *Heroic Stanzas*, which was quickly followed by odes celebrating the return of monarchy and Charles II, *Astraea Redux*. With the theaters reopened, Dryden soon gained success as a popular and prolific dramatist and mentor collaborating with other young writers; over his long literary career, he wrote literary criticism, collected his and his associates' verses into miscellanies, published poems on important public occasions, and translated the works of Virgil (1697). In his appreciation of the popular taste of his readers and his canny negotiations with his publishers, Dryden established one of the patterns for becoming a professional literary author in a print culture, while still enjoying the benefits of a manuscript one.

Notes

1. Lucien Febvre and Henri-Jean Martin, *The Coming of the Book: The Impact of Printing 1450–1800*, trans. David Gerard (London: Verso Printing, 1976), p. 11; Elizabeth L. Eisenstein, *The Printing Press as an Agent of Change* (Cambridge: Cambridge University Press, 1979; repr. 1980), vol. 1, p. 30.

2. Eisenstein, *Printing Press*, vol. 1, pp. 43–44.

3. Ibid., pp. 71–88, 113–26.

4. Adrian Johns, *The Nature of the Book: Print and Knowledge in the Making* (Chicago: University of Chicago Press, 1998), p. 5.

5. Anthony Grafton, "The Importance of Being Printed," *Journal of Interdisciplinary History*, 11.2 (1980), 265–86, p. 273.

6. Ibid., p. 279.

7. Roger Chartier, "The Printing Revolution: A Reappraisal," in *Agent of Change: Print Culture Studies after Elizabeth L. Eisenstein*, eds. Sabrina Alcorn Baron, Eric N. Lindquist, and Eleanor F. Shevlin (Amherst: University of Massachusetts Press, 2007), pp. 397–408, p. 398.

8. Brian Richardson, *Printing, Writers and Readers in Renaissance Italy* (Cambridge: Cambridge University Press, 1999), pp. 8–9. See also Brian Richardson, *Manuscript Culture in Renaissance Italy* (Cambridge: Cambridge University Press, 2009).

9. Antonio Castillo Gómez, *Cultura escrita y clases subalternas: una mirada española* (Oiartzun: Sendoa 2001); David Ólafsson, "Post-Medieval Manuscript Culture and the Historiography of Texts," in *Mirrors of Virtue: Manuscript and Print in Late Pre-Modern Iceland*, eds. Margrét Eggertsdóttir and Matthew James Driscoll (Copenhagen: Museum Tusculanum Press, 2017), 1–30.

10. Margaret J. M. Ezell, *Social Authorship and the Advent of Print* (Baltimore, MD: Johns Hopkins University Press, 1999), p. 2.

11. Raymond Gillespie, *Reading Ireland: Print, Reading, and Social Change in Early Modern Ireland* (Manchester: Manchester University Press, 2005), p. 55; Margrét Eggertsdóttir, "Script in Seventeenth- and Eighteenth-Century Iceland," in *Mirrors of Virtue*, pp. 127–166, p. 128.

12. Gillespie, *Reading Ireland*, p. 57.

13. Colm Lennon, "The Print Trade 1550–1700," in *The Oxford History of the Irish Book, Volume III: The Irish Book in English*, eds. Raymond Gillespie and Andrew Hadfield (Oxford: Oxford University Press, 2006), pp. 61–73, p. 67.

14. Nessa Ní Shéaghdha, "Irish Scholars and Scribes in Eighteenth-Century Dublin," *Eighteenth-Century Ireland*, 4 (1989), 41–54.

15. Matthew J. Driscoll, *The Unwashed Children of Eve: The Production, Dissemination and Reception of Popular Literature in Post-Reformation Iceland* (Enfield Lock, UK: Hisarlik Press, 1997).

16. See Gudrún Ingólfsdóottir, "Women's Manuscript Culture in Iceland, 1600–1900," in *Mirrors of Virtue*, pp. 195–224, p. 222, 203; Susanne

Miriam Arthur, "The Importance of Marital and Material Ties in the Distribution of Icelandic Manuscripts from the Middle Ages to the Seventeenth Century," *Gripla*, 23 (2012), 201–13.

17. E. Ann Matter, "The Canon of Religious Life: Maria Domitilla Galluzzi and the *Rule* of St. Clare of Assisi," in *Strong Voices, Weak History: Early Women Writers and Canons in England, France, and Italy*, ed. Victoria Kirkham (Ann Arbor: University of Michigan Press, 2005), pp. 78–98.

18. Meredith K. Ray, "Letters and Lace: Arcangela Tarabotti and Convent Culture in *Seicento* Venice," in *Early Modern Women and Transnational Communities of Letters*, eds. Julie D. Campbell and Anne R. Larsen (Burlington, VT: Ashgate Publishing, 2009), pp. 45–74; Kate Lowe, *Nuns' Chronicles and Convent Culture in Renaissance and Counter-Reformation Italy* (Cambridge: Cambridge University Press, 2003), pp. 19–20.

19. Heather Wolfe, "Introduction," *Elizabeth Cary, Lady Falkland: Life and Letters*, ed. Heather Wolfe (Tempe, AZ: Arizona Center for Medieval and Renaissance Studies, 2001), p. 45. See also Jenna Lay, *Beyond the Cloister: Catholic Englishwomen and Early Modern Literary Culture* (Philadelphia: University of Pennsylvania Press, 2016).

20. J. W. Saunders, "The Stigma of Print: A Note on the Social Bases of Tudor Poetry," *Essays in Criticism*, 1.2 (1951), 139–64, p. 140.

21. Ibid., p. 139.

22. George Puttenham, *The arte of English poesie Contriued into three bookes: the first of poets and poesie, the second of proportion, the third of ornament* (London, 1589), p. 16.

23. Hyder Edward Rollins, ed., *The Phoenix Nest (1593)* (Cambridge, MA: Harvard University Press, 1931), p. xvi.

24. *The Devonshire Manuscript: A Women's Book of Courtly Poetry*, ed. Elizabeth Heale (Toronto: Centre for Reformation and Renaissance Studies, 2012); *A Social Edition of the Devonshire Manuscript (BL MS Add 17,492)*, eds. Raymond Siemens, Karin Armstrong, and Constance Compton et al., an open access on-line edition demonstrating "collaborative technologically mediated scholarly editing." http://dms.itercommunity.org/a-note-on-this-edition.

25. Nicola Shulman, *Graven with Diamond: The Many Lives of Thomas Waytt, Courtier, Poet, Assassin, Spy* (London: Short Books, 2011), p. 142.

26. Daniel Traister, "Reluctant Virgins: The Stigma of Print Revisited," *Colby Quarterly*, 26 (1990), 75–86, p. 85, n. 39.

27. *Studies on Women's Poetry of the Golden Age: Tras el espejo la musa escribe*, ed. Julián Olivares (Woodbridge: Tamesis, 2009). For editions, see also *Tras el espejo la musa escribe. Lírica femenina de los Siglos de Oro*, eds. Julián Olivares and Elizabeth S. Boyce (Madrid: Siglo XXI de España, 1993).

28. Gavin Alexander, *Writing After Sidney: The Literary Response to Sir Philip Sidney 1586–1640* (Oxford: Oxford University Press, 2006), p. 128.

29. H. R. Woudhuysen, *Sir Philip Sidney and the Circulation of Manuscripts 1558–1640* (Oxford: Clarendon Press, 1996), p. 218.

30. Ibid., p. 219.

31. Ibid., p. 90.
32. Margaret J. M. Ezell, "Invisibility Optics: Aphra Behn, Esther Inglis and the Fortunes of Women's Works," in *A History of Early Modern Women's Writing*, ed. Patricia Phillippy (Cambridge: Cambridge University Press, 2018), pp. 27–45, p. 37.
33. Betty Travitsky, ed., *The Paradise of Women: Writings by Englishwomen of the Renaissance* (New York: Columbia University Press, 1989), p. 24.
34. Esther Inglis, *Argumenta singulorum capitum Geneseos per Tetrasticha* (1605), fol. 1ʳ, Harvard University, Houghton Library MS 428.
35. Arthur F. Marotti, *John Donne, Coterie Poet* (Madison: University of Wisconsin Press, 1986), p. 19.
36. Ted-Larry Pebworth, "John Donne, Coterie Poetry, and the Text as Performance," *Studies in English Literature*, 29. 1 (1989), 61–75, p. 75.
37. Ted-Larry Pebworth, "Manuscript Poems and Print Assumptions: Donne and His Modern Editors," *John Donne Journal*, 3 (1984), 1–21, p. 20; Peter Beal, ed., *Index of English Literary Manuscripts, Volume 1: 1475–1625 (2 parts)* (London: Mansell, 1980–1993), pt. 1, p. 245.
38. Arthur F. Marotti, *Manuscript, Print, and the English Renaissance Lyric* (Ithaca, NY: Cornell University Press, 1995), p. 149.
39. Marotti, *John Donne,* pp. 16–17.
40. John Donne, *Letters to Severall Persons of Honour* (London, 1651), p. 22.
41. Peter Beal, *In Praise of Scribes: Manuscripts and their Makers in Seventeenth-Century England* (Oxford: Oxford University Press, 1998), p. 35.
42. Donne, *Letters*, pp. 196–97.
43. Ibid., p. 197.
44. *The Works of John Wilmot, Earl of Rochester*, ed. Harold Love (Oxford: Oxford University Press, 1999), p. xxiii.
45. Harold Love, *Scribal Publication in Seventeenth-Century England* (Oxford: Clarendon Press, 1993), p. 46.
46. Harold Love, *English Clandestine Satire 1660–1702* (Oxford: Oxford University Press, 2004), pp. 286–302.
47. For the view that Shakespeare was indifferent or hostile to the idea of print publication for his plays, see David Kastan, *Shakespeare and the Book* (Cambridge: Cambridge University Press, 2001), and for an investigation of Shakespeare's conscious engagement with the book trade, see Lukas Erne, *Shakespeare and the Book Trade* (Cambridge: Cambridge University Press, 2013).
48. *The Variorum Edition of the Poetry of John Donne: The Anniversaries and the Epicedes and Obsequies*, ed. Gary A. Stringer (Bloomington: Indiana University Press, 1995), pp. 283–85.
49. Elizabeth H. Hageman, "The 'False Printed' Broadside of Katherine Philips's 'To the Queens Majesty on Her Happy Arrival,'" *Library*, 17.4 (1995), 321–26.
50. Beal, *In Praise of Scribes*, p. 155.
51. Steven K. Galbraith, "English Literary Folios 1593–1623," in *Tudor Books and Readers: Materiality and the Construction of Meaning*, ed. John N. King (Cambridge: Cambridge University Press, 2010), pp. 46–67.

52. Steven W. May, "Tudor Aristocrats and the Mythical 'Stigma of Pint,'" *Renaissance Papers*, 10 (1980), 11–18.
53. Woudhuysen, *Sir Philip Sidney*, p. 210.
54. On Cavendish's rejection of the "stigma of print," see Tina Skouen, "Margaret Cavendish and the Stigma of Haste," *Studies in Philology*, 111.3 (2014), 547–70.
55. Margaret Cavendish, *Observations upon experimental philosophy to which is added The description of a new blazing world* (London, 1666), "To the Reader."
56. Stephen B. Dobranski, *Milton, Authorship, and the Book Trade* (Cambridge: Cambridge University Press, 1999), p. 95.

CHAPTER 9

The Eighteenth Century
Print, Professionalization, and Defining the Author

Betty A. Schellenberg

We shall next declare the occasion and the cause which moved our poet to this particular work. He lived in those days, when (after Providence had permitted the invention of printing as a scourge for the sins of the learned) paper also became so cheap, and printers so numerous, that a deluge of authors covered the land: [. . .] At the same time, the licence of the press was such, that it grew dangerous to refuse them either [applause or money]; for they would forthwith publish slanders unpunished, the authors being anonymous, and skulking under the wings of publishers. (Alexander Pope, "Martinus Scriblerus of the Poem," *The Dunciad*, 1728)

I expect shortly to see my sett of all letters compleat, a matter of no small enjoyment, for beside the pleasure of perusing many ingenious performances in common with but few; there is the vanity of looking upon oneself as a small part of an author; for it is being in print that the self complacency must generally arise from & not the number of readers. (John Heaton to Philip Yorke, 9 March 1741)

The present age, if we consider chiefly the state of our own country, may be stiled with great propriety The Age of Authors; for, perhaps, there never was a time, in which men of all degrees of ability, of every kind of education, of every profession and employment, were posting with ardour so general to the press. (Samuel Johnson, *The Adventurer* No. 115, 1753)

I had written my little Book simply for my amusement, I printed it [. . .] merely for a frolic, to see how a production of my own would figure in that Author like form [. . .] [But I] destined [*Evelina*] to no nobler habitation than a circulating library. (Frances Burney, 1778 journal entry)[1]

The statements about authors in the epigraphs to this chapter range in date from 1728 to 1778; they are found in private correspondence and in publications designed for a wide readership; they range in tone from the irritable to the facetious to the self-deprecating. Yet they share a conscious interest in "author" as an identity, and they all explicitly associate that identity with the printing press – whether the hired press of a coterie, in the case of the strictly controlled *Athenian Letters* publication to which John Heaton is a contributor, or the unregulated fountain of slander lamented by Pope, or the democratic instrument of enlightenment fed by Johnson's laboring-class writers. This chapter will consider the interlinked changes in the general idea of authorship that occurred when it became a widespread assumption that to be an author was to have composed material that had been typeset and reproduced by the printing press. The saturation of British society by the print medium, then, with its accompanying trade apparatus, distribution mechanisms, and regulatory regimes, will figure as the provocative agent, directly or indirectly, in this account.[2]

My goal, however, is less to establish a coherent narrative of cause and effect than to historicize authorship as it appears to have been understood by writers in Britain in the eighteenth century. From this perspective, authorship was a loose collection of multi-valent practices, less a matter of necessity and a common endpoint than a variable practice dependent on the values and situations of individual actors within different media economies. Thus I will note the existence of certain determinants and the resulting emergence of a number of patterns that became dominant over the course of the century – professionalization, originality, and copyright – while giving space as well to alternatives, both traditional and newsprung – disinterestedness, hackwork, amateurism, anonymity, and sociable or coterie authorship – whose shaping force in the period was very real, and indeed generated the greater proportion of authorial activity in the period. The series of vignettes I will present circles back repeatedly to the figures of Samuel Johnson and Frances Burney. Together, the declarations and practices of these self-conscious "authors" and their peers demonstrate general trends, but also provide a glimpse of just how broad and unstable the category of authorship was in the eighteenth century.

Print in the Marketplace

The most powerful material circumstance determining the production of new printed texts in eighteenth-century Britain was the growth of a commercial market for them. A significant increase in literacy and in disposable income, especially in urban areas,[3] was accompanied in the late seventeenth century by the dismantling of any form of pre-publication state regulation, most definitively in the 1695 lapse of the Licensing Act (14 Charles II. C.33). Thus print production in principle became a matter of supply and demand like any other market, although monopolistic practices continued under the auspices of the Stationers' Company and through consortiums of booksellers, or congers, that controlled copyrights (the considerable influence of this reality is discussed further below). The growing market created a need for copy to feed the presses; much of this was supplied by reprints of classical, religious, and popular texts that needed no involvement of an author. But booksellers (who played the role of publishers in our modern-day sense) also responded to a desire for accessibility, novelty, and contemporaneity, and so there was a need for translators, abridgers, and compilers of pre-existing texts as well as creators of original content. As Johnson outlined the matter bluntly in a 1751 *Rambler* essay, in this trade, such authors formed useful links in the chain of production:

> Of [the authors of London] only a very few can be said to produce, or endeavour to produce new ideas, to extend any principle of science, or gratify the imagination with any uncommon train of images or contexture of events; the rest, however laborious, however arrogant, can only be considered as the drudges of the pen, the manufacturers of literature, who have set up for authors, either with or without a regular initiation, and like other artificers, have no other care than to deliver their tale of wares at the stated time.[4]

Not surprisingly, the majority of "authors" in this system were those who could efficiently turn their hand to many forms of writing when called upon by a bookseller to meet a need. While often termed "hacks" because of their writing for hire and taunted as slaves to the booksellers by the likes of Alexander Pope in his mock-epic poem *The Dunciad* and Henry Fielding in his 1730 play *The Author's Farce*, the most versatile and reliable of these authors were arguably highly valued in the trade. They included, for example, Thomas Birch, an indefatigable biographer, compiler, and editor who worked closely through the 1730s to 1750s with large consortia of leading booksellers such as Nicholas Prevost and Andrew Millar, and was influential in furthering wide-ranging projects like the standard English edition of Bayle's *General Dictionary*, a History of the Royal Society, and the collected works of John Milton, Robert Boyle, and the then-forgotten playwright and philosopher Catherine Trotter Cockburn. One might further include in this group of expert manufacturers Johnson himself, whose *Dictionary of the English Language* and critical biographies that came to be known as the *Lives of the Poets* are only the most well-known outcomes of almost five decades in the employ of the booksellers. While a number of these individuals – in addition to Johnson, Oliver

Goldsmith, Charlotte Lennox, Tobias Smollett, and Frances Brooke come readily to mind – have earned a place in literary history for works of imaginative writing, their effective production over a much wider range of formats and genres earned them significant contemporary recognition and respectable middle-class status.

The Professionalization of Authorship

If a majority of the trade's "drudges of the pen" could aspire to no more than minimal remuneration as cogs in the wheel of an often-precarious production system, the authors of whom I have been speaking formed a self-conscious class of workers who, although never organized and self-regulated to the extent that lawyers or the clergy were, had by the end of the century developed a professional identity based on a sense of specialized skill and concomitant claims to remuneration and social recognition. Thus Samuel Johnson in 1780, acknowledging to the young Frances Burney, newly published author of the novel *Evelina*, that he has never "paid his respects to" Grub Street, proposes that they go together: "we have a very good *right* to go, so we'll visit the mansions of our Progenitors, & take up our own Freedom!"[5] We hear in that jocular comment the sense of a collective and ascendant history. James Ralph speaks for this self-identified group in his 1758 pamphlet *The Case of Authors by Profession or Trade, Stated*, which argues vigorously for the right of the "Writer by Trade" to be remunerated fairly for his "Mastery in Matter, Method, Stile and Manner," just like any other professional practitioner who "plead[s] for Money, prescribe[s] or quack[s] for Money, [...] [or] fight[s] for Money." While Ralph positions himself as a cynical adversary of the booksellers, like Birch and Johnson he makes it clear that such issues are to be resolved most effectively within the structures of the print trade, through recognition of common interests and mutual dependency.[6]

Ralph in fact places some of the blame for tensions between impoverished authors and mercenary booksellers on society's assumption that the "Art of Writing" is one practiced by "Voluntier, or Gentleman-Writer[s]," set above the need to earn a living. Unlike the masters of their trade already described, these "Holiday-Writers" "write just enough to shew They can read; and having so done, throw away the Pen."[7] Ralph, who began his London career as a writer in the 1720s, is pinpointing the way in which the interests of authors and booksellers in late seventeenth- and early eighteenth-century Britain were often seen as inherently opposed because they were mapped onto the received status differential between the elite gentleman-writer and the book-seller. If an aristocrat, the writer was possessed of *virtù* and elegant taste, if a classically educated scholar, he was armed with superior learning; although both perhaps needed a publisher to disseminate their wit or knowledge beyond their immediate circles, neither acknowledged any interest in pecuniary rewards. The bookseller, on the other hand, was subject as an entrepreneur to all the clichés of the money-grubbing tradesman, including the intention of taking advantage of his hapless author. One reason for the longevity and success of this adversarial model was undoubtedly its brilliant deployment by Alexander Pope. Inhabiting a no-man's land between the elite amateur and the man of letters because of his marginalized status as a Roman Catholic in post-1688 England, Pope managed to parley his connections with aristocratic patrons and gentleman-authors into successful contract negotiations with booksellers that enabled him to make a comfortable fortune as an author while distinguishing himself from other denizens of the trade. He was the disinterested Horatian satirist "TO VIRTUE ONLY and HER FRIENDS, A FRIEND," whereas they were all Grub-Street hacks, deserving of the scourging and mockery he subjected them to in his various editions of *The Dunciad*.[8]

By mid-century, however, there was considerable resistance to this model of the disinterested author removed from the commercial marketplace – Johnson, for example, was happy to describe the booksellers as his patrons, and the printer-novelist Samuel Richardson and a number of his correspondents who had been the targets of Pope's satire (Aaron Hill and Colley Cibber, for example) had little tolerance for the hypocrisy of Pope's insistence on his aristocratic friendships and disdain for his print-based audience in light of his commercial success.[9] In addition, the dichotomous fiction had little relevance for the many respectable amateur writers – well-educated clergymen, impoverished gentlewomen, provincial poets, laborers whose intelligence and ambition gave them voice, and numerous others – needing to supplement meager incomes through their authorial efforts. Nevertheless, as a trope this association of authorship with elevation above pecuniary concerns persisted through the eighteenth century, to be caught up with an emerging discourse of original genius that gave it new potency in the latter decades of the period. Thus Burney's elderly correspondent Samuel Crisp, himself a failed dramatist, urges her on in the task of composing her monumental novel *Cecilia* using the language of genius to counter her own complaints about exhaustion:

my dear Fanny, for God's sake dont talk of *hard Fagging*! It was not *hard Fagging*, that produced such a Work as Evelina!—it was the Ebullition of true Sterling Genius! you wrote it, because you could not help it!—it came, & so you put it down on Paper!—leave *Fagging*, & Labour, to him

> who high in Drury Lane,
> Lull'd by soft Zephyrs thro the broken pane,
> Rhymes ere he wakes, & prints before Term Ends,
> *Compell'd by Hunger & request of Friends.*
> Tis not sitting down to a Desk with Pen, Ink & Paper, that
> will command Inspiration.[10]

Crisp's invocation of Pope's satiric sketch of the literary hack from his 1735 *Epistle to Dr Arbuthnot* is no accident. It illustrates the influence of that poet's insistent separation of the true author from the hard labor of Grub Street, a separation that Burney well knew was patently false after her own experiences as a novelist and playwright, not to mention her previous initiation to the print trade as her father's amanuensis and copyist. The terms of Crisp's invocation, however, draw not on the model of status distinctions upon which Pope's binary was based, but rather on that of inspiration and genius, some mystical force that either boils up from within or is breathed into the author, eliding the physical means by which a composition is produced, page after manuscript page, by sitting at a desk with pen, ink, and paper.

The Author as Genius and Proprietor

This genius, as has often been noted, is something rather different – at once more indistinct and more capacious – than that characteristic spirit or talent to which Pope referred when he wrote about a landscape's "Genius of the Place" or an individual author's "Genius" that is fit only for "One Science," proving thereby "So *vast* is Art, so *narrow* Human Wit."[11] One of the most succinct articulations of this broad concept is found in the poet Edward Young's 1759 treatise *Conjectures on Original Composition*. Young follows Joseph Warton's 1756 demotion of Pope to the second rank of poets through a narrowed definition of poetry as that which is produced by "a creative and glowing IMAGINATION" rather than striving for "the most solid observations on human life, expressed with the utmost elegance and brevity"; the author of such observations may be "a MAN OF WIT" and "a MAN OF SENSE," but is not a true poet.[12] In this vein, Young's *Conjectures*, which also arise out of the Richardson circle's reaction against Pope's legacy, divorce imitation firmly from originality through a series of binaries. Where imitations are initially flowers "of quicker growth, but fainter bloom" than originals, they ultimately become "a sort of *Manufacture* wrought up by those *Mechanics, Art*, and *Labour*, out of pre-existent materials not their own," while "an *Original* may be said to be of a *vegetable* nature; it rises spontaneously from the vital root of Genius; it *grows*, it is not *made*."[13]

As the concurrence of these mid-eighteenth-century arguments indicates, such thinking was not the work of one aesthetic theorist alone. In fact, Martha Woodmansee has traced in *The Author, Art, and the Market*, her important study of the rise of a European philosophy of aesthetics in the eighteenth century, a current of ideas flowing through France and Germany as well as Britain that culminated in the notion of the work of art as distinct, self-enclosed, and non-utilitarian, the creation of a solitary genius ideally elevated above, but more likely pushed to the margins by, the forces governing increasingly complex societies with a lucrative commercial marketplace for literature. In *ancien régime* France, these ideas existed in perpetual negotiation with uneven interpretations of the royal privilege system until they were completely disrupted by the Revolution's deregulation of the book trade, but in Germany, they culminated in the philosophy of Immanuel Kant and the success of Goethe's *Werther*; and in Britain, their effects included the idolization of William Shakespeare as inspired, untutored genius and the isolated suffering of the Romantic genius as represented by the poetic personas of Thomas Chatterton, the young William Wordsworth, Samuel Coleridge, and Percy Shelley.

Woodmansee's inquiry is motivated by the question of why such a discourse should have arisen in the eighteenth century; her answer focuses on a specific episode in the commercialization of print: the development of the idea of copyright. The process by which this concept emerged in English law over the course of the century did indeed grant legal personhood to the identity of "author," although this was not the original intention or immediate effect. With the 1695 lapse of the Licensing Act noted above, members of the Stationers' Company, the guild that had over time acquired the privilege of registering ownership of "copies," and therefore the rights to print and distribute works, found themselves without recourse in the case of piracy of works to which they believed they held exclusive right. After various attempts to obtain a replacement law were resisted by an anti-monopolist Parliament, a law now known as the Statute of Anne (8 Anne c.19) was enacted in April 1710. By means of this statute, the right in a work belonged to its author, or to those to whom the author might assign that right, for the period of fourteen years, renewable for another fourteen if the author was still alive at the expiration of the original period. As already mentioned, the majority of booksellers' properties at the time would have been in titles whose authors were long dead (in these cases, the copyright was set at twenty-one years from the statute's enactment); established practice for new works was for the author to sell the copy outright to the bookseller who was to publish it. Thus the appearance of the author in this statute had little practical import; it simply served as the starting point for the right of a member of the print trade to control production of the work. Adding to the complication, members of the trade believed all along that their true claim to their copies lay in a common-law right of property that was held in perpetuity, and they acted in that belief throughout much of the century in defending their lucrative rights to the works of Shakespeare, Ben Jonson, James Thomson, and others from the entrepreneurial incursions of the growing trade in reprints.

Nevertheless, over the ensuing decades after 1710, numerous cases brought before various courts required them to rule on the nature of the proprietorship in a newly printed or reprinted work; as a result, the concepts of literary property in general, and the nature of an author's relation to her or his work in particular, were canvassed repeatedly. Since these cases tended to be fought between established booksellers and those they viewed as interlopers on their property, authors themselves frequently aligned with the establishment through which they gained their bread – as we have seen, often by abridging, editing, or otherwise repackaging the works these proprietors believed themselves entitled to in perpetuity. The 1774 decision of *Donaldson* v. *Becket*, in which the House of Lords ruled in favor of the appeal of the Scottish reprint publisher Alexander Donaldson that perpetual copyright based in common law did not exist, has been viewed in retrospect as definitive in upholding the concept of a limited-term copyright, and thereby, of the initial property right of an author in a work that she or he has created. Furthermore, since the book trade was opened up thereby, and publishers now had a greater incentive to acquire new copyrights rather than to rely on much-reprinted work over which they no longer held legal control, it has often been argued that this decision is a landmark in the history of authorship in Britain.[14]

If the decision did affect the likes of Samuel Johnson and Frances Burney, besides creating more work for Johnson (he proceeded shortly thereafter to provide his biographical prefaces for a consortium of London booksellers seeking to create a saleable product out of poetry that was now definitively out of copyright), it may have served to enhance the confidence they felt in their professional identities as authors by buttressing their right to remuneration for the produce of their intellectual labors. In the short term, however, *Donaldson* v. *Becket* did not improve the terms that Burney was able to negotiate when, as an anonymous and unpublished author, she deputed her brother Charles to sell the copyright of *Evelina* to bookseller Thomas Lowndes for the very modest sum of twenty guineas. But when Crisp later wrote indignantly that Lowndes "would have *made an Estate* had he given [Burney] 1100 pounds for it, & [. . .] *ought not* to have given less!,"[15] the proprietary right of the author of an original work to build herself an estate is assumed, in line with arguments in favor of authorial copyright privileges.

Alternative Modes of Authorship

In pursuing print publication as a novelist, Burney was following the lead of her father, the musician-author Charles Burney, and others in the rising class of author-professionals found in urban centers throughout Europe. She was also being realistic about the best means of achieving recognition and earning a living, especially given her desire to maintain a degree of privacy not available to a stage author. But her choice was not as inevitable as it might retrospectively seem, given the extent to which competing and viable models of authorship co-existed in her own milieu. In positioning herself with professionals such as her father and Samuel Johnson, Burney was also setting herself apart from Bluestocking friends such as Hester Thrale (later Piozzi), Elizabeth Montagu, and Mary Delany, who culti-vated scribal, sociable, and collaborative forms of authorship.[16] As an immediate favorite in these women's salons, Burney was aware that they would have been only too happy to stand as patrons of "The Witlings," the stage comedy she composed as a follow-up to *Evelina*. She frets about

> the interference of the various Macaenas's [i.e. patrons] who would expect to be consulted,—of these, I could not confide in *one*, without disobliging all the rest;—& I could not confide in *all*, without having the play read all over the Town before it is acted. Mrs. Montagu, Mrs. Greville, Mrs. Crewe, Sir Joshua Reynolds, Mrs. Cholmondeley, & many inferior &cs, think they have an *equal* claim, one with the other, to my confidence.[17]

Instead, Burney boldly uses her playscript to satirize the modes of amateur coterie authorship, mocking them as insular and irrelevant, yet possessed of the cultural power to interfere with the combination of influential readers and widely circulating texts on which the print author of the day depended to build a reputation. Burney's ridicule of the coterie's misattributions and blatant plagiarisms suggests the period's general move away from the anonymous and collaborative modes of sociable authorship toward the more proprietary and individualist notions of emerging professional and legal paradigms. But the fate of the play offers ironic evidence that the literary professional was far from autonomous: her father and Crisp quickly put an end to the fantasy by urging her to suppress the play, apparently out of fear of the reaction of Montagu and her circle and how they might damage Burney's career prospects.

These were not idle concerns. Montagu's network, for example, had been able to mediate the effective transition of the relatively impoverished Hester Mulso Chapone, another of Burney's admired Bluestocking fore-bears, from coterie fame to more lucrative print-publishing success. In the 1740s and 1750s, Chapone had won a wide reputation among intercon-nected literary coteries as an intelligent and spirited writer of manuscript poetry and polemics; endorsed and edited by Montagu, her 1773 *Letters on the Improvement of the Mind*, followed by a volume of those long-ago poems and miscellaneous works, were an immediate and long-lasting publishing success.[18] On the other hand, social ostracism appears to have been a factor in the declining fortunes of the accomplished Charlotte Lennox, an early author-friend of Johnson about whom Burney remarks, "her Female Quixote is very justly admired here; indeed, *I* think *all* her Novels far the best of any *Living* Author,–but Mrs. Thrale says that though her *Books* are generally approved, Nobody likes *her*."[19]

More evidence for the ongoing vitality of modes of authorship other than print-based professionalism is found in the example of the Birmingham-area poet and landscape artist William Shenstone. Through his relationship with leading bookseller Robert Dodsley, Shenstone was able to live a retired life as a coterie writer exchanging manuscript verse and watercolor illustrations with an intimate circle of correspondents and a wider range of visitors to his *ferme ornée* The Leasowes, while ensuring that the group's compositions, as a coterie whole, featured as the dominant portion of volumes four (1755) and five (1758) of Dodsley's famous *Collection of Poems by Several Hands*. At least eight other members of the coterie were featured along with Shenstone in these volumes, and the authorial careers of several of them were launched through the Dodsley connection. Yet Dodsley's and Shenstone's correspondences reveal prac-tices that diverged significantly from the developing norms of professional authorship: materials came to Dodsley as part of their circulation in manuscript, usually transcribed by Shenstone, often revised by him and others, and neither identified by individual author nor accompanied by permission to print. In fact, at times Shenstone seems to have lost track of, or did not know, who the authors of some of the poems were.

Shenstone's story should not be dismissed as a mere throwback to that earlier time of gentlemanly disdain for print as a trade. The Yorke-Grey coterie of the early 1740s produced the collaborative *Athenian Letters* in the form of a carefully guarded set of a dozen printed copies; for all group-member John Heaton's pride in appearing as an author in print, cited in the second epigraph to this chapter, the printing press here merely served the private ends of the coterie. Shenstone, on the other hand, was nothing if not ambitious of wide recognition as a poet and leader of taste. He accomplished both of these ends through an authorial practice that in retrospect appears anachronistic, but proved to be very modern in its trajectory. His work in the ballad form, his aesthetic of rural simplicity as a rejection of complex urban culture, and his poetic persona of isolation and melancholy influenced the poetic forms of Romanticism and the authorial persona of the isolated Romantic genius – through their wide-spread propagation by the Dodsley publishing firm.[20]

Conclusion

In the series of authorial positions I have outlined in this chapter, only Samuel Johnson and Frances Burney appear self-consciously to practice what has often been characterized as "modern" authorship: the former by aligning himself with the booksellers as his "patrons" and the latter by representing herself as heir to a nascent professional tradition while repu-diating links with patrons and coterie writers.[21] In the later decades of the eighteenth century, the years immediately after *Donaldson* v. *Becket*, there seems to have been a range of authorial models or identities on offer, whether professional or amateur, individual or sociable, original or imita-tive, proprietary or anonymous. What was not necessarily clear was which mode was the way of the future. Frances Burney aligned herself with a largely masculine circle of literary professionals, negotiating a professional identity at a crucial moment in the establishment of a print-based authorial model, choosing print over manuscript, self-determination over the immediate social rewards of patronage, professional association over the increasingly feminized model of the amateur – but also hard fagging over poetic genius.[22] In this she largely followed her chosen mentor Samuel Johnson. But to complicate matters further, in publishing her third novel, *Camilla*, in 1796, Burney chose the subscription method, a kind of distributed patronage that saw her drawing on her Bluestocking connections to maximize her profits, just as Pope had, decades earlier, deployed his aristocratic networks to great success in the *Iliad* translation. At the broadest level, then, the multiplicity of authorial positions I have traced in this chapter raises further questions for consideration: is this instability a reflection of the fact that modern authorship, along with the cultural phenomena that produced it (print, copyright, the commodification of literature, the rise of professional specializations, the articulation of aesthetic theory), was just emerging at this juncture? Or is it possible that "authorship" is always a various, fragmented, and contested entity that eludes our categories?

Notes

1. Alexander Pope, *The Dunciad, in The Poems of Alexander Pope*, ed. John Butt (London: Methuen, 1963), p. 344; John Heaton to Philip Yorke, 9 March 1741, British Library Add. Ms. 35605, f. 77; Samuel Johnson, *The Adventurer*, no. 115, 1753, in *The Yale Edition of the Works of Samuel Johnson*, vol. 2, eds. W. J. Bate, John M. Bullitt, and L. F. Powell (New Haven, CT: Yale University Press, 1963), p. 457; *The Early Journals and Letters of Fanny Burney, Vol. III: The Streatham Years, Part 1 (1778–79)*, eds. Lars E. Troide and Stewart J. Cooke (Montreal: McGill–Queen's University Press, 1994), p. 32.

2. With the exception of a few general references, I will focus my account on Britain, where the commercialization of print was particularly influential. (Because, strictly speaking, Britain did not exist until the Act of Union between England and Scotland in 1707, brief references to pre-1707 events apply to England only.) Other European states experienced similar trajectories, but with greater involvement of regulatory systems (France) and a more philosophically oriented debate about free access to knowledge and the nature of aesthetic creation (the Germanic states). For fuller accounts of eighteenth-century authorship in these two regions, see David Saunders, *Authorship and Copyright* (London: Routledge, 1992), chs. 3 and 4, and Martha Woodmansee, *The Author, Art, and the Market: Rereading the History of Aesthetics* (New York: Columbia University Press, 1994), chs. 2 and 3.

3. J. Paul Hunter, *Before Novels: The Cultural Contexts of Eighteenth-Century English Fiction* (New York: W.W. Norton, 1990), ch. 3; for a detailed discussion of the interplay between the marketplace and monopoly interests in the eighteenth-century British book trade, see James Raven, "The Book as Commodity," in *The Cambridge History of the Book in Britain, Volume V, 1695–1830*, eds. Michael F. Suarez, S. J., and Michael L. Turner (Cambridge: Cambridge University Press, 2009), pp. 85–117.

4. Samuel Johnson, *The Rambler*, no. 145, *The Yale Edition of the Works of Samuel Johnson*, vol. 5, eds. W. J. Bate and Albrecht B. Strauss (New Haven, CT: Yale University Press, 1969), p. 10.

5. Frances Burney, *The Early Journals and Letters of Fanny Burney, Vol. IV: The Streatham Years*, Part 2 *(1780–81)*, ed. Betty Rizzo (Montreal: McGill–Queen's University Press, 2003), p. 209. Burney's journals and letters make frequent use of emphases; italics in quotations follow the original.

6. James Ralph, *The Case of Authors by Profession or Trade, Stated* (London, 1758), pp. 8–9, 2. In an examination of the same phenomena in this transitional period as those I am treating, Dustin Griffin draws a distinction between the concept of the "author by profession" as used by Ralph and the notion of the author as a professional author, which he sees as anachronistic (Dustin Griffin, "The Rise of the Professional Author?", in *Cambridge History of the Book in Britain*, vol. 5, eds. Suarez and Turner, pp. 137–43).

7. Ralph, *Case of Authors*, pp. 2, 6, 8.

8. Pope, *The First Satire of the Second Book of Horace*, in *The Poems of Alexander Pope*, l. 121. The foundation for Pope's ability to live as a gentleman-poet was the lucrative contract for his 1715–20 translation of Homer's *Iliad*, negotiated with the bookseller Bernard Lintot in 1714, but throughout his career Pope continued to manipulate – and perhaps collude with – his bookseller "adversaries." For an account of the *Iliad* contract, see David Foxon, *Pope and the Early Eighteenth-Century Book Trade: The Lyell Lectures, Oxford 1975–1976* (Oxford: Clarendon, 1991); for Pope's various court actions against booksellers and their significance to the developing model of author as proprietor, see Mark Rose, *Authors and Owners: The Invention of Copyright* (Cambridge, MA: Harvard University Press, 1993), pp. 58–66.

9. Johnson declared, for example, that "Doddy [bookseller Robert Dodsley] is my patron, you know" (letter to Bennet Langton, January 9, 1759, *The Letters of Samuel Johnson*, 5 vols., ed. Bruce Redford (Princeton, NJ: Princeton University Press, 1992–92), vol. 1, p. 173). Dodsley had published Johnson's first solo performance, his poem *London*, and was a leading member of the consortium that had conceived of and funded the *Dictionary*. Richardson's extensive discussions of the legacy of Pope with Aaron Hill, Thomas Edwards, Colley Cibber, and Edward Young can be found in Thomas Keymer and Peter Sabor, eds., *The Cambridge Edition of the Correspondence of Samuel Richardson*, 11 vols. (Cambridge: Cambridge University Press, 2013–).

10. Burney, *Early Journals and Letters*, vol. 3, p. 352.

11. Pope, "To Richard Boyle, Earl of Burlington: Of the Use of Riches," in *The Poems of Alexander Pope*, p. 590, l. 57; *An Essay on Criticism*, in *The Poems of Alexander Pope*, p. 146, ll. 60–61.

12. Joseph Warton, *An Essay on the Writings and Genius of Pope* (London, 1756), pp. iv–v.

13. Edward Young, *Conjectures on Original Composition* (London, 1759), pp. 9, 12.

14. For a useful timeline reviewing the history of "custom, law and practice" related to intellectual property in English-speaking texts from the sixteenth to

the twentieth centuries, see "Appendix 2" in William St. Clair, *The Reading Nation in the Romantic Period* (Cambridge: Cambridge University Press, 2004), pp. 480–89.

15. Burney, *Early Journals and Letters*, vol. 3, p. 65; see also Rose, *Authors and Owners*, pp. 5–8, on the trope of the landed estate as a metaphor for copyright in eighteenth-century legal discourse.

16. It should be noted that other Bluestocking women, such as Hannah More, Elizabeth Carter, and Hester Mulso Chapone (the latter discussed later in this section), also built remunerative careers as print authors.

17. Burney, *Early Journals and Letters*, vol. 3, p. 264.

18. Chapone's modern editor has located seventy editions or reprints up to 1851; see Rhoda Zuk, ed., *Bluestocking Feminism: Writings of the Bluestocking Circle, 1738–1785, Vol. 3: Catherine Talbot & Hester Chapone* (London: Pickering & Chatto, 1999), pp. 195–99. Zuk further identifies eighteen publications of the letters in company with other works of instruction in the nineteenth century.

19. Burney, *Early Journals and Letters*, vol. 3, pp. 105–6.

20. As Shenstone's literary executor, Dodsley published a two-volume edition of his friend's works in 1764, followed by a third volume of coterie correspondence in 1769; in addition to six editions of the *Works*, at least sixteen publications authored by Shenstone's friends were issued by the firm between 1764 and 1791. See Betty A. Schellenberg, *Literary Coteries and the Making of Modern Print Culture, 1740–1790* (Cambridge: Cambridge University Press, 2016), ch. 4. Chapter 1 of this study also offers a fuller discussion of the Yorke-Grey coterie.

21. As in the case of Charlotte Lennox noted above, Burney also avoids identification with her female professional predecessors, despite opportunities both in print and in her social life to do so; see Betty A. Schellenberg, *The Professionalization of Women Writers in Eighteenth-Century Britain, 1740–1780* (Cambridge: Cambridge University Press, 2005), ch. 6.

22. For an argument about the gradual gendering of professional versus amateur authorship in eighteenth-century Britain, see Linda Zionkowski, *Men's Work: Gender, Class, and the Professionalization of Poetry, 1660–1784* (Houndmills, UK: Palgrave Macmillan, 2001).

CHAPTER 10

The Nineteenth Century
Intellectual Property Rights and "Literary Larceny"

Alexis Easley

In his preface to *Lyrical Ballads* (1802), William Wordsworth claimed that the "poet binds together by passion and knowledge the vast empire of human society, as it is spread over the whole earth, and over all time."[1] This notion of the Romantic author as a transformational genius played a foundational role in the development of modern copyright, which defined the author as an individual who deserved special recognition and protection under the law. The Copyright Act of 1814 held that copyright rested with the author for twenty-eight years or the author's lifetime, whichever was longer, and over the course of the century these rights were further extended and refined. Thomas Talfourd took up the cause for reform in 1837, putting forward a bill that was designed "to insure to authors of the highest and most enduring merit a larger share in the fruits of their own industry and genius."[2] After five years of parliamentary debate, a bill was finally passed that extended the length of copyright protection to forty-two years from the date of publication or the author's life plus seven years, whichever was greater. The legal construction of the author as a named, individual subject went hand in hand with the professionalization of authorship – the rise of author societies and literary agents, as well as the development of trade journals, clubs, and handbooks for writers.

While in the book trade the author was defined as an individual with legal rights, in contemporaneous journalistic media the notion of authorship was defined in radically different terms. The rapid expansion of the press during the nineteenth century relied on anonymous publication, collaborative models of authorship, and the free exchange of content between newspaper and periodical titles. Section 18 of the 1842 Copyright Act acknowledged that periodical publications should be

* I gratefully acknowledge the assistance of independent scholar Raymond Blair, who provided valuable information about Frances Brown's life and work.

treated differently under the law. It assigned copyright for journalistic content to the publisher of the periodical rather than to the author. When authors were paid by the publisher, they technically handed over their copyright for a period of twenty-eight years, with the proviso that publishers could not reprint contributors' work without permission. The twenty-eight-year period of copyright protection for periodical contributions does not seem to have been enforced. Authors often republished their poems and essays in volume editions shortly after they appeared in periodicals and newspapers. Nevertheless, journalistic publications seemed to fall into the gray area between original, protected forms of authorship and the collaborative, ephemeral productions associated with the public domain. The unsure status of periodical publications reflected the broader instability of the author as a cultural and legal entity during the nineteenth century. As Clare Pettit notes, there was an ongoing tension between the "model of the solitary individual as artist" and the "social production of art and aesthetic forms" within nineteenth-century print culture.[3]

This tension was especially apparent in the widespread practice of scissors-and-paste journalism – the republication of poems, paragraphs, and other content from one paper to another, with or without attribution. This practice was a longstanding convention in journalistic networks, which assumed that news, poetry, and other ephemeral content was in the public domain and thus did not fall under legal definitions of intellectual property. Nevertheless, newspapers and periodicals that paid reporters, foreign correspondents, and other contributors to produce original content viewed scissors-and-paste journalism as a form of literary piracy since the proprietors of these periodicals did not pay for the snippets they chose to reprint. As Bob Nicholson points out, the "'authors' of scissors-and-paste texts were marked out as lacking creativity, originality, imagination and taste," and the periodicals that published their work were defined as being less respectable than those that printed original content.[4]

As a result of the differing status of books and periodicals under copyright law, a single poem or article might have copyright protection in one publishing medium and unsure copyright status in another. For example, a poem might be published in a newspaper as a stand-alone contribution, republished in a book collection, reprinted as part of a book review published in a monthly magazine, and adapted into a popular song by a purveyor of sheet music. Each form of publication was governed by different legal definitions and professional conventions regarding the fair use of copyrighted material. Thus, the notion of the author as an individual with copyright protection was contingent on the publishing conventions associated with the media in which his or her work appeared. A writer might achieve consecrated status as the author of a copyright-protected volume edition but also publish contributions in cheap periodicals, which were then cut and pasted into a host of provincial newspapers, with or without authorial attribution. As much as the law defined authorial rights in increasingly precise terms, the products of literary labor could not easily be contained within these definitions. As we will see, this was especially the case for publications in the newspaper press, which were not specifically mentioned in the 1842 Copyright Act and thus assumed a particularly ambiguous status under copyright law.

In this chapter, I first discuss the practice of scissors-and-paste journalism, using this as a case study to examine the complex status of the author in the newspaper press. The unauthorized reprinting of material from one paper to another was considered, at best, a breach of professional propriety and, at worst, a violation of copyright law. Yet the practice was so ubiquitous and necessary within a rapidly expanding popular press that it was rarely policed. As Will Slauter notes, "[r]eprinting would not have thrived for so long if writers, printers, booksellers, and readers had not derived benefits from it. [. . .] [C]opying not only enabled news (true and false) to spread, it also facilitated commentary and analysis."[5] When cases of copyright infringement did go to court, they revealed the unsure legal status of newspapers, which relied on collaborative, corporate models of authorship instead of the notion of the author as a proprietary individual. I explore these issues by examining a specific legal case, *Walter* v. *Steinkopff* (1892), which highlighted the unsure status of newspaper content under existing copyright law and provided an opportunity for one literary pirate, Sidney Low (1857–1932), editor of the *St. James's Gazette*, to define the parameters by which scissors-and-paste journalism might be practiced in professional, respectable ways.

Within debates over scissors-and-paste journalism, poetry assumed a rather contradictory status. The concept of the poet-genius was crucial to the early development of copyright law, and signed books of poetry held a consecrated status within the literary marketplace. Sometimes the idea of the poet as original genius was reflected in periodical publications such as literary annuals, which relied on the celebrity status of paid contributors, even while technically assuming the copyright of this purchased content. However, most poetry was published anonymously in periodicals and newspapers. Poetry was often poached and republished from one periodical to another, with or without attribution to the author or the original publication source. In the second part of this chapter, I focus on the case study of Irish poet Frances Brown (1816–79), whose careful navigation of the market for poetry reveals the importance of different media forms (along with their differing levels of copyright protection) in fashioning a poetic career.[6] Even though Brown's poetry was often repurposed by scissors-and-paste journalists as if it were free content within the public domain, she was successful in establishing a celebrity identity and publishing her work in book form. However, with time her poetic fame diminished, and she turned to writing children's stories, only to fall subject to a high-profile case of plagiarism after her death. Her case reveals the vagaries of a literary marketplace which, as Meredith McGill points out, had a "tendency [. . .] to shift the ground on which [writers] stood."[7] Authors like Brown were forced to contend with changes and ambiguities in copyright law, both domestically and internationally, and often their works were absorbed into the public domain without their permission or control. Brown's case thus reveals how one author was able to navigate a complex literary marketplace in order to achieve consecrated status as an author of copyright-protected works, while at the same time highlighting the limitations of the "author" as a unifying concept for a body of work that was reprinted and repurposed without copyright protection or authorial control.

"Literary Larceny": Scissors-and-Paste Journalism

In 1855, *Punch* published a comic article titled "Literary Larceny" recounting the trial of Paul Jones, proprietor of the *Literary Pirate*, who is charged with being in possession of stolen goods. A search of his home leads to the discovery of a "large pair of scissors, with a paste pot," along with clippings from the *Times* and the *Daily News*.[8] Jones pleads his case, arguing "that all he had done was for the good of the public, and his only object was to supply the public with good articles at the lowest prices."[9] In response, the magistrate notes that a pickpocket or burglar might similarly claim to rob "people of their goods in order to supply them to other people as cheaply as possible."[10] Jones is ultimately found guilty and sentenced to two months of prison with hard labor.

The notion that literary pirates like Jones might be brought to justice was comic because it so rarely occurred. During the 1850s, "literary larceny" was common practice: sub-editors regularly snipped poetry, articles, crime reports, and other material from other papers, using these snippets to meet the pressing demand for content from week to week. Unlike the *Times* and *Daily News*, provincial and cheap metropolitan periodicals could not afford to hire a staff of professional writers or foreign correspondents. They did employ low-paid reporters (penny-a-liners) to produce original content, but they just as often relied on scissors and a pot of glue. The sub-editor was charged with composing snippets from other papers into columns that would engage and inform their readers. As journalists, they were valued more for their powers of selection than for their production of original content. As *Chambers's Journal* noted in 1867, the sub-editor had a "peculiar journalistic instinct – the faculty which enables him to see at once what is important and what is unimportant – what is likely to interest, not a class merely, but the public at large."[11]

Other periodicals viewed the sub-editor's "instinct" as a criminal impulse, and the readers who purchased stolen material were sometimes imagined as unwitting collaborators in a shady enterprise. An 1853 article in *Eliza Cook's Journal*, for example, proclaims, "All that read, enjoy the literature of our day; yet perhaps the very ease with which people obtain information frequently renders them forgetful of those whose labours have afforded them so much pleasure and gratification."[12] Undergirding the expansion of popular print culture, it reminded readers, was an illegal trade in pirated material that relied on the labor of reporters and writers who were paid by the editors who commissioned their work but not by those who poached this material for rival publications.

By the end of the century, the publication and pirating of paragraphs, poems, and other snippets came to be associated with the New Journalism – a new style of sensationalist press work designed to appeal to a mass-market audience. Magazines such as *Tit-Bits* provided short articles, prize competitions, engaging fiction, and entertaining paragraphs that appealed to busy, easily distracted readers. In 1890, *Punch* satirized these readers in a poem titled "Literature and Lottery." It begins,

> Yes, I've "a literary taste,"
>   And patronise a weekly journal;
> 'Tis what is called *Scissors and Paste*,
>   The paper's poor, the print's infernal.
> But what of that, when, week by week
>   High at the sight of it hope rises?
> What in my Magazine I seek
>   Is just – a medium for Prizes![13]

With the spread of the New Journalism, the demand for scissors-and-paste content expanded significantly. As *Tit-Bits* put it in 1881, "[t]here is scarcely a newspaper which does not give some extracts."[14] This included a robust exchange of content between British, American, European, and colonial newspapers and periodicals. The 1886 Berne Convention guaranteed that the authors in participating countries would receive reciprocal copyright protection for their book-length works, but this did not apply to articles from periodicals and newspapers, which could be "reproduced in original or in translation in the other countries of the union, unless the authors or publishers [had] expressly forbidden it."[15] Thus, journalistic content was clearly distinguished from other, more consecrated forms of work in an international publishing context. Although the United States was not part of the 1886 pact, it nevertheless eagerly participated in this free exchange of journalistic content.[16]

By 1892, the conflict over scissors-and-paste publishing practices in Britain came to a crisis point, resulting in a high-profile lawsuit, *Walter v. Steinkopff*. In this case, the *Times* demanded redress for the unauthorized reprinting of four of its articles in the *St. James's Gazette*, including news reports published under the bylines "Our Correspondent" and "Dalziel," as well as an article by Rudyard Kipling titled "In Sight of Monadnock." According to the 1842 act, the *Times* assumed the copyright of these pieces when it paid the authors for their contributions. Nevertheless, Sidney Low, editor of the *Gazette*, defended his employer by claiming that the reprinting of such material was a well-established journalistic practice that operated according to a set of implicitly understood conventions. A newspaper article could rightfully be reprinted from another paper, he argued,

> [f]irst, if the source of the quotations or information is acknowledged; secondly, if the paper copying or the paper copied from are not direct rivals or competitors; [...] thirdly, if the paper copied from has at some time annexed and published matter appearing in the other paper, thereby implying that it agrees to the free interchange of literary and other matter; fourthly, if the editor of the paper copied from has taken no steps to inform the editor of the other paper that he objects to this use being made of his matter.[17]

In this passage, Low not only attempts to delineate the sort of scissors-and-paste practices employed by respectable newspapers but also defines the parameters of a journalistic public domain that is produced through the "free interchange" of material between consenting, non-competing newspaper titles. The judge in the case did not find that Low's list of conditions had been satisfied, ruling that the articles in question were clearly protected under copyright law. However, he noted that the three news reports were too "trivial" to warrant damages, presumably because they lacked the full authorial name that had been clearly appended to the Kipling article.[18] Indeed, the judge asserted that the bulk of the paragraphs that the *Gazette* routinely reprinted from the *Times* were not protected and could be "reproduced by the defendants with impunity."[19] Thus, even though all paid contributions were covered under copyright law, only those with literary merit would be actively protected by the courts. The judge in the case made a fine distinction between the sort of literary content associated with named authors and the greater mass of ephemeral content published anonymously or under a pseudonym.

The decision in the *Walter* v. *Steinkopff* case was duly reported in the press and garnered a variety of responses. *Judy*, a comic weekly, reflected, "There is sorrow to-day, among subeditors; [. . .] their great God, Scissors and Paste, has gone forth discrowned and disanointed."[20] It then offered a satiric poem in their honor, "The Pressman's Sorrow":

> We are weeping, we are weeping,
>   For a Judge has said us "No,"
> Said we must not go on reaping
>   Things that other people sow.
> Yes, we're weeping and we're wailing,
>   And we suffer from "the pip,"
> For it isn't easy sailing
>   When you aren't allowed to clip.[21]

Of course, as the decision in *Walter* v. *Steinkopff* had indicated, subeditors had no real reason to weep. They were still allowed to poach unsigned, ephemeral material from other papers as long as it was deemed "trivial." In reflecting on the court's decision against the *St. James's Gazette*, Sidney Low published an article in the *National Review* which drew attention to the ambiguous status of newspaper content under the "unsatisfactory and confused" system of copyright law.[22] He asks, "Who are the 'authors' with whom Fleet Street is concerned? They are as the sands of the sea-shore for multitude."[23] He then proposes that a new law be devised that would require newspaper "proprietors or publishers [. . .] [to register] as the owners of all the copyrights" in their publications rather than seeking copyright protection for individual articles.[24] Such a suggestion recognized that all publishing media did not operate under the same definition of authorship. The corporate model adopted by many periodicals and newspapers did not easily fit within existing copyright law.

Ironically, at the same time that Sidney Low alluded to the "multitude" of newspaper journalists whose individual rights did not merit individual copyright protection, he indirectly made an argument for his own status as a high-profile editor whose opinions and identity were worthy of being singled out within the literary establishment. His testimony in *Walter v. Steinkopff*, followed by his high-profile essay published in the *National Review*, seemed to recast the literary pirate in respectable terms – as a man of letters whose work was governed by rules of professional propriety and who aimed to reform the very laws he had been accused of violating. A year after the case was decided, Low was interviewed in "Journals and Journalists of To-day," an illustrated series in the *Sketch* magazine that aimed to illuminate the lives and professional opinions of influential editors and writers. The interviewer begins by referring to editors as the "most important beings on earth" and provides opportunities for Low to define himself as a respectable member of the profession.[25] "Notwithstanding the taste for tit-bits publications and the like," he notes, "there is a public which likes newspapers with a literary feeling."[26] While Low admits that he has "gone as far as to use cross-headings, interviews, [. . .] and [has] even assimilated the 'personal paragraph,'" his larger aim is to reach "men of the world and people of education."[27] In this way, Low defines his own professional status along respectable lines, positioning the *Gazette* in opposition to "tit-bits publications," which engage in the same sorts of scissors-and-paste practices he had been accused of employing just months before. His article and his interview can be seen as attempts to shore up his own reputation as a respectable editor within a literary marketplace rife with less legitimate forms of literary larceny and bad taste. Editorial work might not rise to the status of authorship under copyright law, but it nevertheless could be imbued with authority and cultural importance.

Newspaper Poets and Copyright: The Case of Frances Brown

Periodical poetry would seem to fall under the category of "literary," rather than "trivial," newspaper content, as defined by *Walter v. Steinkopff*. The poet, unlike the editor, would seem to have no difficulty establishing the right to retain ownership of original content. Informed by Romantic definitions of the author as a poet-genius, the 1842 Copyright Act was premised on the notion that the literary legacy and intellectual property of literary writers were deserving of protection. However, since most poetry was published in periodicals and newspapers, rather than in volume editions, its status as intellectual property was somewhat unclear. Periodicals and newspapers printed and reprinted millions of poems during the nineteenth century, with and without authorial signature.[28] As Kirstie Blair notes, most poets were not paid for their work, but aspiring authors enjoyed the "cachet of being known in their community as a published poet [and] [. . .] used newspaper publication to form relationships of patronage with influential editors and critics and as a stepping-stone toward volume publication (which usually required both sponsorship by a patron and enough local reputation to attract subscribers)."[29] Thus, the culture of reprinting could work to a poet's advantage. While unpaid contributions to newspapers were not protected under copyright law, they could nevertheless be used to construct an identity that might lead to a more consecrated status as the paid author of a copyright-protected book of poetry.

Within literary culture, the term "newspaper poetry" was often used pejoratively. As a contributor to the *Ladies Repository* proclaimed in 1859, "newspaper poetry is not *poetry* at all."[30] Critics believed that poems published in newspaper columns lacked quality and originality in part because they were unremunerated and thus did not have the same status as copyright-protected content. As the poet T. C. Harbaugh put it in 1888, "[s]o many papers can fill their poetic niches with clipped or gratuitous matter, that their editors do not think of paying for even meritorious work."[31] Disparaging views of newspaper poetry did not hamper the genre's immense popularity among nineteenth-century readers. Poems were among the most frequently reprinted material in periodicals and newspapers, sometimes appearing with the name of the author and original source publication but sometimes without these markers of attribution.

In the following pages, I will provide a case study of a particular poet, Frances Brown (1816–79), whose career reveals the complex negotiations of authorship and copyright status writers faced in the literary marketplace during the 1840s. Brown was born into a working-class family in Stranorlar, a remote village in the north of Ireland. She lost her sight to smallpox when she was eighteen months old and learned about the world by listening to her siblings' lessons and having family members read aloud to her. In 1840, she published her first poem in an unnamed provincial paper and a handful of other verses in the *Irish Penny Journal* (1840–41). Like many women writers making a debut in the literary world, she developed her love of poetry in part from reading provincial newspapers.[32] So it made sense for her to choose cheap weekly papers as her first publication outlet. Having achieved some success publishing her work in an Irish penny paper, Brown next placed her work in a high-profile metropolitan journal, the *Athenaeum*. Such a move was necessary for relocating herself from the periphery to the center of the literary world. Indeed, she later noted that publishing in the *Athenaeum* "gratified a wish which had haunted [her] very dreams."[33] In June 1841, her poems appeared in the *Athenaeum* under the initials "F.B.," but in January 1842 her full name and home location, Stranorlar, were appended to her contributions, which signaled her desire to establish a reputation as a named poet. This strategy proved to be successful. "From that period," she later notes, "my name and pretensions have been more before the public – many poems of mine having appeared in the pages of that publication, in Mr. Hood's *Magazine*, and in the *Keepsake* edited by the Countess of Blessington."[34]

The publication of Brown's poem "The First" in the *Keepsake* annual in the autumn of 1842 was a particularly fortunate step in her career. As Susan Brown notes, the annuals paid well and "fostered a network of women's writing."[35] The prominence of the *Keepsake* in the literary marketplace meant that poems published in its pages were frequently reprinted. An investigation of the reprinting history of "The First" reveals a great deal about how poetry copyright was understood by writers and editors during the 1840s. It was during this period, Meredith McGill argues, that "texts achieved a remarkable mobility across elite and mass-cultural formats," and authors were continually forced to adjust to the "shifting conditions of literary production," especially where copyright protection was concerned.[36] The initial re-printings of "The First" occurred in reviews of the *Keepsake* published in the *Mirror of Literature*, the *Literary Gazette*, the *Examiner*, and the *Sporting Review* in November and December of 1842. The excerpting of complete poems in reviews easily fell within the guidelines for fair use, and in each case, the editor clearly identified both the poem's author and source publication.

"The First" was also reprinted as a standalone contribution in two British papers, the *Hampshire Telegraph* (December 5, 1842) and the *Manchester Guardian* (March 1, 1843), as well as in a New York weekly, the *Albion* (January 28, 1843). In the two British papers, editors were careful to note Brown's name and to include the phrase "from the *Keepsake*" in the header to the poem. The *Hampshire Telegraph* took the additional step of enclosing the entire poem in quotation marks, perhaps hoping that this would provide extra protection against a potential breach of copyright. As an annual serial publication, the *Keepsake* most likely fell into the gray area between book and periodical publication, which made it somewhat unclear whether the editor or the publisher was the copyright holder of the publication. When reprinting Brown's poem, the *Manchester Guardian* mentions that the *Keepsake* is edited by Lady Blessington, perhaps assuming that she is the annual's "author." After all, her name, rather than proprietor Charles Heath's, appears on the periodical's cover page. The *Albion* also notes Blessington's name along with her biographical footnote on Brown; however, it does not mention the *Keepsake*, which suggests that it may view Blessington as the editor-author (and thus the copyright holder) of the "book" in which Brown's poem had originally appeared. Thus, these editorial annotations, while attempting to carefully and tactfully respect copyright, do so in such a way that demonstrates the ambiguity of the law where periodical publications were concerned. Was Blessington, Brown, or the journal itself the true copyright holder of "The First"? Although Brown's name is always included, she is not foregrounded as the author whose intellectual property rights are in most need of protection.

It is likely that Brown was paid for the original publication of "The First" in the *Keepsake*; however, she received no remuneration for the subsequent reprinting of the poem in periodicals and newspapers. Still, the reprinting of her work in newspapers and periodicals helped her develop a recognizable name in the literary marketplace. As Ellen Gruber Garvey notes, publishing houses "noted an author's popularity in newspaper exchanges as a sign that the writer's reputation was substantial enough to carry a collection of the pieces into a book."[37] Indeed, just one year after "The First" appeared in the *Keepsake*, Brown published her first collection of poems, *The Star of Attéghéi* (1844), and four years later, her second book appeared, *Lyrics and Miscellaneous Poems* (1848). In both instances, she uses prefaces to reclaim her poems as literary property. The "Editor's Preface" to *The Star of Attéghéi* includes a long biography of Brown that recounts the tale of her humble beginnings, struggle with blindness, and eventual triumph. The biography also mentions the titles of the periodicals that had published her poems – the *Irish Penny Journal, Hood's Magazine*, the *Keepsake*, and the *Athenaeum* – thus establishing Brown's own authorial identity as the unifying concept for this scattered body of work. The editor notes that she was a paid author, whose "talent [came] back to her in the shape of money," thus implying that she was no amateur and that the periodicals that published her work could sue for copyright protection.[38] The "Editorial Introduction" also notes that ten of the poems Brown published in the *Athenaeum* were reprinted in *The Star of Attéghéi*. Brown is quoted as saying that only ten were selected since most of the others "were so widely copied into the journals of the day, that

I feared they might be too familiar for repetition."[39] If the reprinting of poems in newspapers could help a writer develop a public identity, it could also de-value her work, placing it in the maligned category of "newspaper poetry."

In the preface to *Lyrics and Miscellaneous Poems*, Brown once again reminds readers that the "present publication is composed of her poetical contributions to various periodicals – 'The Athenaeum,' 'Fulcher's Poetical Miscellany,' 'Chambers' Journal,' 'Hood's Magazine,' and others."[40] She notes that she was motivated to collect these works in volume form because of the worry that "scattered poems become, in process of time, liable to the risk of controverted authorship; and proprietors in general wish to retain their rights, though they should extend over nothing more valuable than rocks and sand."[41] Here she alludes to the practices of scissors-and-paste journalists, who might reprint her work without attributing the author or original source publication. Her ambiguous use of the word "proprietors" is telling because it on one hand suggests that she, as the author of a book collection, has a proprietary right to her intellectual property. At the same time, it draws attention to the periodical proprietors who originally paid for and published some of the poems in the collection and thus technically share the copyright. Amusingly, she undercuts the value of that copyright by comparing her poems to rocks and sand – substances that are valueless because they are so ubiquitous.

Brown's commentary in the preface to *Lyrics and Miscellaneous Poems* is undoubtedly an instance of self-effacing humor, but it is also an acknowledgment of the loss of value produced by the frequent printing, reprinting, and mass consumption of poetry in the periodical and newspaper press. Interestingly, "The First" was one of the poems reprinted in *Lyrics and Miscellaneous Poems*, but the editorial introduction does not make note of the *Keepsake* as the poem's original source publication. Nor does it provide the details of where other poems in the collection were originally published. This can perhaps be interpreted as a self-authorizing gesture that elides the collaborative editorial process that informed the production of the poems the author has now chosen to claim as her own.

It may have been the republication of "The First" in *Lyrics and Miscellaneous Poems* that led to another round of reprintings. In September 1854, *Eliza Cook's Journal* included the poem in a biographical essay on Brown. Even though over a decade had passed since the poem's original date of publication, the article carefully notes the *Keepsake* as the original publication source. Two months later, "The First" was republished in an American monthly, the *Eclectic Magazine*

(December 1854), as part of a reprint of the essay from *Eliza Cook's Journal*, and the poem also appeared as a standalone contribution in the American *Living Age* (October 1854). In both instances, editors carefully identified *Eliza Cook's Journal* as the source publication, thus demonstrating their careful navigation of British copyright law, which identified the periodical as the copyright holder. As American publications, they did so as professional courtesy, rather than as a legal requirement, since in 1854 there was no copyright protection for British authors or works in the American literary marketplace. Of course, the *Keepsake*, as the poem's original publication source, was part of this complex chain of attribution: the *Eclectic's* reprint of the essay on Brown attributes *Eliza Cook's Journal* as the source, and the reprinted essay includes an attribution of the poem to the *Keepsake*.

The *Living Age* takes a shortcut by simply citing *Eliza Cook's Journal* as the poem's source. Neither *Eliza Cook's Journal*, the *Eclectic*, nor the *Living Age* mentions Brown's *Lyrics and Miscellaneous Poems*, even though it had published the most recent, and presumably the most authoritative, version of the poem. Other American periodicals dropped attributions entirely. When "The First" appeared in a literary supplement to the *Connecticut Courant* (November 19, 1853) and the Philadelphia *German Reformed Messenger* (April 1854), neither Brown's name nor the original site of publication was indicated. Perhaps these provincial papers viewed the poem as filler that did not require attribution – or assumed that enough time had passed or a sufficient number of reprintings had occurred so as to meld the poem into the public domain.

As much as Brown was successful at claiming copyright protection for her work through book publication, this was not enough to support her financially. Consequently, she turned to writing for the more lucrative prose fiction market. In an 1844 letter to a Glasgow correspondent, she writes, "You are perhaps aware that I am not blessed with independent circumstances. I have latterly turned to the more profitable line of Prose though it is not a labour of love as the composition of Poetry ever was to me. Yet taste must at times be sacrificed to interest and I have been very successful in my new pursuit."[42] She went on to publish her first novel, *My Share of the World*, in 1861, and wrote a number of works for children, including her most famous work *Granny's Wonderful Chair*, which first appeared in 1856 and was reprinted in several editions.

The publication of books would seem to have provided Brown with the copyright protection that had been so unsure in the poetry marketplace during the 1840s. However, after her death in 1879, a story from *Granny's Wonderful Chair* was plagiarized by none other than Frances Hodgson

Burnett, the famous children's book author, who published a thinly disguised version of Brown's "The Story of Fairyfoot" in an American
children's periodical, *St. Nicholas*. Burnett's plagiarized version of the
story, "The Story of Prince Fairyfoot," appeared in three parts, 1886–7,
just seven years after Brown's death. Did Burnett assume that the copyright
of *Granny's Wonderful Chair* had expired, not realizing that the 1842 act
protected copyright for forty-two years or the author's lifetime plus seven
years, whichever was greater? In any case, a reader of *St. Nicholas* called out
the plagiarism, and the editor of the journal, Mary Mapes Dodge, published a note explaining that she had mistakenly omitted part of the story's
title, "Stories from the Lost Fairy-Book," which identified "Prince
Fairyfoot" as a retelling of a story Burnett had "faint recollections" of
having read as a child but whose author was unknown to her.[43] Burnett, she
notes, also claimed to have asked a friend in the "Congressional Library at
Washington" to help her find the source text, but to no avail.[44]
Acknowledging that a "correspondent" identified *Granny's Wonderful
Chair* as the source text, Dodge duly attributes the book to its proper
author, Frances Brown, and apologizes to her British and American
publishers.[45] In 1887, such an apology was a courtesy, rather than an
attempt to forestall litigation, given that there was no copyright agreement
between the United States and Great Britain and the pirating of British
books by American authors was still common practice.

   Three years later, when a new edition of Brown's book was published,
the *Spectator* took Burnett to task for not making a greater attempt to
identify the source text of her plagiarized story: "But the strange thing is
that, considering new editions of the book had appeared in 1881, 1882, 1883,
and 1884, Mrs. Burnett's inquires [sic] led to no discovery. Perhaps if she
had asked someone to look in the catalog of the British Museum, instead of
going to 'a friend in the Congressional Library at Washington,' they might
have been more successful."[46] An article in the *Fortnightly Review* went
further, accusing Burnett of "calmly [taking] a complete story belonging to
Messrs. Ward, Lock, and Co., and [publishing] it in America as her
own."[47] Given the long and contentious history of literary piracy in
America, Burnett's publication of a plagiarized British story in an
American periodical had clearly hit a sore spot. It is no accident that the
reviews calling out her plagiarism of *Granny's Wonderful Chair* were
published around the same time as debates over the Chace Act (1891),
which established copyright protection for British authors in America.

   In 1904, seventeen years after publishing "Prince Fairyfoot," Burnett
published a new edition of *Granny's Wonderful Chair* along with an

editorial introduction explaining her inadvertent plagiarism of Brown's work. In this account, she notes that she "asked people both in England and America" if they could help her find the source book, "but no one seemed ever to have heard of it."[48] At the same time that she attempts to explain her mistake, she also exerts a kind of ownership over Brown's text. She begins the preface by asserting, "I shall always feel that it belongs to me and that they [children] have only borrowed it from me."[49] Speaking directly to a juvenile audience, she blames the fairies for making her lose Brown's book in the first place and allowing it to be rediscovered by her in the present. *Granny's Wonderful Chair*, she explains, "was of course really a thing invented by the fairies," and when the source text was finally identified by a reader of *St. Nicholas*, who "no doubt felt wronged and robbed" by the publication of "*her*" Fairyfoot," the "fairies did what they had planned to do" and saved the book from obscurity for all to enjoy.[50]

Burnett clearly chose to publish her edition of *Granny's Wonderful Chair* just after the book's copyright had expired. Originally published in 1856, the text was now, forty-eight years later, finally within the public domain, and Burnett was free to profit from its republication. Even though Burnett gave credit to Brown as the author, she blurred any sense of her ownership: the contents of the book "belong" to Burnett, the fairies, and children everywhere. This was technically true, given that *Granny's Wonderful Chair* was now in the public domain, but Burnett's lighthearted account of her earlier plagiarism elides the uncomfortable truth – that Brown's obscurity, femininity, and Anglo-Irishness, as well as her choice of the seemingly ephemeral/collective genre of the fairy tale, made her work seem as if it was "free" long before the copyright had expired.

Conclusion

In her account of Burnett's plagiarism and subsequent reprinting of *Granny's Wonderful Chair*, Gretchen Holbrook Gerzina argues that "Frances was in fact delighted to have recovered something so important to her, writing a new introduction to the book and publishing it under the correct author's name."[51] Interpreting Burnett's actions through the lens of Romantic authorship, Gerzina imagines her as an original, individual author who is "delighted" to give credit to a fellow writer. A closer investigation of the case reveals that Burnett carefully manipulated copyright law to her own advantage by poaching a British story, republishing it in an American magazine (where it had no legal protection from literary piracy), and then republishing the book as her "own" (and for her own profit) once the British copyright had expired. Interpreting Burnett's actions through the lens of copyright law does not diminish our appreciation of her work as a professional author. Rather, it provides a more complex picture of her negotiation of the literary marketplace at the *fin de siècle*, where competing definitions of the author created uneven terrain and where literary texts were defined as "free" content just as often as they were classified as intellectual property belonging to an original, copyright-protected author.

The uneven construction of authorship during the nineteenth century was in part due to the ambiguous status of periodicals and newspapers under British copyright law and the absence of an international copyright agreement between Britain and the United States for most of the century. Practices of literary piracy and scissors-and-paste journalism challenged the notion of the author as a proprietary, copyright-protected individual, even as the rights of authors were becoming increasingly delineated under the law. In 1891, the Chace Act finally provided reciprocal copyright protection for British works published in the United States, and the 1911 Copyright Act in Britain, which extended the period of copyright to fifty years, provided further protection to authors of newspaper and periodical publications. However, the history of the author, like the history of copyright, is always under formation. In the twentieth and twenty-first centuries, the development of new media – film, television, radio, and now digital textualities – has continually challenged existing definitions of the author, necessitating further legislative and cultural redefinition of the boundaries between proprietary authorship and fair use. The author is perpetually redefined according to national and international law and in response to the development of new media, which continually construct – and elude – authorial control.

Notes

1. William Wordsworth, "Preface to *Lyrical Ballads* (1802)," in *William Wordsworth*, ed. Stephen Gill (Oxford: Oxford University Press, 1984), pp. 595–615, p. 606. For further background on Wordsworth's influence on the development of copyright law, see, for example, Martha Woodmansee, "The 'Romantic' Author," in *Research Handbook on the History of Copyright Law*, eds. Isabella Alexander and H. Tomás Gómez-Arostegui (Cheltenham, UK: Elgar, 2016), pp. 53–77.
2. Thomas Talfourd, "Speech on the Motion for the Second Reading of the Bill to Amend the Law of Copyright," in *Critical and Miscellaneous Writings of T. Noon Talfourd* (Philadelphia: Carey and Hart, 1846), pp. 165–71, p. 165. For

further background on the 1842 law, see Catherine Seville, *Literary Copyright Reform in Early Victorian England: The Framing of the 1842 Copyright Act* (Cambridge: Cambridge University Press, 1999).

3. Clare Pettit, "Legal Subjects, Legal Objects: The Law and Victorian Fiction," in *A Concise Companion to the Victorian Novel*, ed. Francis O'Gorman (Oxford: Blackwell, 2005), pp. 71–90, p. 79.

4. Bob Nicholson, "'You Kick the Bucket; We Do the Rest!': Jokes and the Culture of Reprinting in the Transatlantic Press," *Journal of Victorian Culture*, 17.3 (2012), 273–86, p. 276.

5. Will Slauter, "Upright Piracy: Understanding the Lack of Copyright for Journalism in Eighteenth-Century Britain," *Book History*, 16 (2013), 34–61, p. 56.

6. Frances Brown was born Frances Browne yet dropped the "e" when publishing her work in most instances. Only after her death was the "e" restored in biographical accounts that acknowledged her Irish roots.

7. Meredith L. McGill, *American Literature and the Culture of Reprinting, 1834–1853* (Philadelphia: University of Pennsylvania Press, 2003), p. 13.

8. [Gilbert a'Beckett], "Literary Larceny," *Punch*, May 12, 1855, 192.

9. Ibid.

10. Ibid.

11. "Scissors and Paste," *Chambers's Journal*, December 14, 1867, 785–88, p. 787.

12. "The Claims of Literature and the Law of Copyright," *Eliza Cook's Journal*, January 1, 1853, 151–53, p. 151.

13. "Literature and Lottery (by a Patron of the Popular Press)," *Punch*, August 30, 1890, 107.

14. "Tit-bits," *Tit-Bits*, 1.1 (October 22, 1881), 1.

15. "The Order in Council as to International Copyright," *Law Journal*, 22 (1887), 654–57, p. 655.

16. The United States did not agree to reciprocal copyright protection for foreign authors until 1891. For background on the transatlantic movement leading to this breakthrough, see Robert A. Colby, "Authors Unite!: An Anglo-American Alliance," *Victorian Periodicals Review*, 26.3 (1993), 125–32.

17. "Walter v. Steinkopff," *Law Journal Reports for the Year 1892*, eds. John G. Witt and Frederick H. Colt (London: F. E. Streeten, 1892), pp. 521–29, p. 523.

18. Ibid., p. 529.

19. Ibid., p. 525.

20. "Our Harmonic Club," *Judy*, June 15, 1892, 287.

21. Ibid.

22. Sidney Low, "Newspaper Copyright," *National Review*, 19 (July 1892), 648–66, p. 648.

23. Ibid., p. 654.

24. Ibid., p. 666.

25. "Journals and Journalists of To-day: III. Mr. Sidney Low and the 'St. James's Gazette,'" *Sketch*, 4 (November 22, 1893), 178–79, p. 178.

26. Ibid., p. 179.

27. Ibid.
28. Andrew Hobbs estimates that there were five million poems published in the provincial press alone. Andrew Hobbs, "Five Million Poems, or the Local Press as Poetry Publisher, 1800–1900," *Victorian Periodicals Review*, 45.4 (2012), 488–92.
29. Kirstie Blair, "'A Very Poetical Town': Newspaper Poetry and the Working-Class Poet in Victorian Dundee," *Victorian Poetry*, 52.1 (2014), 89–109, p. 91.
30. "Notes and Queries," *Ladies' Repository*, 19 (June 1859), 369.
31. T. C. Harbaugh, "Does Newspaper Poetry Pay?," *Writer* 2 (November 1888), 263–64, p. 263.
32. See "Editor's Preface," *The Star of Attéghéi; the Vision of Schwartz, and Other Poems* (London: Moxon, 1844), pp. vii–xxii, p. xvii.
33. Quoted in "Editor's Preface," *Star of Attéghéi*, p. xix.
34. Ibid., pp. xix–xx.
35. Susan Brown, "The Victorian Poetess," in *The Cambridge Companion to Victorian Poetry*, ed. Joseph Bristow (Cambridge: Cambridge University Press, 2000), pp. 180–202, pp. 190–91. See also Patricia Pulham, "'Jewels—delights—perfect loves': Victorian Women Poets and the Annuals," in *Victorian Women Poets*, ed. Alison Chapman (Cambridge: Brewer, 2003), pp. 9–31.
36. McGill, *Culture of Reprinting*, pp. 13, 12.
37. Ellen Gruber-Garvey, *Writing with Scissors: American Scrapbooks from the Civil War to the Harlem Renaissance* (Oxford: Oxford University Press, 2013), p. 35.
38. "Editor's Preface," p. xx.
39. Ibid.
40. Frances Brown, Preface to *Lyrics and Miscellaneous Poems* (Edinburgh: Sutherland and Knox, 1848), pp. 7–8, p. 7.
41. Ibid., p. 8.
42. Quoted in Patrick Bonar, *The Life and Works of Frances Browne: Novelist, Journalist and Poetess, 1816–1879* (Stranorlar: Bonar, 2000), p. 7.
43. Editorial note, *St. Nicholas*, 14 (Feb. 1887), 318.
44. Ibid.
45. Ibid.
46. "Current Literature," *Spectator*, December 19, 1891, 892–95, p. 893.
47. James Runciman, "King Plagiarism and His Court," *Fortnightly Review*, 47 (March 1890), 421–39, p. 435.
48. Frances Hodgson Burnett, "The Story of the Lost Fairy Book," in *Granny's Wonderful Chair, by Frances Browne* (New York: McClure Phillips, 1904), pp. ix–xxxvi, pp. xxv–vi.
49. Ibid., p. ix.
50. Ibid., p. xxix, xxxii.
51. Gretchen Holbrook Gerzina, *Frances Hodgson Burnett: The Unexpected Life of the Author of The Secret Garden* (New Brunswick: Rutgers, 2004), pp. 236–37.

CHAPTER 11

Industrialized Print
Modernism and Authorship

Sean Latham

Introduction: Ubiquitous Authorship

We now imagine ourselves to be living in an age of nearly frictionless authorship, one in which ideas – both wild and mundane – can be instantly published on a blog, in a Facebook comment, or on platforms from Reddit to Amazon that thrive on what we still awkwardly refer to as "self-published" manuscripts. Authorship – whether defined broadly as the mere production of text or more narrowly as the creation of a work of art – has become ubiquitous. Rapid developments in the field of artificial intelligence, moreover, have eerily extended authorship into the realm of objects and machines: nefarious "bots" flood Twitter streams and, in 2016, an algorithmically generated science-fiction novel advanced past the first round of cuts for the Hoshi Shinichi Literary Award.[1] The origin of such ubiquitous authorship cannot be dated exactly, but its effects registered vividly on the cluttered newsstands of the 1920s, where hundreds of magazines, newspapers, paperbacks, gazettes, pamphlets, and books jostled with one another for attention. In late Victorian Britain, mail could be delivered up to five times each day, making the notecard and the letter nearly as pervasive and accessible as emails and text messages. Printing presses churned tirelessly, fed by ever-cheaper kinds of paper, no longer derived from cotton but from wood pulp – much of it harvested from the rich forests of Canada and the United States.[2] Steamships carried huge cargoes of books and other printed material across global trade networks, while regional and national mail systems created legal and financial incentives designed to encourage periodical publication.[3] Free libraries, compulsory education, and the sheer proliferation of print on hoardings, in pubs, and nearly all public spaces led to a ravenous demand for writing of every sort.

Once a relatively staid and carefully regulated industry, publishing and authorship suddenly began to expand at the turn of the twentieth century, creating what Mike Ashley has called "the age of the storytellers."[4]

Periodicals, in particular, called out from their pages to aspiring authors of all types, encouraging them to clip advertisements, participate in contests, send letters, and even offer contributions of their own – sometimes in exchange for lucrative rewards. Popular magazines were filled with advertisements for the tools of the writing trade, including file cabinets, fountain pens, and typewriters, while correspondence and extension schools offered aspiring artists courses in how to make a living as a journalist, short-story writer, or novelist. The vast universe of pulps, weeklies, slicks, and newspapers all demanded huge streams of new material, including journalistic features, formulaic detective fiction, and advertising copy. Amid this industrialization of authorship, a countervailing movement began to take root – one that often sought to restrict the supply of writing by affirming new standards of aesthetic rigor and romanticizing creativity as a mystical gift. Loosely interconnected coteries turned to small presses like the Hogarth Press, specialized bookshops like Shakespeare and Company, and, perhaps most famously, little magazines like *Broom* that might reach only a few hundred people. Authorship in what we now pragmatically call the modernist period – roughly 1890 to 1940 – navigated between these extremes: between the Scylla of a ravenous mass culture where writing came to resemble the Taylorist assembly line and the Charybdis of an elite culture where, as Pierre Bourdieu famously argues, economic failure became the sign of aesthetic success.[5]

The history of authorship in the twentieth century turns on this new but persistent split between the radical expansiveness of mass culture on the one hand and a tightly restrictive economy of prestige on the other. This division, furthermore, emerged within a complex economic, legal, social, and technological ecology that accompanied the rise of industrialized print. Together, these interdependent systems produced a distinctive and historically contingent "author function," a concatenation of regulations, practices, and processes that helped shape what we now call modernism.[6] This chapter will offer a broad overview of these distinct yet interlocking systems, while also attending to the historical realities of individual writers, including those who thrived within such structures and those who sought to challenge their constraints. In doing so, I will draw on actor-network theory (ANT), which urges us to temporarily bracket big concepts like authorship in order to examine the faint "trail of *associations* between heterogeneous elements," which might include everything from the chemical bonds in paper to corporate boards and copyediting standards.[7] The goal of this chapter, in other words, is to provide a broad overview of modernist textual production, while also pausing at a few key moments to crawl along the intricate trails that guided a particular writer's practices and decisions. Such detailed sampling reminds us that concepts like modernism and even authorship are critical heuristics that can never fully capture the complexity of the immense system for producing texts that emerged at the end of the nineteenth century and continues to make writing an ever more ubiquitous aspect of our modernity.

Everyone's a Writer

What exactly did it mean to be a writer at the start of the twentieth century? In the West, at least, writing – indeed, literacy more generally – was no longer a technology confined to a specially educated elite, but had instead become part of the web of imperial bureaucracies charged with regulating global flows of goods and capital. Writers like Charles Dickens and Herman Melville had already incorporated clerks into their fictions and by the twentieth century, such figures formed an essential part of both the real and imagined capitalist system. E. M. Forster's *Howards End* (1910), for example, turns on the story of Leonard Bast, an office worker with modest aesthetic aspirations who is literally crushed at the novel's end by a bookcase laden with the icons of symbolic capital he can read but never fully possess. T. S. Eliot's *The Waste Land* (1922) details the awkward lovemaking of a clerk and a typist that concludes when the latter reaches out "with automatic hand / And puts a record on the gramophone."[8] Franz Kafka, more than any other writer, focused on the clerk as the quintessential modern figure whose endless production of mindless text could itself become a form of torture. We do not think of characters like these as authors, and their writing offers no special access to culture or art; instead, it has become little more than a trade, a technology not very different from the gramophone, which mechanically reproduces "that Shakespeherian Rag" – in this case, a poor substitute for the real thing.[9]

This transformation of writing from a carefully cultivated talent into an industrialized trade fundamentally redefines the very concept of authorship. Indeed, the characters Eliot, Kafka, and Forster create are defined, in part, by their own doomed attempts to romanticize writing, to make it into something more than mere drudgery. By the early decades of the twentieth century, such romance had grown faint as authorship became pervasive. Thousands of magazines filled the mails and newsstands, each promising a unique mix of fiction, reporting, and memoir. The editorial content was often surrounded by hundreds of pages of advertisements, with dozens of those pages dedicated to selling print matter of all kinds, from encyclopedias and dictionaries to novels and other magazines. It could be overwhelming, and services quickly popped up to help readers manage the deluge. The January 1911 issue of *Harper's Magazine*, for example, carried over thirty-five pages of ads for books and magazines promising things like "The Work of Making Men" (*Harper's Magazine*), "A New Sherlock Holmes Story!" (*The Strand Magazine*), "The Railroads and the Public" (*The World To-Day*), "Dr. Cook's Confession" about his trip to the North Pole (*Hampton's*), a new serialized novel by Robert Hichens (*Scribner's*), and "Masterpieces of American Galleries" (*The Century Magazine*).

We also find on offer here a prominent notice for a novel called *Molly Make-Believe* by the now forgotten Eleanor Hallowell Abbott. The ad itself promises a sensation, stating that the "40th Thousand [is] Ready (and may be the 50th or 60th by the time this appears)." If we recall that Faulkner's *Go Down, Moses* sold only 4,000 copies for Random House and that his *Intruder in the Dust* was considered a breakthrough with 23,000, then *Molly Make-Believe* seems like it must be the work of a superstar. Abbott, however, was something of an amateur who had won an open contest for writers at *Collier's Weekly*. This ad, in other words, is selling not just the book of an amateur writer, but the very idea of authorship itself. Anyone, it suggests, might hit it lucky by sending in a story to the magazines and winning not only one of the many prizes on offer, but possibly a book contract as well. The pulp magazines, in particular, ran contests to attract potential authors and featured ads like this one from the June 5, 1915 *All Story Weekly*: "Poets, Authors! Make good money writing short stories, poems, etc. Mss. sold on commission. Our system unexcelled. Prompt service: quick returns."[10] Magazines of all sorts, in short, offered not only their own distinctive letterpress, but often the promise that anyone might become a writer by taking a course, participating in a contest, or just firing off a submission.

These advertisements and contests clearly hold out authorship as a readily accessible career for the rising generations of clerks and typists in the almost fully literate West. Yet they also conceal the fact that writing itself was undergoing a radical transformation from a relatively autonomous and self-regulated profession to a fully industrialized activity fueled by corporate capital.[11] Here, let's pause a moment and take an ant-like view of how James Joyce, in his early fiction, attempted to represent this change in the nature of writing and its potential consequences for those, like himself, who feared their word-smithing talents might be wasted. Given the largely autobiographical nature of Joyce's fiction, it is surprising to realize that there are relatively few scenes of literary creation in his work.

In fact, one of the first professional writers we encounter in his fiction is Farrington, the drunken, abusive clerk in "Counterparts" (1914). In this story, we see writing at its most modern, its most instrumental, and its most austere. Joyce's narrator becomes a sociological observer who looks closely at the law offices of Crosbie and Alleyne. Here are the opening lines:

> The bell rang furiously and, when Miss Parker went to the tube, a furious voice called out in a piercing North of Ireland accent:
>
> —Send Farrington here!
>
> Miss Parker returned to her machine, saying to a man who was writing at a desk:
>
> —Mr Alleyne wants you upstairs.[12]

We learn a great deal in these few sentences. This appears, for example, to be a fully modernized office with carefully distinguished roles, reporting duties, and hierarchies. The "tube" connects the manager to different pieces of the system, allowing him to oversee and intervene in its various processes. In addition to this mechanical device, he employs a secretary who receives his instructions, then transmits them to others. Here, she simply turns to Farrington and relays the order to go upstairs. But she is also seated at a "machine," that is, a typewriter and, as Lawrence Rainey and others have noted, the word *typewriter* could refer both to the device and to the person (usually a woman) operating it.[13] Is Miss Parker an author? She is producing text in the literal sense of impressing letters on a piece of paper in a meaningful sequence, but she writes (and indeed speaks) only in the voice of another person. Far from a mystical act of creation or a deeply ideological structure, in other words, writing here is a densely structured node in the larger network of the modern, bureaucratic office.

If we see "Counterparts" as a Joycean experiment in mapping the actors and networks of a modern office, then what might we learn about Farrington? In this period, legal documents were not considered valid unless written by hand, and he is essentially a copyist who works amid the mess of others' words without any sense of agency, inspiration, or ownership. The larger story itself actually turns on this brewing tension between writing and agency, as Farrington's mind wanders constantly away from the words he is actually producing:

> The man listened to the clicking of the machine for a few minutes and then set to work to finish his copy. But his head was not clear and his mind wandered away to the glare and rattle of the public-house. It was a night for hot punches. He struggled on with his copy, but when the clock struck five

he had still fourteen pages to write. Blast it! He couldn't finish it in time.
[...] He was so enraged that he wrote *Bernard Bernard* instead of *Bernard
Bodley* and had to begin again on a clean sheet.[14]

There are many ways to read the story's enigmatic title, most of which
focus on the cycles of violence and humiliation that spin from the work-
place into the pub and finally into the darkened family home. Readers have
generally overlooked the fact, however, that Farrington and the typewriter
are counterparts as well in an office transitioning to mechanization.
The clacking keys, the disembodied voices, and the new machines all
point to a radical change in writing as an activity, a technology,
a profession, and a practice. Authorship, in this story, gets cut off from
genius, from inspiration, from creativity, and from originality.

Professionals

Joyce was by no means alone in his allergic reaction to the new realities of
writing. Ezra Pound, too, marveled at the explosion of magazines in the
early twentieth century and their overwhelming demand for copy. He
published a series of articles in *The New Age* called "Studies in
Contemporary Mentality," in which he attempted to provide short studies
of individual magazines and what they might reveal about their readers and
contributors.[15] Borrowing a phrase from Flaubert, he called this series
a *sottisier*, that is, a collection of stupidities that would reveal the tainted
nature of both industrialized writing and the degradation of culture he
believed it created. "You can't know an era," he argued in *Make It New*,
"merely by knowing its best."[16] Thus he set out to dig into the array of print
material that readers of the relatively highbrow *New Age* might ignore on
"the noose-stands" – that huge swath of print that he believed was choking
the intellectual life out of the West.

Pound, of course, played a key role in both imagining and marketing
what we now call modernism, a loosely defined movement that arose, in
part, as a reaction against the deprofessionalization of authorship and the
industrialization of writing. Drawing on the same technologies that made
print increasingly cheap to produce and distribute, the individuals and
coteries we now group under this hazy aesthetic label founded their own
modest publications – the so-called "little magazines" – which aimed to
reach only a small audience and almost never managed to pay their
contributors. Lewis's brilliant *Blast* (1914–1915), for example, ran to only
two issues, while *Rhythm* (1911–1913), founded by John Middleton Murry

and Katherine Mansfield, managed to print only fourteen issues in its two years of existence. The most famous of these periodicals, *The Little Review* (1914–1929), proved hearty enough to last for twelve years, but teetered constantly on the edge of bankruptcy while struggling with American censors. Pound and Eliot believed that the most successful small magazines should "fail into obscure glory," their struggles a paradoxical sign of their attempts to resist the "mental mush and otiose habit" chronicled in "Studies in Contemporary Mentality."[17] Would *Ulysses*, for example, have become such a critical success if the magazines in which it appeared had not become infamously entangled with the American courts? More significantly, as Rainey argues, the book's expensive first edition in 1922 was aimed almost exclusively at an elite audience of collectors, who purchased the object by special subscription and could pay even more to get a copy printed on hand-made paper and signed by the author himself.[18] Amid the tidal waves of print, furthermore, a new emphasis fell on manuscripts, and Joyce's own writing of *Ulysses* was partially financed by a New York attorney named John Quinn, who quietly purchased the author's pages.[19] In the age of industrial print, such manuscripts became (as they still are) fetish objects, promising authenticity, originality, and genius – the literal mark of the author as an individual rather than a mass-produced commodity. Nor was Joyce the only one to depend on support from patrons and collectors. The experimental and often obscure writing of H. D. was financed by Bryher (Annie Winifred Ellerman), a wealthy shipping heiress and magazine editor who effectively insulated the poet from the demands of the literary marketplace. Such patronage, in fact, helps defines a modernism where private capital flowed outside of the marketplace to innovative writers from people like Peggy Guggenheim, Nancy Cunard, Lady Ottoline Morrell, and Scofield Thayer.

Modernism could thrive on this strangely archaic form of support, in large part, because the same technologies and intellectual infrastructure that drove the explosion in mass print culture also made it relatively easy to publish magazines and books. This enabled the creation of the famous little magazines, but it also spawned a new genre of periodicals – the pulps – which derived their name precisely from the cheap stock on which they were printed. As David Earle has revealed, these magazines represent the still largely submerged iceberg of early twentieth-century print culture. When combined, he claims, the little magazines and the more familiar quality magazines like *Vanity Fair* make up "less than 5 percent of actual literary output" in the period.[20] He thus urges literary historians to attend more carefully to publications like *All-Story, Weird Tales, Snappy Stories,* and *The Black Mask*. These periodicals not only published the vast majority of the era's fiction, but they also generated popular genres like science fiction, horror, fantasy, and the hard-boiled detective story – genres that would themselves then shape the emergent new media, including radio, film, and eventually television.

The sheer volume of this publishing venture helped move authorship to a newly industrialized scale, one which essentially transformed writers into workers paid by the word rather than professionals living off royalties or a salary. The opportunities for authorship became increasingly pervasive, in short, but the work paid so poorly that writers had to churn out huge quantities of copy to make a living. L. Ron Hubbard claimed to have written over 100,000 words a month for magazines like *Unknown* and *Astounding Science Fiction*, while Frederick Schiller Faust (who wrote under the pseudonym Max Brand) published more than 500 serialized novels.[21] This evokes the reviled ideal of the eighteenth-century hack writer toiling wretchedly on Grub Street (see Betty Schellenberg's chapter "The Eighteenth Century" in this volume), but translated to a vast, indeed global scale. This makes it clear why Virginia Woolf advised aspiring authors in the late 1920s and early 1930s to seeks rooms of their own in order to avoid the "brain prostitution" that the industrialized writing of the era demanded.[22]

In part to fight this perceived threat, Virginia and Leonard Woolf began printing their own books in 1917 with a small machine they purchased for £19 and set up in their dining room. The Hogarth Press proved exceptional since it eventually grew into a large-scale operation that earned thousands of pounds a year before becoming part of Chatto and Windus and (eventually) Random House. Other similar ventures took advantage of cheap paper and technology as well, many of them designed to produce only a few works of a particular author, circle, or movement. After nearly every commercial house had turned down Joyce's *A Portrait of the Artist as a Young Man* (1916), for example, Harriet Shaw Weaver set up the Egoist Press to publish the novel, alongside a few other then relatively obscure works, including poetry by Pound and Eliot, Wyndham Lewis's *Tarr* (1918), and poetry translated by H. D. Later, when *Ulysses* too failed to find a publisher, Sylvia Beach, the owner of a small expatriate bookshop in Paris, published it under her own imprint. Numerous other small presses sprang up as well in order to support all kinds of politically, sexually, and aesthetically controversial writing. In Dublin, for example, Elizabeth Yeats founded the Cuala Press to publish the work of her brother William Butler Yeats as well as other Irish Revival poets and novelists including St. John

Gogarty, J. M. Synge, and Lady Augusta Gregory. In Paris, Harry and Caresse Crosby created the Black Sun Press in 1928 to publish first their own work and then experimental writing by Hart Crane, Archibald MacLeish, and Eugene Jolas. Other examples include Nancy Cunard's Hours Press (France), John Rodker's Ovid Press (London), Robert McAlmon's Contact Editions (Paris), and Harold Monro's Poetry Bookshop (London).[23]

Everyone, it seemed, was writing something, whether it was personal letters, business correspondence, avant-garde poetry, prize-winning magazine stories, or pulp fictions. Writing quickly changed, in short, from a cultured pursuit to an industrialized and – with the rise of machines like the typewriter and dictaphone – an increasingly mechanized activity. The experimental poet Stevie Smith attempted to describe this newly complex world of writing and authorship in her own ant-like way at the start of *Novel on Yellow Paper* (1936). Pompey, the book's autobiographical protagonist, works as a secretary and typist for Sir Phoebus, the owner and publisher of a large press that turns out all kinds of periodicals. Indeed, the novel opens with Pompey trying to make sense of the kind of writing she is actually doing and how it differs from that all around her: "Beginning this book (not as they say 'book' in our trade – they mean magazine), beginning this book, I should like if I may, I should like, if I may (that is the way Sir Phoebus writes), I should then like to say: Good-bye to all my friends, my beautiful and lovely friends."[24] Struggling to find her own voice as a writer, Pompey has to separate herself from both the titles being churned out in the rooms all around her and from her boss's voice, the man from whom she takes dictation each day. Clearly aspiring here to a conception of authorship rooted in romantic genius, Pompey realizes that her own work will be a concatenation of all the print around her. She warns us directly that she is not fully in command of her own materials and that she is thus not fully responsible for the book. That is, she is not exactly its author: "Read on, Reader, read on and work it out for yourself."[25] Writing here is a partial, uncertain, even hybrid process that will bring together different pieces of Pompey's life as well as the many different voices she hears within herself, ranging from that of Sir Phoebus to those of her mother, her lover, and her friends.

The complexity and paradoxes of authorship Pompey explores are made manifest by the actual physical object itself. The book was famously printed on yellow paper, a material allusion to the dictation tablets Smith herself used to draft the novel during spare moments in her work as a secretary for Sir Neville Pearson at Newnes Publishing Company, a conglomerate that produced periodicals like *The Strand, Tit-Bits, Lady's Companion*, and *Practical Mechanics*. The book also included a series of Smith's own line drawings, making it look at least somewhat like the illustrated fiction magazines being created around her. For both Smith and Pompey alike, in short, authorship is no longer a self-evident category; it has become so commercialized, mechanized, and distributed that the book itself can no longer be clearly distinguished, from the memos, advertisements, articles, and correspondence that constitute the new surround of writing. Thus we are indeed left simply to work it out for ourselves.

Although Smith certainly looks on the pervasiveness of authorship with concern, this same explosion in print culture also opened up the publishing world to a rich new array of voices. From one vantage, modernist authorship can be defined by the "great divide" between the mass culture of pulp magazines on the one hand and the economy of prestige defined by the little magazines on the other. Seen another way, however, modernist authorship might instead be understood as the arrival of previously suppressed narratives from newly educated and literate people. The *New Age* (1907–1922), for example, was edited by A. R. Orage, one of the newly rising members of a literate, intellectual class in Britain who made their way through red-brick universities and trade schools rather than through Oxford and Cambridge. While working as a schoolteacher in Leeds, Orage became deeply interested in socialist politics and, with the help of George Bernard Shaw and Holbrook Jackson, he acquired the *New Age* and transformed it into one of Britain's leading intellectual organs. It succeeded, in part, because he opened the weekly's pages to a new cadre of young and innovative writers. This group included Anthony Ludovici, an arch conservative who played a key role in introducing the works of Friedrich Nietzsche to the English-speaking world; the leading Suffragist, "truculent" Teresa Billington-Greig; and Marmaduke Pickthall, a deeply Christian man who translated the Quran into English and wrote regular columns about Egypt and the larger complexities of the Middle East.

The magazine's most important contributor, however, was Beatrice Hastings. Her real name was Emily Alice Haigh, and Hastings was actually only one of over two dozen different pseudonyms she used to sign pieces in the magazine. She was born in South Africa and attended school in Kent before taking up a relatively itinerant life that led her to Paris and London where she became the lover of the painter Modigliani as well as Orage himself. She reveled in the power and pleasure writing offered and she often pitted her various pseudonyms against one another in the correspondence as well as the editorial sections, setting up elaborately staged debates with herself about feminism, economics, and art. We see this same energized engagement with an exploding print culture in the emergence of other writers, magazines, and presses explicitly devoted to revolutionary art and politics. The feminist and suffrage press in Britain and the United States, for example, opened up new opportunities for women to enter the public sphere as authors and activists – an intervention that often took place at the intersection of art and politics. The *Egoist* (1914–1919), for example, which published Joyce's work in Britain, began its life first as the *Freewoman* (1911–1912) and then the *New Freewoman* (1913) under the editorship of Dora Marsden. Similarly, Margaret Anderson's *Little Review* may have gained fame for serializing *Ulysses* (1922), but it started out as an Anarchist journal dedicated to the political ideas of Emma Goldman. As Mary Chapman argues, "by affiliating themselves with the new, the news, and noise, [. . .] suffragists fashioned themselves and their print cultural products not as marginal, but as central, indeed as representative voices of modern America."[26] The ready access to publishing and to authorship that defined the era opened up precisely this opportunity to be heard – and new voices resonated powerfully first in magazines and then in print culture more generally.

For many aspiring writers, the idea of imagining oneself as an author created both challenges as well as opportunities for experimentation. Hastings's use of pen names might have been prodigious, but it was by no means unique, since pseudonyms played an important part in the larger culture of the era (see also Robert J. Griffin's chapter "Anonymity and Pseudonymity" in this volume). Some writers like George Orwell (Eric Blair), AE (George Russell), and Ayn Rand (Alisa Rosenbaum) simply adopted professional pen names and almost never published anything under their own signature. Others, however, used this convention in the way Hastings did: to conceal their identity or separate one aspect of their writing lives from another. Pound, for example, wrote music and art criticism in a number of little magazines under the name William Atheling, while the art critic Willard Huntington Wright published his fabulously successful Philo Vance detective stories as S. S. Van Dine. Others used pen names to encapsulate cooperative or collaborative projects. The detective novels and story anthologies published under the pseudonym Ellery Queen, for example, were jointly written by two American cousins, Daniel Nathan and Emanuel Lepofsky.[27] Such partnerships included more avant-garde writers as well, including the lesbian lovers Katherine Bradley and Edith Cooper, who published as Michael Field.[28] In some cases, the idea of anonymous or collaborative co-authorship went to extremes, as with the pornographic novel *Teleny* (1893), which is sometimes attributed to Oscar Wilde but was written by a close circle who shared the charged manuscript.[29] These experiments with pseudonymous and collaboratively written works are counterparts to the awareness shared by Joyce's tales about clerks and Smith's *Novel on Yellow Paper* that writing and authorship might be severed from one another. This division opened up all kinds of new possibilities for experimentation, for the creation of different personas, for the expression of otherwise suppressed desires, and for the invention of authorial brands that could be used to enter different political, economic, and aesthetic segments of the literary marketplace.

Deregulation

While often productive, such experiments also posed unusual challenges for the existing legal frameworks that defined authorship. Some of modernism's foundational mythography turns on charged courtroom encounters, such as Oscar Wilde's trial for gross indecency, *The United States v. One Book Called Ulysses*, and *Regina v. Penguin Books Ltd* (the 1960 English prosecution of *Lady Chatterley's Lover* under the Obscene Publications Act). Although Wilde was eventually found guilty, the latter two trials shaped a reassuring liberal narrative about the steady advancement of free speech and the rights of authors to explore the full richness of human experience. This deregulation of artistic production, however, took place alongside the development of a vast new regulatory regime designed not to control speech but to govern the national and international flow of writing now redefined as property (cf. also Alexis Easley's chapter "The Nineteenth Century" in this volume). Put another way, as restrictive legal structures like obscenity and libel law slowly receded, an even more complex set of rules and norms evolved to take their place. Modernist authorship was and remains essentially a legal construct – a way of defining ownership in a global capitalist system where texts no longer circulated under special license from the state but instead became merely one more commodity among others.

Wilde's legal troubles began when he launched a libel prosecution against the Marquess of Queensberry after receiving a truculent message that accused the famous playwright of "posing as a somdomite [*sic*]." Libel laws are complex, but in this case, Queensberry's only practical defense was to assert both the truth of his accusation and that such practices made Wilde a threat to public morality. This meant that Wilde's published works and private letters could be admitted into evidence. Wilde succeeded initially in deflecting their homoerotic charge through an array of witty strategies designed to separate the writing from authorship. That is, Wilde effectively argued that, although he had created some erotic letters and sent them to Queensberry's son, the works themselves might actually be read as works of art, as "prose sonnets" whose exact meaning depended more on the interpretation of the reader than on the intent of the writer. Wilde and his attorney were on solid legal ground here, since most of the statutes surrounding the creation of text did not recognize the actual intentions of the writer. Queensberry's counsel thus only managed to seal Wilde's fate when he turned away from questions about books and letters and instead called witnesses who could attest to unambiguous sexual acts. This resulted not only in disaster for one of the country's most notable celebrities, but it also led some writers, like Max Beerbohm, to move abroad and others, like E. M. Forster, to suppress novels about their own sexuality.

The provisions of libel and obscenity law that separated the writer from his or her text, however, played a key role in a number of subsequent trials and thereby shaped the contours of an unfolding modernism. For nine years, Joyce failed to find a publisher for his first book, *Dubliners*, in part because by naming real people and places in Dublin he invited a host of possible lawsuits. Wyndham Lewis, who pushed the boundaries of the law harder than any other modern novelist, became involved in six libel actions as he morphed from an avant-gardist into "the Enemy." The law's division of the writer from his or her text, and its foundational principle that authorial intention is inadmissible at trial, led to a growing number of lawsuits and criminal actions – though often directed at publishers and even books rather than at the writers themselves. In the United States, the First Amendment right to free speech helped check the expansion of the state's regulatory powers and the ability of enterprising claimants to file suits. In the United Kingdom, however, the courts effectively called into question the legality of fiction itself in the 1909 case *E. Hulton and Co.* v. *Jones*, which held that writers, printers, and publishers could be sued even in cases of accidental libel. The particulars of the case turned on a man named Artemus Jones, who sued the *Sunday Chronicle* for a somewhat fanciful story that included his name – despite the fact that the author had picked it at random. Since the actual intentions of the author were inadmissible, the plaintiff only had to show that someone had confused the real Jones with the fictional one and consequently thought less of him. The Court of Appeal declared the judgment a "terror to authorship," but still found themselves forced to concur with the lower court's decision.

This finding opened the floodgates for libel actions of all sorts, which were slowed only by subsequent legal reforms.[30]

Even as libel courts sought to separate authors from their texts, an entirely different set of legal mechanisms began to take shape that enshrined writing as a piece of valuable but intangible property owned by the writer. Copyright has a long history in the West and is written directly into Article I of the US Constitution in order to protect the state's interest in promoting "the Progress of Science and useful Arts." Amid the industrialization of writing at the start of the twentieth century, however, the once relatively simple idea of a writer or publisher owning a limited-term interest in a work became increasingly complex. "Bookleggers" rushed pirated books hastily into print, leaving it to rights holders to seek costly redress in the courts. Each country, furthermore, had their own copyright regimes and often included, as was the case in the US, a manufacturing clause that required works to be printed in the jurisdiction almost simultaneously with its initial publication. Such measures were designed to protect unions, printers, and publishing houses, but they created a confusing patchwork of irreconcilable copyright laws that made intellectual property theft both commonplace and profitable. This dizzying array of rights and restrictions grew more complicated as texts circulated internationally and then as new media industries like film and radio sought adaptation rights. The huge magazine industry posed challenges as well. Some publications asked authors to sign away rights, while others licensed work from authors for a whole array of interlocking publications. Furthermore, a great deal of written work – both literary and bureaucratic – was done "for hire" and thus owned by the corporations and firms that paid for it rather than by its creators.

Amid this confusion, two key innovations occurred that profoundly shaped the professionalization of authorship. First, at the turn of the century, an enterprising magazine publisher named Samuel S. McClure devised one of the first and most lucrative literary and press syndicates. He and his agents fanned out across Britain, seeking work by both new and established writers. They then negotiated deals to purchase the rights to re-publish this work in the United States, charging the sweeping array of local magazines, newspapers, and periodicals a flat fee to use it. This model caught on quickly and contributed to the international fame of authors like H. G. Wells, Rudyard Kipling, and Jack London, among others. Keeping track of all these intellectual property rights became the responsibility of a new kind of professional: the literary agent. A. P. Watt is considered the first agent and he charged his authors a percentage of their royalties, a now standard practice that effectively invested the agent first and foremost in the financial success of his or her client. This new class of professionals moved in a sometimes shady space between publishers and writers, but played an essential role in helping to regulate the movement of capital between the two and in managing the public persona of the author.

Even with the assistance of agents, lawyers, and syndicates, however, the vast industrialized print culture of the early twentieth century largely managed to outpace the legal structures set in place to regulate it. The law tends to be slow and reactive, which is why so much of the experimental writing associated with modernism found itself entangled with statutes governing morality, copyright, and free speech. As Robert Spoo argues, print culture was therefore often regulated predominantly by a series of shared but informal norms rather than by contracts and laws.[31] American publishers, for example, took advantage of the manufacturing clause to essentially steal and print even new work by prominent Anglophone writers. After one American firm got such a work into print, however, the others would voluntarily refrain from reprinting it themselves – even though it lacked copyright protection (see also Alexis Easley's chapter "The Nineteenth Century" and Daniel Cook's chapter on "Copyright and Literary Property" in this volume). The industry itself established and policed these norms through an array of mechanisms that ran parallel to the law but nevertheless existed outside it. Aware of the enormous costs associated with attempting to regulate the industrialized print industry, governments too turned to quasi- or extra-judicial organizations as a way of outsourcing their regulatory function. In the United States, for example, an NGO, the New York Society for the Prevention of Vice, actually inspected the mails, and their agents called the attention of postal agents to the potentially obscene work that appeared in *The Little Review*. Similar vice organizations operated in Ireland and the United Kingdom and often had standing to bring suits or at least call in local prosecutors.[32] Thus, although governments played an essential role in defining authorship as a statutory and legal entity, there was simply too much writing to be fully controlled or surveilled (see also Trevor Ross's chapter "Censorship" in this volume). Extra-judiciary bodies and informal norms rushed in to fill the gaps, but even this provided only a limited degree of control. The mythology of modernism might have been shaped by its often dramatic trials, but authorship in the twentieth century was defined instead by an excess that ran far ahead of the legal structures set in place to regulate it.

Print Modernity

The explosion of print culture that emerged from the industrialization of writing continues apace; indeed, it has become ever more ubiquitous in an age when digital textuality flows readily beyond national borders and international regulatory schemes (see Adriaan van der Weel's chapter "Literary Authorship in the Digital Age" in this volume). Writing is now more pervasive than it has ever been, and although governments still attempt to regulate some of its aspects, much of this work has fallen outside of the law and into the complex private contracts called end-user license agreements that we click through to access things like Twitter and Facebook. The use of pseudonyms, which once seemed so creative in the hands of someone like Beatrice Hastings, has become pervasive thanks to the screen names that shape our engagement with social media. The entire universe of magazines that helped redefine the very idea of authorship as a profession at the start of the twentieth century has sharply contracted, but the subsequent vacuum has been filled by the Internet and its effectively infinite supply of text.

Modernist authorship emerged, in part, as a response to the explosion of print culture and functions, in some cases, as an essentially atavistic attempt to preserve the idea that writing is special and authorship a unique, even autonomous professional practice. Thus could pulp writers be separated from modernist authors and a highbrow canon carefully preserved from the static buzz of mass culture. The cultural boundaries modernism once sought to inscribe, however, have largely fallen asunder amid the heightened deluge of our digital flood. Consider, in closing, a writer like Neil Gaiman, who began his career steeped in pulp fiction and first made a name for himself as a comic-book writer. He has since gone on to write for television and film while publishing critically admired and best-selling novels like *American Gods* (2001) and *The Graveyard Book* (2008). Much of his work, in fact, alludes constantly to the once largely marginalized authors from the modernist era, including Rudyard Kipling, G. K. Chesterton, and even Aleister Crowley. No one would confuse Gaiman with a modernist, but we see in his work and career the return of much that has been forgotten about the radical transformation in writing and authorship that defined the first half of the twentieth century. The legal, cultural, economic, and ideological problems posed by the industrialization of writing, in short, remain with us still as authorship becomes less a professional calling than an everyday activity that defines a modernity awash in text.

Notes

1. Michael Schaub, "Is the Future Award-Winning Novelist a Writing Robot?", *Los Angeles Times*, March 22, 2016. Curiously, the story was about a computer trying to write a novel.
2. For more on the importance of North American and especially Canadian forests to the rise of mass publishing, see J. Matthew Huculak, "Reading Forensically: Modernist Paper, Newfoundland, and Transatlantic Materiality," *Journal of Modern Periodical Studies* 6.2 (2015), 161–90.
3. For a detailed history of the international trade in magazines, see Patrick Belk, *Empires of Print: Adventure Fiction in the Magazines, 1899–1919* (New York: Routledge, 2017), especially pp. 16–62.
4. Mike Ashley, *The Age of the Storytellers: British Popular Fiction Magazines, 1880–1950* (London: British Library and Oak Knoll Press, 2006), p. 1.
5. On the rapidly changing definition of modernism and its pragmatic usefulness to literary history, see Sean Latham and Gayle Rogers, *Modernism: Evolution of an Idea* (London: Bloomsbury, 2016). On the inverted economies of modernism, see Pierre Bourdieu, *Rules of Art: Genesis and Structure of the Literary Field* (Palo Alto, CA: Stanford University Press, 1996).
6. Michel Foucault, "What Is an Author?", in *Language, Counter-Memory, Practice*, ed. Donald F. Bouchard (Ithaca, NY: Cornell University Press, 1977), pp. 113–38.
7. Bruno Latour, *Reassembling the Social: An Introduction to Actor-Network Theory* (Oxford: Oxford University Press, 2005), p. 5 (emphasis original).
8. T. S. Eliot, *The Annotated Waste Land with Eliot's Contemporary Prose*, ed. Lawrence Rainey, 2nd edn (New Haven: Yale University Press, 2006), p. 65 (ll. 255–56).
9. Ibid., p. 61 (l. 128).
10. *All Story Weekly*, 45.4 (June, 1905), 4.
11. The category "little magazine" is somewhat hazy and critics still cannot agree on a clear definition. Eric Bulson describes them convincingly as "decommercialized, decapitalized, and decentered" in *Little Magazine, World Form* (New York: Columbia University Press, 2017), p. 14.
12. James Joyce, *Dubliners* (New York: Viking, 1969), p. 86.
13. Lawrence Rainey, "Pretty Typewriters, Melodramatic Modernity: Edna, Belle, Estelle," *Modernism/modernity*, 16.1 (2009), 105–22.
14. Joyce, *Dubliners*, p. 90.
15. The series ran in *The New Age* from August 1917 to January 1918 and is reprinted in Robert Scholes and Robert Wulfman, *Modernism in the Magazines: An Introduction* (New Haven, CT: Yale University Press, 2010), pp. 223–326.
16. Ezra Pound, *Make It New* (New Haven, CT: Yale University Press, 1935), p. 16.
17. Ezra Pound, "Small Magazines," *English Journal*, 19.9 (Nov. 1930), 693, 699.
18. Lawrence Rainey, *Institutions of Modernism: Literary Elites and Public Culture* (New Haven, CT: Yale University Press, 1999), pp. 42–76.

19. This proved a wise investment and Quinn's fair-copy of the manuscript rests at the heart of the Rosenbach Museum in Philadelphia.

20. David Earle, *Recovering Modernism: Pulps, Paperbacks, and the Prejudice of Form* (New York: Ashgate, 2015), p. 65.

21. L. Ron Hubbard, "By L. Ron Hubbard," in *Writer: The Shaping of Popular Fiction* (Commerce, CA: Bridge Publications, 2012), p. 123. This is Hubbard's own estimate and, though almost certainly inflated, it does give a sense of the scale of production.

22. Virginia Woolf, *Three Guineas* (New York: Houghton Mifflin, 1966), p. 94.

23. For a useful study of the modernist small presses, see Roderick Cave, *The Private Press* (New York: Bowker, 1983). For a comprehensive overview of publishing in the era, see Faye Hammill and Mark Hussey, *Modernism's Print Cultures* (London: Bloomsbury, 2016).

24. Stevie Smith, *Novel on Yellow Paper* (New York: New Directions, 1994), p. 9.

25. Ibid, p. 10.

26. Mary Chapman, *Making Noise, Making News: Suffrage, Print Culture, and U.S. Modernism* (Oxford: Oxford University Press, 2014), p. 23.

27. To further complicate matters, Nathan published his individually authored work as Frederic Dannay, while Lepofsky wrote as Manfred Bennington Lee.

28. For an authoritative study of how women have collaborated in innovative ways to transform the idea of writing, see Holly Laird, *Women Coauthors* (Champaign: University of Illinois Press, 2000).

29. Oscar Wilde and others, *Teleny* (London: Gay Men's Press, 1986).

30. For more on the ways libel law shaped modern authorship, see Sean Latham, *The Art of Scandal: Modernism, Libel Law, and the Roman a Clef* (New York: Oxford University Press, 2009), especially pp. 69–88.

31. Robert Spoo, *Without Copyrights: Piracy, Publishing, and the Public Domain* (New York: Oxford University Press, 2013). For a wide-ranging overview of how intellectual property law shaped modern literary production see Paul K. Saint-Amour, ed., *Modernism and Copyright* (New York: Oxford University Press, 2010).

32. For more on the role of non-governmental regulation of the mails and of vice societies, see Katherine Mullin, *James Joyce, Sexuality, and Social Purity* (Cambridge: Cambridge University Press, 2003) and Celia Marshik, *British Modernism and Censorship* (Cambridge: Cambridge University Press, 2009).

CHAPTER 12

Postmodernist Authorship

Hans Bertens

Introduction

Any discussion of postmodernist authorship must proceed from a reasonably firm understanding of postmodernism, or at least postmodernist literature. Unfortunately, there is not much of a consensus on these concepts and their implications. Before approaching postmodernist authorship, it is therefore necessary to provide a brief overview of the most influential attempts to define postmodernist literature to create not only some order but also a historical and conceptual foundation.

If we simplify things somewhat, we may place the most important theorizations of (especially literary) postmodernism into two major categories. In the first category, we find those critics and theorists who define postmodernism in terms of the new narrative strategies and stylistic innovations that characterized much of the fiction of the 1960s and 1970s. This view of postmodernism, however, is not exclusively concerned with form. It focuses in equal measure on the way those formal developments were used to address a number of new and pressing concerns that almost simultaneously came to preoccupy literary critics on both sides of the Atlantic. Central in these concerns is a fundamental distrust of language, a deep-rooted suspicion – inherited from modernism – that language has no direct access to the real, to reality as it truly *is*. If that is the case, then literary realism, in spite of its pretensions, never presents the real itself. It either presents new – and by definition unfounded – representations of reality, or it echoes existing representations. From this perspective, literature and its authors will never be able to establish true contact with the real world. Perhaps paradoxically, this makes issues of representation more important than ever. If representations of reality are not truly grounded, they must inevitably present a subjective view of reality, a view that equally inevitably will have a political dimension. Representation will then become narrative, story. And since we live with and inside representations, we live with and inside narratives: large-scale ones – the narrative of capitalism, that of socialism, of humanism, of Christianity, and so on – and small-scale, personal ones. What is more, to the extent that we embrace such narratives, we *embody* them, *are* such narratives. From this enthusiastically embraced but also fiercely contested perspective, what we regard as our unique inner self is, to some extent – and perhaps even wholly – a linguistic construct. And, finally, we can only represent ourselves to ourselves in terms of narrative: we tell ourselves a story – inevitably a distorted one – about our past, our identity, about who and what we are. These issues inform much of the more experimental literature of the 1960s, 1970s, and 1980s, and it is that literature, dealing with issues of language, representation, historiography, and individual identity, that for an influential theorist such as Linda Hutcheon constituted literary postmodernism.[1]

For the theorists in the other camp, the innovations of the 1960s and 1970s were not so much the product of the internal dynamics of the literary system and of new themes that demanded new forms, but were rather triggered by the rapid socio-economic and socio-cultural developments of the 1960s and early 1970s. For Fredric Jameson, this camp's most influential critic, the emergence of postmodern art was intimately tied up with a major reorientation of Western capitalism. Capitalism had moved into a new, "late" phase, and postmodernism was, as Jameson put it, "the cultural logic of late capitalism."[2] Jameson's linking of postmodernism with capitalism found strong support in, for instance, the work of the social geographer David Harvey, who saw postmodernism as ultimately caused by the "time-space compression" that characterized 1970s capitalism.[3] Although Jameson, Harvey, and other like-minded critics did not ignore the formal innovations of postmodern art, their focus was on what they saw as its willful lack of authenticity and depth, its fundamentally ahistorical attitude, and its intimate and uncritical collusion with late capitalism.

However, not all critics for whom postmodernism more or less directly reflected the great changes of the 1960s and the 1970s saw things in that light. For those who welcomed those changes, postmodern literature did indeed include the formally innovative literature of the 1960s and beyond, but they were more interested in the mostly not formally innovative feminist literature of those decades and in the emerging literary self-empowerment of ethnic and cultural minorities that they saw as quintessentially postmodern. For them, postmodernism heralded a long overdue recognition of cultural diversity, of the literary self-expression of all those who until then had been ignored by the mainstream. To offer an example, for the editors of *Postmodern American Fiction: A Norton Anthology* of 1997, the work of feminist, African American, Mexican-American and Chinese-American writers is unequivocally postmodern, no matter how traditional it may be.

How well have these views, mostly formulated in the 1980s, stood the test of time? Although still widely seen as authoritative, Jameson's and Harvey's analyses of postmodernism as the cultural logic of late capitalism have become deeply problematic. In the twenty-five years after Jameson first articulated his position, late capitalism has boomed while, inexplicably (from Jameson's perspective), postmodern literature passed its high-water mark and then, in the 1990s, was rejected by a new generation of writers who argued for a return to more traditional ways of storytelling. Harvey's "time-space compression" suffered a similar loss of credibility. Two years after Harvey published his *The Condition of Postmodernity* (1989), Tim Berners-Lee put the world's first website online, unleashing a time-space compression that dwarfed the developments Harvey had thought responsible for postmodernism's emergence (see also Adriaan van der Weel's chapter "Literary Authorship in the Digital Age" within this volume). But while time-space compression ran rampant, postmodernism kept losing ground. It is hard to see how these contradictory developments could be reconciled. How can the intensification of late capitalism of the 1990s (neo-liberalism, the implosion of Soviet socialism, the Internet) explain the gradual demise of postmodernism? But the positive view of postmodernism – postmodernism as the cultural logic of social and ethnic diversity – is also problematic. Feminist literature and the literatures of ethnic and cultural minorities have become so commonplace that calling them "postmodern" no longer makes much sense. They are here to stay and are, moreover, both thematically and formally so diverse that lumping them together is not very useful. The only view that has really held up and is still of practical use is that of postmodern literature as dealing – by specific structural and formal means – with the crisis in representational practices that I have sketched above. And that is just as well because it is that view with which the discussion of postmodernist authorship is closely tied up.

The Theorists

In the late 1960s, two essays appeared that drastically reoriented all ongoing discussions on authorship. In 1967, the French critic Roland Barthes published "The Death of the Author" in the American avant-garde journal *Aspen*. Two years later, Michel Foucault published "Qu'est-ce qu'un auteur" ("What Is an Author?"), an analysis of what he calls "the author-function" that is an oblique response to Barthes's essay but approaches authorship from a completely different angle. Foucault's essay was not translated until 1977, so that for a whole decade Barthes's radically anti-authorial position was the largest single influence in the Anglophone debate on authorship. When "What Is an Author?" appeared, Barthes remained a formidable influence, not least because Foucault, too, sub-scribed to a generally anti-authorial view. Between the two of them, Barthes and Foucault set the terms for the discussion of authorship in the decades that followed. As Andrew Bennett noted in 2005: "Barthes's and Foucault's essays constitute the founding statements of much subse-quent critical and theoretical work on the author: almost forty years later we are still caught up in debates about the problem of authorship instigated by Barthes and Foucault in the late 1960s."[4]

So what does Barthes mean when he talks about the author's death? We must see his essay – and later texts such *S/Z* (1970), "From Work to Text" (1971), and *The Pleasure of the Text* (1973) – within the context of his radical rejection of phenomenological and existential humanism, a rejection that was shared by Foucault, Derrida, and a good many other Parisian intellectuals who came to the fore in the 1960s. Barthes's target is what he sees as the prevailing humanist view of the author: the author as creator, as the sole originator of a text. Authors have traditionally been seen, Barthes claims, as fully aware of themselves and their intentions – they are fully present to themselves – and as the source of the meanings their texts have, meanings which they ultimately control. However, for Barthes, who takes a radically anti-humanist and anti-authorial position, the modern author is merely a "scriptor," a sort of amanuensis whose text is not original at all, but a "multi-dimensional space in which a variety of writings, none of them original, blend and clash." Every text, Barthes argues, is a "tissue of quotations drawn from the innumerable centers of culture"[5] – quotations whose origin is almost invariably obscure. What Barthes has in mind here is not intertextuality in the sense of textual borrowings that derive their effect from our awareness of their sources, but an intertextuality that practically coincides with language itself: we cannot use language without being intertextual, without drawing on linguistic resources that others have drawn on before us. Obviously, if authors simply cannot help recycling textual material that has been reworked countless times before them, their role is much reduced. What is left, Barthes tells us, is the "power to mix writings, to counter the ones with others, in such a way as never to rest on any of them."[6] Postmodernist authorship seizes upon this power with great gusto, so what for Barthes is more or less a dead end becomes a powerful tool for authors who, rather paradoxically, now feel liberated from all sorts of constraints and give free rein to their imagination.

For Barthes, authors are not unique individuals, graced with a full understanding of themselves and fully conscious of the authorial intentions that give their writings their unique meanings. On the contrary, our supposedly unique individuality is itself constituted by myriad borrowings from countless sources: the "I [. . .] is already itself a plurality of other texts, of codes [. . .]."[7] We are what we are because of what we have borrowed and appropriated and wrongly see as having originated within ourselves. As Barthes put it in *Roland Barthes by Roland Barthes* (1975), *"the subject is merely an effect of language."*[8] If that is indeed the case, then one of Barthes's most radical statements, "[i]t is language which speaks, not the author,"[9] does make sense (if we forget for a moment about language's indispensable conduit). This is clearly as far as anti-authorialism and anti-intentionalism can go. What Barthes is after is the liberation of the text from the controlling presence of the author, that is, the author's subjectivity and intentions as presupposed in traditional criticism. We must get rid of our authorial illusions because "[t]o give a text an Author is to impose a limit on that text, to furnish it with a final signified, to close the writing."[10] For Barthes, such a limit, such closure, is unacceptable – ideally a text should accommodate an infinite number of readings. Critics of Barthes's position have pointed out that he merely replaces the unifying subjectivity of the author – which guarantees the coherence of the text – by that of the reader ("a text's unity lies not in its origin but in its destination,"[11] as Barthes himself declares). That does not alter the fact, however, that the balance of power has radically shifted and that it is now a text's readers who create its unity and meaning, with the result that any given text may have as many meanings as it has readers.

Although Michel Foucault's "What Is an Author?" approached the author and authorship from a wholly different angle, Foucault was not fundamentally at odds with Barthes's anti-humanist, anti-authorial views. On the contrary, he too had little patience with the humanist view of the subject as the origin of meaning and value. For Foucault, what we take to be our autonomous and uniquely individual subjectivity is in fact the product of "discourses," of systems of interrelated but ultimately unfounded claims that interpret and order the world for us and that give us the false illusion of individual autonomy. Thus Foucault, too, seeks to take the author out of the picture.

Unlike Barthes, Foucault does not directly attack the author as the unique subject whose intentions control the text, but instead draws our attention to the "author-function." For Foucault, a major aspect of this "author-function," which is historically and culturally contingent, is that it is bound up with legal and institutional systems, with matters of ownership, copyright, etc. Foucault's embedding of the "author-function" in historical and contemporary discourses suggested new and important approaches to authorship in general, leading to studies of the world of publishing, of censorship, of copyright law, of authorial representations in the various media, and other author-related topics. But more pertinent here is how Foucault severs the relation between the author-function and the actual author, and how he effectively makes that author disappear. The author-function, he tells us, "does not develop spontaneously as the attribution of a discourse" – in this context, the literary text – "to an individual." On the contrary, it is "the result of a complex operation which constructs a rational being that we call 'author.'" Granting that we try to give such a "construction" of an author a "realistic status," he maintains that "these aspects of an individual, which we designate as making him an author are only a projection, in more or less psychologizing terms, of the operations that we force texts to undergo."[12] For Foucault, the author is a projection, superimposed upon the text by us readers. It is a necessary projection because the author is "the principle of thrift in the proliferation of meaning." The projected author provides the "necessary and constraining figure" that the text needs in order to be seen as meaningful and coherent, but this projected author is not the real author because that real author is emphatically not the "source of significations which fill a work." The projected author is "the ideological figure by which one marks the manner in which we fear the proliferation of meaning."[13] A text inevitably contains signs that refer to its author, but those signs only reveal "a plurality of egos" that never allows us to picture a unified author-subject: the author-function "does not refer purely and simply to a real individual, since it can give rise simultaneously to several selves, to several subjects."[14] And with this, the author in the traditional sense disappears from Foucault's radar.

It should be clear that there is a good deal of affinity between these views on authorship and the postmodernism that fundamentally questions our representational practices. For postmodern critics, too, language is far more of an autonomous force than the traditional view of the author had ever imagined. Even if postmodern criticism did not fully buy into the view that the author was dead, it certainly recognized that authors could never be fully in control of their texts. Those texts reflected representations that their authors were not aware of, and the inherent polysemy of language inevitably created meanings independent of its users' intentions. What is more, those intentions no longer were intentions that had originated in a unique autonomous subject. Since every author's self was pervaded by language, there was no telling where the echoing of internalized representations ended and originality began. Although the theorists of literary postmodernism were less convinced that the days of the humanist subject were numbered and that the traditional author was indeed dead, they did agree that, in postmodern literature, the balance had shifted from author to reader. But this does not necessarily mean merely a shift from one authority to another so as to reach a firm footing outside the vagaries of omni-textuality. For Christine Brooke-Rose, for instance, "[a]ll, all is language, even the reader [. . .] all, all is text."[15]

Intermezzo: Public and Publishers

The argument that authors and readers were "text" did not have much of an impact outside of avant-garde literature and theory. The death of the author should have led to a notable falling off of interest in authors' biographical details – or opinions, for that matter – but the opposite is true. Biographies, autobiographies, memoirs, and so-called autofiction sold better than ever. As Kate Douglas noted in 2001, in an article on the ever-increasing visibility of authors, "publishers and critics agree that, for better or worse, the production and popular consumption of life writing, and interest in the biographical details of contemporary authors, are experiencing a notable boom." Indeed, "[a]t a time when two, perhaps even three generations of literary theorists have primarily been raised on the notion that the biography of the author is almost irrelevant to the text [. . .] the author has if anything become even more crucial to a book's success."[16] The author, presented "as an engaging human figure who is socially observant and uniquely creative,"[17] played a central role in the marketing of literature, and there is no reason to assume that things have changed much since then. Douglas's suggestion that the author, symbolizing "the existence of individual, autonomous creativity," was mobilized to neutralize "the threat posed by the postmodernists,"[18] gives the impression that postmodern theory was purposefully undermined by self-serving publishers, but it is far more plausible that publishers, who after all deal with authors in person, had little patience with postmodern theory and saw their authors just as they saw themselves, as autonomous and creative individuals. That is, in any case, how authors were perceived in general and they were given more opportunities than ever before to present themselves as such. Authors were interviewed in newspapers, in weeklies, on television. They appeared as keynote speakers in academic conferences, were welcomed in talk shows, and were jetted around the world as cultural ambassadors. Wherever they went, they drew fascinated audiences who would have laughed off the notion of the author's death. They were awarded literary prizes in Oscar-like settings, with speeches that invariably praised their originality and unique achievements. While across the channel the author was already terminally ill, in the United Kingdom the Geoffrey Faber Prize was established (1963), to be followed by the Alice Hunt Bartlett Prize (1966) and the Cholmondeley Award (1966). In the same year that Barthes declared the author dead, the Winifred Holtby Memorial Prize (1967) was founded, soon followed by what is now called the Man Booker Prize (1969) and a bit later by the National Poetry Competition (1979). The 1980s saw the inauguration of the Betty Trask Award (1984) and Commonwealth Writers' Prize (1987), while in the 1990s the Forward Prizes (1992), the T. S. Eliot Prize (1993), and the Orange Prize (1996; now Women's Prize for Fiction) were established. No doubt marketing played a role in this proliferation of prizes (some of which are actually sponsored by the Society of Authors in the United Kingdom). But in the increasingly neo-liberalist climate of the 1970s and after, publishers did not have to convince the public that their authors were uniquely creative individuals. What publishers responded to was the ever-growing interest in the personal, an interest that later was to be exploited by reality television and other forms of entertainment that pretended to offer authentic reality. The news of the author's death, if heard at all, was never taken seriously by the average reader.

The Authors

However, that news was most certainly heard – and taken quite seriously – by many of the authors who came to prominence in the 1960s and after. British authors such as John Fowles (*The French Lieutenant's Woman*, 1967) and A. S. Byatt (*Possession*, 1990) playfully worked postmodern theory into their fiction; in the United States, John Barth, Robert Coover, William Gass, and other writers demonstrated their familiarity with postmodernism in interviews and essays. Barth even seemed to echo Barthes: "no one has claim to originality in literature; all writers are more or less faithful amanuenses of the spirit, translators and annotators of preexisting archetypes."[19] But what

Barthes called the "power [...] to mix writings, to counter the ones with others,"[20] a power that he does not see as the expression of a unique subjectivity, let alone a source of transcendental meaning, is for Barth and other postmodernist writers far from inconsequential. That power is, in fact, at the core of postmodernist authorship. But let us first look at some of the mixing strategies that postmodernist writers developed or borrowed from literary history.

Paradoxically, with those strategies, authors become more visible than ever in their own texts. Take, for instance, metalepsis – the intrusion of the world of the telling into the narrated world. The reader can, after all, not very well miss the presence of an author who openly enters his or her text and so mixes real life (the world of the telling) with the fictional world (the world that is narrated). Authors may make cameo appearances, as in Kurt Vonnegut's *Slaughterhouse-Five* (1969), where the narrator remarks of one of his protagonist's fellow soldiers: "That was I. That was me. That was the author of this book."[21] Similar examples of metalepsis appear in the novels of Philip Roth, Paul Auster's *City of Glass* (1985), W. G. Sebald's *Austerlitz* (2001), Amélie Nothomb's *Life Form* (2010), and a host of other novels. Or we may have indirect intrusions as in Muriel Spark's *The Comforters* (1957) or Nicola Barker's *In the Approaches* (2014), in which one of Barker's characters fumes at what his creator – that "cow Author" – would seem to have in store for him.[22] But authors may also function as full-fledged characters, as in John Barth's *LETTERS* (1979), or as intradiegetic narrators, telling the story from within the fiction, as in J. G. Ballard's *Crash* (1973) or Iain Sinclair's *Downriver* (1991). Such transgressions of the ontological boundary between the world of the telling and the narrated world tell us that the narrated world should not be taken as a faithful representation of reality but that it is a linguistic construct that functions on a different ontological level. And they hint at the possibility that the real world, too, is at least partly a linguistic construct – in any case, they did so before transgressing the boundary between the real world and the fictional world became so commonplace that readers now take it in their stride.

The authorial presence may even dominate the narrative, as in Richard Powers's *Galatea 2.2* (1995), in which we have a first-person narrator called Richard Powers, who is also the novel's main character and who has authored a number of novels that are recognizably those of the real-world Richard Powers. Still, the Powers character operates in what clearly is a fictive space and we may assume that the intimate letter of his former long-time girlfriend that we read at a certain point is not lifted from the author's files, and we may also assume that he has not trained a self-learning computer to read and understand Shakespeare. In spite of that, it is hard to know where autobiography ends and fiction begins. We know that at a certain point the author transgresses the boundary between reality and fiction, but we do not know where because that boundary is intentionally blurred. Such novels, in which author and protagonist (who may or may not be an intradiegetic narrator) share a name, are often called autofictions. According to Gérard Genette, autofiction implies an explicit or implicit pact with the reader: "I, the author, am going to tell you a story of which I am the hero but which never happened to me."[23] But things are not as clear-cut as this suggests. We do not know to what extent Powers's account of his failed relationship (some of which is definitely autobiographical) is fiction. We face the same problem in Michael Chabon's *Moonglow* (2016), which is the eventful story, narrated by the intradiegetic Chabon, of Chabon's grandparents. *Moonglow* comes with an "Author's note" that issues a strong warning: "In preparing this memoir, I have stuck to facts except when facts refused to conform with memory, narrative purpose, or the truth as I prefer to understand it." Whatever liberties have been taken, Chabon assures us, "they have been taken with great abandon."[24] To complicate things further, there is autofiction that goes beyond this and that purports to represent the author/narrator/protagonist's real world even if it uses the narrative possibilities offered by fiction to do so. In such cases, the boundary between autobiography and fiction has dissolved to the point where they cannot possibly be disentangled. In *Fils* (1977) and later autofictions, Serge Doubrovsky, who coined the term, presents a protagonist called Serge Doubrovsky and apparently stays so close to his own life that his work led to a number of enraged responses from his immediate environment. In fact, a second cousin, Marc Weitzmann, in his novel *Chaos* (1997), took a not so subtle revenge in what presented itself as another autofiction. Doubrovsky's confessional type of autofiction – which might be seen as a radicalization of the long tradition of confessional writing (see also Christian Badura and Melanie Möller's chapter "Authorship in Classical Rome" within this volume) – regularly meets with responses ranging from disbelief to outrage. Chris Kraus's *I Love Dick* (1997) detailed her real-life obsession with the British media critic Dick Hebdige, much to Hebdige's discomfort, and Karl Ove Knausgård's exhaustive portrayal of his father and grandmother led to a permanent alienation from his father's side of the family. Knausgård's *Min Kamp* (*My Struggle*, 6 volumes; 2009–11) is probably the most extreme, at least the most notorious contemporary example of autofiction.[25] *My Struggle* records the smallest detail, no matter how confrontational or nauseating, in a sober prose that suggests that nothing is invention. But of course there is invention. No one has total recall, and so much of what we read must be fictionalized reconstruction, if not outright construction. Autofiction, then, has a narrative effect that is markedly different from those of autobiography and memoir, where we also find identity of name between author, narrator, and protagonist, but where we expect the author to be truthful (while allowing for subjectivity). The reader of autofiction cannot help wondering where the author crosses the boundary between fact and fiction or if there is such a boundary at all. Autofiction inevitably reminds us of the extra-textual, real-life author. In his unfinished novel *The Pale King* (2011), we find David Foster Wallace playing with the inevitable curiosity that autofiction generates, to the point of giving his address and Social Security number to emphasize the real-life basis of his story. Autofiction takes us out of the world of the fiction to the extra-textual, real-life author and indirectly emphasizes the author's creative (and confusing) powers.

Metalepsis and autofiction tell us that the death of the author was not necessarily accepted by those it concerned most. But they also tell us that authors recognize that the relations between their fictions and reality are far from unproblematic. For Doubrovsky, autobiography cannot help having a fictional component – it is based on fictions we have constructed about ourselves – which does not mean, however, that it should be dismissed as fiction: "On se raconte comme on raconte un personage de fiction, pour communiquer sa propre vie."[26] In a sense, Doubrovsky wants to have it both ways, just like Jeanette Winterson, who in the introduction to the 1996 reissue of her *Oranges Are Not the Only Fruit* (1985) tells us that she "wanted to use myself as a fictional character – an expanded 'I.'"[27] In fact, having it both ways is exactly what all postmodernist authors are after. It is central to their conception of authorship and it explains their generally disruptive tactics, their deliberate mixing of discourses or ontological levels (as in metalepsis). Postmodernist authors consciously create contradictions. They present us with two (or more) representations of reality that we cannot reconcile with each other. One of these representations will be familiar to us. It may be a fictional story that we know quite well or it may be what we take to be a "realistic" picture of the real world – it will in some way represent a state of affairs that we experience as given, as natural, and that functions as a natural background. The other representation will take great liberties with the first: the story that we know so well will be drastically rewritten, or we will be bewildered, upset, or fascinated by an alternative reality that is at odds with the reality we know. In both cases representations are played off against each other, a design that inevitably reminds the reader that there is an author who manipulates our response. If we have both a "realistic" and an "unrealistic" representation of reality, the text will present us with two incompatible sets of reading instructions. On the one hand, we will find textual elements that create the illusion that we are dealing with the real world, as in realistic fiction, and that will persuade us to see the text as referential. But on the other hand, we will find elements that expressly counteract that illusion, elements that tell us *not* to see the novel or story as referential, as having bearing upon the real world. To put this in different terms, we have textual elements that suggest depth and meaning and invite traditional interpretation, while almost simultaneously other elements will deny depth and meaning and actively obstruct interpretation. The author sets up a conflict or, to say it in more positive terms, a dialogue between two representations of reality – one representation that we are tempted to see as referential and another that seems non-referential, a linguistic construct – and then leaves things to the reader.

Metalepsis clearly sets up such a conflict. Let us briefly look at some other striking strategies. Fictional characters may be lifted out of their original textual environment and be put to work in a new setting. In Guy Davenport's 1993 story "Christ Preaching at the Henley Regatta" – the title itself an allusion to Stanley Spencer's famous series of paintings "Christ Preaching at Cookham Regatta" – we meet both P. G. Wodehouse's Bertie Wooster and Dorothy L. Sayers's Lord Peter Wimsey. In E. L. Doctorow's *Ragtime* (1975) we are puzzled by the first name of one of its main characters, Coalhouse Walker, until we realize that he, together with the subplot in which he features, has been lifted from Heinrich von Kleist's novella *Michael Kohlhaas* (1804). But it is also possible to leave characters in their original environment and rework the text in question (although not too radically because the original text must still be recognizable in order for the reworked text to have its desirable effect). Donald Barthelme's *Snow White* (1967) rather drastically rewrites the familiar fairy tale, although he himself would not seem to be aware of that in explaining his strategy: "the usefulness of the Snow White story is that everybody knows it and it can be played against [. . .]. Every small change in the story is momentous when everybody knows the story backward."[28] Angela Carter's *The Bloody Chamber* (1979) uses the same strategy in giving us feminist versions of not one fairy tale but a whole batch of them. In *Foe* (1986), J. M. Coetzee's rewriting of Defoe's *Robinson Crusoe*, Crusoe and Friday (who in this supposedly "true" version is mute because his tongue has been ripped out) are at some point joined by a shipwrecked woman, Susan Barton.

When Crusoe dies on their way back to England, Barton is the only one who can tell the story of their life on the island. She tells it to the writer Defoe (born Daniel Foe) who then cynically proceeds to write her out of her own history. Coetzee's rewriting of the story obliquely hints at the way women have for the most part been written out of history, while the voice of Africans was never heard. Such rewritings of familiar stories set up a confrontation between the rewritten version and the original one and thereby invite us to reflect on both of them and on the way representations govern the world we live in (see also Daniel Cook's chapter "Copyright and Literary Property" within this volume).

Rewritings may spread their wings and take on history itself. In Robert Coover's *The Public Burning* (1977), Ethel and Julius Rosenberg, sentenced to death for high treason (which is historically correct), are executed on New York City's Times Square as the high point of carnivalesque festivities (which of course never happened), with then Vice President Richard Nixon anticipating postmodern views in his (fictional) final words to Ethel Rosenberg: "We've both been victims of the same lie, Ethel! There *is* no purpose, there *are* no causes, all that's just stuff we make up to hold the goddam world together."[29] Philip Roth's *The Plot Against America* (2004) takes on American history of the late 1930s and puts not Franklin Delano Roosevelt but the antisemite and Nazi sympathizer Charles Lindbergh, of aviation fame, in the White House. Even more alarming are the new administration's antisemitic measures and the pogroms that begin to take place in major American cities. In Michael Chabon's *The Yiddish Policemen's Union* (2007), re-imagined history is so far removed from actual history that the novel was nominated for various science fiction/fantasy awards (and went on to win them). In Chabon's novel, the United States has acted on a (historical, but rejected) 1938 proposal to allow Jewish refugees to settle in Alaska so that in the early twenty-first century we have a teeming Yiddish-speaking metropolis on an island just off Alaska. The predicament that Chabon then creates for those Alaskan Jews, and which I will not discuss here, is unpleasantly pertinent to the world we live in. In any case, Chabon sets up a confrontation between history as it has come down to us and history as re-imagined by the author, a confrontation that forces us to reflect on important current problems. We may of course read *The Yiddish Policemen's Union* as an autonomous linguistic construct, as fantasy. Postmodernist literature very deliberately offers the reader that option. As William Gass, speaking for himself and for his colleagues, once said: "What you want to do is to create a work that can be read non-referentially."[30] But that option is a by-product of their strategy of preventing unproblematic referential readings. Postmodernist authors put robust obstacles in the way of such readings. And their motives are familiar. As Robert Coover put it, the writer is "the creative spark in this process of renewal: he's the one who tears apart the old story, speaks the unspeakable, makes the ground shake, then shuffles the bits back together into a new story."[31] In the early stage of literary modernism (see Chapter 10 "The Nineteenth Century" in this volume) Ezra Pound told his colleagues to "make it new." Postmodernist writers still heed that call, but with a difference.

John Barth once called his parodic 1960s novels *The Sot-Weed Factor* (1960) and *Giles Goat-Boy* (1966) "novels which imitate the form of the Novel, by an author who imitates the role of the Author,"[32] and his use of the lower case is a felicitous illustration of what is at the heart of post-modernist authorship. Postmodernist novels and authors do not claim the sort of authority with which novels and authors have been invested ever since Romanticism. This is not false modesty. Rather, it points to the awareness that the author cannot help drawing on a "variety of writings," on being intertextual in Roland Barthes's sense, and that all representations of reality will always be shot through with involuntary borrowings and echoes. Fully aware of those limitations and of the fate of supposedly timeless, universal truths that once were central to now rejected represen-tations of reality, postmodernist authors know that their truths are perso-nal and situational – no matter how strong their personal beliefs.

Paradoxically, the loss of faith in representational practices leads to unexpected freedom. It releases the author from the obligation to stay as close as possible to reality or, for that matter, history. And so authors feel free to enter the fictional worlds they create, to lift characters – both fictional and historical – from their original environment, to re-imagine history, or to expand the possibilities of our own world with rather startling innovations. In Thomas Pynchon's *Gravity's Rainbow* (1973), the American soldier Tyrone Slothrop calls baffled attention to himself because his erections in wartime London accurately predict direct hits by German V-2s, while in the same author's *Against the Day* (2006) travel from pole to pole is greatly facilitated by the unexplained existence of a direct channel. As John Barth once said, "such a simple premise as the comic mode, or the parodic, or a fantastical mode, rather than a realistic mode, already, it seems to me, unties you, sets you free."[33] However, postmodernist fiction's compelling narrative energy and the obvious delight that it takes in its own inventiveness always serve an ulterior purpose. In their conscious rework-ing and manipulation of representations, postmodernist authors confront us with vital questions. Who has constructed the narratives and discourses that we internalize when we grow up? What was their purpose? Who controls them and to what ends? Who are excluded from certain narratives or discourses and who benefit from others? Such questions are not only political, they are also deeply moral. It has been argued that fiction that willfully undermines its referentiality, as postmodern fiction routinely does, inevitably also undermines its credibility and that such fiction is therefore incapable of taking up a convincing moral stance. That argument ignores the moral indignation that fuels much postmodernist fiction, as for instance Robert Coover's *The Public Burning*, and fiction that takes its cue from its postmodernist precursors, as, for example, Colson Whitehead's *The Underground Railroad* (2016).

Contemporary Authorship

Colson Whitehead would probably object to having his novel associated with postmodernism and he would be right – but only up to a point. *The Underground Railroad* is representative of an important strand within contemporary fiction that borrows freely from the postmodernist repertoire without being worried by postmodern doubts about representation. But the liberties such fiction allows itself are a direct continuation of those of postmodernist fiction.[34] *The Underground Railroad* takes us back to pre-Civil War America, to the degradations, the brutalities, and the violence of life on a Georgia plantation. Its protagonist, the black slave Cora, suffers all the humiliations, including rape, that we are familiar with from nineteenth-century slave narratives. Indeed, the almost fiercely realistic first part of Whitehead's novel strongly reminds us of the fact that such historical narratives must have been a major source for his own narrative and calls our attention to Roland Barthes's argument that all the author can do is to rework and rearrange textual material that history has handed down to us. But then, in a literally and figuratively fantastic move, Whitehead belies Barthes's claim. The underground railroad of the title, a metaphor for the network of abolitionists who helped escaped slaves to reach free territory, turns into an actual underground railroad and Cora, who is now on the run, is picked up by an actual underground train on which she begins her long voyage toward freedom. It must be emphasized that Whitehead's sudden swerve into the fantastic, and his rewriting of history, both of which are standard features of the postmodernist repertoire, in no way diminish the moral force of his novel, which clearly invites us to look critically at contemporary race relations in the United States.

The ease with which the fantastic and the referential can now be combined and, more importantly, reconciled with each other in a morally compelling harmonious whole is perfectly illustrated by *The Underground Railroad*'s critical success: the novel did not only win the (American) National Book Award and the Pulitzer Prize but also the Arthur C. Clarke Award, the most prestigious British science fiction prize.

The postmodern disposition to disbelief has not spared authorship itself and has reduced Authors to authors, fully aware of their indebtedness to a tapestry of texts that reaches back to prehistoric times. But that does not turn them into Roland Barthes's "scriptors" who merely create new arrangements of already existing textual fragments. Post-1960s authorship may rest on a diminished, or at any rate cautious, humanism, but it is still driven by moral seriousness and still proud to give full rein to the human imagination. It is committed to an open, all-embracing aesthetic attitude that does not rule out contradiction, discontinuity, incoherence, or the arbitrary. And because it willingly accepts, or even welcomes, such sins against realistic representation, the author's hand is more visible than ever. A mid-nineteenth century underground railroad network, a tunnel from pole to pole, an Orthodox Jewish metropolis off the coast of Alaska, a public execution on Times Square, Charles Lindbergh in the White House – the list of impossibilities and of events that never happened is endless and they all remind us that there is an author pulling the strings and manipulating our responses, an author who is, moreover, not at all afraid of being seen. The author's incontrovertible presence demonstrates beyond any doubt that authors are still creators, that they still make it new.

But this post-1960s authorship does not privilege the imagination in the expectation that it will arrive at lasting insights or truths. For these authors, the imagining subject is not a superior fountain of transcendental insight. As William Gass remarked, "I distrust people, including artists, who make pretentious claims for literature as a source of knowledge."[35] But even if they cannot see their work in such terms, postmodernist authors and the contemporary authors that follow in their wake do believe that they have an important contribution to make, that they can and must expose the illusions and false truths with which our world is riddled.

Notes

1. Linda Hutcheon, *The Poetics of Postmodernism: History, Theory, Fiction* (New York and London: Routledge, 1988).

2. Fredric Jameson, "Postmodernism, or the Cultural Logic of Late Capitalism," *New Left Review*, 146 (1983), 59–92.
3. David Harvey, *The Condition of Postmodernity: An Enquiry into the Origins of Cultural Change* (Oxford: Blackwell, 1989).
4. Andrew Bennett, *The Author* (London: Routledge, 2005), p. 11.
5. Roland Barthes, "The Death of the Author," in *Authorship: From Plato to Postmodernism: A Reader*, ed. Seán Burke (Edinburgh: Edinburgh University Press, 1995), pp. 125–30, p. 128.
6. Ibid.
7. Roland Barthes, *S/Z*, trans. Richard Miller (London: Cape, 1974), p. 10.
8. Cited in Max Saunders, *Self Impression: Life-Writing, Autobiografiction, and the Forms of Modern Literature* (Oxford: Oxford University Press, 2010), p. 506.
9. Barthes, "Death of the Author," p. 126.
10. Ibid., pp. 128–29.
11. Ibid., p. 129.
12. Michel Foucault, "What Is an Author?", in *Textual Strategies: Perspectives in Post-Structuralist Criticism*, ed. Josué Harari (Ithaca, NY: Cornell University Press, 1979), pp. 141–60, p. 150.
13. Foucault, "What Is an Author?", p. 159.
14. Ibid., p. 153.
15. Christine Brooke-Rose, *Stories, Theories and Things* (Cambridge: Cambridge University Press, 1991), p. 25. See also Debra Malina, *Breaking the Frame: Metalepsis and the Construction of the Subject* (Columbus: Ohio State University Press, 2002).
16. Kate Douglas, "'Blurbing' Biographical: Authorship and Autobiography," *Biography*, 24.4 (2001), 806–26, p. 806.
17. Ibid., p. 820.
18. Ibid., p. 813.
19. John Barth, *The Friday Book: Essays and Other Nonfiction* (New York: Putnam, 1984), p. 80.
20. Barthes, "Death of the Author," p. 128.
21. Kurt Vonnegut, *Slaughterhouse-Five, or The Children's Crusade: A Duty-Dance with Death* (New York: Dell, 1991), p. 125.
22. Nicola Barker, *In the Approaches* (London: Fourth Estate, 2015), p. 84.
23. Gérard Genette, *Fiction & Diction* (Ithaca, NY: Cornell University Press, 1993), p. 76.
24. Michael Chabon, *Moonglow* (London: Fourth Estate, 2017), n.p.
25. Less well-known examples include Tomas Espedal, *Against Art* (2011); Rachel Cusk, *Aftermath* (2012); Delphine de Vigan, *Based on a True Story* (2017); and the novels of Andreas Maier, beginning with *The Room* (2014), to name but a few. One of their modernist ancestors is Gertrude Stein's *Autobiography of Alice B. Toklas* (1933).
26. Cited in Elizabeth H. Jones, "Serge Doubrovsky: Life, Writing, Legacy," *L'Esprit Créateur*, 49.3 (2009), 1–7, p. 2.

27. Jeanette Winterson, *Oranges Are Not the Only Fruit* (London: Virago, 1996), p. xiii.
28. Donald Barthelme in *Anything Can Happen: Interviews with Contemporary American Novelists*, eds. Thomas LeClair and Larry McCaffery (Urbana: University of Illinois Press, 1983), p. 42–43.
29. Robert Coover, *The Public Burning* (New York: Viking, 1977), p. 436.
30. *Anything Can Happen*, eds. LeClair and McCaffery, p. 164.
31. Geoffrey Wolff, "An American Epic," *New York Times*, August 19, 1977, 48–57, p. 54.
32. Barth, *Friday Book*, p. 79.
33. In Joe David Bellamy, *The New Fiction: Interviews with Innovative American Writers* (Urbana: University of Illinois Press, 1974), p. 16.
34. To mention some other examples: Nicola Barker's *Darkmans* (2006) and David Mitchell's *The Bone Clocks* (2014), both of which effortlessly combine realistic characterization with impossibly supernatural elements, and Kate Atkinson's *Life After Life* (2013), whose otherwise realistically presented main character routinely dies and goes on living.
35. In Bellamy, *New Fiction*, p. 33.

CHAPTER 13

Chinese Authorship

Kang-i Sun Chang

Authorship in Confucian Classics

The modern Chinese term "zuo zhe" (author) is derived from the ancient word "zuo," meaning to compose, to do, or to engage in – all commanding a notion of power and authority. These semantic threads collectively underpin the long-standing contention that Chinese authorship began with Confucius. Mencius (390–305 BCE) was the first person to claim that Confucius was the author of the *Spring and Autumn Annals*: "When the world declined and the Way fell into obscurity, heresies and violence again arose. [...] Confucius was apprehensive and composed [zuo] the *Spring and Autumn Annals*."[1] The Han historian Sima Qian (*c*.145–*c*.86 BCE) inherited this concept of "zuo," acknowledging that "when Confucius was in straits he wrote (zuo) the *Spring and Autumn Annals*."[2] Sima Qian was the first person to claim both that Confucius compiled the *Classic of Poetry* by choosing 305 poems out of 3,000 songs,[3] and that Confucius was responsible for writing the earliest commentaries on the *Book of Changes*.[4]

For more than two thousand years, the Chinese followed Sima Qian's lead, believing that Confucius (551–479 BCE) compiled, edited, transmitted, and partially composed the Six Confucian Classics: the *Classic of Poetry* (*Shijing*), *Classic of Documents* (*Shujing*), *Book of Changes* (*Yijing*), *Book of Rites* (*Liji*), *Book of Music* (*Yuejing*), and *Spring and Autumn Annals* (*Chunqiu*). But since the early twentieth century, some scholars have debated and expressed skepticism over Confucius's role in authoring or editing the ancient classics.[5]

Nonetheless, archaeologists and paleographists continue to document the transmission of Confucian texts, largely focusing on manuscripts excavated in China during the early 1990s. Western sinologists have paid particular attention to such newly discovered manuscripts as *Kongzi shilun* (*Confucius' Discussion of the Classic of Poetry*), written around 375 BCE,[6] and "Zi yi" ("Black Jacket"), a text attributed to Confucius's grandson Zi Si (483–402 BCE).[7] Meanwhile, younger scholars such as Michael Hunter have questioned the traditional status of the Confucian *Analects* and argued that the text was not compiled until early Western Han (i.e., between the 150s and 130s BCE), as a product of the later political, intellectual, and textual milieu.[8] All these studies point to a surge of new interest in authorship problems regarding ancient Confucian texts.

As diverse as they are, most modern studies agree on one point: before the Western Han, transmissions of works were largely oral.[9] However, as modern critic Haun Saussy has shown, "oral tradition is a means of inscription in its own right, rather than an antecedent made obsolete by the written word."[10] In general, most sinologists consider the concept of authorship in ancient China fluid and elusive, encompassing broad traditions of wisdom that were transmitted over many generations. Some modern scholars, such as Christian Schwermann and Raji C. Steineck, call such authorship "composite authorship," referring to the "different author functions" that were "distributed among several individuals" who shared the responsibility of "weaving elaborate tapestries of intertextual references."[11] Similarly, Alexander Beecroft labeled the authorship of the *Shijing* (The *Classic of Poetry*) as "authorship in performance," for in ancient times it was "performance rather than composition" that revealed "the essential meaning of a poem."[12]

In this regard, the canonization of the ancient Chinese classics stemmed from the authority of Confucius, in his role as a cultural sage. For example, although some modern scholars, including *Shijing* translator James Legge, question the attribution of Confucius as the editor and compiler of the *Classic of Poetry*,[13] Confucius's hermeneutic tradition still secured a long cultural legacy for the *Shijing* anthology. Martin Kern said it most succinctly: "Whether or not Confucius was indeed the compiler of the *Poetry*, the hermeneutic approach attributed to him in the Shanghai Museum manuscript of *c.* 300 BC [referring to the recent archaeological find, *Confucius' Discussion of the Poetry*] was the dominant one that carried the anthology into the early empire. Without it, the 'three hundred songs' might have disappeared just like almost all other poetry from pre-imperial times."[14]

Authorship in Biographies and Poetry

Sima Qian was the first writer in ancient China to be keenly preoccupied with the notion of authorship, for he believed in the power of writing as the ultimate salvation for individual writers. In both his "Preface" to *The Record of the Historian* and his famous letter to his friend Ren An, Sima Qian demonstrated how individual authors used writing to bear witness not only to their own experiences of suffering and pain, but also to their literary triumphs. He noted that King Wen of Zhou began working on the *Book of Changes* when he was in captivity in Youli; Confucius wrote the *Spring and Autumn Annals* while suffering great trauma in Chencai; Qu Yuan composed "Encountering Sorrow" (Lisao) after his banishment; Zuo Qiuming wrote *Conversations from the State* (*Guoyu*) after losing his sight; Sunzi began work on his *Art of War* (*Bingfa*) only after his feet were cut off by his enemy.[15] Most importantly, Sima Qian's notion of empowering authorship born out of misfortune came from personal experience. In 98 BCE, he offended emperor Wu in his defense of his friend, general Li Ling, and was then sentenced to castration, a humiliating experience that could have driven him to take his own life. But Sima Qian chose to continue living, simply because he wanted to finish writing his *Record of the Historian.*

It is no coincidence that Sima Qian was the first person to write a biography of China's earliest poet Qu Yuan (*c.*340–278 BCE). Although Jia Yi (200–168 BCE) was the first to mention Qu Yuan in a literary work (in his "Lament for Qu Yuan"), and Liu An (175–122 BCE) was the first to write an introduction to Qu Yuan's famous poem "Encountering Sorrow" (Lisao), Sima Qian was the first to establish Qu Yuan as China's first poet. In his double biography of Qu Yuan and Jia Yi, Sima Qian told the story of Qu Yuan with the greatest sympathy, elaborating on the tragic circumstances that led to Qu Yuan's banishment and eventual suicide by drowning.[16] According to Sima Qian, Qu Yuan wrote "Lisao," a long poem lamenting the injustice of his exile, immediately following his dismissal from the Chu court. Sima Qian also claimed that Qu Yuan wrote his last piece, "Embracing Sand" (Huai sha), before drowning himself in the Miluo river.

Thus, throughout Chinese history, Qu Yuan's "Lisao" was invariably invoked as a model in both exile literature and martyrdom discourse. China's first poet became a perennial cultural hero; even today, the Chinese regarded Qu Yuan as the "People's Poet."[17] Although almost all Chinese readers accept Qu Yuan's authorship of his "autobiographical" poem "Lisao," some modern scholars disagree with Sima Qian's attribution of other pieces – such as the "Summons of the Soul" (Zhao hun), the "Lament for Ying" (Ai Ying), and "Embracing Sand" (Huai sha) – to Qu Yuan, thinking that they might be works of later imitators.[18] Still more recently, some scholars, especially Western sinologists, have questioned Qu Yuan's authorship of "Lisao" as well as "the biographical reading of the text."[19] However, it is easy to understand why most Chinese readers do not want to doubt Qu Yuan's authorship of those works traditionally attributed to him. Qu Yuan was China's first poet to be known by name, and he established the cultural model for later poets to imitate. Moreover, modern readers are increasingly inclined to accept the fluidity of the concept of authorship; for them, the "author" does not have to be a single person, as can be seen in the "posited identity" of Cold Mountain (Han Shan, *c.* seventh to ninth century), to whom a body of anonymous verse by numerous authors were attributed.[20]

It was Sima Qian's reading of Qu Yuan that created the paradigm for later Chinese readers and critics: poems should be read as autobiographies. In his critical text *The Literary Mind and the Carving of Dragons* (*Wenxin diaolong*), Liu Xie (*c.*465–522) explains the rationale for this kind of reading: "In the case of composing literature, the affections are stirred and words come forth; but in the case of reading a work of literature, one opens the text and enters the affections [of the writer]. [. . .] None may see the actual faces of a remote age, but by viewing their writing, one may immediately see their minds."[21] Several centuries before Liu Xie, Mencius (390–305 BCE) said that "an understanding reader can read the minds of the author" (*yi yi ni zhi*).[22] This type of reader's response is closely connected with the Chinese notion of poetry-writing, for "writing poetry is to express one's innermost feeling" (*shi yan zhi*). Through the perpetuation of the notion of *shi yan zhi*, the author can always expect to be understood by future readers, despite distances in time and space. Thus, although the ancient poet Qu Yuan could not be appreciated by his contemporaries, Liu Xie, as an understanding reader, is able to "perceive what is rare" in Qu Yuan.[23]

Liu Xie's argument is the best explanation for why Chinese authors always treasure past models, especially through allusions, as a way of connecting with their predecessors and learning from their brilliance. By extension, an author is confident that he has attained literary immortality when future readers remember him and define their works in terms of his. Meanwhile, Chinese poets also developed the habit of writing poems to each other and sharing their *shi yan zhi* as a way to form friendship and literary identity.[24]

Premodern Chinese authors adopted different modalities of impersonation. Over the centuries, Qu Yuan's allegorical adoption of the female persona in voicing his personal political grievances became an especially important tradition for later literati to emulate. As Wai-yee Li wrote: "When the poetic 'I' in *Encountering Sorrow* [...] declares, 'The throng of women, jealous of my fair brow / Slander me with charges of licentiousness' [...] most readers readily decode this as a lament that jealous rivals block the poet's access to his ruler."[25] From ancient times, Chinese male poets learned to borrow the voice of the abandoned woman from Qu Yuan. Thus, when the prince Cao Zhi (192–232) describes the desperate situation of the deserted wife in his poems – such as "The Forsaken Wife" (Qi fu pian) and "Seven Sorrows Poem" (Qi ai shi) – readers can see that they are meant as political allegories, intending to convey the author's frustration at being ignored by his emperor brother, as well as his "banishment from court."[26] Countless other male writers in premodern China have also adopted the voice of the ill-fated beauty as a metaphor for their political setbacks.

Later, during the traumatic dynastic transition from the Ming (1368–1644) to the Qing (1644–1911), some male poets went to the extent of faking female authorship by using feminine pseudonyms for their writings about the suffering women. One such case is Wu Zhaoqian (1631–1684), who used a female persona, and signed his works under different feminine names, to produce a long series of poems pretending to be the poetic testimonies of victimized women, many of whom were abducted during the dynastic war. He posted these poems – one of which contained as many as one hundred quatrains – on walls near cities such as Suzhou, and Zhuozhou in Hubei.[27] Readers, male and female, believed that women had written the poems, and responded enthusiastically.[28] Wu's use of the female voice, including his use of feminine pseudonyms, for his wall poems is an excellent example of gender crossing, and was not merely a case of a marginalized intellectual during dynastic transition masking his frustration. In general, traditional Chinese male poets, especially in late Imperial China, did not view women as the "other"; instead, they used the female voice to invent a feminine ideal that transcended gender binaries.

The device of impersonation does not apply only to the usage of female voice, however. In pre-modern China, poets often impersonated famous individuals of the past, especially if that "famous individual" left few poetic works to posterity. For example, one of the most memorable episodes recorded in Ban Gu (32–92) and Ban Zhao's (c.49–c.120) *History of the [Former] Han* (*Han Shu*) describes the parting of Li Ling (the failed general who surrendered to the Xiongnu, and whom Sima Qian once risked his own life to defend) and Su Wu (the Han envoy who refused to surrender to the enemy and was called back to China after nineteen years of suffering as a prisoner of war). The "Three Poems for Su Wu" later attributed to Li Ling (d. 74 BC) were often read as parting poems which Li wrote when he bade farewell to Su Wu (d. 60 BC). However, most modern scholars believe that the "Three Poems for Su Wu" were poems of impersonation, possibly written by someone later in the Eastern Han.

Women Poets and Authorship

Our consideration of Chinese authorship would be incomplete, however, if we did not include women writers in the discussion as well. Women writers (especially women poets) were a significant part of Chinese literature since ancient times; works by women were continuously read, alluded to, and ranked by readers of both sexes.[29] No other civilization in the world has produced more women poets than Imperial China. During the Ming and Qing eras alone, the proliferation of women's anthologies and collections (including works of ancient women and contemporary women) reached the stunning number of some 3,000 titles, although about one-third of these works have unfortunately been lost. In traditional China, many learned women shared a world with men; they acted not as auxiliary attachments to a male sphere, but often as full-fledged participants in the literary traditions and expressions that defined the larger cultural and social context. There were various types of eminent women writers – so-called "talented women" (cai nv) – who served as models for later women, and even men. The legendary Ban Zhao of the Eastern Han was famous as a historian, teacher, and court poet: she was summoned to the imperial court to continue writing the History of the [Former] Han after her brother Ban Gu, the original author of the project, died in 92 CE. At court, she taught male scholars as well as Empress Deng. Ban Zhao's written works, such as "Rhapsody on a Journey to the East" (Dongzheng fu) and "Precepts for My Daughters" (Nv jie), became models of "admonition literature" for sons and daughters, promoting ethical education as a tool for empowerment.[30] Li Qingzhao (1084–c.1155), known as the greatest woman poet in premodern China, confidently presented a critique of the major male writers of the Northern Song period in her essay "On Song Lyrics" (Ci lun), demonstrating why her ci songs were more genuine and far better than men's.[31] In the Preface to her famous anthology of women's poetry, Mingyuan shiwei (Classic Poetry by Famous Women, 1667), Wang Duanshu (1621–before 1685) argued that women's poems "complement their predecessors and form a classic in their own right – a complementary canon [wei] answering to the Six Classics."³² Like Ban Zhao and Li Qingzhao, Wang Duanshu and the writers she anthologized are examples of women who acquired literary immortality mainly through literature.

These women received the same classical education as their male counterparts, and they often used historical allusions in their poetry, establishing connections with previous literary models. Thus, when Lady Ban Jieyu (*c*.48–*c*.6 BCE), the great-aunt of Ban Zhao, wrote her "Rhapsody of Self-Commiseration" (Zidao fu) after losing favor with emperor Cheng, she opened the poem with an image that immediately invoked the opening lines of Qu Yuan's "Encountering Sorrow." Like Qu Yuan, who went back to his ancestor "the high lord Gao Yang" for moral support, Ban Jieyu wrote: "Heir to virtue bequeathed by my ancestors / Endowed in life with a noble genius."³³ But unlike Qu Yuan's tone of defiance, Ban Jieyu's voice is one of stoic acceptance and perseverance. Her poem is a statement of moral power and remembrance for her many stages of self-realization. The power of authorship allows her to express her moral approach to abandonment, and eventually canonizes her. Ban Jieyu was later included in the Confucian classic *Lienv zhuan* (*Biographies of Exemplary Women*), a standard handbook for the ethical education of women in traditional China. The story of the virtuous and long-suffering Ban Jieyu as an abandoned woman won much sympathy from later readers, such that one reader (who probably lived a century or so later) even forged a fan poem, entitled "Song of Resentment," under Ban Jieyu's name. In the poem, the abandoned woman compares herself to a fan of white silk, which is discarded by her lord in the cool autumn once the summer heat is over. This poem has been most famously attributed to Ban Jieyu, even though it should be classified under the category of "unknown authorship." The tension between the veracity of authorship and the function of imputed authorial identity is well expressed by Stephen Owen: "Even a reader who did not believe in her authorship of the poem would still expect to find her name in the usual chronological position in the table of contents of the compilation and to find the poem under her name."³⁴ In other words, this chronological method of authorship classification is powerful because it serves both as a preservation mechanism and a way of canonization.

Another distinctive phenomenon of Chinese literary culture is the male literati's general support of women poets. Especially during the Ming-Qing periods, the male literati, harboring a growing dissatisfaction with the political system, gradually withdrew from the conventional world of public service. These "marginalized" men often took up the responsibility of canonizing women writers, publishing anthologies of women writers in unprecedented numbers. Many of these anthologies were edited or sponsored by male literati who had dedicated life-long careers to vigorously supporting women's writing. Of course, the flourishing of women's publications was also the making of Ming-Qing women themselves, who showed an unprecedented "eagerness to preserve their own literary works and to participate, through publication, manuscript circulation, and social networks, in the building of a female literary community."[35] But male literati, with their keen interest in reading, editing, compiling, and evaluating the works of women, helped create China's first episode of "women's studies," without which the concept of "Chinese authorship" would rest on much thinner ground. One of their strategies in canonizing women writers was to compare their anthologies of women poets to the classical canon, the *Shijing* (*Classic of Poetry*), the earliest poetic anthology reputedly compiled by Confucius. Similarly, they looked up to Qu Yuan's "Lisao" ("Encountering Sorrow") as a model for women's works; Qu Juesheng even named his anthology of women's poetry the *Female Sao* (*nü sao*, 1618).

Several other factors contributed to the sudden explosion in the publication of women's works during the Ming: the spread of printing; the rise of literacy among women and the merchant class; and the demands of commercial publishing. In her book *Teachers of the Inner Chambers*, Dorothy Ko discusses the commercial publishing boom and the birth of a new reading public that began in the mid-sixteenth century during the second half of the Ming dynasty, when "the supply of and demand for books soared."[36] Under such circumstances, commercial presses greatly popularized women writers by printing women's anthologies for mass production, expanding the readership for women's works to unprecedented levels.

At the same time, women's anthologies suffered from a laxity in their criteria for selection, which led later scholars to doubt the authenticity of some works included in Ming anthologies. Due to the competition of commercial publications, many book dealers might have felt it necessary to pad the anthologies with additional material. Even Li Qingzhao, the famous Song dynasty woman poet who lived four hundred years before the mid-Ming, underwent a drastic process of textual reconstruction when Ming scholars could no longer determine the authenticity of many of the song lyrics (*ci*) attributed to her. All the original collections of Li Qingzhao's writings had been lost by Ming times, and only twenty-three poems or so were thought to be truly hers. But beginning in the Ming, publishers kept adding new attributions to Li Qingzhao. As the modern scholar Ronald Egan notes, "[a]n anthology that included a few 'new' pieces by Li Qingzhao [...] would attract attention and potential buyers."[37] No wonder that "by the end of the Qing dynasty, the number of song lyrics variously attributed to Li Qingzhao had swelled from the 36 attributed to her in surviving Southern Song sources to 75, more than double the number of early attributions."[38] Thus, to this day, the authenticity of some of Li Qingzhao's works is still being questioned.

While the entire book publishing industry became obsessed with this new genre of "women's writing," poems attributed to contemporary women were often invented under these conditions. For example, poems that may have been based on fictional accounts ended up in Zhong Xing's (1574–1624) anthology *Poetic Retrospective of Famous Ladies* (*Mingyuan shigui*).[39] Zhong Xing was famous for championing a quality of "purity" in women (*qing*); in his anthology, Zhong Xing specifically urged readers to open their eyes to the distinctive power of "purity" in women's poetry.[40] In his view, while women were naturally endowed with this innate quality, contemporary male poets had already lost this essential poetic sense in their pursuit of artificiality and worldly success. Later, another Ming writer, Zou Yi, even said that "the humor of the cosmic *qing shu* [the pure and the gentle] does not occur in males, but it does in females."[41] Such comments on women, especially coming from eminent poet-scholars like Zhong Xing, might have encouraged the printing presses to bring out more poems by women, even if the poets' authorship was in doubt.

New Concepts of Authorship in Drama and Fiction

Even more fluid and capacious than authorship in poetry is authorship in Chinese drama and fiction during the late Ming and early Qing, when re-writing and re-packaging became the norm. In her book *Theaters of Desire*, Patricia Sieber discusses how Ming scholars and editors rewrote texts of plays and songs from earlier periods to create what she calls "reproductive authorship."[42] This kind of authorship does not emphasize originality in the same way that writers today prize originality for reasons of copyright and intellectual property. For example, the Ming writer Li Kaixian (1502–1568) devoted much of his life to rewriting the texts of "Northern Drama" from the previous dynasty and published sixteen rewritten plays under the title *Revised Plays by Distinguished Yuan Authors* (*Gaiding Yuan xian chuangqi*).[43] Ming readers credited Li with partial authorship of these reworked texts. As for Li himself, he considered his "rewriting" of Yuan plays as one of his most important contributions, for he was proud to be recognized as the greatest expert of the time in dramatic texts. "Originality" was not an issue; what counted was his contribution toward textual transmissions.

Jin Shengtan (1608–1661) provides a similar example in the field of fiction. Jin revised the novel *Water Margin* (*Shuihu zhuan*) from its original one hundred and twenty chapters into a seventy-chapter version and, in the last year of the Ming, published his "new" *Water Margin* with copious commentaries, some of which are longer than the "original" text. Jin was also the first person to attribute the authorship of the "original" novel to a single writer named Shi Nai'an (dates unknown); previously, the novel was often credited to multiple authors, including Luo Guanzhong (fl. 1330–1400). According to the modern scholar Tina Lu, "Jin Shengtan's commentaries are acts of creative writing in every sense."[44] Jin not only "put his name to his commentary," but also "couched his editorial additions" as "restorations" of the original text, such that his commentary served as a "self-conscious composition."[45] More recently, Roland Altenburger called attention to the commercial aspect of Jin Shengtan's rewriting and commentary project: "[Jin] invented individual authorship as a strategy of appropriating the *Shuihu zhuan* to win scholarly fame, and perhaps even more importantly, to achieve commercial success."[46] That Jin came from Suzhou, one of the major centers of book publishing, makes this theory about Jin's "commercial" enterprise very convincing.

Authorship of the *Dream of the Red Chamber*

In sharp contrast to Jin Shengtan, who took a public and commercial approach in printing his *Water Margin*, the author of the eighteenth-century novel *Dream of the Red Chamber* (also known as *The Story of the Stone*) favored a private and non-profit-oriented approach by circulating his text only in manuscript form among his close relatives and friends. It was not until three decades after the death of the author (assuming the later constructed authorship is correct), when the *Dream* was printed by a publisher and an editor, that the novel finally reached a "mass distribution" and gradually came to be known as China's greatest novel.[47]

The introduction to the first chapter of the *Dream of the Red Chamber* seems to indicate that the author intended for the novel to be somewhat personal and autobiographical, recording the deeds of those "wonderful girls" whom he knew in his youth:

Having made an utter failure of my life, I found myself one day, in the midst of my poverty and wretchedness, thinking about the female companions of my youth. As I went over them one by one, examining and comparing them in my mind's eye, it suddenly came over me that those slips of girls – which is all they were then – were in every way, both morally and intellectually, superior to the "grave and mustachioed signior" I am now supposed to have become. The realization brought with it an overwhelming sense of shame and remorse, and for a while I was plunged in the deepest despair. There and then I resolved to make a record of all the recollections of those days I could muster – those golden days when I dressed in silk and ate delicately, when we still nestled in the protecting shadow of the Ancestors and Heaven still smiled on us. I resolved to tell the world how, in defiance of all my family's attempts to bring me up properly and all the warnings and advice of my friends, I had brought myself to this present wretched state, in which, having frittered away half a lifetime, I find myself without a single skill with which I could earn a decent living. I resolved that, however unsightly my own shortcomings might be, I must not, for the sake of keeping them hid, allow those wonderful girls to pass into oblivion without a memorial.[48]

But who was the author of this novel, who used such a confessional voice? Although the author did mention in chapter one a certain Cao Xueqin, who in his Nostalgia Studio worked on the novel for ten years, one could not be certain if Cao Xueqin was the real name of the author, for Cao did sound more like someone who merely transmitted the story. So what was the true identity of the author?

In 1792, when Gao E and Cheng Weiyuan published a printed edition of the novel in 120 chapters, claiming that "no one knows for sure who wrote this book," readers speculated wildly on the identity of the author.[49] It was not until 1927, roughly one hundred and thirty-five years later, that an important Red Inkstone manuscript was discovered, and the authorship issue for the first eighty chapters of the novel was more or less settled. The manuscript clearly contains the original commentator Red Inkstone's note: "Xueqin, having run out of tears, departed this life on the last day of ren-wu [12 February 1763], leaving his book unfinished."[50] Red Inkstone, whose name also appears in chapter one of the novel, was obviously a person very close to the author. Throughout the 80-chapter manuscript (titled *The Story of the Stone*), Red Inkstone and another commentator, Old Tablet, repeatedly reminded the author of remembered facts, sometimes even demanding a change in plot to spare the name of a certain relative. In this sense, this novel is an instance where traditional Chinese commentators and readers can be considered "co-authors." In fact, in an early section of the novel, the authorial persona suggests precisely such an idea, when he describes how consecutive readers, including himself, continually changed the title of the novel from "The Story of the Stone" to "The Tale of Brother Amor," and then to "A Mirror for the Romantic," "A Dream of Golden Days," and "The Twelve Beauties of Jinling." Finally, Red Inkstone restored the original title, "The Story of the Stone," when he "recopied the book and added his second set of annotations to it."[51] Clearly, this account, though presented in the context of fiction, reveals a close community of readers (or co-authors) who worked together to refine the title and content of the novel.

To this date, however, the authorship of the last forty chapters of the novel remains a puzzle. So far, every Red Inkstone manuscript that has been found contains only eighty chapters. What troubles scholars most is the fact that the 120-chapter edition, published almost thirty years after Cao Xueqin's death, which Gao E claimed to have edited, contains forty final chapters whose plot drastically diverges from how the novel should end according to Red Inkstone's commentary. Could Gao E's forty chapters be a forgery, or, as Gao E himself claimed in his Preface to the 120-chapter edition, merely a reworking of an old defective manuscript acquired by his friend Cheng Weiyuan?[52] With no clear evidence, we may never solve this mystery of authorship. Perhaps these questions are part of the author's fictional design. Throughout the novel, the author cleverly uses the device of fiction (*xiaoshuo*) to mingle remembered fact with a fictional framework. When he says, "Truth becomes fiction when the fiction's true / Real becomes not-real when the unreal's real," he is already guiding us to a Reality that could be both real and illusive.[53]

Western Sinologists' Detective Work on Authorship

Perhaps inspired by this concept of the "real" and "illusive," Western sinologists engage obsessively in detective work regarding Chinese authorship, using the methods of historicism. An example is Paul Ropp, whose interest in Shi Zhenlin's (1693–1779) *Random Notes from Xiqing* (*Xiqing sanji*), a memoir about the talented peasant woman poet Shuangqing, led him to trace the evolution of Shuangqing's story, from the initial publication of Shi's book in 1737 to the present day. During his research, Ropp developed skepticism about Shuangqing's very existence, for he found Shi Zhenlin's recollection of the talented woman poet and her interactions with Shi and his friends unconvincing as a historical document. Furthermore, were the poems cited in Shi Zhenlin's memoir really by the peasant woman Shuangqing?

Ropp was not the first person to doubt the identity of Shuangqing. As early as the 1920s, Hu Shi was already claiming that Shuangqing might be a total fabrication of Shi Zhenlin's.[54] In the early 1990s, another Chinese scholar, Zhengguo Kang, published in-depth research about the circuitous textual transformation surrounding the image of Shuangqing. Yet in modern Chinese literary history, Shuangqing continues to be a cultural icon, widely acclaimed as China's only great peasant woman poet and certainly the greatest woman poet of the eighteenth century. At the same time, Shuangqing has appeared widely in women's poetry anthologies, including a modern English anthology compiled by the American poet Kenneth Rexroth and his co-translator Chung Ling.[55]

Ropp thus felt undecided on the issue of Shuangqing. Finally, in 1997, along with the two Chinese scholars Du Fangqin and Zhang Hongsheng, he took a three-month investigative trip to the rural counties of Jintan and Danyang in Jiangsu, China, where the poet supposedly lived. His main goal was to discover whether Shuangqing was a real historical figure or merely Shi Zhenlin's fictional creation. For the purpose of the trip, Ropp even drew a detailed map based on Shi Zhenlin's description of the various sites in Jin Tan. In their visit to Jintan and Danyang, Ropp and the two Chinese scholars also interviewed many local people, collecting oral retellings of the Shuangqing story. Ropp's book *Banished Immortal: Searching for Shuangqing, China's Peasant Woman Poet* (2002) was largely based on his findings and reflections from this trip. Ultimately, Ropp became even more skeptical about Shuangqing's historical existence. To Ropp, none of the sites they had visited, or the oral retellings they had collected, could provide historical evidence for Shuangqing's identity.

In sharp contrast, the Chinese scholar Du Fangqin drew a totally different conclusion. Du Fangqin is a renowned expert of Shuangqing studies in China and the author of the *Collected Poems of He Shuangqing* (*He Shuangqing ji*, 1993). Unlike Ropp, Du felt even more strongly about Shuangqing's historical existence after the trip. According to her argument, even if the peasant woman's name were not Shuangqing, her image as a talented woman poet must have been based on a real person, especially because the highly cultivated Jintan region produced many contemporary women poets.[56] Du had no doubt that the poems attributed to Shuangqing were genuine. Also, judging from the writing style in Shi Zhenlin's memoir, Du was not convinced that Shi had the ability to produce the high-caliber poems supposedly written by Shuangqing. Indeed, Du was so inspired by this trip to Jintan and Danyang that she produced a *Biography of Shuangqing* (*Tong ju nai he shuang: Shuangqing zhuan*), which was so well received that it was serialized on the Chinese Internet in 1999. (The book was published in 2001.)

The story of Shuangqing's reconstructed authorship reminds us of many other similar examples in Chinese literature. For example, the Chinese regard Zhu Shuzhen (1135?–1180?) as one of the two greatest women poets in the Song dynasty (the other being Li Qingzhao), and her poems are popular among Chinese readers to this day. But in recent years, Western sinologists Ronald Egan and Wilt Idema questioned Zhu Shuzhen's historicity, suggesting that "it is likely that most if not all of the poems attributed to Zhu Shuzhen were written by men."[57] Many Chinese scholars these days appreciate the painstaking research of Western sinologists, which has led to valuable insights and questions about authorship. But most Chinese readers still find it difficult to question the very existence of writers who hold such important places in Chinese literary tradition. To them, what matters is the voice, the personality, the persona, and the energy that are associated with the "author." Even when authorship is full of ambiguities, it is still important to have an author, for it is a name that functions as a certain organizing power. Perhaps Foucault's idea of "an author" assuming a "classificatory function" – by permitting one "to group together a certain number of texts, define them, differentiate them from and contrast them to others"[58] – can best describe the Chinese notion of what an author means.

Notes

1. *Mencius*, trans. D. C. Lau (London: Penguin, 1970), p. 114.
2. Sima Qian, "Letter to Jen An (Shao-ch'ing)," trans. J. R. Hightower, in *Anthology of Chinese Literature*, ed. Cyril Birch, vol. 1 (New York: Grove Press, 1965), p. 101. For questions regarding the authorship of Sima Qian's letter, see Stephen Durrant, Wai-yee Li, Michael Nylan, and Hans Van Ess, *The Letter to Ren An & Sima Qian's Legacy* (Seattle: University of Washington Press, 2016).
3. Sima Qian, *Shiji*, 10 vols. (Beijing: Zhonghua shuju, 1959), *juan* 47, p. 1936.
4. Ibid., p. 1937.
5. Wai-yee Li, *The Readability of the Past in Early Chinese Historiography* (Cambridge, MA: Harvard University Asia Center, 2007), p. 31; Edward L. Shaughnessy, *Before Confucius: Studies in the Creation of the Chinese Classics* (Albany, NY: State University of New York Press, 1997), pp. 1–2.
6. Alexander Beecroft, *Authorship and Cultural Identity in Early Greece and China: Patterns of Literary Circulation* (Cambridge: Cambridge University Press, 2010), pp. 177–78.

7. Edward L. Shaughnessy, *Rewriting Early Chinese Texts* (Albany, NY: State University of New York Press, 2006), pp. 63–64.

8. Michael Hunter, *Confucius Beyond the Analects* (Leiden: Brill, 2017). See also Mark Csikszentmihalyi, "Interlocutor Collections, the *Lunyu*, and Proto-*Lunyu* Texts," ch. 8 in *Confucius and the Analects Revisited: New Perspectives on Composition, Dating, and Authorship*, eds. Michael Hunter and Martin Kern (Leiden: Brill, 2018), pp. 218–40.

9. David Schaberg, "Orality and the Origins of Zuozhuan and Guoyu," in his *A Patterned Past: Form and Thought in Early Chinese Historiography* (Cambridge, MA: Harvard Asia Center, 2001), pp. 315–24; see also Li, *Readability of the Past*, p. 49.

10. Haun Saussy, *The Ethnography of Rhythm: Orality and Its Technologies* (New York: Fordham University Press, 2016). Quoting from the synopsis on the back of the book.

11. Raji C. Steineck and Christian Schwermann, "Introduction," in *That Wonderful Composite Called Author: Authorship in East Asian Literatures from the Beginnings to the Seventeenth Century*, eds. Christian Schwermann and Raji C. Steineck (Leiden and Boston: Brill, 2014), pp. 20–22.

12. Beecroft, *Authorship and Cultural Identity*, p. 3.

13. James Legge, *The She King*, vol. 5 of *The Chinese Classics* (Oxford: Clarendon, 1871), p. 4.

14. Martin Kern, "Early Chinese Literature, Beginnings Through Western Han," in *The Cambridge History of Chinese Literature*, eds. Kang-i Sun Chang and Stephen Owen (Cambridge: Cambridge University Press, 2010), vol. 1 (ed. Stephen Owen), p. 39.

15. Sima Qian, *Shiji, juan* 130, p. 3300. See also Sima Qian, "Letter to Jen An (Shao-ch'ing)," in Birch, ed., *Anthology of Chinese Literature*, vol. 1, p. 101.

16. Sima Qian, *Shiji, juan* 84, p. 2503.

17. David Hawkes, trans., *The Songs of the South: An Ancient Chinese Anthology of Poems by Qu Yuan and Other Poets* (Harmondsworth, UK: Penguin, 1985), p. 64.

18. Ibid., pp. 36–51.

19. Kern, "Early Chinese Literature, Beginnings Through Western Han," in *The Cambridge History of Chinese Literature*, eds. Chang and Owen, vol. 1 (ed. Owen), p. 79. See also Stephen Owen, "Poetry and Authorship," in *How to Read Chinese Poetry in Context: Poetic Culture from Antiquity through the Tang*, ed. Zong-qi Cai (New York: Columbia University Press, 2017), pp. 30–47.

20. Paul Rouzer, *A Buddhist Reading of the Hanshan Poems* (Seattle: University of Washington Press, 2016), p. 10.

21. Stephen Owen, *Readings in Chinese Literary Thought* (Cambridge, MA: Council on East Asian Studies, Harvard University, 1992), p. 290. For the complete translation of *Wenxin diaolong*, see Vincent Yu-chung Shih, *trans.* and annotated, *The Literary Mind and the Carving of Dragons: A Study of*

Thought and Pattern in Chinese Literature (Hong Kong: The Chinese University Press, 1983).

22. *Mencius*, trans. Lau, p. 142.

23. Owen, *Readings in Chinese Literary Thought*, p. 291.

24. Anna M. Shields, *One Who Knows Me: Friendship and Literary Culture in Mid-Tang China* (Cambridge, MA: Harvard University Asia Center, 2015).

25. Wai-yee Li, *Women and National Trauma in Late Imperial Chinese Literature* (Cambridge, MA: Harvard University Asia Center, 2014), p. 13.

26. Lawrence Lipking, *Abandoned Women and Poetic Tradition* (Chicago: University of Chicago Press, 1988), p. 133.

27. Li, *Women and National Trauma*, pp. 14–24.

28. Ibid., pp. 17–24.

29. See Haun Saussy, "Introduction: Genealogy and Titles of the Female Poet," in *Women Writers of Traditional China: An Anthology of Poetry and Criticism*, eds. Kang-I Sun Chang and Haun Saussy (Stanford, CA: Stanford University Press, 1999), pp. 1–14.

30. Wilt Idema and Beata Grant, *The Red Brush: Writing Women of Imperial China* (Cambridge, MA: Harvard University Asia Center, 2004), p. 26.

31. Ronald Egan, *The Burden of Female Talent: The Poet Li Qingzhao and Her History in China* (Cambridge, MA: Harvard University Asia Center, 2013), pp. 75–90.

32. Haun Saussy, trans., "Wang Duanshu and her Anthology *Mingyuan shiwei*," in *Women Writers of Traditional China*, eds. Chang and Saussy, p. 693.

33. David R. Knechtges, trans., "Rhapsody of Self-Commiseration," in *Women Writers of Traditional China*, eds. Chang and Saussy, p. 19.

34. Stephen Owen, *The Making of Early Chinese Classical Poetry* (Cambridge, MA: Harvard Asia Center, 2006), p. 2.

35. See Saussy, "Introduction: Genealogy and Titles of the Female Poet," p. 8.

36. Dorothy Ko, *Teachers of the Inner Chambers: Women and Culture in Seventeenth Century China* (Stanford, CA: Stanford University Press, 1994), pp. 34–41.

37. Egan, *Burden of Female Talent*, p. 99.

38. Ibid., p. 92.

39. Kang-i Sun Chang, "Literature of the Early Ming to Mid-Ming," in *The Cambridge History of Chinese Literature*, eds. Kang-i Sun Chang and Stephen Owen (Cambridge: Cambridge University Press, 2010), vol. 2 (ed. Kang-I Sun Chang), p. 49.

40. Longxi Zhang, trans., "Zhong Xing's Preface to *Mingyuan shigui*," in *Women Writers of Traditional China*, eds. Chang and Saussy, pp. 739–41.

41. Kang-I Sun Chang, "Gender and Canonicity: Ming-Qing Women Poets in the Eyes of the Male Literati," in *Hsiang Lectures on Chinese Poetry*, vol. 1 (Montreal: McGill University, 2001), p. 5.

42. Patricia Sieber, *Theaters of Desire: Authors, Readers, and the Reproduction of Early Chinese Song-Drama, 1300–2000* (New York: Palgrave Macmillan, 2003), p. 84.

43. Kang-i Sun Chang, "Literature of the Early Ming to Mid-Ming," in *The Cambridge History of Chinese Literature*, eds. Kang-i Sun Chang and Stephen Owen (Cambridge: Cambridge University Press, 2010), vol. 2 (ed. Chang), p. 57.

44. Tina Lu, "Literary Culture of the Late Ming (1573–1644)," in *The Cambridge History of Chinese Literature*, ed. Chang and Owen, vol. 2 (ed. Chang), p. 113.

45. Lu, "Literary Culture," p. 114.

46. Roland Altenburger, "Appropriating Genius: Jin Shengtan's Construction of Textual Authority and Authorship in His Commented Edition of Shuihu Zhuan (The Water Margin Saga)," in *That Wonderful Composite*, eds. Schwermann and Steineck, p. 78.

47. Cheow Thia Chan, "Readership, Agency in Mass Distribution and Fiction as a Literary Field: The Case of the Story of the Stone," unpublished paper, pp. 9–21.

48. David Hawkes, trans., *The Story of the Stone: Volume 1*, by Cao Xueqin (London: Penguin, 1973), p. 20.

49. Haun Saussy, "Authorship and the Story of the Stone: Open Question," in *Approaches to Teaching the Story of the Stone (Dream of the Red Chamber)*, eds. Andrew Schonebaum and Tina Lu (New York: Modern Language Association, 2012), p. 143.

50. Hawkes, trans., *The Story of the Stone*, vol. 1, p. 35.

51. Ibid., p. 51.

52. Ibid., p. 41.

53. Ibid., pp. 44–45.

54. Paul Ropp, *Banished Immortal: Searching for Shuangqing, China's Peasant Poet* (Ann Arbor: The University of Michigan Press, 2001), pp. 252–56.

55. Kenneth Rexroth and Ling Chung, *Women Poets of China* (New York: A New Directions Book, 1972), pp. 66–67, 124–25.

56. Ropp, *Banished Immortal*, p. 255.

57. Egan, *Burden of Female Talent*, p. 35.

58. Michel Foucault, "What Is an Author?", in *Textual Strategies: Perspectives in Post-Structuralist Criticism*, ed. Josué V. Harari (Ithaca, NY: Cornell University Press, 1979), pp. 141–60, p. 147.

CHAPTER 14

Literary Authorship in the Digital Age

Adriaan van der Weel

Throughout the history of text technology, the impetus of innovation has always been the faster production of more texts, to be consumed by more readers. But the effects have never been confined to merely quantitative change. The introduction of new technologies has also inspired new writers to take up the pen, writing about new subjects, inventing new genres, and reaching new social strata of readers. This happened after Gutenberg's invention of printing with movable type, when entrepreneurial printers started to cast around for fresh writing to print and sell. It happened again in the nineteenth century after a quick succession of printing innovations made books cheaper and more widely available, leading to such new genres as detective fiction and popular romance. The mass education revolution of the second half of the nineteenth century enabled large groups of the population to emancipate themselves socially and intellectually. Everyone who had a mind to do so could turn to reading for knowledge, culture, and entertainment. Thanks to the growing size of the print economy, authorship could become a profession.

Today there is a screen revolution underway, and once again more texts are being produced, to be distributed still faster, to be consumed by yet more readers. And once again more people are writing than ever before in history – writing about new subjects, inventing new genres, and reaching new social strata of readers. One of the most fascinating and best-documented cases in recent times to illustrate this is that of E. L. James. Having started her *Fifty Shades* trilogy as web-based fan fiction, James went on in 2011 to self-publish it as an e-book and print-on-demand paperback after there had been complaints about its sexually explicit nature. Snapped up by a commercial publisher, it subsequently turned into one of the greatest publishing successes ever. In August 2013, the trilogy's earnings of $95 million brought James to the top of the *Forbes* list of highest-earning authors. By June 2015 she had sold over 125 million copies worldwide.

The E. L. James trilogy success story constitutes living proof of the brave new world of egalitarian twenty-first-century publication possibilities. The economic investment in production and distribution required in the case of paper-based self-publishing easily led to it being equated with vanity publishing. Paying for publication was tantamount to blowing one's own trumpet. If James managed to remove that vanity stigma, she was aided in no small measure by one of the unique properties of the digital medium: the ability to keep copying a text endlessly at virtually zero marginal cost means that no investment is required beyond the cost of creating the first copy.

There is much to be said about the phenomenon of the *Fifty Shades* trilogy. It may perhaps have made pornography more mainstream than it had already become in the permissive 1960s and 1970s. It may have helped to emancipate its readers, inspiring them to dare to express their fantasies. But in the present connection probably the most interesting question to ask is how – and more precisely, when – E. L. James became a published author. Clearly, she wasn't one when she first put tentative fingers to keyboard to explore her private sexual fantasies. Few would contend that she should be called one today. Whatever we may think the answer to that question should be, it is clear that it would have been a lot harder – if not impossible – for her to rise to the ranks of published authorship without the publication opportunities offered by the digital medium. Desiring to express her fantasies in public is not the same thing as being *able* to do so. But might she even have had that desire: might the thought have occurred to her in a more than desultory way if a fan fiction platform had not been available to her? It is in offering to anyone and everyone the ability to express oneself in public that the digital element can be most truly called revolutionary. Here, *Fifty Shades* represents of course merely the tip of a vast iceberg.

The fascinating thing to observe is that the social consequences of the digital medium, as is always the case with technological innovation, not only extend far beyond the merely quantitative: they are very often not even intended. Indeed, when they first occur they may even be deemed undesirable, for instance because they upset, or threaten to upset, established social power relations. These social effects are so insidious precisely because they are unintended: we are rarely aware of them before they have taken effect. This is exactly what is happening now in the case of the current screen revolution. Even as today we find ourselves still in the midst of an ongoing transformation, it is only natural that we should wish to understand the nature of the changes. But what we should really aim for is to understand their *implications*. When attempting to understand and explain the mechanisms underlying these bewildering contemporary developments, it is helpful to take a longer historical perspective so as to avoid the disorienting feeling of being caught up as observers in the rapidly moving stream of current events.

From the first discovery of the power of writing, the concept of authorship, along with that of readership – and even literacy – has been repeatedly transformed and redefined. The twenty-first-century screen revolution is once again bringing home just how historically contingent such concepts actually are. The paper world is essentially hierarchical and top-down. Only the privileged have access to print to reply to anything they have read. Others are confined to making approving or disapproving notes in the margins of their reading. Online, the author–reader relationship essentially swivels by 90 degrees to become horizontal and "democratic." But in the meantime, the hierarchical print world with all its access barriers has not vanished. Since it is almost impossible to maintain a clear demarcation between notions of pre-digital authorship and digital writing practices, and since both occur in parallel in our hybrid analog–digital media world, this is effectively setting adrift the concept of authorship in its entirety.

In this hybrid world, all of the conventional publication channels are still in operation, even if the output is no longer confined to paper products. The majority of books are still sold in their familiar paper form, though they are increasingly complemented by e-books. But no doubt as a consequence of their more ephemeral nature, a large number of newspapers have migrated to Web-only publication, though many follow a hybrid paper–digital strategy. In addition to these existing, let us call them formal, publishing outlets, however, the Web offers new and widely accessible opportunities for the public expression of ideas hovering between the formal and the informal in countless shades of grey.

Self-publishing actually so called is available, both in paper and digital forms, from platforms such as Lulu, Blurb, Kobo (Writing Life), or Amazon (Kindle Direct). A multitude of Web and app-based opportunities to make one's writings public are also offered by, for example, WattPad; www.xianxiaworld.net (Chinese fantasy); archiveofourown.org or fanfiction.net. Fanfiction.net is where E. L. James, disguised as "Snowqueen's Icedragon," started to write off her midlife crisis in what was to become the *Fifty Shades* trilogy. In the process she launched herself, almost accidentally, into a career as an author. Online, one does not necessarily have to think of oneself as a writer to be able to share one's thoughts and opinions with a wider readership. Web 2.0-based social media such as Facebook, Reddit, WhatsApp, or Tumblr have so far democratized the means of publication that the most ephemeral utterances may now be communicated on public platforms. In the Web 2.0 environment absolutely everything is geared – socially and technologically – toward making it easy for readers to contribute to the conversation. It is hard to imagine a more level field for author and reader to meet. Indeed, one may well wonder how their roles may be distinguished. E. L. James, we may recall, set out on her writing career as a reader – and a very devoted one at that – as a fan of the *Twilight* vampire series by Stephenie Meyer.

What makes the evolution of this democratized online writing environment especially fascinating is the extent to which the social impetus and the technological impetus are intertwined. On the technology side, there is the history of the Internet and the World Wide Web: the history of how electronic text forms came to be produced, distributed, and consumed on a global network of digital screens. Digital technology has come with a range of inherent properties, from the infinite and lossless copyability of digital files, already mentioned, to their machine readability, multimodality and ultimate fluidity. Thus, digital technology made a perfect match with an ideological drive toward "free knowledge," succinctly expressed in the countercultural slogan "information wants to be free." This in turn must be understood in the context of the Internet's origin in the secluded, even rarefied, environment of the military and academic communities, in both of which the profit motive was markedly absent. Contrary to the cut-and-paste techniques used in the analog print production process, the truly revolutionary copy-and-paste potential of the digital environment was actually able to deliver on that oft-repeated rallying cry.

At roughly the same time, there was also a strong impetus toward "liberation" of the reader from the "dictates of a tyrannical author." The poststructuralist disposition to deprecate the author's authority stands out in particular. In their various ways, Barthes, Foucault, and Derrida had long been skeptical of authorial authority. Going back a little further, that poststructuralist stance, incidentally, may well itself have been a response to the modernist sensibility, which asserted the author's position as a member of an intellectual elite – while modernism in its turn had been, at least in part, a reaction to the much feared and much derided democratization and vulgarization of reading in the mass education revolution of the second half of the nineteenth century that we already encountered earlier.[1]

In the early 1990s, a group of influential American academics became fascinated by hypertext as a promising technology to help undermine the author's power. Following the lead of Barthes and the other French poststructuralist theorists, they seized on hypertext as the technological implementation of the theoretical notion of the readerly literary text. The term "hypertext" had been coined by Theodor Nelson in the 1960s, but the technology's concept had many fathers, also including Vannevar Bush, Andries van Dam, and Douglas Engelbart. What they shared was a deep motivation to empower the reader as the user of an information system. As one of the academics who recognized hypertext's potential early on, Jay David Bolter, astutely remarks in *Writing Space: The Computer, Hypertext, and the History of Writing* (1991), the New Criticism – itself a distinctly Modernist phenomenon – had been squarely based on fixity as an inherent property of the printed text, "self-sufficient, perfect, and untouchable" (149). Similarly, he goes on to note, "[n]ot only the reader-response and spatial-form but even the most radical theorists (Barthes, de Man, Derrida, and their American followers) speak a language that is strikingly appropriate to electronic writing" (161).

Bolter was perhaps the first to be struck by the remarkable parallels between French critical theory and American digital technology. But it was George Landow who explored this notion most fully, in his *Hypertext: The Convergence of Contemporary Critical Theory and Technology* (1992). More than Bolter, Landow seemed to exult in the opportunity technology held out to him to dance on the author's grave. The last section of *Hypertext*, entitled "The Politics of Hypertext: Who Controls the Text?", celebrates the reader's liberation from all unwarranted yet institutionalized exercise of power. There are unmistakable overtones here of the Marxist notion that the socialist revolution would eventually bring the means of production under the control of the people. The belief in the advent of a new era of liberation in which the consumer would achieve complete hegemony over the text by taking full control of its production has a similarly religious tinge to it.

The historical irony is that the prophets turned out to be right, only not in the way they had envisaged. Yes, hypertext did indeed go on to become a great success. In the form of HTML, it has seen a tremendously popular implementation on the WWW, instigated by Tim Berners-Lee in 1990. Hyperlinking turned out to be perfectly suited to the Internet's inherent property of two-directionality on which its client-server architecture was based from its inception. Given the current popularity of the Web, the hypertextual transformation of our textual world could thus be said to have been more thorough than even Landow, for all his revolutionary ideology, foresaw. However, it left the way literary fiction was written and read – the central focus of the fervid American theorizing of the early 1990s – almost entirely untouched. Not only has it done remarkably little to inspire authors' literary imagination, from their side, readers too have shown hardly any interest in electronic literature.[2] Whether discouraged by its cold reception or because of their own lack of enthusiasm, few serious authors ever bothered to explore hypertext's potential. Today the Electronic Literature Organization maintains a small and languishing presence on the Web.

That the history of hypertext is also that of a failed political project of denigrating the author's role does not mean, however, that democratization of authorship has not in fact happened. It just happened differently from how the theorists predicted it would. More importantly than professional authors ceding to the reader a significant portion of their authorial power (notably the final responsibility for the narrative that the theorists coveted so much), the newly empowered readers have seized the opportunity provided by technology to be in even fuller control. They elevated themselves to the rank of published authors. This technology was not just hypertext per se. Crucially, the technology that readers adopted with unprecedented speed and enthusiasm was that of Web 2.0, from 2006. Hypertext may have been designed to place the existing, conventional author–reader relationship on a more equal footing, but it wasn't enough. Authorship still required access to the means of production – a server connected to the Internet. It was Web 2.0, incidentally making grateful use of hypertext technology, that enabled the person formerly known as the reader to morph into a "wreader" or "prosumer." Now anyone with an Internet connection could truly be a published author.

Social attitudes to authorship and textuality on the one hand and revolutionary digital technology on the other jointly made for a heady, not to say explosive mixture. It gave rise, for example, to the ethic that now goes by the name of "remixing." This started as a rather subversive practice in a pioneering spirit, but once Creative Commons licensing took care of legalities it went on to flourish in the mainstream. Creative Commons must therefore not just be understood as the attempt it certainly also was to bring copyright into the networked world of the twenty-first century. Creative Commons was also emphatically intended as a way of breaking down existing barriers to the reuse of creative expressions that would be protected and reserved under conventional copyright paradigms. Creative Commons licensing was and still is the ready solution for those who wish on principle to refrain from exploiting their intellectual property rights, not seeking monetary remuneration but expressly wishing to share with other makers around the globe.

The complex socio-technical process we have just observed at work in the example of hypertext leads to the observation that effects were only partly planned. While a more equitable relationship between author and reader was a conscious aim, the explosion of public online writing in the Web 2.0 arena today was neither planned nor foreseen. Even Mark Zuckerberg could not have predicted just how much intimate information people could be enticed to divulge online about themselves and the vicissitudes of their daily lives. For all that it was unplanned, though, this explosion of writing has managed to upset one of the core elements of the conventional notion of authorship. At least for the last hundred and fifty years, authorship has been closely tied up with publication. Publication was distinctive precisely because it was not available to all and sundry. Once achieved, publication could become a source of prestige, be it economic or symbolic (or a combination) – based on copyright and later intellectual property right (see Alexis Easley's chapter "The Nineteenth Century" and Daniel Cook's chapter "Copyright and Literary Property" in this volume). In the digital domain, by contrast, professional authors rub shoulders with rank amateurs. An important mark of distinction has thus largely fallen away, blurring the boundaries between authorship and "mere" writing.

Given Web 2.0 affordances, "publication" (as in "making public") is becoming contested as an adequate criterion for authorship. The resulting digital confusion has led to a frantic search for new certainties, for example by tightening the definition of authorship. There is a scramble for reasons – whether quantitative or qualitative – to exclude from the criteria for authorship the act of making public through "mere" social media. In an attempt to close the digital sluice gates, it has also been suggested that a text cannot properly be called published unless it has been "read" a given number of times.[3] However understandable the impulse to stem the massive and fast-moving tide of change and by any means instill order in the chaos, any such criteria would amount to no more than stop-gap measures. Rather than attempting new definitions, at this stage it may be more helpful to try to understand more fully the mechanism of socio-technical change that we already saw illustrated in the case of hypertext. What we need to account for is how technology, once employed, always delivers more than it was consciously designed to deliver. Such unlooked-for social side effects tend to be more diffuse than the deliberately sought direct quantitative effects, but not less pervasive for that.

As has become clear by now, this mechanism is not unique to digital technology, let alone to the case of hypertext. All major technological milestones in text production, such as printing with individual movable type in the fifteenth century, the mechanization of print production in the nineteenth, and now digital text forms, were consciously looking to achieve immediate quantitative effects – more texts, faster and more convenient multiplication, more readers. Not surprisingly, from the outset it was one of the frequently voiced laments about the printing press that it caused a deluge of books to be read. The Web has met with exactly the same criticism. Information overload is a timeless concern. Yet these same technological milestones have also been followed at a distance by other, more diffuse but pervasive social consequences: for the type of writing being produced, for the economic position of the author, and for the social role and status of the author. With every technological innovation, reading and literacy have gained a more central place in society. The challenge is to establish a convincing link between the immediate and desired – usually primarily quantitative – effects and the longer-term, unintended, social consequences.

Many critics have been at pains to dismiss McLuhan's apodictic pronouncements of the 1960s about the power of the medium to affect the nature and content of the message. How, the rhetorical question goes, could a mere technology, created and controlled by humans, constitute an active force in its own right? But rather than taking the question as rhetorical, it makes sense to try to answer it seriously. Elsewhere I have suggested that technology can constitute a shaping force on how we act and even think without any human intention or forethought through the mechanism of technological properties and their affordances.[4] Thus the fluidity of digital text enables, as we have seen, remixing and copy-and-pasting. The same property allows the verbal message to remain always computable under the surface shown on the screen.[5] Similarly, the fact that all media and modalities (or data types) are computable on the same screen space comes with the affordance of being able to make messages multi-medial as easily as they can be just textual. Another particularly salient example is the Web's two-directional infrastructure (based in the original client-server architecture of the Internet). Among the many relevant affordances of this salient property is the constellation of web practices that we have already encountered under its popular appellation Web 2.0. Powering the concept of social media, Web 2.0 in its turn is the chief digital development responsible for the unbridled increase in the quantity of published texts.

Crucially, these affordances do not fully derive from conscious and deliberate initial invention. The Web 2.0 affordance of the Internet's two-directional architecture, for example, was not immediately apparent, but was *discovered* in a slow socio-technical process. Yet it is part of the constellation of affordances that shape the authorial message as well as the social position of authors in all sorts of subtle and not so subtle ways. The medium – always a technology – is never neutral, but always affects the content of the message. In other words, the socio-technical environment in which authors work strongly affects the nature and social position of their authorship. Phrased differently, the social position of authorship is always founded in a particular socio-technical constellation of a particular dominant technology for the dissemination of texts and the particular literate mentality it engenders. Let's survey some of the notable social consequences of the current, digital, constellation and describe them more fully.

For the first time in history, technology is offering to make "wreadership" available to all and sundry. That is to say that anyone can make public one's own writing, but equally that it has never been easier to appropriate and repurpose the writings of others. To begin with the latter, this has raised more than a few eyebrows, and led some to ask the question who is in charge? As Frank Rose has observed, "[i]n a command-and-control world, we know who's telling the story; it's the author. But digital media have created an authorship crisis. Once the audience is free to step out of the fiction and start directing events, the entire edifice of twentieth-century mass media begins to crumble."[6] When John Updike, in 2006, responded with horror to Kevin Kelly's vision of a digital library to eclipse all previous attempts to collect the world's knowledge and culture, it was not the scope of Kelly's ambition that he objected to but the implications of the blatant shift in power distribution that it represented. Underneath the strident tone of his writing, it is not hard to detect a note of a certain aggrieved powerlessness. Updike feels the victim, if not of technology, then at least of the unfamiliar mindset – alien even – fostered by digital technology. Updike considers himself a professional author who relies on his writing for an income. Yet here were upstarts and amateurs claiming the right to consider his work fair game for "remixing." One gets the sense that he felt almost humiliated by mere readers encroaching on his, the writer's, territory. The two sides of remixing are pride that someone thinks highly enough of one's work versus the ignominy that one's work is apparently not valued enough in its original form.[7]

Of course, appropriation of the authorial text by the reader has happened throughout all times. As the French critics we encountered earlier have long claimed, readers have always made an active contribution to the communication process, regardless of medium. Another French critic,

Michel de Certeau, referred to this as the reader acting as a nomad, "poaching" the writer's game.[8] This is not just a matter of readers being whimsical and wayward in their interpretation. A lifetime of reading inevitably amounts to "bricolage." The point is not just that it is always the reader who makes the final decision about what to read, but that the meaning derived from the reading depends to such a large extent on the accidental context. Choice may be limited in the compulsory part of one's education, but once that has been completed, there are no more normative expectations. In the absence of a reading "program" for life, each reader's reading comes eventually to resemble a patchwork quilt, with each quilt being the outcome of a unique set of reading experiences. The greater the choice and the smaller the units, the patchier the quilt.

Appropriation, then, is not a new phenomenon, but digital technology adds an array of further possibilities – if not incentives – to recalibrate the power balance between author and reader. By constantly presenting fresh menus and new links, leading to any number of (frequently short) texts, the Web has only added to the fragmentation and patchiness of reading. Hypertext, in the original narrow sense envisaged by Nelson, extends the readers' power to make final decisions even within the individual unitary text. Especially copying-and-pasting, remixing, fan-fiction and so on are explicit expressions of appropriation facilitated in the digital realm. The more power the reader is offered, or arrogates to him- or herself – thus the more active the reader is as an agent in the process – the more responsible he or she becomes for its outcome, as a corollary diminishing the author's role.

But the conflict between authors' and readers' interests has, perhaps paradoxically, been intensified most by Web 2.0 and its utter democratization of access to the means of publication. While it is easy to see how remixing or otherwise repurposing materials written by others – in particular by "professional authors" – can be constructed as an attack or invasion, online technology does not just make it easy to borrow or steal, but offers new power to write publicly. This power is widely and greedily embraced. Though no reliable figures exist, it is likely that more people than ever before in history are now recording their thoughts in words to share them with the world. The very ease with which the upstarts can make their voice heard in public has been widely decried by professional authors, journalists, and cultural critics of all stripes.[9] Particularly the fact that professional and dilettante authors may mingle in the same screen-space is hard to accept. Instead of the solidity of, say, a hardcover book, the only marks of distinction available there are virtual, such as a different Web address.

One of the supposedly deleterious effects of this has been called "the cult of the amateur."[10] It has been often remarked that in the unrestricted online publication environment there are no quality barriers.[11] There is indeed what Eugene Volokh has called a "cheap speech" effect.[12] With a great deal of foresight, Volokh saw the Web's fabulous potential for solving "media scarcity," giving consumers greater choice of what to see, watch or hear. What Volokh did not (could not) foresee, though, was the unintended consequence of the democratization represented by the Web, which he had then only observed in its 1.0 form. Once Web 2.0 appeared on the scene, it started hollowing out many writing professions – most notably journalism – to an extent that it began in effect to pose a threat to democracy.[13] This may serve as a grim example of a side effect that is not just unintended but undesirable.

One cannot help but surmise that the intensification of appropriation and the democratization of the means of publication can only serve in the longer run to diminish the authority of authorship. But this power shift has economic implications, too. The competition for earnings, deriving from readers as buyers, increases. This applies to actual income, but even if no money should flow into the pockets of the upstarts, indirectly any competition for attention – for which read "valuable reading time" – potentially detracts from an author's earning capacity. Exploitation of the affordances of the printing press enabled patronage of the wealthy elite to be replaced with patronage by the consumer. Successful authors like Charles Dickens managed to establish a direct economic relationship between the author and his public. Just as the printing revolution of the nineteenth century caused intellectual property right to become the chief factor in the professionalization of authorship, so the screen revolution may well turn out to be a similar harbinger of major economic change, but this time in the reverse direction, away from professionalization. To add injury to insult, not only does status and attention get siphoned off but digital value is lower, too. Authors' earning capacity is under severe strain as a result of the competition for attention by amateurs.

Another characteristic of the online publication environment is that the bulk of everything that is written there is made public by default. Humans have been called the storytelling species. We like to tell stories to make sense of the world as it presents itself to us. We can do so privately, using words and writing as tools to help us think, or to share our doubts and convictions, our feelings and emotions with a friend. We can also, for any number of reasons, seek a public audience for our writings. As we have found, this distinction is one of the chief casualties of the increasing digitization of our daily lives. Technology, especially in the shape of Web 2.0, has enabled almost frictionless ways of making text public. The effect that is most notable in the present context has been the creation of a vast gray area of "authorship" where writing is made public that would have remained private under a paper dispensation. There have always been manuscripts languishing in drawers; there have always been diaries that were not intended for public consumption. Now, partly perhaps from an intrinsic desire to assert one's opinions in public, but probably especially as a result of the social pressure to join in the opportunities offered by the new technological facilities, more and more of these previously private writings are becoming public.

The Web is a virtually unregulated and uncensored, minimally semi-public but always potentially fully public space. Messages intended as private, and conveyed in the closed sphere of, for example, email or texts can be easily made public at any time. If texts are *not* to be made public, or *not* to be made copyable, this requires resorting to special measures, such as locking them behind paywalls or using Digital Rights Management (DRM). With texts thus becoming public by default, the barrier between public and private threatens to vanish. Indeed, in the digital world people appear to experience little tension between the public nature of the Web and the private and ephemeral nature of much of their writings. From the perspective of the Order of the Book[14] – that is, from a paper-based perspective – we can only conclude that the Web environment represents a very different mindset. To the paper-formed mind, the fact that there are no editors, publishers, booksellers, librarians to curtail one's liberty to share anything publicly online would, depending on one's ideological bent, either call for responsibility and restraint or be experienced as a relief from oppressive forces impeding the free flow of information. But the Web-formed mind, not recognizing the distinction between public and private, appears neither to see any need for responsibility or restraint nor to think very hard about the status quo as representing freedom newly gained.

Essentially this is no different from the cultural clash that occurred between Socrates' perspective on writing, decisively shaped by the chiefly oral society in which he grew up, and the perspective of those who believed in the power of that new-fangled medium. According to Plato, one of the chief complaints that Socrates had about writing was that once words are set down they are on their own, left to their own devices, without support from their "father," the author. That, once made public, a text ceases to be under the author's control is not an issue to the digital mind. A new medium fosters a new and very different mindset and new writing conventions. In a hybrid world, it takes time for new habits, formed to suit new and unique inherent technological properties, to become accepted as conventions.

With the unbridled increase in volume, the range of writing being made public broadens significantly in terms of genres and concerns. The less economic investment is required for the act of making public, the lower the bar in terms of urgency. A whole unsuspected range of subjects that would never have moved anyone to set pen to paper for the purpose of public consumption is now brought into the light of day. Facebook timelines filled with a record of the ephemeral minutiae of people's private lives, fan-fiction, blogs, and the Trump tweet: they are all entirely new genres of writing made public.

Not only in terms of subject matter but also as a result of the medium's natural fluidity, such texts on screen are experienced as more ephemeral. Digital texts are fleeting presences on a screen, here today and gone tomorrow. This does not of course do much for the style or precision of the textual expression. In Plato's time, the demands made by the public nature of an utterance set down in writing were not self-evident. David Olson has explained how writers have had to learn over time to take greater responsibility for the reader's understanding of their texts.[15] This caused authors to take greater care in expressing themselves. It would appear that the digital medium is reversing that trend. The more ephemeral the posting, the less polishing appears to be called for. Neither readers nor authors appear to take digital texts as seriously as they tend to do texts on paper across the board.[16] Paradoxically the sense of ephemerality coincides with the experience that texts may persist for a much longer period than their authors expected or might, at second thought, consider desirable – again emphasizing the lack of authorial control over a text once it has been made public. The finding that texts online are experienced as ephemeral and not to be taken very seriously may also be linked to the oft-lamented tendency toward more fragmented reading habits. In a vicious spiral, authors are often reminded that brevity and publication in easily digestible chunks are the appropriate strategy to deal with the shortening of readers' attention spans.

Another answer to shortening attention spans, incidentally, is to avoid text and the effort of reading involved altogether. Technologically speaking, it is easier than ever to take recourse to other modalities than text. In the personal sphere of one-to-one communication and social media, a tendency to use photos, short films, and spoken messages instead of text can indeed be discerned. When it comes to books, there has been greater reserve. There was a brief time when the CEOs of large publishing companies could be heard to declare that e-books that were no more than digitized paper books were "dead." The future was supposed to belong to so-called "enhanced" or "enriched" books. However, in spite of the amount of experimentation that has taken place, lately for example with augmented reality, the oft-proclaimed enhanced book revolution has yet to take place. Authors have been no more eager to embrace multimodal authorship than they were to experiment with hypertext.

We can only speculate about the reasons for this lack of enthusiasm, but it does not seem too far-fetched to surmise that one significant factor may be the very different skill-set required. In the book industry as a "content industry" the boundaries are fluid in principle. Yet the conceptual shift involved in the enhancement of books may be a bridge too far. Multimodality is easily associated with gaming, and so may be too much at variance with the familiar concept of the book. By dint of its long history, this is still preponderantly textual, with illustrations thrown in as occasion demands. Certainly, the digital nature of such hybrid products would provide a technological challenge not just to authors but to all players in the book chain, which is still largely analog. Interestingly, there are actually signs of a reverse trend in which the offline nature of (print) books has started to become part of the appeal of reading. The text-only character of the conventional book may continue, at least for the time being, to offer readers a welcome respite from the digital – and in particular the online – onslaught. If this trend to find ways to escape from the screen world persists, it looks like the creation of fully textual universes to be consumed offline may be becoming a strength rather than a weakness of authors of a more conventional breed.

Diametrically opposed to this stand those who maintain that the paper book is in serious danger of being increasingly marginalized in the larger digital media arena and have high expectations of more multimodal expression. They like to hammer on the argument that, led by the media, the world is becoming increasingly digital. It is just a matter of time before books, too, will be forced to follow the path to the future and to submit ineluctably to the dictates of the digital. In this perspective, e-books have the future, but they still need to come into their own. Coming into their own means obeying the inherent properties of the digital element. In the hybrid world of books, competing pressures are now strongly felt by all parties involved: authors as well as their readers and the publishing industry. There is a great deal of uncertainty and it is impossible to predict which scenario has the greatest likelihood of coming about. But there are some observations we can make.

If we regard the authorship-production-distribution-consumption chain from a longer historical perspective, authorship, though the first link in the chain, is the last link to be "democratized" with the arrival in the twenty-first century of Web 2.0. In neat biblical symmetry, the last – consumption (reading) – was democratized first, in the nineteenth century. In the intervening period, the means of production went through a slower process, starting in the twentieth century with offset lithography, mimeographing, and photocopying and continuing with the same digital revolution in the twentieth century that also revolutionized distribution through the Internet and the Web in the twentieth and twenty-first centuries. While the longer-term consequences may still need to become clear, where the changes that the digital world has brought so far clearly converge is in the way they are affecting the social position of the author and the prestige of authorship. Taken together, in the hybrid digital–analog world of authorship the quantitative explosion, followed by a whole range of more indirect social changes, leads *ipso facto* to a devaluation of that prestige. Social effects like these are so powerful precisely because they are unintended.

Is there any redress? Or are there ultimately limits to the power of the democratized author that there are not for professional authors: platform restrictions? Could the level of control over the form and distribution of one's writings be a decisive factor in a definition of authorship in the digital era? Could we say that it is the possibility to escape restriction that constitutes the essential distinction between amateur and professional authors?

Whether evaded or overcome, these restrictions show the intimate connection of authorship with (economic) power. Only "real" authors have access to that exclusive print world where some form of restrictions still hold. Might it be – however paradoxically and in spite of all orthodoxies about the democratization of the means of publication – the very restrictions of that print world that both authors and readers continue to seek?

Can we – should we – redefine authorship in some way? Can we – should we – exclude certain categories of writers from authorship? We have already observed that the public *versus* private nature of writing fails to be a usable criterion. However, aren't there plenty of other conventional formal criteria: membership of authors' societies; publication contracts; remuneration; ISBNs; a form of selection, for example by a "recognized" publisher? None of these would seem to do full justice to the E. L. James case that we started out with. Isn't the point that we cannot continue to judge the digital with the criteria from the analog world? Given the current hybridity of authorship, aren't the boundaries permeable by definition? What is more to the point is that, given the nature of the digital revolution, none of those criteria would do anything to alter the changing *perception* of authorship.

The same applies to the distinction between "real" and – what, "pretend"? – authorship in our digital world. No criterion is going to stop the concept of authorship from being unstable – from the perspective of the Order of the Book, that is. Ultimately, it may come down less to the question of whether it is tenable to make a distinction than to the question of whether it is necessary or even desirable to do so. What purpose would it serve? It is only useful (if useful is indeed the word) as a label for critics and academics to wield. It may be more realistic to accept that confusion simply comes with the digital territory. We may thus need to prepare for the slow but inexorable hollowing out of the existing concept of authorship. But for whom is that a problem?

Notes

1. One need only think of Nietzsche's, Flaubert's, D. H. Lawrence's, or Huxley's often-voiced distaste for the mass literacy made possible by education and the printing press.
2. See Anne Mangen and Adriaan van der Weel, "Why Don't We Read Hypertext Novels?", *Convergence: The International Journal of Research into New Media Technologies*, 23.2 (2017), 166–81.
3. Denis G. Pelli and Charles Bigelow, "A Writing Revolution," *Seed Magazine*, 20 October 2009, http://seedmagazine.com/content/article/a_writing_revolution/
4. In my book Adriaan van der Weel, *Changing our Textual Minds* (Manchester, UK: Manchester University Press, 2011), but see also Adriaan van der Weel, "Pandora's Box of Text Technology," *Jaarboek voor Nederlandse Boekgeschiedenis*, 20 (2013), 201–4. As far as the agency of inanimate subjects is concerned, compare also for example the Actor-Network Theory (ANT) perspective (of Bruno Latour and others), and the embodied-cognition perspective of Lambros Malafouris, *How Things Shape the Mind: A Theory of Material Engagement* (Cambridge, MA: MIT Press, 2013).
5. See Adriaan van der Weel, "Feeding our Reading Machines: From the Typographic Page to the Docuverse," in "Beyond Accessibility: Textual Studies in the Twenty-First Century," eds. Brent Nelson and Richard Cunningham, *Digital Studies / Le champ numérique*, 6 (2015–16), DOI: http://doi.org/10.16995/dscn.15
6. Frank Rose, *The Art of Immersion: How the Digital Generation Is Remaking Hollywood, Madison Avenue, and the Way We Tell Stories* (New York: Norton, 2011), p. 83.

7. See Kevin Kelly, "Scan This Book," *New York Times*, 14 May 2006, and John Updike's reply, "The End of Authorship," *New York Times*, 25 June 2006.

8. Michel de Certeau, *The Practice of Everyday Life* (Berkeley: University of California Press, 1988), p. 174.

9. See, for example, the thoughtful and incisive book by Michael P. Lynch, *The Internet of Us: Knowing More and Understanding Less in the Age of Big Data* (New York: Norton, 2016).

10. Andrew Keen, *The Cult of the Amateur: How Blogs, MySpace, YouTube and the Rest of Today's User Generated Media Are Killing Our Culture and Economy* (London: Nicholas Brealey, 2008).

11. Perhaps it is better to speak of market barriers, in the sense that in the book trade publication decisions are primarily based on the suitability of a given text for the market a given publisher is able to reach.

12. Eugene Volokh, "Cheap Speech and What It Will Do," *Yale Law Journal*, 104 (1995), 1805–1850.

13. Richard L. Hasen, "Cheap Speech and What It Has Done (to American Democracy)" (11 August 2017). *First Amendment Law Review*, 2018, forthcoming; UC Irvine School of Law Research Paper No. 2017–38. Available at SSRN: https://ssrn.com/abstract=3017598.

14. See *Changing our Textual Minds*, 27; 67–103

15. David Olson, *The World on Paper: The Conceptual and Cognitive Implications of Writing and Reading* (Cambridge: Cambridge University Press, 1996).

16. There is a huge and growing body of scientific evidence that bears this out. It applies to all ages. Two recent large-scale meta-studies independently come to the same conclusion: L. M. Singer and P. A. Alexander, "Reading on Paper and Digitally: What the Past Decades of Empirical Research Reveal," *Review of Educational Research*, 87.6 (2017), 1007–41, and Pablo Delgado, Cristina Vargas, Rakefet Ackerman, and Ladislao Salmerón, "Don't Throw Away Your Printed Books: A Meta-Analysis on the Effects of Reading Media on Comprehension," *Educational Research Review*, 25 (2018), 23–38.

PART II

Systematic Perspectives

CHAPTER 15

Literary Authorship in the Traditions of Rhetoric and Poetics

Kevin Dunn

To begin with the obvious: the terms "literary" and "authorship" are bound to their histories – at some points of their history bound to each other – and a survey of literary authorship in rhetorics and poetics cannot work from overly granular definitions given the shifts in the signification of these concepts. Material changes (e.g., the shift from manuscript culture to the printed book and from printed book to electronic transmission), social conditions of literary production (e.g., the concentration of textual transmission in monastic settings during the Middle Ages and the emergence of authorial copyright in the eighteenth century), and conceptual shifts (e.g., the development of a notion of authorial subjectivity) all complicate the creation of definitions, and the temptation to construct definitions teleologically is powerful. I will therefore work from the broadest possible starting place: authorship exists where there is acknowledged *enunciative responsibility*, where the writer is taken to "back" his or her words and their promulgation, and where the writer's name "marks off the edges" of the work, to use Michel Foucault's formulation.[1] The classical rhetorical tradition acknowledges this sense of origination in the body and voice of the orator, and it continues to be present, though transformed, in Romantic assumptions of our concept of authorship: "How many authors are there among writers?" Friedrich Schlegel asks, and then defines his terms: "Author means originator."[2] "Literary" in this context is not a matter of genre but of mode: literature is written, backed by authorship, and intended to last beyond any immediate rhetorical context. I acknowledge that these definitions, though sweeping and general, are only beginning to be woven into a consistent picture at the beginning of Western literary history, and that they are now noticeably fraying, but they do describe the landscape in which rhetorics and poetics have moved for most of their history.

"Rhetoric" and "poetics" are also moving targets, but much more transparently so. Even in antiquity, the landscape is varied, including the prescriptive (the handbook or *enchiridion*), the pedagogic (*institutio*), the descriptive (Aristotle's *Rhetoric* and *Poetics* might be considered in this category), and the critical (Longinus's *On the Sublime*, for instance, which proposes interventions into the established practice of the orator or poet). All of these categories have a relative stability up to the eighteenth century, when prescriptive and pedagogic poetics (and rhetorics) lose some of their cultural currency. At that time, the final category – what we would now simply call literary criticism – takes off, particularly with the Romantics. Within a hundred years, the modern research university canonizes this mode as an academic discipline.

There is, in addition, an important sense in which rhetoric as an institution is directly opposed to the claims of authorship. This is undoubtedly what Roland Barthes meant when he argued that Valéry's "taste for classicism" and "the lessons of rhetoric" led him to be ceaselessly "calling into question and deriding the Author."[3] Classical rhetoric provides a discursive automaticity that circumscribes the need for authorial subjectivity. It provides a system of language and gesture that contains and contextualizes the originating *auctor*. The appeals to the voice and character of the individual orator, which I will discuss in a moment, are themselves calculated and codified strategies of the law court, a more limited, less subject-oriented, articulation of authorship. The *fons et origo* of these appeals is the handbook, not the heart. Not surprisingly, the heyday of the author and the heyday of rhetoric as a prescriptive system have very little overlap. I therefore end this survey with the full emergence of literary authorship in the philosophical criticism of the Romantics. The story does not, of course, end there. Modernism and postmodernism, as is evident in Valéry, challenged the centrality and even the reality of authorship, and rhetoric re-emerges as a subject of theoretical interest.

Classical Antiquity

Theorists of authorship have generally treated it as constituted by two conceptions absent from Greco-Roman thought: literary ownership and an articulated sense of the "subject." Literary ownership in anything like our contemporary sense cannot really emerge before the invention of printing and the development of a book trade, when copyright takes on financial value, as I will discuss below. Before the printing press, there was potential gain in acquiring patronage through the dedication of a literary work, but the gain was mostly a one-time matter; the copying and dissemination of such work held little added monetary value for the writer except in the enhancement of reputation. Unsurprisingly, the legal foundation for authorial ownership and for authorship itself does not emerge until the eighteenth century.

Subjectivity is an even more slippery concept, but there is no reason to question historian Paul Veyne's assessment: "[N]o ancient, not even the poets, is capable of talking about himself. Nothing is more misleading than the use of 'I' in Greco-Roman poetry."[4] And, in fact, almost all Greek and Roman oratory was practiced in very specific social and political contexts, with very specific ends. Speeches in the law courts or the forum, civic celebrations, advice to rulers, all produced their own forms and modes that were not literary (in the sense of autotelic *belles lettres*) nor authored, in that the orator's ownership of his spoken word was never a matter of interest (although I will go on to qualify that assessment in a moment).[5] Poetry is a more complicated matter, but it remains close to the contexts of recitation and performance throughout antiquity.

And yet ownership, considered simply in the frame of possessive individualism, and the related concept of the autonomous subject, may also be construed more generally as a subset of enunciative responsibility. Which is to say, classical rhetorics take several discursive directions that form the basis for a theory of authorship. Most fundamentally, the orator cannot ignore the presentation of the self. Most ancient theorists agree that with a strong case, the pleader need only lay out the facts. With a weaker case, however, more work is needed. Aristotle articulates four "remedies" for the pleader, appeals that go beyond the mere presentation of an honorable and straightforward case. These four are: appeals to the judge and jury; appeals to the strength of one's case; attacks on the opponent's character; and, finally, the appeal to one's own ethical strength.[6] This last remedy, ethical proof, becomes the centerpiece in rhetorical theory for winning the audience's good will, the *captatio benevolentiae*. If an orator can convince the audience of his own integrity, he is that much closer to having it regard his case with favor. One often-articulated theme of ethical proof is the contrast between the leisured activities (usually philosophical) that need to be set aside to handle the public business of appearing before the court. This grudging agreement to perform a public duty dispels, at least in theory, any sense that the advocate might be seeking self-gain. But it also creates a second dimension, a depth, to the persona of the author, a glimpse into a private backstory of an individualized and subjectively realized owner of discourse who sits in his garden contemplating his own

philosophical or poetic thoughts. This oratorical persona lays the foundation for a theory of rhetorical authorship. The persona, however, is not the
equivalent of the early modern or romantic author whom we will examine
in a moment. Rather, it is built around a well-defined set of calculated self-
presentational conventions that encouraged modesty. Quintilian, for
instance, advises his orator: "[T]here is [. . .] a certain tacit approval to be
won by proclaiming ourselves weak, unprepared, and no match for the
talents of the opposing party."[7]

Rhetorical treatises balanced the practical advice to orators – that they
present themselves as weak – with the theoretical position that historian of
rhetoric George Kennedy calls "the image of the ideal orator leading society
to noble fulfillment of national ideals."[8] The trope of the ideal orator is all
but ubiquitous in the tradition of rhetorical theory, providing the backbone of Quintilian's compendious *Institutio Oratoria* and the central
subject of Cicero's dialogues and treatises on rhetoric (*Orator, Brutus, De
Oratore*). The ideal orator becomes a particularly potent theme in the
Roman tradition, adduced in service first to the Republic and then to the
Empire. This political implication may seem to carry rhetoric further from
questions of literary authorship, but in fact the obsession with the figure of
the orator produced a version of enunciative responsibility, the focus on
the orator's role in articulating and then owning discourse. The discussion
of the ideal orator returns again and again to questions of nature and
nurture. Does the perfect orator possess innate qualities of persuasion, or
may these be learned? Ancillary to this question is another: must the orator
be a master of all bodies of knowledge and discourse? Must he, in other
words, fully incorporate his society? If the nature versus nurture debate
does not evidence a fully constituted "subjectivity," it does show clear
interest in what defines the rhetorical "author" as the origin and the
"backer" of discourse. We must resist the conviction that we have here
a fragment of a fully formed conception of literary authorship, but that
does not mean denying the connections with later versions of the author.

Far fewer treatises on poetics survive from antiquity than do rhetorical
tracts. The most famous and influential of these is Aristotle's *Poetics*, which
is a descriptive account of tragedy and epic poetry. Even though the text
that comes down to us is incomplete, it seems clear from Aristotle's method
that he is uninterested in issues that we might consider connected to
authorship. There is little discussion of the poets themselves; Aristotle
focuses on genre and attendant structures and effects. The audience is
central to his account, but not the author. Implicit in his account is
a response to Plato's attack on the moral and philosophical faults of poetry,

but this response is oblique and couched as an objective taxonomy rather than as a defense of the poet.[9] The one surviving monument in this relatively barren landscape is Horace's verse treatise *Ars Poetica*, which had a powerful influence on subsequent poetics. It is, once again, not much interested in the idea of poetic subjectivity, but it does assume and argue from the category of what we might consider the "professional poet." Horace attacks poetic amateurism, and with it the idealizing of undisciplined inspiration. Even though in his own verse he felt free to invoke the role of ecstatic *vates* (for instance in *Odes* 2.20), as theorist he stressed careful revision and sober judgment. Real poetry comes from hard work: "such is the power of order and connexion [*iunctura*]" (242). His own role as critic is to serve as the "whetstone" [*cotis*] (304) to sharpen the verse of others.[10]

Many of the themes and issues in both rhetorics and poetics of antiquity converge in the treatise *Peri hypsous* or *On the Sublime*, of unknown authorship but traditionally attributed to Cassius Longinus. It presents a logical culmination to any discussion of classical literary authorship, and it played a profound role in the history of aesthetic theory and the establishment of literary criticism as an independent genre when it was translated in the seventeenth century. *Peri hypsous* begins with the premises of a rhetorical treatise, in the mode of Quintilian's *Institutio* or the *Rhetorica ad Herennium*. The author of the work offers prescriptive advice to the aspiring orator to improve his impact on the audience. However, he replaces the traditional goal of oratory, persuasion, with a more lofty, Platonic, or even Neoplatonic one, "transport" [*ekstasis*]: "For the effect of genius is not to persuade the audience but rather to transport them out of themselves."[11] Just as importantly, he comes down clearly and distinctively on one side of the nature-nurture debate. The orator must certainly master the *techné* of his discipline, which can enhance his ability to produce transport, but the congenital element of oratorical power is primary, because a work that can transport its listener or reader is the product of natural genius. The effects that this genius can produce cannot be constrained by or boiled down to any craft, but belong to the "great nature" of the consummate orator: "Perhaps it is inevitable that humble, mediocre natures, because they never run any risks and never aim at the heights, should remain to a large extent safe from error, while in great natures their very greatness spells danger."[12] This concept of genius gets us much closer to the idea of the author that we now take as normative: the solitary writer, taking full enunciative responsibility for a work. Longinus's emphasis on ecstatic effects circles back to the subjectivity that produces those effects.

"Sublimity is the echo of a noble mind" (9.2). The orator's own emotions will always be the origin of rhetorical power: "For it is impossible that those whose thoughts and habits all their lives long are petty and servile should produce anything wonderful, worthy of immortal life. No, a grand style is the natural product of those whose ideas are weighty. This is why splendid remarks come particularly to men of high spirit" (9.3–4). Perhaps not surprisingly, *Peri hypsous* interests itself less in the spoken than the written and less in oratory than in poetry, and much of it is devoted to the effects that poets like Homer produce in their verse. Yet Longinus disappoints if we expect him to lay out a full-blown theory of poetic originality that chimes with post-romantic pictures of creativity. "Here is an author [i.e., Plato] who shows us, if we will condescend to see, that there is another road [. . .] which leads to sublimity. What and what manner of road is this? Zealous imitation of the great prose writers and poets of the past" (13.2). If rhetorical-ecstasy-as-imitation does not fit well with modern notions, it does work well with medieval and early modern ones. *Auctor*, after all, means "grower" rather than originator, and nurturing the seeds of the tradition becomes its own version of originality.

The Middle Ages and Renaissance

In the course of the Middle Ages, rhetoric and its sister art, poetry, came to hold an ancillary place to dialectic. Nonetheless, the period saw the production of many rhetorical and poetic treatises. Medieval writers tended to construe the *auctor* less as author and more as authority, less as a continuing place of origination than one of canonical closure. In poetic practice, at least, this schema could produce a rich interplay between authoritative sources and a writer's manipulation of them. Chaucer's narrator in *The Parliament of Fowls* tells the reader that he requires literary authority even to experience love: "I knowe nat Love in dede," but nonetheless "ful ofte in bokes reede / Of his myrakles and his crewel yre."[13] He then falls asleep reading Cicero and has what one might consider an *authorized* dream vision, certainly a faux-naïve deference to his authorities. When Shakespeare's Gower intones "I tell you what mine authors say,"[14] he is sketching a picture of the poet balanced between a medieval deference to authority and the early modern sense of history and invention. Rhetorical and poetical theory from the period, however, does not engage in questions that touch on literary authorship. With few exceptions, these works were prescriptive handbooks on the arts of letter writing, sermonizing, and versifying, prescriptions based largely on antique sources, notably

Cicero and Horace.[15] The agora and the forum, the sites that subsumed the orator in public discourse, also provided the space for developing his voice and authority, and those spaces atrophied with the decline of the Western Roman Empire.

Like their predecessors, Renaissance rhetorical and poetic theorists also relied heavily on the classical canon, but that canon was gradually expanding with the recovery of ancient texts. This expansion helped complicate the reliance on authorities with a more flexible and nuanced understanding of imitation. As we saw in Longinus, imitation bears a paradoxical relationship to the authorial subject, cancelling it in the abstract but, in practice, serving as a tool for constructing it. As Thomas M. Greene puts it, "*Imitatio* [. . .] contained implications for the theory of style, the philosophy of history, and for conceptions of the self." Greene continues, "it assigned the Renaissance creator a convenient and flexible stance toward a past that threatened to overwhelm him."[16] While imitating ancient poets and orators could produce sterile and derivative work, it also created a means for navigating authoritative models, charting a course that for some – Petrarch, Poliziano, Erasmus, du Bellay, Rabelais, Jonson, to name a few – produced a powerfully individualized style and, with it, the structures of authorial subjectivity.

Humanism, therefore, joined rhetorical and poetic practice to theory. The expansion of the ancient canon bred a self-consciousness about the historical place of the writer, and this self-consciousness was translated into the theory of *imitatio*. At the same time, nascent state formation and the expansion of monarchical power in many European countries meant that eloquence and literary skill had new purposes. Humanist learning came to be seen as indispensable to bureaucracies that conducted their business in Latin. More articulated governmental and civic structures meant an ever more important place for the law, which relied both on the eloquence of the orator and the interpretive skills of a literary scholar. Increasingly elaborate state apparatuses required more regulations, legislation, and diplomatic correspondence, all of which increased the importance of rhetoric. Beginning in the city states of Italy and then spreading north and to Spain, the sense of the authority of the man of letters grew. For figures such as Coluccio Salutati, Erasmus, and Thomas More, literary skill translated into public authority.

Something similar happened in the realm of poetry and poetics. In a striking departure from both classical and medieval precedent, the Renaissance produced a large number of works on poetics both in Latin and in the vernacular languages. In part, the upsurge registers the sense that the ability to compose poetry was a useful skill for the aspiring courtier. If oratorical skill was seen as indispensable to the public servant, then poetry was viewed as an important tool for someone wishing to demonstrate his social credentials. Castiglione's *Book of the Courtier*, the de facto handbook for the social-climbing courtier, makes *de rigeur* "the knowledge and the ability to serve them [princes] in every reasonable thing, winning their favour and the praise of others."[17] If poetry, like oratory, was often a means to a well-defined end, it was also the vehicle for self-fashioning, and for the first time the "author" is celebrated in theoretical literature. George Puttenham, in *The Arte of English Poesie*, extols the powers of the poet in lavish terms, devoting a chapter to "How Poets were the first Philosophers, the first Astronomers and Historiographers and Oratours and Musitiens of the world."[18] But he also lauds what might be considered its more practical uses, relating the story of Alain Chartier, who was kissed while sleeping by the French queen, who says, "we may not of Princely courtesie passe by and not honor with our kisse the mouth from whence so many sweete ditties and golden poems have issued."[19]

The large number of works on poetry also took impetus from the growth of what might be called literary nationalism. Along with philosophical maxims, stylistic features, and commonplaces, Renaissance authors found in classical literature a strong sense of political purpose that coalesced in the movement we have come to call civic humanism. Dante's *On Vernacular Eloquence* and Joachim du Bellay's *The Defense and Enrichment of the French Language* are only two of the better-known examples. William Webbe, in *A Discourse of English Poetry*, strikes a common note when he expresses the hope to "reform" poetry, reclaiming it "from the rude multitude of rustical rhymers."[20] Looking back to the democracy of Athens and to republican Rome, writers from Petrarch onward yearned to use their newly honed literary and oratorical skills in the public sphere. It is no wonder that this movement blossomed in the communes of fourteenth- and fifteenth-century Italy, which could cast themselves as the inheritors of the Roman Republic, vestiges of which they could see all about them. When these fragile political structures began to crumble under the pressure of autocracy and growing national powers, humanists found themselves in possession of a body of literary skills and a body of ideological values that no longer could work in easy concert. One result was the increased value placed on the belletristic and apolitical. But the public values of humanism also found an outlet in service of the nation state itself. This service could take the form of populating a civil service with literate students of classical literature, the *studia humanitatis*, but more importantly for our purposes, it led some humanists to create manifestos for the literary legitimacy of their countries and of their national languages and literatures.

Could one, for instance, write worthy poetry in French? Could a dramatist write a play in English that could stand beside the tragedies of Seneca? The early versions of this question were, once again, Italian, and involved the apotheosizing of Dante, Petrarch, and Boccaccio into the so-called *Tre Corone*, the three crowns. The French, English, Spanish, and others followed suit, each constructing their own chauvinistic literary histories. In England, handbooks on poetry usually worked through the same lists with the same narrative: Chaucer first pulled English verse from barbarity, Sir Thomas Wyatt and the Earl of Surrey provided polish, Edmund Spenser gave it the intellectual heft to match European vernacular poetry – but the point is less the list itself than establishment of a tradition of authorship to counter a tradition of authorities. The narrative validates the present and suggests a trajectory for the future. The praised poets are not exemplars to be repeated or even imitated; rather, they are now part of literary history, a history that can and should change, be supplemented.

One final aspect of early modern poetics is worth considering, in part because of its influence on Romantic conceptions of the poet. Renaissance philosophers took a strong interest in Plato and the Neoplatonists, often in explicit contrast to Aristotle (associated with the dialectic of the Scholastics). In poetics, this interest produced the model of the vatic poet, the divinely inspired solitary voice. As Sir Philip Sidney notes, "[a]mong the Romans a poet was called *vates*, which is as much as a diviner, foreseer, or prophet [. . .] so heavenly a title did that excellent people bestow upon this heart-ravishing knowledge."[21] This poetic stance, certainly not unknown in antiquity (epic invocations, after all, assume such a framework), is often connected to the mythical figures of Musaeus, Amphion, and especially Orpheus, who could with their poetry move stones, tame wild beasts, and even harrow hell. Even a poet as hard-headed and resolutely classical as Ben Jonson partook of this persona: poetry "riseth higher, as by a divine instinct, when it contemns common, and known conceptions. It utters somewhat above a mortal mouth. Then it gets aloft, and flies away with his rider [. . .]."[22] Sidney, exalting the poet above the historian and philosopher, goes further: "Only the poet, disdaining to be tied to any such subjection, lifted up with the vigour of his own invention, doth grow in effect another nature [. . .]."[23] The poet's vigorous, unfettered imagination separates him from nature itself and grants him an authority never imagined in classical poetics.

The Rise of Literary Criticism

But this freedom from "subjection" had to wait for social and legal developments to catch up to its idealization of the poet-author. When Ben Jonson published his *Works* (1616) in the folio format and with the title usually reserved for classical authors, contemporaries regarded the gesture as a risible pretension.[24] It made, however, a clear enough statement about Jonson's status as an *author*, about what Joseph Loewenstein has called Jonson's "bibliographic ego."[25] His outlandishness was a prophetic anticipation of authorial ownership and the commercial grounding of literary authority. In unprecedented fashion, he explored every avenue for profiting on his literary labor: patronage, publication, fees from theatrical companies for composing plays, payment for collaborating on court masques. It was not, however, until the late seventeenth century, particularly in England, that our own prevailing definition of authorship solidified.[26] The basis for – or at least the sign of – this definition was a dramatic change in copyright law. With the Statute of Anne (1710), British writers now owned the right to their "copy" and no longer had to hand this right over to a publisher along with the manuscript, the material "copy," in order for the book to see print.[27] Concomitant with this market definition of authorship came the definition of the author that quickly came to seem intuitive rather than a contingent innovation: the author is the *person* who produces an *original* textual artifact from the materials of the world.

When the author became a legally entitled entity, the story of literary authorship entered a new chapter. But how was this shift reflected in rhetorics, poetics, and in the genre that increasingly came to encompass and supersede them, literary criticism? Pure rhetoric, in the sense of a system that could produce discourse from its own rules, had entered a long period of decline and increasing disregard. Although we often associate classicism with a dry, rule-bound form of invention, the theorists of the period rarely embraced this "classicism" without an awareness of the new claims of authorial personhood. John Dennis encapsulates this uncertain relation between the subjectless speech of rhetoric and the personality of the true author. On the one hand, as he puts it baldly, "there are proper means for the attaining of every end, and those proper means in poetry we call the rules."[28] On the other, he shows himself a true Longinian by seeing the end of poetry as "an art by which a poet excites passion" or enthusiasm (which he connects to "religious and divine ideas").[29] Like Longinus, he supports the idea of genius, "that happy elevation of thought which alone can make a great poet,"[30] but simultaneously holds that the manifestation of genius can be bound to follow regulations. Likewise, Joseph Trapp, in his *Lectures on Poetry*, captures this tension by creating a sort of Venn diagram: "Every ingenious thought, then, is well founded, but every thought that is well founded is not an ingenious one."[31]

The new institution of authorship quickly occludes its origins in the market. As Mark Rose puts it, "the sense of the commercial is, as it were, the unconscious of the text."[32] "[T]he task," he continues, "was to differentiate true authorship from mechanical invention and to mystify and valorize the former."[33] Pope's mock rhetorical treatise *Peri Bathous*, which inhabits Longinus as a means of satirizing his bathetic contemporaries, would seem to be part of this project. He follows closely Longinus's interest in natural genius versus learned craft, although the ideological heart of his work is Horatian: real poetry is created through the decorous application of talent. More importantly, the work serves as an intervention in the creation of authorship out of the book market. Pope's apologist for bathos says his purpose is to "procure a farther vent for our own product,"[34] but rather than a mechanistic and dry sort of production, the speaker imagines the author created by the market ("vent") engaging in another kind of venting, with poetry becoming the "laudable vent of unruly passions."[35] In true mock-epic fashion, Longinus becomes not just the tool for satirizing poetasters, but himself the focus of criticism, with Longinian sublimity looking like an unseemly airing of authorial subjectivity.

Pope would seem to validate, avant la lettre, Terry Eagleton's claim that the cult of genius takes off "just when the artist is becoming debased to a petty commodity producer."[36] Romanticism embraces the critique, but without letting go of the notion of "transcendent genius." That is, Romantic thinkers fought hard against the commodification of poetry, but they did not worry that it may have been market forces themselves that created the hegemony of the vatic poet. By the time Matthew Arnold states that "[i]t is undeniable that the exercise of a creative power, that a free creative activity, is the highest function of man,"[37] the claim does in fact feel uncontroversial, even "undeniable."

The Romantics would thus seem to be the logical end-point of a discussion of authorship. M. H. Abrams, in his foundational work contrasting the "lamp" of the Romantic imagination with the "mirror" of mimetic theory, outlines the "expressive theories" of the Romantics that defined poetry as "the overflow, utterance, or projection of the thought and feelings of the poet."[38] Abrams's echo of Wordsworth's famous definition of poetry does capture something near the core of Romantic theory.

In Shelley, for instance, the language of authorship and origin would seem to be clear enough:

> But Poets, or those who imagine and express this indestructible order, are not only the authors of language and of music, of the dance, and architecture, and statuary and painting: they are the institutors of laws, and the founders of civil society and the inventors of the arts of life and the teachers, who draw into a certain propinquity with the beautiful and the true that partial apprehension of the agencies of the invisible world which is called religion.[39]

But Shelley skates between a vision of poetry as purely imaginative and as an "apprehension" of an "invisible" but real "indestructible order." Poetry as pure imagination might escape all rules for achieving its goal; the originating author stands above and beyond any prescriptive exercise or rhetorical automaticity. And yet "apprehension," even if of an "invisible world," continues to tie the poet to a function that, if not merely mimetic, is more than expressive solipsism.

In Wordsworth, the ambivalence is even more pronounced. In the Preface to the *Lyrical Ballads*, he substitutes for rhetorical exercise the work of "a man who being possessed of more than usual organic sensibility had also thought long and deeply."[40] Wordsworth hedges his measured view of a poet's natural capacity even further when he compares it to the reality of human suffering: "However exalted a notion we would wish to cherish of the character of a Poet, it is obvious, that, while he describes and imitates passions, his situation is altogether slavish and mechanical, compared with the freedom and power of real and substantial action and suffering."[41] He stands Shelley's poetic monarch on his head; Wordsworth's "mechanical" poet is a slave to the human content that governs his work. The great poet is therefore the one with the greatest powers of empathy and identification, tutored by the suffering and feelings of those around him. Romantic theory, then, allows for a continuity with a socially attuned mimetic theory, but it also changes the mode of poetics and rhetorics from the prescriptive to the philosophical, creating a mode practiced by the Victorian sages and continental figures such as Hugo and Tolstoy.

Perhaps the most significant contribution of Romantic criticism to the topic, then, is its shift in thinking about the role of the critic and about the relationship between poetics and poetry. In a pronouncement that is also a performative utterance, Friedrich Schlegel describes the passing of criticism from the prescriptive application of rules to an active participation in a philosophical project shared with poetry: "It is not necessary for anyone to sustain and propagate poetry through clever speeches and precepts, or, especially, to try to produce it, invent it, establish it, and impose upon it restrictive laws as the theory of poetics would like to."[42] "[T]he sublime discipline of genuine poetry" is instead an art of intellectual commerce between critic and poet and within the critic-poet: "the poet cannot be satisfied with leaving behind in lasting works the expression of his unique poetry as it was native to him and which he acquired by education. He must strive continually to expand his poetry and his view of poetry [. . .]."[43] The Romantics created a new model of the poet-critic. Goethe, Wordsworth, Shelley, Schlegel, Arnold, Wilde, Yeats, Eliot, all in different ways work within Schlegel's project "to put poetry in touch with philosophy and rhetorics."[44]

Literary authorship therefore enters directly into poetics. The critic becomes a point of creative origin. Schlegel himself grounds this project through an aphoristic style. He laments: "As yet there is nothing which is aphoristic in matter and form, altogether subjective and individual, simultaneously completely objective, and a necessary part in the system of all sciences."[45] Anticipating Nietzsche and Benjamin, Schlegel considers the aphorism a building block of philosophical criticism – "[a] dialogue is a chain or a wreath of aphorisms,"[46] the melding of the subjective and objective, each a poem and a maxim. It is not hard to find other examples of the phenomenon during the period. Blake's *The Marriage of Heaven and Hell*, with its "Proverbs of Hell," is only the most explicit example in his work, which is shaped around a poetics of prophetic pronouncement. The aphoristic joining of poetry and criticism stands behind a central characteristic of continental literary criticism that culminates in Deconstruction. Responding directly to Schlegel, Paul de Man identifies a "subterranean path" that links "the critical and poetic [. . .] so closely [. . .] that it is impossible to touch the one without coming into contact with the other." This connection creates the conditions in which "critics can be granted the full authority of literary authorship."[47] De Man's explicit claim of literary authority for the critic could be considered one end of a pendulum's long swing that begins with the socially embedded conception of rhetoric in the Forum and ends with a claim for the autotelic role of the philosopher-critic. And this arc, while it hardly captures the complex historical movement of poetics and rhetorics, does perhaps capture the range of positions articulated across the *longue durée* of critical history.

Although this survey ends with Romanticism, it must be remembered that British and American criticism – despite the Emersonian tradition –

did not fully embrace the Romantic philosopher-critic. Geoffrey Hartman's claim that "criticism is *within* literature,"[48] "not outside of it looking in,"[49] never became orthodoxy, or at least not for long. The Anglo-American tradition is better described by Kenneth Burke, who sets as his task a "job of reclamation" against "pure poetry."[50] The key term in his analysis of persuasion is "identification," which can include the sometimes temporary filiations between speaker and audience or the more profound one between political actors. This concern drives a good deal of literary criticism today and defines a different brand of authority for the critic. Social and political identification, in the form of race studies, gender studies, disability studies, and many other subfields, is not, of course, couched in terms of classical rhetorical analysis. Nor is it a return to Valéry's "taste for classicism" and "the lessons of rhetoric" that led him to "[call] into question and [deride] the Author," with which we began. Yet it does place the authority of the critic outside of his or her expressive powers, outside of philosophy, outside of literature itself. To generalize broadly, the positioning of the critic is figured as less a matter of rhetorically garnered authority than it is from identification with the victims of social injustice. It may seem strange to align Cicero and the contemporary critic, but rhetoric has in a sense returned to the advocacy of the Forum, even if in a vastly different form and context.

Notes

1. Michel Foucault, "What Is an Author?", in *Aesthetics, Method, and Epistemology*, vol. 2, ed. James D. Faubion, trans. Robert Hurley et al. (New York: The New Press, 1998), pp. 205–222, p. 211.

2. Friedrich Schlegel, *Dialogue on Poetry and Literary Aphorisms*, trans. Ernst Behler and Roman Struc (University Park: Pennsylvania State University Press, 1968), p. 128.

3. Roland Barthes, *Image – Music – Text*, trans. Stephen Heath (New York: Hill and Wang, 1977), p. 144.

4. Paul Veyne, "Roman Empire," *A History of Private Life, vol. 1: From Pagan Rome to Byzantium*, ed. Paul Veyne, trans. Arthur Goldhammer (Cambridge, MA: Belknap Press, 1987), p. 231.

5. Foucault describes the interest in the "care of the self" that arises during antiquity, but this concern has little bearing on the institution of authorship; nor does another aspect of the period traced by Foucault, the valorization of private life. While leisure (*otium*) was seen as requisite for certain kinds of production – mostly philosophical and poetic – such production did not create a concomitant picture of individualized accomplishment. See Michel Foucault, *The History of Sexuality, vol. 3, The Care of the Self*, trans. Robert Hurley (New York: Vintage, 1988), pp. 39–68.

6. Aristotle, *Rhetoric*, 3.14.7.

7. Quintilian, *The Orator's Education*, 5 vols., ed. and trans. Donald A. Russell (Cambridge, MA: Harvard University Press, 2001), vol. 2, p. 183, 4.1.8.

8. George Kennedy, *Classical Rhetoric and its Christian and Secular Traditions from Ancient to Modern Times*, 2nd edn (Chapel Hill, NC: University of North Carolina Press, 1999), p. 14.

9. I do not treat Plato here since he did not produce anything that we could label a rhetoric or a poetics. His suspicion of both poetry and rhetoric, however, provides the backdrop for much subsequent discussion.

10. *Horace on Poetry: The "Ars Poetica,"* ed. C. O. Brink (Cambridge: Cambridge University Press, 1971).

11. Longinus, *On the Sublime, in Aristotle Poetics; Longinus On the Sublime; Demetrius On Style*, ed. and trans. Doreen C. Innes (Cambridge, MA: Harvard University Press, 1999), 1.4.

12. Longinus, *On the Sublime*, 33.2–3.

13. *The Works of Geoffrey Chaucer*, 2nd edn, ed. F. N. Robinson (Boston: Houghton Mifflin, 1957), p. 83, ll. 8, 10–11.

14. William Shakespeare, *Pericles*, First Chorus, l. 20. *The Norton Shakespeare, Romances and Poems*, gen. ed. Stephen Greenblatt (New York: Norton, 1997), p. 90.

15. See Kennedy, *Classical Rhetoric*, ch. 9, for an overview.

16. Thomas M. Greene, *The Light in Troy: Imitation and Discovery in Renaissance Poetry* (New Haven, CT: Yale University Press, 1982), p. 2.

17. Baldesar Castiglione, *The Book of the Courtier*, trans. George Bull (Harmondsworth, UK: Penguin, 1976), p. 39.

18. George Puttenham, *The Arte of English Poesie* (Kent, OH: Kent State University Press, 1970), p. 24.

19. Ibid., p. 35.

20. William Webbe, *A Discourse of English Poetry*, ed. Sonia Hernández-Santano (Cambridge: The Modern Humanities Research Association, 2016), p. 61.

21. Sir Philip Sidney, *The Major Works*, ed. Katherine Duncan-Jones (Oxford: Oxford University Press, 1989), p. 214.

22. Ben Jonson, *The Complete Poems*, ed. George Parfitt (New Haven, CT: Yale University Press, 1975), pp. 446–47.

23. Sidney, *Major Works*, p. 216.

24. In "A Session of the Poets," a satire of his contemporaries, Sir John Suckling famously described Jonson's pretense: "And he told them plainly he deserved the bays, / For his were called works, where others were but plays" (ll. 21–2); *The Works of Sir John Suckling in Prose and Verse*, ed. A. Hamilton Thompson (New York: Russell and Russell, 1964), p. 10.

25. Joseph Loewenstein, "The Script in the Marketplace," in *Representing the English Renaissance*, ed. Stephen Greenblatt (Berkeley: University of California Press, 1988), pp. 265–78, p. 265,

26. For a countervailing argument, suggesting that the connection between intellectual property law and Romantic authorship is very difficult to establish

given the differing epistemologies of law and aesthetics, see Erlend Lavik, "Romantic Authorship in Copyright Law and the Uses of Aesthetics," in *The Work of Authorship*, ed. Mireille van Eechoud (Amsterdam: Amsterdam University Press, 2014), pp. 45–93.

27. The new law aligned with John Locke's definition of property in the *Second Treatise of Government* as defined by an individual's labor: "[. . .] every Man has a *Property* in his own *Person*. This no Body has any Right to but himself. The *Labour* of his Body, and the *Work* of his Hands, we may say, are properly his" (ch. 5, sec. 27). John Locke, *Two Treatises of Government*, ed. Peter Laslett (Cambridge: Cambridge University Press, 1988), pp. 287–88.

28. Scott Elledge, *Eighteenth-Century Critical Essays* (Ithaca, NY: Cornell University Press, 1961), vol. 1, p. 101.

29. Ibid., pp. 103, 108.

30. Ibid., p. 117.

31. Ibid., p. 230.

32. Mark Rose, *Authors and Owners: The Invention of Copyright* (Cambridge, MA: Harvard University Press, 1993), p. 118.

33. Ibid., p. 119.

34. *The Prose Works of Alexander Pope*, ed. Rosemary Cowler, (Hamden, CT: Archon Books, 1986), vol. 2, p. 187.

35. Ibid., p. 189.

36. Quoted in Rose, *Authors*, p. 120.

37. Matthew Arnold, *Essays in Criticism. First Series*, ed. Sister Thomas Marion Hoctor (Chicago: University of Chicago Press, 1968), p. 10.

38. M. H. Abrams, *The Mirror and the Lamp: Romantic Theory and the Critical Tradition*. (New York: Oxford University Press, 1953), pp. 21–22.

39. Percy Bysshe Shelley, *Shelley's Poetry and Prose*, eds. Donald H. Reiman and Sharon B. Powers (New York: Norton, 1977), p. 482.

40. William Wordsworth, *Lyrical Ballads and Other Poems, 1797–1800*, eds. James Butler and Karen Green (Ithaca, NY: Cornell University Press, 1992), pp. 744–45.

41. Ibid., p. 751.

42. Schlegel, *Dialogue on Poetry*, p. 54.

43. Ibid., pp. 53, 55.

44. Ibid., p. 140.

45. Ibid., p. 138.

46. Ibid., p. 137

47. Paul De Man, *Blindness and Insight: Essays in the Rhetoric of Contemporary Criticism*, 2nd edn (Minneapolis: University of Minnesota Press, 1983), p. 80.

48. Geoffrey Hartman, *Criticism in the Wilderness: The Study of Literature Today* (New Haven, CT: Yale University Press, 1980), p. 6.

49. Ibid., p. 1.

50. Kenneth Burke, *A Rhetoric of Motives* (Berkeley, CA: University of California Press, 1969), p. xiii.

CHAPTER 16

Authors, Genres, and Audiences
A Rhetorical Approach

James Phelan

I will begin this scholarly chapter in literary criticism and theory with examples of another genre, the joke, more specifically, the subgenre of "X-walks-into-a bar" jokes. Although such an opening isn't standard practice, it isn't shocking either: I'm far from the first to begin a scholarly chapter with a joke or two (or four), and I certainly won't be the last. I'm confident that you are not inferring that I've completely misread my assignment for this volume, even as you withhold other judgment until you see me use the jokes in the service of my argument about genre. In other words, though my beginning with this meta-commentary and going on to the jokes slightly bend the generic boundaries of the scholarly chapter, you and the genre itself can readily accommodate that bending.

Here are the jokes:

> 1. A bear walks into a bar and says, "I'd like a beer . . . . and some of those peanuts." The bartender says, "Sure, but why the big paws?"
>
> 2. A horse walks into a bar. The bartender says, "Hey." The horse says, "You read my mind, buddy."
>
> 3. Some bacteria walk into a bar. The bartender says, "We don't serve your kind here." They reply, "But we're staph."
>
> 4. The bartender says, "We don't serve your kind here." A time traveler walks into a bar.

My first use of the jokes is to link this opening to the following theses: authors and audiences rely on genres as loose organizing principles, broad frames within which to construct and reconstruct literary communications. Furthermore, because genres offer loose rather than rigid organizing principles, they leave authors room for maneuver, and that room in turn makes it possible for authors to bend genres further than I have done with my opening – indeed, to the point that new genres emerge.

In general, genre theory itself falls into two main kinds: lamentation or advocacy. The lamenters include such prominent theorists as Benedetto Croce, Maurice Blanchot, and, in a characteristically more complicated fashion, Jacques Derrida.[1] These theorists bemoan the ways genre constrains or confines individual works, operating as a kind of border police that keep individual works within pre-set boundaries. Indeed, some lamenters, including Croce and Blanchot, would like genre just to go away so that we could all focus on the singularity – and power – of the individual work. Blanchot, for example, writes: "The book is all that matters, just as it is, far from genres, outside of the rubrics, prose, poetry, novel, testimony, under which it refuses to place itself, and to which it denies the power to fix its place and to determine its form."[2]

The advocates include such prominent theorists as Aristotle, Northrop Frye, Bruce Robbins, and Jonathan Culler.[3] These advocates view genre as not only an all-but-inevitable category (our kind categorizes things into kinds) but also an enabling concept. Genre contributes to an author's construction and an audience's reconstruction of individual works; it makes possible productive comparisons among works; and it adds a significant dimension to literary criticism's strong interest in history. As Culler puts it, "if literature is more than just a succession of individual works, it is at the level of genre that it has a history: the modifications of genres, the rise of new genres, and the eclipse of the old."[4] Culler goes on to justify his more specific interest in the genre of lyric this way:

> The notion of lyric as a genre [. . .] embodies a claim that *poetry* as a whole [. . .] is in various ways a less useful category for thinking about poems than is *lyric*; that there is a Western tradition of short, nonnarrative, highly rhythmical productions, often stanzaic, whose aural dimension is crucial; that thinking about such productions in relation to one another both highlights features that might otherwise be neglected or obscured and brings out similarities and differences that are crucial for both poets and readers.[5]

My rhetorical view aligns with those of the advocates, but its emphases are different. Where most advocates, like Culler, focus on the recurrent features of genres, I want to subsume that focus within a larger conception of literary works as rhetorical actions. For example, in *Somebody Telling Somebody Else*, I explore the consequences of viewing narrative as rhetoric and defining it as somebody telling somebody else on some occasion and for some purpose(s) that something happened.[6] Culler calls his book *Theory of the Lyric*, and he offers a primarily text-based description of it: lyric is short, nonnarrative, rhythmic, and has a significant aural dimension. If I were to take on Culler's project, I would shift the focus from the textual features to authors and audiences and title it "How Authors and Audiences Work with Lyric." In this view, authors use the resources of literature – character, speaker, thought, event, temporality, space, and more; or in the case of lyric, brevity, non-narrativity, rhythm, and sound – in some ways rather than others in order to influence an audience in some ways rather than others. Genre, then, is another resource at an author's disposal. This view of genre responds to the lamenters by saying, "not to worry." Genres help organize but they need not determine the shape of individual works, and, indeed, authors often work with existing genres in order to develop new ones that they find more responsive to their engagement with particular issues of human experience.

Let me elaborate. Raymond Williams nicely articulates the case for the power that genre ("literary form" is his term) exerts upon authors:

> When I hear people talk about literature, describing what so-and-so did with that form – how did he handle the short novel? – I often think we should reverse the question and ask, how did the short novel handle him. Because anyone who has carefully observed his own practice of writing eventually finds that there is a point where, although he is holding the pen or tapping the typewriter, what is being written, while not separate from him, is not only him either, and of course this other force is literary form.[7]

I note, first, that Williams slides from a question giving greater agency to genre than to the author ("how did the short novel handle him") to a more reciprocal description of the relation between the two. I share Williams's idea that genres have some agency, but I contend that this agency has multiple possible relations to authorial agency. In addition to cases in which genres handle authors or in which each handles the other, there are cases in which the author mishandles genre and cases in which the author dominates the genre – even to the point of revising it into something new. Furthermore, each of these varied author–genre relations typically has consequences for readers' aesthetic judgments. The author who mishandles genre typically produces a flawed work. The author who is handled by the genre typically produces an unoriginal work. The author in a reciprocal relation with genre is likely to produce an effective work, and the author who dominates the genre is likely to produce an innovative work.

Although Franco Moretti is a champion of distant reading, and my approach is one rooted in close reading, his analysis of the early detective story supports this view of authorial and generic agency.[8] In seeking to explain why Arthur Conan Doyle's tales of Sherlock Holmes became canonical and those of his contemporaries writing detective stories did not, Moretti notes that Doyle makes more use of clues than others do. But he goes on to note that only four of Conan Doyle's stories work with clues that are decodable by the reader, a feature that comes to define the detective story. Why? Because at this early stage of the development of the genre, Conan Doyle stumbles upon the value of clues as he pursues his dominant interest in making Holmes omniscient. Clues decodable only by Holmes support that omniscience, while clues also decodable by the reader work against it. Dominant interest wins – and so Conan Doyle handles the emerging genre. But at the same time, his handling leads to the development of certain features (clues in general and decodable clues in particular) that subsequent authors put at the center of the genre even as they preserved the singularity (if not the omniscience) of the detective.

In what follows, I develop these theoretical positions by revisiting and expanding some previous proposals I've made about narrativity, lyricality, and portraiture and by then analyzing John Edgar Wideman's generically innovative fiction "Everybody Knew Bubba Riff."[9] But first I need to return to my opening jokes.

Authors, Audiences, and Room for Maneuver: "X Walks into a Bar" Jokes

Jokes 1–3 exhibit the recurrent features and conventions of the "X walks into a bar" subgenre. Such jokes are short and highly stylized, with minimal characterization of X and the bartender, and with just three simple moves culminating in a punny punchline. The jokester's purpose is to evoke laughter at the cleverness of the pun (or in some cases to evoke a groan at how labored it is). The first move is the set-up (X walks into a bar); the second move is a single line of dialogue – either from X or the bartender. This line introduces a small narrative instability in the relationship between X and the bartender, provoking the audience's interest in the other character's response. The third move resolves this instability via another line of dialogue that delivers the punny punchline designed to evoke the appropriate laughter (or groan).

In subsuming these features under a conception of "jokes as rhetoric," I home in on how the authors both rely on the grooves of the subgenre and make particular choices within those grooves to achieve their desired effects. In Joke #1, for example, one authorial choice that stands out is the adjective "big" in the punchline, since the more common and more appropriate adjective for a pause of some duration is "long." Does this choice weaken the joke, making the pun on "pause" too much of a stretch? (Note that the puns on "hey" and "staph" in Joke #2 and Joke #3 respectively are more straightforward.) I think not for two reasons. (1) The particular progression of the joke makes the pun a clever surprise. By following the pause in the first line of dialogue with the unusual move of the bear's ordering something in addition to a drink, the jokester introduces a misdirection of the audience's attention: away from the pause and toward "those peanuts." The jokester continues that misdirection with the bartender's "Sure," and only then makes the sudden switch to the punny focus on the ellipsis in that order. (2) The jokester relies on the grooves of subgenre – and the audience's knowledge of those grooves. More specifically, the jokester relies on the audience's expectation of a punny punchline as more important than strict fidelity to common usage. (Anyone who hears the joke and objects "but the bartender should say '*long* pause'" will come across as a pedant.) In these ways, then, the jokester makes the conventions of the subgenre work hand-in-hand with the particulars of this joke.

So far, so standard. But let's now consider Joke #4, where the jokester uses the subgenre as a resource in a significantly different way. First, she deviates from the standard conventions in several ways. She writes a two-move rather than a three-move joke, and she reverses the usual order of the set-up and the dialogue. Perhaps most remarkably, she does not end with a pun. By deviating in these ways, she runs the risk of having the joke fall flat – as, indeed, it would for anyone who does not have some familiarity with the subgenre. But the jokester relies on her audience's knowledge of the subgenre and ability to use that knowledge to navigate her construction of the joke. It's as if she asks, "how can I make the conventions of the subgenre part of my joke's subject matter?" Her most outrageous answer is to make the standard set up "X walks into a bar" the actual punchline of the joke – or better, the completion of the punchline. In other words, she makes the two moves of the joke part of the same extended punchline. The humor of the line depends on the intersection of the conceit of time travel with the meta-communication about playing with the conventions of the subgenre, the jokester's implied "do you see what I did there?" As a meta-joke, #4 offers a different kind of humor, one focused more on the cleverness of the authorial performance than on the humor generated by the punny punchlines of the non-meta-jokes. In using the subgenre as a resource in this way, the author also does something more formally innovative than the authors of Jokes #1–3.

I don't want to oversell the innovation of Joke #4: it's a simple joke after all, and its deviations from the standard conventions ultimately reinforce those conventions. Nevertheless, this analysis of Joke #4 points the way toward a recognition that authors often engage in more radical uses of the room for maneuver provided by genres, uses that can lead to more substantial innovation at the level of both genre and individual work.

Genres: A Heuristic Taxonomy

As I now turn from jokes to literature, I want to further sort out meanings of the term "genre." I have referred to it as "a loose organizing principle or a broad frame" that authors and audiences draw on in their construction and reconstruction of individual works. But I also find it useful to distinguish among these principles and frames according to their level of generality (or degrees of looseness). I propose five different generic categories, going from the most general to the most specific. I design this taxonomy as a pragmatic tool, useful for basic distinctions, rather than a comprehensive and rigorous account of the ontology of genres.

Category 1: widely accepted designations of general literary expression such as poetry, prose, drama; fiction or nonfiction.

Category 2: modes of literary expression such as lyricality, narrativity, portraiture, and essay.

Category 3: more specific but still broad instantiation of these modes such as epic, novel, history, biography, autobiography, lyric poem, character sketch, and argument.

Category 4: more specific kinds within such modes, such as the novel of action, the Bildungsroman, the allegorical novel, the memoir, the dramatic lyric, the dramatic monologue, and so on.

Category 5: common structures harnessed to a set of affective and thematic effects such as tragedy, comedy, tragicomedy, satire, utopia, dystopia, and so on.

In considering individual works, all categories are relevant. Ernest Hemingway's *A Farewell to Arms*, for example, is a tragic fictional Bildungsroman in prose, while Robert Frost's "Out, Out – " is a tragic fictional narrative poem, and William Shakespeare's *Othello* a fictional tragic drama. In addition, these categories can be inflected by movements in literary history. Shakespeare's play is a Renaissance tragedy, while Hemingway's novel and Frost's poem are modernist ones.

Narrativity, Lyricality, Portraiture, and Authorial Innovation

In previous work,[10] I have focused on some relations between individual works and the loose organizing principles of Category 2. More specifically, I have tried to distinguish among narrativity, lyricality, and portraiture as distinct modes, while also suggesting that attention to what makes each one distinct helps illuminate its relation to the other two. Consistent with my view of literature as rhetoric, I have proposed the following conceptions that pay attention both to the authorial shaping of resources and to readerly responses to that shaping. Narrativity, the mode devoted to storytelling, is rooted in the rhetorical action of somebody telling somebody else on some occasion and for some purpose(s) that something happened. Furthermore, this rhetorical action involves the authorial shaping of one or more characters experiencing change over time, a shaping that invites audiences to observe, affectively respond to, and judge those experiences. In *A Farewell to Arms*, Hemingway has Frederic Henry tell the tragic story of his coming to love and lose Catherine Barkley against the backdrop of his slowly evolving understanding of the destructiveness of World War I and of the world in general. In addition, Hemingway ties the trajectory of Frederic's experiences to a trajectory of audience response rooted in ethical judgments about and affective reactions to those experiences. This trajectory culminates in the audience's deep sorrow over Frederic's loss of Catherine and his recognition that there was nothing he – or anyone – could have done to prevent it, even as that sorrow is offset by small signs that he will be able to cope with both his loss and his hard-won knowledge about the destructive world.[11]

Lyricality, the mode devoted to the representation of thoughts and feelings, is rooted in one of two rhetorical actions: (1) somebody telling somebody else (or even oneself) on some occasion and for some purposes that something is, where that something is a situation, an attitude, an emotion, a belief, or a truth claim (example: Robert Frost's "Nothing Gold Can Stay"); (2) somebody telling somebody else (or even oneself) on some occasion for some purposes about his or her meditations on something, or to put it another way, his or her process of coming to terms with something (example: Frost's "Stopping by Woods on a Snowy Evening"). Furthermore, these rhetorical actions involve the authorial shaping of the speaker's telling so that it invites the audience not to judge the speaker and her thoughts, attitudes, or beliefs but rather to enter wholly into the speaker's perspective. The difference between Frost's "Out, Out—" and his "Stopping by Woods" illustrates the difference between narrativity and

lyricality. In "Out, Out—" Frost not only depicts a radical change in
a short time but also invites his audience to observe and judge the boy who
loses his hand and his life as well as those in his community who witness
those losses and then, "since they / Were not the one dead, turned to their
affairs" (ll. 33–34).[12] In "Stopping by Woods," by contrast, as Frost depicts
the process by which the speaker works through his temptation to lie down
in the snow, Frost invites his audience not to judge the speaker (as vain,
self-absorbed, brilliantly sensitive, or anything else) but rather to participate in his thoughts and feelings.

Portraiture, the mode devoted to the representation of character, is
rooted in the rhetorical action of somebody telling somebody else on
some occasion and for some purposes that someone is. This rhetorical
action involves an authorial shaping of the unfolding revelation of character that invites the audience to judge that character. Indeed, the ethical
judgment is tied to the purpose. In "My Last Duchess," Robert Browning
not only wants to create the impression that "there [he—the Duke of
Ferrara—] stands as if alive" but he also wants to convey his layered,
though mostly negative, evaluation of the Duke's remarkable combination
of vanity, imperiousness, possessiveness, and rhetorical skill.[13]

We can comprehend the similarities and differences of these broad
genres by thinking about correspondences among fundamental elements
of each. With narrativity, those elements are character, event, and change
plus judgment, affect, and ethics. With lyricality, character is replaced by
speaker; event by situation, thought, emotion, attitude, or belief; and
change yields to the revelation of an essentially static situation or to the
process of the speaker coming to terms with something. Furthermore,
judgment of the speaker is replaced by entering into his or her perspective,
or to put it another way, whereas narrativity relies on sequential judgments
of characters, lyricality invites an increasingly deeper merging between
speaker and audience. To be sure, readers will make judgments of that
merging, but these are post-experience judgments of the poem as a whole
rather than building blocks in the construction of the rhetorical action.
With portraiture, character returns and occupies the dominant place in the
rhetorical action; event recedes or is subordinated to the function of
revealing character; and change is replaced by the freeze-frame of the
portrait – this person in this moment. Moreover, built into the unfolding
revelation of that character is a series of sequential ethical judgments just
like those in narrativity.

I want to emphasize two other features of this view. (1) It does not tie any
mode to any Category #1 genre. Authors can deploy narrativity, lyricality,

and portraiture in prose, in poetry, or in drama. Authors can also deploy the modes in works of fiction or of nonfiction. Nevertheless, at different historical moments, some Category #2 genres will be more or less closely linked with Category #1 genres. For example, at least since the Romantic period, lyricality has been associated with poetry, and narrativity with prose. Consequently, authors can enhance the power of individual works by going against the grain of these primary links. When Frost publishes "Out, Out—" in 1916, the link between poetry and lyricality is sufficiently strong that his abandoning that link enhances the power of his narrative poem. Indeed, that power is connected to the way in which his narrative eschews such typical features of the traditional lyric as the detailed revelation of a speaker's thoughts and perceptions. Instead, Frost focuses on the extraordinary quality of the combination of characters and events. Similarly, when Hemingway experiments with lyricality within the short story in works such as "A Clean, Well-Lighted Place" and "Now I Lay Me," his experiments take on added force because he conducts them in prose. In that (restricted) sense, Hemingway becomes the Short Story Writer as Lyric Poet.

(2) The rhetorical view of genre as a resource that authors can deploy in some ways rather than others leads to the dual recognition that authors can construct hybrids from these generic modes – and from the more specific instances of them denoted in Category #4 – and that such hybrid constructions can be a significant source of formal innovation. Sometimes the hybrids evolve into their own recognizable Category #4 genres and sometimes the hybrids remain remarkable experiments that may or may not get picked up on and further refined by future authors. As an example of the first development, I shall discuss the establishment of the genres of the mask lyric and the dramatic monologue in Victorian England. As an example of the second situation, I shall analyze Wideman's "Everybody Knew Bubba Riff."

In discussing the mask lyric and the dramatic monologue, I build on the work of Ralph W. Rader, who is primarily concerned with the relation of poet to speaker in such works.[14] For Rader, the essence of the mask lyric is that the poet adopts a persona but uses that persona to express his or her own feelings, thoughts, attitudes, and/or beliefs. Rader's main examples are Alfred Tennyson's "Ulysses" and "Tithonus." For Rader, the essence of the dramatic monologue is that the poet constructs a speaker radically distinct from himself and puts that speaker's self-expression on display for the audience. His main example is Browning's "My Last Duchess." I build on Rader by relating these two Category #4 genres to the Category #2 genres of lyricality, narrativity, and portraiture. While individual works may contain elements of all three Category #2 genres, lyricality is the dominant mode of the mask lyric, and portraiture the dominant mode of the dramatic monologue. This view, I believe, more fully captures the differences for authorial construction and readerly reconstruction between the mask lyric and the dramatic monologue, and, thus, goes even further than Rader does in showing that the surface similarity of poems such as "Ulysses" and "My Last Duchess" can obscure the significant differences in their purposes.

I now propose a schematic and speculative account of how Tennyson and Browning developed these Category #4 genres. To move beyond speculation, this account would need to be much longer, since it would require more discussion of historical context, including the work of other poets, and of the biographies of Browning and Tennyson. But I am less concerned with getting all the details right than I am with illustrating how the rhetorical view of genre helps explain the role of authors in generic innovation, especially how authors draw upon previous generic modes as they establish new ones. As readers in the tradition of English poetry, Browning and Tennyson were familiar with the general mode of the dramatic lyric in which a speaker other than the poet addresses some other text-internal audience on a particular occasion. Seduction poems such as John Donne's "The Flea" and Andrew Marvell's "To His Coy Mistress" constitute one line in this tradition of the dramatic lyric. Browning and Tennyson were also familiar with the dramatic device of the soliloquy, in which a character's aside to the audience often took the form of a lyric meditation, as it does in two of the most famous examples, Hamlet's "To be or not to be" and Macbeth's "Tomorrow and tomorrow" speeches. Browning and Tennyson were also familiar with the Romantic lyric in which the poet expressed his or her own feelings and attitudes, as, for example, in Wordsworth's "Composed upon Westminster Bridge," Keats's "On First Looking into Chapman's Homer," and many other individual poems.

What Tennyson saw in these existing Category #4 genres was the possibility of having his own feelings be expressed by another recognizable speaker addressing a text-internal audience. Thus, in "Ulysses," Tennyson uses the mask of Homer's wanderer to express his own interest in going on after the death of Arthur Henry Hallam, the friend who is the subject of *In Memoriam*:

> Tho' much is taken, much abides; and tho'
> We are not now that strength which in old days
> Moved earth and heaven, that which we are, we are;
> One equal temper of heroic hearts,
> Made weak by time and fate, but strong in will
> To strive, to seek, to find, and not to yield. (ll. 65–70)[15]

What Browning saw in these Category #4 genres was the possibility of taking on the ideas and perspectives of a figure significantly different from himself. More than that, he saw the possibility of using the speaking situation not in the service of the lyric ends of the persona's speech but rather in the service of the construction of the character of the speaker. Thus, the dramatic monologue effects a shift from lyricality to portraiture. In "My Last Duchess," "The Soliloquy of the Spanish Cloister," and other poems, Browning uses the speaker's monologues in particular situations to reveal – and invite the audience to judge – those characters.

Wideman's Generic Experiment in "Everybody Knew Bubba Riff"

Wideman's "Everybody Knew Bubba Riff" is a ten-page medley of voices with no punctuation until it ends with a period. Here's how it begins.

> Voices are a river you step in once and again never the same Bubba here you are dead boy dead dead dead nigger with spooky Boris Karloff powder caked on your face boy skin lightener skin brightener and who did it to you I'm talking to you boy don't roll your eyes at me don't suckee teeth and cutee eye look how that boy's grown come here baby give me some sugar[16]

Here's how it ends:

> you got to remember today's today and yesterday shit yesterday's long gone we was kids back then you and me and Bubba playing kid games then time runs out is spozed to run out it spozed to change and we sure ain't babies no more Big Bubba a dinosaur man wasn't even in the right century man living by the wrong clock man he was Bubba all right your man Bubba Bubba Bubba everybody knew Bubba.[17]

As these excerpts indicate, reading the piece without the benefit of any generic frame makes it very puzzling. Just who speaks to whom when? How many speakers and listeners and how many temporal points are introduced in these opening lines, and who is speaking to whom at the end? Where are the syntactic breaks in this continuous stream of prose? And how do the answers to these questions relate to a larger frame of intelligibility? Fortunately, Wideman's title – and the ideas about narrativity, lyricality, and portraiture that I have sketched here – help us begin to answer this last question, and that answer in turn can help us understand how Wideman, influenced by postmodernism and its penchant for destabilizing categories of all kinds, engages in his own generic innovation.

Wideman uses the title not only to give an abstract of the piece but also to initiate his audience into the layering of voices and meanings produced by the continuous stream of prose. "Riff" works both in conjunction with "Bubba" – it could be his surname – and as a broad generic designation for the piece, a signal that what follows will be a riff on the phrase "everybody knew Bubba." By using that designation from the realm of jazz, Wideman invites his audience to consider the piece in relation to lyricality. More specifically, he signals that his continuous stream of prose is analogous to a continuous stream of musical notes. At the same time, "Everybody Knew Bubba" invites the audience to consider the piece in relation to portraiture. Riffing on "knowing Bubba" (or "knowing Bubba Riff") promises to generate a rich character sketch. In addition, while such riffing is unlikely to generate a narrative progression following the pattern of instability-complication-resolution, such riffing should lead to multiple mini-narratives about Bubba. Let's take a closer look.

I start with the through-line of the piece, the backbone of character and event upon which Wideman builds his riff, and elements of which are present in the excerpts from the beginning and ending I quoted above. The medley of voices speaks in response to Bubba's death at some unspecified age in adulthood; the temporal present of that speaking is at a memorial service for him; he died as a result of his involvement in the drug trade in the Homewood section of Pittsburgh. But as the excerpts also indicate, this through-line is often subordinated to Wideman's riffing. More than that, the riffing is the means by which Wideman infuses the piece with considerable affective force, as it provides the strong affect of the speakers and invites Wideman's audience to respond affectively in turn.

As with the analysis of Joke #4, it's helpful to attend to how Wideman both follows and deviates from the standard conventions of the relevant genres and then turn to how he harnesses all those elements of construction into this remarkably distinctive piece. With lyricality, rather than using a single lyric voice or even a clear sequence of juxtaposed voices, Wideman for the first half of the piece gives his audience multiple overlapping voices with no clear hierarchy among them. About halfway through, however, Wideman introduces an "I," Bubba's best friend, whose voice dominates the rest of the piece. But this "I" does not simply focus on Bubba and his life. Instead, his comments about Bubba lead him to digressions about other things, including his own first love, and the story of Charley Rackett, which Bubba himself loves. Charley was a slave ancestor of the "I," a man who was also known as Bubba, and who had the stubbornness to insist that he go to the fields every day, even long after he could work in them. In addition, rather than locating his medley of voices at a single temporal occasion in the first half of the piece, Wideman disburses those voices across different moments in Bubba's life – with the kind of shifts evident in the excerpt from the beginning. Furthermore, although Wideman does locate the "I" of the second half at Bubba's memorial service, that "I" frequently narrates from his perspective in the past. Finally, Wideman uses both the medley of voices and the discourse of the "I" to explore multiple aspects of African American life in the Homewood area of Pittsburgh where Bubba lived: family, church, ancestry, gender differences, the drug trade and the ravages it has wrought on the men of Homewood. Wideman's deviating from the standard conventions of a lyric with a single speaker in a fixed situation offering a particular take on some aspect of experience introduces a significant communal and thematic element to the piece. Bubba is being mourned and remembered by the Homewood community and especially by a particular representative of that community. Bubba too represents that community, someone who grew up there and was subject to all the forces that led to his death. Wideman's work with the other generic modes will shed further light on these effects.

Wideman does give his audience many mini-narratives: the infant Bubba breastfeeding with his mother; the adolescent Bubba warning his mother's drug supplier not to lay a hand on her; the young adult Bubba who wants to hear the story of Charley Bubba Racket; the story of Bubba the enforcer with the baseball bat in the drug trade. Strikingly, Wideman also moves beyond Bubba to sketch the outlines of a larger narrative about the drug trade and how it led to Bubba's murder:

> everybody gets what they want plenty to go round if your shits tight it's these free-lance Rambo motherfuckers fucking things up just a matter of time before somebody waste Bubba don't care how big he is how many bad brothers he busted up with his bare hands his big bat Bubba go down just like anybody else you bust a cap in his chest no man the word on the set is nobody knows who did it but nobody in business don't care neither[18]

Nevertheless, Wideman doesn't use these mini-narratives to offer a coherent cause-and-effect account of Bubba's life. "Everybody Knew Bubba Riff" is not a Bildungsroman. At the same time, the resulting fragmentary narrative of Bubba's life humanizes him, even as it keeps the thematic issues of family, church, ancestry, and, above all, the drug trade central to Wideman's audience's understanding of Bubba's life.

As for portraiture, I agree with Tracie Guzzio[19] that Wideman works to ironize his title by emphasizing the gap between the voices talking to and about Bubba and anybody's substantially knowing him. In this way, what

Wideman does with portraiture works together with the fragmentary quality of the narrativity. While Wideman does give us elements of Bubba's adult character, such as his interest in and similarity to Charley Rackett, and his identity as a stubborn enforcer who wields a baseball bat and who fails to change with the times, Wideman does not do for Bubba what Browning does for his subjects: produce a full word portrait. Bubba's best friend refers to "the streets where Bubba's known where they say his names *Junior June Juney Junebug JB J Bub Bubby Bubba* all the silent names hidden behind curtains and blinds,"[20] and this reference itself is noteworthy for what it leaves out. The "I" never explains the relations among these names, never identifies one of them as the given name, never definitely indicates that all are just nicknames, and never ties any of them to particular character traits. By listing the names in this series, Wideman suggests how the sound of each gradually morphs into the sound of the next one in the series. Thus, the names become signifiers without strong ties to an ostensible signified. Everybody was acquainted with Bubba, but nobody knew Bubba.

Wideman combines his through-line and the various ways he works with lyricality, narrativity, and portraiture to construct a very moving work. The piece is a communal elegy for Bubba that places his life and death into the larger social context of Homewood, and especially the context of the drug trade. This elegiac quality makes lyricality prominent but Wideman also invites his audience to judge various aspects of that communal elegy just as the author of a dramatic monologue invites his audience to judge the speaker. The community genuinely mourns Bubba, and so does Wideman's audience: the overwhelming affective response to the piece is a sense of loss. But Wideman's audience feels a different, arguably deeper, sense of loss than those in his community because of what the audience knows and doesn't know about Bubba, this once bouncing baby boy who has died too soon. Wideman's audience knows that the community doesn't know Bubba the way it thinks it does. It knows that there's more to Bubba – without being able to specify exactly what – than what the various voices of the community have commented on. It knows that Bubba's character and his story have been shaped by all those forces operating in Homewood, and it knows especially that Bubba is just one of many men lost to the drug trade. Above all, Wideman's audience recognizes the limitations of the community's passive acceptance of the violence of the drug trade, an acceptance evident in the best friend's account of Bubba's death.

In this connection, consider once again the concluding lines, where Bubba's best friend speaks to another mutual friend.

> you got to remember today's today and yesterday shit yesterday's long gone
> we was kids back then you and me and Bubba playing kid games then time
> runs out is spozed to run out it spozed to change and we sure ain't babies no
> more Big Bubba a dinosaur man wasn't even in the right century man living
> by the wrong clock man he was Bubba all right your man Bubba Bubba
> Bubba everybody knew Bubba. (73)

These lines are poignant for Wideman's audience because they combine genuine truths – things change and people need to change with them – with blaming the victim: Bubba didn't change and so he died. The lines are especially poignant because the speaker ends with what Wideman has guided his audience to recognize as empty consolation. The gap between Bubba's best friend's reaching for that consolation and the audience's even fragmentary knowledge of Bubba's life and death makes the ending affectively powerful.

In sum, then, Wideman uses the room for maneuver provided by lyricality, narrative, and portraiture to construct a remarkable hybrid. He fuses lyricality (the communal elegy) and narrativity (the story of Bubba and the drug trade and the judgments accompanying it) and juxtaposes that fusion with the negative energy of his portraiture (what Wideman doesn't reveal about Bubba's life signifies as much as what he does reveal) in a way that leaves his audience deeply mournful, albeit in different ways, about both Bubba and the community in which he lived and died. In short, Wideman constructs a tragic lyric.

Conclusion

Stepping back from the particular analysis of Wideman's work, I offer the following general points about the relations of authors, genres, and audiences. Authors and audiences rely on genres because they provide fundamental systems of intelligibility, ways of relating the diverse particulars of individual works to larger structures of meaning and feeling. At the same time, genres are not rigid systems that confine and constrain authors and audiences. Instead, they leave room for maneuver, and skillful authors often do innovative things with that room, and perceptive audiences adapt to those innovations. Furthermore, sometimes those innovations develop into their own recognizable genres, which in turn set up new kinds of room for maneuver. Consequently, tracking these developments can add substantially to our understanding both of individual works and of the history of forms. If I am right about "Everybody Knew Bubba," then Wideman has made a bid for generic innovation with his new hybrid form. It will be worth watching to see if another author picks up on that bid and either reinforces it or takes it in a new direction.

Notes

1. Benedetto Croce, *Aesthetic as Science of Expression and General Linguistic* (New York: Noonday, 1953); Maurice Blanchot, *Le livre à venir* (Paris: Gallimard, 1959); Jacques Derrida, "The Law of Genre," trans. Avital Ronell, *Critical Inquiry*, 7 (1980), 55–81.
2. Blanchot, *Le livre à venir*, p. 243, as quoted in Jonathan Culler, *Theory of the Lyric* (Cambridge, MA: Harvard University Press, 2015), p. 41.
3. Aristotle, *Poetics*, trans. S. H. Butcher (New York: Macmillan, 1895); Northrop Frye, *Anatomy of Criticism* (Princeton, NJ: Princeton University Press, 1957); Bruce Robbins, "Afterword," *PMLA*, 122.5 (2007), 1644–51; Culler, *Theory of the Lyric*.
4. Culler, *Theory of the Lyric*, p. 89.
5. Ibid.
6. James Phelan, *Somebody Telling Somebody Else* (Columbus: Ohio State University Press, 2017).
7. Raymond Williams, "The Writer: Commitment and Alignment," 1980, in *The Raymond Williams Reader*, ed. John O. Higgins (Malden: Blackwell, 2001), pp. 208–17, p. 216.
8. Franco Moretti, "The Slaughterhouse of Literature," *Modern Language Quarterly* 61 (2000), pp. 207–27.
9. John Edgar Wideman, "Everybody Knew Bubba Riff," in *All Stories Are True* (1992; New York: Vintage, 1993), pp. 64–73.
10. James Phelan, *Living to Tell about It* (Ithaca, NY: Cornell University Press, 2005); James Phelan, *Experiencing Fiction* (Columbus: Ohio State University Press, 2007).
11. For a fuller analysis, see James Phelan, *Reading the American Novel, 1920–2010* (Malden: Wiley-Blackwell, 2013), pp. 85–104.
12. *The Poetry of Robert Frost: The Complete Poems*, ed. Edward Connery Latham (New York: Henry Holt, 1969), pp. 136–37.
13. Cf. Robert Browning, "My Last Duchess," *The Works of Robert Browning* (Ware, UK: Wordsworth Editions), pp. 469–70, ll. 50–51: "There she stands / As if alive." What the Duke says about the portrait of the duchess also applies to Browning's portrait of the Duke.
14. Ralph W. Rader, "The Dramatic Monologue and Related Lyric Forms," in *Fact, Fiction, and Form: Selected Essays of Ralph W. Rader*, eds. James Phelan and David H. Richter (Columbus: Ohio State University Press, 2011), pp. 134–54.

15. Alfred Tennyson, *The Works of Alfred, Lord Tennyson* (Ware, UK: Wordsworth Editions, 1998), p. 148.
16. Wideman, "Everybody Knew Bubba Riff," p. 64.
17. Ibid., p. 73.
18. Ibid.
19. Tracie Guzzio, *All Stories Are True: History, Myth, and Trauma in the Work of John Edgar Wideman* (Jackson: University Press of Mississippi, 2011), pp. 87–88.
20. Wideman, "Everybody," p. 71.

CHAPTER 17

The Author in Literary Theory and Theories of Literature

Jakob Stougaard-Nielsen

We have become accustomed to regarding the question of the author in literary criticism and theory in anti-authorial terms. It is a quaintness of modern literary theory that the author, whom we would, commonsensically, expect to be the central agent in the production of the literary work, has, for the most part of the past century, been considered a liminal character of minor importance to literary criticism, and, if not completely dead, then at least a ghost haunting the limits of the literary work of art.

The turn away from the author in literary criticism to the literary text itself was, in the first half of the twentieth century, a way to bestow credibility and objectivity on the burgeoning professionalization of literary criticism and a way to distance "modern" literary criticism from the connoisseurship and biographical positivism that had dominated the critical appreciation of literature in the nineteenth century.

The discourse of "the death of the author," associated with Roland Barthes and his famous 1967 essay with that title, has been widely accepted by shifting theoretical currents and in pedagogical practices, as "reading the last rites over the corpse of the idea of the author."[1] However, apart from the fact that repeated anti-authorial pronouncements have had the ironic effect of keeping the question of the author at the center of shifting theoretical debates, the ghostly figure of the author already haunted author-critics in the late nineteenth century.

In France, the dominant mode of criticism became associated with Charles Augustin Sainte-Beuve's biographical method, the contention that the literary work of art gives access to the values of the author. In spite of the fact that contemporary admirers such as Henry James considered Sainte-Beuve "the acutest critic the world has ever seen," and that he has more recently been revived as a "father [. . .] of modern literary criticism," his afterlife was sealed by Marcel Proust's posthumously published collection of essays *Contre Sainte-Beuve* (1895–1900; publ. 1954), which furiously refuted his biographical method of reading for the author, and by Proust's own *À la recherche du temps perdu* (1913–27), for which his essays against Sainte-Beuve provided a programmatic critical framework.[2] In this decisively modern work, Proust blurred the distinction between author and narrator by portraying an author figure who is only able to write once the novel has ended. As Barthes summed up Proust's achievement: "[I]nstead of putting his life into his novel, as is so often maintained, he made of his very life a work for which his own book was the model."[3]

Proust's poetics represented a break with nineteenth-century connoisseurship and with what he called "literary gossip," and pointed toward formalist and narratological notions of "literary personas" and "implied authors," who are neither wholly inside nor wholly outside the literary work. According to Christopher Prendergast, the Proustian aesthetic that supplanted Sainte-Beuve's biographism insists "on the rift or incommensurability between the social persona of the author and his creative self [. . .]: 'a book is the product of a self other than that which we display in our habits, in company, in our vices.'"[4] Where the nineteenth-century narratorial subject was generally associated with the voice of the actual author, which was made accessible to the reader through the literary work, toward the end of the century "a sense of a growing distance and impersonality" began to alter the relationship between authors and readers, as well as the way in which critics and writers understood the relationship between the written and the writing self, the "private" creative work and the "public" persona of the author.[5]

Henry James's artist-tales from the 1890s are particularly illustrative of this gradual transformation not only of the relationship between authors and readers but also of the very "purpose" of literary criticism and its preference for the autonomous work of art. James famously allegorized what would later become known as "the intentional fallacy," committed by critics practicing the biographical method. In "The Figure in the Carpet" (1896) and "The Aspern Papers" (1888), James illustrates the trappings of a reader's ambition to "get at the author" through the literary work; in the latter tale, this is exemplified in the absent God-like author Jeffrey Aspern, who appears as a "bright ghost" only accessible through "a morsel of papers."[6]

In James's "The Private Life" (1892), the problem of attributing the literary work to a living author is turned into a Gothic mystery haunted by a "ghost writer" creating his solitary art in the dark. While searching for a play the celebrity author Clare Vawdrey may or may not have written, the narrator enters the author's dark room, and is startled by a figure seated at a table in a writer's pose. The narrator believes this figure to be the author himself, but when calling him, he receives no reply. The writer does not turn from his writing pose, and does not reveal why he is writing in the dark. The narrator discovers that the writer could not, in fact, have been Vawdrey, since he was at the same time declaiming a scene from his play on the balcony. Symptomatically, this divorce of the private writer from the public celebrity author leaves the "reader" with "an insane desire to see the author."[7] Looking for the author in the literary work leads to a ghostly encounter with a figure who both is and appears not to be the "actual" author; and it is precisely the mystical separation of the voice of the "biographical" author from the hand that writes which results in a desire to see the author, who now no longer exists outside of the written text. Never quite inside, yet neither wholly outside the text, writers and literary critics have continued to explore the relationship between the writer and the written, the author and her literary inscription.

Seán Burke maintains that the question of the author is *the* question of literary theory. According to Andrew Bennett, the author "is an inescapable factor in criticism and theory, not least when she is most firmly being pronounced dead."[8] Bennett and Royle, picking up on a rich narrative tradition of ghost-writers and Barthes's late-modern pronouncement of "the death of the author," conclude that the author remains "a kind of ghost" in literary theory: "the author cannot die precisely because [. . .] the author is – always has been and always will be – a ghost. Never fully present or fully absent, a figure of fantasy and elusiveness, the author only ever haunts."[9]

Against Biographical Positivism: New Criticism and Russian Formalism

Writer-critics such as Proust and James came to play an important role in the burgeoning professionalization of literary criticism in the early decades of the twentieth century. James's championing of impersonality in narration ("as a narrator of fictitious events [the novelist] is nowhere"),[10] pointing toward Wayne C. Booth's conception of the "implied author," defines novelistic narrators not as coterminous with the empirical author, but as "the impersonal author's concrete deputy or delegate, a convenient substitute or apologist for the creative power otherwise so veiled and disembodied."[11] James's early critical considerations of novelistic discourse were echoed in T. S. Eliot's formulation of an ideology of authorial self-effacement, a poetic "extinction of personality" or depersonalization, which to him pushed the appreciation of poetic art closer to a more objective evaluation of the literary work of art.[12]

To Eliot, poetry "is not the expression of personality, but an escape from personality," and the poet has "not a 'personality' to express, but a particular medium."[13] The poet, in Eliot's famous 1919 essay "Tradition and the Individual Talent," is properly understood as "individual," "original," and creative when evaluated aesthetically and placed, "for contrast and comparison, among the dead" – as a medium that not only recalls but also eventually transforms the tradition of dead poets and artists.[14]

Literary-critical studies of narrative soon took up the mantle from the modernist aesthetic of impersonality. Percy Lubbock's proto-New Critical *Craft of Fiction* (1921), one of the first works of Anglo-American literary criticism to focus on the techniques of modern writers and the novel as a form, engages explicitly with the question of "impersonal narration" and asks of James's use of authorial delegates in *The Ambassadors* (1903): "How is the author to withdraw, to stand aside, and to let Strether's thought tell its own story?"[15] In exploring the author's "craft" through the intrinsic workings of fiction, Lubbock makes a distinction between two modes of writing: the "pictorial" and the "dramatic." The first describes the way "the reader faces toward the story-teller and listens to him," while in the latter "the recording, registering mind of the author is eliminated."[16] The Jamesian "unobtrusive" authorial technique, Lubbock's ideal form, is a hybrid of the two: it is "the method by which the picture of a mind is fully dramatized."[17] While not discounting that some works may be more "pictorial" than others, Lubbock rejects as irrelevant the question of an author's biography, the external consciousness or intentions of the author, or indeed any other social context: "there is no authority at the back of a novel, independent of it, to vouch for the truth of its apparent wilfulness."[18]

If the Anglo-American New Critics were generally against turning criticism into an "objective" science, the Russian Formalists in the 1910s and 1920s set out to conceptualize the literary work as an autonomous aesthetic object available for rigorous scrutiny without recourse to its author's biography, authorial intentions, or social context. Common to Viktor Shklovsky, Boris Eikhenbaum, Boris Tomashevsky, Yury Tynyanov, and Roman Jakobson was a methodological concern to lay bare the linguistic and aesthetic devices that defined "literariness" as a phenomenon clearly divorced from the communicative properties and intentions associated with everyday speech. This preoccupation with literary devices, literary forms, and their universal application would influence European structuralisms and narratologists such as Gérard Genette.

If the author was largely ignored by the early Formalists, the question of intentionality took center stage in postwar New Criticism. W. K. Wimsatt and Monroe Beardsley most persuasively countered the still prevalent tendency in literary criticism toward historical contextualization, biographism and moralization with their seminal 1946 essay "The Intentional Fallacy," a central reference point for the elusive movement of New Criticism that rose to prominence in the US in the 1930s and 1940s and subsequently found local expressions throughout Europe. Beyond a rejection of authorial intentions ("the design or intention of the author is neither available nor desirable as a standard for judging the success of a work of literary art"[19]), New Critics were joined in their primary concern with the close reading of texts: examining a poem's "technical elements, textual patterns, and incongruities."[20] An early statement regarding the New Critical method is found in Cleanth Brooks and Robert Penn Warren's *Understanding Poetry* (1938), where the poem itself is seen to dramatize themes exclusively in terms of textual characteristics such as situation, character, imagery, rhythm, and tone. Brooks's *The Well-Wrought Urn* (1947), devoting several pages of close analysis to a short poem, makes no reference to the poet's biography or historical contexts, and does not present any "speculation on the mental processes of the author."[21]

The notion of "intentional fallacy" has been instrumental in shaping the legacy of New Criticism's anti-authorialism, yet, as Bennett has argued, the strong focus on this aspect of Wimsatt and Beardsley's work amounts "to something of a misreading."[22] While often taken to suggest that the literary work as such is bereft of authorial intentions, Wimsatt and Beardsley actually leave much more room for the author: "A poem does not come into existence by accident."[23] But if the critic is to understand what "the poet tried to do," only the successful poem itself will show: "if the poet did not succeed, then the poem is not adequate evidence, and the critic must go outside the poem – for evidence of an intention that did not become effective in the poem." The poet's "aim" or intention, therefore, "must be judged at the moment of the creative act [...] by the art of the poem itself."[24] The poem "is detached from the author at birth and goes about the world beyond his power to intend about it or control it. The poem belongs to the public. It is embodied in language, the peculiar possession of the public, and it is about the human being, an object of public knowledge."[25]

Booth's narratological study *The Rhetoric of Fiction* (1965) adopts a less dogmatic view of the function of the author in the production of meaning without incriminating critics and readers for committing fallacies when evoking the figure of the author. He takes as his starting point Lubbock's modes of presenting events in narrative, and terms them instead "telling" and "showing."[26] In Booth's perspective, "[e]verything [the author] *shows* will serve to *tell*; the line between showing and telling is always to some degree an arbitrary one."[27] The author is not so easily exiled from the premises of the literary work as impersonal aesthetics, Russian Formalism, or early New Criticism may have hoped: "we must never forget that though the author can to some extent choose his disguises, he can never choose to disappear."[28] This not-quite-exiled author is what Booth names the "implied author" – an author who, much like Wimsatt and Beardsley's intra-textual author, is not visible as the work's origin but veiled as the creation of writing: "As he writes, he creates not simply an ideal, imperson-al 'man in general' but an implied version of 'himself' that is different from the implied authors we meet in other men's works. To some novelists it has seemed, indeed, that they were discovering or creating themselves as they wrote."[29]

Booth's "implied author" is an "effect" of reading: "However imperso-nal he may try to be, his reader will inevitably construct a picture of the official scribe who writes in this manner."[30] According to Carla Benedetti, Booth aimed to counter a fallacy closer to his own interest in narrative fiction, namely the fallacy of readers' "naïve identification" of "narrators with the author who creates them."[31] His answer was to maintain a principled distinction between author and narrator, and the implied author is introduced "in a negative way" to sustain this distinction. The instance of the implied author is perhaps most apparent in the case of "unreliable narration," where "the reader becomes aware of the existence of another instance beyond that of the narrator: a mute instance [. . .] which is, nonetheless, indicating something. This instance is the implied author."[32] The implied author is a virtual author created by the reader based on the work; an amalgam of "core norms and choices" that govern a work's style, technique, narrators, characters, actions, and world-view.

In these formal approaches to the literary work, which came to dominate literary theory and education from the 1920s to the 1960s, the author is, however, not entirely dismissed from the literary work of art; authors still haunt the limits of the text and find a new form as discursive or interpretive constructs in the reader's inevitable desire to "see" the author in the literary text as impersonal, an author's delegate, an implied or a disembodied literary persona created between an external authorial consciousness, an autonomous verbal art, and the reader's creative and interpretive imagination. While the author's return in literary criticism and theory as an intra-textual phenomenon would be drawn further into disrepute by poststructuralists in the late 1960s, it is also here, in the second half of the twentieth century, possible to see that authors are not easily dismissed; they will return in similar gestures with Foucault's "author-function" and with a significant political function in feminist criticism.

The Death of the Author: Structuralism and Poststructuralism

The question of the author resurfaced in literary theory, ironically, with two authors, literary critics and philosophers, who came to embody a particular late-modern anti-authorialism associated with French Structuralism and Poststructuralism: Roland Barthes and Michel Foucault. Barthes's "The Death of the Author" was originally published in English in 1967, in the American avant-garde magazine *Aspen*. The issue consisted of a box "containing twenty-eight artefacts, including movies, records, diagrams, cardboard cut-outs, as well as more conventional texts."[33] Dedicated to Mallarmé, it was "aimed at confronting and subverting conventional ways of thinking about, of approaching or theorizing, literature and art."[34] Peggy Kamuf relates the programmatic and montage-like quality of Barthes's brief "performative" contribution, written in a "polemical style, favoring reductive summary and rapid judgments to any more patient procedure," to the original context of its publication and its intended readership.[35] Its bombastic title, and many quotable assertions, have arguably played a decisive role in its subsequent academic canonization, while its frontal attack on authority came to coincide, when it was republished in French in 1968, with a year of seismic social and political change, civil rights movements in the United States, political assassinations, protests, and revolutions in Europe.

Barthes insists that, in a historical view, the history of the Author (with capital A, to refer to the "Author-God") and the attendant critical and cultural preoccupation with the Author's biography are a historical parenthesis. He finds in Mallarmé and Proust evidence that writers themselves have fervently disavowed the Author figure: Mallarmé's "entire poetics consists in suppressing the author in the interests of writing."[36] Just as Proust's attack on Sainte-Beuve at the beginning of the century functioned as a poetics for his own creative work, Barthes's essay could, in a similar vein, be viewed as a theoretical statement prefacing and preparing for *S/Z* (1970) – his study and minute disassembly of textual codes in Balzac's novella "Sarrasine" (1830).

It is precisely with a brief discussion of a short passage from "Sarrasine" that "The Death of the Author" opens. The eponymous "enamored sculptor" is wooing the singer La Zambinella, who, the reader will later discover, is a castrated man dressed as a woman. Barthes quotes the phrase: "This was woman herself, with her sudden fears, her irrational whims, her instinctive worries, her impetuous boldness, her fussings and her delicious sensibility,"[37] and asks:

> Who is speaking thus? Is it the hero of the story bent on remaining ignorant of the castrato hidden beneath the woman? Is it Balzac the individual, furnished by his personal experience with a philosophy of Woman? Is it Balzac the author professing "literary" ideas on femininity? Is it universal wisdom? Romantic psychology?[38]

Is it, in other words, the character in the story, Balzac the author, dominant ideologies or the socio-cultural context that is speaking thus? The question clearly presupposes a formalist or New Critical insistence on the non-identity of empirical author, extra-textual phenomena, and words on the page.

In light of the widespread disregard for the author in dominant critical schools of the early part of the twentieth century, it is curious that Barthes should frame his question with the assertion: "[t]he *author* still reigns in histories of literature, biographies of writers, interviews, magazines, as in the very consciousness of men of letters anxious to unite their person and their work through diaries and memoirs."[39] It would appear little has changed since the New Critics made a similar complaint against the profession of criticism and a wider culture of "authorism." Barthes asserts, without providing much in terms of evidence or discussion, that "the sway of the Author remains powerful (the new criticism has often done no more than consolidate it)."[40]

It is certainly possible to view New Critical anti-authorialism as paradoxically maintaining a desire for the author even as its method professes a preoccupation with "the text itself." It is similarly possible to consider the modern aesthetic of impersonality as promoting the author as a transcendental figure not dissimilar to a Romantic Author-God. However, Barthes's initial answer to the question of who is speaking thus takes the theoretical question of authorship in a more radical direction: "We shall never know, for the good reason that writing is the destruction of every voice, of every point of origin. Writing is the neutral, composite, oblique space where our subject slips away, the negative where all identity is lost, starting with the identity of the body writing."[41] An attention to "the text itself" does not, then, merely sever the empirical author from her literary work; writing *itself* is an activity that radically obliterates any sense of a stable subject, an originating voice. Barthes continues:

> No doubt it has always been that way. As soon as a fact is *narrated* no longer with a view to acting directly on reality but intransitively, that is to say, finally outside of any function other than that of the very practice of the symbol itself, this disconnection occurs, the voice loses its origin, the author enters into his own death, writing begins.[42]

Barthes's anti-mimetic theory of narrative fiction, and its consequential renunciation of the Author, fits within a wider and ongoing contemporary "decentering" of the subject, as noted by Foucault, in psychoanalysis, linguistics, and anthropology, "in relation to the laws of its desire, the forms of its language, the rules of its actions, or the play of its mythical and imaginative discourse."[43] The subject, determined by "a series of systems," as Jonathan Culler puts it, is, then, "decentered" as "it is not a source or centre to which one refers to explain events."[44] For instance, Émile Benveniste held that "[i]t is in and through language that man constitutes himself as a *subject*, because language alone established the concept of 'ego' in reality, in *its* reality which is that of the being."[45] In his early writing on the mirror stage (1949), Jacques Lacan had already stated what would become a Poststructuralist mantra: namely, that human identity is "decentered," and perceived the unconscious as "structured like a language," which echoes in Claude Lévi-Strauss's 1962 dictum that "the goal of the human sciences" is not to constitute "but to dissolve man."[46]

Foucault agrees with the necessity to move beyond the typical "questions" of how a "free subject penetrate[s] the substance of things and give[s] it meaning" and how it "activate[s] the rules of language and thus give[s] rise to the designs which are properly its own." However, dissatisfied with simply noting the subject's disappearance, skeptical about the transcendental connotation of writing implicit in the Poststructuralist notion, and insisting that "it is not enough [...] to repeat the empty affirmation that the author has disappeared," Foucault's essay is centrally preoccupied with locating "the space left empty by the author's disappearance." His implicit riposte to Barthes's dramatic authorcide asks instead:

under what conditions, and in what forms can something like a subject appear in the order of discourse? What place can it occupy in each type of discourse, what function can it assume, and by obeying what rules? In short, it is a matter of depriving the subject (or its substitute) of its role as originator, and of analyzing the subject as a variable and complex function of discourse.[47]

Foucault agrees, therefore, with the basic tenet of modern literary theory that the author-as-originator is a "dead subject," but he also insists that literary theory must instead consider the various ways in which the author remains and returns as a "function of discourse." One such way is through the peculiar classificatory function of authors' proper names, which occupy a liminal space between the inside and outside of the literary work. Author names, systems of ownership, and the question of what kinds of texts may be designated as having been authored pertain to what Foucault names the "author function": a "characteristic of the mode of existence, circulation, and functioning of certain discourses within a society."[48] Rather than thinking of the author as originator, Foucault posits that the author is:

a functional principle by which, in our culture, one limits, excludes, and chooses; in short, by which one impedes the free circulation, the free manipulation, the free composition, decomposition, and recomposition of fiction. In fact, if we are accustomed to presenting the author as a genius, as a perpetual surging of invention, it is because, in reality, we make him function in exactly the opposite fashion.[49]

The author is "an ideological product," a discursive construction, whose transcendental veil of creativity and innovation is a mere cover for a cultural or institutional anxiety about "the cancerous and dangerous proliferation of significations within a world where one is thrifty not only with one's resources and riches, but also with one's discourses and their significations." The author is, quite simply, "the principle of thrift in the proliferation of meaning."[50] With this ideological critique of the "author function," Foucault inserts the question of the author into a much wider discursive, social, and philosophical context, which Barthes had already gestured toward with his celebration of a textual "proliferation of meaning" beyond the death of the author and his deconstruction of the originating subject through writing.

At roughly the same time, Jacques Derrida began to develop what would later become known as a "deconstructive" critique of ideas of origins, or a "metaphysics of presence," which he regarded as central to the Western philosophical tradition, including linguistics. One influential strain of

Derrida's critique was his deconstruction of the ingrained notion of writing as a mere supplement to or substitute for the absence of the "original" spoken word and the "presence" it implies, as expressed in the work of, for instance, Rousseau ("often credited with helping to bring into being the modern notion of the individual self").[51] However, Derrida demonstrates that Rousseau, in his *Confessions*, repeatedly refers to writing and supplements as necessary in order to correct the misunderstandings of his self as it appears in conversation, in speech, presumably when most "present." Therefore, writing and speech, absence and presence, follow a logic of supplementarity, according to Derrida, in which the origin, the self, the thing itself are constantly deferred: "ineluctably multiplying the supplementary mediations that produce the sense of the very thing they defer: the mirage of the thing itself, of immediate presence, of originary perception. Immediacy is derived. That all begins through the intermediary is what is indeed 'inconceivable' [to reason]."[52]

Barthes's enigmatic phrase "the voice loses its origin, the author enters into his own death, writing begins" resembles Derrida's notion of deferred origins, and the consequential dismantling of the idea of the author as an origin preceding the written: "there has never been anything but writing; there have never been anything but supplements, substitutive significations which could only come forth in a chain of differential references."[53] To conceptualize what this authorial instance of deferred origins may mean to a theory of authorship, Barthes employs another "supplement" and recasts, in a decidedly Derridean manner, the author as a "scriptor," or copyist, for whom "the hand, cut off from any voice, borne by a pure gesture of inscription (and not of expression), traces a field without origin – or which, at least, has no other origin than language itself, language which ceaselessly calls into question all origins."[54]

Barthes's modern "scriptor," who "is born simultaneously with the text" and "is in no way equipped with a being preceding or exceeding the writing," is related to Derrida's figure for the literary critic in the guise of Lévi-Strauss's mythopoetic *bricoleur*.[55] In his 1966 essay "Structure, Sign and Play in the Discourse of the Human Sciences," Derrida explains that the *bricoleur* is one who uses the "means at hand": "the instruments he finds at his disposition around him, those which are already there, which had not been especially conceived with an eye to the operation for which they are to be used and to which one tries by trial and error to adapt them." Derrida equates the work of *bricolage* with "critical language itself" and determines that "every discourse is *bricoleur*."[56] This may partly explain why Barthes saw the role of the critic as having been conceived as a mirror-image of the Author-God, as one who imposes a limit: "Once the Author is removed, the claim to decipher a text becomes quite futile. To give a text an Author is to impose a limit on that text, to furnish it with a final signified, to close the writing." What we need, Barthes suggests, is a criticism of *bricolage* that rejects any notion of deciphering and probing texts for singular meanings and instead understands its task as an activity of "disentangling."[57]

This view of the absence of hidden ciphers below the surface of the text and the removal of the Author-Critic from the center of signification would lead Alexander Nehamas to reconsider the author as wholly "separated from metaphors of depth" and instead "conceived in terms of breadth and expansion."[58] Nehamas's author "has no depth," he is a "character" or an "agent postulated to account for construing a text as an action."[59] Instead of probing for the Author's covert meaning beneath a text's surface, Nehamas's Foucaultian "postulated author" is the manifestation of "juxtaposed surfaces," of texts generating and made possible by other texts.[60]

This "author without depth" or "*bricoleur* critic" is what Barthes, at the end of his essay, defines as the "reader"; not an empirical reader outside of the text, but a destination holding together "all the traces by which the written text is constituted": "The birth of the reader must be at the cost of the death of the Author."[61] In the end, then, the answer to the question of who speaks thus is surprisingly none of the options Barthes initially proposed, but the less imposing "reader," who may, nevertheless, merely substitute one origin, one authority (Author or Critic) for another (Reader). To Burke, "it remains unclear that Barthes's Reader is any less mystifying than the author (s)he (it?) would replace."[62]

While mostly ignored by literary theory, the figure of the "reader" began to attract wider attention with reader-response criticism, which became influential from the 1970s onwards. Wolfgang Iser's aesthetics of reception argued for the active and creative participation of what he termed *The Implied Reader* (1972) in the production of meaning in convergence with the text, while Stanley Fish's *Is There a Text in This Class?* (1980) proposed that the interpretation of literary texts is determined and constrained by readers' situatedness within varying "interpretive communities."

While some mystification remains in Barthes's notion of the "birth of the reader," his is arguably a well-chosen figure to encapsulate the overturning of authorities, of Authors and Critics, and the democratizing forces underway in the late 1960s. Barthes's "reader" is a product of writing and discourse, a "scriptor" who exists as a "multi-dimensional space in which a variety of writings, none of them original, blend and clash," "a tissue of quotations drawn from the innumerable centres of culture."[63] The montage-like quality of "The Death of the Author" is not merely a stylistic device fitting its publication format, but a performance of its own attempt to script its theory of unoriginal authorship and practice of a radical intertextuality in which multiple and disjointed discourses flicker as quotations without quotation marks.

Conclusion: Resurrections of the Author

The "Death of the Author" thesis promised to "liberate us from the interpretively restrictive views of literature," views, according to Barthes, that are "tyrannically centred on the author, his person, his life, his tastes, his passions," where the Author, according to Foucault, plays the role of a "functional principle" that "impedes the free circulation, the free manipulation, the free composition, decomposition, and recomposition of fiction."[64]

Postcolonial and feminist theory has on the one hand continued and modified this deconstruction of the subject and the literary canon in its "universalized" state as significantly Western, white, and male. The death of this subject, "with his implications in racism, sexism and imperialism, can therefore be seen as part of a strategy of political liberation."[65] On the other hand, as Maurice Biriotti reminds us, "the Author's death denied authorship precisely to those who had only recently been empowered to claim it," anonymizing and disembodying the very voices it had helped to liberate, such as "black voices, women's voices, the voices of those in the margins."[66]

In *The Madwoman in the Attic* (1979), Sandra Gilbert and Susan Gubar asked: "What does it mean to be a woman writer in a culture whose fundamental definitions of literary authority are [...] both overtly and covertly patriarchal?"[67] Struggling against a patriarchal literary canon, women writers had suffered, according to Gilbert and Gubar, from a debilitating "anxiety of authorship":

> Handed down not from one woman to another but from the stern literary "fathers" of patriarchy to all their "inferiorized" female descendants, it is in many ways the germ of a dis-ease or, at any rate, a disaffection, a disturbance, a distrust, that spreads like a stain throughout the style and structure of much literature by women, especially [...] throughout literature by women before the twentieth century.[68]

If women writers in the second half of the twentieth century began to claim their own sense of authority through writing, they stood on the shoulders of generations who struggled in "isolation that felt like illness, alienation that felt like madness," attempting to overcome the "anxiety of authorship."[69] Gilbert and Gubar's challenge to the unequal regime of authorship was one that insisted on a counter-discourse to both the paternal lineage of the institutionally legitimized (male) canon, and to the silencing of all subjectivities, a universal author figure, as proclaimed by the "death of the author" discourse. Nancy K. Miller has argued that such a feminist non-alignment with a Poststructuralist attack on authorship, agency, and subjectivity arises out of a realization that a theoretical anti-authorism does not necessarily hold for women:

> Because women have not had the same historical relation of identity to origin, institution, production that men have had, they have not, I think, (collectively) felt burdened by *too much self*, ego, cogito, etc. Because the female subject has juridically been excluded from the polis, hence decentred, "disoriginated," deinstitutionalised, etc., her relation to integrity and textuality, desire and authority, displays structurally important differences from that universal position.[70]

However, rather than resurrecting a new universal "feminist" Author, modeled on an already thoroughly debunked discourse of patriarchal author(ity), as maintained also by Toril Moi, Rita Felski has pointed out that feminist critics may opt for a "third position" that "does not naively assert that the author is an originating genius, creating aesthetic objects outside of history, but does not diminish the importance of difference and agency in the responses of women writers to historical formations."[71] Such a view involves the recognition that "female authors have themselves been authored" within, against, and by a "multiplicity of social and cultural forces that exceed their grasp" (a view commensurate with Foucault's understanding of the author function). Yet such forces do not exclude the possibility and ability for the subject "to act and create." Viewed from this "third position," authorship is not depersonalized, ignored, eliminated, or feared, but is, according to Felski, just "one strand in the weave of the text rather than a magic key to unlocking its mysteries."[72] This position does not easily move from questions of authorship and agency to theoretical laws and generalizations – thus avoiding a trap of universalization into which poststructuralist as well as New Critical and formalist theories of authorship have arguably fallen too easily.

Whether deemed self-contradictory, too reductive, counter-productive, or simply products of their own time, Barthes and Foucault ensured that the question of the author would remain central to literary theory beyond poststructuralism. Foucault's historicization of the "author function" influenced New Historicism and book history. These theories or disciplines proceeded, in the words of Roger Chartier, to "reconnect the text with its author," albeit with the caveat that the author is perceived to be dependent (he or she is "not the unique master of meaning," and his or her intentions are not necessarily imposed on the producers or readers of the work) and constrained (by the organization of the social space of literary production).[73] In what may appear as an ambiguous return to biographism and the Author-God, Stephen Greenblatt's New Historicist work on, for instance, William Shakespeare considers the "apparently isolated power of the individual genius" to be "bound up with collective, social energy."[74]

Foucault's and Barthes's essays not only continue to be central reference points for theories of authorship and literary theory more generally, they have also been instrumental to theorizing writing in a digital age. In the twenty-first century, the writer-critic Kenneth Goldsmith has explored the potential of "uncreative writing" (drawing on Marjorie Perloff's notion of the author as an "unoriginal genius") by considering "an explosion of writers employing strategies of copying and appropriation [. . .] with the computer encouraging writers to mimic its workings."[75] Perhaps there is no great difference between Barthes's "scriptor" and Goldsmith's uncreative writer as programmer: "While the author won't die," Goldsmith suggests, "we might begin to view authorship in a more conceptual way: perhaps the best authors of the future will be ones who can write the best programs with which to manipulate, parse and distribute language-based practices."[76] Whether the author-as-programmer will continue to function as a bulwark against the proliferation of meaning or as a Barthesian "scriptor," thriving in an anonymous and uncontrollable web of texts and writing, is a pressing question for literary theory in the twenty-first century.

Notes

1. Andrew Bennett, *The Author* (London: Routledge, 2005), p. 10.
2. Christopher Prendergast, *The Classic: Sainte-Beuve and the Nineteenth-Century Culture Wars* (Oxford: Oxford University Press, 2007), pp. 3, 1.
3. Roland Barthes, "The Death of the Author," in *Image–Music–Text*, trans. Stephen Heath (London: Fontana Press, 1977), pp. 142–48, p. 144.

4. Prendergast, *Classic*, p. 2.

5. Barbara Hochman, "Disappearing Authors and Resentful Readers in Late Nineteenth-Century American Fiction: The Case of Henry James," *ELH*, 63.1 (1996), 177–201, p. 177.

6. Henry James, "The Aspern Papers," in *The Aspern Papers and Other Stories*, ed. Adrian Poole (Oxford: Oxford University Press, 2013), pp. 3–88, p. 27.

7. Henry James, "The Private Life," in *Aspern Papers,* ed. Poole, p. 219.

8. Bennett, *Author*, p. 72.

9. Andrew Bennett and Nicholas Royle, *An Introduction to Literature, Criticism and Theory*, 4th edn (Harlow, UK: Pearson, 2009), p. 23.

10. Henry James, "Anthony Trollope," in *Partial Portraits* (London: Macmillan, 1894), pp. 116–17.

11. Henry James, "The Golden Bowl," in his *Literary Criticism*, vol. 2. (New York: Library of America, 1984), p. 1322.

12. T. S. Eliot, "Tradition and the Individual Talent," in *Authorship: From Plato to the Postmodern. A Reader*, ed. Seán Burke (Edinburgh: Edinburgh University Press, 1995), pp. 73–80, p. 76.

13. Ibid., pp. 80, 78, 78.

14. Ibid., p. 74.

15. Percy Lubbock, *The Craft of Fiction* (London: Jonathan Cape, 1960), p. 156.

16. Ibid., p. 111.

17. Ibid., p. 156.

18. Ibid., pp. 12, 132.

19. W. K. Wimsatt and Monroe C. Beardsley, "The Intentional Fallacy," in *The Verbal Icon: Studies in the Meaning of Poetry*, ed. W. K. Wimsatt (Lexington: University of Kentucky Press, 1954), pp. 3–20, p. 3.

20. Vincent B. Leitch, ed., *The Norton Anthology of Theory and Criticism* (New York: Norton, 2001), p. 1352.

21. Cleanth Brooks, "The Formalist Critics," in *The Norton Anthology of Theory and Criticism*, ed. Leitch, pp. 1366–1371, p. 1367.

22. Bennett, *Author*, p. 77.

23. Wimsatt and Beardsley, "Intentional," p. 4.

24. Ibid., quoting J. E. Spingarn, "The New Criticism," in *Criticism in America: Its Function and Status*, by Irving Babbitt et al. (New York: Harcourt, Brace, 1924), pp. 9–45, pp. 24–25.

25. Ibid., p. 5.

26. Wayne C. Booth, *The Rhetoric of Fiction* (Chicago: University of Chicago Press, 1961), p. 24.

27. Ibid., p. 20.

28. Ibid.

29. Ibid., pp. 70–71.

30. Ibid., p. 71.

31. Carla Benedetti, *The Empty Cage: Inquiry into the Mysterious Disappearance of the Author*, trans. William J. Hartley (Ithaca, NY: Cornell University Press, 2005), p. 62.

32. Ibid., p. 63.
33. Bennett, *Author*, pp. 13–14.
34. Ibid.
35. Peggy Kamuf, *Signature Pieces: On the Institution of Authorship* (Ithaca, NY: Cornell University Press, 1988), p. 8.
36. Barthes, "Death," p. 143.
37. Ibid., p. 142; italics removed.
38. Ibid.
39. Ibid., p. 143.
40. Ibid.
41. Ibid., p. 142.
42. Ibid.; emphasis original.
43. Quoted. in Jonathan Culler, *Literary Theory* (New York: Sterling, 2009), p. 150.
44. Ibid.
45. Émile Benveniste, *Problems in General Linguistics*, 1966, trans. Mary Elizabeth Meek (Coral Gables, FL: University of Miami Press, 1971), p. 224.
46. Seán Burke, *The Death and Return of the Author: Criticism and Subjectivity in Barthes, Foucault and Derrida* (Edinburgh: Edinburgh University Press, 1998), p. 13; Claude Lévi-Strauss, *The Savage Mind* (Oxford: Oxford University Press, 2004), p. 247.
47. Michel Foucault, "What Is an Author?," in *The Death and Resurrection of the Author*, ed. William Irwin (Westport, CT: Greenwood Press, 2002), pp. 9–22, p. 12, 21.
48. Ibid., p. 14.
49. Ibid., pp. 21–22.
50. Ibid., p. 21.
51. Culler, *Literary Theory*, p. 9.
52. Jacques Derrida, *Of Grammatology*, trans. Gayatri Chakravorty Spivak (Baltimore, MD: Johns Hopkins University Press, 1998), p. 157.
53. Ibid., p. 159.
54. Barthes, "Death," p. 146.
55. Ibid., p. 145.
56. Jacques Derrida, "Structure, Sign and Play in the Discourse of the Human Sciences," in *Writing and Difference*, trans. Alan Bass (Chicago: University of Chicago Press, 1978), p. 285.
57. Barthes, "Death," p. 147.
58. Alexander Nehamas, "What an Author Is," *The Journal of Philosophy*, 83.11 (1986), 685–691, p. 687.
59. Ibid., p. 689, 688.
60. Ibid., p. 690.
61. Barthes, "Death," p. 148.
62. Burke, *Authorship*, p. 69.
63. Barthes, "Death," p. 146.

64. Jason Holt, "The Marginal Life of the Author," in *The Death and Resurrection of the Author?*, ed. William Irwin (Westport, CT: Greenwood Press, 2002), pp. 65–78, p. 66; Barthes, "Death," p. 143; Foucault, "What Is an Author?", p. 21.

65. Maurice Biriotti, "Introduction: Authorship, Authority, Authorisation," in *What Is an Author?*, eds. Maurice Biriotti and Nicola Miller (Manchester, UK: Manchester University Press, 1993), pp. 1–18, p. 4.

66. Ibid., p. 6.

67. Sandra M. Gilbert and Susan Gubar, *The Madwoman in the Attic: The Woman Writer and the Nineteenth-Century Literary Imagination* (1979; New Haven, CT: Yale University Press, 2000), pp. 45–46.

68. Ibid., p. 51.

69. Ibid.

70. Nancy K. Miller, "Changing the Subject: Authorship, Writing and the Reader," in *Authorship*, ed. Burke, pp. 193–212, p. 197.

71. Rita Felski, *Literature after Feminism* (Chicago: University of Chicago Press, 2003), p. 91, quoting Cheryl Walker, "Feminist Literary Criticism and the Author," *Critical Inquiry*, 16.3 (1990), 551–71, p. 560.

72. Felski, *Literature after Feminism*, p. 91.

73. Roger Chartier, *The Order of Books: Readers, Authors, and Libraries in Europe Between the Fourteenth and Eighteenth Centuries*, trans. Lydia G. Cochrane (1992; Stanford, CA: Stanford University Press, 1994), p. 28.

74. Stephen Greenblatt, *Learning to Curse: Essays in Early Modern Culture* (1990; New York: Routledge, 2012), p. 221.

75. Kenneth Goldsmith, *Uncreative Writing: Managing Language in the Digital Age* (New York: Columbia University Press, 2011), p. 5; Marjorie Perloff, *Unoriginal Genius: Poetry by Other Means in the New Century* (Chicago: University of Chicago Press, 2010).

76. Goldsmith, *Uncreative Writing*, p. 11.

CHAPTER 18

Gender, Sexuality, and the Author
Five Phases of Authorship from the Renaissance to the Twenty-First Century

Chantal Zabus

The aim of this chapter is to highlight the way in which gender and sexuality have inflected conceptions of authorship. Several categories such as that of author, language, and text (with a special emphasis on the latter) come to bear on the criticism of literature produced by individuals reflecting the spectrum of gender diversity. I here examine a wide array of English-language fictional texts, mostly from England and the US, but also autobiographies or other forms of life-writing from the English Renaissance to the beginning of the twenty-first century, with one incursion, at the end, into a non-Western context. I distinguish between five phases of authorship: (1) Fathering the text; (2) (M)Othering the text; (3) En-gendering the Text; (4) Queering the text and the author; and (5) Transgendering the text.

Fathering the Text

The male gendering of writing during the English Renaissance is best encapsulated in Thomas Dekker's coy declaration that it was "not [his] ambition to be a man in print."[1] In the lingo of the time, "in print" meant "thoroughly." Despite the author's conventional sense of modesty at a time when most publications, especially in poetry, were posthumous, "in print" implicitly conveyed a full masculine authorship. Dekker's almost reluctant form of print authorship, in tune with the attitude of his peers, reveals the tensions between manuscript coterie writing and the new print practices of the emerging marketplace with its rising literacy rates and a growing female readership in the second half of the sixteenth century. Aspiring female writers were no longer celebrated as muses of a manuscript culture but condemned as prostitutes in print culture, because public expression defied the notions of chastity, domestic piety, silence, and obedience as female virtues. Through print publication, which was labeled as a lower-class activity for both men and women, a "fallen" woman fell from grace a second time by associating with the non-elite. As John Davies reportedly told the Countess of Bedford, the Countess of Pembroke, and Elizabeth Cary, "you presse the Presse with little you have made," hinting at their daring intimacy with the printing press.[2] According to Wendy Wall, "Presse" also referred in Elizabethan slang to "undergo a pressing," that is, "to act the lady's part and be pressed by a man."[3] While querying "how women's writing provided counter-models to dominant modes of authorization,"[4] Wall confirms that the category of author is a masculinized one. Writing was therefore a sexualized and gendered activity.

When not twice fallen, the educated, married woman writer had license to author a form of "life"-writing only when she was dying, or a solicitous husband anticipated her death, very often in childbirth; to wit, the "prayers" and "blessings" by, e.g., Elizabeth Jocelin and Dorothy Leigh in their "legacies."[5] Dying female authors are thus powerful in death, a bit like medieval witches who were found innocent after drowning in the ordeal by water. Among the women who did write while still in good health,[6] the poet Lady Mary Wroth, author of *Pamphilia to Amphilanthus* and *The Countess of Montgomery's Urania*, created her own sonnet sequence. About her, however, letter-writer John Chamberlain wrote with irritation that she "takes great libertie or rather licence to traduce whom she please,/ and thinks she daunces in a net."[7] These Renaissance women managed to "presse the Presse" and, when not dying or "dauncing," found niches to express the "ambition to be a (wo)man in print." Religious writing was such a legitimate niche for women. The title of Margaret Hannay's 1985 critical collection is telling: *Silent but for the Word: Tudor Women as Patrons, Translators, and Writers of Religious Works.*[8] If grieving husbands were willing to publish their wives' books after the latter's death in childbirth, the converse example of a woman writer's freedom to write after a male relative's death is to be found in Mary Sidney, who co-authored with her brother Philip Sidney a translation of the psalms, "revising his forty poems and writing ninety of her own after his death."[9] Mary is here inverting the role of the muse since Philip is cast as the muse that inspired the moment of joint literary production to then give up the ghost.

Joint authorship between siblings can be extended to literary couplings in the nineteenth century. Upon the death of her father, Samuel Taylor Coleridge, in 1834, Sara Coleridge, in collaboration with her husband and first cousin, Henry Nelson Coleridge, found it incumbent upon herself to reconstruct the corpus of her father's work. She tellingly called it "the body of my father's writings, which I have taken great pains to bring into one."[10]

Her painstaking efforts were, however, put under erasure, as Henry Nelson Coleridge is the only editor mentioned on the cover. Following Henry's death and after an editorial interlude with her brother Derwent, Sara completed the 1847 edition of the *Biographia Literaria*, in which she is listed not by name but as Henry's "widow" on the title page. In her editions of her father's *Notes and Lectures upon Shakespeare* (1849) and the three-volume *Essays on His Own Times* (1950), Sara again appears not by name but by filiation as "his daughter."

In her correspondence, Sara Coleridge refers to her editorial task as a complex "filial phenomenon."[11] Sara was not only the biological daughter of an individualized genius such as Samuel Taylor Coleridge but also the figurative heiress of William Wordsworth and "Uncle Southey," Coleridge's brother-in-law. Alison Hickey has aptly framed Sara as "an heir to all three men, eminently qualified to be the consolidator of the fragmentary Coleridge that Southey and Wordsworth failed to unify – and arguably helped to fragment."[12] The burden of Sara Coleridge's authorial inheritance, especially if the author is considered a genius yet an absent father, is obviously complicated by Sara's gender. Throughout the eighteenth and nineteenth centuries, the genius was, in Christine Battersby's words, "a male author whose act of creation echoes a male God's eternal 'act of creation in the infinite I AM'."[13] Here Battersby is quoting Coleridge's celebrated definition of the imagination, which unconditionally endorsed the fertility of the *gens* or male clan. As in monotheistic belief systems, the God of creative authorship engenders the wor(l)d without female collaboration, even if Coleridge engaged in collaborative authorship with fellow male members of the Romantic pantheon. The immediate fellow-God William Wordsworth, to whom Sara Coleridge dedicated her edition of the *Biographia*, dismissed her as not "knowing anything about [her father]" and therefore unqualified "for such an Employment, ... nor could her judgment be free from bias."[14] Wordsworth's wife, Mary (Hutchinson) Wordsworth, also dismissed her as "poor dear indefatigable Sara";[15] yet Sara referred to her tiring labor as an act of "bringing forth" her father's work. Even if the metaphor of childbirth is striking and turns her into "mother of the man,"[16] her en-gendering of her own father-cum-creator perversely returns us to the Romantic notion of authorship and of the Oedipal struggle for literary paternity.

(M)Othering the Text

The Romantic notion of authorship underwent a change as British and American women were given entrance into the public sphere, complete with its legal rights. For instance, the American law of coverture, which meant that the intellectual property rights that writing women might gain from copyright automatically went to their husbands, ended in the 1860s. The International Copyright Act was passed in the US in 1891, some forty years after the Married Women's Property Act of 1848. This Act granted women the property they owned before their marriage except for, for instance, in Louisiana, where the Napoleonic code and Clause 1388 still applied, as in Kate Chopin's *The Awakening* (1899). In addition to these legal shifts away from the common law in England, the American Civil War augured definite change for American women writers. Whereas neither male nor female authorship was considered a profession in the antebellum period, the Civil War provided opportunities for women writers like Louisa May Alcott and Elizabeth Stuart Phelps, who launched their careers by writing war stories, as well as for female journalists who ended up owning their own newspapers or converted the parlor into a site of writing.

A quick survey of nineteenth-century American fiction writers supports Fanny Fern's statement in *Ruth Hall* (1857) that "no happy woman ever writes," confirming that women writers wrote out of economic necessity rather than artistic passion.[17] While taking care of her six children, Harriet Beecher Stowe provided amateur domestic sketches based on imitation, which were supposedly characteristic of female writing, before she wrote her anti-slavery novel *Uncle Tom's Cabin; or, Life Among the Lowly* (1852) "out of a clear sense of 'call.'"[18] Only after the war did Stowe make the transition to professional authorship and "mother" her own texts. Nathaniel Hawthorne bitterly lamented that "America is now wholly given over to a damned mob of scribbling women, and I should have no chance of success while the public taste is so occupied with their trash."[19] Susan Williams registers the fact that female writers "were just as unhappy" as their male counterparts, such as Hawthorne, Herman Melville, and Henry James.[20] This female unhappiness has a theoretical corollary in "the artistry of anger" that was held to be characteristic of Black and White American women's literature in the nineteenth century.

This American "artistry of anger" is directly traceable to Victorian novels like *Jane Eyre* (1847), the genealogy of which Sandra M. Gilbert and Susan Gubar charted in *The Madwoman in the Attic*. At the time of its publication in 1979, Gilbert and Gubar's critical ur-text vented women writers' anger by challenging the dominant conception of literary paternity and taking a stab at Harold Bloom's postulate that the historical relationship between literary artists is one of filiation between father and son, whereby a "strong poet" is inexorably involved in an Oedipal struggle with his precursor. Reflecting on Bloom's definition of the poetic process as a sexual encounter between a male poet and his female muse, Gilbert and Gubar ask the famous question: "Does [the female poet] have a muse, and what is its sex?"[21] For the female author, the impossibility of becoming a precursor in the male literary economy transforms the Bloomian "anxiety of influence" into what Gilbert and Gubar dub "the anxiety of authorship." Yet they refused to lock the female writer in an "Electra pattern" to match Bloom's Oedipal struggle and to feed the "cult of invalidism" to which women artists allegedly adhere.[22] Short of writing "silly novels," as George Eliot sarcastically put it,[23] or disguising their female identities, as the Brontë sisters and George Eliot herself famously did, British and American women writers in the nineteenth and the early twentieth century revised the male writers' images of women. In questioning the paradigmatic polarities of angel and monster, they also freed women characters from the female Gothic.

Bertha Mason, "the madwoman in the attic" in Gilbert and Gubar's book title, illustrates Jane Eyre's Gothic double in enacting in her stead the suppressed destructive rage of plain Jane, and in embodying the "female schizophrenia of authorship,"[24] which causes the text to be "othered" rather than "mothered," as it were. Meanwhile, the other madwoman, confined to the nursery room, in Charlotte Perkins Gilman's "The Yellow Wallpaper" (1892), associates authorship or "the writing itch" (after Juvenal's *cacoëthes scribendi*) with confinement, madness, and isolation. This other Jane indeed attempts to write her own script on the wallpaper of her chamber, which acts as Gilman's retort to her physician Weir Mitchell, who had prescribed the post-partum rest cure to her.

Before Gilbert and Gubar, *Jane Eyre* had given rise to extensive criticism such as Patricia Beer's *Reader, I Married Him* (1974), after Jane's famous address to the reader about her eventual marriage to a maimed Rochester. But Beer's work is not necessarily feminist. More assertively feminist, *The Madwoman in the Attic*, along with Ellen Moers' *Literary Women* (1976) and Elaine Showalter's *A Literature of Their Own* (1977), belongs to the second wave of the women's movement. Significantly, Showalter's book takes its title from Virginia Woolf's influential essay "A Room of One's Own" (1929) and thus moves away from the attic as a site of authorial schizophrenia and othering. This choice gave rise to a few spin-offs, including Susan Gubar's own *Rooms of Our Own* (2006). This womanly continuum confirms that authorship is also linked to "the room," that is, to spatiality, and that female authorship is in a tense relation with space within the domestic sphere and *a fortiori* in the public sphere. In Alice Munro's short story "The Office" (1968), the unnamed female protagonist rents an office outside of her home until she is driven out by her landlord's false allegations of sexual misconduct at seeing his toilet walls disfigured with obscenities written in lipstick. She had earlier reflected that "[a] house is all right for a man to work in. He brings his work into the house, a place is cleared for it. [...] So a house is not the same for a woman. She is not someone who walks into the house, to make use of it, and will walk out again. She *is* the house."[25] However, Munro's writerly act of penning the landlord down by "arrang[ing] words" enables her "to be rid of him."[26] The "writing itch" has turned into a cathartic release for the woman writer who, in the mid-twentieth century, continues to write *dialectically*, against the male grain. Concurrently, women critics, from the late 1960s to the late 1970s, initiated a critical trend that views female writers as a separate group or subculture, a trend that may hark back to Betty Friedan's *The Feminine Mystique* (1963), written – significantly – in the heyday of the Civil Rights movement. In French academe, the equivalent of that trend is the Althusserian perception of women as a class, which goes back to the Marxist-Feminist Literature Collective, *Questions féministes* (1977), founded by Simone de Beauvoir and taken up by Marxist-Leninist sociologist Christine Delphy and semiotician Julia Kristeva.

En-gendering the Text

Two decades before Susan Williams toned down Gilbert and Gubar's postulate of the female writer's unmitigable rage, Toril Moi had, in her *Sexual/Textual Politics* (1985), deemed "reductionist" Gilbert and Gubar's premise that "the mad double" of female creativity as well as her "*feminist rage*"[27] are present in *all* nineteenth-century novels. In Moi's new genealogy, Gilbert and Gubar, along with Ellen Moers and Elaine Showalter, represent the coming-of-age of Anglo-American feminist criticism. Moi lifted her book's title from Kate Millett's *Sexual Politics* (1969), which is contemporaneous with Mary Ellmann's *Thinking about Women* (1968), but added "Textual Politics." This slashing effect in *Sexual/Textual Politics* is a diacritic tell-tale sign that the *text* matters. Moi urges feminists to disentangle the author/character as well as the "female"/"feminine" confusion. Her prose sounds like a summons: "[Feminists] must insist that though women undoubtedly are female, this in no way guarantees that they will be feminine."[28] Even though Moi had in mind female feminists, she unwittingly opens a portal to transgender theory, of which more later.

Meanwhile, the process of excavation has already begun. In her poem, "Diving into the Wreck" (1972), Adrienne Rich, who posited a female diaspora and a lesbian continuum, charts the protagonist's slow diving into the wreck of women's *herstory*, where "our names do not appear." When approaching the place of the wreck, the protagonist becomes an androgynous creature, or rather two halves of one:

> And I am here, the mermaid whose dark hair
> streams black, the merman in his armored body
> We circle silently
> about the wreck
> we dive into the hold.
> I am she: I am he[.][29]

Before Rich, Hélène Cixous, who had written her doctoral dissertation on the Penelope chapter of *Ulysses* (1922), in which Joyce attempts to penetrate the mind of Leopold Bloom's adulterous wife, concluded that "to be signed with a woman's name doesn't necessarily make a piece of writing feminine."[30] However, Cixous's premise of an *écriture féminine*, which could be used by both sexes on the Derridean – and later, Butlerian – ground that masculinity and femininity have to be deconstructed as binaries, is belied by her notion of the female body as a site of writing, a pre-Oedipal, primeval space flooded by milk and honey, which is the source of "[t]he Voice, before the Law [of the Father]."[31] *La venue à l'écriture* describes writing as a libidinal act whereby Cixous is visited by the "disinterested power" of books and her body is "traversed and fertilized" by them, so that it is impossible to "have closed [herself] up in silence."[32] Nancy K. Miller, among others, has been critical of an *écriture féminine* existing outside of the language women share with men.[33]

More therefore than did "the sex" of the author, the *language* of authorship signaled the gender of the writing. Yet, the paradox in Cixous's theory and practice is also perceptible in the writing of Luce Irigaray. Irigaray opposed Freud's *Penisneid* – the girlchild's alleged penis-envy – and postulated a multiple *jouissance* born out of a woman's genital anatomy, whereby her very sex is "double," that is, her vagina is girdled by two lips which embrace continually.[34] But the vagina continues to be read as a Freudian absence. More generally, the alleged confusion between the sex of the author and the sex of the writing points to the advent of increased subjectivity and the questioning of a fixed, immutable identity.

Already, questions about identity, subjectivity, and gender had been raised in relation to autobiography in the 1970s, often referred to as the "Me-decade."[35] Philippe Lejeune's influential *Le pacte autobiographique* (1975), according to which the pact between author and reader is predicated upon a single identity shared between a real person, the narrator, and the object of narration, was disowned by himself later on when he acknowledged the many (dis-)simulations in miming such a contract and, perforce, identity.[36] To this already complex, growing field, we have to add the multiple terminological instabilities surrounding the term "autobiography": e.g., "autofiction" (Doubrovsky), "surfiction" (Federman), "postmodern auto-biography" (Sukenick), "global novel" (Hong Kingston), *nouvelle autobiographie* (Robbe-Grillet), "biomythography" (Lorde), "gynography" (Brée), or even *fiction autobiographique post-coloniale* (Boudjedra). The seeming consensus is that the "I" writes his/her autobiography when the cohesion of that "I" is most uncertain.

One recalls that in Elaine Showalter's gynocriticism, the assumption was that women's writing is "bitextual," that is, "in dialogue with both masculine and feminine literary traditions," unless, as Myra Jehlen argued, they find "an alternative base" or "fulcrum" after Archimedes, who "lifted the earth with his lever, yet required "someplace else on which to locate himself."[37] Yet there seems to be no space outside of panoptical patriarchy, unless one considers black or lesbian or black-lesbian feminist criticism to have created a "room" outside of the white heterosexual paradigm. When Alice Walker famously claimed that "womanist is to feminist what purple was to lavender,"[38] she clearly questioned feminisms of white manufacture and their pretensions to universality. Likewise, the gay, lesbian, and bisexual writers of the early (LGB) Western liberation struggles can be argued to be in dialogue with both heterosexual and homosexual literary traditions, the way later transgender writing was to be in dialogue with cisgender and transsexual literary traditions.

Queering the Text and the Author

Among the poststructuralist challenges to the primacy of the author, the most famous ones are certainly male, French, and date back to the late 1970s: Roland Barthes's fateful pronouncement on the death of the author and Michel Foucault's essay on the author as function.[39] The fact that these two theorists were homosexual has helped twin the author with the homosexual. In the 1990s, Richard Dyer, one of the first openly gay professors in Britain, reminded us that – all authorship and all sexual identities being "performances" – "the study of (gay/lesbian) authorship is the study of those modes and the particular ways in which they have been performed in given texts."[40] In *Search for a Method* (1968), Jean-Paul Sartre said of Paul Valéry that he was "a petit-bourgeois intellectual, no doubt about it. But not every petit-bourgeois intellectual is Valéry."[41] Indeed, Dyer reasons there would be few lesbian and gay texts if the text alone had to bear the burden of being lesbian or gay. On the one hand, authorship is not only performed, it is also multiple and hierarchical. On the other hand, "the homosexual," as Michel Foucault has argued, emerges in fin-de-siècle clinical literature and it is in medical texts that it becomes "a type of person rather than a sexual activity, such as buggery," and that "inversion" becomes a marker of homosexuality, which becomes "a species,"[42] thereby moving homosexuality from performing an act to becoming an identity.

In Joseph Bristow's *Sexual Sameness/Textual Differences in Lesbian and Gay Writing* (1992), besides the slash that harks back to Toril Moi, the conjunction "and" between "Lesbian" and "Gay Writing" signals "the overlapping concerns of discrete subcultures."[43] Gay Studies and Lesbian Studies can indeed be paired off politically and critically, because of their origins in Western liberation struggles, but gay and lesbian individuals' concern with sameness may be variously performed. Same-sex desire may be differently expressed in the fiction of Virginia Woolf and James Baldwin or in the poems of Langston Hughes, Adrienne Rich, and Audre Lorde. Also, Clarissa in *Mrs. Dalloway* (1925) is by no means Virginia Woolf, and Sally Seaton is not Woolf's partner, Vita Sackville-West, even though Vita inspired Woolf's androgynous *Orlando* (1928). Likewise, Oscar Wilde's *The Picture of Dorian Gray* (1891) presents a puzzling relationship between the Walter Pater-like Henry Wotton, the painter Basil Hallward, and Dorian Gray, but that relationship is not contiguous with the relationship that Wilde had with Lord Alfred Douglas aka Bosie or Wilde's late-Victorian rent-boys. E. M. Forster's *A Passage to India* (1924) hints at same-sex desire and so does Forster's *Maurice* (1971), which was published fifty-seven years after its completion, but not for the same reasons. It is therefore not so much an alleged pre-existing social or biological reality that creates "sexual difference," a term that came into play in the 1970s, as the way subjectivity is enacted or "semioticized"[44] in the work of representation.

At a time when theories of sexuality drove a wedge between a straight original and its inverted mirror-image, the novelist was split in two. Henry James's 1893 short story tellingly titled "Collaboration," written after his offer to work with H. G. Wells was turned down, points to the double writing strategies among British authors and the implicit specter of homosexuality lingering in such collaborations. In *Double Talk* (1989), Wayne Koestenbaum singles out four such co-authorships or "manuscript affairs":

between Robert Louis Stevenson and his stepson Lloyd Osborne in "romances" with a "pederastic intent" hidden behind the boyish tale of adventure; H. Rider Haggard and Andrew Lang in *The World's Desire* (1890); Michael Field, the twinned pseudonym of Katharine Bradley and her niece Edith Cooper in their lesbian poetry; and Joseph Conrad and Ford Madox Ford in *Romance* (1898).[45] Tellingly, Ford said of Conrad's words that they "crepitate from the emasculated prose like fire-crackers amongst ladies' skirts."[46] While not being avowed homosexual writers, these male monarchs of letters certainly wrote books about men and created worlds without women, possibly to counter women's fiction, which had been growing since the 1840s. The most emblematic of these texts is Stevenson's *Strange Case of Dr. Jekyll and Mr. Hyde* (1896), which he wrote in collaboration with his wife, Fanny Osborne, whom he managed to erase.[47]

The Well of Loneliness* (1928) by Radclyffe Hall may well be the supreme test case for queer authorship. Hall's novel is on "congenital sexual inversion," a phrase coined by sexologist Havelock Ellis, who wrote a note endorsing and almost "author-izing" her novel as an authoritative sexological narrative. Hall allegedly wrote her novel for a reason: "I wished to offer my name and my literary reputation in support of the cause of the inverted."[48] Authorship is thus used to support a "minority" cause. The subject of sexual inversion is written into fiction by a self-designated insider, for who else would be "better qualified"?[49] Although Hall, in her own "Notes" to *The Well*, seems to have internalized contemporaneous theories of craniology and its predecessor, phrenology, she nonetheless presents her protagonist, Stephen Gordon, as "the finest type of the inverted woman" while claiming that Gordon exists side by side with "the weaker members." Not Stephen Gordon but Radclyffe Hall wishes to speak for the "inverted" subaltern, even though Hall as a "transgendered butch" *avant la lettre* – unlike the uncoupled Gordon – had two successful queer relationships with women. What is more, the sympathy of the British working classes was extended to Hall, not Gordon, upon the British government's prosecuting order that the book be suppressed. Hall's authorship is thus very much enmeshed with the law, as in the Oscar Wilde trials of 1895, during which excerpts from *The Picture of Dorian Gray* were read by the Defense Attorney, Carson, as if the novelist rather than the person was to be indicted. However, even though inversion is the marker of homosexuality in *The Well*, the heterosexual ending of the novel is commensurate with the fact that Stephen Gordon is masculine and a potential trans man rather than a mannish lesbian or "a lesbian in male body drag."[50] Both Stephen Gordon and Radclyffe Hall have since been claimed by transgender theory. Trans-historically, therefore, the category of inversion is instrumental in the emergence of what Jay Prosser calls "the interlinked literal and literary construction of the transsexual."[51]

Unlike gay and lesbian narratives, queer or queered narratives are supposed to propound an identity without essence or a suspension of identity, with claims to be more inclusive than the historically determined gay and lesbian movements and to dissolve the binary gender system. Yet, gay, lesbian, and even queer narratives differ from transsexual narratives in that the latter reject same-sex relations as same sex. This is where transgender and queer theory part even though they are aligned in the ever-expanding spectrum now known as LGBPTQI2A+: Lesbian-Gay-Bisexual-Pansexual-Transgender-Queer-Intersex, to which "2" or Two-Spirit and "Asexual" and "+" or Others have lately been added.

A queer text like Jamaican-American Michelle Cliff's *No Telephone to Heaven* (1987) highlights the contentious dialogue between queer theory and transgender theory, in that it portrays the enmeshed lives of Clare Savage, a bisexual, light-skinned *tragic mulatta* who can pass as white and straight, and Harry/Harriet (or H/H), a non-operative transgendered cross-dresser raised as male, who ends up surviving guerilla warfare against American imperialism as well as living and working as Harriet, a woman nurse in a Kingston hospital. Cliff claimed in an interview that H/H was "the novel's lesbian."[52] Indeed, Clare has sex with two men and never with a woman but because she has sex with H/H who is a female-identified man at the time of intercourse, Clare turns out to be "the novel's lesbian." Cliff has "split" – a statistically recurrent term in the novel – the true biracial lesbian of the novel into Clare Savage and H/H. H/H's queerness and campiness therefore act as a foil to Clare's repressed lesbian identity, which is part of Cliff's semi-autobiographical investment in her character, as an avowed lesbian and Adrienne Rich's partner, who left Jamaica, lived in England, and resided in the US until her death in 2016. H/H's future as a trans woman still has to be written.

Transgendering the Text

The fin-de-siècle invert's autobiographical narrative – which is the sexologist's means of diagnosis, as in *The Well of Loneliness* – augurs later accounts by trans individuals. The most famous transsexual autobiography is undoubtedly that of Christine Jorgensen, born George William Jorgensen, whose "trip to Denmark," the country of her forebears where she underwent surgery, became shorthand for undergoing sex reassignment surgery (SRS). *Christine Jorgensen: A Personal Autobiography* (1967) became the template of medically legitimized transsexuality before the term "transsexual" became widespread. By contrast, *Michael née Laura* is the memoir (recounted by Liz Hodgkinson) of the first trans man – Michael Dillon – to have undergone a full transition as early as 1946, in the wake of e.g., "the Danish Girl,"[53] that is, Lilli Elbe née Einar Wegener. Transsexual narratives have thus been dominated by one genre – autobiography – partly on account of the medical script that trans individuals have to provide to endocrinologists and other members of the medical profession to secure approval for SRS or what is increasingly called *gender confirmation surgery*.

The novelty in transsexual autobiographies is that the original "I" who starts the autobiography is gendered according to the sex assigned at birth and then slowly transitions into the targeted sex after hormonal treatment and/or SRS. Even if, most of the time, the first-person pronoun hosts both the assigned and targeted genders/sexes, it is not always stable and the MTF "she" and the FTM "he" are used to refer to this other person struggling to be born both in life and in the narrative, a bit like the creature behind Gilman's "Yellow Wallpaper." In *The Testosterone Files* (2006), Max Wolf Valerio, an American trans man poet, comments in gender-split style that "I probably cried more as Anita in six months than I have as Max in four years."[54] The "I" behind both Max and his former lesbian-identified self, Anita, is "another," complicated by ethnicity (Blackfoot), race (Latino), and faith (Sephardic), that Philippe Lejeune could not have anticipated when he revised his pact between the reader and the author in *Je est un autre* (1980), after Arthur Rimbaud's famous 1871 statement.

In *Canary: The Story of a Transsexual*, both Danny O'Connor, who was raised as a boy, and MTF Canary Conn, one and the same person, vie for the ownership of the "I" in a scene of rare violence. Fighting for her life at the hands of a mentally disturbed woman in a Hollywood restaurant's toilets – toilets being always a site of binary ambiguity in transsexual writing – Conn writes as in a dissociation or *Spaltung*: "Danny had never had a fear of anyone female; *he* was too busy warding off male assaults. Canary had never had to deal with situations like this. *She, I,* wasn't afraid of anyone yet, and *I'*d not developed the sort of sixth sense women have of recognizing situations and people who threaten them."[55] In Beemyn and Rankin's *The Lives of Transgender People* (2011), pronouns undergo some sort of sex change as well: "Because ze has struggled to get others to see hir as genderqueer and to stop using hir birthname, 'Ron thinks that ze may change hir name entirely to break with hir gendered past."[56] The apostrophe in "'Ron" indicates that his new name is severed from a previous name and therefore I-dentity. In *The Making of a Man* (2013), Maxim Februari mentions a common *faux pas*: "People can present themselves as '(s)he,' but if someone calls himself 'he,' why would you say '(s)he', or even worse, 'a (s)he'?"[57]

FTM autobiographies by British trans men such as Mark Rees's *Dear Sir or Madam* (1996) or Rico Adrian Paris's *Transman* (2006), and by American trans men like Jamison Green's *Becoming a Visible Man* (2004), break with the earlier medical-autobiographical script by focusing on gender expectations and violations, thereby turning from author/autobiographer to chronicler of a movement, a travelogue documenting a yearning for the "hominess" of the recovered gender and a sense of arrival. However, behind most transgender autobiographies, whether FTM or MTF, the individual authorship is doubled by the collective voice of activist groups, academic networks, and even transgender nations. The "I" embraces a spectral "we," the way African women's autobiographies and pathographies or what I have called elsewhere "experiential texts"[58] around the traumatic experience of excision or female genital mutilation, for instance, did and still do.

In the new South Africa, with its 1996 clause (9/3) against discrimination on the basis of sexual orientation, transgender and transsexual individuals' homing desires are of a different order. The autobiography of Zulu traditional healer or *sangoma* Nkunzi Zandile Nkabinde, *Black Bull, Ancestors and Me: My Life as a Lesbian Sangoma* (2008), adds complexity to the Western shift from transgender to transsexualism, for her selfhood as a "male woman" dominated by a powerful male ancestor finds earlier avatars in imported words such as "lesbian" and "butch." As her narrative of transgendered "possession" by a dominant male ancestor transitions into the transsexual narrative, the "I" is also possessed by the amanuensis, that is, the American-trained anthropologist Ruth Morgan, who solicited Nkabinde's story and helped her write it down.

When Anastacia Thomson came out, shed her "deadname" and the burden of maleness as a practicing medical doctor in Johannesburg, her outing was quickly followed by her autobiography, *Always Anastacia* (2015). Unlike Zandile, now Zaen, Nkabinde's autobiography, it is conversant with the most up-to-date vocabularies that have trickled down from the West. To wit, this entry of 22 October 2014: "I heard about the support group from a friend I'd met at a dinner party. Originally, I had thought that *she* was a cisgender lesbian. I later learned that *they* (a chosen gender-neutral pronoun) were in fact genderfluid, and non-binary, and self-identified as 'hella queer'." These are words that Staci has to master; she learns "to become skilled at avoiding the use of gendered pronouns or epithets when talking about myself and others."[59] These two autobiographies are, like the new South Africa, in the making, leaving the "imprint of gender" on nation-building conventionally gendered as male.

When Mary Wroth wrote her own sonnet sequence in a man's world and was accused of "dauncing in a net" in seventeenth-century England, she was a woman writer cross-dressing as a male sonneteer. Wendy Wall surmises that this transgression, even if performed within the safety of a net, "probably forced her out of the arena of authorship."[60] Authorship has since then definitely become all-inclusive and polymorphously perverse.

Notes

1. Thomas Dekker, "To the Reader," in *The Gull's Hornbook* (London, 1609), ed. R. B. McKerrow (rpt. New York: AMS Press, 1971), p. 3; and his address "To the Reader" in *The Wonderfull Yeare, in The Plague Pamphlets of Thomas Dekker*, ed. F. P. Wilson (Oxford, Clarendon Press, 1925), pp. 4–7.
2. Quoted in Wendy Wall, *The Imprint of Gender: Authorship and Publication in the English Renaissance* (Ithaca, NY: Cornell University Press, 1993), p. 279.
3. Ibid., p. 1.
4. Ibid., p. 6.
5. Elizabeth Jocelin, *The Mothers Legacie, To her vnborne childe* (London, 1624); "The Praiers made by the right Honourable Ladie Frances Aburgauennie, and committed at the houre of hir death, to the right Worshipfull Ladie Marie Fane (hir onlie daughter) [...]", in Thomas Bentley, *The Monument of Matrones* (London, 1582), pp. 139–213; Dorothy Leigh, *The Mothers Blessing: or the godly counsaile of a Gentle-woman, not long since deceased, left behind her for her children* (London, 1616).
6. See also Isabella Whitney's *The Copy of a letter, lately written in meeter, by a yonge gentilwoman: to her vnconstant louer* (1567) and her *A sweet nosgay, or pleasant posye* (1573).
7. Quoted in Wall, *Imprint*, p. 279.
8. Margaret Hannay, ed., *Silent but for the Word: Tudor Women as Patrons, Translators, and Writers of Religious Works* (Kent, OH: Kent State University Press, 1985).
9. Wall, *Imprint*, p. 312.
10. Quoted in Earl Leslie Griggs, *Coleridge Fille: A Biography of Sara Coleridge* (London: Oxford University Press, 1940), p. 164.
11. Sara Coleridge, *Memoir and Letters of Sara Coleridge*, ed. Edith Coleridge (New York: Harper, 1874), p. 300.
12. Alison Hickey, "'The Body of My Father's Writings': Sara Coleridge's Genial Labor," in *Literary Couplings: Writing Couples, Collaborators, and the Construction of Authorship*, eds. Marjorie Stone and Judith Thompson (Madison: University of Wisconsin Press, 2006), pp. 124–50, p. 125.

13. Christine Battersby, *Gender and Genius: Towards a Feminist Aesthetics* (Bloomington, IN: Indiana University Press, 1989), p. 44.

14. *The Letters of William and Dorothy Wordsworth*, ed. Alan Hill (Oxford: Clarendon Press, 1988), vol. 7, p. 813.

15. Ibid., pp. 888–89.

16. Hickey, "'Body,'" p. 143.

17. Quoted in Susan Williams, *Reclaiming Authorship: Literary Women in America, 1850–1900* (Philadelphia, PA: University of Pennsylvania Press, 2006), p. 17.

18. Quoted ibid., p. 26.

19. Nathaniel Hawthorne, "Female Authors," *North American Review*, 72 (January 1851), 162.

20. Williams, *Reclaiming*, p. 18.

21. Sandra M. Gilbert and Susan Gubar, *The Madwoman in the Attic: The Woman Writer and the Nineteenth-century Literary Imagination* (New Haven, CT: Yale University Press, 1979), p. 47.

22. Ibid., pp. 49–50, 54. Cf. Harold Bloom, *The Anxiety of Influence: A Theory of Poetry* (1973), 2nd edn (Oxford: Oxford University Press, 1997).

23. George Eliot, "Silly Novels by Lady Novelists," *Westminster Review*, 64 (1856), 442–61.

24. Gilbert and Gubar, *Madwoman*, p. 78.

25. Alice Munro, "The Office" (1968), in *Dance of the Happy Shades and Other Stories* (London, Vintage, 2000), p. 60.

26. Munro, "The Office," p. 74.

27. Toril Moi, *Sexual/Textual Politics: Feminist Literary Theory* (1985; London: Routledge, 2002), p. 61 (original italics).

28. Ibid., p. 64.

29. Adrienne Rich, "Diving into the Wreck" in *The New Oxford Book of American Verse*, ed. Richard Ellmann (New York: Oxford University Press, 1976), pp. 1020–22, p. 1022.

30. Hélène Cixous, "Castration or Decapitation?" (1970), in *Feminist Literary Theory: A Reader*, ed. Mary Eagleton (Oxford: Wiley-Blackwell, 2011), pp. 314–18. p. 315.

31. Hélène Cixous and Catherine Clément, *The Newly Born Woman*, trans. Betsy Wing (Minneapolis: University of Minnesota Press, 1986).

32. Hélène Cixous, *Coming to Writing and Other Essays*, ed. Deborah Jenson (Cambridge, MA: Harvard University Press, 1991), p. 13.

33. See Nancy K. Miller, "Changing the Subject, Authorship, Writing, and the Reader," in *Feminist Studies/Critical Studies*, ed. Teresa de Lauretis (London: Macmillan, 1988), pp. 102–21.

34. Luce Irigaray, *This Sex Which is Not One*, trans. Catherine Porter (Ithaca, NY: Cornell University Press, 1985).

35. Tom Wolfe, "The 'Me' Decade and the Third Great Awakening," *New York Magazine*, August 23, 1976.

36. Philippe Lejeune, "Le Pacte autobiographique (bis)," *Poétique* 56 (1983), 416–34.
37. Moi, *Sexual/Textual*, p. 191 and notes p. 4.
38. Alice Walker, *In Search of Our Mothers' Gardens: Womanist Prose* (New York: Harcourt Brace Jovanovitch, 1983), p. xii.
39. Michel Foucault, "What Is an Author?", in *Textual Strategies: Perspectives in Post-Structuralist Criticism*, ed. Josué V. Harari (Ithaca, NY: Cornell University Press, 1979), pp. 141–160; and Roland Barthes, "The Death of the Author," in *Image – Music – Text*, ed. Stephen Heath (New York: Hill and Wang, 1977), pp. 142–148.
40. Richard Dyer, "Believing in Fairies: The Author and the Homosexual," in *Inside/Out: Lesbian Theories, Gay Theories* (New York: Routledge, 1991), pp. 185–204, p. 188.
41. Jean-Paul Sartre, *Search for a Method* (New York, Vintage, 1968), p. 56.
42. Michel Foucault, *The History of Sexuality: An Introduction*, trans. Robert Hurley (Harmondsworth, UK: Penguin, 1981), p. 43.
43. Joseph Bristow, *Sexual Sameness: Textual Differences in Lesbian and Gay Writing* (London: Routledge, 1992), p. 2.
44. Mandy Merck, "Difference and Its Discontents," *Screen* 28.1 (1987), 2.
45. Wayne Koestenbaum, *Double Talk: The Erotics of Male Literary Collaboration* (New York, Routledge, 1989), pp. 143–147.
46. Ford Madox Ford, "Working with Conrad" (1929); rpt. in *The Yale Review*, Autumn 1985, 13–28.
47. See Koestenbaum, *Double Talk*, p. 150.
48. Radclyffe Hall, "From 'Notes on The Well of Loneliness,'" in *Gender in Modernism: New Geographies; Complex Intersections*, ed. Bonnie Kime Scott (Urbana: University of Illinois Press, 2007), p. 325.
49. Ibid.
50. Esther Newton, "The Mythic Mannish Lesbian: Radclyffe Hall and the New Woman," in *Palatable Poison: Critical Perspectives on The Well of Loneliness*, eds. Laura Doane and Jay Prosser (New York: Columbia University Press, 2001), pp. 99–128.
51. Jay Prosser, "'Some Primitive Thing Conceived in a Turbulent Age of Transition': The Transsexual Emerging from The Well," in *Palatable Poison*, ed. Doane and Prosser, pp. 129–44, p. 130.
52. Quoted in Judith Raiskin, *Snow in the Cane Fields: Women's Writing and Creole Subjectivities* (Minneapolis: University of Minnesota Press, 1995), p. 191.
53. David Ebershoff, *The Danish Girl* (London, Weidenfeld & Nicholson, 2000).
54. Max Wolf Valerio, *The Testosterone Files: My Hormonal and Social Transformation from Female to Male* (Berkeley, CA: Seal Press, 2006), p. 304.
55. Canary Conn, *Canary: The Story of a Transsexual* (New York: Bantam Books, 1974), p. 229 (my italics).

56. Genny Beemyn and Susan Rankin, *The Lives of Transgender People* (New York: Columbia University Press, 2011), p. 152.

57. Maxim Februari, *The Making of a Man: Notes on Transsexuality*, trans. Andy Brown (London: Reaktion Books, 2015), p. 32.

58. Chantal Zabus, *Between Rites and Rights: Excision in Women's Experiential Texts and Human Contexts* (Stanford, CA: Stanford University Press, 2007).

59. Anastacia Tomson, *A Transgender Life in South Africa* (Johannesburg: Jonathan Ball, 2015), p. 7, 130.

60. Wall, *Imprint*, p. 338.

CHAPTER 19

Postcolonial and Indigenous Authorship

Mita Banerjee

Involved as they necessarily are in the social and economic contexts of literary publishing, authors can cater to the "dictates" of the market or set out to subvert these dictates. As Graham Huggan has argued with regard to Arundhati Roy, for instance, an author – in this case, an Indian or "postcolonial" author – may seemingly cater to the expectations of a Western audience by providing an "exoticist" description of a far-away country, but she may at the same time weave into her text a questioning of the politics of exoticism.[1] At the same time, the reception of a given literary text may be informed not only by the politics of the literary marketplace or a mass audience, but also by the academic reception of this text. Here, too, authorship and scholarly criticism have often worked in tandem: literary authors have taken up, responded to, or resisted certain "turns" in criticism. Much has been made of this "symbiotic" relationship between literary writing and academic analysis, and it has often remained unclear whether writing precedes new developments in literary criticism or whether academic discussion in turn inspires new conventions of writing. Moreover, one field that also pertains to notions of authorship but is only beginning to be studied in an academic context is the process and politics of editing literary texts. Such editing practices may make a manuscript "palatable" for a mass audience; they may add to the "selling power" of the text, but they may also substantially distort its original message. At the same time, paratexts[2] such as titles or blurbs are crucial for both the publication and reception of a literary text; prefaces or dust jacket descriptions, for instance, may serve to authenticate and legitimate the authorship of this narrative. Moreover, there is a close connection between authorship and genre; to the extent to which some genres – for instance, the domestic novel in the nineteenth century – were dismissed as popular and catering to the taste of a mass readership, the writers of such domestic fiction (mostly women) were similarly relegated to a lower rank of authors. Finally, conceptualizations of authorship are central to the embeddedness of a literary work in a social, historical, cultural and political context. By establishing, for instance, members from minority communities as literary authors, literary texts can become vehicles for social change; conversely, texts can justify political regimes in which certain communities have little or no political representation by representing these communities as "childlike" and hence as being unable to "represent themselves."[3]

Authorship is thus inextricably connected to concepts of personhood, but also to concepts of social belonging. The act of writing, on a number of different levels, can be seen as bringing subjectivity and personhood into being, both with regard to the internal perspective of the writing subject and in relationship to an external audience to this writing. Given this link between authorship, subjectivity, and personhood, it is by no means surprising that the concept of authorship has been central to an understanding of postcolonial and indigenous literatures.

A Piece of Chattel as a Literary Author: Personhood and the Slave Narrative

Authoring a literary text – a novel, an autobiography, a short story, a poem – can thus be understood as an act of emancipation. This is especially true of instances – historical, political, or cultural – where there is a discrepancy between the concept of authorship and the legal or political status of the person writing a given literary text. Nowhere was such a discrepancy as pronounced as in the genre of the American slave narrative. At the time when the slave narrative emerged as a genre – with Olaudah Equiano's *The Interesting Narrative of the Life of Olaudah Equiano, or Gustavus Vassa, an American Slave, Written by Himself* (1789) as one of the first modern English-language narratives authored by a black writer – African Americans were defined as "chattel" by the "peculiar institution" of slavery in the United States. As far as legal definition was concerned, then, African American slaves were not persons in the first place; defined as non-human by law (as well as in cultural and political rhetoric), they could hardly have qualified as authors. Thus, the political potential of the slave narrative as a literary genre resided precisely in the intersection between personhood and the law: its power could be located in the very difference between a legally ascribed lack of humanity and the idea of authorship, which at the same time implied the existence of a human (and intellectually capable) subject. The act of authoring a slave narrative, for the African American author, thus constituted an act of emancipation, of writing herself into being (for similar considerations in the field of feminist literary studies, see Chantal Zabus's chapter "Gender, Sexuality, and the Author" within this volume).

Such an act of literary (if not literal) emancipation was especially difficult for most African Americans under slavery because they were legally forbidden to learn to read and write in the first place. This legal prohibition might well be taken to indicate the power of the pen: so powerful was the act of acquiring literacy, and so dangerous for the political system was a black person's literacy, that it was sought to be prevented by law. Ultimately, the task that the black author of a slave narrative had to perform was to call, *through the humanity which he or she established in the text*, for a change in the legal status of black subjects. Literature and the law were hence intricately connected: through the prohibition of black literacy, the law sought to prevent black authorship and hence to perpetuate the relegation of African Americans to the realm of the non-human. Inversely, literary texts authored by black writers, by establishing their authors' humanity, could call for a change in law and the legal definition of African American personhood.

As this example shows, concepts of authorship can be tied to legal definitions of citizenship. As Ian Haney López has argued, there is a double bind between the legal and the social spheres: the law may translate social conventions into legal practice; as legal practice, it also shapes social conventions.[4] At this juncture between society and the law, literary texts contribute to changing, for instance, the social perception of members of minority communities. By portraying African American characters as fully human, literary texts may in time make a mass readership aware of discriminatory legal practices. Thus, US president Abraham Lincoln is alleged to have once referred to Harriet Beecher Stowe, the author of *Uncle Tom's Cabin* (1852), as "the little woman who wrote the book that made this great war [i.e., the Civil War]."[5] The paternalistic tone of this phrase notwithstanding, what this anecdote recognizes is the power of Stowe's text and hence, implicitly, the political potential of her authorship. Using the genre of domestic fiction and appealing to the moral sensibilities of a large female audience, *Uncle Tom's Cabin* urged white readers to sympathize with black mothers and fathers who were unable to prevent their children being sold "down the river," and, through the "colorblind" potential of the literary novel to make substantial numbers of white readers identify, for the first time in American literary history, with black characters. It is through the possibility of such identification that Stowe caused her white audience to revolt against the institution of slavery. What this instance demonstrates is the relationship between an author, the literary marketplace, and society at large. Even as Stowe herself could not have foreseen the social avalanche that her novel would unleash, and although then, as now, the politics of the literary marketplace are often unpredictable, it can nonetheless be argued that Stowe's choice of genre was well taken. Through the genre of the domestic novel, she succeeded in mobilizing a mass audience of women readers; at the risk of being dismissed as the producer of mere sentimental fiction, she used, as the vehicle for her call for abolitionism, a genre whose political potential had largely been underestimated. In so doing, she was able to influence the political debate of her time, completely under the radar of nineteenth-century political rhetoric and discussion.

The example of Beecher Stowe also illustrates the relationship between authorship and the literary marketplace, which in the United States in the nineteenth century was only beginning to emerge. The debate surrounding the reception of *Uncle Tom's Cabin* testifies to the connections between author and genre. Both, it can be argued, are mutually constitutive: the legitimacy and the validity as well as the economic and cultural success of a given genre will have profound effects on our understanding of the "authorship" of the person who writes a text within a specific genre (see James Phelan's chapter "Authors, Genres, and Audiences" within this volume). Thus, women's writing in the nineteenth century was often confined to the genre of domestic fiction. The lower status of this genre, in turn, had repercussions on the assumed qualification of its authors. These were, as Nathaniel Hawthorne famously argued, mere "scribbling women"; they were by no means seen as literary authors in their own right. Yet, as Stephanie Browner has suggested, by dismissing female authorship and by linking this dismissal to the disregard of sentimental fiction, Hawthorne was in fact also trying to defend his own status – and that of male writers – in a literary marketplace of increasing complexity, a marketplace in which women writers had come to be more successful than men.[6]

To return to the slave narrative, then, the act of authorship and the representation of characters within literary texts such as the novel could serve as a form of intervening in the political debate. At the core of understanding the reception of *Uncle Tom's Cabin*, from a contemporary perspective, is the relationship between character, narrator, and author. Stowe chose domestic sentimental fiction to further the cause of abolitionism; by having her narrator describe black characters capable of the full range of human emotions – love, shame, morality – her narrative proved a powerful tool in the political call for the abolition of slavery. Yet, powerful as Stowe's text may have turned out to be in the public debate, it remained an outside representation of the African American community under slavery; it was thus substantially different from the emergence of black authorship in the United States.

As the example of the slave narrative illustrates, the act of constituting black authorship through the genre of the slave narrative was multi-layered. First, it required a black subject who had attained literacy. Second, this author had to be educated enough to be able to master, inhabit (and potentially, subvert) the codes of literary writing at the time; third, this author had to find a white person who would vouch, in the preface, to the "authorship" of the slave narrative itself; fourth, the black author, supported by the white patron, needed to have access to the publishing industry.

Black authorship hence required both literacy and an awareness of the social, literary, cultural, and moral conventions of the time. The task the author of the slave narrative had to perform, then, was to enlist his or her (predominantly white) audience in the cause of abolitionism while at the same time being careful not to offend the moral sensibility of his white readership by dwelling on the atrocities of slavery in too much detail. This balancing act between the slave narrative's political impetus and its moral implications was especially pronounced for black women authors such as Harriet Jacobs, the author of *Incidents in the Life of a Slave Girl* (1861). For female slaves, the atrocities of slavery as a political and economic system often involved the slave's being raped by her master; to dwell on such a violation, however, seemed almost impossible in the moral codes of nineteenth-century social and literary conventions. As Jacobs writes,

> No pen can give an adequate description of the all-pervading corruption produced by slavery. The slave girl is reared in an atmosphere of licentious-ness and fear. The lash and the foul talk of her master and his sons are her teachers. When she is fourteen or fifteen, her owner, or his sons, or the overseer, or perhaps all of them, begin to bribe her with presents. If these fail to accomplish their purpose, she is whipped or starved into submission to their will.[7]

As this example illustrates, the concept of authorship is closely bound up with notions of readership; there is a sense in which the two are mutually constitutive. As Frederick Douglass's *Narrative of the Life of Frederick Douglass, an American Slave, Written by Himself* (1845) also demonstrated, a slave narrative was especially effective when it succeeded in inhabiting, and *bending* to its own purposes, the codes of literary convention to the extent that it established its author not only as a human subject but as an African American intellectual. If the slave narrative is read as a "postcolonial" text in that it resists the internal colonization of African Americans in the United States, then understanding the politics underlying the authorship of a narrative such as Douglass's may shed light on some of the parameters of authorship in a postcolonial context. First and foremost, there is a sense in which black and postcolonial authorship may be defined by an act of "writing back"[8] or of resisting through writing the literary codes and the political and social assumptions of the dominant culture. Authorship as a concept is hence central to understanding the complex enmeshment between the realms of the social and the literary. Even as the literary text never merely mirrors the social sphere, the two are nonetheless intricately related.

In the case of the slave narrative, black authorship emerges as a call not only for the recognition of black humanity and the abolition of slavery, but also for citizenship. At the same time, this authorship was qualified in multiple ways. In order to testify to the fact, unimaginable for white readers at the time, that a black person was intellectually capable of authoring a literary text, this text had to include, in its title, a guarantee that it was indeed a narrative written by this black person herself; this promise contained in the title, moreover, had to be substituted by the preface of a white patron who further vouchsafed the text's authenticity. Both these ways of authenticating the slave narrative, in turn, would open up the possibility of publication. Yet to focus only on the question of authenticity would fall short of capturing the full complexity of the slave narrative as a genre. Rather, the careful tailoring of the narrative to the expectations, but also the moral sensibilities, of a large, predominantly white readership implies the cultural and intellectual proficiency of the black writer in "reading" the dominant culture. Black authorship is hence inseparable from what W. E. B. Du Bois called "double consciousness": black authors must be able to read their own narrative, as it were, from the perspective of a white audience; only through such an act of looking at themselves as another will they be able to censor their own narrative to an extent that it will not offend the moral sensibilities of their audience.[9] What is true of any literary text and the task of any literary author – to write in such a way that his or her writing is amenable to the taste of a larger audience – may thus be particularly true of writers from minority contexts. The study of authorship as a concept is hence also central to a field that has only begun to emerge: the investigation of the politics of taste, especially with regard to class dimensions, but also ethnic specificities as they inform the reception process.[10]

Madwomen in the Attic: Postcolonial Authorship and the Act of "Writing Back"

As the example of the slave narrative illustrates, literary texts have the potential to emancipate members from minority communities by helping to change the public perception of literary characters from such communities. Acts of authorship may hence be subversive of the dominant order both in inventing such characters and by establishing a member from a minority community as a literary author in his or her own right. In the field of postcolonial literature, such emancipatory potential also pertains to the relationship between the literary text and the nation at large.

Postcolonial writing, as it emerged, for instance, in former British colonies in Asia, Africa, and the Caribbean, is also an attempt, by postcolonial authors, to come to terms with the legacy of colonialism. As in the case of the slave narrative, postcolonial authors find themselves trapped in a language and a cultural and literary system not originally their own. In India, for instance, Thomas Babington Macaulay's 1835 "Minutes on Education" set out to create an education system in what was then British India that sought to displace both Indian languages (termed mere "vernaculars" in Macaulay's diction) and Indian cultural, literary, and religious practices by transplanting, as it were, the system of British education onto British India. The aim of this imposition was nothing short of creating a "race" of what Homi Bhabha and V. S. Naipaul have termed "mimic men": Indian colonial subjects, Macaulay announced, were to be transformed into Englishmen, if not in color, then at least in character.[11]

Such a mimetic emphasis inherent in an entire education system leaves authors with a troublesome burden: how are they to achieve, after political decolonization, a truly postcolonial literature? This signature question has been addressed, for instance, by Salman Rushdie. His 1981 novel *Midnight's Children* can be read on a number of levels. Through the innocent eyes of young Saleem Sinai, it portrays a narrator's coming to terms with the legacy of British colonialism in India. At the same time, it addresses the link between "writing [the] self and writing [the] nation," as Elaine Kim has put it in another context.[12] The narrator's predicament can be seen to metaphorize that of the postcolonial author. In this respect, the symbolism of Saleem's birth at the precise moment of Indian independence is particularly apt because it implies that the narrating subject, the postcolonial author, and the postcolonial nation are mutually constitutive. However, there is an added burden of representation. As Rushdie playfully illustrates in *Midnight's Children*, individual and collective voices cannot be separated. Precisely because writing the self *is* writing the nation, Saleem Sinai, even though he is the narrator telling the story, cannot be conceived of solely as an individual: his narrative, rather, sets out to capture an "Indian" epic and communal voice. As Saleem himself puts it, "Who what am I? My answer: I am the sum total of everything that went before me, of all I have been seen done, of everything done-to-me. [. . .] [T]o understand me, you have to swallow a world."[13] What emerges here is an aspect that has been central to both postcolonial and indigenous concepts of authorship: first, individual and collective notions of authorship converge; and second, texts such as *Midnight's Children* set out to connect both the literary conventions of the novel and the (Indian) tradition of (oral) storytelling. As in many indigenous literary narratives, oral traditions and written conventions are by no means diametrically opposed; rather, they are juxtaposed in an aesthetic that seeks to create an alternative, a "postcolonial" literary tradition.

At the same time, the convergence between individual and communal voices creates a dilemma for the postcolonial author, a dilemma she shares with many "minority" authors from a variety of contexts. The postcolonial writer sets out, through his literary text, to represent "the postcolonial condition," just as, for instance, African American writers such as Toni Morrison have been said to represent "the African American experience." Such an assumption of representativeness at once seems to qualify and modify the notion of authorship as such. To the extent that authors are seen as representative of an entire culture or nation, they lose their individuality, paradoxically, in the very moment of writing. This predicament is a burden that virtually all authors from "minority" communities have had to grapple with. The relationship between "minority writers" (itself a controversial term) and national self-definition has been central to the notion of authorship. As Patricia Storace has written about Toni Morrison: "To read her work is to witness something unprecedented, an invitation to a literature to become what it has claimed to be, a truly American literature."[14] Thus, African American writers can be said to remind the nation of the democratic potential it has not yet fulfilled; in the work of "ethnic" writers in particular, writing the nation comes to fruition as these writers refuse to be relegated to the margins of the canon of national literature, but – as the awarding of the Nobel Prize to Morrison suggests – they are at its center.

Taking the same assumption of a minority author's representativeness as a case in point, Native American (Coeur D'Alene) writer Sherman Alexie titles one of his novels *The Absolutely True Diary of a Part-Time Indian* (2007). In this very title, Alexie addresses, in minute detail, the predicament of the minority writer. First, the audience at large wants his writing to be "authentic"; the choice of the "diary" as a genre is thus particularly apt for an audience in search of an "unfiltered," "true" account of native sensibilities. This very expectation is subverted in Alexie's postmodernist fiction. His novels and short stories stress the fact that no writer can ever represent his or her entire community, and that neither can this author be fully defined by his or her community. In its debunking of authenticity, Alexie's title also implies that every form of writing, even autobiographical writing, will always be mediated and hence, in some sense, fictional.[15] At the same time, the assumption of representativeness also emphasizes the political implications of a text over its literary and aesthetic qualities.[16]

In both postcolonial and indigenous contexts, the concept of authorship is especially fraught. At one end of the spectrum, the postcolonial author has been reduced to mere political activism, the aesthetic and literary merits of her text having been dismissed; at the opposite end, postcolonial and indigenous authors have stressed that, *pace* the "death of the author," they cannot dispense with the notion of authorship and the *social location* of the author[17] (see Jakob Stougaard-Nielsen's chapter "The Author in Literary Theory" and Hans Bertens's chapter "Postmodernist Authorship" within this volume). At the same time, the "death of the author" gave rise to numerous schools of thought and ways of interpretation that stressed the embeddedness of a given text in a particular social and historical context. Thus, arguably, the emergence of the term "discourse" worked in tandem with the demise of the author; each individual text was now seen to be woven into a discourse it served to illustrate and perpetuate. The notion of discourse, in turn, was especially important in the unveiling of power structures and the workings of the dominant culture. In Michel Foucault's work, discourse (in the sense of a network of ideas arising at a particular historical moment in time in a specific society) takes precedence over authorship; even more importantly, the author becomes a function of discourse and not vice versa. Looking back at the use of "authorship" in his own work, Foucault admits that he had used the authors' names as a form of shorthand, without intending to enshrine the individual of the author as such: "I wanted to locate the rules that formed a certain number of concepts and theoretical relationships in their works [...].

I wanted to determine the functional conditions of specific discursive practices."[18] He goes on to note that literary criticism has been in the habit of ascribing authorship to some texts but not to others, thus privileging some genres at the expense of others. In this vein, once the position and the function of the author no longer entail a hierarchy between different narratives, we can trace certain discourses in a given society by referring not only to literary works, but a plethora of different narratives and texts.

Thus, approaches to literary writing after Barthes and Foucault, such as the New Historicism, refused to privilege a literary narrative over other, presumably more trivial genres; they read newspaper articles alongside novels and poems. From a postmodernist vantage point, anything could now be read as a "text." The notion of the text, in turn, became all-encompassing, dismissing in its wake the attention to aesthetic and genre specificities of the entity that was now being "read." Similarly, American Beat Generation writers such as Jack Kerouac and William S. Burroughs experimented with "spontaneous prose" and the cut-up technique; they set out to turn off their own conscious minds, through drugs or meditation, in order let the text "flow" into the world seemingly without a source. Paradoxically, texts were now said to write themselves rather than being deliberately shaped by an author-genius. In many different ways, the death of the author had democratic potential; postmodernist and poststructuralist forms of writing and of literary criticism de-emphasized formal education by allowing for an unlimited range of writing styles, many of them experimental. By killing off the author, these schools of thought paradoxically gave rise to infinite numbers of authors, who would previously not have been acknowledged as such, or who would previously have been excluded from the sphere of "letters." One field that can be seen to have evolved from such developments in the early twenty-first century is the "material turn" in literary criticism. In line with the idea that anything could be a "text," critics now proceeded to focus on forms of "writing" that previously would not have been recognized as such. Thus Alice Walker argued that, never having had access to formal education, her mother "wrote" her own life through sculpting her garden; her own genealogy as a writer, Walker suggested, would have been impossible without her mother's authorship, in the material form of her garden as a "text" in its own right.[19] The challenge for contemporary literary criticism, then, may lie in reconciling the "death of the author" with her presence. To be sure, the demise of the author as the sole authority of textual meaning may have been both necessary and empowering; yet, minority authors in particular have argued that such a demise must not occur at the expense of taking into account the social location from which a text – and its author – emerge.

In the wake of poststructuralist emphases on discourse (as opposed to the individuality of a specific text) and the demise of the author, postcolonial and indigenous writers have argued that a poststructuralist turn risks depoliticizing minority literatures. Indigenous authors in particular have stressed the fact that their writing emerges from particular histories, and from particular locations, socially, culturally, geographically, and historically. Even as the aesthetic aspects of indigenous or postcolonial texts must never be disregarded, the practice of placing the sole focus on the aesthetic or discursive qualities of a text runs the risk of undermining its political implications and implicit call for social change. Thus, it may be especially fruitful to revisit the notion of authorship from a postcolonial or indigenous perspective precisely because such a revision may reveal the potentially normative assumptions, and the cultural implications, of such concepts. Postcolonial and indigenous texts have appropriated the concept of authorship and have challenged the idea that authorship – in its associating an individual writer with a specific text – is only a "Western" convention. In so doing, they have inquired into the elasticity of authorship as a concept. Just what forms of authorship or ownership of ideas, they have asked, can this concept accommodate? It can be argued, then, that postcolonial and indigenous literary texts inhabit two definitions of authorship simultaneously: the text's author, even as her name may appear on the book's cover, is at once evocative of a communal voice that is captured within the text, and that absolves authorship from its sole mooring in Western traditions.

Moreover, the particular locations from which these authors write are themselves highly significant. Thus, critics and writers alike have stressed the difference between "indigenous" and "postcolonial" writing. The inclusion of indigenous writers into the paradigm, both in terms of production and reception, of "postcolonial literature" may have contributed to the "mainstreaming" of indigenous writers, but such inclusion certainly comes at a cost. In order to capture notions of authorship, particularly with regard to minority writers, it may thus be important to employ multiple frameworks simultaneously. Concepts such as "divergent indigeneities," then, stress both the place-based particularities of specific indigenous communities across the globe, and the similarities that these communities may have to other minority or postcolonial groups within a given nation-state.[20]

At the same time, the practice of "writing back" may also have profound repercussions for notions of authorship as such. If, as Edward Said has argued, culture (and, by implication, literary texts) constitutes the under-pinnings of empire, then the attempt to create a postcolonial literary tradition is inextricably bound up with the literary act of writing back. In Salman Rushdie's memorable formulation, "the Empire writes back" to the center,[21] thus subverting the canon of British literature from within. There is a sense in which the literary practice of writing back may lead to a doubling of authorship. Each newly emerging postcolonial text that rewrites a canonical novel from the perspective of the colonial subject, who occurs as a mere extra in this novel's literary universe, bears an intertextual relationship to the original work. Seen from this perspective, the work of the postcolonial author becomes an echo of the British colonial author; but his is an echo that at the same time sets out to distort the original voice (see also Daniel Cook's chapter "Copyright and Literary Property" within this volume).

As in the case of Frederick Douglass and the slave narrative, postcolonial authors first have to "master" the literary canon of the dominant culture; without such mastery, their subversion of this canon, in their own writing, would be impossible. The minority writers' own authorship, in this con-text, depends on their proficiency as readers of the canon of the erstwhile "mother country." As creators of a new tradition, postcolonial authors proceed to transform their readerly comments on the original colonial text into their own work. It is important to note, however, that this newly created text is not a mere copy of the canonical original; postcolonial authors are by no means "mimic men." Rather, they turn Macaulay's legacy – an education system that insisted on turning Indians into Englishmen – against the former colony. The link between culture and imperialism is severed as authors adapt and bend the literary canon of the former colonizer to their own purposes. One of the most significant moments of postcolonial authorship is the deliberate unfaithfulness to the colonial original, which, in the context of rewriting, ceases to be an "original" in the first place.[22] The postcolonial author, in this sense, deliberately displaces colonial notions of authorship and the cultural own-ership they imply. If the colonial education system sought to turn its subjects into a race of "mimic men," postcolonial authors revel in the imperfection of their literary mimicry and their unfaithfulness to imperial "master narratives." As Jean Rhys's novel *Wide Sargasso Sea* emphasizes in its re-writing of Charlotte Brontë's *Jane Eyre*, reading and writing are inextricably intertwined. In Brontë's novel, Rochester's Caribbean wife,

Bertha, has to die in order for his love to Jane to be fulfilled. To make this turn in the narrative's plot possible, the text has to relegate Bertha, who is conveniently mad, to the attic, both literally and metaphorically; the attic, as feminist as well as postcolonial critics have argued,[23] becomes a space marginal to the social fabric the novel envisions. Postcolonial writers such as Jean Rhys, in "writing back" to the center, and to the literary canon of the (former) center, thus re-write canonical texts such as *Jane Eyre* from the margins, turning the tables on the colonizer and her colonialist mind-set. In *Wide Sargasso Sea*, it is Bertha who has turned into the protagonist; the madness, in this postcolonial narrative, is that of the colonizer who is unable to comprehend systems of cultural signification other than her own. In this context, the postcolonial author emerges as a reader (or, rather, re-reader) of colonial texts, and as the author of literary narratives that endeavor to set the lopsided logic of colonialism straight. At the same time, it has been argued that for a genuinely postcolonial writing to emerge, the act of "writing back" can only be a first step; unless other forms of engagement follow, the postcolonial writer will continue to be mesmerized by her colonial past.

The Politics of Literary Recognition: Kim Scott's *Benang*

Postcolonial writing, as well as indigenous literature, hinges on stressing the extent to which it is an alternative system of signification. In this context, the work of Australian Nyoongar writer Kim Scott can be used as an example of an "indigenous" novel that subverts and modifies established notions of authorship on a number of levels. First and foremost, Scott's novel *Benang* (1999) illustrates the interweaving of genre and the literary marketplace. For in settler colonies such as Australia, New Zealand, Canada, and the United States, notions of indigeneity have been central to defining the concept of the nation-state as such. In these national contexts, the act of nation-building is inseparable from colonial conquest; the founding myths of the settlers, and the literature that has subsequently been produced, have often served to displace indigenous notions of inhabiting this land now turned into a Western nation-state. Such displacement, in turn, occurred in tandem with "writing out" or excluding indigenous presences from the archives of national historiography. The task of the literary author, in this context, becomes manifold. First, they may set out, through their novels, to set the archives straight, and to fill the gaps left in "official" historiography; second, in order to fill these gaps, they must rely on oral accounts and testimonies rather than written documents; third, they must acknowledge that their own authorial voice is in fact a communal one and cannot be divorced from the culture from which it emerges. Crucially, such an effacing or transcending of the individuality of the author is vastly different from "automatic writing"; it is, rather, a sharing of the ownership of a given text and the refusal to privilege the author over the community of which they are a part.

In *Benang* (1999), Scott juxtaposes the conventions of the novel with history writing; in so doing, he links oral and literary traditions: the novel "speaks to the present and a possible future through stories, dreams, rhythms, songs, images and documents mobilized from the incompletely acknowledged and still dynamic past" (dust jacket, inside flap). Indigenous writers such as Kim Scott thus address, head-on, the idea of "multiple ontologies."[24] At the same time, since Kim's novel spans both the nineteenth and the twentieth centuries, it pits different forms of personhood against one another: a time when indigenous Australians had not yet been given citizenship or civil rights and could be killed with impunity, as in the murder of two indigenous women described in the text, and a time when both citizenship and literary authorship may serve as the basis of literary conventions and official historiography alike. From the very beginning, the novel effaces the identity of the narrating subject, who is poised in between individual and collective identities, between indigeneity and the desire to belong in the dominant culture. It may be indicative of notions of authorship that the narrative will ultimately refuse to distinguish between the two, let alone favor one over the other. Rather, in telling his version of the killing, the narrator turns historian in what could be termed an indigenous version of Linda Hutcheon's "historiographic" metafiction; oral narratives thus contain information excluded from the archives. Regarded in the light of authorship, Scott's text refuses to distinguish between "major" and "minor" genres, between "authentic" and illegitimate sources. Notions of postcolonial and indigenous authorship here hinge, it could be argued, on the notion of faithfulness or legitimacy. Scott writes Aboriginal subjects into being at a time when legally they did not yet possess citizenship rights and their status as persons or human beings was a contested one. In literary retrospect, his writing grants them citizenship where, historically, they would not have been given such privilege. His role as a literary writer using and transforming the conventions of novel writing is thus instrumental in emancipating subjects, dismissed from nineteenth-century Australian historiography, from his own Nyoongar perspective.

What does it imply, then, that in 2000 Scott received Australia's highest literary honor, the Miles Franklin Award, for this novel, as the first writer of Aboriginal descent to win this prize? What emerges here is the nexus between authorship and recognition, as well as between authorship and national self-definition. Literary prizes, and national literary awards in particular, serve to validate, legitimate, and recognize some practices of authorship and literary writing while dismissing or ignoring others. In this context, indigenous authors are now recognized for the hybrid texts they create, for their fusion of elements from indigenous and settler cultures, and for showing that different forms of authorship must not be mutually exclusive but can in fact be fruitfully fused, allowing new forms of national belonging to emerge. When Keri Hulme was awarded the Booker Prize in 1985 for *The Bone People,* the jury emphasized that her novel could be seen as central to the project of reconciliation between Maori and Pakeha in New Zealand. Similarly, Kim Scott's novel *That Deadman Dance,* which won the Miles Franklin Award in 2011, was hailed by the jury as a "novel for reconciliation."

At the same time, we may have reason to be wary of wholeheartedly celebrating the politics of literary awards. By awarding literary honors to indigenous authors, the nation may strive to prove its liberalism; and it may substitute literary recognition for a more profound inclusion of indigenous voices and political agendas on levels other than literary. Moreover, the aesthetic qualities of award-winning novels may themselves be reason for the wide success of these novels. As has been indicated above, juries are especially welcoming of "hybrid" texts which, in postmodern fashion, fuse indigenous and settler voices. Narratives that do not conform to such aesthetic (and cultural) hybridity may thus continue to be marginalized. In this context, it is especially important to note that Kim Scott has written a number of other texts in formats other than the novel, which were directed at indigenous audiences in particular.

Indigenous and postcolonial concepts of authorship may be central to our understanding of the notion of authorship, precisely because they question and often unsettle its mooring in a Western tradition of letters. As authors like Kim Scott illustrate, the concept of authorship must always be read in tandem with the authors whom it excludes or dismisses, and the texts of whose authorship it is unaware: of the gardens "authored" by illiterate creators such as Alice Walker's mother, or of texts that never had access to the publication industry. Only if we simultaneously inscribe and question different notions of authorship, then, will the concept of authorship be fruitful precisely in its historical evolution and in its malleability. This malleability, in turn, will owe much to a creative dialogue between processes of reception and creation. As Walker so vividly illustrates through the image of her mother's gardens, for instance, disenfranchised communities will strive to find outlets for their creativity, whether or not such creativity is recognized as literature or art. As literature continues to evolve, then, so does literary criticism. This necessary symbiosis between creation and reception is especially important for our attempts at continuing to define and redefine the notion of authorship.

Notes

1. Graham Huggan, *The Postcolonial Exotic: Marketing the Margins* (New York: Routledge, 2001).
2. Gérard Genette, *Paratexts: Thresholds of Interpretation* (Cambridge: Cambridge University Press, 1997); Georg Stanitzek, "Texts and Paratexts in Media," *Critical Inquiry*, 32.1 (2005), 27–42.
3. Edward Said, *Orientalism: Western Conceptions of the Orient* (New York: Pantheon, 1978), pp. 40, 293, 335.
4. Ian Haney López, *White By Law: The Legal Construction of Race* (New York: New York University Press, 1996).
5. Quoted in Cindy Weinstein, "Introduction," *The Cambridge Companion to Harriet Beecher Stowe*, ed. Cindy Weinstein (Cambridge: Cambridge University Press, 2004), p. 1. On the questionable origin of this famous anecdote, see Daniel R. Vollaro, "Lincoln, Stowe, and the 'Little Woman/ Great War' Story: The Making, and Breaking, of a Great American Anecdote," *Journal of the Abraham Lincoln Association*, 30.1 (2009), 18–34.
6. Nathaniel Hawthorne, *Letters 1853–56*, ed. Thomas Woodson, *Centenary Edition of the Works of Nathaniel Hawthorne*, vol. 17 (Columbus, OH: Ohio State University Press, 1987), p. 304. Stephanie Browner, *Profound Science and Elegant Literature: Imagining Doctors in Nineteenth-Century American Literature* (Philadelphia: University of Pennsylvania Press, 2003).
7. Harriet Jacobs, *Incidents in the Life of a Slave Girl: Written by Herself,* 1861, ed. Nell Irving Painter (New York: Penguin, 2000), p. 57.
8. Salman Rushdie, "The Empire Writes Back with a Vengeance," *The Times*, 3 July 1982.
9. W. E. B. Du Bois, *The Souls of Black Folk*, 1903 (Oxford: World's Classics, 2008).
10. See Michelle Lamont and Marcel Fournier, eds., *Cultivating Differences: Symbolic Boundaries and the Making of Inequality* (Chicago: University of Chicago Press, 1992); and Kathy Davis, "Intersectionality as Buzzword: A Sociology of Science Perspective on What Makes a Feminist Theory Successful," *Feminist Theory*, 9.1 (2008), 67–85.
11. Cf. Homi Bhabha, *The Location of Culture* (London: Routledge, 1994).
12. Elaine Kim, ed., *Writing Self, Writing Nation* (San Francisco, CA: Third Women Press, 1994).

13. Salman Rushdie, *Midnight's Children* (London: Picador, 1982), p. 383.

14. As quoted in Hilton Als, "Ghosts in the House: How Toni Morrison Fostered an Entire Generation of Black Writers," *The New Yorker*, October 27, 2003.

15. Alfred Hornung, ed., *Autobiography and Mediation* (Heidelberg: Winter, 2010).

16. Ulla Haselstein and Klaus Benesch, eds., *The Power and Politics of the Aesthetic in American Culture* (Heidelberg: Winter, 2007); Rocio Davis and Sue-Im Lee, eds., *Literary Gestures: The Aesthetic in Asian American Writing* (Philadelphia, PA: Temple University Press, 2005).

17. Seán Burke, *The Death and Return of the Author: Criticism and Subjectivity in Barthes, Foucault, and Derrida* (Edinburgh: Edinburgh University Press, 2010).

18. Michel Foucault, *Language, Counter-Memory, Practice: Selected Essays and Interviews*, ed. Donald F. Bouchard (Ithaca, NY: Cornell University Press, 1980), p. 114.

19. Alice Walker, "In Search of Our Mothers' Gardens," in *In Search of Our Mothers' Gardens: Womanist Prose* (1972; New York: Mariner, 2004), pp. 231–43.

20. Anna Tsing, "Indigenous Voice," in *Indigenous Experience Today*, eds. Marisol de la Cadena and Orin Stan (Oxford: Berg, 2007), pp. 33–67, p. 33.

21. Rushdie, "Empire"; Bill Ashcroft, Gareth Griffiths, and Helen Tiffin, *The Empire Writes Back: Theory and Practice in Postcolonial Literatures* (London: Routledge, 1989).

22. Linda Hutcheon, *A Poetics of Postmodernism* (London: Routledge, 1988).

23. Sandra Gilbert and Susan Gubar, *The Madwoman in the Attic: The Woman Writer and the Nineteenth-Century Literary Imagination* (New Haven, CT: Yale University Press, 2011); Edward Said, *Culture and Imperialism* (New York: Vintage, 1994); Ashcroft et al., *Empire*.

24. See Mario Blaser, "Ontological Conflicts and the Stories of Peoples in Spite of Europe: Toward a Conversation on Political Ontology," *Current Anthropology*, 54.5 (2015), 547–68; Dipesh Chakrabarty, *Provincializing Europe: Postcolonial Thought and Historical Difference* (Princeton, NJ: Princeton University Press, 2007); Mary Louise Pratt, "Afterword: Indigeneity Today," in *Indigenous Experience*, eds. de la Cadena and Stan, pp. 397–404.

PART III

Practical Perspectives

CHAPTER 20

Attribution

John Burrows and Hugh Craig

The matter of attribution has to do with identifying the author (or even the most likely candidates) for a text whose authorship is doubtful, collaborative, or unknown. Such work has been practiced down the centuries, most often for the rectification of literary history but also in political and theological disputation where the authenticity of a document is at issue. Its apparent value in legal inquiry is limited by the fact that few criminals offer a substantial corpus of their writings. The notorious US Unabomber, who might well have written himself into gaol without benefit of other evidence, was a striking exception.

External evidence of the provenance and physical characteristics of a document can be decisive but is often wanting. Internal evidence as yielded by stylistic analysis is the area of our own work and of the following discussion. It is providing increasingly accurate results whenever there is a sufficient body of appropriate material to admit the necessary comparisons. The advent of the computer has made it possible to cover more ground more quickly and accurately; and, accordingly, success rates in tests where the truth is known have risen from around 80 percent to over 95 percent under acceptable conditions.

It is worth noting that this success is surprising, given the many circumstances militating against identifying a constant authorial signal amidst all the competing noise. The materials for attribution are created by independent, reasoning, imaginative human beings, who are not only free to write something different today from what they wrote yesterday, but (if they are professional writers) actually under pressure to come up with something different from what they have done before. There must be variation for readers to keep reading and for spectators to keep coming to performances. There may be a large element of deliberate, structural variation. Authors may decide to write a pastiche of an existing style, to write in a new style under a new name, or to produce a forgery of someone else's style.[1] As well as this inherent drive toward innovation there are many other reasons to expect striking variation. Audiences' tastes change, and the viewpoints of writers change, as does their life experience.

There are structural reasons for variation even within the same mode. In plays, writers seek to differentiate one character from another, giving each a certain style in behavior and in speech to provide the essential contrasts to make interesting and enjoyable drama.[2] Within a novel, there is generally dialogue, fundamentally different from the rest, and within the other parts differences between narrative, reflection, and description. Internal contrasts are part of what keeps readers and spectators entertained, surprised, and disconcerted. There is another set of differences between genres, such as between comedies and tragedies; between first-person and third-person novels; between lyric poems and epics; and between modes like prose fiction and non-dramatic verse.

When we try to judge if a new work is by a particular author or not, we are asking if it would be possible for the author to write that way – is it within their range? We have to make this judgment from what we know they have written, but bear in mind that they can always extend their range and strike into new territory. In statistical terms we have a collection of samples of what J. K. Rowling has written, but what is the population, the ultimate underlying set of possibilities, of what she might or could write, in the sense of her capability and inherent limits? Then if this work is deemed to be within her range, i.e., possibly by her, we have to work out if it is also outside the range of a set of other candidates, and, to be really sure, outside the range of all other writers as well.

Besides the universal conditions for the activity of detecting authorship in literary language there are especially difficult cases, and shortcomings in the way authorship tests are designed and carried out. The law of large numbers means that more is always better. Yet there are inherent limitations in many attribution problems. We need good samples of the background classes, good in the sense that they represent the class as a whole, because they are of a similar text type to the disputed work, and all the variation we might anticipate is present.

This may not be available for a given problem. *A Lover's Complaint* was published under Shakespeare's name, but is quite unlike his other non-dramatic verse in style, and his authorship of this example of the genre of female complaint has often been doubted. Yet he left no corpus of work in this genre to provide a model for any testing. The only sizeable comparison corpus would be dramatic dialogue. Thomas Nashe may or may not have written part of the tragedy *Dido, Queen of Carthage*, but his surviving canon includes only one play, an odd one at that. We are compelled to work out how we would expect Nashe to write dramatic dialogue, judging from his style in prose fiction. We cannot elicit more writing in a given category from authors of the past, and hardly from living authors either. While we are fortunate that more and more well-curated digital text is becoming available for older authors, what they wrote, and what survives from what they wrote, often makes for severe limitations. For writers of our own time, copyright is often a disabling restriction on assembling control sets.

Tests must be applied with consistency. It is difficult to maintain precisely the same method and parameters all the way across the samples, and this can lead to a hidden bias. Focusing on a single candidate author makes it hard to distinguish a genuine resemblance or difference from an apparent one, arising from restricting the context. In a multi-author comparison, known rival candidates may be eliminated, but a candidate not in the original field is often a possibility.

Attribution is more like a prediction about an uncertain future than it may seem. We are interested in the authorship of an anonymous text so must relate the patterns of language use in it to what we know of the patterns of candidate authors. This is a judgment about likelihoods, extrapolating from the incomplete knowledge we have, as when we judge which of two policies is least likely to lead to war, or which of two solutions to a pressing social problem will bring the greatest benefits in the future.

In these circumstances intuition, even in very widely read and perceptive scholars, is probably an unreliable guide since it has an inbuilt tendency to overlook the inherent variation in the background sets, and exaggerate fancied resemblances, as research in the psychology of the "hunch" has shown.[3] Literary scholars are used to dealing with exceptional phrases and passages, and placing most interpretive weight on these, but in attribution it may be the commonest elements – the function words, for example – which are the most reliable authorship markers. It may be the absence or comparative scarcity of a particular feature that is the best evidence for authorship, but that sort of signal may not be as noticeable for a reader. Readers may sense that parallel passages are so similar that they must be the product of one mind, but it may be that just as many good parallels could be found in another writer, if the search in other candidates was as assiduous as within the favored author. If there is only one horse in the race, it is bound to win.[4] Statistics and literary studies are disciplines with deep differences in methods. This is reflected in the resistance in some scholars to the idea that quantitative attribution can provide reliable findings and can detect and analyze signals that are not necessarily available to readers or listeners.

Fortunately, we can now harness a greatly expanded volume of data, and analytical tools of great precision and reach. This means we can test whether attribution works in particular circumstances, with works of known provenance. We do not need to remain at the level of *a priori* statements about the reliability or otherwise of quantitative attribution. We can apply the methods to samples where we already know the author and observe the outcome. If we take a sample, withdraw it from our control set, and treat it as anonymous, where does the method place it? How often do we see the right result?

To emulate the conditions for the attribution of samples of unknown or disputed provenance, the test sample should play no part in forming the classifier, i.e., no part in selecting markers or thresholds for one class or the other. If the sample is part of a work, the rest of the work should be excluded from the control set. This reflects the typical situation for mystery samples – they are from an unknown work, or constitute an unknown work. The resemblances between the test sample and the rest of the work it comes from are likely to be strong, stronger than resemblances by genre or era for instance, so including some or all of the rest of the work is biasing the control set toward being hospitable to the test sample. If we keep doing this – withdrawing works from the control sets and watching where the method places them, in samples which closely resemble the mystery case in size and composition – we can estimate the underlying reliability of the method.

We can also check any result by a second method, which is independent of the first. Even if we stay within the data provided by language, there are different ranges of markers to be found, e.g., words that occur only a handful of times even in a large authorial canon, on one side, and, on the other, words that can almost always be found even in a short sample. There may of course be hidden factors that link the two areas, and compromise this independence, but there are ways of checking for these. If two methods both provide a composite variable that separates Goethe from Schiller, yet the two methods array the Goethe and Schiller samples in an uncorrelated order, we can be confident the methods are truly independent.

The agreement of two methods sharply reduces the overall error rate. Where the attribution is the same in two independent methods, it is much less likely to be in error than with just one method. If both methods are typically wrong once in ten trials, the chance that an attribution is one of the mistakes we expect from the first method is one in ten, but the chance that it happens also to be one of the mistakes we expect from the second independent method is a tenth of that, one in a hundred.

Good attribution studies include a testing phase that is closely aligned to the case at hand. In addition, the accumulated experience of attribution studies can provide a broader context. We can consult work on how quickly the performance with a given method deteriorates as samples get shorter, following the law of large numbers in which the larger the sample, the greater the chance of finding a true underlying mean, through the cancelling out of local aberrations.[5] Where the variation between genres needs to be taken into account, previous work comparing the strength of that variation with the strength of the contrasts between authors is relevant. Other published work will help show whether a given method gives good results when applied across time spans and sharply different modes like personal letters and poems and other contrasting text types that the researcher will need to include in control sets.

Several decades of testing have shown that the authorial signal is remarkably strong, providing a foundation for reliable attribution. The fact that a great many tests of this type have shown reliability rates at 90 percent or greater, despite the inherent variability of language, suggests that there is a powerful effect operating to transcend the centrifugal forces, a human propensity to individualize language. This has been observed in popular romance writers as well as in classical philosophers.[6] Language production is too complex a task to be done consciously, so much of this individuation must occur as our brains construct comprehensible sentences at a deep level. Even in editing, we alter our writing to fit a voice we wish to be known by and according to deep-seated preferences. This matches individuation in other areas like dress, approaches to games, and the myriad other choices of daily life.[7] It is safest to assume for attribution purposes that writing is a mixture of conscious and unconscious activity. Subtle and consistent continuities in the use of very common words may seem to defy conscious control, but the larger structures that bring more or fewer instances with them – from the choice of third-person narration to a rhetorical stance of downrightness versus one of open speculation – are within the reach of artistic control.

In the first instance attribution is a quantitative and forensic activity, which serves the purposes of a separate, more synthetic practice, interpretation and literary history. Practitioners aim at the best answer to specific questions about the authorship of a work or a part of a work, knowing that this determines an important part of the context for the object of their study. It matters whether "The Disappointment," a Restoration poem about impotence, was written by the woman playwright Aphra Behn, as the modern consensus has it, or by the libertine male poet John Wilmot, Earl of Rochester, under whose name it was first printed. If the latter was the true author, both the poem and our notions of Rochester as a poet would be changed.[8] *Timon of Athens* (discussed further below) appears in the Shakespeare First Folio, but scenes in it read quite differently if we know they are not by Shakespeare but by Thomas Middleton. The outlines of a literary tradition are clearer if we are sure about the innovations and influences of particular creators, and the nature and degree of collaboration on individual works if that is the reigning *modus operandi*.

Attribution is in this sense merely quantitative and purely utilitarian. It also has other, more theoretical consequences as well. The close attention that attribution pays to style has brought with it new illustrations of the role played by the grammatical words in a passage, and of the deep interconnectedness of different parts of language. It also confronts literary scholars with the incontrovertible fact that in comparing works on similar genres, authorship is generally the strongest factor in overall patterns of likeness and contrast. Attribution draws attention to the contest between authorial individuation and the variability born of pressures to innovate and to match expectations of genre and local text type, and provides a calibrated analysis of that process. Attribution is a mix of disciplines. That gives it its fluidity and indeterminacy, its ability to offer more definitive results than are available any other way, and its capacity to surprise and illuminate.

In principle, any recurring feature can serve as the basis for attribution. Word length; the use or otherwise of contractions; metrical patterns like internal pauses, extrametric syllables, feminine rhymes, and enclitics; rare phrases; and word adjacency networks, have all been employed, if not always tested with full rigor, especially where hand counting is required and datasets are correspondingly small. The commonest feature to count has been word frequencies – usually the relative frequencies of an appropriate set of word-types (the variables) in a chosen set of texts (the specimens). The term "word-type" denotes the word-form regarded as an entity comprising as word-tokens all the instances of its use. Hence the sentence "The cow jumped over the moon" embraces six tokens but only five types.

We offer an example of this kind of attribution below, with a new method that takes advantage of the correlations between word-frequencies as well as their individual, independent fluctuations.

The underlying postulate is that, by virtue of human individuality, our styles of writing form distinctive idiolects or *paroles*, personal (though not necessarily conscious) selections from *langue* as a general system. (The distinction between *parole* and *langue* was first drawn by Ferdinand de Saussure in 1907.) These *paroles* display a great many properties. Among them three major features, all quantifiable, enable us to model the styles of written texts with considerable accuracy and to compare them with each other. The three are measures of abundance, of consistency, and of interrelationship. Relative abundance, ranging from high frequencies down to zero, is easily calculated and can yield potent contrasts. But abundance is of little use for our purposes unless it is consistently sustained across a range of texts. Taken together, these two determinants bear much weight. Their limitation, however, is that they treat the language as a mere list of chosen word-types or, at best, as an aggregation of them. But, as everybody knows, language functions through the *interrelationship* of words.

Those who have sought to go further by choosing word-types that tend to "go together" have taken sequence and close proximity as their determinants. But many words display similar fluctuations in their patterns of frequency without necessarily meeting those requirements: sets of grammatical associates and syntactic partners among the function words or of pervasive features like archaism, colloquialism, Latinism, and many others among the lexical words. Lexical words are those that bear one or more dictionary meanings. They include common nouns, main verbs, and most adjectives and adverbs. Function words, including pronouns, auxiliary verbs, and connectives lack that kind of meaning but provide much information when their relative abundance is assessed. They are nowadays regarded as the more stable source of stylistic information. (It is true, however, that many authors have favorite lexical words that they carry with them from one topic to another.) Consider such examples as I/you, hath/doth, and could/would.

Such sets, moreover, often have negative corollaries, the alternatives consistently *not* chosen: has/hath, you/thou, and so forth. Across a range of texts appropriate to whatever case may be in hand, both positive resemblances and direct contrasts of frequency can be identified by Spearman's method of correlation. The coefficients (or rho-scores) for many of the pairs united in this way show very high levels of statistical significance. These pairs or "rho-grams" can be gathered in sets embracing all the partners of a given member, with separate subsets for positives and negatives. When, for example, "the" is taken as a "headword," it yields both positive and negative sets, "THE_p" and "THE_n." Such "rho-sets," as we call them, can then be treated as compound variables and employed as data in much the same ways as single-word variables have been used. The trials so far undertaken (and to be illustrated here) suggest that this approach gives unusually accurate measures of stylistic difference, especially with very short texts. Many of the rho-sets themselves are of considerable philological interest and help to explain how the study of word frequencies can be so rich in stylistic information.

As an illustration, let us compare the plays of Shakespeare with those of Thomas Middleton. We can then glance at their respective contributions to *Timon of Athens*. Such "two-horse races" are familiar ground. In recent years, they have yielded considerable, though seldom perfect, success. They offer a useful proving ground for a new procedure like that of rho-sets.

The first step is to establish one or more training-sets. Twenty-eight plays of Shakespeare and eighteen of Middleton are regarded as of sole authorship. For equitable comparison and for corroboration, the former are divided into two effectively random subsets by arranging them all in alphabetical order of title and then forming one group from the odd-numbered and another from the even. So we have "14ShakespeareA" and "14ShakespeareB." Each of them can be compared with "16Middleton." The next requirement is for independent test-specimens, texts that do not participate in the training phase but are matched against its outcome. We take two of Middleton's plays for this purpose and add two in which Shakespeare is thought to have played a dominant but not exclusive part, with Middleton as putative minor author. These four are *The Revenger's Tragedy; Hengist, King of Kent; Macbeth*; and *Measure for Measure*. And, finally, we introduce our target-text, *Timon of Athens*, which is also kept apart from the training.

A suitable list of word-variables can be derived from the training-set itself or from some larger archive. We have chosen to use the most frequent function words of Craig's archive of over two hundred English Renaissance plays. The topmost 191 of them are ranked in descending order of frequency, from "the" and "I" to "sith."

The raw word-counts for all these variables in each of the training-texts were tabulated. They were then standardized in such a way as to prevent the longer texts or the most frequent words from dominating the outcome. The first object is attained by calculating "text-percents," where each score is expressed as a percentage of its text. The second object is attained by transforming all the text-percents for a given word-variable into "set-fractions." The total of the text-percents for each variable in this range of texts is transformed to a common base of 1.00. The text-percents for its components are then expressed as decimal fractions thereof. The comparative parity of these set-fractions allows them to be added together or averaged out, tasks better not undertaken with either raw scores or text-percents where high scores engulf the low.

It is at just this point that the new rho-set procedure departs from most of the more familiar tests. Each of the Shakespeare subsets, A and B, is matched with the Middleton set and submitted to Spearman's form of correlation. This yields two vast matrices in each of which our 191 variables are correlated, each with every other, across the range of thirty specimens. There are almost forty thousand coefficients in each matrix. Thanks to the computer, these are easily sifted and ranked. We are then able to determine which of all the word-variables form statistically significant partnerships (whether positive or negative) with any or all of their fellows. Those that qualify in only one matrix are discarded as unreliable. The remainder are true "rho-grams" and they make up the rho-set for each chosen "headword."

Correlation coefficients reflect the degree to which the standardized scores, whatever their actual size, across a given range of texts vary in unison or counter-unison. Perfect matches and mismatches yield coefficients of 1.00 and −1.00 respectively. Coefficients on either side of 0.00 show that there is no meaningful relationship between the variables in question. Coefficients beyond 0.46, whether positive or negative, are "highly significant" when, as in each of our present matrices, thirty specimens are being compared. At our chosen level of significance, one in two hundred of them is likely to be a chance event. Our requirement that any instance must qualify in both matrices greatly reduces the incidence of chance events.

We have now identified the members of each rho-set as all those associated at a significant level with each head-word. Most of the stronger rho-sets will comprise between a dozen and twenty members. Accordingly, we can set the correlation matrices aside and return to the table of set-fractions as the scores to be compared. At this point, moreover, we can reunite 14ShakespeareA with 14ShakespeareB and match all twenty-eight against Middleton's sixteen.

For the purposes of philological inquiry, any desired variables can be taken as headwords, their rho-sets assembled, and their membership studied. Any of them is likely to shed an interesting light on a particular corner of the vast web of interrelated words that are at work in any text.

For the purposes of attribution, however, we take a different course. We now wish to select as headwords those word-types that yield the

strongest contrasts of all between the training sets. The established procedure for this purpose is Student's *t*-test. The *t*-scores produced by this test
show, for each variable in turn, the likelihood that the specimens under
comparison all come of a single population. All of the variables are then
ranked by *t*-score and the strongest discriminators selected as the headwords to be pursued. In the present case, we chose to work with ten of the
top-ranking variables, including the twelfth, the indefinite article, but
passing over the tenth and the eleventh, "on" and "somewhat."
The scores for the last-named were much more erratic than those for "a."
The inclusion of "on" would have meant that six of the chosen ten favored
Shakespeare. With the initial of the favored author attached to each, the list
of chosen headwords ran: hath (S), has (M), all (M), doth (S), and (S), now
(M), thus (S), never (M), did (S), a (M).

In the case of Shakespeare versus Middleton, these are all very strong
discriminators. The weakest, "a," shows a likelihood of less than one
chance in a thousand that the two sets come of one population. With the
strongest, "hath," the likelihood extends to one chance in many trillions.
That is because Shakespeare uses it, on average, more than fifty times in
a play whereas Middleton averages less than four.

Each of these ten headwords forms useful rho-sets, positive and
negative, numbering between eight and twenty members in either
case. The headword "hath," for example, yields "HATH_16p" and
"HATH_18n."

The set-fractions for each member of a given rho-set are added and then
averaged, yielding an overall rho-score on that variable for each of the
forty-four training-texts. These rho-scores for the ten pro-Shakespeare
variables are then added to each other and their grand average is calculated.
The ten "pro-Shakespeare" rho-sets comprise the five Shakespeare-
positives and the five Middleton-negatives. The converse group comprises
the ten pro-Middletons.

The grand averages for the ten pro-Shakespeares are set out as a column-
graph in Figure 20.1.

The perfect accuracy of Figure 20.1 in separating the two authorial sets
need occasion no surprise: these forty-four texts, in authorial groups,
supply the data that distinguish them from each other. (It is true, however,
that an occasional aberration might have arisen.) The four horizontal
"benchmark lines" across the graph add greatly to its force. The topmost
and the lowest of these represent the mean set-fraction for each author and
show the gulf between the two sets. The other two lines, close to each other
and near 0.018, represent the likely extremity of each set: three units of

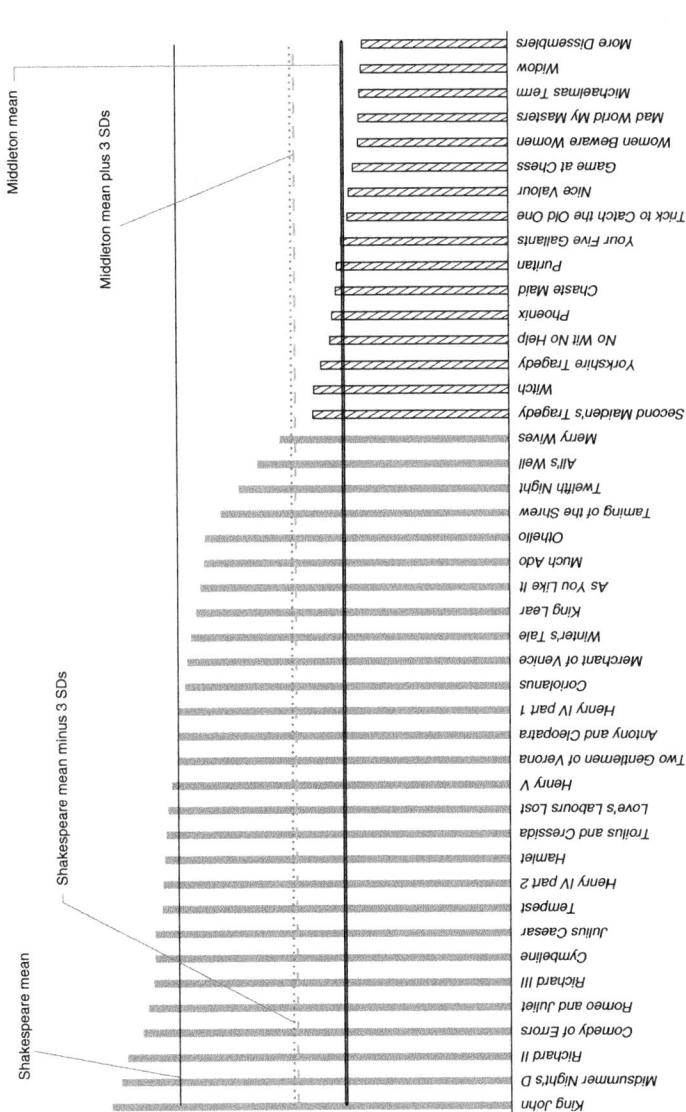

Figure 20.1 Rho-set scores for forty-four plays by Middleton and Shakespeare. Gray columns: Shakespeare; striped columns: Middleton.

standard deviation below Shakespeare's mean and three such units above Middleton's.

In a normal distribution curve, 99.7 percent of all cases are likely to lie between +3 and −3 standard deviations from the mean, half of them on each side of it. In other words, the likelihood that a genuine Shakespeare entry will score below about 0.018 is only 0.15 percent, or one chance in over six hundred. The same proportion of Middleton entries will lie above 0.018. In work like ours, the probabilities are indicative rather than binding because the distribution curves of scores for our variables are not normal. They tend to form two peaks and they tend to skew toward the negative because the mean is usually closer to zero than to the topmost score. (Take a sentence like "The remains of the rat lay on the mat by the fire in the claws of the cat with the . . . " It is meaningful and correctly formed – but the incidence of "the" rises from between 3 and 8 percent to 33 percent of all the word-tokens.) It remains the case, nevertheless, that, if the boundary-lines are breached, it is better to acknowledge an error and seek to understand it than to declare it a mere freak of chance.

Figure 20.2 replicates the scores of Figure 20.1 but also includes scores for our four independent test-specimens and three blocks of our target-text.

As has been said, these seven entries play no part in constructing our model but are now registered against it. All four of the test-specimens are sorted accurately and the three entries for *Timon of Athens* behave in a most interesting fashion.

Current scholarly opinion, well represented in the *New Oxford Shakespeare* (2016), attributes three thousand words of the play to Shakespeare and six thousand to Middleton. Nine thousand words are unassigned. We have united the various scenes so described into three continuous blocks and assessed their behavior. To the extent that our evidence holds good, it appears that current opinion is well-founded for the putative Shakespeare and the putative Middleton. But the unassigned block leans so firmly toward Shakespeare that it seems well worth a closer scrutiny.

Are we equipped for this demanding task? Figure 20.3 certainly suggests so.

We have broken each of our four test-plays into successive segments of only 500 words and tested them in the same way as we tested the whole plays. Of the 154 segments, we have taken every fifth member of each set to form Figure 20.3 – the first, sixth, eleventh, and so on amounting in all to

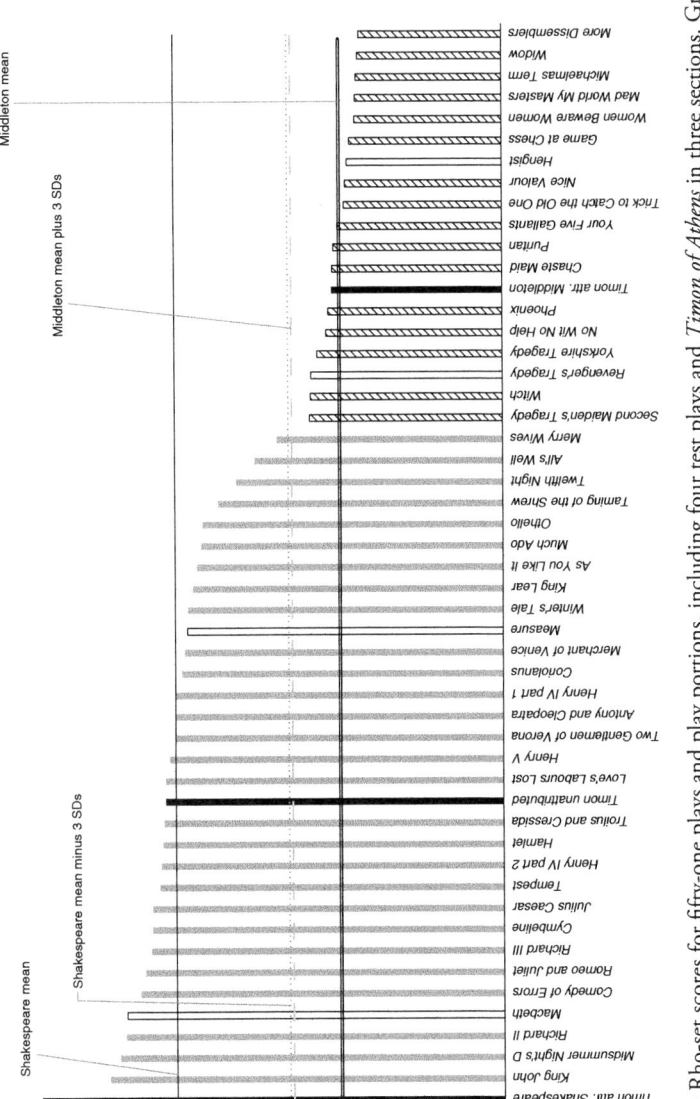

Figure 20.2 Rho-set scores for fifty-one plays and play portions, including four test plays and *Timon of Athens* in three sections. Gray columns: Shakespeare; striped columns: Middleton; white columns: test plays; black columns: portions of *Timon of Athens*.

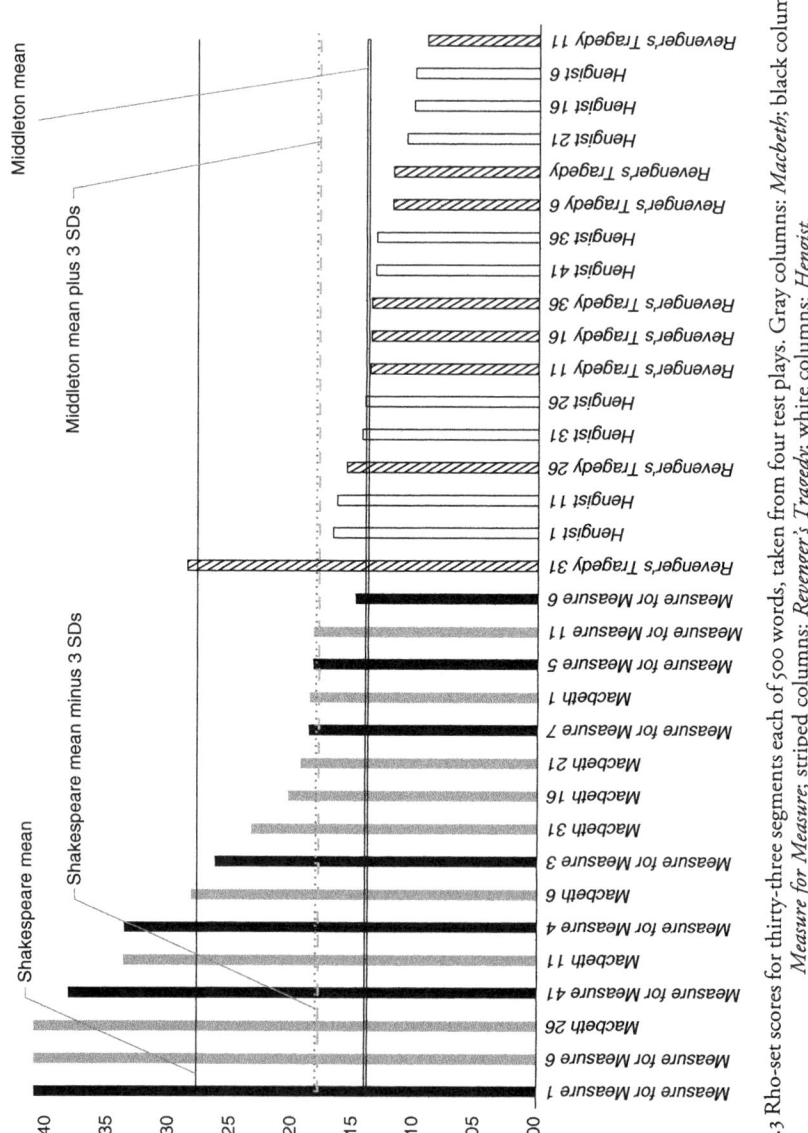

Figure 20.3 Rho-set scores for thirty-three segments each of 500 words, taken from four test plays. Gray columns: *Macbeth*; black columns: *Measure for Measure*; striped columns: *Revenger's Tragedy*; white columns: *Hengist*.

thirty-three. We have grouped them according to author to establish whatever level of authorial contrast they may display.

As Figure 20.3 shows, only two entries breach the authorial boundaries. The specimen from *Measure for Measure* need occasion no surprise and hardly qualifies as an error because it is accepted that Middleton had a hand in this play and is thought to have interpolated some passages. The aberrant entry for *The Revenger's Tragedy*, segment 31, is a different matter. It is a true error of classification and it represents a limitation in our model of Middleton's *parole*. It is a villain's narrative, speaking of two seductions and seeking to commission a murder. It is not a monologue but the main speaker is dominant and the flow of his language is far removed from Middleton's characteristic staccato, his brisk dialogic intercourse.

One error in thirty-three represents an accuracy rate of 97 percent, a remarkable outcome in work where two thousand words is usually accepted as a lower working limit. As it happens, our choice of every fifth specimen proves to be a little favorable. Allowing for Middleton's hand in *Measure for Measure*, the only aberration in the Shakespeare entries is segment 29 of *Macbeth*, the sleep-walking scene, where the unhappy woman's piteous, broken cries are like little else in Shakespeare. The two Middleton plays, however, yield a sprinkling of errors and reduce the overall rate of accuracy to a fraction above 90 percent.

Ninety percent, remarkable as it is for these short passages, is not enough to yield serious attributions. But all such work needs corroborative support from other tests and the present result suggests that we should undertake it, albeit in another forum. As for the rho-set procedure, we may hope that this promising early version can be modified and improved, perhaps by ourselves, perhaps by other scholars.

Notes

1. Wayne McKenna and Alexis Antonia, "Intertextuality and Joyce's 'Oxen of the Sun' Episode in *Ulysses*: The Relation between Literary and Computational Evidence," *Revue informatique et statistique dans les sciences humaines*, 30 (1994), 75–90; Vina Tirvengadum, "Linguistic Fingerprints and Literary Fraud," *Computing in the Humanities Working Papers* A.9 (1998), http://projects.chass.utoronto.ca/chwp/tirven/.
2. John Burrows and Hugh Craig, "Authors and Characters," *English Studies*, 93.3 (2012), 292–309.
3. Amos Tversky and Daniel Kahneman, "Judgment under Uncertainty: Heuristics and Biases," *Science*, 185 (1974), 1124–31.

4. Samuel Schoenbaum, *Internal Evidence and Elizabethan Dramatic Authorship: An Essay in Literary History and Method* (London: Edward Arnold, 1966); MacDonald P. Jackson, "One-horse Races: Some Recent Studies," in *The New Oxford Shakespeare: Authorship Companion*, eds. Gary Taylor and Gabriel Egan (Oxford: Oxford University Press, 2017), pp. 48–59.

5. Maciej Eder, "Does Size Matter? Authorship Attribution, Small Samples, Big Problem," *Literary and Linguistic Computing*, 30.2 (2015), 167–82.

6. Jack Elliott, "Patterns and Trends in Harlequin Category Romance," in *Advancing Digital Humanities: Research, Methods, Theories*, eds. Paul Arthur and Katherine Bode (London: Palgrave Macmillan, 2014), pp. 54–67; Harold Tarrant and Terry Roberts, "Appendix 2: Report of the Working Vocabulary of the Doubtful Dialogues," in *Alcibiades and the Socratic Lover-Educator*, eds. Marguerite Johnson and Harold Tarrant (Bristol: Bristol Classical Press, 2012), pp. 223–36.

7. John Burrows, "All the Way Through: Testing for Authorship in Different Frequency Strata," *Literary and Linguistic Computing*, 22.1 (2007), 27–47.

8. John Burrows, "Computers and the Idea of Authorship," in *Rückkehr des Autors. Zur Erneuerung eines umstrittenen Begriffs*, eds. Fotis Jannidis, Gerhard Lauer et al. (Tübingen: Niemeyer, 1999), pp. 133–44.

CHAPTER 21

Anonymity and Pseudonymity

Robert J. Griffin

Anonymous authorship can be defined as encompassing any publication that appears without the author's name printed either on the title page or in any other paratext such as a preface or dedication. Pseudonymous authorship, it follows, is a form of anonymity; the author's name is concealed, while a false name is presented to the public. Anonymity, in this definition, is constituted formally by the absence of a name, or the presence of a false name, in the medium of publication. Friends, family, colleagues, editors, and publishers, naturally, are frequently aware of the identity of an anonymous author (but they are also frequently kept in the dark). The anonymity of a publication, as I define it, is not affected by whether a few people are in on the secret, or whether the identity of the author is in fact an open secret to many. For example, consider a first edition that has been published anonymously while the second edition has been signed; the author is now known, but the first edition continues to be an anonymous publication. This formal distinction allows us to recover the material literary and cultural history of earlier periods when anonymity was a widely practiced strategy in the literary system, while allowing us also to reflect on our own system, in which anonymity and pseudonymity continue to be operative but in different proportions and in media other than manuscript and print. The project of recovering the original contexts of anonymity that are obscured by modern named editions has driven much of the scholarship in the field.

From the introduction of print technology in the late fifteenth century up to the late nineteenth century, books published anonymously and pseudonymously in Britain were familiar to readers. To take one example: from 1750 to 1830, the classic period of the rise of the novel as a new genre, roughly 70 to 80 percent of all new novels were published either without any indication of the author's name or under a false name.[1] It was not only the obscure novels that were anonymous when they first appeared and quickly forgotten, but most of the great and lasting ones as well. What *we* have largely forgotten, or simply neglected as a significant fact, is that nearly all of the famous authors in the current canon who wrote before 1900 originally published at least some of their works (if not all, as Jane Austen did) without their names on the title page. This is not to say that anonymity subsequently vanished, not at all, only that its dominance has waned. Given the predominance of literary anonymity, including journalism, in earlier times, as well as its persistence in the literary field and on the Internet today, it is not an extravagant claim to assert that the history of authorship, as well as the history of the book, is incomplete and cannot be accurately assessed without an understanding of anonymity and its subset pseudonymity as literary and cultural practices. When they are taken into account, many of our received ideas about authorship and its history are called directly into question.

This chapter presents a brief overview of the theory and history of anonymous publication, with several admitted limitations, in part because of space and in part because the range of instances is so large that only a fragment of them can be compassed. First, although I will be referring to many examples to illustrate particular points, surveys of the multiple modes of anonymity and pseudonymity, and of the motives of authors, are available elsewhere.[2] Second, references to scholarly works are not meant to be comprehensive but as indicators of trends in the field. Third, my examples in most cases inevitably derive from the field with which I am most familiar, British literature and culture. Given, moreover, that we have already learned enough to be able to see how anonymity varies widely at different times according to period, genre, and location, there is much research yet to be done within even this delimited field. Nonetheless, research on anonymity in one area may at the very least be taken as a point of comparison for research on anonymity in other areas. Scholarship on early modern France and Germany, for example, as in England during this period, shows that anonymity in all three cultures was driven, among other motivations, by attempts to avoid prosecution for political and religious offenses, and by an aristocratic avoidance of publicity, either feigned or genuine.[3] While each history will take different paths, certain structural similarities such as the restrictions placed on print and speech under absolute governments, or the exclusivity of class identities, appear to produce similar social, legal, and cultural environments.

Sustained scholarly attention to anonymity in British literary history has recently achieved the required critical mass for it to be called by the general title "anonymity studies."[4] An older version of literary history, with its roots in the nineteenth-century drive to establish national literary traditions, put its energies into decoding manuscript hands, determining the succession of editions of texts, and writing authoritative biographies of authors, etc., before the emphasis shifted to aesthetic criticism in the early to mid-twentieth century with arguments along the lines of R. S. Crane's in 1935.[5] In those contexts – at first the recovery of a literary tradition, and subsequently literary history as background for critical assessment – anonymous works were viewed primarily as a problem of attribution. As an illustration, prefacing his 1870 edition of an Elizabethan anthology of sixteenth-century poetry, Tottel's *Songs and Sonnets*, Edward Arber sees his purpose as an attempt "to restore – in a just measure of fame – not a few of our *best English Poets* to their places in our National Literature." Once all lost poetry has been "brought to light, *verified*, and collated," Arber reasons, then "may we hope to solve the whole host of Initials and Pseudonyms which are, but often vainly supposed to attest the authorship of so many extant poetical pieces."[6]

With the same goal in mind, a large-scale reference work of attribution such as Halkett and Laing's *A Dictionary of the Anonymous and Pseudonymous Literature of Great Britain* was first published in four volumes in the 1880s and revised into nine volumes in the twentieth century (whose reliability has recently been severely challenged);[7] similarly, William Prideaux Courtney's comprehensive bibliographic and anecdotal survey *The Secrets of our National Literature* appeared in 1908. In the early twentieth century also, many writers took stock in various ways of the recent, relative disappearance of literary anonymity, among them E. M. Forster, in *Anonymity: An Enquiry* (1925), and Virginia Woolf, not only in *A Room of One's Own*, but also in the unpublished essay "Anon." The waning of anonymity was gradual, but a measure of its momentum by 1865 can be found in Anthony Trollope's "should" in an article in *The Fortnightly Review*: "It is, I think, now generally presumed that all literature of a high class [...] should present itself accompanied by the name of its author."[8]

The return to prominence of historical scholarship at the end of the 1970s led to a different kind of attention being paid to anonymous publication. First, the problem of anonymity was taken up by feminist literary history, which has affinities both with the older literary history's interest in recovery and attribution, and with the new history's critical edge. Under the stimulus of Virginia Woolf's *A Room of One's Own* (1929), feminist scholars perceived anonymity as an obstacle to be overcome: it stood not just for textual anonymity, but for the social condition of women in general, and for the neglect of women writers in an academy dominated by male professors in particular. But the emphasis on anonymity as privation, which was and is real enough, explained only so much. What does one do, for instance, with the phrase "By a Lady" on the title page of a book, a phrase that maintains anonymity while advertising gender together with class status?[9] Attention thus shifted to the agency, ingenuity, and professionalism of women writers, while anonymity came to be described as strategic.[10] Further, an important line of self-reflexive criticism emerged within this field to argue that, in the many cases in which the author's gender cannot be recovered, or in which a male writer deployed a female pseudonym, feminist literary history needed to consider female-*voiced* works as a natural extension of their concerns. Marcy North's chapter on "Reading the Anonymous Female Voice," for instance, surveyed discussion of this vexed issue and called for a recognition that "the female voice and female authorship [are] two different conventions that do not always work together."[11] Jennie Batchelor, in a recent essay on the fluidity of authorial identities in the long-running monthly *Ladies Magazine* (1770–1832), re-emphasized the point that Anon "troubles us by reminding us that the goal of recovery will always be, in part, illusory."[12]

Second, the project of feminist recovery converged, or found common ground, with three other movements: New Historicism on the one hand and Cultural Materialism on the other, both of which deployed ideological demystification to critique traditional historical narratives, and whose influence was felt on a third methodology, the cultural-historical emphasis of an emerging History of the Book. The compatibility of methodologies can be illustrated by setting a quotation by Raymond Williams, the Marxist critic, next to one by D. F. McKenzie, the book historian. Williams defines "cultural materialism" as "the analysis of all forms of signification, including quite centrally writing, within the actual means and conditions of their production."[13] McKenzie, in turn, calls for an expanded sense of bibliography as "the discipline that studies texts as recorded forms, and the processes of their transmission, including their production and reception."[14] The focus on production, distribution, and reception – that is, on the material genesis and circulation of objects in the world – opened the way to studying the historical contexts of authorship, including anonymity and pseudonymity, quite apart from any drive toward attribution. Attribution is a perennial issue, nonetheless (see John Burrows and Hugh Craig's chapter "Attribution" within this volume), and has recently claimed attention by means of young scholars who have taken anonymity's opacity seriously and have challenged attributions long taken for granted.[15]

Finally, a third line of inquiry that has stimulated work on anonymity is postwar French theory. The two most influential writers on this topic, Roland Barthes and Michel Foucault, viewed modern authorship as a cult of the individual compatible with capitalist society (see Jakob Stougaard-Nielsen's chapter "The Author in Literary Theory and Theories of Literature" within this volume).[16] Their central point is that writing is essentially anonymous, in two related senses, even when it is signed.

First, anonymity figures the separation between the living writer and the written text effected by the process of writing itself, the separation that Barthes calls the "death" of the author. In a related essay, Barthes refers to the subject of writing, who exists only in the continuous, performative, present tense of the writing itself, as a "paper-*I*": "the *I* which writes the text, it too, is never more than a paper-*I*."[17] An illustration brings the precept home. John Banville, in an article on "Benjamin Black," the pseudonymous author of Banville's crime thrillers, distanced himself equally from the writing subjects "Black" and "Banville": "When I stand up from my writing desk, 'John Banville', or 'Benjamin Black' – that is, the one whose name will appear on the title page – vanishes on the instant, since he only existed while the writing was being done."[18]

Barthes, of course, is not the only one to understand the author as absent in this sense. In their early work on narrative in the 1960s, both Tzvetan Todorov and Julia Kristeva used the term "anonymity" to refer to the gap between author and text. Todorov: "The author is unnameable: if we want to give him a name, he leaves us a name but is not to be discovered behind it; he takes eternal refuge in anonymity." Kristeva: "[The author] becomes an anonymity, an absence, a blank space, thus permitting the structure to exist as such [...]. On the basis of the anonymity, this zero where the author is situated, the *he/she* of the character is born."[19] In "What Is an Author," Foucault goes beyond Barthes by calling attention to what is left behind when the author disappeared: the cultural and economic imbrication of the *name* of the author that functions discursively after the author has departed. The author function is, above all, a cultural role, or subject position, within an existing discourse, which subjects individuals to its own rules and exclusions:

> Consequently, we can say that in our culture, the name of an author is a variable that accompanies only certain texts to the exclusion of others: a private letter may have a signatory, but it does not have an author; a contract can have an underwriter, but not an author; and, similarly, an anonymous poster attached to a wall may have a writer, but he cannot be an

author. In this sense, the function of an author is to characterize the existence, circulation, and operation of certain discourses within a society.[20]

The second sense of the anonymity of authorship shared by Barthes and Foucault correlates the split between author and text with the effacement of the writer within a larger system. For Foucault, for example, the analysis of the historicity of the author function, how it operates differently in different times and places, allows us "to imagine a culture where discourse would circulate without any need for an author," and which "would unfold in a pervasive anonymity."[21] Beyond this distancing of present norms by historical perspective, Foucault posits the immanent structural anonymity of *all* discourse as a precondition – the vocabulary, grammar, and syntax, as it were – of any possible statement within a discursive formation (a discipline). The author, or speaker, is absent from any statement because it is the discourse that establishes rules both for statements and for subject positions within discursive formations that individuals assume and inhabit. The system, we are told countless times, is *anonymous*: The rules of discursive formations, for instance, operate "according to a uniform anonymity, on all individuals who undertake to speak in this discursive field."[22]

To illustrate what might appear to be abstract notions, we can compare the theorists' version of collectivity (discourse in general) to other, more nostalgic or romantic anonymous collectivities, such as Virginia Woolf's Anon, who is understood as the voice of the folk, and who is killed off by the printing press.[23] Or we could turn to Herman Melville's famous essay, written after reading a collection of stories by Nathaniel Hawthorne: "I know not what would be the right name to put on the title-page of an excellent book, but this I feel, that the names of all fine authors are fictitious ones, far more so than that of Junius, – simply standing, as they do, for the mystical, ever-eluding Spirit of Beauty, which ubiquitously possesses men of genius."[24] Closer to the theorists, but not in its affect, is the "distinctive anonymity" that Robert Wells explains as the relation between a writer and the traditions of the language:

> In this view our language is what we have in common, an inheritance, the creation of all the dead whoever spoke it, the embodiment of what they knew. Language carries the individual voice, but it does so because of this larger anonymity. What I value in poetry – in all art – most, I think, is this quality of distinctiveness and anonymity together, a distinctive anonymity;

and so far as they are separable I value the anonymity above the distinctiveness. The voice must fit the language before the language fits the voice.[25]

However, a more recent version of distinctive anonymity, which also illustrates Foucault's notion of the primacy of discursive formations, emerged from experiments in search of the defining elements of style at Franco Moretti's Stanford Literary Lab. Through analysis of a database of the nineteenth-century British novel, the group sought the most basic unit that conveyed style, noticing how different sentence constructions tended statistically to be related to particular cognitive tasks (sequencing, predicating, coordinating, etc.). They discovered further that particular constructions also tended to be related to certain narrative functions and, on a higher level, to literary genres. The correlation between the sentence type and the genre is not necessary, they observed; it followed, they surmised, from stylistic choices made either consciously or unconsciously. Style, however, when it did emerge became "typical and recognizable: it distinguished an author, a genre, or a literary movement in the most direct and unambiguous way." The category of the author to them remained "decisive." Yet the author's style also merged with the genre in such a way that the author could be seen "as *the highest embodiment* of the genre."[26] The key text for them was George Eliot's *Middlemarch*.

We can see this fundamental relation – the collectively developed features of a genre (or a tradition) and the emergence within that tradition of the author that embodies it – in a different light by examining the paradigmatic case of Homer, which includes questions as to whether a Homer actually existed, whether the poems attributed to "Homer" were written by the same person, and whether the poems as we have them in their current form were stabilized in sixth-century BCE Athens or in third-century BCE Alexandria. In this case, we have not a known historical author (George Eliot) who embodies a genre, but poems that emerge from a series of anonymous bards working in an oral-formulaic tradition. Some scholars believe the *Iliad* and the *Odyssey* were composed at the end of this tradition by a single genius whom they call Homer, while others see the poems "as the product of a long series of compositions and re-compositions which gradually reached a stage of fixation."[27] Gregory Nagy holds to the second line of thinking, proposing a sociological explanation for the individualization, in the figure of the pseudonymous Homer, of a collective oral tradition that was shaped over centuries. From Nagy's sociological perspective, epic originated as the poetry of praise for heroes (with Pindar's victory odes a later development) and thus encoded the values of honor and sacrifice. The singers were originally entertainers at feasts, with each performance adapted to its audience, and thus the poems developed their panhellenic character, reaching a point at which they were no longer improvisations adapting and adding to earlier versions. A "crystallization" of Greek culture, they came to be recited by the Homeridai (sons of Homer) at annual festivals.[28] Thus an individual with a name (whose origin is mythical) was assigned to what had developed as a collective generic social and cultural function. Moreover, what is posited about the life of "Homer," Mary Lefkowitz has argued, follows a pattern of constructing out of the text the person who is supposedly behind the text.[29] Foucault's point about the function of the modern author as "a privileged moment of individualization in the history of ideas, knowledge, and literature," holds also for the way "Homer" came to represent the culture of classical Greece.[30]

Over the past several decades, developments in theory, book history, and feminist literary history have stimulated work in many directions. But of the work that has focused on anonymous and pseudonymous authorship, and is ongoing, the greatest impact, in my view, has been on our understanding of the history of authorship. The first lesson, brought home most forcefully by Marcy North, is that the history of authorship is not linear: there were named authors in the medieval period on the one hand, while anonymity found a place in burgeoning print culture on the other.[31] We can extend this to say that anonymity, pseudonymity, and signed authorship exist simultaneously in every period, including the twentieth and twenty-first centuries.[32] We arrive at a more accurate picture of literary history, therefore, if we think in terms of dominant and alternative formations, rather than taking a dominant practice as representing the totality.

If we begin to think in terms of overlapping author functions, current controversies over which functions are more pertinent than others in relation to Shakespeare are a good case in point. Was Shakespeare a collaborative writer for the stage? Or was he a literary author with an eye to print publication?[33] It is the overlapping models of authorship during this period (and in others) I wish to call attention to. Colin Burrow's synopsis of Richard Helgerson's work outlines three models available in the late sixteenth and early seventeenth century: a courtier-poet such as Sir Philip Sidney, who circulated manuscripts among his friends and whose writings fell into the hands of booksellers after his death; a professional writer of pamphlets and plays such as Robert Greene, who lived from hand to mouth; and the laureate poets such as Edmund Spenser and Ben Jonson, who aspired to royal patronage.[34] Burrow adds a fourth version: the author who posed as an editor, only to emerge later, as many of the editor's functions were absorbed by the author. If we add to the list the man of theater we see not only multiple models, but also the possibility of one writer inhabiting more than one role. Shakespeare's company enjoyed royal patronage and gave command performances at court. Jonson wrote for the theater, published his *Workes*, and wrote masques for James I and Charles I.

Furthermore, because more than one model of authorship exists in any particular time, a writer has the possibility of resorting to multiple publication strategies. Over half of what Percy Shelley published in the early nineteenth century appeared either anonymously or pseudonymously, under such rubrics as "By a Gentleman at Oxford," or "Edited by John Fitzvictor," or "By Philopatria, Jun." There is also the case of "Epipsychidion," which Shelley instructed his publisher to print without his name because it represented a part of himself that was dead. These instances reinforce our claim that anonymity is not replaced by the signature in a straight historical sequence.[35] Anonymity did not disappear with commercial publication because there were, and are, various uses for it in a market economy. Mary Robinson, who was responsible for many of the poems published in the *Morning Post* in 1800, resorted to a variety of pseudonyms to disguise the fact that so many of the newspaper's poems were coming from the same hand.[36] More recently, Stephen King published several novels in the 1970s and 1980s under the name "Richard Bachman" to ward off the appearance that he was flooding the market. A secondary motive was the curiosity to see whether his novels would sell without the Stephen King brand, an experiment used by Doris Lessing as well in two books authored by "Jane Somers" (1983–84). Female pseudonyms have been adopted by male authors writing novels directed at a female readership.[37] Evan Hunter, a pseudonym for Salvatore Lambino, wrote crime novels under the name Ed McBain, very much like actors adopting a stage name, but in this case two stage names to fit different genres; J. K. Rowling adopted the name Robert Galbraith, also to publish crime novels. There are pseudonyms that call attention to themselves, such as Peter Pindar, and others that pass unnoticed, at least at first. Other motives for anonymity can include the hope of an unprejudiced reception from readers who will be forced to focus on the work and not on the author (Mary Astell, George Eliot); modesty and privacy (Jane Austen, Elena Ferrante); the avoidance of prosecution for sedition and other offenses (John Wilkes, Junius); and the desire to deceive (Pope's *An Essay on Man,* Forrest Carter's *The Education of Little Tree*). Thackeray's use of pseudonyms is particularly varied and creative.[38] Inquiring into authors' motivations for going invisible is necessary for understanding the historical breadth of anonymity and pseudonymity, but Mark Vareschi has argued cogently for a shift of attention away from motive and toward intention, by which he means "the collective agencies at work in textual and literary production" available to be read in the way the work manifests itself in the world.[39]

As an extension of the insight into the simultaneity of multiple publishing practices, we have also learned that the relation of anonymity to named authorship varies widely according to genre, as well as from period to period, and from place to place. Published plays are mostly anonymous (65 percent) in the last decade of the sixteenth century, for example, but from 1611 to 1642 they are mostly attributed on the title page (90 percent). This trend continues in the period 1660–1712 with only 11.5 percent published anonymously, which becomes the norm for the genre.[40] It is quite the opposite for the novel. The norm for the novel up to 1830, beyond which we do not have reliable statistics, averages above 70 percent unsigned.[41] In mid-eighteenth-century Scotland, however, *both* drama and fiction were more than 80 percent anonymous, with all other genres combined less than ten percent anonymous.[42]

In the Anglo-Saxon era, poetry is mostly anonymous, whereas prose is mostly signed.[43] The same remains true of the early modern period; as Nita Krevans observes: "anonymity is more common for books of verse than for other types of writing."[44] In the late eighteenth to early nineteenth century (1770–1835), however, poetry moved from being predominantly anonymous to being predominately signed, at a time when the norm for the novel continued to be anonymity.[45] Walter Scott, for instance, signed his poetry but not the Waverley novels. Journalism, including book reviewing, was 96 percent anonymous before 1865, then 57 percent for the period between 1865 and 1900; the *TLS* remained anonymous until the 1970s.[46] These variations are merely a sample that may be used as a heuristic for further exploration.

Notes

1. James Raven, "The Anonymous Novel in Britain and Ireland, 1750–1830," in *The Faces of Anonymity: Anonymous and Pseudonymous Publication from the Sixteenth to the Twentieth Century*, ed. Robert J. Griffin (New York: Palgrave Macmillan, 2003), pp. 141–66.

2. See, for instance, Gérard Genette, "The Name of the Author," *Paratexts: Thresholds of Interpretation*, trans. Jane E. Lewin (Cambridge: Cambridge University Press, 1997), pp. 37–54; John Mullan, *Anonymity: A Secret History of English Literature* (London: Faber and Faber, 2007); and William Prideaux Courtney, *The Secrets of our National Literature: Chapters in the History of the Anonymous and Pseudonymous Writings of our Countrymen* (London: Constable, 1908).

3. "Anonymity," special issue of *MLN*, 126.4 (2011), ed. Wilda Anderson; Anne Green, *Privileged Anonymity: The Writings of Madame de Lafayette* (Oxford: Legenda, 1996); Geoffrey Turnovsky, *The Literary Market: Authorship and Modernity in the Old Regime* (Philadelphia: University of Pennsylvania Press, 2010); Martin Mulsow, "Practices of Unmasking: Polyhistors, Correspondence, and the Birth of Dictionaries of Pseudonymity in Seventeenth-Century Germany," *Journal of the History of Ideas*, 67 (2006), 219–50.

4. Janet Wright Starner and Barbara Howard Traister, eds., *Anonymity in Early Modern England: "What's in a Name?"* (Farnham, UK: Ashgate, 2011), p. 3.

5. R. S. Crane, "History vs. Criticism in the Study of Literature," in *The Idea of the Humanities and Other Essays, Critical and Historical*, vol. 2 (Chicago: University of Chicago Press, 1967), pp. 3–24.

6. *Tottel's Miscellany; Songs and Sonnets*, ed. Edward Arber (London, 1870), p. iii.

7. Leah Orr, "The History, Uses, and Dangers of Halkett and Laing," *Papers of the Bibliographical Society of America*, 107.2 (2013), 193–240.

8. Anthony Trollope, "On Anonymous Literature," *The Fortnightly Review*, 1 (1865), p. 491.

9. Margaret J. M. Ezell, "'By a Lady': The Mask of the Feminine in Restoration, Early Eighteenth-Century Print Culture," in *The Faces of Anonymity*, ed. Griffin, pp. 63–79.

10. Jean DeJean, "Lafayette's Ellipses: The Privileges of Anonymity," *PMLA*, 99.5 (1984), 884–901.

11. Marcy North, *The Anonymous Renaissance: Cultures of Discretion in Tudor-Stuart England* (Chicago: University of Chicago Press, 2003), p. 256.

12. Jennie Batchelor, "Anon, Pseud and 'By a Lady': The Spectre of Anonymity in Women's Literary History," in *Women's Writing, 1660–1830: Feminisms and Futures*, ed. Jennie Batchelor and Gillian Dow (London: Palgrave Macmillan, 2016), pp. 69–86, p. 72.

13. Raymond Williams, "Marxism, Structuralism, and Literary Analysis," *New Left Review*, 129 (1982), 64–5.

14. D. F. McKenzie, *Bibliography and the Sociology of Texts* (Cambridge: Cambridge University Press, 1986), p. 12.

15. Leah Orr, "The Basis for Attribution in the Canon of Eliza Haywood," *The Library*, 12.4 (2011), 335–75; Leah Orr, "Attribution Problems in the Fiction of Aphra Behn," *The Modern Language Review*, 108.1 (2013), 30–51; Ashley Marshall, "Did Defoe Write *Moll Flanders* and *Roxana*?" *Philological Quarterly*, 89.2–3 (2010), 209–41; P. N. Furbank and W. R. Owens, "On the

Attribution of Novels to Daniel Defoe," *Philological Quarterly*, 89.2–3 (2010), 243–53; Robert J. Griffin, "Did Defoe Write Roxana? Does it Matter?", *Philological Quarterly*, 89.2–3 (2010), 255–62.

16. Roland Barthes, "The Death of the Author," in *Image – Music – Text*, trans. Stephen Heath (New York: Hill and Wang, 1977), pp. 142–48; Michel Foucault, "What Is an Author?" in *Language, Counter-Memory, Practice*, ed. Donald F. Bouchard (Ithaca, NY: Cornell University Press, 1977), pp. 113–38.

17. Barthes, "From Work to Text," in *Image – Music – Text*, trans. Stephen Heath (New York: Hill and Wang, 1977), pp. 155–64, p. 161.

18. John Banville, "John Banville on the Birth of his Dark Twin, Benjamin Black," *The Guardian*, July 22, 2011. For similar reflections, see also Jorge Luis Borges, "Borges and I," and Henry James, "The Private Life."

19. Tzvetan Todorov, *Introduction to Poetics*, trans. Richard Howard (Minneapolis: University of Minnesota Press, 1981), p. 39; Julia Kristeva, "Word, Dialogue and Novel," in *Desire in Language: A Semiotic Approach to Literature and Art*, ed. Leon S. Roudiez, trans. Thomas Gora, Alice Jardine, and Leon Roudiez (New York: Columbia University Press, 1980), pp. 64–91, p. 75.

20. Foucault, "What Is an Author?", pp. 123–24.

21. Ibid., p. 138.

22. Michel Foucault, *The Archaeology of Knowledge and the Discourse on Language*, trans. A. M. Sheridan Smith (New York: Pantheon Books, 1972), p. 63.

23. Virginia Woolf, "Anon," in Brenda Silver, "'Anon' and 'The Reader': Virginia Woolf's Last Essays," *Twentieth Century Literature*, 25 (1979), 382–85.

24. Herman Melville, "Hawthorne and His Mosses," in *The Piazza Tales and Other Prose Pieces, 1839–1860*, eds. Harrison Hayford, Alma A. McDougall, G. Thomas Tanselle et al. (Evanston, IL: Northwestern University Press and the Newberry Library, 1987), pp. 239–53, p. 239.

25. Robert Wells, "Distinctive Anonymity," in *The Poet's Voice and Craft*, ed. C. B. McCully (Manchester: Carcanet, 1994), p. 176.

26. The Stanford Literary Lab (Sarah Allison, Marissa Gemma, Ryan Heuser, Franco Moretti, Amir Tevel, and Irena Yamboliev), "Style at the Scale of the Sentence," *n+1*, 17 (2013), p. 138.

27. Barbara Graziosi, *Inventing Homer: The Early Reception of Epic* (Cambridge: Cambridge University Press, 2002), p. 15.

28. Gregory Nagy, "Early Greek Views of Poets and Poetry," in *The Cambridge History of Literary Criticism*, vol. 1, *Classical Criticism*, ed. George A. Kennedy (Cambridge: Cambridge University Press, 1989), p. 31.

29. Mary Lefkowitz, *The Lives of the Greek Poets* (Baltimore, MD: Johns Hopkins University Press, 1981).

30. Foucault, "What Is an Author?", p. 115.

31. North, *Anonymous Renaissance*, pp. 1–55. On manuscript culture's coexistence with print in the late seventeenth and early eighteenth century, see also Margaret Ezell, *Social Authorship and the Advent of Print* (Baltimore, MD:

Johns Hopkins University Press, 1999); for a slightly later period, see Betty Schellenberg, *Literary Coteries and the Making of Modern Print Culture* (Cambridge: Cambridge University Press, 2016).

32. See, for example, Emily Kopley, "Anon Is not Dead: Towards a History of Anonymous Authorship in Early-Twentieth-Century Britain," *Mémoires du livre* 7.2 (2016).

33. See "Forum: The Return of the Author," with an introduction by Patrick Cheney and essays by Lukas Erne, David Kastan, Jeffrey Knapp, Wendy Wall, Richard Wilson, Heather James, Leah Marcus, Brian Vickers, Richard Dutton, and Michael Bristol, in *Shakespeare Studies*, 36 (2008).

34. Burrow, Colin, "Fictions of Collaboration: Authors and Editors in the Sixteenth Century," in *Medieval and Early Modern Authorship*, eds. Guillemette Bolens and Lukas Erne (Tübingen: Narr Francke Attempto, 2011), pp. 175–98, pp. 175–76.

35. Robert J. Griffin, "Anonymity and Authorship," *NLH*, 30.4 (1999), 877–95, p. 890.

36. Griffin, "Anonymity," p. 886.

37. Raven, "Anonymous Novel," p. 145.

38. Mullan, *Anonymity*, pp. 247–50. Marysa Demoor re-evaluates Thackeray's overlapping motives in *A Very Special Relationship: Discursive Constructions of Britishness in Belgium in the Long Nineteenth Century*, unpublished book manuscript.

39. Mark Vareschi, "Motive, Intention, Anonymity and *Evelina*," *ELH*, 82 (2005), 1135–58, p. 1136.

40. Judith Milhous and Robert D. Hume, *The Publication of Plays in London, 1660–1800: Playwrights, Publishers, and the Market* (London: British Library, 2015), pp. 16–19.

41. Raven, "Anonymous Novel."

42. Richard B. Sher, *The Enlightenment and the Book: Scottish Authors and Their Publishers in Eighteenth-Century Britain, Ireland, and America* (Chicago: University of Chicago Press, 2006), p. 149.

43. For more nuance than I can convey here, see Mary Swan, "Authorship and Anonymity," in *A Companion to Anglo-Saxon Literature*, eds. Phillip Pulsiano and Elaine Treharne (Oxford: Blackwell, 2001), pp. 71–83; and Thomas A. Bredehoft, "Introduction: Authorship and Anonymity in Old English Verse," in *Authors and Audiences in Old English Verse* (Toronto: University of Toronto Press, 2009), pp. 1–38.

44. Nita Krevans, "Print and the Tudor Poets," in *Reconsidering the Renaissance: Papers from the Twenty-First Annual Conference*, ed. Mario A. Di Cesare (Binghamton, NY: Medieval & Renaissance Texts & Studies, 1992), p. 301–13, p. 312.

45. Lee Erickson, "'Unboastful Bard': Originally Anonymous English Romantic Poetry Book Publication, 1770–1835," *NLH*, 33.2 (2002), 247–78, p. 247.

46. Mullan, *Anonymity*, p. 324, n. 70, pp. 181–2.

CHAPTER 22

Plagiarism and Forgery

Jack Lynch

The study of literary deception – which the US Library of Congress calls "literary forgeries and mystifications" in its catalog of subject headings – has plenty of attractions. We can treat the thief or the faker as an embodiment of the mythological trickster figure wreaking havoc on a staid establishment, or the crafty *pícaro* mischievously showing up his betters. Literary malefactors are adored for their chutzpah in embarrassing the self-important and revealing they are gullible fools and knaves.

The real value of the study of deception, though, lies not in providing after-dinner stories but in making us pay attention to the competing conceptions of authorship that operate among the fakers and their audiences. Nearly all the high-profile "crimes of writing," to use Susan Stewart's resonant phrase, are "crimes" because they highlight fault lines between conflicting notions of the nature of authorship.[1] In this chapter, I examine a few exemplary episodes of plagiarism and forgery and ask what they reveal about authorship. My examples might have been drawn from any era – literary deception is perennial – but my focus is on English-language literature from the seventeenth to the twenty-first centuries, with eighteenth-century Britain providing the bulk of the evidence. This is the tradition I know best and the one that has produced the most scholarly commentary; furthermore, it is the period in which some of the most significant transformations of the conception of authorship took place (see also Betty A. Schellenberg's chapter "The Eighteenth Century" within this volume).

All varieties of literary offense involve some violation of a shared understanding of the proper relationship of author, world, audience, and work. "Whether a thing is a forgery," Michael Wreen writes, "depends on what kind of thing it is."[2] It may be more accurate to say "what kind of thing it purports to be." Exactly the same act – the publication of a text – might be perfectly innocent or flagrantly felonious, depending entirely on the claims made for the text by the author, the editor, and the bookseller. Whenever the author's understanding of these matters differs from the audience's, we are in the realm of literary criminality.

The most widely discussed of the crimes of writing is plagiarism. "The concept of 'plagiarism,'" writes Thomas McFarland, "cannot stand the stress of historical examination."[3] That may be true: the moral tale of unambiguous good and evil that informs a million earnest lectures to first-year students becomes harder and harder to justify once we begin probing what actual authors understand by "original" and "copy." Our academic handbooks tell young writers that originality is essential and all borrowings must be acknowledged; real-world authors draw on countless works consciously or unconsciously, meticulously or sloppily, with or without acknowledgment. No professional writer could ever live up to our supposed standard.

In cases of plagiarism, putative authors present the work of others as their own. The Latin *plagiarius*, "kidnapper," was famously applied to literary theft by Martial in *Epigram* 1.52, when he criticized someone who had stolen his verses (see also Christian Badura's and Melanie Möller's chapter "Authorship in Classical Rome" within this volume).[4] Since the end of the sixteenth century, the English language has used variations on that word (*plagiary*, attested from 1598; *plagiarism*, from 1621; *plagiarize*, from 1660; *plagiarist*, from 1674) to refer to writers who claim others' words as their own. An early modern example shows a particularly brazen plagiary at work. In 1602 was published *The Christian Navy: Wherein is playnely described the perfit course to sayle to the Hauen of eternall happinesse*. The title page is clear: the poem is "Written by Anthony Nixon." And readers turning to the first page of text would come across these lines:

> He that amidst the raging Ocean Seas,
> With sayling Barke doth seeke the happy Port,
> No leysure hath to giue himselfe to ease,
> Nor respite, for due-season-losing sport;
> Each time-delaying calme doth him displease,
> In nothing ioyes, in nothing pleasure finds,
> Saue in the blasts of prosperous happie winds.[5]

A very few readers with very good memories, however, might have been struck by the sensation that they had seen these lines before. And perhaps a few might have looked around to discover a work by Barnabe Googe, *A newe Booke called the Shippe of safegarde*, which was published in 1569 and began this way:

The wandring wight that in the raging seas
Wyth sayling Barke doth seke the happy port,
No leysure hath to giue himselfe to ease:
Ne time he findes wherein to play or sport.
Eche long delay, eche calme doth him displease,
Hym listeth not to lynger in such sort,
In nothing ioyes, in nothing pleasure findes,
Saue in the blastes of prosperous happie windes.[6]

And so on, through nearly 1,800 lines. Googe, dead for eight years when this plagiarism appeared, was in no position to object. But his ghost surely had reason to resent those responsible for stealing his literary property.

The proprietary relationship implicit in Martial's metaphor of the *plagiarius* became ever more explicit in the seventeenth and eighteenth centuries – not coincidentally, the time in which economic changes were making it possible for authors to earn a living from their publications. As Daniel Defoe put in in 1710, the year the world's first copyright statute went into effect: "A Book is the Author's Property, 'tis the Child of his Inventions, the Brat of his Brain; if he sells his Property, it then becomes the Right of the Purchaser; if not, 'tis as much his own, as his Wife and Children are his own."[7] Though Defoe uses the word "property," he means something more than goods and chattels: for another to lay claim to his works is to abduct his child or seduce his wife.

Unmistakable in these arguments over plagiarism is the widely shared sense that a plagiarized work, though perhaps *verbatim et litteratim* identical to the work from which it was copied, is still inferior to that original. Both copyright law and a concern about plagiarism, therefore, ground value – financial in the one case, aesthetic in the other – in *originality*. Copyright violations and plagiarism are not the same thing: copyright infringement is a violation of statutory rights, can occur whether or not a source is acknowledged, and can happen only during a limited term, whereas plagiarism is generally not covered by statutes, requires a lack of proper citation, and has no expiry date. Still, both take for granted the bond between the creator and the created, and both treat the labor of the author's brain as a kind of property that needs to be defended.

Edward Young's *Conjectures on Original Composition* marks an epoch in its theorizing about the value of originality and imitation. Of course, "originality" was a literary virtue long before 1759, but the word's meaning was changing. What had once applied to works that harkened back to some kind of origin increasingly came to be used for works that were their own origins – works that had origins nowhere beyond the author's mind.

The *Oxford English Dictionary* suggests that the linguistic shift took place in the eighteenth century: sense A.6.a., "Having the quality of that which proceeds directly from oneself; such as has not been done or produced before; novel or fresh in character or style," dates from 1756. Where once authors were praised for the effective use they made of familiar material, they were now expected to produce something genuinely new. For Young, this difference in kind structures a hierarchy of value: "*Originals* are, and ought to be, the great Favourites, for they are great Benefactors; they extend the Republic of Letters, and add a new province to its dominion: *Imitators* only give us a sort of Duplicates of what we had, possibly much better, before."[8] Imitation, he writes, "is inferiority confessed; Emulation is superiority contested, or denied; Imitation is servile, Emulation generous; That fetters, this fires; That may give a name; This, a name immortal."[9]

No actual writer could ever hope to live up to this extreme conception of originality, but the creative ideal has hung over discussions of literary composition for centuries. Theorists of originality have usually sought a balance between creating *ex nihilo* and drawing freely on the cultural patrimony without acknowledgment. Robert Macfarlane invokes George Steiner's distinction of *creation* from *invention* – "Creators bring entirely new matter into being. Inventors, however, permute pre-existing material into novel combinations" – and places our own ideas about originality somewhere on the spectrum between these "two poles of making." One pole consists of the "so-called 'Romantic' theories of literary creation," modeled on "divine creation," in which originality is "an immanent or transcendent value which inheres in the text, rather than being ascribed to it." The other pole consists of those conceptions of originality "which refuse to believe in the possibility of creation out of nothing, or in the uninfluenced literary work," which "assume that the writer is merely a rearranger of bits and pieces: an administrator rather than a producer."[10] It is fair to say that no writer, not even any work, manages to be entirely one or the other, and yet discussions are often conducted in Young's absolutist terms. Young's conceptual framework, one of the first unambiguous statements of the "Romantic" theory of uninfluenced authorship, inevitably involved him in contradictions. Shakespeare makes an instructive example. Young needs Shakespeare to be maximally admirable, and to be admirable in Young's mind is to be original: as God is the unmoved mover, so is the ideal Youngian author the uninfluenced influencer. And yet, by post-Youngian standards, Shakespeare can hardly be considered "original" at all.[11] There are few original plots in his entire canon, and some stretches of the plays are virtually lifted intact from earlier works. As Edward Capell admitted in 1768 with obvious discomfort, "the historians of that time [. . .] are pretty closely follow'd; and that not only for their matter, but even sometimes in their expressions: The harangue of the archbishop of *Canterbury* in 'Henry V,' that of queen *Catherine* in 'Henry VIII' at her trial, and the king's reply to it, are taken from those chroniclers, and put into verse."[12] And yet, even as evidence mounted that Shakespeare's works were often derivative, he was celebrated ever more intensely as original. "*Shakespeare* mingled no water with his wine, lower'd his Genius by no vapid Imitation," Young insisted. "*Shakespeare* gave us a *Shakespeare*, nor could the first in antient fame have given us more. *Shakespeare* is not their Son, but Brother; their Equal, and that, in spite of all his faults."[13]

The conviction that a derivative work was inferior to a newly conceived one was weaponized in one of the most curious episodes of literary deception. In 1747, William Lauder – supposedly angered by the shabby treatment his beloved Arthur Johnston suffered at the hands of the Miltonophilic Alexander Pope – launched an attack on *Paradise Lost*, identifying unacknowledged borrowings that would be enough to disqualify it from serious consideration. He reproduced an extract from Jacob Masen's poem *Sarcotis* (1654) and demonstrated that a long stretch of Milton's masterpiece is nothing more than a servile translation of Masen's original Latin. The similarities were too great to explain away: "whoever [. . .] can imagine, that *Milton* could possibly write as he has done, without seeing this author's performance, may, with equal reason, suppose, that a limner can draw a man's picture, exactly like the original, without ever viewing his person."[14] That was just one of many parallels: one beloved passage of *Paradise Lost* after another was revealed to be taken from Latin works by Masen, Hugo Grotius, Caspar Staphorstius, or Andrew Ramsay. Lauder even put his finger on Milton's precise offense: "nor do I blame him for this unlimited freedom [in copying authors], but for his industriously concealing it."[15] As the saying goes, the problem is not the original crime but the cover-up. Milton bore the marks of conscious guilt.

It seemed an open-and-shut case: Milton's poem was unmistakably an English version of the Latin passages Lauder adduced, and he was therefore "not the original author of any one single thought in *Paradise Lost*; but has only digested into order the thoughts of others, and cloathed them in an elegant *English* dress."[16] The charge seemed likely to stick until John Douglas, the Bishop of Salisbury, set out to examine those passages that Lauder had identified as Milton's sources. Unable to get his hands on a copy of Masen or Grotius's *Adamus Exul* – the books were extraordinarily rare – he did manage to locate Staphorstius's *Triumphus Pacis*, and was "resolved [. . .] to collate this Quotation with the printed Edition from which it is pretended to be taken."[17] And yet, when he looked at the passage Lauder identified, he discovered that the quotation was doctored:

> Now if any one will but take the Trouble to compare the above Lines [. . .] with those which the Critic of *Milton* quotes as his, a very remarkable Difference will appear at first Sight. He will observe several Lines omitted [. . .]; and not only this, but he will be surprized to find eight Lines quoted as *Staphorstius*'s, which have no Existence in that Author.[18]

The brazenness of the stunt was remarkable and led Douglas to conclude that all the dozens of passages which Lauder quoted as Milton's originals appeared in none of the books where he claimed to have found them. Lauder had counted on the inaccessibility of the obscure mid-seventeenth-century poets he quoted and, to prove Milton had stolen from them, he stole from Milton. The passages that seemed so close to *Paradise Lost* were in fact taken from William Hog's Latin translations of Milton, *Paraphrasis poetica in tria Johannis Miltoni, viri clarissimi, poemata* (1690).

The hoax makes sense only when we recognize how thoroughly notions of literary worth were tied up with notions of originality. And while this was a particularly extreme and pathological case, squabbles over originality and imitation have persisted through the eighteenth century, into the nineteenth, and even to the present. By the end of the eighteenth century, originality was a cardinal literary virtue, as John Aikin instructed his son: "surely it is more desirable that a poet of original genius should give full scope to his inventive powers, under the restrictions of such laws only as are founded on nature, than that he should fetter himself with rules derived from the practice of a predecessor."[19] The solitary creative genius is among the commonplaces taught to undergraduates in overviews of the Romantic period, and a literary culture so devoted to originality and so averse to imitation would seem to be the ideal environment for clear-cut definitions of originality and plagiarism. And yet the practice remains terribly complex. Tilar J. Mazzeo sets out to answer "a deceptively simple question: What constituted plagiarism in Britain during the late eighteenth and early nineteenth centuries?"[20] "In many ways," she acknowledges, "the subject is a treacherous one." In fact, in the age that so emphatically fetishized originality and dismissed imitation, Mazzeo finds a "'poetical' plagiarism," distinct from the "'culpable' plagiarism" we are accustomed to, and raises the seemingly paradoxical possibility that a work might "be considered implicitly acknowledged or 'avowed' if a 'well-versed' reader could be expected to recognize the original. Ironically, the more extensive the

borrowing the more likely it was to have been considered acknowledged."
A brilliant poet can get away with some kinds of theft, since "a successful
improvement justified any borrowing, regardless of extent."[21]

This kind of "poetic" plagiarism is not the result of either laziness or
malice. John Ferriar, writing in 1798, thought he had scored a hit against
Laurence Sterne when he accused him of lifting passages from Robert
Burton's *Anatomy of Melancholy*. "It is very singular," Ferriar writes, that

> Sterne should take occasion to abuse plagiarists. "Shall we forever make new
> books, as apothecaries make new mixtures, by pouring only out of one vessel
> into another? Are we for ever to be twisting and untwisting the same rope?
> for ever in the same track – for ever at the same pace?" And it is more
> singular that all this declamation should be taken, word for word, from
> Burton's introduction.[22]

Ferriar might have recognized that this "very singular" plagiarism of
a lament about plagiarism was not a fault in which he caught Sterne, but
Sterne's postmodern joke *avant la lettre* – he was consciously plagiarizing
Burton's warning against plagiarism with a knowing wink. Milton had
done something similar in the opening of *Paradise Lost*, with his promise of
"Things unattempted yet in Prose or Rime" – the poet's proud declaration
of his originality – being a translation of Ludovico Ariosto's "Cosa non
detta mai in prosa nè in rima."[23] More recently, Bob Dylan has been
known to appropriate others' writing into his own songs without acknowledgment, while giving authorship credit to others for things they did not
write. For example, his song "Sugar Baby," from the album *"Love and
Theft"* (2001), takes the melody, chord structure, and many of the words
from Gene Austin's "Lonesome Road" (1927), but Dylan withholds song-
writing credit from Austin. The same album contains a number of small,
unacknowledged quotations of Junichi Saga's *Confessions of a Yakuza*,
a learned account of Japanese organized crime. Dylan's next album,
Modern Times (2006), is riddled with snippets lifted from a translation of
Ovid's *Tristia* and the obscure nineteenth-century American poet Henry
Timrod. Confronted by an interviewer with accusations of literary theft –
"Some critics say that you didn't cite your sources clearly" – Dylan replied
bluntly: "Wussies and pussies complain about that stuff."[24] The so-called
"voice of his generation" proves to be a playful and puckish one that
incorporates many other voices. Or, as Jonathan Lethem puts it,
"Dylan's originality and his appropriations are as one."[25]

Lethem himself, as it happens, is playing at the same game. At the end of
his article on originality and appropriation comes a key to "every line [he]

stole, warped, and cobbled together,"[26] including many of the most important parts of "his" essay. He calls the resulting piece "a collage text,"[27] a genre he traces back to Walter Benjamin's *Arcades Project*, Graham Rawle's *Diary of an Amateur Photographer*, and Eduardo Paolozzi's *Kex*. Even the gimmick of plagiarizing an essay on plagiarism is plagiarized – at the end Lethem acknowledges David Edelstein, whose "Where Have I Read That Before?", an investigation into a largely plagiarized novel, was in turn a plagiarized pastiche of a variety of sources. Edelstein came clean a week after his original publication in a follow-up article.[28]

The genre of the cobbled-together plagiarism can be followed back further still, to the *cento*, an ancient literary genre in which lines from distinguished poets, especially Homer and Virgil, are rearranged and repurposed into a new work. The cento has struggled for respectability and has typically been found "on the fringes of the canon and curricula, where it resides amid other literary curiosities."[29] But it usefully reveals how conceptions of originality and adaptation have varied over time. Ancient poets seem to have viewed the form as an opportunity to show off their own ingenuity, but later poets have seen it as somehow beneath true poetic dignity, and occasionally even as an assault on the person of the source poet. Elizabeth Barrett Browning, for example, chides Aelia Eudocia Augusta's fifth-century Greek cento as an insult to Homer: "The reader, who has heard enough of centos, will not care to hear how she did it. That she did it, was too much; and the deed recoiled."[30]

Lethem draws a lesson about the impossibility of complete originality, noting that *every* act of creation is ultimately an act of reworking disparate source materials. "Invention," he writes, "it must be humbly admitted, does not consist in creating out of void but out of chaos." As he surveys some of the truly great works of art and literature that seem to take us close to the line of plagiarism, he declares: "If these are examples of plagiarism, then we want more plagiarism."[31] And yet, as we may have come to expect by now, neither of these sentences is his; the first is "borrowed" – he might prefer "stolen" – from Mary Shelley's introduction to *Frankenstein*, and the second from legal scholar Richard Posner.

Given that even the most original creator is always making use of a shared cultural patrimony, with or without explicit acknowledgment, the line between tribute and plagiarism is constantly being negotiated both as a matter of ethics and as a matter of law. Copyright, Lethem observes, "is taken as a law, both in the sense of a universally recognizable moral absolute [. . .] and as naturally inherent in our world, like the law of gravity. In fact, it is neither. Rather, copyright is an ongoing social negotiation, tenuously forged, endlessly revised, and imperfect in its every incarnation." It "is a 'right' in no absolute sense; it is a government-granted monopoly on the use of creative results."[32]

US law, typical of much international copyright legislation, protects "original works of authorship fixed in any tangible medium of expression, now known or later developed, from which they can be perceived, reproduced, or otherwise communicated, either directly or with the aid of a machine or device." The statute goes on to say that "[i]n no case does copyright protection for an original work of authorship extend to any idea, [...] concept, principle, or discovery."[33] Still there have been accusations, both in courtrooms and in the periodical press, about thievery of things less "tangible" than strings of distinctive words. Edgar Allan Poe, for example, brazenly accused Longfellow of plagiarism, even while admitting that his words had not been stolen. Still, he maintained, Longfellow was guilty of "the most barbarous class of literary robbery; that class in which, while the words of the wronged author are avoided, his most intangible, and therefore least defensible and least reclaimable property, is purloined."[34] No court would countenance that sort of claim today in a copyright case, but we certainly would be prepared to acknowledge that an author who "borrows" tone, style, settings, and characters from another would deserve some disapprobation.

The law has long held that originality might consist in the novel rearrangement of other people's work: as Judge Leon Yankwich held in an influential legal opinion in 1947, "taking commonplace materials and acts and making them into a new combination and novel arrangement [...] is protectible by copyright."[35] How far does this extend? In 2018, Roger Rix faced challenges and accusations of plagiarism, or at least copyright violation, over his republication of some of Philip Larkin's letters as "poems" of a sort, and then claiming the copyright in the resulting publication. The book bears the title *Philip Larkin: The Secret Poems*, with Rix's name as the only author. A blurb describes Rix's scissors-and-paste method: "Using only Larkin's words placed in the sequence in which they occur he has eliminated unwanted phrases while providing judicious line breaks to faithfully mirror the poet's unique rhythm and style" – and even invokes Larkin's own authorization from beyond the grave with the quotation, "I think there is a poem to be made out of the letters."[36] True, we often resort to the metaphor of "rearranging" others' words and ideas when we speak about literary composition, but Rix's contribution to Larkin's source material was the most literal kind of rearrangement imaginable, accomplished by little more than the enter key in his word processor. We seem to be only a few steps away from Jorge Luis Borges's famous meditation on the paradoxes of originality, "Pierre Menard, Author of the *Quixote*," in which a "new" work of literature consists of a verbatim copy of the whole of an older one and manages to be not merely good but better than its original.[37] Not everyone has found violations like Sterne's, Dylan's, and Lethem's charming, either in the eighteenth century or today, but there is a logic behind these episodes. Sterne and Dylan can get away with violations that would send an undergraduate before a disciplinary review board because both have a solid reputation for originality that long predates and dominates their pranks. Only figures whose originality is unimpeachable have the luxury of toying with notions of originality and turning unacknowledged appropriation – under normal circumstances a sin – into a creative act in its own right.

Meanwhile, "culpable" plagiarism continued – and continues – to flourish, especially in contexts that are not generally thought of as especially "literary." In eighteenth- and nineteenth-century periodical culture, plagiarism was the norm, with Edward Cave giving the genre its lasting name, the *magazine*, from a storehouse or armory in which others' works were collected. While a few publishers were scrupulous about identifying their sources, most reprinted freely. History books are another genre in which unacknowledged copying was close to universal; before the age of large databases of texts, it was always risky for modern scholars to attribute quotations from a work of history to the author on a work's title page, since there was always a substantial chance that the relevant passages were copied from an unacknowledged source.[38] A more complex variety of intellectual theft, if theft it be, comes in the reappropriation of characters, plot points, even ill-defined notions like "style" or "mood," and the creation of a new work that participates in the same literary universe of an original (see Daniel Cook's chapter "Copyright and Literary Property" within this volume). Whether this kind of reworking constitutes "theft," either in the eyes of the law or the public, is difficult to answer. Some rights-holders have been more and some less vigilant in "protecting" their property. Some actively encourage audiences to become co-creators; some tolerate it by pretending to ignore it; others actively prosecute every real or perceived infringement.

The odds of plagiarism seem to rise as the writing process becomes more collaborative. Today academic publications in fields where collaboration is the norm seem to see a higher rate of plagiarism than those dominated by single-author publications. A recent study of presentations at a major management conference, for example, revealed that one in four articles had "some amount of plagiarism," and more than one in eight "exhibited significant plagiarism."[39] And even in fields where authors typically work solo, tremendous commercial success often leads authors to cut corners. Stephen Ambrose and Doris Kearns Goodwin, for instance, had to counter high-profile plagiarism charges in 2002.[40] Both followed a familiar script by blaming inattentive research assistants, hoping that by sharing responsibility for the texts' creation they would mitigate their own guilt. While the moral logic of the gesture may not be convincing, it does at least acknowledge the fact that Ambrose and Goodwin in their late careers are not authors in the solitary-genius mold so much as project managers in a writing factory. Publish-or-perish academics – who, entrusted with teaching young people to write, often imagine themselves as the guardians of the institutions of intellectual property – have been known to steal work from others, usually the less powerful, and often including their own students.[41] The catalog of plagiarized politicians' speeches is long. Two high-profile American examples are Joe Biden, who plagiarized Neil Kinnock in 1987, and Senator Rand Paul, who in 2013 copied much of a speech from the Wikipedia pages for the film *Gattaca*. Again, these public figures are not authors so much as employers of staffs of writers. Modern corporate communications are routinely plagiarized, and more than one university's academic integrity office has been caught appropriating another university's academic integrity policy without attribution.[42] Students are routinely exhorted about the dangers of plagiarism in a plagiarized work.

The motives for plagiarism, at least in its common or garden varieties, are easy to understand: we have no trouble imagining how someone might benefit from it. The reverse, however, is harder to comprehend. The plagiarist claims the work of another as his or her own; the forger, on the other hand, disavows his or her work and attributes it to someone else. An author who attributes his or her original work to another seems to be giving away potentially valuable intellectual property without recompense. Rather than a metaphorical kidnapped child, the forged work seems to be a baby abandoned at birth. Why?

The forger often gains attention for his or her work, aware that a forged work by Homer or Shakespeare will get a kind of reading denied to a work by an unknown modern writer. The forger need not attribute his or her work to an actual historical author. Two of the most famous literary forgers of the eighteenth century, Thomas Chatterton and James Macpherson, attributed their works to the fifteenth-century cleric Thomas Rowley and the third-century blind bard Ossian, authors who had either no existence or, at most, a shadowy legendary one. But the dynamic of manipulating an author's identity is clearer when the illusory source is already known as an author, and there was no source better known than Shakespeare. In the 1790s, William Henry Ireland infamously foisted new works on him. He began by "discovering" legal documents bearing Shakespeare's signature, moved on to personal letters to and from Shakespeare, and eventually worked his way up to two entire pseudo-Shakespearean plays (*Vortigern* and *Henry II*), the first of which was produced on the London stage in April 1796 in one of the great theatrical disaster stories of all time. The potential appeal of the plays is obvious, but the less obviously literary finds also did important work in sustaining the forgery. Ireland shrewdly predicted the way many people thought about these minor papers: no one, they reasoned, would bother to forge something as trivial as a playhouse receipt. The presence of these seemingly negligible documents – the receipts, the marginal annotations in books supposedly owned by Shakespeare, the commonplace book – therefore served to authenticate the more literary finds by providing a back-story for the creative genius.

One of the most remarkable of the fraudulent discoveries, which provoked much discussion at the time, was a "deed of gift" in which Shakespeare disposed of his most valuable literary property to someone who had saved his life. Shakespeare – in his imagined secretary hand and his preposterously archaized orthography – details the events "onne or abowte the thyrde daye of the laste monethe," August 1604, when he had "taene boate neare untowe myne house afowresayde," along with a group of friends. These friends, "beynge muche toe merrye throughe Lyquorre," managed to "upsette oure fowresayde bayrge." Most of the company swam to shore, but Shakespeare struggled for life in the water. Fortunately for him – and, of course, fortunately for all of us who are beneficiaries of the genius's survival – one of the party realized "that I was drownynge onn the whyche he pulledd off hys Jerrekynne and Jumpedd inn afterre mee withe muche paynes he draggedd mee forthe I beynge then nearelye deade and soe he dydd save mye life." The name of this selfless benefactor, who risked his life to save Shakespeare's? "William henrye Irelande."[43]

This bizarre insertion of himself – in the person of a previously unknown ancestor and namesake – into Shakespeare's story allows Ireland to imagine himself not merely as a friend of Shakespeare but as his savior. And for preserving the Bard's life, this Ireland ancestor received "mye writtenn Playe of Henrye fowrthe Henrye fyfthe Kyng John Kyng Leare," along with "mye written Playe neverr yett impryntedd whych I have named Kyng henrye thyrde of Englande" (Shakespeare's savior

was to receive "alle the profytts" for this previously unheard-of play).[44]
Here Ireland was imposing his own age's conception of a playwright's
proprietary relationship to his works: the actual Shakespeare, under contract to his theatrical company, was almost certainly in no position to
assign the profits of one of his plays to a friend.

The recklessness of summoning a namesake into being raised eyebrows,
not least those of Edmond Malone. His huge scholarly *Inquiry into the
Authenticity of Certain Miscellaneous Papers* made a convincing case that the
papers were riddled with contradictions, both external, where they were
inconsistent with the known facts about the early seventeenth century, and
internal, where they were inconsistent even with themselves. His critique
of the "William henrye Irelande" episode was among the more damning
arguments he laid out. Malone admitted that there was, in fact, a historical
William Ireland who had connections with Shakespeare's biography. But it
was not William *Henry* Ireland, and "his zeal to serve his friend, (enkindled
by so valuable an acquisition as that good estate which he has lately
recovered, or *discovered*,) greatly outran his discretion, and that no other
three words in the language could [have] been selected more unpropitious
to the cause of imposture than the names – WILLIAM HENRY Ireland. –
The deed in which they are found is [. . .] perfectly a *felo de se*."[45]

Shakespeare of course stands at the topmost rank of admired authors,
but authors need not be so beloved as Shakespeare to attract forgers. To the
faker the infamous can be as appealing as the famous. The most notorious
literary forgery of the twentieth century caught the world's attention
in April 1983, when *Stern* magazine announced the discovery of Adolf
Hitler's diaries, said to have been pulled from a burning airplane
in April 1945 and secretly passed from hand to hand for decades.
The diaries contained just the right combination of the expected and the
surprising to promote the illusion of authenticity. *Stern* acquired sixty-two
volumes of diaries for 9.3 million Deutschmarks, and London's *Sunday
Times*, freshly acquired by Rupert Murdoch, bought the UK and
Commonwealth serialization rights for £250,000.

It turned out, of course, that the discovery of the century was a forgery –
and, as we can see in retrospect, a clumsy forgery at that. The creator,
Konrad Kujau, an unscrupulous art dealer with a fondness for Nazi
memorabilia, made mistakes in interpreting typefaces; he copied passages
verbatim from published sources; he used expressions that were not current
in the 1930s and 1940s; he even used postwar synthetic materials. Hans
Booms, director of the Bundesarchiv in Koblenz, called the diaries "a
grotesque, superficial forgery." He was put off by the "'great banality' of

the Hitler who emerges from the forged diaries. 'If you read these diaries for two evenings, as I have, you get the impression of very limited emotion and understanding.'"[46] Still, even though the fakes were riddled with inconsistencies that should have definitively discredited the discoveries, they managed to fool the right people, at least for a while. Critics were persuaded, as were William Henry Ireland's dupes, by the sheer volume of the discoveries, and the improbability that anyone would forge so many documents of such little intrinsic interest. The historian Hugh Trevor-Roper permanently damaged his reputation by too hastily authenticating the diaries.

Forgery, which seems to be the opposite of plagiarism – not the claiming of someone else's work as one's own, but the attribution of one's own work to someone else – turns out to demonstrate the same obsession with originality. Forgers strive to insert themselves into history, to become the originals from which giant talents like Shakespeare or Milton make their imitations. Fakers put a major literary or historical figure under their own control, and therefore get the opportunity to change the understanding of literature or history. The forger also gets the thrill of competing, as it were, with great figures of the past, and – at least for as long as the forgery is believed – gets to feel a double joy: the first is being mistaken for the greatest figures in history and seeing one's own original compositions praised as the equal of Shakespeare's; the second comes from pulling the wool over the eyes of the critical establishment. The humiliation of the critics seems to loom large in many forgers' psyches, and it is no coincidence that many literary forgers had been failures in one way or another before they turned to deception: Macpherson's Scottish epic was ignored; Ireland was dismissed as a blockhead by his teachers and his father; Kujau spent much of his early adulthood behind bars for petty theft. When they were at the top of their game, though, they got to look down on the very critics who had once dismissed them, or, worse, ignored them altogether.

These joys, however, come at a price. The forgers can take intense pride in their handiwork, but they are obliged to conceal their authorship from history. Apart from a few confidants sworn to secrecy, fakers must keep their triumphs to themselves. And their only hope for recognition comes through failure: we know history's great forgers only because they failed to conceal themselves. Ireland and Kujau have joined the ranks of the legendary forgers, which is to say the failed forgers – who are, of necessity, the only forgers we know about, a reminder that there may be countless fakes in our canon of great works of literature that are unsuspected by anyone. The successful ones bought literary immortality at the cost of literary oblivion; the ones who achieve the dream of recognition as an original author are the ones who failed in their deception.

Notes

1. Susan Stewart, *Crimes of Writing* (Oxford: Oxford University Press, 1991; reprinted Durham, NC: Duke University Press, 1994).
2. Michael Wreen, "Is, Madam? Nay, It Seems!", in *The Forger's Art: Forgery and the Philosophy of Art*, ed. Denis Dutton (Berkeley: University of California Press, 1983), pp. 188–224, p. 193.
3. Thomas McFarland, *Coleridge and the Pantheist Tradition* (Oxford: Clarendon Press, 1969), p. 45.
4. See J. Mira Seo, "Plagiarism and Poetic Identity in Martial," *American Journal of Philology*, 130.4 (Winter 2009),567–93, and Scott McGill, *Plagiarism in Latin Literature* (Cambridge: Cambridge University Press, 2012), esp. ch. 3.
5. Anthony Nixon, *The Christian Navy. Wherein is Playnely Described the Perfit Course to Sayle to the Hauen of Eternall Happinesse* (London, 1602), sig. A3^r.
6. Barnabe Googe, *A Newe Booke Called the Shippe of Safegard* (London, 1569), sig. B1^r.
7. Daniel Defoe, *Review*, 2 Feb. 1710.
8. Edward Young, *Conjectures on Original Composition. In a Letter to the Author of Sir Charles Grandison* (London, 1759), p. 10.
9. Ibid., pp. 65–66.
10. Robert Macfarlane, *Original Copy: Plagiarism and Originality in Nineteenth-Century Literature* (Oxford: Oxford University Press, 2007), pp. 1–4.
11. The most recent and thorough consideration of the subject is John Kerrigan, *Shakespeare's Originality* (Oxford: Oxford University Press, 2018).
12. *Mr William Shakespeare his Comedies, Histories, and Tragedies*, ed. Edward Capell, 10 vols. (London, 1768), vol. 1, pp. 53–54.
13. Young, *Conjectures*, p. 78.
14. William Lauder, *An Essay on Milton's Use and Imitation of the Moderns in His "Paradise Lost"* (London, 1750), p. 47.
15. Ibid., p. 77.
16. Ibid., p. 155.
17. John Douglas, *Milton Vindicated from the Charge of Plagiarism, Brought against him by Mr. Lauder, and Lauder himself convicted of several Forgeries and gross Impositions on the Public* (London, 1751), p. 29.
18. Ibid., p. 31.
19. John Aikin, *Letters from a Father to his Son* (London, 1793), p. 160.
20. Tilar J. Mazzeo, *Plagiarism and Literary Property in the Romantic Period* (Philadelphia: University of Pennsylvania Press, 2006), p. ix.
21. Ibid., pp. 2–3.
22. John Ferriar, *Illustrations of Sterne: with Other Essays and Verses* (London, 1798), pp. 66–67. Ferriar quotes Laurence Sterne, *Tristram Shandy*, eds. Melvyn New

and Joan New, 3 vols. (Gainesville: University Presses of Florida, 1978–84), 5.1.279. Sterne, in turn, quotes Robert Burton, *The Anatomy of Melancholy* (Oxford, 1621), p. 8. See also H. J. Jackson, "Sterne, Burton, and Ferriar: Allusions to the *Anatomy of Melancholy* in Volumes Five to Nine of *Tristram Shandy*," *Philological Quarterly*, 54.2 (1795), 457–70, and Jonathan Lamb, "Sterne's System of Imitation," *Modern Language Review*, 76.4 (1981), 794–810.

23. See Daniel Shore, "Things Unattempted ... Yet Once More," *Milton Quarterly*, 43.3 (2009), 195–200, p. 195.

24. Mikal Gilmore, "Bob Dylan Unleashed," *Rolling Stone*, 27 September 2012.

25. Jonathan Lethem, "The Ecstasy of Influence: A Plagiarism," *Harper's Magazine* (February 2007), 59–71, p. 60.

26. Ibid., p. 68.

27. Ibid., p. 71.

28. David Edelstein, "Where Have I Read That Before?: The Scourge of Plagiarism Is Plaguing All Writers: Thanks to Kaavya, Everyone's a Suspect," *New York Magazine*, 15 May 2006; Edelstein, "A Stunt Explained," *New York Magazine*, 22 May 2006.

29. Scott McGill, "Tragic Vergil: Rewriting Vergil as a Tragedy in the Cento *Medea*," *The Classical World*, 95.2 (2002), 143–61, p. 161.

30. Elizabeth Barrett Browning, *Essays on the Greek Christian Poets and the English Poets* (New York, 1863), p. 67.

31. Lethem, "Ecstasy," p. 61.

32. Ibid., pp. 63–64.

33. 17 U.S. Code § 102 (a).

34. *Burton's Gentleman's Magazine*, February 1840, 103.

35. *Universal Pictures Co.* v. *Harold Lloyd Corporation*, 162 F.2d 354 (9th Cir. 1947).

36. See J. C., "Man of Letters," *Times Literary Supplement*, 29 Nov. 2017, and Rix's letter to the editor in *TLS*, 3 Jan. 2018. I have been frustrated in my attempts to locate a copy of Rix's (self-published) book, which is listed as unavailable on all the major bookselling sites and does not appear in the catalogs of the British Library, the Library of Congress, or WorldCat.

37. Jorge Luis Borges, "Pierre Menard, Author of the *Quixote*," in *Collected Fictions*, trans. Andrew Hurley (New York: Viking Penguin, 1998), pp. 88–95.

38. See, for instance, Giovanna Ceserani, "Narrative, Interpretation, and Plagiarism in Mr. Robertson's 1778 *History of Ancient Greece*," *Journal of the History of Ideas*, 66.3 (2005), 413–36.

39. Benson Honig and Akanksha Bedi, "The Fox in the Hen House: A Critical Examination of Plagiarism among Members of the Academy of Management," *Academy of Management Learning & Education*, 11. 1 (2012), 101–23.

40. See David D. Kirkpatrick, "2 Say Stephen Ambrose, Popular Historian, Copied Passages," *New York Times*, 5 Jan. 2002, and Kirkpatrick, "Historian Says Borrowing Was Wider than Known," *New York Times*, 23 Feb. 2002.

41. For a first-person account from a victim of scholarly plagiarism, see "Anonymous Academic," "Plagiarism Is Rife in Academia, So Why Is it Rarely Acknowledged?", *The Guardian*, 27 Oct. 2017.

42. In 2009, for instance, the committee charged with formulating a plagiarism policy for Southern Illinois University lifted its 139-word definition of plagiarism from a plagiarism policy written by Indiana University. See Adam Testa, "Is Draft of Plagiarism Policy Plagiarized?", *The Southern Illinoisan*, 30 Jan. 2009.

43. [William Henry Ireland], *Miscellaneous Papers and Legal Instruments under the Hand and Seal of William Shakspeare* (London, 1796), sig. B2^{r-v}.

44. Ibid., sig. B2^v.

45. Edmond Malone, *An Inquiry into the Authenticity of Certain Miscellaneous Papers and Legal Instruments, Published Dec. 24 M DCC XCV, and Attributed to Shakspeare, Queen Elizabeth and Henry, Earl of Southampton* (London, 1796), p. 227.

46. James M. Markham, "Bonn Says Tests Show Diaries Aren't Hitler's," *New York Times*, 7 May 1983.

CHAPTER 23

Authorship and Scholarly Editing

Dirk Van Hulle

In his famous lecture "Qu'est-ce qu'un auteur?" Michel Foucault para-doxically refers to the author Samuel Beckett when he quotes the line "Qu'importe qui parle," which Foucault interprets in terms of indiffer-ence. The full quotation is "Qu'importe qui parle, quelqu'un a dit qu'importe qui parle" ["What matter who's speaking, someone said what matter who's speaking"][1] – which adds an important nuance. For even though the gist of the line is that the biography of the author may be irrelevant, it does indicate that even the questioning of author-ship involves a "speaker" or "writer." If one chooses not to include biographical research in literary criticism, this usually implies the exclu-sion of the "bio-" element; but it is harder to ignore the "graphical" facet, the fact that writings are *written*, by "someone." Take for instance the author of "What Is an Author?": Michel Foucault presented his lecture at the Collège de France on 22 February 1969, but also a modified version at the University at Buffalo (SUNY) in March 1970. In this second version, he still discussed the proliferation of meaning, but he also argued that "as our society changes, at the very moment when it is in the process of changing, the author-function will disap-pear, and in such a manner that fiction and its polysemic texts will once again function according to another mode, *but still with a system of constraint.*"[2] Apparently the author of the Buffalo version thought it was necessary to write a version that differed from that of his younger self. Even if one were to conclude that it does not matter who is speaking, one might want to know which of the two textual versions one is reading or listening to. This leads us from the question of authorship to scholarly editing.

* The research leading to these results has received funding from the European Research Council under the European Union's Seventh Framework Programme (FP7/2007–2013) / ERC grant agree-ment nr. 313609.

Authorial Intention and the "Authoritative" Text

Historically, textual scholarship tended to value the mature author over his or her younger self. In the long tradition of German *Editionswissenschaft*, the paradigm was Goethe. He lived long enough to oversee the Complete Works edition, the *Gesamtausgabe* (1827–1830). The programmatic subtitle *Vollständige Ausgabe letzter Hand* had a huge impact on the subsequent editorial treatment of his works, as Rüdiger Nutt-Kofoth notes.[3] The aim of the first critical edition (the so-called *Weimarer Ausgabe*) of his works, which comprised 143 volumes and was finished in 1919, was to render what was known to be Goethe's own wish ("was uns als Goethes selbstwillige Verfügung bekannt ist").[4] In this tradition, the editor was seen as an executor of the author's (last) will, a "*Testamentsvollstrecker.*"[5] The underlying assumption was that the mature and experienced author has the last word.

This principle of the author's last will is still applied once in a while. For instance, in the late twentieth century, James Knowlson wrote in his General Editor's Note to the Theatrical Notebooks of Samuel Beckett, which contain "revised texts": "The texts are now as close as possible to how Beckett wanted them to be."[6] It is interesting to note that in this statement "Beckett" is silently assumed to be the mature Beckett, the author in the last years of his career. The texts of his plays were revised accordingly: the editor takes into account what Beckett marked in his production notebooks and in the copies of his published texts whenever he directed his own plays. As a result, for instance, the stage directions for *Krapp's Last Tape* in the revised text indicate that the actor is supposed to look over his left shoulder, as if death (the "grim reaper") were standing behind him. This gesture was not yet part of the original edition of the play as it was published in 1958.

This may seem a minor detail, but the changes quickly add up. Similarly, in Goethe's case, when he had the chance to revise his text for a complete works edition in 1787, he seized the opportunity to seriously revise the text of some of his early works, including *Die Leiden des jungen Werthers* (*The Sorrows of Young Werther*), originally published in 1774. With hindsight, from the later Goethe's perspective, there was apparently much to be improved on the original text, but whereas the 1774 text of *Die Leiden des jungen Werthers* is the icon of "Sturm und Drang," the question is whether that can still be said of the 1787 text, since Goethe revised the text precisely because he had taken a distance from his younger self. During the twentieth century, there was a growing sense that the "ultima manus" approach was not self-evident, even in Goethe studies. From a historical point of view, the text of *Die Leiden des jungen Werthers* was the one that shook the world in 1774, causing a notable rise in suicides.

Similarly, in 1993, the text of James Joyce's *Ulysses* was reprinted the way it was published in 1922,[7] warts and all, because that was the text that had changed literature forever. This edition was a statement because it came after the famous 1984 edition of *Ulysses* by Hans Walter Gabler, Wolfhard Steppe, and Claus Melchior.[8] Gabler's edition was special because it combined elements from both the German and the Anglo-American traditions of scholarly editing. These two schools had evolved quite differently, partly due to their totally divergent paradigms: whereas Goethe served as paradigmatic author in the German tradition, Shakespeare played this role in the Anglo-American school. Goethe kept almost all of his manuscripts, while almost no manuscripts by Shakespeare are extant. As a consequence of this basic difference, the German approach is generally more historically oriented, choosing a historical document as base text and emending it only in cases of obvious textual error (*Textfehler*). Whereas this German approach was designed to deal with an *abundance* of manuscript material, the Anglo-American school initially developed an editorial strategy to deal with the *lack* thereof. As a consequence, the role of the editor in this tradition was generally more prominent. Nonetheless, one of his or her main jobs remained the same: to find out which of the transmitted texts was the most "authoritative."

In his *Prolegomena for the Oxford Shakespeare*, Ronald B. McKerrow defined the most authoritative text as "that one of the early texts which, on a consideration of their genetic relationship, appears likely to have deviated to the smallest extent in all respects of wording, spelling, and punctuation from the author's manuscript."[9] He spoke of an "ideal text," which "should approach as closely as the extant material allows to a fair copy, made by the author himself, of his plays in the form which he intended finally to give them."[10] In *The Editorial Problem in Shakespeare* (1951), W. W. Greg came up with an alternative set of "rules," which according to him "should govern the procedure of an editor of Shakespeare."[11] Especially in the third rule Greg introduced his new ideas, but the first two rules followed McKerrow's principles. The first rule was: "The aim of a critical edition should be to present the text, so far as the available evidence permits, in the form in which we *may suppose* that it would have stood in a fair copy, made by the author himself, of the work as he finally intended it."[12] And in the second rule, he called the most *authoritative* text of the early prints the "copy-text."[13] So, final authorial intention was still the guideline, and the editor was given a lot of freedom to make an educated guess as to what this intention was.

In the United States, Fredson Bowers further developed what came to be known as the "copy-text theory" and in 1970 he defined "the aim of textual criticism" as "the recovery of the initial *purity* of an author's text and of any revision (insofar as this is possible from the preserved documents), and the preservation of this *purity* despite the usual *corrupting* process of reprint transmission."[14] The emphasis on "purity" versus "corruption" illustrates the then prevailing view that textual agents other than the author were, almost by definition, regarded as introducers of textual "corruption." This corruption was seen as an obstacle to what the author intended, the text as the author wanted it to be. In "The Editorial Problem of Final Authorial Intention" (1976), G. Thomas Tanselle noted that, in literary criticism, influential writings on authorial intention on both sides of the spectrum – on the one hand, Wimsatt and Beardsley's "The Intentional Fallacy" (1946), on the other hand E. D. Hirsch's *Validity in Interpretation* (1967) – differed enormously in their opinion on authorial intention, but they shared an underlying assumption: "the question of the bearing of authorial intention on interpretation would hardly arise unless the text is assumed to be what its author wished."[15] From a textual-critical and editorial point of view, this assumption is not self-evident. In order to establish a text that reflected the author's final intention, the copy-text theory allowed the editor to select readings from various versions. This approach, however, resulted in what – in German editorial theory – was disparagingly called "an eclectic (contaminated) text."[16] The Swiss editorial theorist Hans Zeller doubted "whether the sum of authoritative readings yields an authoritative text."[17] He objected to this approach arguing that an "eclectic editor contaminatingly synchronizes that which occurred diachronically," thus establishing a text that has never existed before, "in the name of authorial intention."[18] When Hans Walter Gabler and his team made the above-mentioned edition of *Ulysses*, this event confronted the two schools with their respective orientations to text. With hindsight, from a twenty-first-century perspective, Patrick Sahle calls this editorial feat "the climax of the traditional method," attempting to reconcile the reality of the documents with the ideality of the author's will.[19]

Many of the hot debates on authorial intention and textual authority were prompted by the printed medium's limitations of space and the consequential focus on establishing a single reading text. The digital medium has relativized the urgency of these issues. As a result, the traditional schools of scholarly editing are interacting and merging more freely, and instead of talking about "schools" or "traditions," it seems more suitable to speak of "orientations to text."[20] Each orientation is a particular approach to texts, determining the way the narrative of the genesis, revision history, and publication is framed. There is no "right" or "wrong" orientation. What matters is that, whatever orientation is chosen at the beginning of an editorial project, it should be applied consistently. Thus, (1) a *material orientation* focuses on the documentary evidence. Authority, from this perspective, resides in the material document. (2) A *causal orientation* focuses on the involvement of every agent of textual change (not only the author, but also any other agent involved in the composition, revision, and production of texts). Both the "authorial" and the "social" subsets within this orientation regard the work as a record of human actions. (3) A *temporal orientation* emphasizes the moment when a text was produced and investigates whether there are, for instance, elements in the text that do not fit the period of its production. From this perspective, authority resides in periods of (re-) inscription. (4) A *genetic orientation* is interested in the dynamics of the composition as implied by the extant versions, their chronology, and the changes within them (deletions, additions, substitutions) and between them (variants or rewritings). (5) A *performance orientation* pays special attention to the way a work's instructions for performance are carried out. (6) An *aesthetic orientation* is anything ranging from an editor's subjective revamping of a text based on his or her aesthetic preferences to an edition that tries to respect the known aesthetic principles of an author or of a historical publisher.[21]

A facet of textual scholarship that has become more prominent thanks to digital editing is textual "fluidity." In *The Fluid Text,* John Bryant defines the critical edition as "a genre of scholarly editing in which a text is constructed usually after the inspection, and sometimes the conflation, of significant versions of the work; it is also a text that is invariably emended along certain principles so as to bring it closer to an announced notion of intentionality."[22] Bryant brilliantly moves the discussion beyond Wimsatt and Beardsley's notion of the "intentional fallacy" by introducing the "Intentional Fallacy Fallacy":

> It is, of course, a truism that we cannot retrieve the creative process, nor, according to the "intentional fallacy," can we use some magically derived sense of a writer's intentions as a validation of or substitute for an interpretation of a text. But in the past century, some advocates of this tenet have grown so doctrinaire as to commit what might be called the Intentional Fallacy Fallacy, which is essentially to imagine that because intentions have no critical relevance they are not even discussable.[23]

In scholarly editing, authorial intention is a question about what the author intended the text to *do* (i.e., what character or punctuation mark was intended to be inscribed), not about what he or she intended the text to *mean*.[24] Determining what an author intended will always be controversial since it implies a critical act, but in textual scholarship – as Paul Eggert notes – the subjectivity of this act is "hedged in at every point by whatever can be ascertained or inferred about the history of the work's writing and early production."[25] Especially in the digital age, it becomes increasingly clear that an author's intentions, whether they are taken into account or not, are eminently changeable.

Multiple Intentions

This plurality of intentions over time is reflected in various editorial solutions to particular problems. In the case of *Die Leiden des jungen Werthers*, for instance, the problem of the young versus the more mature Goethe was solved both elegantly and inexpensively in the double edition by Reclam, which prints the two texts in parallel presentation, the 1774 text on the left, the 1787 version on the right.

The digital medium also facilitates research into changing intentions, including not only revisions *after* but also *before* publication. This is an area of interest that is most prominent in French genetic criticism (*critique génétique*). Whereas textual criticism traditionally did pay attention to changing intentions during the genesis of the work, it did so mainly at the service of scholarly editing, that is, the establishment of a single reading text used to be the main goal. French genetic criticism (the study of the dynamics of – usually literary – writing processes) emancipated the study of modern manuscripts by regarding it as a discipline in its own right. While most literary theories were increasingly focusing on the reader, Louis Hay advocated a renewed interest in the author and later wrote a collection of essays explicitly called *La littérature des écrivains*. As early as 1967, he wrote an article in the French newspaper *Le Monde* called "Des manuscrits, pour quoi faire?" ["Manuscripts, what for?"], in which he noted that literary criticism (in those days dominated by structuralism) tended to privilege the finished product and that the study of a text's genesis could be an end in itself.[26]

From this perspective, editing thus becomes a tool to study the manuscripts rather than the other way round. Good examples are the Beckett Digital Manuscript Project, the Jane Austen Fiction Manuscripts, Woolf Online, and Faustedition (a historical-critical edition of Goethe's *Faust*).

The digital genetic edition of the novel *Molloy*,[27] for instance, shows that Beckett originally wrote a long passage on the so-called Molloy country, "Ballyba," whose economy was based on the excrements of its citizens. The passage may have been intended as a parody of Ireland's protectionist policy under Éamon de Valera in the 1930s,[28] but eventually Beckett changed his mind and decided to cut the passage. Similarly, on a micro-level, there are intertextual references to Dante, Verlaine, or Shakespeare that Beckett considered including, but eventually deleted again. Thus, for instance, a dramatic fragment referred to as "Bare room" in one of Beckett's late notebooks (UoR MS 2934) refers explicitly to Shakespeare as the author of two sonnets in particular:

> Where are you?
> Here. (P.) At the window. (P.) The snow has ceased.
> The what?
> The snow.
> P.
> Come & read to me.
> What?
> That sonnet we ~~once so~~ used to loved.
> You mean "No longer weep ... "
> What? (P.) No longer what?
> Weep. (P.) "No longer weep ... "
> No no.
> We ~~loved~~ used to love it too.
> Yes, but not ~~now. tonight~~ this evening.
> "Let me not ~~to~~ – "
> Yes. "Let me not ~~to~~ – " How did it go on?
> ~~P.~~
> I ~~can't remember~~ have forgotten.
> We used to know it by heart. One would say the first
> quatrain, then the other the second. Then the one
> the ~~next ... what do you call it~~. third. Then the
> other the geegee
> [...] Geegee? [...]
> The couplet. We used to call it the geegee.[29]

Eventually, Beckett never published this dramatic fragment, but even so, the manuscript shows an interesting change of intentions. Beckett first introduces two of Shakespeare's sonnets mentioning the author explicitly. Then he "undoes" the author's name, in accordance with his self-proclaimed poetics of ignorance, eliminating all the erudition, and still rebelling against the Joycean pose of alleged omniscience, but also literally erasing the greatest authority in English literary history. The idea of erudition in ruins is further emphasized by the misremembered line "No longer weep" instead of "No longer mourn for me when I am dead" (Sonnet 71), and by the manner in which the line "Let me not to the marriage of true minds / Admit impediments" (Sonnet 116) is only partially remembered, first the opening four words: "Let me not to – " until even four is considered one too many: "Let me not to – ."

These erasures are the literary equivalent of what are called *pentimenti* in the visual arts. Paisley Livingston defines the term as follows:

> A *pentimento* is, first of all, an artist's intentional action of non-trivially reworking, replacing, or covering over some expressive or representational feature of an artifact or design that had previously and provisionally been established, either *intentionally or not*, by that artist as part of a work in progress. The reworking or replacing in question is motivated by the artist's dissatisfaction with the provisional results achieved so far, and the altering or replacement of those results amounts to a change of mind regarding the projected work's eventual features. The notion of reworking here covers both process and product: "pentiment" refers not only to the prior, provisional creation of features, but also to the features thereby created, as they stand in relation to the artist's subsequent action of deleting, replacing, or covering them over.[30]

Even though the notion of intention is employed more cautiously in literary studies, the kind of intention meant by Livingston is closer to "intention" as used in textual scholarship than "intention" as used in literary criticism, that is, what the author/artist intended to *do*, not what he or she intended the text/painting to *mean*. The interest in this erasure as a moment of regret is connected to a view of the author as someone who develops cognitively and the erasure as the literary equivalent of *pentimenti* is also defined in terms of a change of intentions, even a change of identity on the part of the author. The author who crosses out a word is no longer the same as the one who wrote it. This interval opens up the space in which genetic criticism operates, as Nicholas Donin and Daniel Ferrer note.[31] In other words, every author is seen as a succession of selves, a multiplicity of authors.

Multiple Authorship

In addition to this multiplicity of selves and of intentions, there are numerous other agents that are part of what Jack Stillinger has dubbed "multiple authorship." Stillinger mentions on the one hand the theorists who speak of the disappearance, banishment, or "death" of the author and on the other hand those who invest the author with a significance approaching apotheosis or deification. But as he observes:

> It is noteworthy that both of these theoretical extremes share the concept of *an* author – singular – as creator of a text. In many cases such a concept does not accord with the facts of literary production; numerous texts considered to be the work of single authorship turn out to be the product of several hands. It may, therefore, advance our thinking to expand the question to include, in effect, *how many* authors are being banished from a text or apotheosized in it.[32]

The examples are legion. Some authors, such as Jane Austen, relied on their publisher to correct their spelling mistakes, as Kathryn Sutherland pointed out.[33] Others "inoculated" their own work by incorporating, and responding to, criticism. For instance, Charles Darwin not only hesitated many years before he decided to publish *On the Origin of Species*, but as soon as it was published he responded to criticism by revising each successive edition to such a degree that the critics can be regarded as agents of textual change. James Joyce used to read parts of *Finnegans Wake* (when it was still called "Work in Progress") to friends before he published them and he also incorporated phrases from bad reviews of his previous book, *Ulysses*, thus allowing external agents to shape the text to some extent. An author's "typical" style sometimes turns out to be mainly due to the interventions of an editor, as in the case of Raymond Carver and his editor Gordon Lish. Especially for playwrights, the role of actors and other agents of textual change cannot be underestimated. After having had the chance to direct a few of his plays, Samuel Beckett came to realize that he actually needed to see his play in performance before it could be published. As he wrote to the publishing house Suhrkamp in 1964: "I shall never give another theatre text, if there ever is another, to be published until I have worked on it in the theatre."[34] Beckett was also a self-translator (translating his French texts into English or vice versa), but he sometimes received help from co-translators or native speakers of French who assisted him to various degrees.

To conclude, the multiplicity of authorship comes to the fore in textual scholarship and genetic criticism, notably in the digital age. A digital genetic edition such as the Beckett Digital Manuscript Project enables readers to discover the contributions of the various agents of textual change from one version to the next. New developments in (digital) textual editing facilitate the comparison of all these versions by means of automatic or computer-assisted collation. So far, collation software has been created mainly as a tool *for editors* (the way for instance TUSTEP was already used as a tool by the editors of the 1984 synoptic edition of *Ulysses*). The editors first need to correct the output before it can be presented as a critical apparatus. Thanks to recent research in collation software development (by such experts as Barbara Bordalejo, Ronald Haentjens Dekker, Nick Laiacona, Vincent Neyt, Peter Robinson, and Desmond Schmidt) it becomes conceivable to propose a different model and offer automatic collation as a tool *for readers*, to highlight variants. Instead of turning the so-called "critical apparatus" into the least exciting part of a critical edition (listing all the variants), this model enables readers to compare textual versions using a "collation engine" in a similar way as looking up a word with a "search engine." As collation algorithms are still in the process of being developed and fine-tuned, there will always be a margin of error, but users of a collation engine would quickly develop the same degree of ingenuity as users of a search engine. To draw readers' attention to textual fluidity, they are offered a set of digital tools that enable them to highlight variants between versions.[35] Apart from its traditional functions, a printed critical edition also increasingly becomes a tool for readers to find their way to the digital archive and explore the intricacies of the writing process. In this way, both genetic criticism and (digital) scholarly editing can play their role in serving as "the ferryman between the universe of writers and the universe of readers."[36]

Notes

1. Samuel Beckett, *Texts for Nothing and Other Shorter Prose 1950–1976* (London: Faber and Faber, 2010), p. 11.
2. Michel Foucault, "What Is an Author?", in *Textual Strategies: Perspectives in Poststructuralist Criticism*, ed. Josué V. Harari (Ithaca, NY: Cornell University Press, 1979), pp. 141–60, p. 160; emphasis added. Foucault's conclusion follows on his argument that "[t]he author is therefore the ideological figure by which one marks the manner in which we fear the proliferation of meaning. In saying this, I seem to call for a form of culture in which fiction would not be limited by the figure of the author. It would be pure romanticism, however, to imagine a culture in which the fictive would operate in an absolutely free state, in which fiction would be put at the disposal of everyone and would develop without passing through something like a necessary or constraining figure" (ibid., p. 159). For the

differences between the two versions, see also Michel Foucault, *Dits et Écrits* vol. 1 (Paris: Gallimard, 2001), p. 839.

3. Rüdiger Nutt-Kofoth, "Goethe-Editionen," in *Editionen zu deutschsprachigen Autoren als Spiegel der Editionsgeschichte*, eds. Rüdiger Nutt-Kofoth and Bodo Plachta (Tübingen: Niemeyer, 2005), pp. 95–116, p. 96.

4. Bernhard Suphan, "Vorbericht," in *Goethes Werke, herausgegeben im Auftrage der Großherzogin Sophie von Sachsen*, vol. 1 (Weimar, 1887), pp. xviii–xxv, p. xviii.

5. Georg Witkowski, "Grundsätze kritischer Ausgaben neuerer deutscher Dichterwerke," in *Funde und Forschungen: Eine Festgabe für Julius Wahle zum 15. Februar 1921* (Leipzig, 1921), pp. 216–26, p. 225.

6. Samuel Beckett, *The Theatrical Notebooks of Samuel Beckett: "Waiting for Godot"* (New York: Grove Press, 1993), p. v.

7. James Joyce, *Ulysses*, ed. Jeri Johnson (Oxford: Oxford University Press, 1993).

8. James Joyce, *Ulysses: A Critical and Synoptic Edition*, eds. Hans Walter Gabler, Wolfhard Steppe, and Claus Melchior (New York: Garland, 1984).

9. Ronald B. McKerrow, *Prolegomena for the Oxford Shakespeare: A Study in Editorial Method* (Oxford: Clarendon Press, 1939), pp. 7–8.

10. Ibid., p. 6.

11. W. W. Greg, *The Editorial Problem in Shakespeare: A Survey of the Foundations of the Text* (Oxford: Clarendon Press, 1951), p. ix.

12. Ibid., p. x; emphasis added.

13. Ibid., p. xii.

14. Fredson Bowers, "Textual Criticism," in *The Aims and Methods of Scholarship in Modern Languages and Literatures*, ed. James Thorpe (New York: Modern Language Association, 1970), pp. 23–42, p. 24; emphasis added.

15. G. Thomas Tanselle, "The Editorial Problem of Final Authorial Intention," *Studies in Bibliography*, 29 (1976), 167–211, p. 172.

16. Hans Zeller, "A New Approach to the Critical Constitution of Literary Texts," *Studies in Bibliography* 28 (1975), 231–64, p. 235.

17. Ibid., p. 237.

18. Hans Zeller, "Structure and Genesis in Editing: On German and Anglo-American Textual Editing," in *Contemporary German Editorial Theory*, ed. Hans Walter Gabler, George Bornstein, and Gillian Borland Pierce (Ann Arbor: University of Michigan Press, 1995), pp. 95–123, p. 106.

19. Patrick Sahle, *Digitale Editionsformen. Teil 1: Das typografische Erbe* (Norderstedt: Books on Demand, 2013), p. 129, my translation.

20. Peter Shillingsburg originally defined five orientations (documentary, sociological, authorial, bibliographical, and aesthetic) in *Scholarly Editing in the Computer Age*, 3rd edn (Ann Arbor: University of Michigan Press, 1996). They were recently "revisited" to add a "genetic orientation" and fine-tune the other orientations: Dirk Van Hulle and Peter Shillingsburg, "Orientations to Text, Revisited," *Studies in Bibliography*, 59 (2015), 27–44.

21. For a more elaborate discussion of these orientations, see Van Hulle and Shillingsburg, "Orientations."

22. John Bryant, *The Fluid Text: A Theory of Revision and Editing for Book and Screen* (Ann Arbor: University of Michigan Press, 2002), p. 20.

23. Ibid., p. 8.

24. Peter Shillingsburg, *Scholarly Editing in the Computer Age: Theory and Practice* (Athens: University of Georgia Press, 1986), pp. 36–37.

25. Paul Eggert, "Apparatus, Text, Interface," in *The Cambridge Companion to Textual Scholarship*, eds. Neil Fraistat and Julia Flanders (Cambridge: Cambridge University Press, 2013), pp. 97–118, p. 104. Eggert sees the life of a literary work as a negative dialectic in Adorno's terms between the material medium (the documentary dimension) and meaningful experience (the textual dimension). This dynamic is brought to life through reading and performing, but also through editing. See also Paul Eggert, *Securing the Past: Conservation in Art, Architecture and Literature* (Cambridge: Cambridge University Press, 2009).

26. Louis Hay, "Des manuscrits, pour quoi faire?", *Le Monde*, 8 Feb. 1967.

27. Samuel Beckett, *Molloy: A Digital Genetic Edition*, eds. Magessa O'Reilly, Dirk Van Hulle, Pim Verhulst, and Vincent Neyt (Brussels: University Press Antwerp, 2016), www.beckettarchive.org.

28. Adam Winstanley, "'Grâce aux excréments des citoyens': Beckett, Swift and the Coprophagic Economy of Ballyba," *Samuel Beckett Today / Aujourd'hui*, 26 (2014), 91–106.

29. Samuel Beckett, *Stirrings Still / Soubresauts and Comment dire / what is the word: A Digital Genetic Edition*, eds. Dirk Van Hulle and Vincent Neyt (Brussels: University Press Antwerp, 2011), www.beckettarchive.org: UoR MS 2934.

30. Paisley Livingston, "Pentimento," in *The Creation of Art: New Essays in Philosophical Aesthetics*, eds. Berys Gaut and Paisley Livingston (Cambridge: Cambridge University Press, 2003), pp. 89–105, p. 92.

31. Nicolas Donin and Daniel Ferrer, "Auteur(s) et acteurs de la genèse," *Genesis*, 41 (2015), p. 24: "l'écrivain qui rature un mot et le remplace n'est pas exactement le même que celui qui l'a inscrit, même dans le cas d'une correction intervenant presque instantanément. Si celui qui relit avait exactement la même perspective que celui qui a écrit, il n'y aurait pas de ratures, pas de corrections, pas de nouvelles versions. C'est l'intervalle qui s'ouvre entre les deux positions qui crée l'espace dans lequel peut opérer la critique génétique."

32. Jack Stillinger, *Multiple Authorship and the Myth of Solitary Genius* (Oxford: Oxford University Press, 1991), p. v.

33. Kathryn Sutherland in William Garner, "Jane Austen Could Write – But Her Spelling Was Awful," *The Independent*, 22 October 2010: "Austen's unpublished manuscripts unpick her reputation for perfection in various ways: we see blots, crossings out, messiness, we see creation as it happens, and in Austen's case, we discover a powerful, counter-grammatical way of writing. She broke most of the rules for writing good English. In particular, the high degree of polished punctuation and epigrammatic style we see in *Emma* and

Persuasion is simply not there. This suggests somebody else was heavily involved in the editing process between manuscript and printed book." The editor William Gifford (working for the publisher John Murray II) is probably responsible for most of the corrections.

34. *The Letters of Samuel Beckett, vol. III, 1957–1965*, eds. George Craig, Martha Dow Fehsenfeld, Dan Gunn, and Lois More Overbeck (Cambridge: Cambridge University Press, 2011), pp. 598.

35. As a recent study at the University of Utrecht has shown, readers who read a story from a print edition are better at reconstructing the plot than readers who read it from an e-book.

36. Louis Hay, *La Littérature des écrivains: Questions de critique génétique* (Paris: José Corti, 2002), p. 30; my translation.

CHAPTER 24

Copyright and Literary Property
The Invention of Secondary Authorship

Daniel Cook

"... there is no law that a sequel should be necessarily self-written."
Gérard Genette[1]

The world's first copyright act established a contradiction between access to content and the rights of the creator (or the purchaser of his or her copies) that has yet to be resolved more than three hundred years later.[2] The right to print and reprint books as recognized in the Statute of Anne (1710) only lasted for a limited period (fourteen years if the book was new; a further fourteen if the author remained alive at the end of the initial period), though this gradually increased in the ensuing centuries. The 1842 Copyright Act provided *post mortem* protection to authors for the first time – this was further strengthened in Britain under the 1911 Copyright Act, which gave protection for fifty years after the author's death, and which was extended to seventy years in 1995, in line with EU legislation. Various international treaties, such as the Berne Convention (1886) and the Agreement on Trade-Related Aspects of Intellectual Property Rights (1994), have expanded the geographical scope of intellectual property to include most of the globe.

Generally speaking, modern writers also retain certain moral rights regardless of the legal status of their rights in copy. Under the UK's 1988 Copyright Act, for instance, authors have a "paternity right" (the right to be identified as the text's author), an "integrity right" (the author's right to object to any derogatory treatment of his or her work), and the right not to have a work falsely attributed to them. Publication, for the jurist Marcel Plaisant, "extends the personality of the author and thus exposes him to further injuries because the surface of his vulnerability has been enlarged."[3] Against the personhood school of copyright law, Peter Baldwin has argued that the authors' moral rights ideology (*droit d'auteur* in French, *Urheberrecht* in German, *diritto d'autore* in Italian, and *derecho de autor* in Spanish) "is elitist and exclusive, while copyright is democratic and egalitarian."[4] At issue here is a debate about whether writers ought to retain any sort of paternal rights over their work if they have lost or relinquished their economic claims over it. Should personality-based rights exist independently of copyright limitations? Have copyright holders "adopted" the work that also belongs, through a figurative bloodline at least, to an author-parent?

Legal historians and literary scholars alike have often endorsed Roland Barthes's critique of the myth of filiation in which "[t]he Author is thought to *nourish* the book, which is to say that he exists before it, thinks, suffers, lives for it, is in the same relation of antecedence to his work as a father to his child."[5] Novelists have long literalized the familial metaphor by playfully claiming that their narrator or authorial alter ego is the offspring or some sort of relative of an established text (*John Buncle, Junior, Gentleman*; *Joseph Andrews*; *Mr Dalloway*; or *Mrs Osmond*, for example). Many imitative writers in this mode present their new work as a revisionary "supplement," even when the novel radically re-orientates the focus of the action or the participating characters to the point of losing sight of the original (as happens with Curtis Sittenfeld's *Eligible* and J. M. Coetzee's *Foe*). The protagonist of Peter Carey's *Jack Maggs* (1997), in Beverly Taylor's reading, is a sort of "post-birth abortion" that irritably seeks out a relationship with its parent text, Charles Dickens's *Great Expectations* (1860) – or what Ankhi Mukherjee calls "a vexed author-to-author filiation."[6] "I have wondered if Miss Brontë does not *want* her book tampered with!," so Jean Rhys noted, when recounting her struggles with writing her prequel, *Wide Sargasso Sea* (1966).[7] The original work (*John Buncle*; *Pamela*; *Mrs Dalloway*; *The Portrait of a Lady*; *Pride and Prejudice*; *Robinson Crusoe*; *Great Expectations*; and *Jane Eyre*, to expand in order the examples under erasure given above) is left intact, physically at least, but nevertheless secondary authors have been alternately described as fair-users or thieves (kidnappers, in many eighteenth-century complaints).[8] Even now, rewriting can be seen as "sabotage" as much as a "symbiosis," as Christian Moraru reminds us.[9]

This chapter is interested in the legality of supplementary writing in a metaphorical sense, and the implications a "secondary" form of production has for authorship studies at large.[10] Linda Hutcheon provides the spirit I wish to trace: "to be second is not to be secondary or inferior; likewise, to be first is not to be originary or authoritative."[11] An author's "aftering," as Julie Sanders avers, "can mean finding new angles and new routes into something, new perspectives on the familiar."[12] Michael Worton and Judith Still similarly argue that "every literary imitation is a *supplement* which seeks to complete and supplant the original and which functions at times for later readers as the pre-text of the 'original.'"[13] Here, supplementary is taken in the Derridean sense of being a vital substitute, giving a different version of life to an established work without defeating it. Fan fiction (or attentive rewriting, we might say) extends the literary property – it fills in "missing scenes," redoes endings, expands the book's timeline, and elaborates the background stories of minor or additional characters, or creates cross-overs with other pieces. Hutcheon's and Sanders's in-depth studies of adaptation cover a wide range of transmedia maneuvers, but I am limiting my focus to examples with a largely explicit relationship between a hypertext (the rewrite) and the hypotext (the rewritten), to adopt Gérard Genette's terms. These examples will be full-length novels (rather than short stories, poems, plays, or comics and graphic novels), as such works typically include an author's note or paratextual manifesto of some kind. Often, these publications offer a small, informal acknowledgment of debt to a favorite author or – in rarer cases – a declaration of authorial parricide set amongst a goading, emulous imitation. Novels in the secondary mode revisit the origins of the property, often by reconfiguring the first author as a character struggling with his or her own material.

One significant reason why, in this account, I am setting aside playtexts and comics (visual productions, in short) is because their authorship is largely collaborative (often in very different, immeasurable ways) and therefore raises a different set of research questions about in-text boundaries and ownership, among other things.[14] The copyright of comic-book characters is particularly fraught territory, as best exemplified by the decade-long battle between Neil Gaiman (the scripter) and Todd McFarlane (the original artist) over Medieval Spawn, Cogliostro, and Angela, all of whom first appeared in *Spawn* #9. In 2004, the Seventh Circuit Court of Appeals effectively granted the scripter and the artist joint custody of the characters; but the issue was further complicated by the fact that, in Gaiman's view, three later creations for the *Spawn* series (Dark Ages Spawn, Domina, and Tiffany) were derivative (a legal term) of the three earlier characters. The case is complicated further still because Gaiman's paternity right (the right to be acknowledged as an author) seems to have been set in tension against his right not to have a work credited to him, insofar as a comic series is subject not only to unique collaborative practices but also to ongoing corporate concerns.

That said, any study of novelistic hypertextuality must also take account of what we might call belated collaboration (or, less gently, enforced co-authoring): Seth Grahame-Smith's facetiously co-authored (with Jane

Austen) *Pride and Prejudice and Zombies* (2009) provides an infamous illustration of this type of authorship, even if it is in fact an extension of a prominent eighteenth-century tradition of textual engraftment, to use John Cleland's somewhat dismissive term in his anonymous review of an unofficial follow-up to Henry Fielding's *Tom Jones*, namely, *Tom Jones in His Married State* (both 1749): "[sequels are] spurious, mercenary ingraftments."[15] By reorienting the study of copyright and literary property in terms of the theory and practice of secondary authorship, we can seek to contextualize such value judgments more fully, and perhaps open up the fictional archive to include a larger body of work than is often allowed. We could also address certain blind spots in authorship studies. For instance, the English Short Title Catalogue defines *The Comical Adventures of Roderick Random and His Friend Strap* (1776) as an abridgment of Tobias Smollett's *Roderick Random* (1748) – is it merely an abridgment, though, or is it a sort of understated type of adaptation? Is it a derivative or a transformative work (to use the language of current US copyright law)? To what extent might the act of abridging more generally be considered a specific form of authorship? In the case of *Gyles* v. *Wilcox* (1741), Lord Chancellor Hardwicke explained that "abridgements may with great propriety be called a new book," lest we forget, and therefore outside of normal copyright restrictions.[16]

So-called supplementary writing can amount to a redaction or an overwriting from which a text might not recover, as happened with French literature's most famous fictional giants, Gargantua and his son Pantagruel, who now belong to Rabelais, author of the pentalogy *La Vie de Gargantua et de Pantagruel* (c. 1532–64), at the expense of the first author of the anonymous *Les grandes et inestimables chroniques du grand et énorme géant Gargantua* – or in a rivalrous sense, as in Fielding's contemptuous abbreviating of Richardson's *Pamela* (1740) as *Shamela* (1741). Some secondary texts actively seek to replace the original outright, as in the case of *The Life of Pamela* (1741), an early reboot of *Pamela* that distinctly relegated the first author to the position of the mere compiler of a dubious "other account."[17] A more recent publication, one that is decidedly not affected by copyright limitation, Lyndsay Faye's *Jane Steele* (2016) creatively toys with its status as a modern mimicry of a frequently rewritten Victorian classic: the narrator writes, "I have been reading over and over again the most riveting book titled *Jane Eyre*, and the work inspires me to imitative acts."[18] Imitation here signals a clear departure from the source, moving away from the infamously bathetic line "Reader, I married him" delivered at the dénouement of Charlotte Brontë's tale to a more violent confession upfront: "Reader, I murdered him." Sherri Browning Erwin's *Jane Slayre* (2010) performs the same trick, incidentally: "Reader, I buried him." In such cases, Faye, Browning Erwin, and countless others are not "rewriting" an established property so much as they are relocating it within a horizon of expectations shaped, in these examples, by recent trends in young adult Gothic and horror fiction.

Secondary authorship is not an invention of the copyright era. Arguably the most celebrated European example of belated collaboration is the thirteenth-century allegorical poem *Le Roman de la Rose*. Jean de Meun picks up the narration at the point at which the first author, Guillaume de Lorris, orphaned it about forty years previously, using the explicit marker "In this place . . . ." Sir John Suckling similarly recounts how he came across "an imperfect Copy" of *The Rape of Lucrece* to which he was adding his own "Supplement." "Thus far Shakespear," he notes in the margin. Like *Le Roman de la Rose*, Philip Sidney's *The Countess of Pembroke's Arcadia* was left unfinished at the time of the author's death in 1586. In the tenth edition of *Arcadia* appeared a counterfeit burlesque titled "A Remedie for Love." Incredibly, it remained there, falsely attributed to Sidney, in subsequent reprints until the 1950s. Popular works (or charismatic texts, to use Paul Budra and Betty A. Schellenberg's phrase) have always attracted subsequent authorial engagement.[19] Robert Henryson, the fifteenth-century Scottish makar, recalls reading by the fire one winter a book "Writtin be worthie Chaucer glorious, / Of fair Creisseid [*sic*] and worthie Troylus."[20] And he tells us that when he had finished reading the poem, which ends with Troilus mourning his faithless love but does not say what becomes of her, that he took up another book, in which he found "the fatall destenie / Of fair Cresseid" fully outlined. This latter book does not really exist – he's about to write it, *The Testament of Cresseid* (first published in 1532), as a sequel to Chaucer's poem. In this maneuver, Henryson pays homage to his forebear, propelling us back into the familiar text and moving it forward at the same time. Spenser's *Faerie Queene* (1590–96) instead unashamedly updates the "labors lost" in Chaucer's *The Squire's Tale*, a seemingly abandoned piece.

Some secondary works are playful homages, some are antagonistic reboots. In the preface to *The Old English Baron* (1778), Clara Reeve calls her novel "the literary offspring" of Horace Walpole's *The Castle of Otranto* (1764). William Godwin, by contrast, satirized the decadence of the cult of sensibility expressly by rewriting (or overwriting, perhaps) Henry Mackenzie's popular novella *The Man of Feeling* (1771) as *Fleetwood: or, The New Man of Feeling* (1805). Not merely does a secondary author knowingly encroach upon established literary estate, he or she can deceitfully mimic another author, corrupting the moral right not to have a work falsely credited to them. The anonymous author of *Tom Jones in His Married State* anxiously alerts readers to the fact that "HENRY FIELDING, *Esq; is not the* Author *of this Book, nor in any Manner concerned in its Composition or Publication*."[21] He nevertheless proceeds to give a recap of Fielding's characters (Mr. Blifil, "you have read, was covetous, proud, hypocritical, and malicious towards Mr. *Jones*") as though he has an equal stake in their fates. Secondary authorship, in short, might be viewed as a species of co-authorship, though often belated, or an invasive form of rewriting that seeks to challenge (sometimes outwardly, sometimes secretly) the original creator.

A Brief History of Proprietary Authorship

In a famously aggressive article written at the outset of the copyright era, Daniel Defoe fears that secondary authors could unfairly seize his literary offspring: "A Book is the Author's Property, 'tis the Child of his Inventions, the Brat of his Brain; if he sells his Property, it then becomes the Right of the Purchaser." If not, he continues, "'tis as much his own, as his Wife and Children are his own – But behold in this Christian Nation, these Children of our Heads are seiz'd, captivated, spirited away, and carry'd into Captivity, and there is none to redeem them."[22] Honoré de Balzac later relied on another familial metaphor when attacking dramatic adaptations of novels – a playwright, he said, would steal your materials, feeling as little guilt as if he had taken your wife. When Samuel Richardson heard that a continuation of his own *Pamela* was to be published before he had concluded the story, he described himself as the wronged party; his plan had been "[r]avished out of my Hands, and, probably my Characters depreciated and debased."[23] Implicit in these claims over literary property is an authorial complaint that goes back to at least Martial: plagiarism (from *plagiarius*, "kidnapper, slave-stealer"; see also Jack Lynch's chapter "Plagiarism and Forgery" in this volume).

Such claims also treat print culture as what Simon Stern calls an economy of scarcity: "Talk of misappropriation and pilfering suggests that texts are diminished through copying, as if the novelist who 'borrows' a plot has removed something from the book, leaving it incomplete."[24] Miguel de Cervantes made such a claim in the world's first novel (in the modern sense of the term), *Don Quixote* (1605): "Abundance, even of good things, prevents them from being valued; and scarcity, even in the case of what is bad, confers a certain value."[25] So he eventually kills his hero. In the final paragraph of *The Adventures of David Simple. Volume the Last* (1753), the darker follow-up to *The Adventures of David Simple* (1744), Sarah Fielding's narrator imagines that false sequels might attempt to drag her titular character back from the dead and prolong his sufferings further: "if any of my Readers chuse to drag *David Simple* from the Grave, to struggle again in this World, and to reflect, every Day, on the Vanity of its utmost Enjoyments, they may use their own Imaginations, and fancy *David Simple* still bustling about on this Earth." "But," she continues, "I chuse to think he is escaped from the Possibility of falling into any future Afflictions."[26] Fielding grants the author and the reader equal claims over her creation – though, in light of her speech, surely no one would be willing to put the long-suffering hero into harm's way yet again. David Simple belongs to everyone and no one, all the same.

Modern authors are no less protective. In Kurt Vonnegut's *Breakfast of Champions* (1973), the first-person narrator (often taken to be a fictional version of the author, with whom he happens to share a birthday) makes a point of stressing his artistic control over his characters: "I do know who invented Kilgore Trout. I did. I made him snaggle-toothed. I gave him hair, but I turned it white. I wouldn't let him comb it or go to a barber. I made him grow it long and tangled."[27] James Gill, representing the Evelyn Waugh estate, expressed such a view about author–character relations in 2003 when opposing Michael Johnston, author of the unauthorized *Brideshead Regained*: "You cannot just wander into someone else's property and take their characters."[28] Some estates, such as Daphne Du Maurier's, J. M. Barrie's, and Ian Fleming's, it must be said, have embraced "official" sequels (including Sally Beauman's *Rebecca's Tale*, Geraldine McCaughrean's *Peter Pan in Scarlet*, and William Boyd's *Solo*, respectively). But as David Roh rightly recognizes, "[p]rotected by law, author estates have little incentive to tolerate ideologically divergent takes on their works."[29] Lord Chancellor Northington had warned against such an occurrence back in the 1760s, when he remarked that it might be "dangerous to determine that the author has a perpetual property in his books, for such a property would give him not only a right to publish, but to suppress too."[30] Lawrence Lessig has become a powerful advocate for fewer controls: "The opportunity to create and transform becomes weakened in a world in which creation requires permission and creativity must check with a lawyer."[31] Or, to return to Stern, we might look to an economy of abundance, "a world of endlessly recyclable material, forever mutating into new variants 'original' enough to distinguish them from their precursors."[32]

Global copyright law largely focuses on individual stakeholders (typically "the creator" or "the inventor"). However, writing is a social product; as Adam D. Moore puts it: "individuals should not have exclusive and perpetual ownership of the works that they create, because these works are built upon society's shared knowledge" – indeed, the encouragement of learning is enshrined in the foundational 1710 Copyright Act.[33] Margaret Atwood's *The Penelopiad* (2005) will never displace Homer (nor does it seek to do so), but it does challenge his proprietary hold over the myths with which he is associated: "The story as told in *The Odyssey* doesn't hold water: there are too many inconsistencies. I've always been haunted by the hanged maids."[34] Daniel Levine's *Hyde* (2015) opens up an influential modern myth in cannily retelling Robert Louis Stevenson's *Strange Case of Dr Jekyll and Mr Hyde* (1886) from the perspective of the otherwise muted demonic alter ego. Levine treats this as a kind of tandem authoring when he thanks his forebear "for the use of his haunting yarn and his fantastic dream," which, he adds, "belongs, in the end, to us all" – indeed, his publisher literally gifts the earlier, out-of-copyright novella to the reader by binding it with Levine's own book.[35] What precisely is the status of collaboration, particularly when it is unannounced, enforced, or even posthumous? Can characters, plots, myths, or other storied properties be seized or borrowed in any legal sense?

Enforced collaboration gets played out in the courts if the original author is alive or otherwise represented. Pia Pera's *Lo's Diary* (*Diario di Lo* in the original Italian, 1995) purports to be the true journal of the titular character of Nabokov's *Lolita* (1955), a bestselling novel under copyright until at least 2030. The Nabokov estate, represented by the author's son, Dmitri, filed suit in 1998 in order to block an upcoming American edition of Pera's revisionary supplement. Leon Friedman, the lawyer representing Farrar, Straus & Giroux, claimed the new novel fell within fair use standards set by the Supreme Court. He lost the case. In the somewhat unusual settlement, Dmitri allowed Pera to publish her work subject to the allocation of some royalties (which were donated to PEN) and the inclusion of a preface publicly granting his permission for *Lo's Diary* to exist in print – and railing against writerly thieves ("Is *Lolita* to pay this price because it is too good, too famous?").[36] Limiting Pera's ability to profit economically from his father's work, Dmitri might be accused of allowing her to unsettle the original novel – after all, the new telling attends in great detail to Lolita's flagrant seductiveness, among other things. To solve the puzzle one might resort to a literary question: to what extent do the novels exhibit the same female character?

In the case of *Salinger* v. *Colting* (2009), similarly, J. D. Salinger filed suit in the United States against a Swedish author and publisher (Fredrik Colting, operating under the pen-name John David California) whom he claimed infringed upon the Holden Caulfield character of *The Catcher in the Rye* (1951) in a new novel titled *60 Years Later: Coming Through the Rye* (2009). The court sided with Salinger, noting that Colting had "reanimated" the teenaged anti-hero in the unlikely form of a septuagenarian narrator: "Mr. C has similar or identical thoughts, memories, and personality traits to Caulfield, often using precisely the same or only slightly modified language from that used by Caulfield."[37] Colting certainly adopts some Caulfieldisms ("and all," "phony") – but is it the same character or, to risk a tautology, a kind of fictional clone? Rather than taking Mr C as a grown-up iteration of the original creation, the court's ruling defines them as separate yet identical characters. The implications of such cases for authorship studies are far from clear. In a sense, these rulings garble Francis Hargrave's influential claim in *An Argument in Defence of Literary Property* (1774) that "a literary work *really* original, like the human face, will always have some singularities, some lines, some features, to characterize it, and to fix and establish its identity."[38] A subsequent reworking of any character, however close to the original (in terms of biographical particulars or vocabulary, and the like), is by necessity an imitation.

Many writers, following in the inky footsteps of Henry Fielding, have capitalized on the uncertainty arising out of the reuse of popular characters. *Shamela* – or *An Apology for the Life of Mrs. Shamela Andrews* – exposes the hidden vagaries of the so-called Virtue in Distress, Pamela Andrews.[39] That is, Fielding extensively tailors the original material of his notional hypotext, *Pamela*, in what Thomas Lockwood calls a "contemptuous abbreviation" of Richardson's novel.[40] Read as a challenge to proprietary authorship, we can more readily appreciate Fielding's bold use of a cut-and-pasting technique as a means of excavating the hypocrisy buried amid Richardson's own language. In Letter VI of *Shamela*, Mr. Booby's gratuitous invective – "Hussy, Slut, Saucebox, Boldface" – consists entirely of words used by his counterpart, Mr. B, throughout *Pamela*: "What a foolish Hussy you are . . . " (Letter XI), "I believe this little Slut has the Power of Witchcraft . . . " (Letter XXII), "by such a Sawcebox as you . . . ," "Very well, Boldface . . . " (both Letter XV). In Letter VI, Mr. Booby mock-bashfully sexualizes the girl's body ("I know not whether you are a Man or a

Woman, unless by your swelling Breasts"), an erotic reworking of Mr. B's contradictory claim that "I know not, I declare beyond this lovely Bosom, your Sex" at the point at which he confesses to harboring "the worst Designs" on her (Letter XXXII). Fielding's authorship is impressively passive to the point of being an unwriting rather than a rewriting of the source.

Like *Shamela, The Comical Adventures of Roderick Random and His Friend Strap* (notionally an abridgment of Smollett's *Roderick Random*) largely sticks with the language used by the first author. Whereas Smollett's opening captures the uncertainty of post-Union identity in Scotland ("I was born in the northern part of this united kingdom in the house of my grandfather, a gentleman of considerable fortune and influence, who had on many occasions signalized himself in behalf of his country"), the later text empties the material of the hero's loss of heritage, an integral theme in the book – "I was born in *Scotland*, in the House of my Grandfather, a Gentleman of great Fortune."[41] This is not to suggest that *Comical Adventures* merely shrinks the novel. On the contrary, it promotes fan favorite Hugh Strap to second billing and, at the conclusion of the story, rewards him with £200 and a job as a steward to the protagonist's father. It is, in short, both an unwriting and a rewriting. A self-titled "plagiarism," Kathy Acker's *Great Expectations* (1982) revisits the famous opening of Dickens's novel – the young protagonist's *lapsus linguae* ("Pip"), a reduction of his true name, Philip Pirrip – only in order to mock the very absurdity of self-naming ("My father's name being Pirrip, and my Christian name Philip, my infant tongue could make of both names nothing longer or more explicit than Peter. So I called myself Peter, and came to be called Peter").[42] The unwriting gesture made, the novella then leaps into Christmas 1978 and begins a dizzyingly creative journey of multifictional cannibalism. Less radically but no less forcibly, Jean Rhys's *Wide Sargasso Sea* agitates against another Victorian text, *Jane Eyre*. Although it crosses paths with Brontë's work (toward the end of Rhys's novel, Bertha Mason describes her attic room at Thornfield Hall, where we find her in the original), most of the action takes us into a different time and space, namely young Rochester's experiences in the West Indies, ahead of his marriage to the first Mrs Rochester. Here Bertha is renamed – or, rather, unnamed, revealing her true identity as Antoinette Cosway – ahead of her diminished life in England as the Madwoman in the Attic.

Many of the cases explored so far rework established property, often by revisiting specific phrases or events, sometimes at a remove. Another significant way in which writers have engaged with classical works is to interrogate the role of the primary authors, many of whom become characters, such as Foe (a fictive version of Defoe) in Coetzee's novel of that name, and Tobias Oates (a fictive version of Dickens) in Carey's *Jack Maggs*, a sideways-reboot of *Great Expectations*. In these secondary novels, the original author is depicted as a scribbling fraud who steals stories and struggles to tell tales – Jack Maggs, for one, is painfully aware that his life story has been "burgled, plundered, and he would not tolerate it."[43] For much of *Foe* (1986), Susan Barton, a survivor of a shipwreck near the island of the reclusive Robinson Crusoe (renamed "Cruso"), searches for an established author of some repute if low in means, Foe, in the hope that he will write the "true" story (*The Female Castaway*). Growing weary of ever finding the would-be chronicler, Susan frequently imagines his death ("you had starved in your lodgings and been given a pauper's burial") and even takes up the tools of his trade ("I sat at your bureau this morning [. . .] and took out a clean sheet of paper and dipped pen in ink – your pen, your ink, I know, but somehow the pen becomes mine while I write with it").[44] But, as Susan recognizes, Foe (and professional writers of the copyright era, by extension) is like a patient spider, sitting in a giant web, waiting for prey; "when we struggle in his grasp [. . .] he opens his jaws to devour us" – a dismissive, brilliant metaphor for authorial appropriation.[45]

Cruso, meanwhile, is quietly rewarded with a novel in his name (*Robinson Crusoe*) as he happily exists within the boundaries of the authored page ("It was as though he wished his story to begin with his arrival on the island"), a textual confinement against which Susan rebels. Foe also asks to record the story of the loss of Susan's daughter, but "I choose not to tell it," she reasons, "because to no one, not even to you, do I owe proof that I am a substantial being with a substantial history in the world."[46] "If there is no place in *Foe* for a mother-daughter reunion," as Radhika Jones argues, "it is because parentage in the novel – such as it exists – is exclusively patrilineal."[47] After all, Susan curtly informs the mysterious girl who claims to be her daughter that she is, oddly, "father-born," that is, a phantom character brought to life by the hack writer in order to trick Susan, so she suspects, into a forced reunion and hence a false narrative closure. *Foe* itself is father-born, a corrupted offspring that both supplants and prefigures the eventual telling of a novel published long ago, *Robinson Crusoe*.

In *Authors and Owners*, Mark Rose observes that the "distinguishing characteristic of the modern author, I propose, is proprietorship; the author is conceived as the originator and therefore the owner of a special kind of commodity, the work."[48] The examples briefly outlined here suggest a caveat to Rose's otherwise useful definition of proprietary authorship is needed: authors have long been, and continue to be, interested in interrogating those boundaries of literary property to a point at which we might suggest the metaphor itself induces authorial traction in a hypotext, that the imaginative act of redoing or supplementing takes on its own textual (if not a legal) reality within and around the original. Implicit in the original copyright term, as Rose recognizes, is the implication that a protected work, like any child, will eventually be emancipated.[49] It isn't clear what literary emancipation would look like, however, or who might be responsible for liberated characters.

Never-endings

Of all the major novelists in English, Jane Austen has attracted, and continues to attract, the most attention from professional sequelists. *Emma in Love* (1996) by Emma Tennant picks up the story four years from the wedding that closes *Emma* (1815). P. D. James's *Death Comes to Pemberley* (2011) is set six years after the events in *Pride and Prejudice* (1813). Jo Baker's *Longbourn* (2013) revisits favorite characters (Elizabeth Bennet and that "great tall fellow in the green," Mr. Darcy). Many novelists have balked at continuations, though. The eponymous hero of Charles Dickens's *Nicholas Nickleby* (1839) protests to a would-be adapter that "you take the uncompleted books of living authors, fresh from their hands [. . .] finish unfinished works, hastily and crudely vamp up ideas not yet worked out by their original projector." "Now," he rants, "show me the distinction between such pilfering as this, and picking a man's pocket in the street."[50] Fearful that other writers would capitalize on the rapid success of *Robinson Crusoe*, Defoe rushed out in the same year, 1719, a continuation that sought to complete the story for good, as the title indicates: *The Farther Adventures of Robinson Crusoe; Being the Second and Last Part of His Life*. In the preface to the latter work, Defoe made clear his thoughts on secondary authors, anticipating the complaint later played out by Dickens: "The Injury these Men do the Proprietor of this Work, is a Practice all honest Men abhor; and [the Author] believes he may challenge them to shew the Difference between that and Robbing on the Highway, or Breaking open a House."[51] Richardson similarly lamented "that a Writer could not be permitted to end his own Work, when and how he pleased without such scandalous Attempts of Ingrafting upon his Plan."[52]

The author's right to end his or her story where and how they choose cannot feasibly be inscribed into statutory law; nevertheless, proprietary authors have used a variety of strategies in their attempts to uphold control over the legacy of their works, which for present purposes we might divide into two broad groups: plotting a future beyond the book (in a self-contained epilogue or in the announcement of a forthcoming sequel or spin-off, for instance) or delivering a definitive conclusion such as major or multiple deaths. Fictional works often eschew a linear plotting from the cradle to the grave, of course, but the founding father of the modern novel, Cervantes, confidently insisted that killing off Don Quixote meant that "no one may dare bring forward any further evidence against him, for that already produced is sufficient."[53] Many authors dared. A better strategy, which he also employs, is to point out the inferior quality of a knock-off, thereby alerting the reader to what we now define as the author's integrity right: "you should bear in mind that this *Second Part of Don Quixote* which I offer you is cut by the same craftsman and from the same cloth as the *First*." Inferior craftsmen or illegitimate children: in both metaphors the rejection of secondary authorship is played out on the page.

Notes

1. Gérard Genette, *Palimpsests: Literature in the Second Degree*, trans. Channa Newman and Claude Doubinsky (Lincoln, NE: University of Nebraska Press, 1997), p. 207. Reproduced from *Palimpsests: Literature in the Second Degree* by Gérard Genette, translated by Channa Newman and Claude Doubinsky, by permission of the University of Nebraska Press. English translation copyright 1997 by the University of Nebraska Press. Copyright 1982 by Editions du Seuil.
2. For pertinent histories of copyright and literary property see Lionel Bently, Uma Suthersanen, and Paul Torremans, eds., *Global Copyright: Three Hundred Years Since the Statute of Anne, from 1709 to Cyberspace* (Cheltenham: Elgar, 2010); and Lyman Ray Patterson, *Copyright in Historical Perspective* (Nashville, TN: Vanderbilt University Press, 1968).
3. Quoted in David Saunders, *Authorship and Copyright* (London: Routledge, 1992), p. 31.
4. Peter Baldwin, *The Copyright Wars: Three Centuries of Trans-Atlantic Battle* (Princeton, NJ: Princeton University Press, 2014), pp. 15–16.
5. Roland Barthes, *Image – Music – Text*, trans. Stephen Heath (London: Fontana, 1977), p. 145; emphasis in the original.
6. Beverly Taylor, "Discovering New Pasts: Victorian Legacies in the Postcolonial Worlds of *Jack Maggs* and *Mister Pip*," *Victorian Studies*, 52.1 (2009), 95–105, p. 96; Ankhi Mukherjee, "Missed Encounters: Repetition, Rewriting, and

Contemporary Returns to Charles Dickens's *Great Expectations*," *Contemporary Literature*, 46.1 (2005), 108–133, p. 126.

7. Jean Rhys, *Letters 1931–1966* (Harmondsworth, UK: Penguin, 1985), p. 175.

8. See Elizabeth F. Judge, "Kidnapped and Counterfeit Characters: Eighteenth-Century Fan Fiction, Copyright Law, and the Custody of Fictional Characters," in *Originality and Intellectual Property in the French and English Enlightenment*, ed. Reginald McGinnis (London: Routledge, 2009), pp. 22–68.

9. Christian Moraru, *Rewriting: Postmodern Narrative and Cultural Critique in the Age of Cloning* (Albany, NY: State University of New York Press, 2001), p. 4.

10. While I shall attend to a long and thin history, from the eighteenth century to the present day, Paul K. Saint-Amour has made a notable contribution to the study of the impact of copyright on the literary imagination in the period 1830–1930: Paul K. Saint-Amour, *The Copywrights: Intellectual Property and the Literary Imagination* (Ithaca, NY: Cornell University Press, 2003).

11. Linda Hutcheon with Siobhan O'Flynn, *A Theory of Adaptation*, 2nd edn (London: Routledge, 2013), p. xv.

12. Julie Sanders, *Adaptation and Appropriation* (London: Routledge, 2006), p. 158.

13. Quoted ibid., p. 158.

14. On dramatic authorship and literary property, see Paulina Kewes, *Authorship and Appropriation: Writing for the Stage in England, 1660–1710* (Oxford: Clarendon Press, 1998).

15. Quoted in Natasha Simonova, *Early Modern Authorship and Prose Continuations: Adaptation and Ownership from Sidney to Richardson* (London: Palgrave Macmillan, 2015), p. 195.

16. On abridgments, see Ronan Deazley, *On the Origin of the Right to Copy: Charting the Movement of Copyright Law in Eighteenth-Century Britain (1695–1775)* (Oxford: Hart, 2004), pp. 79–85.

17. See Thomas Keymer and Peter Sabor, *"Pamela" in the Marketplace: Literary Controversy and Print Culture in Eighteenth-Century Britain and Ireland* (Cambridge: Cambridge University Press, 2005), pp. 51–52.

18. Lyndsay Faye, *Jane Steele* (Croydon, UK: Headline Review, 2016), p. 3.

19. Paul Budra and Betty A. Schellenberg, "Introduction," in *Part Two: Reflections on the Sequel*, ed. Budra and Schellenberg (Toronto: University of Toronto Press, 1998), pp. 3–18, p. 6. See also Debra Taylor Bourdeau and Elizabeth Kraft, eds., *On Second Thought: Updating the Eighteenth-Century Text* (Newark: University of Delaware Press, 2007).

20. Robert Henryson, *The Testament of Cresseid and Other Poems* (London: Penguin, 1973), p. 20.

21. *The History of Tom Jones the Foundling, in His Married State* (London: J. Robinson, 1749), preface.

22. Daniel Defoe, *Review* (2 February 1710). In Joseph Loewenstein, *The Author's Due: Printing and the Prehistory of Copyright* (Chicago: University of Chicago

Press, 2002), Loewenstein convincingly shows that authorial assertions of property had grown common since at least the days of Francis Bacon and Samuel Daniel.

23. *Selected Letters of Samuel Richardson*, ed. John Carroll (Oxford: Clarendon Press, 1964), p. 43.

24. Simon Stern, "'Room for One More': The Metaphorics of Physical Space in the Eighteenth-Century Copyright Debate," *Law and Literature*, 24.2 (2012), 113–50, p. 119.

25. Miguel de Cervantes, *Second Part of the Ingenious Gentleman Don Quixote of La Mancha*, 1615, ed. Joseph R. Jones and Kenneth Douglas, trans. John Ormsby (New York: Norton, 1981), p. 417.

26. Sarah Fielding, *The Adventures of David Simple*, 1744–53, ed. Malcolm Kelsall (Oxford: Oxford University Press, 1994), p. 432.

27. Kurt Vonnegut, *Breakfast of Champions*, 1973 (London: Vintage, 2000), p. 32.

28. Quoted in Nicola Solomon, "Character Reference: Protecting and Exploiting Rights in Characters," *The Author* (Spring 2016), 19–21, p. 19.

29. David Roh, *Illegal Literature: Toward a Disruptive Creativity* (Minneapolis, MN: University of Minnesota Press, 2015), p. 28.

30. Mark Rose, *Authors and Owners: The Invention of Copyright* (Cambridge, MA: Harvard University Press, 1993), p. 94.

31. Lawrence Lessig, *Free Culture: How Big Media Uses Technology and the Law to Lock Down Culture and Control Creativity* (New York: Penguin, 2004), p. 173.

32. Stern, "Room for One More," p. 119.

33. Adam D. Moore, "Concepts of Intellectual Property and Copyright," in *The Book: A Global History*, ed. Michael F. Suarez, SJ and H. R. Woudhuysen (Oxford: Oxford University Press, 2013), pp. 182–196, p. 194.

34. Margaret Atwood, *The Penelopiad* (Edinburgh: Canongate, 2005), p. xxi.

35. Daniel Levine, *Hyde: A Novel* (New York: Mariner Books, 2015), p. 306.

36. Pia Pera, *Lo's Diary*, 1995, trans. Ann Goldstein (New York: Foxrock, 1999), p. ix.

37. Quoted in Samuel J. Coe, "The Story of a Character: Establishing the Limits of Independent Copyright Protection for Literary Characters," *Chicago-Kent Law Review*, 86.3 (2011), 1305–29, p. 1315.

38. Francis Hargrave, *An Argument in Defence of Literary Property* (London: W. Otridge, 1774), p. 7.

39. For detailed textual comparisons, see Charles B. Woods, "Fielding and the Authorship of *Shamela*," *Philological Quarterly*, 25.3 (1946), pp. 248–72.

40. Thomas Lockwood, "*Shamela*," in *The Cambridge Companion to Henry Fielding*, ed. Claude Rawson (Cambridge: Cambridge University Press, 2007), pp. 38–49, p. 41.

41. Tobias Smollett, *Roderick Random*, 1748, ed. Paul-Gabriel Boucé (Oxford: Oxford University Press, 1999), p. 1; *The Comical Adventures of Roderick Random and His Friend Strap* (London: H. Turpin, 1776), p. 3.

42. Kathy Acker, *Great Expectations: A Novel* (New York: Grove Press, 1982), p. 5.

43. Peter Carey, *Jack Maggs* (London: Faber and Faber, 1997), p. 32.

44. J. M. Coetzee, *Foe* (London: Penguin, 1986), p. 107, 67.
45. Ibid., p. 120.
46. Ibid., p. 131.
47. Radhika Jones, "Father-Born: Mediating the Classics in J.M. Coetzee's *Foe*," *Digital Defoe*, 1.1 (2009), 45–69.
48. Rose, *Authors and Owners*, p. 1.
49. Mark Rose, "Copyright and Its Metaphors," *UCLA Law Review*, 50.1 (2002), 1–15, p. 14.
50. Charles Dickens, *Nicholas Nickleby*, 1839, ed. Paul Schlicke (Oxford: Oxford University Press, 2008), p. 633.
51. Daniel Defoe, *The Farther Adventures of Robinson Crusoe; Being the Second and Last Part of His Life* (London: W. Taylor, 1719), preface.
52. Quoted in Keymer and Sabor, *"Pamela,"* p. 56.
53. Cervantes, *Second Part*, p. 417.

CHAPTER 25

Censorship

Trevor Ross

Censorship is the suppression of speech that not everyone considers harmful. Public discourse is regulated through a multitude of mechanisms, from conventions of syntax and address, codes of civility, and professional protocols to laws against defamation, fraud, and theft of intellectual property. Michel Foucault and Pierre Bourdieu have likewise alerted us to how orthodoxies of thought may become so entrenched that they go unrecognized as controls on speech.[1] For these theorists, such tacit acceptance that some speech has already been silenced represents the most insidious form of censorship. Yet their arguments neglect the most important qualitative dimension in how censorship is usually perceived, which is precisely that censorship is experienced as a prohibition. Whether it is an author stymied by state licensers or too afraid to speak plainly, a reader precluded by the church from obtaining heretical or erotic material, or a publisher threatened with violence over the dissemination of satires and caricatures, all confront censorship as a constraint on their liberty. And even if many people believe the prohibition to be just, the point is that the practices of censorship are always sites of conflict over the scope, purpose and legitimacy of the prohibition.

Literary authorship has been the subject of some of the most publicized contests over censorship, and not simply because the works at issue have often been by famous writers. Attention has been drawn to contests involving literary works because, more so than in cases involving other kinds of speech, there is a lack of consensus as to the nature of the harm that may result from either these works or the censoring of these works. Literary authors have not suffered the displeasure of the authorities with the same frequency or severity of penalty than have investigative reporters, political dissidents, or religious controversialists. Yet however much harm literature is thought to cause by comparison with other discourses, literary authors stand out from other public writers in the variety of offenses of speech and representation they have been accused of committing.

Furthermore, and again in a way that sets them apart from writers of most other public genres, literary authors have not had the benefit of a single defense with which to answer these accusations. Journalists and scientists may affirm that the free flow of knowledge is so vital to social and intellectual progress that it ought not, within reason, be impeded in deference to political, economic, or moral interests. Literary authors, by contrast, have had to contend not only with claims that their writings are liable to offend one or more of these interests and may do so in diverse ways, but equally with varying available rationales for either permitting or banning the publication of their works in the face of such claims. More so than in the past, the stakes in contests over literary censorship are unsettled because literature has become a testing ground for arguing over both the role that language and the imagination perform in enabling social value and, more acutely, the felt limits that people are willing to tolerate on what they can say and how they can say it. I will consider this in relation to the three main sets of harms that writings are believed capable of producing.

Public Order Harms

Within democracies no censorship is assumed to pose a greater threat to liberty than restrictions on the press, whose reporting of information and opinion allows for open and robust debate upon which popular sovereignty depends. Only in moments of crisis, such as wartime, it is possible for governments to obtain broad support for curtailing press freedoms. At the same time, modern democratic thinking assumes that no speech is more dangerous to public order than what it perceives as a defining opposite to the knowledge the press provides, namely propaganda, disinformation, "fake news," or other verbal coercion designed to undermine the rationality of public debate. Of late, the threat of coercion has seemed to many people to have increased exponentially with the spread of electronic media, prompting a groundswell of reaction in favor of greater policing through Internet filters, chat room monitors, and moderating algorithms on social media sites. Similarly, some jurisdictions have instituted laws against a newly recognized category of coercion commonly referred to as hate speech. Though hate speech may appear a moral offense in that, as some argue, it compromises the dignity of persons by denigrating their identity, the purpose of hate speech is ideological as its purveyors seek above all to assert the supreme authority of their speech by denying equality and a political voice to other peoples.[2]

Guiding this sensitivity to socially harmful speech is the belief that it has the potential to overwhelm the public's capacity for deliberative judgment, manipulate people into embracing sentiments they might not otherwise assent to, and override a democratic plurality of opinion with groupthink and rage. Whether of political, religious, or other import, coercion agitates the public mind though slanted or distortive speech whose tendentiousness may not be readily apparent because it is delivered in distractingly affecting language, deceitfully presented as truthful and non-partisan, or so aggressively promulgated as to drown out opposing points of view. By this standard, the virulently racist and antisemitic novel *The Turner Diaries* by the American white supremacist William Luther Pierce or the militaristic, ultra-nationalist poetry of the convicted Serbian war criminal Radovan Karadžić constitute literary hate speech that must be banned lest its dissemination incite violence or open the floodgates to more such propaganda. By this same standard, Salman Rushdie's *The Satanic Verses* – however outrageous its mockery of Islam – does not fall to the level of hate speech because, as a comic novel dealing with the immigrant experience of mediating between cultures, its representation of identity and its magical realist irony are too complex to inspire an irrational conformity of opinion.

The trouble with this standard is that it assumes that speech and representation can have great power but leaves unclear how the public can avoid becoming enslaved to this power, such that under its influence we begin to accept as orthodoxy – or complexity, for that matter – what was formerly condemned as offense. A major reason why heated debates over censorship have attended cases like Rushdie's, quite aside from the brutality of the *fatwa*, is that these cases bring to the fore a kind of ambivalence about forceful words and what this force entails for our capacity for self-governance. The ambivalence reflects the fact that there is no readily identifiable way to reconcile belief in the power of the people with recognition of the power of words to change people's minds.

In non-democratic states, including all pre-modern polities, control of the public mind is the desired end of all speech. What renders an utterance unacceptable is not its coerciveness but its content and the ends to which it is directed. Writers are expected to use the persuasive power of their words to instill virtue and faith, honor the community and its leaders, and make eternal truth pleasing and memorable to audiences; these are among the functions that literary writings are felt to perform supremely well, which accounts for the high esteem that poets enjoy in authoritarian regimes like Iran and Russia. Writers who run afoul of these expectations are felt to abuse the license that has been granted to them to speak, and they may be punished for their presumption even as their works remain in circulation. The emperor Augustus banished Ovid from Rome, and the Senate under his successor Tiberius had the minor poet Clutorius Priscus tried and executed for having composed a premature elegy on the emperor's son, but neither had the poets' offending verses officially proscribed.[3] The writer's crime in speaking out of turn is presumed to have effects as injurious to public order as the challenge to authority that may result from the writer's promulgation of heterodox ideas.

The harm is believed the same in either case. Whether attracting converts to radical beliefs, circulating reports that contradict official accounts, or presuming to speak freely and thereby encouraging others to do the same, the writer imperils social harmony by breeding a disabling diversity of opinion. The dissemination of unauthorized ideas as much as the ideas themselves loosens people from the bounds of conscience and certitude. And while some, like Plato, might fear that poetry had a dangerous power to unhinge the mind from the constraints of reason, literary authors in these regimes are not necessarily more subject to persecution for the affectivity of their language than writers of religious, political, or historical polemic. Even otherwise uncontroversial and formally understated writings may be denounced if they are felt insufficiently declarative of official conformity: the novels of Shen Congwen were burnt, and their printing plates destroyed, shortly after the communist takeover in China because his apolitical regionalist fiction was considered reactionary.[4] Offending writers in these regimes may protest the innocence of their intentions or decry the unjustness of the sentence pronounced on their person, yet what is unavailable to them is any recognized defense that either their works can have no bad tendency or the suppression of these works will be detrimental to learning. Only once some measure of diversity begins to be accepted as a condition of liberty is it possible for an author like John Milton, in his *Areopagitica* (1644), to contend that some noxious ideas ought to be left uncensored so that people might learn to perceive and withstand them, though even he drew a line at allowing the circulation of Catholic doctrine.

The long revolution for press freedoms that Milton's tract helped to augur necessitated a reorganization of discourse as a response to the problem of forceful words and their effect on people's judgment. Commentators in Britain and France signaled the change at the end of the eighteenth century by adapting two old words to identify a pair of newly delimited categories of public utterance. The first word, "propaganda," was to be the name for the inappropriate use of rhetorical speech to influence public opinion. The second word, "literature," was the new designation for the old rhetorical category of poetry, which was henceforth to be divided off from rhetoric as a category of affective and imaginative speech that anyone could write, on any subject and in any style, and through which readers could experience the force of words and fiction directly, without state-enforced safeguards yet equally without threat of coercion. Though poets, Immanuel Kant declared in his *Critique of Judgment*, relied on artful devices and stories similar to those orators used, poetry was the greatest of all arts whereas rhetoric was of dubious value. The machinery of persuasion, he recommended, was not to be tolerated in settings where the public met to decide the common good since its application in winning minds over would undermine the integrity of the proceedings. Poetry, by contrast, did not take control of the mind but expanded it by setting the imagination free. By presenting us the full power of its language and representation, it offered us the opportunity to exercise our faculties fully and independently of outside determination, yet, Kant insisted, it could so only on condition of remaining mere aesthetic play that neither roused us to action nor summoned us to a cause.[5]

Ever since, literary authors have felt compelled to disavow using art in the service of power. In being free to write about anything and in any form, they help to emancipate us from received limits on the sayable and imaginable. In transforming us, their work may also paradoxically help us to redefine ourselves continually as a culture. They cannot, however, seek to determine what these limits or the culture ought to be without thereby infringing on people's right of self-determination. If their work is to serve as proof of the mind's freedom over the power of words, literary authors must abjure coercion and affirm a commitment to preserving art's autonomy. Writers of politically liberal persuasion, whether working under repressive regimes or in democratic states, feel especially compelled to declare an aversion to using their art to intervene directly in politics. For André Brink, whose 1973 novel *Kennis van die Aand* (*Looking on Darkness*) was the first Afrikaans book to be banned by the South African government, all great art is offensive but it cannot be great if it offends in order to effect social change. It will defeat the state only by outlasting it, Brink declared, and it will endure only if the writer refrains from deploying verbal weaponry akin to the state's and does "not even try to think in terms of immediate, practical consequences." Similarly, for George Orwell, who encountered what he called "veiled censorship" in struggling to find a publisher for *Animal Farm*, the writer must observe the "frontier" between literature and propaganda, and, as difficult as it is to remain detached from contemporary events, must realize that "you cannot really sacrifice your intellectual integrity for the sake of a political creed – or at least you cannot do so and remain a writer."[6]

Unenforceable as a standard for distinguishing licit speech from coercion, the artist's renunciation of power is no credible defense against the charge that a work has disturbed the peace. It is nonetheless a symbolic gesture that literary authors often make in response to these charges, as though merely insisting on their right of free expression were insufficient as security against censorship. The wages of censorship may not be as high in democracies as they are in other societies, where penning a squib on the sovereign could lead to the pillory or scaffold. Yet where the unfettered circulation of knowledge is considered essential to public decision-making, the peculiar nature of literary writing renders the case for its public value more difficult to mount. In defending their work, literary authors have to respect the public's judgment, as all writers must, while also upholding the potential of their art to move people, provoke them into imagining new things, keep them open to openness as much as help them define themselves as a people. Affirming the priority of art over swaying opinions has become for these writers a way of showing deference to the public's autonomy rather than to the censors who serve the public. José Saramago went into self-imposed exile in protest against what seemed to him an act of censorship when Portugal's ministry of culture, under pressure from the Vatican, withdrew its nomination of his 1991 novel *O Evangelho Segundo Jesus Cristo* (*The Gospel According to Jesus Christ*) for the European Literary Prize on the grounds that the novel did not represent but was instead divisive of the Portuguese people. That a novel can at various times divide and represent a people will not dissuade politicians from banning it, but for Saramago there is no question of the literary author fighting injustice by taking on a political role: "It's not a role. [. . .] The painter paints, the musician makes music, the novelist writes novels. But I believe that we all have some influence, not because of the fact that one is an artist, but because we are citizens. As citizens, we all have an obligation to intervene and become involved, it's the citizen who changes things."[7]

Property Harms

If few have written except for money, countless others have not for lack of it. More than any formal prohibition, financial restrictions have shaped the history of authorship. The illiteracy born of poverty, the caprices of patronage, the vagaries of the book market, the prejudices deterring women and the lower classes from making a living from writing, and the costs of time, space, research, and materials needed for writing have all constrained writers from saying what they have to say. Authors, it seems safe to say, censor themselves far more commonly to attract potential patrons, publishers, and readers than to avoid angering government or church officials. State censorship has regularly been enforced through limits on trade: the Stationers' Company in early modern England and the London theaters under the Licensing Act of 1737 were granted monopolies of publication and performance, respectively, on the condition that they submitted new work for vetting by ministry censors. Copyright statutes, first passed in the eighteenth century, uncoupled anti-piracy protection from pre-publication licensing, but at the price of requiring authors to abide by an economy of fair competition.

This economy is now the most prevalent system of legally enforced controls on public speech in capitalist societies. These controls permit private interests to take legal action against the publication of works that may cause them financial harm. Yet as they function to manage the uses of speech rather than to proscribe whole categories of offensive content or inflammatory utterance, these controls are not usually experienced as censorship, as interdictions on what can be said. Only in exceptional cases has their application been decried as private censorship pernicious in its chilling effect on public discourse. For example, it has become common practice to include rote disclaimers – about resemblances between characters and actual persons living or dead being purely coincidental – on the copyright pages of works of fiction or at the end of the credit rolls in films, television shows, and video games. Though not always taken seriously by the courts, these disclaimers are meant to anticipate possible allegations of defamation, a moral harm, but also increasingly the accusation that a work has infringed on an individual's rights of publicity, a property harm. In 2011, the Tolkien estate called for the destruction of all copies of *Mirkwood: A Novel About JRR Tolkien*, written by the Texas entrepreneur Stephen Hilliard, on the grounds that Hilliard's use of Tolkien as his novel's main character took "unlawful commercial advantage" of the estate's valuable property.[8] Hilliard launched a counter-suit in federal court, arguing that the estate's threat of legal action endangered free speech by potentially stifling the creation of works on historical persons. The claim was withdrawn after Hilliard agreed to release the novel with the disclaimer that his work was not endorsed by the estate.

Hilliard had the means to challenge the action. In other cases, powerful commercial interests have successfully petitioned lawmakers and the courts to have their privileges extended in ways that have progressively narrowed the range of allowable uses or "fair dealing" of protected material. Many jurisdictions now recognize the moral right of authors to object to alterations of their work that they consider prejudicial to their reputation. Entertainment conglomerates and authors' estates have similarly campaigned to have the terms of copyright protection lengthened, allowing them to exercise ongoing authority over not only the commercial but the more broadly cultural reproduction of works whose importance is already well established. Some estates have sought to preserve the prestige of their intellectual properties from being "diluted" through quotation in new contexts, and to do so for reasons that have seemingly little to do with concerns over lost profits or honor. Notoriously, following the 1995 extension of European copyright to seventy years, James Joyce's grandson, Stephen, announced that he would no longer grant permissions to scholars wishing to quote from his grandfather's work and refused to allow the singer Kate Bush to include portions of Molly Bloom's soliloquy from *Ulysses* in a song. The trustees of the Yeats estate similarly blocked the release of Van Morrison's 1985 album *A Sense of Wonder* because they objected to his rock version of the poem "Crazy Jane on God," believing that Yeats's poetry ought to be set only to classical music.[9] It is difficult to see how Bush and Morrison were engaging in unfair competition that might have caused financial harm to the estates, since in paying homage to canonical authors through a popular medium, these artists were helping to broaden the market for these authors' works. Yet, with the weakening of the concept and scope of the public domain, it has become equally difficult to say why adaptations like Bush's or Morrison's might serve the public interest in a way that ought to take precedence over private rights.

A similar process of attenuation is happening to the public commons, that is, the realm of what is not copyrightable. Copyright protects a work's expression while permitting authors to share ideas, facts, themes, plots, and literary techniques, in addition to the entire cultural vocabulary of words, conventions, and beliefs that are the raw ingredients of writing. Recently, courts have begun to grant authors publicity rights in their fictional characters and settings, in the belief that authors should be able to deter others from capitalizing on the name value of their creations. A notable current manifestation of this trend among authors to seek greater safeguards against admirers invading their market is in relation to the phenomenon of fanfiction. Though clearly derivative of its source material, fan fiction is not in any conventional sense in competition with this source, being posted online by its creators with no intent to detract attention from the original author's work and usually with no expectation of monetary gain. To some authors, fan fiction is welcome publicity. To others, it debases their creations. It may seem reasonable for an author like J. K. Rowling to warn her fans against damaging her Harry Potter franchise by depicting her fictional child protagonists in erotic situations. But when the fantasy writer Robin Hobb denounces fan fiction as "personal mas-turbation fantasy" that "isn't healthy for anyone," or when the fantasy novelist Diana Gabaldon argues that "a terrible lot of fan-fic is outright cringe-worthy and ought to be suppressed on purely aesthetic grounds," it may seem that rather different categories of harm are being invoked in support as much of proprietary rights as of a new order of censorship protecting fans from themselves.[10]

Authorial rights have always been defined in accordance with ideological assumptions about the nature and value of creativity. For almost a century after the passage of the first copyright statute in 1710, English courts gave wide latitude to derivative works including abridgments, sequels, and translations. They did so on grounds of public utility, believing that it aided learning to have important ideas rendered in accessible versions and recognizing that imitation was central to much education, particularly training in rhetoric and the arts. Authors were to be rewarded not for creating knowledge but for rendering it persuasive. Only once publishers began complaining about specific types of infringement, such as the copy-ing of maps and charts, did it become incumbent on their advocates to argue for a new legal standard of creativity to determine whether a work was sufficiently transformative to qualify as original. This standard pre-supposed that the primary aim of copyright was not to encourage learning, as the original statute had declared, but to maximize diversity of thought and expression. Whereas previously censorship had enforced conformity of opinion, copyright was now expected to facilitate the opposite.

Since its mechanism of incentive has remained, however, the awarding of monopoly privileges to distinctive expression, the law has ever since promoted the creation of proprietary brands at the expense of the unifying features of culture, such as the possibility that novels like Saramago's may represent a people as much as dissent from prevailing attitudes. Fair use exemptions to the standard are granted only for writing that is demon-strably divergent in purpose and sentiment from the original source, such as criticism and commentary. The law in France and more recently Britain allows parodies, pastiches, and caricatures only if there is evidence of comic intent, as if differences of opinion were more definitively expressed through humor than seriousness. No one, however, may publish a pastiche of an author's work to mock something other than the work. The law does not recognize how a work, well before its copyright lapses, may become a reference point for the public, a cultural document whose meaning and value is stable enough that it may be quoted for new purposes without loss to its integrity. The common culture is not, in principle, amenable to branding. Brand protection may even influence how works in the public domain are treated, as in the recent case of major corporations withdrawing their sponsorship of a controversial adaptation of Shakespeare's *Julius Caesar* in New York.[11] When a corporation pulls its support for a literary festival or theatrical company out of fear that its brand will be tainted by association with scandalous material, it is difficult to come up with arguments that the action is not in the corporation's best interest. The corporation has a right to select what it sponsors and, in not precluding anyone else from patronizing the same event, its action does not amount to censorship. The action is nonetheless bound to have a chilling effect, so it feels like a prohibition, one not so much on any work in particular as on the arts in general.

Private Harms

Peremptory censorship, the banning or redacting of books before they are published, presupposes that the public cannot be trusted to deal with harmful material. In many jurisdictions, obscenity, blasphemy, sedition, and other crimes of speech are classed as public order offenses that the state must police preemptively to prevent offending material from having a volatile effect on the public sensibility. Some anti-pornography campaigners in America and elsewhere have similarly argued that obscenity is as coercive an incitement to violence as hate speech and so ought to be prohibited outright. Censorship is also practiced on the assumption that exposing members of the public directly to bad ideas may be too much for their private consciences to handle. Unless these ideas are mediated through generalized language and accompanied by statements of official condemnation, publishing them, it is feared, will give them a legitimacy that may tempt readers into acting on those ideas. The Irish Republic outlaws any book that advocates the procurement of abortion or miscarriage. Officials in late imperial Japan scoured pulp fiction for details on how to commit a crime. Taboo subjects in Saudi Arabia include alcohol and pork. Editors in East Germany advised authors that plots involving suicide or extra-terrestrials would not get past the censors.[12]

In states without peremptory censorship, the public decides which material is harmful and why. The public enacts consensual norms, either by
acting as jurors who speak for these norms in passing judgment on offenders
or by electing representatives to boards and legislatures who apply these
norms in filtering and prosecuting this material. Believing that the public has
a right to determine what may be damaging to it creates a problem, however,
of perspective: for the public to suffer harm, it must be inside the sphere of an
offending work's malign influence, yet if it is inside this sphere, then it is not
clear how it is in a position to judge or even recognize the harm. In 1727,
Edmund Curll became the first person to be convicted for obscenity under
the common law. The judges in the case believed that the erotic novel Curll
had printed was of "a general immoral tendency" made worse by the fact the
"book goes all over the kingdom."[3] Obscenity, they reasoned, divided the
public by making its members alternately its audience and victim. Yet it was
not clear from their reasoning why a work of general immoral tendency
should necessarily have a divisive rather than a uniform effect on the public.
A new conformity of universal depravity would have been for the judges the
ultimate triumph of evil, incalculably worse than any degree of social
discord. But there was nothing in their rationale for the precedent they
were establishing to explain how the public could act as steward of its moral
virtue if it could not always resist obscenity's corrupting tendency.

The solution later lawmakers devised to address the problem was to
characterize obscenity and other offenses as not wholly public in their
nature and effect. The offenses were deemed to harm people mainly in
their private circumstances and relations or to affect only certain people,
like the young who were yet incapable of informed consent. The public in
this conception could rule on these offenses because it occupied a moral
space at a remove from a private realm where much of the damage was
thought to occur. From this perspective, the public could identify offensive
speech as private knowledge or opinion that was publicly disseminated
with such directness that it deformed individuals to the point of impairing
their capacity to participate fully in public life.

This defining opposition of public authority and private knowledge,
however, laid the groundwork for the liberal counter-argument that the
public was made up of individuals whose right to their own beliefs and
preferences, including possibly a private taste for pornography, was to be
protected under the laws the public enacted. The counter-argument, first
essayed in pleas for religious tolerance, configured the public as a decision-
making body so various in its composition that no individual set of beliefs
could conceivably damage the whole, unless, in acting on those beliefs,

a person threatened this diversity. By the end of the eighteenth century, the counter-argument and the principle of popular sovereignty it presupposed had become sufficiently compelling that, for the first time, lawmakers in England permitted juries to rule on the libelousness of allegedly seditious publications. Thereafter, juries in several jurisdictions were given responsibility for deciding the criminality of blasphemous and ultimately obscene publications. Today, a majority of Western nations have legalized pornography and begun to repeal their laws against blasphemy and seditious libel.

Throughout the history of this change, literary authors have played a central role.[14] Literary writing has always been valued as a creative and expressive art, but from the mid-eighteenth century onward its verbal and fictive inventiveness was felt to put it at odds with conventional modes of public address. In direct correlation to the rise of the periodical press as the most ubiquitous medium of public knowledge, literature's expressiveness would be felt by many as best suited to the representation of private speech, perception, and behavior, in novels, short stories, lyric poems, life-writings, and domestic drama. The role of literary authorship was accordingly transformed, from one of teaching virtue delightfully to one of maintaining public recognition of a diverse realm of inner lives, individual styles, and personal choices, feelings, and fantasies. Literary authors made it possible for the public to know what went on in those private spaces where individuals exercised their liberty, and to understand how individuals might come to suffer injury to their sensibilities, but to know this without seeming to invade those spaces and encroach on its members' liberty. Still more broadly, one of the principal functions of literature, and the arts more generally, within modern democracies is to enable members of the public to experience forms of private knowledge and behavior that otherwise could not be treated in public unless mediated through generalized, impersonal, or scientific language. In enabling this, literature ensures the public's supreme right to know and keeps its discourse free and revisable by making it possible for its members to write publicly about anything in expressive, irrational, even indecent language without reasonable fear of being ejected from the public sphere.

Literary authors are thus implicitly tasked with producing works to serve as test cases in the public's continuing review of its threshold of harm. This threshold has progressively fallen in part because of the cultural importance attributed to these works by those who have sought to prosecute them, bowdlerize them for public consumption, and proscribe them from school libraries and curricula. The high-profile actions against the publication of *Madame Bovary*, *Ulysses*, *Lady Chatterley's Lover*, and others necessitated the introduction of aesthetic claims into the law, by which the transgressive affectivity alleged of these works, and the knowledge they presented of the qualitative dimensions of personal experience, could be re-evaluated as a formative influence on culture and the private sensibility that mere entertainment did not provide.[15] Literary works, it was supposed, made beneficial demands on readers in ways that, though they might not be readily appreciable or explicable in rational terms, were not any the less "serious." This criterion in turn would soon be dropped as redundant, with advocates for the best-known pornographic novel in English, John Cleland's *Memoirs of a Woman of Pleasure*, successfully defending it as "literature" on the basis solely of its author's exploit of sexual metaphor. By then, literature had seemingly fulfilled its purpose in helping the public adjust its sensitivity to sensuous language, and a private taste for erotica could henceforth be a lawful expression of diversity.

Words have hardly lost their power to hurt. Current debates over university speech codes, content restrictions on social media, and bandwidth throttling suggest a sharpening of conflict is happening between the public's commitment to free expression and the prerogatives of corporations and institutions to set internal protocols and protect themselves from scandal. A related realignment of the categories of public order and private harms is likewise underway as public attention focuses increasingly on cultural appropriation and other perceived threats to group identities. This realignment is prompting a corresponding change in literature's public purpose. To the extent that they are now assumed to articulate their identities of origin as much as their own interpretations of experience, literary authors are expected to render the nature of these threats appreciable to the public while also defining, if possible, a perspective for its members to occupy at once inside and outside these identities. Their writings may, as ever, represent a people and challenge the public, and in doing both at once they contribute to the ongoing evolution of the public's self-perception as a people. Yet, as evidenced by the recent controversy over trigger warnings in the teaching of writings that have a power to disturb, the public has not overcome its ambivalence over the force of words. Literary authors must, it appears, continue to aid the public in wrestling with this ambivalence.

Notes

1. Michel Foucault, *History of Sexuality, vol. I: An Introduction*, trans. Robert Hurley (New York: Pantheon, 1978), pp. 15–35; Pierre Bourdieu, *Language and Symbolic Power*, ed. John B. Thompson, trans. Gino Raymond and Matthew

Adamson (Oxford: Polity, 1992), pp. 137–159. Helen Freshwater reviews contemporary theories of censorship in Helen Freshwater, "Towards a Redefinition of Censorship," in *Censorship and Cultural Regulation in the Modern Age*, ed. Beate Müller (Amsterdam: Rodopi, 2004), pp. 225–45.

2. Jeremy Waldron sees hate speech as a dignitary harm, in *The Harm in Hate Speech* (Cambridge, MA: Harvard University Press, 2012). Heather Katherine McRobie argues against regulating literary hate speech in *Literary Freedom: A Cultural Right to Literature* (Alresford, UK: John Hunt, 2013).

3. Peter L. Corrigan, "Rome, Ancient," in *Censorship: A World Encyclopedia*, ed. Derek Jones (London: Fitzroy Dearborn, 2001), p. 2054.

4. Jenny Huangfu, "Roads to Salvation: Shen Congwen, Xiao Qian and the Problem of Non-Communist Celebrity Writers, 1948–1957," *Modern Chinese Literature and Culture*, 22.2 (2010), 39–87.

5. Immanuel Kant, *Critique of the Power of Judgment*, ed. Paul Guyer, trans. Paul Guyer and Eric Matthews (Cambridge: Cambridge University Press, 2000), pp. 203–05.

6. André Brink, "Skrywer en literatuur in die strydperk" (Writer and literature in the time of struggle), 1976, in *Literatuur in die strydperk* (Cape Town, South Africa: Human & Rousseau, 1985), quoted from trans. in J. M. Coetzee, "André Brink and the Censor," *Research in African Literatures*, 21.3 (1990), 61. George Orwell, "The Frontiers of Art and Propaganda," *The Listener*, 29 May 1941, rpt. in *The Collected Essays, Journalism and Letters of George Orwell. Volume II: My Country Right or Left 1940–1943*, eds. Sonia Orwell and Ian Angus (London: Secker and Warburg, 1968), p. 126.

7. Stephanie Merritt, "Still a Street-Fighting Man: Interview with José Saramago," *The Guardian,* 30 April 2006. On Saramago's history of conflict with the Portuguese government, see Sérgio C. Andrade, "Cronologia: As polémicas de José Saramago (actualizada)" (Chronology: The controversies of José Saramago, updated), *Pùblico*, 18 June 2010.

8. Dalya Alberge, "JRR Tolkien Novel *Mirkwood* in Legal Battle with Author's Estate," *The Guardian*, 26 Feb. 2011.

9. Gordon Bowker, "An End to Bad Heir Days: The Posthumous Power of the Literary Estate," *The Independent*, 6 Jan. 2012; Parke Puterbaugh, "Review of *A Sense of Wonder* by Van Morrison," *Rolling Stone*, 9 May 1985.

10. Robin Hobb, "The Fan Fiction Rant" (2005), www.robinhobb.com/rant .html, deleted by the author, available via the Wayback Machine, http://web .archive.org/web/20050630015105/http://www.robinhobb.com/rant.html; Diana Gabaldon, "Fan-Fiction and Moral Conundrums" (2010), http://voyage softheartemis.blogspot.com/2010/05/fan-fiction-and-moral-conundrums.html, deleted by the author, available via the Wayback Machine, http://web .archive.org/web/20100507173749/http://voyagesoftheartemis.blogspot.com/201 0/05/fan-fiction-and-moral-conundrums.html.

11. Liam Stack, "Et Tu, Delta? Shakespeare in the Park Sponsors Withdraw From Trump-Like *Julius Caesar*," *New York Times*, 11 June 2017.

12. Christine Bohan, "Censored: The 274 Books and Magazines Still Banned in Ireland Today," *The Journal.ie*, 21 May 2012; Jonathan Abel, *Redacted: The Archives of Censorship in Transwar Japan* (Berkeley: University of California Press, 2012), pp. 90–91; Trevor Mostyn, "Saudi Arabia," in *Censorship: A World Encyclopedia*, p. 2149; Sonja Fritzsche, *Science Fiction Literature in East Germany* (Bern: Peter Lang, 2006), pp. 90–91.

13. *Rex v.Curll* (Court of King's Bench, 1727), 2 Str. 288, rpt. in *English Reports* (Edinburgh: William Green and Sons, 1904), vol. 93, p. 851.

14. This paragraph is derived from a longer argument I develop in Trevor Ross, *Writing in Public: Literature and the Liberty of the Press in Eighteenth-Century Britain* (Baltimore, MD: Johns Hopkins University Press, 2018).

15. Marisa Anne Pagnattaro, "Carving a Literary Exception: The Obscenity Standard and *Ulysses*," *Twentieth Century Literature*, 47.2 (2001), 217–40; Charles Rembar, *The End of Obscenity: The Trials of Lady Chatterley, Tropic of Cancer and Fanny Hill* (New York: Random House, 1968); Elisabeth Ladenson, *Dirt for Art's Sake: Books on Trial from Madame Bovary to Lolita* (Ithaca, NY: Cornell University Press, 2007).

CHAPTER 26

Publishing and Marketing

Andrew King

This chapter thinks through the implications of authorship for publishing in terms of marketing over the last 150 years, mainly in the UK fiction industry. The UK Chartered Institute of Marketing does not define what marketing is, but the American Marketing Association describes it as "the activity, set of institutions, and processes for creating, communicating, delivering, and exchanging offerings that have value for customers, clients, partners, and society at large."[1] This does not imply that marketing lies entirely in the hands of marketers – or indeed of any one person or organization (such as a publisher): while marketers may devise strategies and objectives, the role of chance in the achievement of results is commonly recognized. Marketing, furthermore, goes well beyond the generation of advertising copy: it embraces product design, pricing, and targeted communications at specific times in particular places so as to manage relationships key for sales. The questions this chapter asks, therefore, concern what, in terms of authorship and publishing since the mid-nineteenth century, marketing activity has comprised, and what might be the activities, processes, and institutions that have both aided and constrained the creation, communication, delivery, and exchange of "offerings that have value."

At all times, it is vital to bear in mind who is marketing what to whom, when, and why. Even in its most basic form, the marketing chain in publishing is long, each link requiring different communications strategies: authors have traditionally marketed their texts to editors or publishers and more recently to agents. But then publishers market to wholesalers; wholesalers to retailers; retailers to potential purchasers (though some will differentiate this as "sales"); readers to potential readers. The direction of this chain is not as fixed as it was thirty years ago. Combining social media with resources like Lulu.com and Amazon's CreateSpace, authors can both publish and market their wares directly to readers. Electronic communications technology such as email means that authors themselves can far more easily arrange with retailers, book festivals and educational establishments to market their work as well as sell directly to readers. Such "disintermediation" – the cutting out of the middleman – is common, if rarely very successful in commercial terms, for the resources of large marketing departments are normally necessary to power a bestseller. Furthermore, as I shall describe toward the end of this chapter, readers can now, either actively or through their demographic profile, influence the development of products. How marketing communications take place and what effect they generate (if any) have dramatically changed from the mid-nineteenth century to today, but there are distinct continuities.

I focus on the marketing of prose fiction of the past 150 years mainly in the UK, for prose fiction is the largest sector of retail publishing. I shall not remain within the marketing category of the "literary," as I wish to show similarities as well as mark differences across market sectors as well as across the last 150 years. As we shall see, George Eliot's *Daniel Deronda* (1876) and Dan Brown's *The Da Vinci Code* (2003) have a surprising amount in common.

Are Authors Needed for Marketing?

If an author can be taken as a named body whose labor we consider to have produced a text and to whom the copyright of a text (at least at first) belongs by virtue of that labor,[2] in marketing terms, an author might have various functions that have little to do with the labor of writing: one thinks of ghost-written memoirs whose sole-named "authors" are celebrities or politicians. In 1957, John F. Kennedy won the Pulitzer Prize for a work on which, it seems, he had considerable help from his aide and speechwriter.[3] It was the Kennedy name that sold the book, not the invisible speech-writer's. Ninety years earlier, an 1867 article in the *London Review* discussed the implications of pseudonymity: "If one man can begin a novel and leave it to be finished by another, why cannot several men begin on various parts of a novel, let some skilful editor join the parts together, and put the name of Lady Caroline Lascelles to the whole?"[4] This, in turn, suggests that an author's name might signal to the consumer less an originating body than a repeatable narrative experience. The point of the *London Review* article is well exemplified by the fate of the nineteenth-century popular English novelist Charlotte Mary Brame (1836–1884), which has been well documented by Graham Law, Gregory Drozdz, and Debby McNally.[5] Late in the century, American publishers pirated Brame's work, renaming its author "Bertha M. Clay" (a name invented on the basis of Brame's initials in reverse) and even added the name to other titles. They found it sold very well. After Brame died, the New York dime-novel publishers Street & Smith began to pay local (male) staff writers to provide romances under the Clay signature, and took other publishers to court for using the signature they openly claimed to have invented. This suggests that, in marketing terms, rather than referring to an origin, an author's name is a marker of the reliability of a product offering experience of a certain kind: it is, in other words, a *brand*.

Until the late nineteenth century, an author's name was not always necessary to signal a brand in fiction publishing. Advertisements for books laid far greater stress on previous and repeat experiences ("a new novel by the author of . . ."). An author's name was simply a supplementary signal of a brand sent to carefully selected sectors of the public at varying times and in various densities according to a media plan. Timing, targeting, and iterability were more important than a name. Furthermore, the main promise of reliability was often contained in the name of the publishing house rather than in the author's, a practice that continued well into the twentieth century. In the mid-1950s, the Honorary Secretary of The Publishers' Advertising Circle, Sydney T. Hyde, complained that relying on a publisher's reputation was old-fashioned and ineffective,[6] but the huge success of publishers' book series throughout the twentieth century and beyond suggests its sustained vitality as an alternative and supplement to the promotion of individual authors or works.[7] If the foregoing seems too casually contrary to the considerable body of work that has been written on star authors and the manufacture of celebrity and "genius" in the nineteenth century and earlier, it is as well to remark the powerful difference between advertisements and reviews. It is the latter, not advertisements, that we turn to in literary and historical analysis, and they operate according to different discursive rules regarding authorship, almost always emphasizing authorial agency in determining the reliability and value of the individual product. Reviews, unlike most nineteenth-century book advertisements, emphasize individuality and the possession or lack of "genius."

Another alternative branding signal to author names comprises characters. Early novel series based on the same characters were not usually planned from the outset or commissioned by publishers as series. Typical in this regard are the American dime novels centering on Buffalo Bill described by Daryl Jones. Buffalo Bill was a character originated by "Ned Buntline" (Edward Zane Carroll Judson) in 1869, and quickly taken up by other writers.[8] Rider Haggard's Allan Quartermain and Ayesha novels, like Conan Doyle's Sherlock Holmes stories in the

Strand, were likewise responses to market demand (though with the author providing the additional material), as was the case with Agatha Christie's Miss Marple and Poirot novels and Raymond Chandler's Phillip Marlowe. In contrast, other character-based series were not led by the market: Anthony Powell's twelve-volume *Dance to the Music of Time* cycle (1951–1975) started with a contract for just two books; it continued because the author himself was interested and was able to convince his publisher Heinemann of the value of his work.[9] There were, of course, examples of planned and contracted series – Tolkien's *The Lord of the Rings* (1954–1955) would now be the best known – but they were rare.

It was only in the 1970s, when individual publishing houses started to be consolidated into giant multi-national media conglomerates, and the power of individual editors was supplanted by that of the marketing departments, that contracts for planned multi-volume series became more and more important, especially when tied in to multi-media deals. Over the last two decades, Stephenie Meyer's *Twilight* (2005–2008), Suzanne Collins's *The Hunger Games* (2008–2010), E. L. James's *Fifty Shades* (2011–2012), and George R. R. Martin's *A Song of Ice and Fire* (1996–) are exceptionally profitable examples, all with hugely lucrative media tie-ins, but there are many more only marginally less well-known series like Philip Pullman's *His Dark Materials* (1995–2000) and Terry Pratchett's *Discworld* (1983–2015). Such series are helpful for publishers as they can promote repeat purchase for a proportionally reduced marketing spend per item, and each component is (at least in theory) an automatic promotion for the others. If, in 1923, Stanley Unwin could claim that the major difficulty for publishers was that they were not manufacturers of standardized repeat-purchase products like soap,[10] the series is the next best thing.

Much of the foregoing can usefully be compared to a case in which publishers have actively sought to loosen branding from authorship and attach it to characters. In 2015 the Swedish publishing company Norstedt released *Det som inte dödar oss* ("That which does not kill us") by David Lagercrantz, a continuation of the Millennium series centering on the journalist Mikael Blomkvist and the hacker Lisbeth Salander.[11] Three novels with these characters had already appeared in Swedish with huge success in 2005 and 2006, all under the signature of the radical journalist Stieg Larsson, who had died in 2004. After Larsson's first novel was published in French, a Swedish film company, Yellow Bird, commissioned a well-known American translator, Steven T. Murray, to make a quick English-language version in order to attract a British scriptwriter to write a Swedish film adaptation. The translation was subsequently sent to several publishers and, in 2007, encouraged by the novel's success in Sweden and France, the veteran publisher Christopher MacLehose accepted the book as an early entrant in a new imprint he was creating for Quercus Books – with the condition that he could edit the translation. This angered Murray so much that he only agreed to appear as translator under a pseudonym.[12] The resultant English-language *The Girl* trilogy (... *with the Dragon Tattoo*, 2008, ... *who Played with Fire*, 2009, ... *who Kicked the Hornets' Nest*, 2009) went on to sell twenty-five million copies between 2005 and 2015 in the US alone,[13] and (to 2017) eighty-two million copies worldwide.[14] Meanwhile, much publicized court cases continued about who owned Larsson's estate, including his copyrights: his common-law partner or his blood relatives.[15] They became part of the publicity for the series, generating yet more print space – for, as the publisher Stanley Unwin well knew, the amount of space a text takes up in reviews and features is often more important than whether the reviews are friendly or hostile.[16]

The questions this example raises concern not only the old cherry of who the "author" was and who owns the intellectual property, but how much the author matters in terms of marketing. When Lagercrantz's continuation came out in English it was careful to maintain the branding of the previous, including the title – *The Girl in the Spider's Web* – and the format of the cover. As with Bertha M. Clay or "by the author of . . .," it was the kind of experience the texts offered that publishers believed was important to consumers, not the text's origin in the labor of particular bodies. This was signaled less by the author's name than by the similarities of title, typography, and cover image, and of course by key properties of the text: plot types, the logic and characteristics of a fictional world, characters, and (to a lesser degree) the style. If typographic prominence on the cover is anything to go by, *The Girl in the Spider's Web* was much more a "Lisbeth Salander novel" than a Stieg Larsson or David Lagercrantz. Unlike in the nineteenth-century case of Brame/Clay (and later, as when Conan Doyle failed to prevent Sherlock Holmes being used in other authors' fiction[17]), these textual properties now enjoy a legal status as trademarks. That in turn enables them to be franchised and to generate brand extensions: the various continuations and rewritings of Ian Fleming's James Bond constitute a famous and profitable example.[18] These textual properties have a life of their own liberated from an author as point of origin while – unlike most fan fiction – still within the control of the major players in the entertainment industries.[19]

Authorship and Relationship Marketing

Despite the contrary cases raised above, authorship continues to matter in the market, not least because it remains a *personal* promise of a specific kind of experience. Unlike a brand of toothpaste, an author's name offers a clearer indication both of a kind of relationship that a reader might have with the text, and of the reader's insertion into a social group. The promise of relationship and identity can be related to a genre (as when we read an "Agatha Christie") but it can also refer to something not obviously confined to one genre: a "Margaret Atwood," for example, promises to educate us through exquisite language in whatever genre she works.

Although Dickens had put a great deal of effort into personal reader engagement with his readings from the 1850s, he was an unusually early adopter, for promoting authors as people to whom readers could relate began in earnest only in the 1870s. This was the time when interviews with celebrities emerged in force: begun in 1876, Edmund Yates's "Celebrities at Home" series in *The World*, for example, included several writers. In such interviews, authors were supposedly writing/speaking as themselves rather than through the masks of characters or narrators, though of course their utterances, like the props of their homes, were as stage-managed as any fiction. It was also the time when author names began to be more prominent in advertising, and printing technology allowed for cheap reproduction not only of author photographs but of their hand-written signatures. By the 1890s, Henry James's "Death of the Lion," a story about a writer whose celebrity is of more interest than his life would seem only an exaggeration, not a fantasy. A decade later, many authors were fully in charge of what Richard Salmon called the "signs of intimacy."[20] Authors were offering apparently authentic and intimate relationships to their readers in which autobiography and fiction melded.

This notion recalls "relationship marketing," a strategy developed in the late 1970s concerned with building long-term loyalty to a brand.[21] Richard Bagozzi suggested that "experiences" between the buyer and seller – and buyer and product – consist above all of emotional states. From the marketer's point of view, these are preferably affection or admiration. Such emotions not only lead to brand loyalty but also to brand advocacy. "Relationship marketing" precisely describes what underlies the word-of-mouth advertising that publishers have long known to be the most reliable way of selling books. It necessarily relies on trust and crucially an interaction of authors with their readers. By the mid-1950s, "autograph parties," a practice that was first used in book marketing in the late 1940s in the USA, were being run by UK publishers in bookshops with scientific precision. Book signings are still liked by publishers not only because they personalize authorship as a body but also because signed copies are rarely returned from bookshops: instead, they find their way into Internet auction sites at higher prices.

One of the most established ways trust can be encouraged is through the bestseller list. Though originating as an aid to booksellers' stocking decisions in the 1890s, bestseller lists have become an implicit endorsement of product reliability. Entry in the lists is far more likely to result in greater advertising spend on a book: the reverse very rarely happens. Another perceived guarantor of quality is the literary prize, of which authors are the figureheads. Some book prizes occasion media spectacles both visual and verbal, usually rendered more newsworthy through the promotion of conflict somewhere along the decision chain. All the best-publicized prizes are for "literary fiction" and create what Joe Moran has called a "kind of premier league of bankable literary names" that determines "contemporary canon formation."[22] As James English has demonstrated, bestsellers no longer win literary prizes, of which there has been a huge proliferation since the 1980s.[23] Although winning a major prize will boost sales, it does so through a demonstration of what Bourdieu-influenced critics call "consecration": unlike the bestseller list, which celebrates commercial success, prizes endorse a book's aesthetic or cultural value. That said, authors are selected by publishing houses to be put forward for these prizes not only on the grounds of abstract literary quality; how personable and photogenic they are is very often another factor. In various ways, then, an author's body, not just their writing, can prove a key weapon in a marketing strategy.[24]

That not all authors are either good at or appropriate for face-to-face interactions is not necessarily a problem for marketing. Some authors deliberately eschew appearing in public, seeking instead to increase their value by cultivating an apparently rebellious opposite – an image of unapproachability and lack of interest in commercial success – even while they carefully manipulate the marketing of their work behind the scenes. Samuel Beckett, "the hottest literary property of the late twentieth century," was especially skilled at this. As several recent studies have shown, he carefully cultivated tastemakers and had them do his marketing for him based on a carefully calculated image of ascetic, troubled aloofness.[25]

The use of tastemakers – people prominent in the media or otherwise influential in target demographics, like book retailers – is by no means confined to the twentieth century or to the aesthetic *avant-garde*.

Publishing has long recognized that enlisting the support of tastemakers is more important than general advertising: tastemakers advocate a brand by validating the promise of a relationship between author and reader. Collectively, tastemakers provide publicity (rather than paid-for advertising) and create "buzz": recommendations by friends and other influencers such as celebrities and booksellers. In the nineteenth century, publishers would send pre-publication copies not only to newspapers, critics, major booksellers, and the principal lending libraries, but also to prominent public figures who they hoped might mention it to others. Blackwood made pronounced use of tastemakers in the "radical experiment" of serializing George Eliot's *Daniel Deronda* in monthly parts in 1876, sending unusually high number of 703 advance copies.[26] He also supplied newspapers with a "gossip paragraph" and primed *The Times* to print a glowing review just before the novel was published.[27] Searches in the British Newspaper Archive suggest that this resulted in over twenty mentions in newspaper features *before* Blackwood started to advertise the novel and then almost three times more mentions than adverts in the year of publication. Besides *The Times*, the *Examiner* printed a review before the first issue came out. Even if it was unfavorable, the many subsequent reviews in high-status periodicals (such as the *Academy*, the *Contemporary Review*, and the *Atlantic Monthly*) marked the novel as something cultured people needed to read. The expense of printing and distributing so many advance copies was never spent on popular authors: their novels were considered to be able to look after themselves (often advertising was minimal as well). Eliot may not have sold in the vast numbers that popular authors did, but unlike fast sellers, Blackwood's careful cultivation of tastemakers was an investment in generating auratic status that turned Eliot into a profitable long-seller: in the 1890s, sales of her works in cheap editions accounted for over fifty percent of Blackwood's income.[28]

It is instructive to compare the marketing of *Daniel Deronda* with that of a twenty-first-century novel at the other end of the cultural scale, Dan Brown's *The Da Vinci Code* (2003). Random House sent out 10,000 advance copies of the novel across the USA, confident that booksellers would willingly promote it if they had read it themselves. The strategy worked. In its first week, *The Da Vinci Code* was top of the *New York Times* bestseller list, helped, similarly to *Daniel Deronda*, by a stage-managed rave review the day before the book was published.[29] There are differences of course. In 2003 Random House targeted wholesalers and retailers rather than an elite circle that would halo the work with reviews and comments over many years. Furthermore, unlike George Eliot's in 1876, the "Dan

Brown brand" had yet to be established even though *The Da Vinci Code* was Brown's fourth novel. In order to establish Brown as a brand, in fact, a chapter from his novel *Angels and Demons* (first published in 2000) was included at the end of *The Da Vinci Code*. Readers were thus shown that Brown had a back catalog and could repeat the experience. Again, this marketing decision worked: at one point in 2004, four of Brown's novels figured in the *New York Times* bestseller list simultaneously.[30]

Designing the Product

In marketing terms, a "product" is not a passive object: it is an active participant that (to varying degrees) will target specific consumers. In publishing this does not equate simply with designing an attractive cover or writing a striking blurb with appropriate celebrity endorsements: novels are published as packages comprising texts, images, time of release, placement in bookstores and social media, author interviews, potential prizes, and so on.

Relations between author, reader, and text have changed dramatically since the rise of the Internet. Now there is a huge amount of data available about readers' interests, preferences, language use, income, and expenditure. We would expect not only publishers to exploit this information to position and promote an author's work but also authors to react to it in the design of their products. Fauzia Burke's recent *Online Marketing for Busy Authors*, for example, makes the need for authors to create a focused readership profile fundamental to successful writing; Catherine Bell, the Joint Managing Director of the very successful Scholastic Press, suggests that the way forward is for authors to research and write for the demographic profile of target readerships through online tracking.[31] Previously authors were almost always told their target reader was an editor rather than a particular social category. Percy Russell's much reprinted 1891 *Author's Manual*, like all its fellows, recommended that writers had to please an editor through demonstrating their hard work by good writing.[32] This in effect meant that authors had to adhere to an absolute standard of excellence which was rarely precisely defined beyond a need for authoritative grammar and lexis, and learning from the "great."

Although already in the nineteenth century, quantitative research on readers had suggested devising products for them, the recommendations always aimed to correct faulty taste, not to sell more by catering to the desires that the research uncovered. Recognizably modern empirical reader research began in the 1920s: the first newspaper reader profiles in the UK

were (probably) conducted by Gallup in 1932, though newspaper readership surveys had preceded that by eight years in the USA.[33] Writers for
newspapers now began to pen what these studies showed readers wanted
(though the continuing power of newspaper editors as mediators of this
knowledge should not be underestimated). It is all the more surprising,
then, that as late as 1957 Hyde lamented of the British book publishing
industry (as opposed to the newspaper industry) that "there is no market
research in the scientific manner that we have become accustomed to when
launching new commodities; no integration of media into one large,
sustained, drive, whether regionally or nationally, and no careful recording
of results."[34] Book publishers and editors were clinging to the nineteenth-
century, gentlemanly belief both in their own expertise as mediators
between author and public and in the value of an author's sheer hard
work and study of the masters to create a quality product. This was
manifested as disdain for the insights of marketing and social sciences
research as much as their dislike of possible new sales venues such as in the
increasingly common supermarkets.

Hyde would no longer be able to complain of a lack of "one large,
sustained, drive" from the late 1960s. Profits now reigned over abstract
standards of literary quality or an editor's expertise. In the 1950s and 1960s,
"best sellers" – books which sold quickly in large numbers in a short space
of time – had already come to dominate the market.[35] Such fast sellers (as
they are more properly called) made more economic sense to multinational
conglomerates than books with long tails: fast-sellers targeting specific
types of consumer tie up less capital in stock and storage. This had an
effect on the kind of advice authors were given by writers' guides. From the
1970s, authors were urged to envisage what readership they were aiming at
before they started writing and to send those reader profiles to publishers
with their manuscripts. That said, most guides were still advocating, with
varying emphases, the traditional combination of learning from the masters and marketing to individual editors, as author guides to publishing
usually still do today. While of course authors have continued to write (and
be very successful) without heeding empirical audience research profiles,
genre authors are more frequently encouraged to do so. In 1993, for
example, Jean Saunders, a successful writer of more than sixty novels,
mainly romances, was urging her colleagues to conduct research on their
readerships as much as research around their topic.[36]

Authors today can make use of social media of various kinds to ensure
the continuity and depth of their relationships with readers. J. K. Rowling
is particularly well known for her use of Twitter (she does not appear in

public). Margaret Atwood, besides blogging and tweeting, lecturing and signing in person, is an advocate of the "LongPen" by which authors can sign books from afar, extending the guarantee of signatory presence through cyberspace (no doubt with some irony).[37] Young Adult authors are particularly fortunate in having a readership characterized by high social media usage: Veronica Roth, for example, is open about how her relations with her readers and her market research coincide, thanking her fans for their ideas and feedback on their experiments in her "Special" to *Allegiant* (2013). Meanwhile, YouTube videos of authors explaining their work either to an audience at an event or directly to camera are a new norm.

A particularly famous example of product design through market research is E. L. James's *Fifty Shades of Grey*. Its exceptional success over 2011–2012 seems to have been considerably helped by the several public iterations the novel went through and the passage of James herself from reader to fan to author. Developed initially as free online fan fiction after Meyer's *Twilight* series and published on FanFiction.net, *Fifty Shades of Grey* was eventually "pulled" [removed] for violating the site's terms of service for adult content. A revised version migrated to James's own site before it was brought out by the Writer's Coffee House, an e-publisher set up by Twilight fans to monetize "pulled-to-publish" fan fiction (that is, fan fiction with trademarked names and descriptions altered or removed, and then published as original work). Over the process, James had developed her own fan base, actively engaging in conversations with readers so as to design her product to match their desires. Previously enjoying tens of thousands of readers, under the Writer's Coffee House *Fifty Shades of Grey* sold 250,000 copies before Vintage (an imprint of the largest book publishing company in the world, Penguin Random House, owned by the transnational media giant Bertelsmann) published it in both electronic and paperback forms in early 2012, with a slickly suggestive cover design and abundant marketing expertise targeting mothers in supermarkets. By the end of the year, *Fifty Shades* had sold almost four million print copies and 1.5 million e-books in the UK alone, and over 65 million copies (print and e-book) of the *Grey* trilogy had been sold worldwide.[38]

Authors, in other words, can now, in theory at least, both extend and deepen their relationships with readers and create products based on the results of their own market research in a cybernetically enhanced form of "buzz." The marketing that publishers do might simply be to channel and extend the product's reach and smooth distribution, exactly mirroring the triumph of marketing and production departments over the editor in this age of conglomerates. But the same technological means allow authors to create not only texts for readers, but also their own readers – and purchasers. That glowing reviews and comments on their own works are contributed online by authors under pseudonyms (sometimes called "sockpuppets") is well known, but bestseller lists have long been compromised as well. Two cases may stand as representative. The first, dating from 1995, involved the purchase by the authors of 10,000 copies of their own marketing book. These figures pushed it to the top of the *New York Times* bestseller lists in the field: the authors hoped to recoup their investment in their purchases by the increased purchases that appearance in the bestseller list promised.[39] A more recent case occurred in July 2017, when Amazon's sales-rankings algorithm was hacked so that the novel *Dragonsoul* suddenly became Amazon's top seller, having been ranked 385,841 just the day before. There had been no previous marketing of any kind. David Gaughran of the *Let's Get Digital* blog site for self-published authors explained that someone had clearly used "clickfarms," which "can download free books, or borrow [Kindle Unlimited] books, and/or page through borrowed books to generate reads – which will then be paid out of the communal [Kindle Unlimited] pot."[40]

It seems that now not just fake authors like Street & Smith's "Bertha M. Clay" worry the triangular relationship of authorship, publishing, and marketing, but fake readers too.

Notes

1. American Marketing Association, www.ama.org/AboutAMA/Pages/Definitio n-of-Marketing.aspx.
2. Hugh Jones and Christophe Benson, *Publishing Law*, 2nd edn (London: Routledge, 1996), pp. 30–31.
3. Godfrey Hodgeson, "Theodore Sorenson: Obituary," *The Guardian*, 1 November 2010.
4. "Lady Caroline Lascelles & Co. (Unlimited)," *London Review*, 14.439 (1867), 282–84, p. 283. My thanks to Ann M. Hale for bringing this article to my attention.
5. Graham Law, Gregory Drozdz, and Debby McNally, "Introduction," in *Charlotte May Brame*, http://victorianfictionresearchguides.org/charlotte-ma y-brame/.
6. Sydney T. Hyde, *Sales on a Shoestring: How to Advertise Books* (London: Deutsch, 1957), p. 28.
7. See John Spiers, ed., *The Culture of the Publisher's Series*, 2 vols (London: Palgrave Macmillan, 2011).

8. Daryl Jones, *The Dime Novel Western* (Bowling Green, OH: The Popular Press, Bowling Green State University, 1978), pp. 61–75.
9. Michael Barber, *Anthony Powell: A Life* (London: Duckworth, 2005), p. 185.
10. Stanley Unwin, *The Truth About Publishing* (London: George Allen & Unwin, 1926), pp. 257–58.
11. My thanks to Charlotta Billström for bringing the following to my notice.
12. See Charles McGrath, "The Afterlife of Stieg Larsson," *New York Times*, 20 May 2010.
13. Sarah Begley, "Here's the Cover for the New Book in Stieg Larsson's Millennium Series," *Time*, 31 March 2015.
14. "David Lagercrantz" at Norstedt's site, www.norstedts.se/forfattare/119997-david-lagercrantz.
15. Anita Singh, "Family Feud over Stieg Larsson Millennium Sequel," *The Telegraph*, 27 August 2015; "The Final Mystery of Stieg Larsson," *ShortList*, [n.d.], www.shortlist.com/entertainment/the-final-mystery-of-stieg-larsson/98425; Kira Cochrane, "Stieg Larsson's Partner," *The Guardian*, 4 October 2011.
16. Unwin, *Truth*, pp. 247–48.
17. Betsy Rosenblatt, "The Great Game and the Copyright Villain," *Transformative Works and Cultures* 23 (2017), http://dx.doi.org/10.3983/twc.2017.0923.
18. James Chapman, *Licence to Thrill: A Cultural History of the James Bond Films*, 2nd edn (London: I.B. Tauris, 2007); Christoph Lindner, ed., *The James Bond Phenomenon: A Critical Reader* (Manchester, UK: Manchester University Press, 2003).
19. Hugh Jones, "Writers and Trademarks," *The Author*, 101.1 (1993), 30–31.
20. Richard Salmon, "Signs of Intimacy: The Literary Celebrity in the 'Age of Interview'," *Victorian Literature and Culture*, 25.1 (1997), 159–77.
21. R. P. Bagozzi, "Toward a Formal Theory of Marketing Exchanges," in *Conceptual and Theoretical Developments in Marketing*, ed. O. C. Ferrell, S. W. Brown, and C.W. Lamb, Jr. (Chicago: American Marketing Association, 1979), pp. 431–47.
22. Joe Moran, *Star Authors: Literary Celebrity in America* (London: Pluto Press, 2000), p. 153.
23. James F. English, *The Economy of Prestige: Prizes, Awards, and the Circulation of Cultural Value* (Cambridge, MA: Harvard UP, 2005).
24. Stephen Brown, "Rattles from the Swill Bucket," in *Consuming Books: The Marketing and Consumption of Literature*, ed. Stephen Brown (London: Routledge, 2006), pp. 1–17, p. 6–7.
25. The quotation is from Bruce Arnold, *The Spire and Other Essays in Modern Irish Culture* (Dublin: Liffey, 2003), p. 90. See also Stephen John Dilks, *Samuel Beckett in the Literary Marketplace* (Syracuse, NY: Syracuse University Press, 2011).
26. Frederick Karl, *George Eliot: A Biography* (London: HarperCollins, 1995), p. 561.

27. Letters from George Henry Lewes to Blackwood (22 November 1875), and from Blackwood to Lewes (28 December 1875) in *George Eliot Letters*, ed. Gordon S. Haight, vol. 6 (London: Oxford University Press, 1955), pp. 192–93, 203–5; "Daniel Deronda," *The Times*, 31 January 1876, 6.

28. David Finkelstein, *The House of Blackwood: Author-Publisher Relations in the Victorian Period* (Philadelphia: Pennsylvania State University Press, 2002), p. 34.

29. Dan Glaister, "The Guardian Profile: Dan Brown," *The Guardian*, 6 August 2005.

30. Alistair Ray, "The Author-Brand Identity," *The Bookseller*, 22 April 2005.

31. Fauzia Burke, *Online Marketing for Busy Authors: A Step-by-Step Guide* (Oakland, CA, Berrett-Koehler, 2016), pp. 19–25; Catherine Bell, "What Lies Ahead for Books in 2016? From Bespoke Publishing to the Continued Rise of Vloggers. Industry Leaders Give Us Their Tips for the Likely Trends in 2016," *The Bookseller*, 6 January 2016.

32. Percy Russell, *The Authors' Manual*, 4th edn (London: Digby and Long, 1891), p. 119.

33. Michael Brown, "Estimating Newspaper and Magazine Readership," in *Measuring Media Audiences*, ed. Raymond Kent (London, Routledge, 1994), pp. 105–44.

34. Sidney T. Hyde, "Sales Promotion," in *The Book World Today*, ed. John Hampden (London: George Allen & Unwin, 1957), p. 189.

35. Gary Hoppenstand, "Genre and Formula in Popular Literature," in *A Companion to Popular Culture*, ed. Gary Burns (Chichester, UK: Wiley-Blackwell, 2016), pp. 101–22, p. 109.

36. Jean Saunders, "Romance in America," *The Author*, 104.4 (1993), 139–40.

37. See Kelvin Smith, *The Publishing Business: From p-books to e-books* (Lausanne: AVA Publishing, 2012), p. 176.

38. Bethan Jones, "Fifty Shades of Exploitation: Fan Labor and *Fifty Shades of Grey*," in *Transformative Works and Cultures* 15 (2014), http://dx.doi.org/10.3983/twc.2014.0501.

39. Patrick M. Reilly, "Publishing: How a Book Makes the Bestseller Lists, And How the Bestseller Lists Make a Book," *Wall Street Journal*, Eastern edition [New York], 7 September 1995, B1.

40. David Gaughran, "Scammers Break the Kindle Store," 15 July 2017, https://davidgaughran.wordpress.com/2017/07/15/scammers-break-the-kindle-store/.

CHAPTER 27

Institutions
Writing and Reading

Jason Puskar

When I was a child I devoured mystery novels about the Hardy boys, two squeaky-clean teen detectives who solved surprisingly serious crimes plaguing the otherwise sleepy small town of Bayside, a fictional locale on the Atlantic coast of the United States. But eventually I learned of a crime in these novels even more shocking than the counterfeiting, smuggling, drug running, and murder that the Hardy boys routinely uncovered: the author, Franklin W. Dixon, was an imposter, a mere pseudonym for many different writers churning out titles for the Stratemeyer Syndicate, a fiction factory that mass-produced novels for children and teenagers. I felt betrayed. And foolish. Frank and Joe Hardy could sniff out an international spy ring in a week, but this ruse operated under my nose for years, and even then someone else blew the whistle on Dixon for me.

To call Dixon a pseudonym is only partly accurate, however, because that implies that he stood for another individual, the real author concealed behind a pen name. There were identifiable writers who composed many of the Hardy Boys books, including Leslie McFarlane, who wrote nineteen of the first twenty-five novels, but even he worked from plot outlines generated by Edward Stratemeyer and his staff. McFarlane later called Stratemeyer "a Henry Ford of fiction for boys and girls,"[1] for in addition to the Hardy Boys series, the Stratemeyer Syndicate also produced the Bobbsey Twins series, the Nat Ridley detective stories, and the Dave Fearless outdoor adventures, as well as roughly 100 other entire *series* before Stratemeyer's death in 1930.[2] McFarlane recalled his own surprise when, newly hired by the syndicate, he discovered that one of his own childhood literary idols, Roy Rockwood, author of *Bomba the Jungle Boy*, was a Stratemeyer creation. "Roy Rockwood had less substance than a puff of smoke," McFarlane said.[3] But there actually was substance behind

---

* I am grateful to Gilberto Blasini for his thoughtful advice on the nature of authorship in film and television, and for his guidance on recent debates about it in film studies.

Rockwood, and behind Franklin W. Dixon too, because their names stood in for an entire institutional arrangement of contract writers, editors, company priorities, market exigencies, contract lawyers, marketing professionals, and even previously published titles, all of which lay concealed behind the pretense of romantic authorship.

If Franklin W. Dixon seemed like a criminal imposter in my childhood, he seems more like the model of authorship today. As many critics have noted over the last several decades, authors get conjured out of collaborations between and among an array of co-producers, both other people and other institutions, none of which can claim sole jurisdiction over the literary work that results. Whatever writers do with paper and ink, they only become authors through a network of editors, publishers, distributors, book stores, reviewers, and universities, to name only a few of the main institutional participants in the process. One great irony of authorship is that people may scribble away as long as they like, but they remain writers, not authors, until institutions like publishers and book stores legitimize their work, and in the process, transform the nature of their own authority.

Naturally, this raises the question of what counts as an institution. The very term "institution" can seem pejorative, a byword for alienating bureaucracy or social control. To say that someone has been "institutionalized" in English means he or she has been locked in an asylum. Of course, in disciplines such as sociology, institutions are more neutral, and as Jonathan Turner has put it, consist of "a complex of positions, roles, norms and values lodged in particular types of social structures and organizing relatively stable patterns of human activity."[4] This often takes the form of a discrete organization, such as the post office, but it can also apply more abstractly to replicable social practices, such as marriage, or even to an entire system of organizations and practices, such as capitalism.[5] Only the first sort of institution will be considered for these purposes, in organizations such as libraries, bookstores, publishers, universities, hospitals, prisons, and newspapers, among many others, even though it is rarely easy to draw a bright line between the various kinds of institutions.

Indeed, authorship itself may be understood as an institution, a role or office that organizes literary production, and that need not be overidentified with any particular person who happens to occupy it. Accordingly, the following is not an attempt to argue that institutions shape and sustain authors, a claim so obvious it scarcely needs stating, but rather an attempt to show how institutional resources lie concealed within the romantic fiction of the individual human author, and thus how authorship in general might be conceived in a more heterogeneous and less anthropocentric form. Roland Barthes famously eulogized the author by calling the text "a multi-dimensional space in which a variety of writings, none of them original, blend and clash," and "a tissue of quotations drawn from the innumerable centers of culture."[6] However, those centers are probably not innumerable, and some of the most conspicuous are easily identifiable institutions. Nor need we unravel the author into something as general as "discourse," as Michel Foucault attempted to do. Foucault's emphasis on discursive practices gets closer to institutions, but even this discerning critic of the prison and the hospital had little to say about actual institutions as they relate to authorship. The goal of the following pages, then, is not to evacuate the author so that only words remain, but to anatomize some of the institutional components of his or her more heterogeneous and hybrid identity.

We might reconceive of the author as an "assemblage," to use Gilles Deleuze and Felix Guattari's term for distributed agency; instead of a single person, the author might better be understood as a constellation of human and non-human actors that combine to accomplish what none could do alone.[7] The English term "assemblage" awkwardly translates Deleuze and Guattari's original French term "*agencement*," which, as Manuel DeLanda has pointed out, more clearly designates not just an ensemble of parts but also the distinctive agency that results.[8] In extending and clarifying Deleuze and Guattari's original formulations, DeLanda insists that an assemblage is not a transcendental generality (like "the market"), but always historically specific, local, and "individual" in the most literal sense: it cannot be divided.[9] For instance, one might isolate for consideration the people in a city, or the buildings, or the urban planning, or the climate, but the city is the irreducible assemblage of all those things, and more. To see the author as an assemblage is thus to understand authorial agency not as fantasy or illusion, but as an assemblage of specific and reconfigurable historical and material parts, including but not limited to people. In what follows, I do not insist on any very specific theoretical application of assemblage theory to authorship, nor do I attempt to extend that theory in any detailed way. I simply offer it as a model that can help recalibrate our expectations about authorship, and reveal its components in a truer relation to each other.

One of the most traditional ways of acknowledging the collaborative nature of authorship has been to consign other factors to the realm of influence. An author might be influenced by another author or authors, but also by cultures, institutions, political systems, literary trends, or anything else in the realm of experience. The liquid metaphor of influence is vague enough that the author need not cede credit to an alleged co-author. Stephen Crane may have been influenced by his early work as a newspaper journalist, but in saying so we do not mean to attribute Crane's fiction to *The New York World* or to any of its editors, nor do we mean to suggest that any newspaper or any person at a newspaper exerted direct pressure on his fiction. Indeed, we only call something "influence" once we conclude that it had "flowed in" to the human author, as if he subsequently incorporated it as part of himself. To use the language of influence is thus to defend a traditional view of authorship as human and individual, and to discount other factors as potentially agentive.

However, Crane did not just write under the influence of newspapers; he also wrote for newspapers, and many of his stories appeared in *The New York World* and in magazines such as *Scribner's*. Accordingly, it is not just that journalism influenced Crane, but also that he adapted his writing to their institutional demands. Scholars have long recognized how directly journalism has shaped fiction.[10] For instance, the advent of the serial novel by Honoré de Balzac and Charles Dickens proved mutually beneficial for writers and magazines alike, and both helped shape the new kinds of narratives that emerged. Serialization itself had direct impact on narrative form, evident in the sheer scale of the Victorian multi-plot novel and in the development of "cliffhanger" chapter endings. Such institutional sources of literary authority need not be quarantined safely outside the category of authorship, but might instead be seen as an integral component of it, a collaboration of sorts that human writers enter into but do not entirely control.

This raises the question of just where to draw the line between the writer's private creativity and the various audiences – including the audience of editors and publishers – that the writer anticipates and even internalizes. To think of authorship as an assemblage may require us to think about the putative author's formal decisions as originating, in part, from some of his readers. At first glance, this can seem more than a little ludicrous. Surely the recipient of a love letter is not also the letter's author, just because the sender anticipated what would please her most. Yet looked at more carefully, sometimes this is precisely the case. In Viktor Shklovsky's modernist epistolary novel *Zoo, or, Letters Not About Love* (1923), the narrator pens letters to his beloved under a stern injunction from her: he may write about anything he likes, except love.[11] The novel is partly autobiographical, but even within the conceit of the fictional world, the letters the narrator writes have been shaped decisively by his beloved's injunction, and in that way, she is one source of the writing that results.

With institutions, the situation may be similar, even when the conditions of writing are generalized or unstated, as writers make creative choices from their publishers' menu of possibilities.

Perhaps we need to think about authorial agency not just as a causal push from the side of composition, but also as a causal pull from the side of publication. That is to say, a literary work may result not just from what Aristotle called an "efficient cause," the activity of the writer, but also from "final cause," the goal or purpose that organizes the activities that precede it. Aristotle's example of a final cause is the goal of health, which causes one to walk about, lose weight, or take medicine.[12] By analogy, then, the goal of publishing a story in *The New York World* is the cause of certain kinds of writing, and as such, functions alongside the writer's determinations. The theory of final cause easily can be abused when applied to natural science, where it is prone to become metaphysical, but perhaps it has more utility in the social analysis of distributed agencies, where purposes need not be imagined as either natural or unchanging.[13] Something like "final authorship" could thus represent structural and institutional conditions that shape writing by exerting causal pull from the destination, rather than just causal push from a supposed point of origin, and thereby recognize them as properly agentive.

The most sweeping account of the institutionalization of literary authorship comes from Michel Foucault, whose analysis of institutions and their discourse led to his well-known claim that discourse produces authors, rather than the other way around. Other works such as *The Birth of the Clinic* and *Discipline and Punish* contend that vast disciplinary systems based in institutions like the hospital and the prison generate subjectivities that may seem natural, but that are in fact produced through systems of power. Surprisingly, however, those institutions are little evident in his influential essay "What Is an Author?" Indeed, Foucault expressly says that his goal is not to "offer here a sociohistorical analysis of the author's persona" roughly equivalent to his analyses of the hospital or the prison.[14] Foucault even confirms that "the author function is linked to the juridical and institutional system that encompasses, determines, and articulates the universe of discourses," even if he shows little interest in tracing discourse back to particular institutions.[15]

The wide influence of Foucault's work has led to various institutional analyses of literary production, some of which retain a rather sweeping association of all institutions with panoptic discipline. Related Marxist accounts of institutions, such as Louis Althusser's theory of the Ideological State Apparatus, have similarly seen institutions as powerful extensions of the state, which reproduce the prevailing political order by interpellating individuals as compliant subjects. For example, Lennard Davis has called the professional institutions that organize the study and teaching of literature "compulsory bureaucracies" associated with "a hegemonic process that dominates the individual."[16] According to Davis, they endure only "because they function to guard powerful interests."[17] However, many critics of both Foucault and Althusser have found their accounts of institutions too levelling, and have charged Foucault especially with leaving too little room for dynamic change or effective resistance. Assemblage theory tends to be similarly skeptical about the naturalness, boundedness, or permanence of the human subject, but also tends to be committed to a more radical fluidity of relations, and this limits its tendency to generalize across different institutions, or to elaborate more rigid explanatory models, systems, or binaries.

If this resistance to generalization limits the explanatory power of assemblage theory, it also opens up much more room for us to discern surprising resistances and reversals. For instance, in Foucauldian terms it can be difficult to explain prison literature as anything other than an effect of power. Yet from Boethius to Malcolm X, the prison has been an especially rich environment for literary, political, and autobiographical writing, and we would do well to avoid ascribing that writing too exclusively to either the prisoner or the prison. Some more dynamic relationship animates the two in concert, further aided by entire cultures that have placed special value on prison writing. To take just one example, Rivkah Zim has suggested that Western societies have deemed the prison a "crucible of suffering that induces self-knowledge and new wisdom," and as a result, prison writers may be inhabiting an established social role, that of the prison prophet, which many readers have been primed to respect.[18] To be this certain kind of author requires a certain kind of institutional legitimation. It seems noteworthy that the hospital has not fostered a similar amount of literary production, for while there is no shortage of literature about hospitals, there seems to be drastically less generated from hospitals. Many of the best known involve confinement in sanatoriums, such as Thomas Mann's *The Magic Mountain* (1924), or asylums, such as Ken Kesey's *One Flew Over the Cuckoo's Nest* (1962), both of which involve long-term stays that resemble imprisonment. In a work like Sylvia Plath's *The Bell Jar* (1963), confinement in a psychiatric hospital is a welcome respite from the crueler conditions outside, but perhaps for Plath confinement also registered as special mode of carceral wisdom.

Only writers who avoid or refuse publication also avoid contact with the powerful institutions that connect them to audiences, such as publishers, literary agents, universities, and book retailers. When an editor who works for a publishing company edits a manuscript in an official capacity, the writer collaborates not just with another person – like T. S. Eliot seeking help from Ezra Pound on *The Waste Land* – but with an entire institutional arrangement. The effects of such relationships can be profound. Maxwell Perkins's heavy editing of Thomas Wolfe's bloated manuscripts drastically reshaped *Look Homeward, Angel* (1929), among other novels, and helped Wolfe win both an audience and critical esteem. Similarly, Gordon Lish's extensive editing of Raymond Carver's fiction, first at the magazine *Esquire* and later for the publisher Alfred A. Knopf, has seemed to many to cross the line from editing to composing, especially after the *New Yorker* published a Carver story without Lish's alterations in 2007. Indeed, what we think of as Carver's own distinctively austere voice seems to have resulted largely from Lish's merciless eradication of Carver's prose.

Still, debates about Carver's and Lish's dueling authority have tended to retain humanist and individualist assumptions about authorship, as they try to gauge whether Carver or Lish is the real genius behind the fiction. For instance, Stephen King says that Lish "imposed his own style on Carver's stories, and the so-called minimalism with which Carver is credited was actually Lish's deal." "It's a total rewrite," King concludes, "and it's a cheat."[19] That may be, but lost in that indictment is the basic fact that Lish worked as an employee of a publishing company that charged him not just with editing the text but with representing the publisher's interests. To see Lish as an institutional representative is not at all to see him as cynically beholden to narrowly commercial standards. Far from it. It is simply to acknowledge that Lish occupied an office within an institutional structure charged with coordinating many different values, some artistic, some commercial, some dully practical. If Lish was especially zealous or talented in his work, the fact remains that the office itself existed as part of the institutional production of literature, and hence, of authors too. Many literary agents have an even greater say over what writers produce, as they informally advise their clients on the direction of the work, suggest alterations, engage in preliminary editing, and guide writers to marketable projects. To hire an agent is to delegate a range of decisions to another expert, and so to displace certain sensitivities to the market onto another person, and at the same time to preserve a role for those sensitivities in the author's overall function. Too great a focus on the people who occupy the office of editor or agent distracts from the fundamental fact that the writer is surrounded by other authorities who have considerable say over the production of a literary work, even if the final results end up bundled, misleadingly, in a category labelled "Raymond Carver."

The apparent individualism of print authorship contrasts with a more openly collaborative model in visual media such as film and television. The rise of the *auteur* in mid-twentieth-century film actually re-appropriated a model of traditional literary authority against the perceived commercialism and factory conditions of the Hollywood studio system. The auteur is allegedly the creative genius behind the entire film, usually the director, a figure such as Alfred Hitchcock or Ingmar Bergman, and he (for the term has been largely reserved for men) receives credit for authoring the film as a whole. One of the more self-conscious auteurs, Jean-Luc Godard, metaphorized his authority over his films specifically as a form of literary writing: "The cinema is not a craft. It is an art. It does not mean teamwork. One is always alone on the set as before the blank page."[20] Godard's claims aside, nobody really disputes that even the most audacious auteur still depends on the creative capacities of a vast array of writers, actors, designers, photographers, editors, producers, and technicians to a degree that most novelists or even editors would find appalling. And although Godard himself is far more dependent on far more people than Carver ever was on Lish, similar controversies about his creative independence seem not to arise.

James Naremore has insightfully correlated the film auteur with more traditional conceptions of authorship. Naremore acknowledges that "French auteurism . . . may be dead, but so are tedious debates about the death of the author."[21] What we need, he alleges, is a way of talking about authorship that neither isolates and individualizes the author, nor eradicates the author completely from the scene of production. "Critics need to understand the phenomenon of the author dialectically, with an awareness of the complicated, dynamic relationship between institutions and artists, and with an appreciation of the aesthetic choices made by individual agents in particular circumstances," he says.[22] Those dynamic relationships are much more visible in film and television than in belletristic print literature, which takes greater pains to over-ascribe creative authority to individual people. To do otherwise in the realm of print is to teeter toward a perceived abyss of banality and commercialism. Precisely because they are less beholden to traditional and belletristic standards of authorship, film and television have been far more candid with their audiences about the circumstances of their production.

The question of whether an institution enhances or impedes creativity is an important one, even if it is not liable to be settled in any sweeping way. Looked at one way, institutional production tends toward the formulaic, as in the case of the Hardy Boys novels and in the vast majority of television series. When the goal of the institution is mass production, we should expect a certain uniformity of results. Moreover, the institutional production of literature often exposes it to excessively commercial interests. However, looked at another way, institutions can have more salutary effects. Some institutions attempt to insulate writers against market pressure, or foster collaborations that can generate new creative possibilities. Some institutions may even help release, refine, or amplify the creative potential otherwise locked too narrowly in an individual's preconceptions and habits. Against the dismal view of the institution as a prison or an auction block, we should acknowledge an equally influential view of the institution as the protector and even incubator of creativity and knowledge. Over the last century, the institution most closely aligned with that role has been the university.

As Mark McGurl has shown, the development of progressive education in the United States led to a new emphasis on the creative capacities of all students, in a Deweyan curriculum that prized curiosity, independent learning, and creativity. Educational institutions changed as a result, de-emphasizing rote learning and devising new ways to respond to each student's individual needs. Several decades later, the rise of New Criticism in the academic study of literature placed new emphasis on close reading and craft, techniques for literary analysis that informed writing too. When universities combined the goals of progressive education with the methods of New Criticism, they had a ready synthesis for new graduate programs in creative writing. As progressive educators "worked to re-gear US schools for the systematic production of original persons," McGurl suggests, creative writing became an exemplary way to perform that mission. And through the workshop model of peer feedback, their new instructional methods attempted to balance imagination with craft. As McGurl notes, more than a few of these students "would actually become the most celebrated form of the self-expressive individual, the writer."[23]

There had been no such thing as a creative writing graduate program before about 1940, but *Poets & Writers* magazine – a professional magazine for creative writers – catalogs 226 different programs that offer a Masters of Fine Arts in creative writing in North America today. The crown jewel of American writing programs for much of the twentieth century was the University of Iowa's Writer's Workshop, which has produced an impressive array of writers, including T. C. Boyle, Jorie Graham, Dennis Johnson, Bharati Mukherjee, Flannery O'Connor, Jane Smiley, and John Edgar Wideman, to name only a few. For many critics, the question has been whether the institutionalization of creative writing has helped or hindered literature. Has it in fact released the creative potential of these writers, helping them augment their imaginative power with the rigor of craft? Or has it homogenized literary production, disciplining graduates in orthodox styles, preserving New Critical canons of taste, and spawning too many identifiable "Iowa writers"? Surely the university does both of those things, unevenly and in ways that would be hard to generalize across all institutions, let alone across all writers. But McGurl is primarily interested in reading American fiction differently once it has been informed by a history of its institutional production. For instance, he argues that the modernist fascination with point of view derives from "an institutional environment engaged on many levels with the problem and promise of cultural difference."[24] Through those kinds of analyses, McGurl has done more than anyone to show how literary authorship, at least in the United States, has come to depend on university sponsorship, and how our understanding of that literature requires us to take stock of its institutional origins.

Universities today have professionalized creative writing to a degree that would have astonished any nineteenth-century novelist. Creative writing students have professional mentors, professional networks, professional journals, and professional conferences, all designed to prepare them not just to write better, but to *be* authors, to perform professionally in relation to established literary institutions and their norms. Within the university, this also involves professionalizing writers to navigate academic tenure requirements and expectations for research productivity, all of which compel creative output and organize it according to academic standards and timelines.

This can change the entire complexion of a literary field, or even preserve a field. If not for university creative writing programs, far fewer books of poetry would be published today, for one struggles to think of any living poets able to support themselves only by the pen. Poets who formerly would have depended on a wealthy patron now depend on the university instead, unless they are fortunate enough to have inherited or married a fortune. Even the most famous poets depend on fellowships, residencies, and visiting appointments, often at universities. Consider the case of best-selling poets today: as of this moment, the list of the top twenty best-selling books of poetry on Amazon.com, updated hourly, contains three children's books and five books by writers who are dead, one of whom is the Greek epic poet Homer. Jalal al-Din Rumi, Lao Tzu, John Milton, Edgar Allan Poe, and the anonymous author or authors of *Beowulf* are also in the top forty. When even best-selling contemporary poets are still struggling to compete against *Beowulf*, I think we can conclude that the poetry market, such as it is, depends on something more than direct connections between writers and readers through published work. It also depends significantly on the institutional support of creative writing programs, on the tuition dollars those programs generate, and on the cultural capital that accrues to universities that have well-known poets on their faculties. Authors may produce books of poetry, but universities produce authors for reasons all their own.

Other institutions have functioned like the university as a sponsor of authorial activity. Wallace Stevens, Franz Kafka, and Ted Kooser all worked for insurance companies while writing on the side, and some critics (including this one) have attempted to understand how their embeddedness in the insurance industry shaped their work. In the pre-modern period, the monastery served as an institutional incubator for literature, followed by the printing shop in the early modern period, and the newspaper or magazine up to the present. Early modern coteries, eighteenth-century coffee houses, aristocratic salons, and even governmental information ministries also fostered productive environments for writers. In the matter of government support, we find the clearest example of that debate about whether the institutional production of literature liberates creativity or suppresses it, whether it diversifies the field of literature or homogenizes it. From one perspective, government support of literary production may seem to be the crassest kind of propaganda, while from another it may seem like a necessary protection against the degrading standards of the mass market.

Such is the complexity and power of modern institutions that purely individual attempts to reach an audience stand little chance of success, and protest against one kind of institution almost always requires an alliance with another. Before she tried to assassinate Andy Warhol, Valerie Solanas was best known for her anti-patriarchal *SCUM Manifesto*, which she sold in mimeographed form on the streets of New York for $1 ($2 for men).[25] No publisher would touch a book that began: "Life in this society being, at best, an utter bore and no aspect of society being at all relevant to women, there remains to civic-minded, responsible, thrill-seeking females only to overthrow the government, eliminate the money system, institute complete automation and destroy the male sex."[26] When the Olympia Press finally did offer to publish her work, Solanas worried that the press's owner, colluding with Warhol, intended to steal it instead. She shot Warhol in the throes of that delusion. Solanas's desire for an audience thus collided with her total distrust of all institutions, and of most people too, but ironically, she became an author at least partly because shooting Warhol brought her own name before the public after all, and eventually attracted publishers to her. Some writers employ the spectacle of violence more deliberately as a publication strategy. The "Unabomber," Theodore Kaczynski, mailed copies of his manifesto *Industrial Society and Its Future* to media outlets in conjunction with his bombings; similarly, Anders Behring Breivik emailed a rambling compendium titled *2083: A European Declaration of Independence* to more than a thousand recipients shortly before his attacks. In both cases, the spectacle of violence compelled the news media to facilitate an alternative mode of publication.

Even those who want to escape all institutions can scarcely escape the institutional origins of their writing instruments. A medieval scribe would have been aware of, and possibly involved with, many stages of making the vellum and ink he would use to copy or compose a text, but he depended on the monastery itself to procure all the necessary materials and to train people in the art of preparing them. To write on vellum required an elaborate institutional system, from the cowherd or shepherd who raised the animals, to those who processed the hides, to those who procured the materials, such as lime, to turn the hides into vellum, not to mention the patronage that supported the monks who performed many of these activities. Unlike writers today who write on paper with little sense of, or interest in, its production history, a medieval scribe would have had a fairly detailed sense that the act of writing was not the first step of making a book, but one of the last. A sheet of medieval vellum is not just a material object, but also the encapsulation of an entire ensemble of production systems, institutions, materials, animals, people, and beliefs.

Today most writers probably use some form of word processing. But the word processor is a "writer processor" too, in that it conditions the writer to work in certain ways, shaping him or her according to its own designs. That is not to say that writing is simply technologically determined, but rather that it is mediated by complex technical systems that have social and political ramifications. As Matthew Kirschenbaum has argued in his literary history of word processing, recent writing technologies reveal "the hybrid, heterogeneous nature of both individual persons and their personalities," along with the circuitous path of text that "morphs and twists through multiple media at nearly every stage of the composition and publication process."[27] For these purposes, it matters most of all that large corporations have scripted these processes to a considerable degree, and that technical script is hardly a utilitarian necessity. In fact, some of it imitates traditional office systems and writing methods, such that an entire pre-computational system remains visible within the digital interface. The main input mechanism imitates a nineteenth-century typewriter, the screen imitates a piece of paper, and many available actions have decidedly pre-digital names, such as "cut," "copy," and "paste." Icons often represent these functions in archaic form, such as a stamped envelope for "mail merge" or a rubber eraser for "clear all formatting." The very serifs on my Times New Roman font imitate the finial cuts that Roman stonecutters used to finish strokes of letters. Older institutional practices persist in our technologies, remediated now in digital form, and these are more than just metaphors. They are also organizational ghosts, the afterlives of older institutions that survive in the digital present.

Yet my computer's file system does not come with a clerk to keep the records straight, a secretary to take my dictation, a manager to coordinate the various functions of storage, processing, and retrieval, a clerk to stamp dates and times on documents, a purchasing agent to buy me more paperclips, folders, ink, paper, or paste, or even a copy editor to correct my spelling and grammar. Those formerly social functions, organized institutionally, are now embedded in the machine, and automated technologically. This has the powerful effect of allowing me to experience writing as a largely private affair. Even as I type these words, a software company has conjured the enabling fiction that an entire office – a Microsoft Office – is entirely under my executive command. If this helps me conceive of the act of writing as an individual activity, it also helps me conceive of the author as very different from that medieval monk, because even though my writing system is vastly more complex than his, I am far less aware of it, so can more easily indulge the illusion that unlike Franklin W. Dixon, authors like me work alone.

It is not impossible to imagine some point in the future when a more candid attitude about authorship will allow us to admit and perhaps even celebrate more institutionally intensive modes of writing, without disguising them behind the names of individual people. Perhaps novels will bear the name of the editor and literary agent alongside the name of the author and publisher, just as films credit many other collaborating producers. We might even imagine some future Stratemeyer Syndicate which, by collectivizing literary production for some goal other than maximum profit and efficiency, generates something salutary, novels or even poems that are better for having been produced by teams of people working within institutional frameworks. Conceived as an assemblage, the author might then appear as the most open kind of fiction, as the name "Boston" or "Berlin" individualizes the collective components of those cities, but does not conceal them in the least. Just as the city is not reducible to its buildings or its people, so too an author might be understood without shock or shame as a name for that creative assemblage of resources, temporally expansive and spatially distributed, fluidly recombinant and historically contingent, that includes but is not limited to the human.

Notes

1. Leslie McFarlane, *Ghost of the Hardy Boys: An Autobiography* (Toronto: Methuen, 1976), p. 9.
2. Deirdre Johnson, *Edward Stratemeyer and the Stratemeyer Syndicate* (New York: Twayne, 1993), p. 6–7.
3. McFarlane, *Ghost*, p. 13.
4. Jonathan Turner, *The Institutional Order: Economy, Kinship, Religion, Polity, Law, and Education in Evolutionary and Comparative Perspective* (New York: Longman, 1972), p. 6.
5. For a useful review of the term "institution," see the entry on "Social Institutions" in the *Stanford Encyclopedia of Philosophy*, https://plato.stanford.edu/entries/social-institutions/.
6. Roland Barthes, "The Death of the Author," in *Authorship: From Plato to Postmodernism: A Reader*, ed. Seán Burke (Edinburgh: Edinburgh University Press, 1995), pp. 125–30, p. 128.
7. Bruno Latour's actor-network theory also could be useful for these purposes, as the agency Latour accords to the non-human is intimately related to social organization, including institutions. See Bruno Latour, *Reassembling the Social: An Introduction to Actor Network Theory* (Oxford: Oxford University Press, 2005). For a study of interpersonal communication in Latourian terms, some of which might be developed further in terms of authorship, see François Cooren, *Action and Agency in Dialogue* (Amsterdam: John Benjamins, 2010).
8. Manuel DeLanda, *Assemblage Theory* (Edinburgh: Edinburgh University Press, 2016), p. 1; cf. Gilles Deleuze and Felix Guattari, *A Thousand Plateaus: Capitalism and Schizophrenia*, trans. Brian Massumi (Minneapolis, University of Minnesota Press, 1987).
9. DeLanda, *Assemblage*, p. 19.
10. Among many others, see Mark Canada, *Literature and Journalism in Antebellum America: Thoreau, Stowe, and Their Contemporaries Respond to the Rise of the Commercial Press* (New York: Palgrave, 2011); Shelley Fisher Fishkin, *From Fact to Fiction: Journalism and Imaginative Writing in*

America (New York: Oxford University Press, 1985); Matthew Rubery, *The Novelty of Newspapers: Victorian Fiction After the Invention of the News* (Oxford: Oxford University Press, 2009); Doug Underwood, *Journalism and the Novel: Truth and Fiction, 1700–2000* (Cambridge: Cambridge University Press, 2008).

11. Viktor Shklovksy, *Zoo; or, Letters Not About Love*, trans. Richard Sheldon (Ithaca, NY: Cornell University Press, 1971).

12. Aristotle, *Physics*, trans. Richard Hope (Lincoln: University of Nebraska Press, 1961), 2.3.

13. For two contrasting views of final cause in the sciences, see Ernst Mayr. "The Idea of Teleology," *Journal of the History of Ideas*, 53.1 (1992), 117–35, and Ernest Nagel, "Teleology Revisited: Goal Directed Processes in Biology," *Journal of Philosophy*, 74 (1977), 261–301.

14. Michel Foucault, "What Is an Author?", in *The Essential Works of Foucault 1954–1984*, ed. James D. Faubion, vol. 2 (New York: New York Press, 1998), pp. 205–22, p. 205.

15. Ibid., p. 216.

16. Lennard J. Davis, "Dancing in the Dark: A Manifesto Against Professional Organizations," in *The Institution of Literature*, ed. Jeffrey J. Williams (Albany, NY: State University of New York Press, 2002), pp. 153–72, p. 155.

17. Ibid., p. 153.

18. Rivkah Zim, "Literary Contexts and the Authority of Carceral Experience," *Huntington Library Quarterly*, 72.2 (2009), 291–311, p. 296.

19. Stephen King, "Strong Poison," *The New York Times*, 22 Nov. 2009, C11.

20. Jean-Luc Godard, *Godard on Godard*, eds. Jean Narboni and Tom Milne (New York: Viking, 1972), p. 76.

21. James Naremore, "Authorship," in *A Companion to Film Theory*, eds. Toby Miller and Robert Stam (Malden, MA: Blackwell, 1999), pp. 9–24, p. 21.

22. Ibid., p. 22.

23. Mark McGurl, *The Program Era: Postwar Fiction and the Rise of Creative Writing* (Cambridge, MA: Harvard University Press, 2011), p. 83.

24. Ibid., p. x.

25. Breanne Fahs, *Valerie Solanas: The Defiant Life of the Woman Who Wrote SCUM (And Shot Andy Warhol)* (New York: Feminist Press, 2014), p. 81.

26. Valerie Solanas, *SCUM Manifesto* (London: Verso, 2004), p. 35.

27. Matthew G. Kirschenbaum, *Track Changes: A Literary History of Word Processing* (Cambridge, MA: Belknap Press, 2016), p. 30.

Select Bibliography

Authorship: General and Theoretical

Agamben, Giorgio. "The Author as Gesture," in *Profanations*. Trans. Jeff Fort. New York: Zone, 2007. 61–72.

"Anonymity." Special Issue of *New Literary History* 33 (2002).

Barthes, Roland. "The Death of the Author." 1967. In *Image–Music–Text*. Trans. Stephen Heath. London: Fontana Press, 1977. 142–48.

Barthes, Roland. "Authors and Writers," in *Critical Essays*. Trans. Richard Howard. Evanston, IL: Northwestern University Press, 1972. 143–50.

Battersby, Christine. *Gender and Genius: Towards a Feminist Aesthetics*. Bloomington: Indiana University Press, 1989.

Benedetti, Carla. *The Empty Cage: Inquiry into the Mysterious Disappearance of the Author*. Trans. William J. Hartley. Ithaca, NY: Cornell University Press, 2005.

Benjamin, Walter. "The Author as Producer," in *Reflections: Essays, Aphorisms, Autobiographical Writings*. Trans. Edmund Jephcott, ed. Peter Demetz. New York: Harcourt Brace Jovanovich, 1978. 220–36.

Bennett, Andrew. *The Author*. London: Routledge, 2005.

Berensmeyer, Ingo. "The Genius and the Hive: Travelling Concepts of Authorship in Literature and Culture." *Cahier voor Literatuurwetenschap* 6 (2014): 33–45.

Berensmeyer, Ingo, Gert Buelens, and Marysa Demoor. "Authorship as Cultural Performance: New Perspectives in Authorship Studies." *Zeitschrift für Anglistik und Amerikanistik* 60.1 (2012): 5–29.

Biriotti, Maurice, and Nicola Miller, eds. *What Is an Author?* Manchester: Manchester University Press, 1993.

Birke, Dorothee, and Tilmann Köppe, eds. *Author and Narrator. Transdisciplinary Contributions to a Narratological Debate*. Berlin: De Gruyter, 2015.

Bloom, Harold. *The Anxiety of Influence: A Theory of Poetry*. 1973. 2nd edn New York: Oxford University Press, 1997.

Booth, Wayne C. *The Rhetoric of Fiction*. 1961. 2nd edn Chicago: University of Chicago Press, 1983.

Bourdieu, Pierre. *Rules of Art: Genesis and Structure of the Literary Field*. Palo Alto, CA: Stanford University Press, 1996.

Buchanan, Judith, ed. *The Writer on Film: Screening Literary Authorship.* Basingstoke, UK: Palgrave Macmillan, 2013.

Burke, Seán. *Authorship: From Plato to the Postmodern. A Reader.* Edinburgh: Edinburgh University Press, 1995.

Burke, Seán. *The Death and Return of the Author: Criticism and Subjectivity in Barthes, Foucault and Derrida.* Edinburgh: Edinburgh University Press, 1998.

Childress, Clayton. *Under the Cover: The Creation, Production and Reception of a Novel.* Princeton, NJ: Princeton University Press, 2017.

Claassen, Eefje. *Author Representations in Literary Reading.* Amsterdam: Benjamins, 2012.

Coelsch-Foisner, Sabine, and Wolfgang Görtschacher, eds. *The Author as Reader: Textual Visions and Revisions.* Frankfurt am Main: Peter Lang, 2005.

Detering, Heinrich, ed. *Autorschaft: Positionen und Revisionen.* Stuttgart: Metzler, 2002.

Dimock, Wai-Chee, and Bruce Robbins, eds. "Remapping Genre." *PMLA* 122.5 (2007).

Donovan, Stephen, Danuta Fjellestad, and Rolf Lundén, eds. *Authority Matters: Rethinking the Theory and Practice of Authorship.* Amsterdam: Rodopi, 2008.

English, James F. *The Economy of Prestige: Prizes, Awards, and the Circulation of Cultural Value.* Cambridge, MA: Harvard University Press, 2005.

Fish, Stanley. *Is There a Text in this Class? The Authority of Interpretive Communities.* Cambridge, MA: Harvard University Press, 1982.

Foster, Don. *Author Unknown: On the Trail of Anonymous.* New York: Holt, 2000.

Foucault, Michel. "What Is an Author?" in *Language, Counter-Memory, Practice.* ed. Donald F. Bouchard. Ithaca, NY: Cornell University Press, 1977. 113–38.

Fox, Alistair. *Speaking Pictures: Neuropsychoanalysis and Authorship in Film and Literature.* Bloomington, IN: Indiana University Press, 2016.

Gagliardi, Caio. "The Problem of *Authorship* in Literary Theory: Deletions, Resumptions and Reviews." *Estudos Avançados* 23.73 (2011): 285–99.

Gallop, Jane. *The Deaths of the Author: Reading and Writing in Time.* Durham, NC: Duke University Press, 2011.

Genette, Gérard. *Palimpsests: Literature in the Second Degree.* 1982. Trans. Channa Newman and Claude Doubinsky. Lincoln, NE: University of Nebraska Press, 1997.

Genette, Gérard. *Paratexts: Thresholds of Interpretation.* Trans. Jane E. Lewin. Cambridge: Cambridge University Press, 1997.

Gray, Jonathan, and Derek Johnson. *A Companion to Media Authorship.* Malden, MA: Wiley-Blackwell, 2013.

Gubar, Susan. *Rooms of Our Own.* Urbana, IL: University of Illinois Press, 2006.

Hadjiafxendi, Kyriaki, and Polina Mackay, eds. *Authorship in Context: From the Theoretical to the Material.* New York: Palgrave Macmillan, 2007.

Hartley, Daniel. *The Politics of Style: Towards a Marxist Poetics.* Leiden: Brill, 2016.

Hayez, Cécile, and Michel Lisse, eds. *Apparitions de l'auteur: Etudes interdisciplinaires du concept d'auteur.* Bern: Peter Lang, 2005.

Haynes, Christine. "Reassessing 'Genius' in Studies of Authorship: The State of the Discipline." *Book History* 8 (2005): 287–320.

Hogan, Patrick Colm. *Narrative Discourse: Authors and Narrators in Literature, Film, and Art.* Columbus: Ohio State University Press, 2013.

Hutcheon, Linda, with Siobhan O'Flynn. *A Theory of Adaptation.* 2nd edn London: Routledge, 2013.

Irwin, William, ed. *The Death and Resurrection of the Author?* Westport, CT: Greenwood Press, 2002.

Iser, Wolfgang. "Auktorialität: Die Nullstelle des Diskurses," in *Spielräume des auktorialen Diskurses.* ed. *Ralph Kray and Klaus Städtke.* Berlin: Akademie Verlag, 2003. 219–41.

Jacques-Lefèvre, Nicole, and Frédéric Regard, eds. *Une histoire de la "fonction-auteur" est-elle possible?* Saint-Etienne: Publications de l'Université Saint-Etienne, 2001.

Jannidis, Fotis et al., eds. *Rückkehr des Autors: Zur Erneuerung eines umstrittenen Begriffs.* Tübingen: Niemeyer, 1999.

Jones, Derek, ed. *Censorship: A World Encyclopedia.* London: Fitzroy Dearborn, 2001.

Kamuf, Peggy. *Signature Pieces: On the Institution of Authorship.* Ithaca, NY: Cornell University Press, 1988.

Kindt, Tom, and Hans-Harald Müller, eds. *The Implied Author: Concept and Controversy.* Trans. Alastair Matthews. Berlin: de Gruyter, 2006.

Koestenbaum, Wayne. *Double Talk: The Erotics of Male Literary Collaboration.* New York, Routledge, 1989.

Kyora, Sabine, ed. *Subjektform Autor: Autorschaftsinszenierungen als Praktiken der Subjektivierung.* Bielefeld: transcript, 2014.

Laird, Holly. *Women Coauthors.* Champaign, IL: University of Illinois Press, 2000.

Lamarque, Peter. "Authors," in *The Philosophy of Literature.* Malden, MA: Blackwell, 2009. 84–131.

Lejeune, Philippe. *Le pacte autobiographique.* Paris: Seuil, 1975.

Lejeune, Philippe. *On Autobiography.* ed. Paul John Eakin, trans. Katherine Leary. Minneapolis, MN: University of Minnesota Press, 1989.

Livingston, Paisley: "Authorship Redux: On Some Recent and Not-So-Recent Work in Literary Theory." *Philosophy and Literature* 35.1 (2008): 191–97.

Longolius, Sonja. *Performing Authorship: Strategies of "Becoming an Author" in the Works of Paul Auster, Candice Breitz, Sophie Calle, and Jonathan Safran Foer.* Bielefeld: transcript, 2016.

Louichon, Brigitte, and Jérôme Roger, eds. *L'auteur entre biographie et mythographie.* Bordeaux: Presses Universitaires de Bordeaux, 2002.

McGill, Meredith L., ed. *Taking Liberties with the Author: Selected Papers from the English Institute.* Cambridge: English Institute, 2013.

Meizoz, Jérôme. *Postures littéraires: Mises en scène modernes de l'auteur.* Geneva: Slatkine, 2007.

Meizoz, Jérôme. *La fabrique des singularités: Postures littéraires II*. Geneva: Slatkine, 2011.

Moers, Ellen. *Literary Women*. New York, Doubleday, 1976.

Mullan, John. *Anonymity: A Secret History of English Literature*. London: Faber and Faber, 2007.

Nehamas, Alexander. "The Postulated Author: Critical Monism as a Regulative Ideal." *Critical Inquiry* 8.1 (1981): 133–49.

Nehamas, Alexander. "What an Author Is." *The Journal of Philosophy* 83.11 (1986): 685–91.

Nesbit, Molly. "What Was an Author?" *Yale French Studies* 73 (1987): 229–57.

Pabst, Stephan, ed. *Anonymität und Autorschaft: Zur Literatur- und Rechtsgeschichte der Namenlosigkeit*. Berlin: de Gruyter, 2011.

Pease, Donald E. "Author," in *Critical Terms for Literary Study*. ed. Frank Lentricchia and Thomas McLaughlin. Chicago: University of Chicago Press, 1995. 105–17.

Pérez Fontdevila, Aina, and Meri Torras Francés, eds. *Los papeles del autor/a: Marcos teóricos sobre la autoría literaria*. Madrid: Arco Libros, 2016.

Phelan, James. *Narrative as Rhetoric*. Columbus: Ohio State University Press, 1996.

Prosser, Jay. *Second Skins: The Body Narratives of Transsexuality*. New York: Columbia University Press, 1998.

Rabinowitz, Peter J. *Before Reading: Narrative Conventions and the Politics of Interpretation*. 1987. Columbus: Ohio State University Press, 1998.

Sanders, Julia. *Adaptation and Appropriation*. London: Routledge, 2006.

Schaffrink, Matthias, and Marcus Willand, eds. *Theorien und Praktiken der Autorschaft*. Berlin: de Gruyter, 2014.

Schönert, Jörg. "Author." Trans. Alexander Starritt. In *The Living Handbook of Narratology*, ed. Peter Hühn et al. Hamburg: Hamburg University Press. http://wikis.sub.uni-hamburg.de/lhn/index.php/Author [Last modified: 6 September 2011]

Simion, Eugen. *The Return of the Author*. 1981. ed. James W. Newcomb, trans. James W. Newcomb and Lidia Vianu. Evanston, IL: Northwestern University Press, 1996.

Spoerhase, Carlos. *Autorschaft und Interpretation: Methodische Grundlagen einer philologischen Hermeneutik*. Berlin: de Gruyter, 2007.

Städtke, Klaus, and Ralph Kray, eds. *Spielräume des auktorialen Diskurses*. Berlin: Akademie Verlag, 2003.

Stillinger, Jack. *Multiple Authorship and the Myth of Solitary Genius*. New York: Oxford University Press, 1991.

Stone, Marjorie and Judith Thompson, eds. *Literary Couplings: Writing Couples, Collaborators, and the Construction of Authorship*. Madison, WI: University of Wisconsin Press, 2006.

van Eechoud, Mireille, ed. *The Work of Authorship*. Amsterdam: Amsterdam University Press, 2014.

Williams, Raymond. "The Writer: Commitment and Alignment." 1980. In *The Raymond Williams Reader*. ed. John O. Higgins. Oxford: Blackwell, 2001. 208–17.

Wimsatt, W. K., and Monroe C. Beardsley. "The Intentional Fallacy," in *The Verbal Icon: Studies in the Meaning of Poetry*. ed. W. K. Wimsatt. Lexington, KY: University of Kentucky Press, 1954. 3–20.

Woodmansee, Martha. *The Author, Art, and the Market: Rereading the History of Aesthetics*. New York: Columbia University Press, 1994.

Woodmansee, Martha, and Peter Jaszi, eds. *The Construction of Authorship*. Durham, NC: Duke University Press, 1994.

Zabus, Chantal, and David Coad, eds. *Transgender Experience: Place, Ethnicity, and Visibility*. New York: Routledge, 2013.

Zwierlein, Anne-Julia, ed. *Gender and Creation: Surveying Gendered Myths of Creativity, Authority, and Authorship*. Heidelberg: Universitätsverlag Winter, 2010.

Historical: Ancient to Medieval

Bakker, Egberg J., ed. *Authorship and Greek Song: Authority, Authenticity, and Performance*. Leiden: Brill, 2017.

Bale, Anthony. "From Translator to Laureate: Imagining the Medieval Author." *Literature Compass* 5 (2002): 918–34.

Beecroft, Alexander. *Authorship and Cultural Identity in Early Greece and China. Patterns of Literary Circulation*. Cambridge: Cambridge University Press, 2010.

Birt, Theodor. *Das antike Buchwesen in seinem Verhältnis zur Literatur*. Berlin: Hertz, 1882.

Bolens, Guillemette, and Lukas Erne, eds. *Medieval and Early Modern Authorship*. Tübingen: Narr, 2011.

Chang, Kang-i Sun, and Stephen Owen, eds. *The Cambridge History of Chinese Literature*. 2 vols. Cambridge: Cambridge University Press, 2010.

Cohen, Mordechai Z. *Opening the Gates of Interpretation: Maimonides' Biblical Hermeneutics in Light of His Geonic-Andalusian Heritage and Muslim Milieu*. Leiden: Brill, 2011.

Ebin, Lois. *Illuminator, Makar, Vates: Visions of Poetry in the Fifteenth Century*. Lincoln: University of Nebraska Press, 1988.

Edwards, Robert R. *Invention and Authorship in Medieval England*. Columbus: Ohio State University Press, 2017.

Enmarch, Roland, and Verena M. Lepper, eds. *Ancient Egyptian Literature: Theory and Practice*. Oxford: Oxford University Press, 2013.

Fisher, Matthew. *Scribal Authorship and the Writing of History in Medieval Literature*. Columbus: Ohio State University Press, 2012.

Foster, Benjamin R. *Before the Muses: An Anthology of Akkadian Literature*. 3rd edn Bethesda, MD: CDL Press, 2005.

Friede, Susanne, and Michael Schwarze, eds. *Autorschaft und Autorität in den romanischen Literaturen des Mittelalters*. Berlin: de Gruyter, 2015.

Gillespie, Alexandra. *Print Culture and the Medieval Author: Chaucer, Lydgate and their Books 1473–1557*. Oxford: Oxford University Press, 2006.

Graziosi, Barbara. *Inventing Homer: The Early Reception of Epic*. Cambridge: Cambridge University Press, 2002.

Griffiths, Jane. *Diverting Authorities: Experimental Glossing Practices in Manuscript and Print*. Oxford: Oxford University Press, 2014.

Halliwell, Stephen. "The Subjection of Muthos to Logos: Plato's Citations of the Poets." *Classical Quarterly* 50 (2000): 94–112.

Houston, George W. *Inside Roman Libraries: Book Collections and their Management in Antiquity*. Chapel Hill: University of North Carolina Press, 2014.

Kim, Lawrence. *Homer Between History and Fiction in Imperial Greek Literature*. Cambridge: Cambridge University Press, 2010.

Lee, Jongsoo. "Netzahualcoyotl and the Notion of Individual Authorship in Nahuatl Poetry." *Confluencia* 20.1 (2004): 73–86.

Longman, Tremper. *Fictional Akkadian Autobiography: A Generic and Comparative Study*. Winona Lake, IN: Eisenbrauns, 1991.

Loprieno, Antonio, ed. *Ancient Egyptian Literature. History and Forms*. Leiden: Brill, 1996.

Marmodoro, Anna, and Jonathan Hill, eds. *The Author's Voice in Classical and Late Antiquity*. Oxford: Oxford University Press, 2013.

McGill, Scott. *Plagiarism in Latin Literature*. Cambridge: Cambridge University Press, 2012.

Meier, Christel, and Martina Wagner-Egelhaaf, eds. *Prophetie und Autorschaft: Charisma, Heilsversprechen und Gefährdung*. Berlin: de Gruyter, 2014.

Minnis, Alastair J. *Medieval Theory of Authorship: Scholastic Literary Attitudes in the Later Middle Ages*. 2nd edn Philadelphia, PA: University of Pennsylvania Press, 1988.

Möller, Melanie. *Talis oratio – qualis vita: Zu Theorie und Praxis mimetischer Verfahren in der griechisch-römischen Literaturkritik*. Heidelberg: Winter, 2004.

Nagy, Gregory. *Pindar's Homer: The Lyric Possession of an Epic Past*. Baltimore, MD: Johns Hopkins University Press, 1990.

Nagy, Gregory. *Poetry as Performance: Homer and Beyond*. Cambridge: Cambridge University Press, 1996.

O'Neill, Mary J. *Courtly Love Songs of Medieval France: Transmission and Style in the Trouvère Repertoire*. Oxford: Oxford University Press, 2006.

Parkinson, Richard B. *Reading Ancient Egyptian Poetry, Among Other Histories*. Chichester, UK: Wiley-Blackwell, 2009.

Partridge, Stephen, and Erik Kwakkel, eds. *Author, Reader, Book: Medieval Authorship in Theory and Practice*. Toronto: Toronto University Press, 2012.

Peirano, Irene. "Authenticity as an Aesthetic Value: Ancient and Modern Reflections," in *Aesthetic Value in Classical Antiquity*. eds. Ineke Sluiter and Ralph M. Rosen. Leiden: Brill, 2012. 215–42.

Radner, Karen. *Die Macht des Namens: Altorientalische Strategien zur Selbsterhaltung.* Wiesbaden: Harrassowitz, 2005.

Rubanovich, Julia. "Metaphors of Authorship in Medieval Persian Prose: A Preliminary Study." *Middle Eastern Literatures* 12.2 (2009): 127–35.

Scheidegger Lämmle, Cédric. *Werkpolitik in der Antike: Studien zu Cicero, Vergil, Horaz und Ovid.* Munich: C.H. Beck, 2016.

Schwermann, Christian, and Raji C. Steineck, eds. *That Wonderful Composite Called Author: Authorship in East Asian Literatures from the Beginnings to the Seventeenth Century.* Leiden: Brill, 2014.

Steiner, Emily. "Authority," in *Middle English.* ed. Paul Strohm. Oxford: Oxford University Press, 2007. 142–59.

Suarez, Michael F., S. J., and H. R. Woudhuysen, eds. *The Book: A Global History.* Oxford: Oxford University Press, 2013.

Suerbaum, Werner. *Untersuchungen zur Selbstdarstellung älterer römischer Dichter: Livius Andronicus. Naevius. Ennius.* Hildesheim: Olms, 1968.

Ziolkowski, Jan. "Cultures of Authority in the Long Twelfth Century." *Journal of English and Germanic Philology* 108 (2009): 421–48.

Historical: Early Modern to Twentieth Century

Adams, Amanda. *Performing Authorship in the Nineteenth-Century Transatlantic Lecture Tour.* Farnham, UK: Ashgate, 2014.

Brake, Laurel. *Subjugated Knowledges: Journalism, Gender and Literature in the Nineteenth Century.* New York: New York University Press, 1994.

Brewer, David. "The Tactility of Author's Names." *Eighteenth Century: Theory and Interpretation* 54 (2013): 195–213.

Buurma, Rachel Sagner. "Anonymity, Corporate Authority, and the Archive: The Production of Authorship in Late-Victorian England." *Victorian Studies* 50.1 (2007): 15–42.

Demers, Patricia. *Women's Writing in English: Early Modern England.* Toronto: University of Toronto Press, 2005.

Dobranski, Stephen B. *Milton, Authorship, and the Book Trade.* Cambridge: Cambridge University Press, 1999.

Dorleijn, Gillis J., Ralf Grüttemeier, and Liesbeth Korthals Altes, eds. *Authorship Revisited: Conceptions of Authorship around 1900 and 2000.* Leuven: Peeters, 2010.

Dutton, Richard. "The Birth of the Author," in *Texts and Cultural Change in Early Modern England.* eds. Cedric C. Brown and Arthur F. Marotti. Houndmills, UK: Macmillan, 1997. 153–78.

Easley, Alexis. *First-Person Anonymous: Women Writers and Victorian Print Media, 1830–1870.* Aldershot, UK: Ashgate, 2004.

Easley, Alexis. *Literary Celebrity, Gender, and Victorian Authorship, 1850–1914.* Newark: University of Delaware Press, 2013.

Egan, Gerald. *Fashioning Authorship in the Long Eighteenth Century: Stylish Books of Poetic Genius*. Basingstoke, UK: Palgrave Macmillan, 2016.

Erne, Lukas. *Shakespeare and the Book Trade*. Cambridge: Cambridge University Press, 2013.

Ezell, Margaret J.M. *Social Authorship and the Advent of Print*. Baltimore, MD: Johns Hopkins University Press, 1999.

Fang, Karen. *Romantic Writing and the Empire of Signs: Periodical Culture and Post-Napoleonic Authorship*. Charlottesville: University of Virginia Press, 2010.

Finkelstein, David. *The House of Blackwood: Author-Publisher Relations in the Victorian Period*. Philadelphia: Pennsylvania State University Press, 2002.

Gallagher, Catherine. *Nobody's Story: The Vanishing Acts of Women Writers in the Marketplace, 1670–1820*. Berkeley: University of California Press, 1994.

Gilbert, Sandra, and Susan Gubar. *The Madwoman in the Attic: The Woman Writer and the Nineteenth-Century Literary Imagination*. 1979. 2nd edn New Haven, CT: Yale University Press, 2000.

Goodrich, Jaime. *Faithful Translators: Authorship, Gender, and Religion in Early Modern England*. Evanston, IL: Northwestern University Press, 2014.

Grasso, Linda. *The Artistry of Anger: Black and White Women's Literature in America 1820–1860*. Chapel Hill: University of North Carolina Press, 2002.

Greene, Thomas M. *The Light in Troy: Imitation and Discovery in Renaissance Poetry*. New Haven, CT: Yale University Press, 1982.

Griffin, Dustin. *Authorship in the Long Eighteenth Century*. Newark: University of Delaware Press, 2014.

Griffin, Robert J., ed. *The Faces of Anonymity: Anonymous and Pseudonymous Publication from the Sixteenth to the Twentieth Century*. New York: Palgrave Macmillan, 2003.

Gruber-Garvey, Ellen. *Writing with Scissors: American Scrapbooks from the Civil War to the Harlem Renaissance*. Oxford: Oxford University Press, 2013.

Hammill, Faye, and Mark Hussey. *Modernism's Print Cultures*. London: Bloomsbury, 2016.

Hannay, Margaret, ed. *Silent but for the Word: Tudor Women as Patrons, Translators, and Writers of Religious Works*. Kent, OH: Kent State University Press, 1985.

Hepburn, James. *The Author's Empty Purse and the Rise of the Literary Agent*. London: Oxford University Press, 1968.

Homestead, Melissa J. *American Women Authors and Literary Property, 1822–1869*. Cambridge: Cambridge University Press, 2005.

Hutcheon, Linda. *A Poetics of Postmodernism*. London: Routledge, 1988.

Jardine, Lisa. *Still Harping on Daughters: Women and Drama in the Age of Shakespeare*. 1983. New York: Columbia University Press, 1989.

Johns, Adrian. *The Nature of the Book: Print and Knowledge in the Making*. Chicago: University of Chicago Press, 1998.

Kewes, Paulina. *Authorship and Appropriation: Writing for the Stage in England, 1660–1710.* Oxford: Clarendon Press, 1998.

Losse, Deborah. "From *auctor* to *auteur:* Authorization and Appropriation in the Renaissance." *Medievalia et humanistica* 16 (1998): 153–63.

Love, Harold. *Scribal Publication in Seventeenth-Century England.* Oxford: Clarendon Press, 1993.

Macfarlane, Robert. *Original Copy: Plagiarism and Originality in Nineteenth-Century Literature.* Oxford: Oxford University Press, 2007.

Mazzeo, Tilar J. *Plagiarism and Literary Property in the Romantic Period.* Philadelphia: University of Pennsylvania Press, 2006.

McGill, Meredith L. *American Literature and the Culture of Reprinting, 1834–1853.* Philadelphia: University of Pennsylvania Press, 2003.

McGinnis, Reginald, ed. *Originality and Intellectual Property in the French and English Enlightenment.* London: Routledge, 2009.

McGurl, Mark. *The Program Era: Postwar Fiction and the Rise of Creative Writing.* Cambridge, MA: Harvard University Press, 2011.

Müller, Beate, ed. *Censorship and Cultural Regulation in the Modern Age.* Amsterdam: Rodopi, 2004,

Peterson, Linda H. *Becoming a Woman of Letters: Myths of Authorship and Facts of the Victorian Market.* Princeton, NJ: Princeton University Press, 2009.

Petrov, Petre M. *Automatic for the Masses: The Death of the Author and the Birth of Socialist Realism.* Toronto: University of Toronto Press, 2015.

Phillippy, Patricia, ed. *A History of Early Modern Women's Writing.* Cambridge: Cambridge University Press, 2018.

Pochmara, Anna. *The Making of the New Negro: Black Authorship, Masculinity, and Sexuality in the Harlem Renaissance.* Amsterdam: Amsterdam University Press, 2011.

Rainey, Lawrence. *Institutions of Modernism: Literary Elites and Public Culture.* New Haven, CT: Yale University Press, 1999.

Richardson, Brian. *Printing, Writers and Readers in Renaissance Italy.* Cambridge: Cambridge University Press, 1999.

Ross, Trevor. *Writing in Public: Literature and the Liberty of the Press in Eighteenth-Century Britain.* Baltimore, MD: Johns Hopkins University Press, 2018.

Ryan, Susan M. *The Moral Economies of American Authorship: Reputation, Scandal, and the Nineteenth-Century Literary Marketplace.* Oxford: Oxford University Press, 2016.

Saunders, Max. *Self Impression: Life-Writing, Autobiografiction, and the Forms of Modern Literature.* Oxford: Oxford University Press, 2010.

Schellenberg, Betty A. *The Professionalization of Women Writers in Eighteenth-Century Britain, 1740–1780.* Cambridge: Cambridge University Press, 2005.

Schellenberg, Betty A. *Literary Coteries and the Making of Modern Print Culture, 1740–1790.* Cambridge: Cambridge University Press, 2016.

Shapiro, James. *Contested Will: Who Wrote Shakespeare?* New York: Simon and Schuster, 2010.

Showalter, Elaine: *A Literature of Their Own: British Women Novelists from Brontë to Lessing*. Princeton, NJ: Princeton University Press, 1977.

Simonova, Natasha. *Early Modern Authorship and Prose Continuations: Adaptation and Ownership from Sidney to Richardson*. London: Palgrave Macmillan, 2015.

Stewart, Stanley. "Author Esquire: The Writer and 'Immaterial Culture' in Caroline and Jacobean England." *Ben Jonson Journal* 20.2 (2013): 241–59.

Stewart, Susan. *Crimes of Writing*. New York: Oxford University Press, 1991; reprinted Durham, NC: Duke University Press, 1994.

Wall, Wendy. *The Imprint of Gender: Authorship and Publication in the English Renaissance*. Ithaca, NY: Cornell University Press, 1993.

Williams, Susan. *Reclaiming Authorship: Literary Women in America, 1850–1900*. Philadelphia: University of Pennsylvania Press, 2006.

Zionkowski, Linda. *Men's Work: Gender, Class, and the Professionalization of Poetry, 1660–1784*. Houndmills, UK: Palgrave Macmillan, 2001.

Contemporary

Busse, Christina. *Framing Fan Fiction: Literary and Social Practices in Fan Fiction Communities*. Iowa City: University of Iowa Press, 2017.

Chakrabarty, Dipesh. *Provincializing Europe: Postcolonial Thought and Historical Difference*. Princeton, NJ: Princeton University Press, 2007.

Dawson, Paul. *The Return of the Omniscient Narrator: Authorship and Authority in Twenty-First Century Fiction*. Columbus: Ohio State University Press, 2013.

DuPlessis, Rachel Blau. "Agency, Social Authorship, and the Political Aura of Contemporary Poetry." *Textual Practice* 23.6 (2009): 987–99.

Fitzpatrick, Kathleen. "The Digital Future of Authorship: Rethinking Originality." *Culture Machine* 12 (2011): 1–26.

Goldsmith, Kenneth. *Uncreative Writing: Managing Language in the Digital Age*. New York: Columbia University Press, 2011.

Lessig, Lawrence. *Free Culture: How Big Media Uses Technology and the Law to Lock Down Culture and Control Creativity*. New York: Penguin, 2004.

Levmore, Saul, and Martha C. Nussbaum. *The Offensive Internet: Speech, Privacy, and Reputation*. Cambridge, MA: Harvard University Press, 2010.

Moraru, Christian. *Rewriting: Postmodern Narrative and Cultural Critique in the Age of Cloning*. Albany, NY: State University of New York Press, 2001.

Perloff, Marjorie. *Unoriginal Genius: Poetry by Other Means in the New Century*. Chicago: University of Chicago Press, 2010.

Rife, Martine Courant. *Invention, Copyright, and Digital Writing*. Carbondale, IL: Southern Illinois University Press, 2013.

Savu, Laura E. *Postmortem Postmodernists: The Afterlife of the Author in Recent Narrative*. Madison, NJ: Fairleigh Dickinson University Press, 2009.

Tsing, Anna. "Indigenous Voice," in *Indigenous Experience Today*. eds. Marisol de la Cadena and Orin Stan. Oxford: Berg, 2007. 33–67.

Van der Weel, Adriaan. *Changing our Textual Minds: Towards a Digital Order of Knowledge*. Manchester: Manchester University Press, 2011.

Attribution

Burrows, John. "All the Way Through: Testing for Authorship in Different Frequency Strata." *Literary and Linguistic Computing* 22 (2007): 27–47.

Craig, Hugh, and Arthur F. Kinney, eds. *Shakespeare, Computers, and the Mystery of Authorship*. Cambridge: Cambridge University Press, 2009.

Juola, Patrick. "Authorship Attribution." *Foundations and Trends in Information Retrieval* 1 (2006): 233–34.

Kestemont, Mike, Justin Stover, Moshe Koppel, Foldert Karsdorp, and Walter Daelemans. "Authenticating the Writings of Julius Caesar." *Expert Systems with Applications* 63 (2016): 86–96.

Love, Harold. *Attributing Authorship: An Introduction*, Cambridge: Cambridge University Press, 2002.

Rybicki, Jan, David L. Hoover, and Mike Kestemont. "Collaborative Authorship: Conrad, Ford and Rolling Delta." *Literary and Linguistic Computing* 29 (2014): 422–31.

Stamatatos, Efstathios. "A Study of Modern Authorship Attribution Methods." *Journal of the American Society for Information Science and Technology* 60 (2009): 538–56.

Taylor, Gary, and Gabriel Egan, eds. *The New Oxford Shakespeare: Authorship Companion*. Oxford: Oxford University Press, 2017.

Book History and the Material Text

Chartier, Roger. *The Order of Books: Readers, Authors, and Libraries in Europe Between the Fourteenth and Eighteenth Centuries*. Trans. Lydia G. Cochrane. Stanford: Stanford University Press, 1994.

Chartier, Roger. *The Author's Hand and the Printer's Mind*. Trans. Lydia G. Cochrane. Cambridge: Polity Press, 2013.

Darnton, Robert. "What Is the History of Books?" *Daedalus* 111.3 (1982): 65–83.

Finkelstein, David, and Alistair McCleery, eds. *The Book History Reader*. London: Routledge, 2006.

Finkelstein, David, and Alistair McCleery. *An Introduction to Book History*. 2nd edn London: Routledge, 2013.

Kirschenbaum, Matthew G. *Track Changes: A Literary History of Word Processing*. Cambridge, MA: Belknap Press, 2016.

Meier, Thomas, Michael R. Ott, and Rebecca Sauer, eds. *Materiale Textkulturen*. Berlin: de Gruyter, 2015.

Olson, David. *The World on Paper: The Conceptual and Cognitive Implications of Writing and Reading*. Cambridge: Cambridge University Press, 1996.

Rohrbach, Augusta. *Thinking Outside the Book*. Boston, MA: University of Massachusetts Press, 2014.

Copyright

Baldwin, Peter. *The Copyright Wars: Three Centuries of Trans-Atlantic Battle*. Princeton, NJ: Princeton University Press, 2014.

Bently, Lionel, Suthersanen, Uma, and Paul Torremans, eds. *Global Copyright: Three Hundred Years Since the Statute of Anne, from 1709 to Cyberspace*. Cheltenham, UK: Elgar, 2010.

Coombe, Rosemary J. *The Cultural Life of Intellectual Properties: Authorship, Appropriation, and the Law*. Durham, NC: Duke University Press, 1998.

Loewenstein, David. *The Author's Due: Printing and the Prehistory of Copyright*. Chicago: University of Chicago Press, 2002.

Rose, Mark. *Authors and Owners: The Invention of Copyright*. Cambridge, MA: Harvard University Press, 1993.

Rose, Mark. "Copyright and its Metaphors." *UCLA Law Review* 50.1 (2002): 1–15.

Saint-Amour, Paul K. *The Copywrights: Intellectual Property and the Literary Imagination*. Ithaca, NY: Cornell University Press, 2003.

Saint-Amour, Paul K., ed. *Modernism and Copyright*. New York: Oxford University Press, 2010.

Saunders, David. *Authorship and Copyright*. London: Routledge, 1992.

Woodmansee, Martha. "The Genius and the Copyright: Economic and Legal Conditions of the Emergence of the 'Author'." *Eighteenth-Century Studies* 17.4 (1984): 425–48.

Woodmansee, Martha. "The 'Romantic' Author," in *Research Handbook on the History of Copyright Law*. ed. Isabella Alexander and H. Tomás Gómez-Arostegui. Cheltenham: Elgar, 2016. 53–77.

Editing

Bein, Thomas, Nutt-Kofoth, Rüdiger, and Bodo Plachta, eds. *Autor – Autorisation – Authentizität*. 2004. Rpt. Berlin: De Gruyter, 2012.

Bryant, John. *The Fluid Text: A Theory of Revision and Editing for Book and Screen*. Ann Arbor: University of Michigan Press, 2002.

Cerquiglini, Bernard. *In Praise of the Variant: A Critical History of Philology*. Trans. Betsy Wing. Baltimore, MD: Johns Hopkins University Press, 1999.

Hay, Louis. *La Littérature des écrivains: Questions de critique génétique*. Paris: José Corti, 2002.

Shillingsburg, Peter: *Scholarly Editing in the Computer Age*. 3rd edn Ann Arbor: University of Michigan Press, 1996.

Tanselle, G. Thomas. "The Editorial Problem of Final Authorial Intention." *Studies in Bibliography* 29 (1976): 167–211.

Van Hulle, Dirk, and Peter Shillingsburg. "Orientations to Text, Revisited." *Studies in Bibliography* 59 (2015): 27–44.

Publishing and Marketing

Bassett, Troy J. "T. Fisher Unwin's Pseudonym Library: Literary Marketing and Authorial Identity." *English Literature in Translation: 1880–1920*, 47 (2004): 143–60.

Baverstock, Alison. *How to Market Books*. 4th edn London: Kogan Books, 2008.

Becnel, Kim. *The Rise of Corporate Publishing and its Effects on Authorship in Early Twentieth-Century America*. New York: Routledge, 2008.

Brier, Evan. *A Novel Marketplace: Mass Culture, the Book Trade and Postwar American Fiction*. Philadelphia: University of Pennsylvania Press, 2010.

Brown, Stephen, ed. *Consuming Books: The Marketing and Consumption of Literature*. London: Routledge, 2006.

Burke, Fauzia. *Online Marketing for Busy Authors: A Step-by-Step Guide*. Oakland, CA: Berrett-Koehler, 2016.

Demoor, Marysa, ed. *Marketing the Author: Authorial Personae, Narrative Selves and Self-Fashioning, 1880–1930*. Houndmills, UK: Palgrave Macmillan, 2004.

Everton, Michael J. *The Grand Chorus of Complaint: Authors and the Business Ethics of American Publishing*. Oxford: Oxford University Press, 2011.

Greco, Albert N., Clara E. Rodríguez, and Robert M. Wharton. *The Culture and Commerce of Publishing in the 21st Century*. Redwood City, CA: Stanford University Press, 2007.

Laquintano, Timothy. *Mass Authorship and the Rise of Self-Publishing*. Iowa City: University of Iowa Press, 2016.

McBride, Erin Ann. *When Books Fly: Social Media Secrets for Bestselling Books*. Spring Ville, UT: Plain Sight, 2016.

Miller, Laura J. *Reluctant Capitalists: Bookselling and the Culture of Consumption*. Chicago: University of Chicago Press, 2006.

Pecoskie, Jen, and Heather Hill. "Beyond Traditional Publishing Models: An Examination of the Relationships between Authors, Readers, and Publishers." *Journal of Documentation* 71 (2015): 609–26.

Smith, Kelvin. *The Publishing Business: From p-books to e-books*. Lausanne: AVA, 2012.

Thompson, John B. *Merchants of Culture: The Publishing Business in the Twenty-First Century*. 2nd edn Cambridge: Polity Press, 2012.

Wilson, Nicola Louise, ed. *The Book World: Selling and Distributing British Literature, 1900–1940*. Leiden: Brill, 2016.

Journals and Other Resources for Authorship Studies

Authorship. Open access online journal. www.authorship.ugent.be

The Author. Quarterly journal of the *Society of Authors* (UK)

Book History. Annual journal of the Society for the History of Authorship, Reading and Publishing (SHARP). www.sharpweb.org/main/

British Book Trade Index (BBTI). http://bbti.bodleian.ox.ac.uk/

East Asian Publishing and Society. Leiden: Brill

Histoire et civilisation du livre. Geneva: Droz

Journal of the Printing Historical Society

The Library. Journal of the Bibliographical Society (UK)

The Library Quarterly. Chicago: University of Chicago Press

Library and Information History. London: Taylor & Francis

Papers of the Bibliographical Society of America

Papers of the Bibliographical Society of Canada

Publishing History

Scottish Book Trade Index (SBTI). www.nls.uk/catalogues/scottish-book-trade-index

Studies in Bibliography

Textual Cultures: Texts, Contexts, Interpretation. Bi-annual journal of the Society for Textual Scholarship

Variants: Journal of the European Society for Textual Scholarship

Victorian Periodicals Review

Index

Glosses of full names in both main and subheadings are to disambiguate the person named from others in the index with the same last name.

Titles beginning with definite or indefinite articles are sorted on the word following. *The Bell Jar* for example is sorted in the Bs. This applies to titles in Romance languages as well.